Library of
Davidson College

PAPERS AND CORRESPONDENCE
OF
WILLIAM STANLEY JEVONS

Volume II

Also by R. D. Collison Black

CENTENARY HISTORY OF THE STATISTICAL SOCIETY
OF IRELAND

ECONOMIC THOUGHT AND THE IRISH QUESTION, 1817–1870

A CATALOGUE OF PAMPHLETS ON ECONOMIC SUBJECTS,
1750–1900

JEVONS'S THEORY OF POLITICAL ECONOMY (*editor*)

THE ECONOMIC WRITINGS OF
MOUNTIFORT LONGFIELD (*editor*)

READINGS IN THE DEVELOPMENT
OF ECONOMIC ANALYSIS, 1776–1848

PAPERS AND CORRESPONDENCE OF WILLIAM STANLEY
JEVONS, VOLUME I (*editor with Rosamond Könekamp*)

William Stanley Jevons
from a photograph taken about 1851–2

PAPERS AND CORRESPONDENCE OF WILLIAM STANLEY JEVONS

Volume II
CORRESPONDENCE 1850–1862

EDITED BY
R. D. COLLISON BLACK

AUGUSTUS M. KELLEY · PUBLISHERS
CLIFTON 1973

© R. D. Collison Black 1973

All Rights Reserved.
No part of this publication may be reproduced
or transmitted, in any form or by any means,
without permission.

Published by
AUGUSTUS M. KELLY · PUBLISHERS
305 ALLWOOD ROAD
CLIFTON, NEW JERSEY 07012

ISBN 0 678 07012 1

LCN 72-77230

Printed in Great Britain by
R. & R. CLARK LTD
Edinburgh

CONTENTS

List of Plates   xv

Preface   xvii

List of Abbreviations   xix

Letter

1	Thomas Jevons to William Stanley Jevons 7 July 1849	3
2	Herbert Jevons to Thomas Jevons 24 September 1850	4
3	Thomas Jevons to William Stanley Jevons 28 October 1850	6
4	Herbert Jevons to Thomas Jevons 13 November 1850	8
5	Thomas Jevons to William Stanley Jevons 19 November 1850	10
6	Herbert Jevons to Thomas Jevons 21 November [1850]	12
7	Herbert Jevons to Thomas Jevons 22 November [1850]	16
8	Herbert Jevons to Thomas Jevons 23 November [1850]	19
9	William Stanley Jevons to Thomas Jevons 11 December 1850	20
10	Herbert Jevons to Thomas Jevons 18 January [1851]	21
11	Thomas Jevons to William Stanley Jevons 18 March 1851	23
12	Thomas Jevons to William Stanley Jevons 28 June 1851	25
13	Thomas Jevons to William Stanley Jevons 26 September 1851	27
14	Thomas Jevons to William Stanley Jevons 14 January 1852	28

Letter

15	William Stanley Jevons to Henrietta and Thomas Edwin Jevons 2 February 1852	29
16	Thomas Jevons to William Stanley Jevons 3 May 1852	31
17	William Stanley Jevons to Thomas Jevons [May 1852]	32
18	Thomas Jevons to William Stanley Jevons 8 June 1852	33
19	William Stanley Jevons to Lucy Jevons July 1852	35
20	Thomas Jevons to William Stanley Jevons 17 November 1852	35
21	Thomas Jevons to William Stanley Jevons 9 February 1853	37
22	Thomas Jevons to William Stanley Jevons 18 February 1853	39
23	Thomas Jevons to William Stanley Jevons 2 April 1853	41
24	Thomas Jevons to William Stanley Jevons 6 May 1853	42
25	Herbert Jevons to William Stanley Jevons 9 July 1853	44
26	Thomas Jevons to William Stanley Jevons 10 July 1853	46
27	William Stanley Jevons to Henry Enfield Roscoe 28 August [1853]	49
28	Thomas Jevons to William Stanley Jevons 17 September 1853	51
29	Thomas Graham and William Allen Miller to Edward Ward 13 October 1853	54
30	Thomas Jevons to William Stanley Jevons 17 October 1853	55
31	Edward Ward to William Stanley Jevons 23 January 1854	57
32	William Stanley Jevons to Henrietta Jevons 7 February 1854	57

Letter

33	Thomas Jevons to William Stanley Jevons 15 February 1854	59
34	William Stanley Jevons to Henry Enfield Roscoe 17 February 1854	61
35	Henry Enfield Roscoe to William Stanley Jevons 21 February 1854	64
36	William Stanley Jevons to Henrietta Jevons 28 February 1854	67
37	William Stanley Jevons to Thomas Jevons 11 March 1854	70
38	Henry Enfield Roscoe to William Stanley Jevons 20 April 1854	71
39	Henry Enfield Roscoe to William Stanley Jevons 25 May 1854	74
40	William Stanley Jevons to Henrietta Jevons 4 June [1854]	76
41	William Stanley Jevons to Henry Enfield Roscoe 25 June 1854	77
42	William Stanley Jevons to Thomas Jevons 3 July 1854	80
43	Thomas Jevons to William Stanley Jevons 6 July 1854	86
44	Thomas Jevons to William Stanley Jevons 1 September 1854	90
45	William Stanley Jevons to Thomas Jevons 11 September 1854	96
46	Thomas Jevons to William Stanley Jevons 30 September 1854	101
47	William Stanley Jevons to Lucy Jevons 16 October 1854	105
48	William Stanley Jevons to Thomas Jevons 16 October 1854	107
49	William Stanley Jevons to Thomas Jevons 12 November 1854	108
50	William Stanley Jevons to Lucy Jevons [November or December 1854]	108
51	William Stanley Jevons to Henrietta Jevons 17 December 1854	109

Letter

52	William Stanley Jevons to Frederick B. Edmonds 26 January 1855	111
53	Thomas Jevons to William Stanley Jevons 31 January 1855	115
54	William Stanley Jevons to Edward Ward 31 January 1855	120
55	Henry Enfield Roscoe to William Stanley Jevons 12 March 1855	121
56	Thomas Jevons to William Stanley Jevons 18 March 1855	125
57	Thomas Jevons to William Stanley Jevons 1 April 1855	132
58	Thomas Jevons to William Stanley Jevons 18 April 1855	137
59	Thomas Jevons to William Stanley Jevons 3 May 1855	141
60	Thomas Jevons to William Stanley Jevons 9 May 1855	144
61	William Stanley Jevons to Lucy Jevons 28 May 1855	146
62	Thomas Jevons to William Stanley Jevons 3 June 1855	147
63	Thomas Jevons to William Stanley Jevons 17 June 1855	153
64	William Brown to Thomas Jevons 24 May 1855	157
65	William Stanley Jevons to Henrietta Jevons 1 July 1855	158
66	William Stanley Jevons to Henry Enfield Roscoe 11 July 1855	159
67	Thomas Jevons to William Stanley Jevons 14 July 1855	163
68	William Stanley Jevons to Thomas Jevons 16 July 1855	170
69	Thomas Jevons to William Stanley Jevons 1 August 1855	170
70	Thomas Jevons to William Stanley Jevons 26 August 1855	173

Letters

71	Thomas Jevons to Henrietta Jevons 2 September 1855	177
72	William Stanley Jevons to Henrietta Jevons 9 September 1855	179
73	Thomas Jevons to William Stanley Jevons 9 September 1855	183
74	Thomas Jevons to Herbert Jevons 25 September 1855	185
75	Henry Enfield Roscoe to William Stanley Jevons 15 October 1855	190
76	William Stanley Jevons to Thomas Jevons 29 October 1855	195
77	Thomas Jevons to William Stanley Jevons 29 October 1855	199
78	William Stanley Jevons to Herbert Jevons 29 November 1855	202
79	William Stanley Jevons to Herbert Jevons 17 December 1855	204
80	William Stanley Jevons to Thomas Jevons 18 January 1856	207
81	William Stanley Jevons to Lucy Jevons 14 February 1856	208
82	William Stanley Jevons to Henrietta Jevons 15 February 1856	212
83	William Stanley Jevons to Herbert Jevons 4 March 1856	215
84	William Stanley Jevons to Herbert Jevons 6 April 1856	218
85	William Stanley Jevons to Thomas Edwin Jevons 2 May 1856	221
86	William Stanley Jevons to Henrietta Jevons 3 May 1856	223
87	Henry Enfield Roscoe to William Stanley Jevons 10 May 1856	227
88	William Stanley Jevons to Herbert Jevons 20 May 1856	230
89	William Stanley Jevons to Herbert Jevons 4 July 1856	233

Letter

90	William Stanley Jevons to the *Sydney Morning Herald* 19 July 1856	235
91	William Stanley Jevons to Lucy Jevons 22 September 1856	237
92	William Stanley Jevons to Herbert Jevons 22 September 1856	238
93	William Stanley Jevons to Henrietta Jevons 1 October 1856	240
94	William Stanley Jevons to Henry Enfield Roscoe 21 October 1856	243
95	William Stanley Jevons to Lucy Jevons 1 January 1857	252
96	William Stanley Jevons to Henrietta Jevons 4 January 1857	255
97	William Stanley Jevons to Herbert Jevons 18 January 1857	259
98	William Stanley Jevons to the *Empire* [10 February 1857]	262
99	William Stanley Jevons to the *Empire* 25 February 1857	268
100	William Stanley Jevons to Herbert Jevons 9 March 1857	270
101	William Stanley Jevons to Henrietta Jevons 4 April 1857	274
102	William Stanley Jevons to the *Empire* 28 March 1857	281
103	William Stanley Jevons to the *Empire* 7 April 1857	282
104	William Stanley Jevons to Lucy Jevons 16 June 1857	288
105	William Stanley Jevons to Henrietta Jevons 17 June 1857	289
106	William Stanley Jevons to Thomas Edwin Jevons [July 1857]	292
107	William Stanley Jevons to Henrietta Jevons 16 July 1857	294
108	William Stanley Jevons to Lucy Jevons 23 August 1857	299

Contents xi

Letters

109	William Stanley Jevons to Henrietta Jevons 7 September 1857	302
110	Henry Enfield Roscoe to William Stanley Jevons 27 September 1857	304
111	William Stanley Jevons to Henrietta and Lucy Jevons 17 November 1857	306
112	William Stanley Jevons to Lucy Jevons 11 January 1858	309
113	William Stanley Jevons to Henrietta Jevons 24 January 1858	311
114	Henry Enfield Roscoe to William Stanley Jevons 1 February 1858	315
115	William Stanley Jevons to Henrietta Jevons 28 February 1858	317
116	Henry Enfield Roscoe to William Stanley Jevons 20 March 1858	322
117	William Stanley Jevons to Henrietta Jevons 9 June 1858	325
118	William Stanley Jevons to the *Sydney Magazine of Science and Art* 23 June 1858	329
119	William Stanley Jevons to Lucy Jevons 9 July 1858	331
120	William Stanley Jevons to Henrietta Jevons 4 August 1858	333
121	William Stanley Jevons to Lucy Jevons 10 September 1858	339
122	William Stanley Jevons to Henry Enfield Roscoe 9 October 1858	342
123	William Stanley Jevons to Lucy Jevons 14 October 1858	348
124	William Stanley Jevons to the *Sydney Morning Herald* [29 October 1858]	350
125	William Stanley Jevons to Lucy Jevons 8 November 1858	352
126	Henry Enfield Roscoe to William Stanley Jevons 14 November 1858	355
127	William Stanley Jevons to Lucy Jevons 9 December 1858	356

Letter

128	William Stanley Jevons to Henrietta Jevons 30 January 1859	358
129	William Stanley Jevons to Lucy Jevons February 1859	364
130	William Stanley Jevons to Lucy Jevons 13 March 1859	366
131	William Stanley Jevons to Lucy Jevons 9 April 1859	370
132	William Stanley Jevons to Lucy Jevons 29 May 1859	373
133	William Stanley Jevons to Henrietta Jevons 21 June 1859	377
134	William Stanley Jevons to Herbert Jevons 25 July 1859	381
135	William Stanley Jevons to Lucy Jevons 1 August 1859	383
136	William Stanley Jevons to Lucy Jevons 17 August 1859	384
137	William Stanley Jevons to Francis Boyer Miller 11 September 1859	385
138	William Stanley Jevons to Lucy Jevons 18 September 1859	388
139	William Stanley Jevons to Herbert Jevons 24 [September] 1859	388
140	William Stanley Jevons to Francis Boyer Miller 5 October 1859	393
141	William Stanley Jevons to Herbert Jevons 15 October 1859	403
142	William Stanley Jevons to Herbert Jevons 27 December 1859	403
143	William Stanley Jevons to Herbert Jevons 27 January 1860	404
144	William Stanley Jevons to Herbert Jevons 1 June 1860	409
145	William Stanley Jevons to Herbert Jevons 25 July 1860	412
146	Herbert Jevons to William Stanley Jevons 6 November 1860	418
147	William Stanley Jevons to Herbert Jevons 28 November 1860	421

Letter		
148	William Stanley Jevons to Lucy and Thomas Edwin Jevons 9 December 1860	422
149	Herbert Jevons to William Stanley Jevons 1 April 1861	423
150	William Stanley Jevons to Herbert Jevons 7 April 1861	425
151	William Stanley Jevons to Sir John F. W. Herschel 21 July 1861	432
152	William Stanley Jevons to Thomas Edwin Jevons 23 July 1861	433
153	Sir John F. W. Herschel to William Stanley Jevons 30 July 1861	433
154	William Stanley Jevons to Henrietta Jevons [September 1861]	434
155	William Stanley Jevons to Thomas Edwin Jevons [3 December 1861]	436
156	Francis James Roscoe to William Stanley Jevons 16 February 1862	438
157	William Stanley Jevons to Henrietta Jevons 3 March 1862	440
158	William Stanley Jevons to Herbert Jevons 3 July 1862	442
159	William Jevons Junior to William Stanley Jevons 14 July 1862	443
160	Williams Jevons Junior to William Stanley Jevons 17 July 1862	444
161	William Stanley Jevons to Herbert Jevons 17 August 1862	446
162	Timothy Jevons to William Stanley Jevons 18 August [1862]	448
163	William Stanley Jevons to Sir Anthony Panizzi 29 August 1862	449
164	William Stanley Jevons to Richard Holt Hutton 1 September 1862	450
165	William Stanley Jevons to Herbert Jevons 14 September 1862	451
166	William Jevons Junior to William Stanley Jevons 11 October 1862	456

Letter
167 William Stanley Jevons to Herbert Jevons   457
       18 November 1862
168 William Stanley Jevons to Thomas Edwin Jevons   460
       28 December 1862

A complete index to the Papers and Correspondence will be contained in Volume IV.

LIST OF PLATES

   William Stanley Jevons   *Frontispiece*
   From a photograph taken about 1851–2

1 Thomas Jevons   *facing page* 12

2 Melting House, Sydney Royal Mint: furnace for rough gold   13
   Photograph taken by Jevons, 25 February 1858

3 'Our cottage from the back' – the house at Double Bay, Sydney, in which Jevons lodged with Mr and Mrs F. B. Miller   13
   Photograph taken by Jevons in March 1858

4 William Stanley Jevons   44
   From a photograph taken in Australia in 1858

5 William Stanley Jevons   45
   From a photograph taken about 1861–2

PREFACE

In the early correspondence of Jevons published in this volume, personal letters predominate and the overwhelming majority of them are addressed to or from members of his immediate family. In selecting letters for publication from amongst the large volume of family papers made available to me by Mrs Könekamp, I have adhered to the criteria indicated in the Preface to Volume I – that only those letters which cast light on the development of Jevons's career or ideas, or on the public affairs of his time, should be included. Consequently a few extracts from letters giving purely personal or family details which Mrs Jevons included in *Letters and Journal* have not been reproduced here; references to those are included when necessary.

The core of the volume consists in the letters exchanged between Jevons and his family, but especially his father, Thomas Jevons, during the years 1854–9, when Jevons was Assayer to the Sydney Mint. Preceding this are the youthful letters of the schoolboy and undergraduate finding his feet in the London of the Great Exhibition. Following it are the letters of the still young, but now experienced and travelled, man who has made up his mind what he wants to do, but is still seeking the means by which to do it. The gradual, but eventually complete, shift of Jevons's interest from subjects such as chemistry and botany to the social sciences and logic can be clearly traced through this correspondence.

The text of the letters has been reproduced in a form which follows the original manuscript as closely as possible. Generally it has not been possible to give any details of the manner in which the letter was addressed unless these appear on the manuscript itself, since in the Jevons Papers the covers have not been kept with the letters except in a few instances.

A complete index to *Papers and Correspondence of William Stanley Jevons* will be included in Volume IV.

In the Preface to Volume I, I have already acknowledged some of the debts which I owe for help in the editorial process. In completing Volume II, the size of some of these debts has been greatly increased, and many new ones have been added. My Research Assistant, Mrs J. Wright, has given indispensable help throughout in searching for the many and wide-ranging references required in editing the letters. In identifying sources in the varied fields which interested the young Jevons, I have had much help from colleagues in other departments at

Queen's University – Mr R. E. Parker, of the Department of Botany, Dr C. Ehrlich and Dr L. A. Clarkson, Economic and Social History, Mr J. W. Herivel and Dr G. R. Talbot, History and Philosophy of Science, and Professor Raymond Warren, Department of Music.

I am also indebted for help in locating and identifying material to Dr G. R. Blainey, University of Melbourne, Australia, Mr P. R. Harris, Deputy Keeper of Printed Books, the British Museum, Mr Desmond Clarke, Librarian of the Royal Dublin Society, Dr F. E. Dixon of the Meteorological Service, Dublin, Mr R. G. Griffin, Librarian of the Chemical Society, London, Miss E. Talbot-Rice of the National Army Museum, London, Dr G. Chandler and Miss Janet Smith of the Liverpool Record Office, Mr Bernard A. Bernier, Jr., Reference Section, Serial Division, Library of Congress, Washington, D.C., Mr H. E. Gibbney, Research Officer of the Australian Dictionary of Biography, and Miss Suzanne Mourot of the Mitchell Library, Sydney, New South Wales. To all of these I am most grateful for their expert help which has always been freely and willingly given.

For permission to make use of manuscript material in their custody, my thanks are also due to the President and Council of the Royal Society and The Trustees of the Mitchell Library, Sydney.

R. D. COLLISON BLACK

Department of Economics,
Queens' University
Belfast
February 1972

LIST OF ABBREVIATIONS
used throughout the volumes

Relating to Jevons material

LJ	*Letters and Journal of W. Stanley Jevons,* edited by his wife (1886).
LJN	Previously published in LJ; manuscript not now in Jevons Papers, or other known location.
LJP	Previously published in LJ, but only in part; fuller text now given from the original manuscript in the Jevons Papers, or other indicated location.
WM	From a manuscript made available by Dr Wolfe Mays, University of Manchester.
Investigations	*Investigations in Currency and Finance,* by W. Stanley Jevons. Edited, with an Introduction, by H. S. Foxwell (1884). All page references to first edition.
Methods	*Methods of Social Reform and other papers,* by W. Stanley Jevons (1883).
T.P.E.	*The Theory of Political Economy* by W. Stanley Jevons (1st ed. 1871, 4th ed. 1911). All page references to fourth edition, unless otherwise stated.

Relating to other material

BM	British Museum, London.
FW	Fonds Walras, Bibliothèque Cantonale de Lausanne.
HLRS	Herschel Letters, Royal Society, London
JRSS	*Journal of the London* (later *Royal*) *Statistical Society.*
KCP	Palgrave Papers in the Library of King's College, Cambridge.
LSE	London School of Economics, British Library of Political and Economic Science.
MA	Archives of Macmillan & Co. Ltd.
NYPL	New York Public Library.
TLJM	Isabel Mills, *From Tinder Box to the 'Larger Light'. Threads from the Life of John Mills, Banker* (Manchester, 1899).
Walras Correspondence	*Correspondence of Léon Walras and Related Papers* edited by William Jaffé (3 vols, Amsterdam, 1965).

Figures following any of these abbreviations denote page numbers.

LETTERS

1. THOMAS JEVONS TO W. S. JEVONS
   [LJP, 9]

Liverpool 7 July 1849

My Dear Stanley

Although I have seen you since you wrote to me yet I must begin this letter to you by thanking you for your manly and excellent note to me. In it I see signs of ripening thought & judgment which gives me great joy. Your other notes to Lucy and the rest are also excellent and give us all pleasure to receive. In this visit[1] you are not only adding vigour to your bodily frame, but I feel satisfied that you are gaining manliness and gaining some little power over that natural timidity of character which is the worst or perhaps I may say almost the only weakness you have. A little more observation of the world, and a habit of looking closely into the origin of the fears that create the timidity or bashfulness which you occasionally display will help you wonderfully to get the better of it. When I have been some times in a low mood I have turned my thoughts to find out what has caused it, and on tracing my feelings from one cause to another I have almost invariably found the lowness of spirits to have no good cause and then immediately succeeds a cheerful self satisfied temper and feeling and I feel sure that if at times when you experience feelings of bashfulness or timidity to interfear[2] with your undertaking any duty if you will ask yourself in thought what occasions it and look through to the consequences of your actions you will at once dissolve the imaginary difficulty before you. As you walk forth before a fellow mortal your presence inspires a feeling of respect in those whom you approach or who approach you, that is *innate!* if you meet that encounter with a correct knowledge of your own deserts you at least keep up that respect in the person you accost, but an erect posture, an open countenance, and a general desire to give pleasure to the individual before you, will increase in him that respect for you which he cannot help at first feeling. If on the contrary you slacken all the nerves of your body, if you avert your eyes and hold down your head and think that somebody more than a fellow mortal is before you and that you are beneath & below the party you meet or if you judge wrongfully of the party believing that they would do you harm then you will lessen in him that very respect for you which as I have before said every mortal

[1] Jevons was staying with his Aunt Jane and her husband, the Rev. Francis Hornblower, at Nantwich.
[2] This is one of many idiosyncrasies of spelling which occur throughout the family correspondence, particularly in the letters of Thomas Jevons; all subsequent instances are denoted by an asterisk.

at first sight must feel towards every other mortal. I wish you to weigh well these thoughts and if you cannot understand some parts of what I have said ask me to explain more fully and it will give me the greatest pleasure to answer you.

This day comes off the great picnic party at Heswall.[3] More than 70 persons are to be there among whom are Lucy & Herbert. Up to this time the day is fine and I hope for their sakes it will continue. There is a fine breeze stirring and they went off in most excellent spirits.

Will you give my kindest love to Henny & Tommy and remember me affectionately and gratefully to your Uncle and Aunt to whom we are all indebted for innumerable acts of kindness which we ought ever to remember and which we can never repay

And believe me my very dear Son
Your most affectionate Father
Thos Jevons

Grandpapa continues pretty well.

2. HERBERT JEVONS TO THOMAS JEVONS

14 Torrington Sq:[1] 24 Sep 1850

Dearest Father

I hope this first letter home will be an earnest of all the following ones for as far as we have gone yet. I have nothing to recount but good news and satisfactory progress. Journey pleasant – Stanley already fixed in his new school with cash paid down – lodgings taken to be entered upon tomorrow, in the consumption of mutton chops – these are the chief things we have done as yet, but you will perhaps like to hear a few particulars of our journey &c. Two of our fellow passengers were I supposed coming home from a residence & travels in America. They seemed in high spirits, very noisy, & discussed the merits of America & the Americans.

We were not overcrowded, as very generally is the case, which made it much pleasanter for us. Thanks to Lucy's presents of a novel & Punch, for they were both very entertaining on the way.

We must have got in before half past seven for we had finished tea before eight having been previously welcomed to the square by Aunt H Harry & Harriet who were all very well & hearty, & glad to see us.

---

[3] This was probably held at the home of relatives since Jevons's aunt, Mrs Timothy Jevons, came from Heswall in Cheshire.

[1] The London home of Mrs Henry Roscoe, Jevons's 'Aunt Henry', mother of Henry Enfield Roscoe – then at University College – and his sister Harriet.

Stanley keeps very hearty & seems pleased, *very much* pleased with the first appearances of his school. I bore the journey a great deal better than I expected, & am pretty well today.

Yesterday Evening was passed in pleasant chat & so to bed, as Mr Pep's* his dairy has.

At about half past nine today I went with Stanley to the school and after waiting for about an hour I should think along with numerous other parties similarly situated, we had an interview with Mr Key[2] the head master. He seemed a very clever, practical, pleasant man, somewhat stoutish & very gentlemanly. Took down the particulars of Stanleys previous acquirements, with his age & health. He said he would he had little doubt be sufficiently advanced to begin *German*.[3]

We dined at Torrington sq: today with Harry, Aunt H & Harriet spending the day at Richmond[4] & sleeping there tonight. Stanley has done no work in the morning & I do not suppose will do any today, & very little for a day or two to come.

After leaving Stanley Harry & I called upon our little Landlady again and settled with her to begin weekly, and she is to receive us tomorrow with a four oclock dinner – You see I am very precise – it helps to fill up the letter, I hope to have more worth writing in my next. I think the lodgings will do very well & they cannot be called dear. The terms are

Lodging with (dinners at home cooking only) & waiting	0.	15.	0
Boots 6d ea: per week	0.	1.	0
Coals 4d per day	0.	2.	4
We shall also have to pay for washing the linen, which she estimates at 1/n, & will be inclusive of our other washing	0.	1.	0
	0.	19.	4

So it will be at the rate of £50. 5. 4 per annum. We shall have a nice little sofa, & can make use of the other part of the drawing room anytime as she will only use it herself and will be principally in the kitchen.

Stanley's *Top Coat* is the only thing forgotten. It will go in the large

---

[2] Thomas Hewitt Key (1799–1875), headmaster of University College School, 1842–75, and concurrently first Professor of Comparative Grammar, University College, London.

[3] Jevons studied German for a year at University College School and later in Australia (see below, Letters 86, p. 225, and 94, p. 251). It would appear, however, that he never became proficient in the language. See Vol. III, Letter 423.

[4] At the home of Jevons's uncle, Dr Richard Roscoe.

Tin box, the key of which I enclose, as the Portmanteau is pretty well stuffed already. Can you in your next letter send back the key & also the duplicate Lucy has of my portmanteau – and the sooner you can send us our other luggage the better. Please do not let them be delayed in coming.

Lucy & I fixed before our leaving that Stanley write one week & I write the other so that you would hear from us every week. Do you like that arrangement? Stanley intends I think to write to day. I will write again next Sunday & then on Monday week Stanley writing on the intervening Wednesday.

You of course will write whenever you have time & inclination. I need not add how much the letters will be valued. I hope Lucy will not be afraid of writing too often. Once a day would not be too much, for if our tables & chimney piece became inconveniently full, waste paper is useful as we shall have no newspapers. Tell her not to spare when inclined to give her pen exercise.

Uncle Dick[5] wishes us to dine with him next Saturday – & Laura's[6] best love was awaiting me here. Today is a very dull day indeed with a thick yellow fog hanging over the city. With best love to each individual member of the now small circle at home, & hoping our absence will not for long affect its usual cheerfulness, I remain ever

Your very affectionate Son
Herbert Jevons.

P.S. Please thank Uncle William[7] for being so kind as to write to me about these lodgings, you can tell him how to all probability, we shall be very comfortably settled.

Our direction is

23 Harrington St
Hampstead Rd

Our Landlady M^{rs} McLellan.

Stanley will write tomorrow as he is going a walk with us this afternoon.

3. THOMAS JEVONS TO W. S. JEVONS

Lpool 28 Oct 1850

My Dear Stanley

I have not forgotten you in the several notes I have despatched for 23 Harrington St[1] but now I think you claim a separate note not how-

---

[5] Dr Richard Roscoe.
[6] Jevons's cousin Laura Roscoe, known as 'Poppy', daughter of Robert Roscoe of Englefield Green. See below, Letter 59, p. 141.   [7] William Jevons Junior (1794–1873).
[1] See Vol. I, p. 115.

ever from my having any answer to give to any letter received from you for you have not addressed one letter to me yet but your claim rests on my unalterable love for you and my desire to do and say what may be for your present happiness and your future welfare. That you are applying all your mind & energy to your studies I gather from hints thrown out in other peoples communications. I never doubted your doing that, but I am pleased indeed to think that you are shewing* other manly qualities, and that your character seems as if it would be really & truly drawn[2] out by contact with so many strangers As to your resolution to carry away some of the prizes at your College School let me warn you that you will have competitors of a very different class to those you have seen before. You will have many as highly qualified as yourself opposed to you and who may perhaps have equal energy and more health I would therefore strongly advise you to weigh well the course you resolve upon. Dont by no means try too much. If you attempt too much you will fail in all. You may safely keep your decision open for awhile but not too long and when you are competent to decide which of the prizes you have the best chance for then drop the others I dont say that you may not try for more than one but I warn you against trying for too many I know nothing of the different branches of education you are studying and am only reasoning with you as a general topic of prudence, but if you require aid to make any decision and Herberts advice wants confirmation by all means write down all you have to say on the subject pro & con and then I shall be able to give you an opinion on your particular case –

We are going on all well at home except that we miss the organ very much[3] Henny makes up as well as she can on the Piano and it is quite surprizing how well she reads music off She can play almost any ordinary piece at sight I am perfectly astonished at it in so young a creature. Tommy gets a little spoiled now being the only lad at home and the youngest son into the bargain I am in the fault always they say but I think others pet him nearly if not quite so much as me

Do you know that one of our greatest privations is not hearing from you or Herbert oftener I think each of you might write once a week and then we should have two letters every week In which case we should know better how you are coming on

I was a little dissapointed* when Herbert told me that he had paid away more than half the last £5 note away [sic] the first payment to

---

[2] 'draw' in the original manuscript.

[3] When Thomas Jevons's father, William Jevons, gave up his house in Park Hill Road, Liverpool, in 1848 and moved in with his son into No. 125, Chatham Street 'he brought with him an organ, on which Stanley used to play a great deal; and he did it well enough to give much pleasure to his grandfather and father, who were both very fond of music, although unable to play any instrument themselves'. (LJ, p. 8.)

M^{rs} McCelland* and that what was left would not pay your next fortnight bill but I suppose at first you have a few more expenses incident to a new Lodgings I therefore enclose the half of a tenpound note ^F_R 2500T dated London 4 Sep 1850 and when you inform me that you have received this then I will enclose the other half but not till then for its quite as well to be perfectly safe in sending cash by post

I am snatching a few moments from business to send you these lines and that must be my apology for writing so fast but as you are a scholar no doubt you can read any writing that is not above 5000 year old and trusting that you can find out my affection for you through every line I remain with love to Herbert also

Ever Yours
Thos Jevons

4. HERBERT JEVONS TO THOMAS JEVONS

London Wednesday Nov 13. 50

My dearest Father

This is the third day, that Prof- Graham has disappointed us by not lecturing,[1] so I have come home to write this note to you with more pleasure than I have done for some time, because I can give you a more cheering account of our doings. I am decidedly better myself & in good spirits. The change we are going to make is both what I like & what will be the very best I could have in all respects.

There are two things in Stanley's change which are not settled. They are the choosing a place for him to live which we could like in every way, & the other whether Stanley will be able to accustom himself to a mode of life so different from what he has been accustomed to before. There is no fear I think that he will like it very much & it will be a great deal better for him than being in lodgings only with me. The way in which we live here at present only fosters his diffident & reserved habits, and he is accordingly quite comfortable and content, except when we go out to any of our friends, which has been but seldom, when he grumbles about it till the visit is over, & which is not very agreeable for me. I will see Aunt Henry & ask her if she could recommend any place for Stanley, & do what I can to find out a place in other ways.

Yesterday as you know I went to Richmond & drank tea with them, there being Mrs Ferniow an old maid there who is a lodger. Uncle Richard had a cold & cough. He offered to take me in for six months

---

[1] See Vol. I, pp. 10 and 115, n. 7.

or so, & as he says "make a man of me", which of course I joyfully agreed to, & you will hear from Aunt Richard[2] about it.

Though there is no need for any hurry in the change yet the sooner done the better I should say, as the fine pure air & cheerful society at Richmond with the Railroad travelling daily will I am confident make quite a different fellow of me in a few days.

Stanley is all right as he will have told you himself. He intends today to visit both the British Museum & National Gallery, as it is his half-holiday. At last we have been to Engle Field Green.

The visit to me was so delightful increased by the beautiful weather, that it was too much for me, and though it did me a great deal of good, yet afterwards I felt exhausted with it.

Talking all day is no joke, except to such as Aunt Jane[3] or Mrs Richard.

We took an omnibus from Staines Station on Sat: night and after engaging a bed, and dispatching a good tea at the Barley Mow, spent the rest of the evening with our cousins. On Sunday we had a hearty breakfast by ourselves again, went to the little chapel in the Park in the morning and were not at home till past eleven oclock, that being partly the fault of the train which came in to Waterloo an hour and a half & more, later than it should have done. How very unfortunate Lucy has been. If I could help her to recover her brooches again I would do my best, but can unfortunately only hope they will turn up at last.

Those that I lost at Bonn were not of much value, but I felt sufficiently mortified then. With very best love to Grandpapa Lucy & all the rest I remain
Your affec Son
Herb^t Jevons.

I shall write again before long, when I have anything to tell you.

---

[2] Mary Ann Hodgson, formerly Bardswell (1801–88), a second cousin of Dr Richard Roscoe, whom she married as her second husband in 1849. In an unpublished letter of 8 November 1850 Herbert commented to his father: '. . . Mrs Richard is of course as usual cheerful & talkative, & vehemently but sincerely expresses her great desire to do anything in her power for us on account of her friendship with mama. . . .' See also below, Letter 24, n. 5, p. 44.

[3] See Vol. I, pp. 59, 88 and 92.

5. THOMAS JEVONS TO W. S. JEVONS
[LJP, 11]

Chatham S^t 19 Nov
1850

My Dearest Stanley

Lucy has gone to a party at the Dawsons a new acquaintance.[1] The young ones & Grandpapa are gone to bed. I am sitting up and being tired of reading a thought has struck me that I might write to you who richly deserve a letter in return for the many nice ones you have sent us home You took quite a wonderful walk on Sunday It must have been at least 12 miles and the sightseeing all the way was quite as tiring as if you had gone 3 miles further When you were at the farther point viz the Thames Tunnel I wonder it did not strike you to take boat and go up right away under all the Bridges until you got to Westminster Bridge where you might have landed and pursued your way afterwards with less fatigue and more zest You have not given us much of the impressions which the sight of each object made upon you Temple Bar, Bow Church are famed in the history of the great City Then you must have gone through Paternoster Row where many a trembling author has dragged his weary footsteps in search of fame and his daily bread without success The Centre of the world Exchange could only have charms for you in the way of Architecture and the Great Bank of England also But one would have thought that the Mansion House famed for Turtle and venison and wine & wassaile* would at least have attracted some attention But all this seems to have passed by you like a panorama and, probably the greatest wonder of them all, the Thames Tunnel even has not drawn from you one expression of wonder. The impression however has been made and let one hope dear Stanley that at no very distant days the glories of that walk will shine out in a more worthy manner than any such crude account as present opportunity would afford you for giving us the moral of your perigrination*

I am delighted to think that you look so philosophically at the prospect of a change of your residence, but I fear that you will not find the new place quite so agreeable If you go to any of the masters there will be a good deal of surveillance over you and no Sunday walks like that you have just taken But as the change is necessary on Herberts account we must not repine I shall have hard work to raise the money to pay for you for instead of about £130 a year for you both I fear it will take

---

[1] Presumably the family of John Dawson, a Liverpool merchant. A pedigree of this family is among Jevons's notes on the Jevons Family History. One of John Dawson's daughters, Catherine, married Jevons's cousin Arthur Jevons, third son of Timothy Jevons, on 18 September 1856. See Vol. III, Letter 247.

at least £250 Tell Herbert that his Aunt Rich^d has consented to allow half the cost of the railway going backwards and forwards to Richmond When the time comes for his going to Richmond he must take out a Ticket Mrs Richard says for a year but perhaps it would be better to take a ticket for a shorter period for perhaps he might not agree so long as a year or a thousand things might happen to interrupt the affair in that time

I have asked Uncle Rich^d to enquire about proper place for you and Aunt Henry will do the same and Lucy has written to Miss Taylor[2] and surely among them all we shall hear of something suitable before long.

I had the expectation that I might have come up to Town this week but instead of that two of our London Firm came down to Lpool without notice on Monday and that has prevented me but I think I shall be able to make an excuse for a journey before the end of next week Still I am not altogether my own master[3] and cannot absolutely controle* my own time as is witnessed by the occurrence I have mentioned of the parties coming down from London instead of me going up – All I can say both to you & to Herbert is that you must have patience but be silently on the lookout in the meanwhile and as soon as I can come with effect I will try to combine my own with my employers business so as to make the expense lighter –

Looking at Herberts P S to your note[4] I find he has been to see a M^r or Mrs Dikins board & lodgings but he does not say what the *charge is* Herbert had better call again & ask the terms and also Mr Cases terms. If they ask as much as *£100* a year I cannot afford it but I will say no more on this head tonight.

So you have seen the Palace of Glass What a wonderful structure it will be when completed Who but Paxton could ever have thought of covering over in a green house Large and Lofty and old Elm Trees and yet this will be done. Paxton read a paper at the Society of Arts containing the history of the invention so to say. It is 20 or 30 years since he first began to study the construction of glass houses. He made one improvement after another until some few years ago he put up the great Concervatory* at Chatsworth At the time that was first erected it was thought a most extraordinary erection of the sort but it is a pigmy to this Crystal Palace. Nevertheless the principle of construction is exactly the same and he had only to stretch his mind so as to make his conception of extent equal the necessity of the occasion and behold what he has

---

[2] Miss Emily Taylor (1795–1872) the writer, who had been a close friend of Jevons's mother. See Vol. I, p. 6.

[3] A reference to Thomas Jevons's employment as the Liverpool agent of John Guest & Co.

[4] This letter does not appear to have survived. The manuscripts of only two of the letters Jevons wrote to his father are among the Jevons Papers. A further manuscript is in the Mitchell Library, Sydney. See below, Letter 76, p. 195.

done⁵ Already there are numerous packages of things arrived for the exhibition. A large quantity from Prussia have arrived in London and some from Russia and the American Government have appointed a large Man of War Frigate to bring over the American articles and they may be expected before long⁶

I am glad to see the first report of your character & progress and standing in your school It is a very good one but only what I expected from you Go on in that good way and you will secure the reward of all good men happiness both here and in an eternity to come

I hear Lucy's car at the door so must conclude Love and every blessing attend you both from

Your aff^{te} Father
Thos Jevons

P.S. Lucy says that she has not written to Miss Taylor When you next go to Hyde Park buy & send me some of the penny pictures of the Palace of Glass.

6. HERBERT JEVONS TO THOMAS JEVONS

London Thursday Nov 21st [1850]

Dearest Father

As yet your beautiful letter has only pleased Stanley by its exterior, whose smiles & gladdened countenance gave evident tokens that it was a true pleasure to him to see your hand writing.

---

⁵ Sir Joseph Paxton (1801–65), gardener and architect. In 1826 he became head gardener at Chatsworth, beginning a long association and friendship with the Duke of Devonshire. In the years 1832–6 he superintended the erection of a greenhouse, orchid house and arboretum at Chatsworth and from 1836–40, the Great Conservatory, followed in 1850 by the Lily House.

His design for a building to house the Great Industrial Exhibition of 1851 was accepted by the Royal Commission after more than 200 others had been rejected. Its most decisive feature was the fact that it was not a permanent structure and thus would not necessitate the destruction of the Hyde Park site. The 'Palace of Glass' captured the public imagination. It was one of the earliest and most famous examples of the use of standardised building techniques and was erected with a speed that amazed contemporaries, taking only seven months. It was not in fact Paxton's idea to include trees within the building. His original design was enlarged to include a transept and as this created siting difficulties the building committee suggested altering the ground plan to bring the trees within the transept, for which Paxton then designed a circular roof, similar to that of the Great Conservatory at Chatsworth. See C. R. Fay, *Palace of Industry 1851* (Cambridge, 1951), pp. 11–17.

⁶ Liberal newspapers, which supported the Exhibition, kept the public informed of the progress of preparations and of the arrival of exhibits from abroad.

Prussian goods were exhibited with those of other states in the Zollverein and included a wide range of manufactures. Most of the exhibits from Russia were delayed by frozen waters *en route*, so that the Russian Section was virtually empty when the Exhibition was opened by the Queen on 1 May 1851. The American exhibits ranged from Colt's revolver and McCormick's reaper to trays of gold from California and an Indian bark canoe. Cf. *The Art Journal Illustrated Catalogue of the Industry of all Nations, 1851*.

PLATE 1   Thomas Jevons

PLATE 2 Melting House, Sydney Royal Mint: furnace for rough gold
Photograph taken by W. S. Jevons, 25 February 1858

PLATE 3 'Our cottage from the back' – the house at Double Bay, Sydney, in which Jevons lodged with Mr and Mrs F. B. Miller
Photograph taken by W. S. Jevons in March 1858

He was just going out to school & not being practised in reading handwriting gave me the letter to read till he came home.

Though any praise of mine on your letter is needless, if not out of place, yet you will not mind my praising the beautiful and impressive manner in which you mention the wonderful sights of London. It will not fail I am sure to make both him & me to desire more profit & pleasure from those sights than before we had done. I should be sorry to be undeceived from the opinion that Stanley observes & stores up in his mind more than what he at present shows. I wish it was more generally known that it is not merely the sightseeing but the spirit in which they are viewed & the power of mind & observation which one exerted besides, that are necessary to give any lasting pleasure & satisfaction.

I find myself however getting into my old habit of philosophysing,* which I have of late overcome.

Prof: Graham has been unwell for a few days & unable to continue his lectures, which I did not like atal*. He began again on Tuesday, & the students took the liberty of showing their pleasure by all stamping their feet. I continue to be quite as much delighted with them, rather more, for I have the additional satisfaction of feeling I am really gaining a little knowledge, a few drops in the ocean of science, I am getting poetical you see. The most disheartening thing in the attainment of Chemistry to me now is the rapid progress in discoveries new theories, new methods, which makes me feel as if I could never get up to it; only feel for I am the same as others & see no reason why I should not get in as quick as they do.

2. P.M. I have just this minute come in, & think I have found a place which will suit Stanley very well. Perhaps the whole round of my peregrinations may interest you a little. I first went to my lecture on Oxygen, which is the 3rd hour nearly that he has occupied on that element alone. I then went to call on Miss Emily Taylor, & saw her for the first time. She was very glad to see me, and our conversation turned altogether on our prospects & views, as they do too much with me. I saw Mrs Martineau,[1] I think, her sister a minute or two, before leaving who asked about Lucy with evident interest. Miss Taylor told me of two places for Stanley Mrs Mackenzie's & a surgeon Dr Bird. I need not tell you any particulars about Dr Bird, merely that Stanley would be a lodger there, & is not old enough for that. I believe Mrs Mackenzie will suit in every respect & the information I have already got puts me in good spirits concerning Stanley whom I have been rather anxious about.

[1] This is probably a reference to Mrs James Martineau who was not in fact a sister of Miss Emily Taylor, having been formerly Helen Higginson of Liverpool. Cf. Vol. I, p. 60, n. 3.

After leaving Miss Taylor I went to call on Aunt Henry, where I met Uncle Richard. Aunt H. who knows Mrs M. went with me to call on her, but she was out & we spoke with the Housekeeper. Aunt Henry thinks it will do & does not see any cause to make an agreement directly. She left word for Mrs M. to call on her this afternoon to talk over it with her, & she wishes you to write to her by return of post after getting this letter to give her orders whether to settle with Mrs M. or not or what to do.

All I know of her at present is that she is the sister of Mrs Egerton Smith, & Miss Wood of Liverpool, was formally a governess at Mrs Cromptons,[2] knows Aunt Henry, who speaks very highly of her. There is a matronly housekeeper, apparently a nice old body. She has at present 3 boys living with her, ages 13 14 & 15. The eldest is a son of Mr Ogden, who himself or relation is the Psalm tune Ogden.[3] He works very hard at his lessons, is next session going to college to study for the law. I fancy one of the Liverpool Boltons[4] is another of the boys. They have a tutor to help them in their lessons every evening. She lives close to the College in Gower St. The terms 60 guineas everything included tutor and all, I think. Do not depend too much on this. I do not know whether Aunt H. will write to you today or atal*, but she will see Mrs Mackenzie & then be sure of all particulars I will see her before post tomorrow & write to you again with more particulars.

If arrangements can be made I do not see why we should not leave here this day week, ie if you settle to put Stanley with Mrs Mackenzie.

I have given M^{rs} McLellan notice so that any Wednesday in future we can leave here. Have you agreed fully with Aunt Richard? I suppose you have settled all that.

If you think our plans hasty & wish things to remain till you come up yourself say so & we will make ourselves comfortable where we are. Of course I am anxious to get to Richmond & will tell you what I think of the change & why I wish it so much.

Lucy will acknowledge to you that before we came here, I felt having Stanley with me in lodgings with his reserved & timid disposition a responsibility.

[2] Mrs Henry Roscoe's sister Caroline (formerly Fletcher) wife of Mr Justice Crompton. Cf. Jevons's remarks in Letter 15, p. 31.

[3] Thomas Bolton Ogden, a pupil at University College School, 1846–51 (see *Register* for 1831–91 by Temple Orme). His father Jonathan Robert Ogden (1806–82) was a composer who had studied in London, Paris and Munich. When James Martineau was compiling his *Hymns for the Christian Church and Home* (1840) he had invited Ogden – who had received part of his education from Rev. Joseph Hutton, father of Richard and John, and who had become a Unitarian – to supply tunes of unusual metre. The result was *Holy Songs and Musical Prayers* (1842) which incurred considerable criticism as it included adaptations as hymn tunes of pieces by Beethoven and other composers.

[4] See Vol. I, p. 100, n. 1.

I believe I exagerate* the responsibility he involves on me, but that is owing to my weak health I believe.

I think he is not at present situated atal* favourably to bring out into action many habits which to him are of the greatest importance. He is timid & reserved & not social, & the manner in which we at present live is only calculated to increase these. He is at present not put out with encountering new faces, seldom interfered with in his daily routine of duties. This solitary bachelor way, is pleasing to him for it gives him no occasion to battle with those failings which will be the chief temptations & struggles of his life, & as his present way of living is but fostering these habits, it will but increase his reserve.[5] There is another thing which I hope will not give you much pain when I say it. It is this. I am his elder brother. He is influenced more or less by living & being so much with me. Now for his sake I am not an example or stay for him. My illness has made me changeable & fretful. I hope you will not think what I have said, is not in my place. I do not know whether you have heretofore weighed these[6] things, & think otherwise. But I shall feel more easy after having laid before you my thoughts openly. As far as you think me then capable of being the only guardian of Stanley, I hope, I shall do all in my power to have a good influence upon him. To do anything towards strengthening & developing Stanleys moral habits would give me the truest happiness.

Perhaps you are thinking my thoughts far fetched & imaginary, & are saying to me in your mind. "Dont trouble yourself about Stanley – he will do very well – if you will leave him to himself".

This is one reason. Another is that though I believe myself much better & hope soon to be comparatively well again, yet at present any change which I thought would relieve me & do me good makes me feel in a hurry to make it. I shall never forget a remark you once made, that when a person is ill in pain he thinks of little else if anything else than a means to gain present comfort, & I can tell you the greatest temptations I have had have been in foregoing means to present comfort & ease from a fear that I was increasing the cause. I do not understand the few words you put in about your arrangements with Aunt Richard. First of all what does she mean, by telling me I had better get an '*annual* ticket for the Railway'. How long do you & she think I shall stay there? I cannot get there before next Wednesday. I have no lectures from the 21st Dec to 8th Jan. From 8th Jan I may continue, if I choose to finish the Chemical sessional course, which other things agreeing I should like very much to do till the 15 April after which I shall have no lectures again till next session in October,[7] if I ought to look forward.

---

[5] See Vol. I, pp. 100 and 131; also below, Letter 93, p. 240.
[6] 'this' in the original manuscript.

I did not think of staying longer than 15 April at longest with Uncle R. for I might return home, then till next session if well enough & in the meantime able to prepare for Matriculating I should like in the beginning of July to matriculate in which case I might fix to live somewhere at the time.

My best plan I should think for Railway tickets would be to subscribe a quarter from 8th Jan to 15 April & pay daily from now till 21st Dec. But when I have the prices we would easily settle which would be cheaper & of course fix that plan.[8]

We shall be at home again in little more than a month, which makes one think of the old man with his sycle.*

What will you think of me when I have to tell you I have not quite enough Cash left to settle this last weeks account. It certainly seems to have disappeared too quickly, but our journey to Engle Field & bed tea & breakfast there, my stay & daily journey at Richmond & other occasional visits there, Port wine, medically ordered, & some medicine which is rather dear, *spectacles* also, will account for a good deal. If we leave so soon I shall of course require some more money.

Aunt Jane in writing to me sent me a most cheering account of Roscoe, & Lucy, too, whose good hopes & opinion I am very glad to receive. I am also glad you have agreed to give only every other Sunday morning to Roscoe.

Whether Roscoe recovers or not you will not indeed have reason to repent your unwearied perseverance in visiting & cheering him up. A fortnightly visit is quite enough tax upon you dearest Father. With love to all, & kind remembrances to Anne & Martha,[9] I remain till next letter tomorrow

Yours &c H.t J.

7. HERBERT JEVONS TO THOMAS JEVONS

London Friday Eving Nov 22 [1850]

Dearest Father

I did not see Aunt Henry soon enough to write to you what she had learned from Mrs Mackenzie by this evening's post, as I intended to do but will post this tomorrow morning. As I wrote you a long letter yesterday I will only write you today what Aunt H & Stanley have

---

[7] See Vol. I, p. 54, n. 1.

[8] He then wrote, 'I often wish I could in any degree return all your forbearance for me and advantages you are giving me' but crossed it out.

[9] Presumably Anne Bolton and another of the family's servants.

together told me. Mʳˢ Mackenzie being out when I & Aunt H. called on her yesterday Mʳˢ M. called in the afternoon on Aunt H. when Uncle R. happened to be there & they had quite a long talk over the matter.

The substance of it is this. You will see by the circular that her charge is 68 guineas, the housekeeper making a mistake. She is wishing to have young lady boarders, when she can get any, when she would give up taking any boys atal,* but not being as yet successful in that she has been obliged to continue keeping boys. She will therefore take Stanley any day and at present to pay weekly or at any rate lodge weekly. She will give due notice if she is going to give up keeping boys so that we should have time to look out for another place if that were to happen.

Mʳˢ Mackenzie is in all respects a most suitable person, and would be as a mother to the boys. She has two young ladies who live there also one a niece of hers. They live all together, getting meals together. There is also a young man, some relation of hers I believe living there who is an engineer. The tutor helps them every evening in their lessons. Stanley would have to keep to the rules laid down for the other boys, which I dont know, but I have reason to think they would not be so strict or particular as Mʳ Case's or boarding schools in general.

I do not know if she has any rules except such as not going out without asking before hand &c. They all dine at 5 p.m. & have some lunch in the middle of the day.

The 3 boys are the only objections that Aunt H. sees, or that I can see either. Ogden the eldest was expelled from Cases for telling a lie they say & then Mʳˢ Mackenzie took him in, being aware that he was rather unruly and wild. She says he is working very hard at his lessons now, as he is going to College when Stanley will go. The next boy is Bolton, brother to the renowned Boltons of Liverpool, & is not liked by the other boys or Stanley atal.* Pusey the youngest is an ignorant little dwarf Stanley informs me.

From what I hear of Ogden, I should not think there could be anything vicious in him.

As far as you like to take Aunt H's judgement she gives it decidedly for Mʳˢ Mackenzie.

Of the others *Cases* is expensive & boarding school like, & Stanley would not like that. Dʳ *Bird*'s the surgeon merely lets his rooms for lodgers & Stanley would be obliged to manage his affairs entirely himself.

There is also another female who takes the boys of the U.C.S. into her house, & I do not know anything about her. Mʳˢ M. is known by our set of acquaintance so well however & is by accounts such a nice lady herself, that it would be unreasonable to think this other person would be equal to her, as neither Aunt H. or Miss Taylor seem to be aware of her being there.

If you think proper to fix upon Mrs M. without seeing her yourself – if you have agreed everything with Aunt Richard – if you send me a fresh remittance & give me orders to move Stanley & myself to our new quarters – we can manage everything very easily & you will not then have the trouble or inconvenience of coming up yourself.

You see I have grown business like. I shall wait anxiously for your answer, for I shall be very glad to get to Richmond. Nevertheless I continue stronger & better.

I went to see the new Nineveh sculptures[1] today & before. They are beautifully carved, & have quite a grand effect. The faces are very mild & amiable. You must not miss seeing them next time you come up here. Today Mr Graham showed us a light which was seen 69 sixty nine miles off by means of a reflector once, when a Lieutenant Drummond[2] was land surveying. It was caused by a flame of oxygen & Hydrogen called the oxi-hydrogen blowpipe, directed against lime, & though from the absence of solid matter in the original flame it was scarcely luminous yet when lime was put in its way it heated it to such an extent as to cause a light more resembling that of the sun than any other ordinary light. The Voltaic light closely resembles it also. The lectures are now full of experiments. He melted a number of metals in the flame such as iron steel copper *Platinum*[3] which stands the heat of a furnace, &c &c. He sent up a small baloon.* With love to all, Lucy in particular, believe me ever

                        Your devoted son
                        Herbert Jevons.

P.S. Stanley wishes me to add, that he does not like my being in such a hurry & settling & changing without your coming up & seeing Mrs M. & settling him there or some other place yourself.

[1] Two bas-reliefs – a winged human-headed lion and a winged human-headed bull – brought to England by Mr (later Sir) Austen Henry Layard (1817–94) from his excavations at the Palace of Nimrud in the ancient city of Nineveh and exhibited at the British Museum.

[2] Thomas Drummond (1797–1840). He entered the Royal Engineers in 1815 and in 1820 joined the work of ordnance survey undertaken by the regiment. Murky weather was one of the greatest difficulties encountered in surveying and led him to invent a limelight, later called the 'Drummond light', which caused a sensation in scientific circles. The incident to which Thomas Graham apparently referred occurred during the survey of Ireland, begun in 1824–5. In the autumn of 1825 two months were spent in unsuccessful attempts to make observations between Divis Mountain, near Belfast, and Slieve Snaght, the highest hill on Inishowen, Donegal, 67 miles away. In October of that year the 'Drummond light' was used with success. In 1829 Drummond was engaged in adapting the limelight for use in lighthouses. It was described as vivid, conspicuous and exquisitely white.

[3] Platinum was prized at this period for use in making laboratory utensils as it was resistant to temperatures produced by the furnaces then available.

8. HERBERT JEVONS TO THOMAS JEVONS

London Saturday Nov 23
[1850]

Dearest Father

This is the third day I shall have written to you in succession. You will not I am sure think that too seldom.

First I have to acknowledge receipt of the two halves of the 5£ notes & send thanks for them also.

The next point is this. I have come to the determination not to change our places or remove atal,* or do anything more until you after receiving this give your decided commands to me to do anything.

The reason is this that Stanley does not like any of the three boys who would be his constant companions, and does not atal* like the prospect of being thrown so much into their company & is in fact uncomfortable about it. He admits that as far as he can judge everything else is perhaps the best that could happen.

I do not know the boys myself & cannot tell you anything of them. I have urged Stanley to write to you himself & tell you what he thinks of them & how he feels himself about the changing altogether, but he says he has nothing to say, but that they are *nasty boys*, boys with tastes & pursuits not congenial with Stanleys.[1] He has no fear that they will lead him into any wrong or vice of any kind. Mrs M. thought it proper to inform Aunt H that Ogden had been expelled from Mr Cases for telling a lie and had taken him in being aware that he was wild & unruly.

There is another thing Stanley is getting timid & finds it rather difficult to bear the idea of living among strangers & under their control altogether, & he naturally feels that to him it would be much more comfortable if the change were left for a week or so until you could come up & see Mrs M. yourself and judge better on it & other places. It is too very natural for him to feel this, and I have set his mind at ease, and told him you would not wish me to proceed any further if you knew he did not like the boys.

We shall therefore stay here until you tell me what to do.

There is not any need for your coming in the changing or making the agreement. As Stanley has been so happy & contented till now, with lodging here with me, if he were not to be happy with Mrs M. my going to Richmond would be partly the occasion of it, so that anything I can do to obviate such chances it is my duty & desire to do, though I think it will be far the best for both of us at present to have the change, – one as much as the other.

[1] See Vol. I, p. 100, n. 1.

Do not let my desire to get to Richmond make you do any different to what you would otherwise do, for it would be odd if I could not wait a few days for that reason. Believe me ever
                    Your very affec Son
                        Herbert Jevons

9. W. S. JEVONS TO THOMAS JEVONS

                                        London
                                        Dec^{er} 11th
                                        1850.[1]

Dearest Papa

I rec. your letter this morning and am now going to tell you, as well as I can about all I have been doing. . . . I got over my visit to M^r. Yates[2] very well, but you will perhaps be a little disappointed to hear that his wife and daughters were away from home, in Scotland or Ireland I believe, so that there were only Mr Yates, ourselves & D. Sadler[3] who preaches at Portland Street Chapel in the evening & his wife to dinner We did scarcely anything but read newspapers, and journals, of which there were plenty – M^r. Yates is a very pleasant gentleman & his house is beautifully furnished. . . . You want me to tell you something about my companions but it is not very easy to tell exactly what I think of them – O. ———[4] is certainly disagreeable and rather bad tempered & I do not know how Annette & M^r. ———s' niece can live near him. He likes teazing B———[5] and P———[6] and making them do as he likes rather, but he has always behaved very well to me – There are one or two things that he pays attention to as chemistry, but generally he does not learn them well but gets M^r B to tell them him and correct his exercises the last of which is very unfair – He is thinking a great deal about the Christmas holidays & his skatings now & says he is going to work hard next term – B——— is the next in age – he is sometimes very disagreeable & plays tricks but as a whole is far the better He is learning the Violin, but never plays more than two hours a week. . . . It has been very foggy here lately and one afternoon it grew so dark that we could not see to read our books in School and strange to say they have no

---

[1] The original manuscript of this letter is not among the Jevons Papers. This extract was copied by Mrs Lucy Hutton into a series of notes entitled 'Recollections of my brother'.

[2] Cf. below, Letter 11, n. 5, p. 24.

[3] Probably Thomas Sadler (1822–91), son of Thomas Sadler, Unitarian Minister of Horsham, Sussex; educated at University College, London; Ph.D. Erlangen, 1844; Unitarian Minister at Hackney, 1845; Minister of Rosslyn Hill Chapel, Hampstead, 1846 until his death; senior trustee of Dr Williams's Library.

[4] Ogden.   [5] Bolton   [6] Pusey.

way of lighting the School I am going on very well at School since my last report —⁷...

I remain y^r lov dutiful Son
W. S Jevons

P.S. I forgot to tell you that M^r. Yates sent his 'respects' or regards or something of that sort to you.

10. HERBERT JEVONS TO THOMAS JEVONS

Twickenham Saturday Jan 18 [1851]

My dearest Father

I have acted very wrong & thoughtless in causing you & Lucy such anxiety, as you could not but have felt at my long silence. My only excuse for it is the debility & weakness I have until lately felt which has made me feel averse to doing anything. But I do not mean to try to excuse myself for I have done wrong & ask you to forget it this time as I think I can promise you it will be the last.

I have little doubt that the dampness & relaxed state of the atmosphere which we have had now for so long a time has done a great deal towards weakening me; however that is of no consequence as it seems to have spent itself & my weakness also for I was better when I wrote you my last short note & have been getting rapidly better since then. At one time I did not intend to go to town to see Stanley till next week, but being so much stronger I went yesterday, & after seeing M^{rs} McKenzie for a few minutes I sat talking over all our affairs for an hour. The enclosed receipt will show you what I have done with the £10 for Aunt Richard, & Stanley gave me two pounds that you gave him for his journey but which he did not use, so I have put it down as a further remittance to myself, having at present £12 in my possession.

What splendid health Stanley appears to be in, and he is evidently very comfortable & happy where he is. I am afraid he does not take *half* the amount of exercise which he ought to do if he wishes to keep that health for long.

He could not make a better rule & habit than to take exercise sufficient every day & if you tell him of it, it will have more weight with him than any other person.

---

⁷ Lucy inserted the following passage here: 'then follows a little school gossip about his schoolfellows which is not interesting to the general reader but would shews [sic] how entirely open & confidential he was with his father how honest and straightforwardly he steered his life through the difficulties that all must meet with in Companionship with all kinds of boys & came out with the esteem if not the love of all whose love and esteem was of any value – he concludes the letter –'.

M^rs McKenzie mentioned to me that she thought he worked too hard & did not go out enough. I mean every now & then to work at him, for I am beginning to consider these things as more particularly my province than others. I was rather disappointed at the 17th. I had hoped to have watched the progress of the eclipse of the moon on that day but just then the clouds had collected & effectually destroyed my observations.

Of all the advantages I lose from separation from you I will mention one. We have abundance of newspapers, but I want your ever ready explanation of the great political & social topics & changes going on. You have other duties & occupations to occupy you or I should value some of your opinions & explanations on those things. We have heard very lately from Aunt Jane & her improvement in health has still no relapse. It is a reason for true rejoicing for she will not long remain quiet when she feels strong & well, and I hope we shall see the floggings of Juvenile offenders, disappear, & some of the gross ignorance in the poor of England, done away with partly by her aid & exertions.[1]

We are having a most beautiful cloudless day, & the sun has sufficient warmth to show us what it intends to exert after a while. It is very extraordinary weather, at any rate in this part of the country & more or less I believe over all the parts.

Uncle Richard who has been not so well until a few days since has now got better which is no less pleasant for ourselves than for him, as he has such cheerful & social spirits when in his usual health, that it makes a great change when he is unwell.

Give my very best love to Lucy & I hope you & she will not let yourselves be anxious about me any more, for you may depend upon me writing if I was very unwell, a thing which is no more or little more likely to happen to me than any other person, for they say a creaking door hangs long.

But it will be my duty & pleasure henceforth not to tax your patience since it arose mainly from inexcusable delay on my part. Ever your
very affec Son
Herb Jevons

[1] 'Aunt Jane' was Jane Hornblower, formerly Roscoe, sister-in-law of Thomas Jevons. No other specific information about her activities as a social reformer appears to be on record, but it is known that one of William Roscoe's two surviving daughters was concerned with the foundation of the Female Apprentices' Library in Liverpool which was added after the Mechanics' and Apprentices' Library was established in 1824; it seems probable that Jane was the daughter concerned and that she continued to play an active part in the movement for social progress. Cf. R. V. Holt, op. cit.; also M. B. Simey, *Charitable Effort in Liverpool in the Nineteenth Century* (Liverpool, 1951) p. 25.

11. THOMAS JEVONS TO W. S. JEVONS
[LJP, 11]

Chatham S^t 18 Mar^1
1851

Dear Stanley

If you begin to think that I have forgotten you you will begin to think wrong for I never have and never can forget you but have you in my thoughts oftener than I can tell. For the last two or three weeks I have not been in quite so good working order as I generally am in perhaps that may have arisen in consequence of not being particularly busy for I find that there is a parity of reasoning in this respect with the saying of Scripture to him that hath shall be given more abundantly and so the more I have to do the more I can do When one's hand is in, as the saying is, one can get along famously but when we have little to do or which is the same in effect are languid in doing what we have we can then with difficulty enter into those duties which we ought to take upon ourselves and do take cheerfully enough under favorable* circumstances but enough of this Sermon

Herbert & Thommy* are gone to Nantwich.[2] Herbert thought it would do him good and we all thought the same and so he is gone We had such a beautiful letter from him this morning that I will enclose it for you and that will save the necessity of giving you any more particulars about him. Thommy* has had a little cough upon him for the last week or two and we thought change of air would remove it so we sent him along with Herbert

We have missed your usual weekly letter last night but suppose you were too much tired on Sunday Evening with your usual walk to the Crystal Pal^{ce} That emporium must now be becoming a most interesting place indeed Did you hear of the great Organs that are to be put up in it One of them as large as the great organ at Harlem.*[3] It will weigh they say 30 Tons One of them is the invention of Colonel Thompson[4] and has been built for his own room The long metal pipes are all discarded and the deep sounds are produced by very broad & short

[1] Jevons incorrectly dates this letter 18 May 1851 when listing his father's letters in the Journal. See Vol. I, p. 116.
[2] See above, Letter 1, n. 1, p. 3.
[3] i.e. the large organ in the Church of St Bavo (known as the Groote Kerk) in Haarlem, built in 1738 by Christian Müller. Of the fourteen organs exhibited at the Great Exhibition, the largest was that shown by Henry Willis (1821–1901) who in 1855 built the organ for St George's Hall, Liverpool; cf. below, Letter 59, p. 142.
[4] Thomas Perronet Thompson (1783–1869) soldier, Radical politician and author, proprietor of the *Westminster Review* from 1829 and author of the *Catechism on the Corn Laws*. His Enharmonic Organ, shown at the Great Exhibition, is now exhibited in the Science Museum at Kensington. Cf. L. G. Johnson, *General T. Perronet Thompson* (1957).

wooden pipes But besides that there are a great many improvements in the fingering or rather keying a much greater number of keys are introduced into the ordinary space many being thin Iron keys where the sharps & flats are placed and many come up through the centre of the ivory keys and are played something like the keys of a flute he has. Whether the object of this system of keying is merely to do away with one or two of the higher setts* of keys which all large organs have or is intended to introduce more notes so as to do away with the imperfection of making one pipe serve for both a flat and a sharp I cannot tell we must have a better description than I have seen to find this out But what a grand thing it will be to play upon these immense instruments when I go to see the Exhibition you shall certainly try these organs for me if I can prevail upon you to summon up the courage.

I was much delighted to hear that you got over your "trouble" at Mr Yates[5] and to find that it even sat rather comfortably upon you like the eels in the hands of the cook you will perhaps get quite used to the operation. The Miss Yates have a true ear[6] for and love of music *it is* music which they play You do not say whether they have an Organ in their house if they have I hope you will let them know a little of your talent on that instrument and then they will like you more and more All people like those who can save trouble and give pleasure at the same time If you can play for them you save them the trouble of playing for you and your playing is sure to give pleasure to all ordinary lovers of music but it will give exquisite pleasure to those who are able to appreciate it and *no mistake!*

I was not a little gratified by the receipt of your "character" as pronounced by your several Masters I have no doubt of its truthfulness and it is highly honorable* to you Go on in like manner and prosper you must in whatever walk of life you select.

Wednesday

I wrote the first part of this letter last evening just before Henry[7] came in then of course we had the usual rubber then supper and then to bed and I thought to myself that I should hear from you but sorry am I to

---

[5] For the Jevons connections with the Yates family see Vol. I, p. 3. It is not clear whether the visit referred to was paid to the Rev. James Yates (1789–1871), the educationalist and classical scholar who lived at Highgate, or to his younger brother John Ashton Yates (1791–1863), a Liverpool broker, literary man, economist and M.P. We know that Jevons had visited John Yates and his family earlier from a reference in a letter written to him by his grandfather William Jevons dated March 1851 (unpublished): '. . . You should be pleased and thankful to be asked to dine with such a worthy family as John Ashton Yates you seem to call it a trouble you should consider it an honor* to be Invited to such a respectable family. . . .' See also above, Letter 9, p. 20.

[6] 'hear' in the original manuscript.

[7] See below, Letter 21, n. 2, p. 38.

find that you have been so poorly as to keep your bed However that was the very best way of getting the mastery & I hope tomorrow we shall have still better accounts Of course I cannot divine how you caught so severe a cold & I can only tell you to take better care of yourself and in one respect in particular always take regular exercise *every day* Dont leave all your exercise for Sunday but have at least one decided long walk every day Stopping in the school room and in the house so many hours makes you rash and in that way you take cold

I am decidedly glad you are going to Mr Taggarts*[8] You seem surprized* why you should be asked out to so many places but you are not asked to more places than Ogden & Bolton I suppose such a galaxy of talent as the three youths possess must necessarily have its effect But you must not forget that your Father is known to these friends and your Grandfather too your Grandfather Jevons but more especially your Grandfather Roscoe and the fact of your being a descendant of the illustrious and good Roscoe cannot fail to be a passport to you into the society of the most eminent of the day and generation to say nothing of your own merits which one day will earn a distinction for yourself alone. We shall be anxious to hear that you are getting on well again in your health and I beg you will write if possible every day until you are quite restored for if we do not hear with good accounts I must come up to see you myself

I left your letter at home so I suppose Lucy will write all the domestic news of this day and as I must now set out for Crown S^t I conclude with my most affectionate Love and the blessing of
Your endeared Parent
Thos Jevons

12. THOMAS JEVONS TO W. S. JEVONS
  [LJP, 11]

Lpool 28 June 1851

Dearest Stanley

It is a long time since I wrote to you but the cause has not been from neglect but from incessant occupation of one sort or another

I received your note about your classes and most certainly agree with you that you ought not to try for too many prizes or else you may lose all Try only for those which you have a well grounded hope of deserving and obtaining.

---

[8] Rev. Edward Tagart (1804–58), well-known minister of the Unitarian Chapel in Little Portland Street, London, 1833–58. He attracted a wide congregation – Dickens at one time attended his services. In 1835 he moved the resolution for the foundation of the London Domestic Mission Society and was its secretary, 1841–4.

Your Cousin Mary Roscoe made a very grand affair of her wedding when she became Mary Hutton.[1] Lucy was one of her *six brides* maids. The bride certainly never appeared in my eyes so lovely as she did that day she was dressed so very becoming The brides maids were lovely in their own personal beauty and their simple dresses sett* that off the more conspicuously There was a grand breakfast after the Ceremony where thirty two sat down to a most sumptuous set out of rich foods and fruits & drinks including almost every sort you can mention of the costly kind She might have had £100,000 to her fortune. Myself and Lucy and Herbert and Henny and Tommy were all at the Chapel and also at the breakfast and the whole affair went off splendidly and Henny was selected to throw the Old Shoe over the heads of the bride & bridegroom for luck as they left the house for their wedding journey

We have had but a poor account of Aunt Janes[2] health the last few days and Lucy has gone over to Nantwich to see her I expect her back on Monday but on tuesday* she is to go with Aunt Timothy[3] to the Lakes for a fortnight and Henny goes with her Lucy's address will be Miss Jevons The Grange Borrodale near Keswick.

What glorious weather we have now, if this continues we shall have one of the finest harvests that can be imagined. But it is too hot for the Crystal Palace They will be all baked there if not sublimed I hope it will be cooler when I pay my next visit there[4]

You will rejoice to hear that Herbert is very much better now in his health & spirits though at times a little uncertain. He is doing nothing but reading abstruce* works which I fear were one great cause of his not recovering sooner, but he is rather more moderate with them now and goes out and enjoys himself a little more than he did. He is very unsettled in his views for the future as yet and whether he will turn to the ministry or stick to medicine or fancy anything else I cannot say. I could not press him on the point while he was so poorly but now I think he is nearly well enough to make a permanent decision however when you come home you may perhaps help to settle him in some degree

Grand Papa has been over to Kenyon Terrace[5] to day which has tired him a good deal but it is certainly wonderful that he keeps up so very well as he undoubtedly is just now.

---

[1] Mrs Richard Holt Hutton. Jevons writes of her death in his Journal entry for 23 January 1853 (see Vol. I, p. 80. See also below, Letter 35, n. 3, p. 64.

[2] See Vol. I, pp. 59, 88 and 92.

[3] Mrs Timothy Jevons (1798–1859). Formerly Catharine Lomax, she was the daughter of John Lomax of Heswall in Cheshire.

[4] Extracts from letters describing two of W. S. Jevons's visits to the Great Exhibition are quoted in LJ, p. 10.

[5] Kenyon Terrace, Birkenhead, was at that time the home of William Jevons Junior.

I shall be very glad when your holidays commence for it seems a long time to be deprived of your society and I shall begin now to look to you for assistance in family affairs by consultation and advice, for Roscoe you know cannot help me, and Herbert does not do much good just now, and Lucy is full of her own affairs and has indeed been a good deal away from home of late so that I need the help of a friend in whom I can trust and I must bring you forward to take part in the battle of life young as you yet are, however, that is a fault which you reply you will mend of every day and wishing you success in your examinations and looking forward with great joy to seeing you at home once more I remain

      Dearest Stanley
      Your aff^{te} Father
      Thos Jevons

13. THOMAS JEVONS TO W. S. JEVONS

                Lpool 26 Sept 1851

Dearest Stanley

Though you have not informed me of your safe arrival at Nantwich yet I will just address this note to you there for the chance of its finding you as I did not hear that any accident happened to the train by which you started from Lpool You may perhaps think that I ought to have written to you before now and so I should only I have been very much engaged my Father requiring so much attention from me and dear Lucy demanding a note a day because she sends a note a day to us You must therefore excuse my seeming neglect and I call it *seeming* advisedly for I assure you that you have been frequently in my thoughts. Deprived as I am of the society of your two elder brothers[1] you may readily conceive that I think the more of you even if I had only common inducements to it but I cannot lose sight of the promise your already acquired honors give of future fame & usefulness and if I have been doomed to disappointment in my cherished hopes of my first born I cling the more to my fond desires for your success in Life. I trust you keep well in health but even Aunt Jane in the two letters I have seen from her since you went there has not mentioned you so that I must trust to providence for any knowledge on that point.

Lucy will be with you tomorrow and that will no doubt add to your enjoyment while you remain at Nantwich but I hope I may see you both at home again on Monday accompanied by your good Uncle and Aunt.

Lucy will know how they are to be accommodated at our house but

---

[1] Herbert had recently sailed for South Africa. See Jevons's summary of this letter, Vol. I, p. 116.

one thing I will name if Lucy can accommodate Betsey also she must ask her for your Aunt does not like to be without her

Grandpapa has been rather low and poorly yesterday and this morning but I hope I shall find him better when I get home for he has got Miss Stokes[2] to keep him company while I am away The rest are all well and hoping you will excuse this rapid scrall* in acc. of my having had a hard day of writing I remain with ever affectionate Love Your parent & friend

Thos Jevons

14. THOMAS JEVONS TO W. S. JEVONS

Lpool 14 Jany 1852

Dearest Stanley

The last letter which my dear Father wrote was addressed to you It was just at the beginning of his declining powers and shewed* this so much that I persuaded him not to send it. I did not think at the time that he would so rapidly go worse or I should not have interfeared* with my advice He is now however numbered with the blest and the circumstances attending this note are such that I resolve to send it you as the best proof possible of his affection for you since it is evident that he must have labored* hard to complete this his last effort at writing You will perceive by the date 22 Nov 1851 that it is exactly 21 days before his death which took place yesterday morning[1] being then 91 years 3 mths & 2 days old. His last few days and nights were anxious ones for all of us here for our feelings of love and duty would not allow us to leave him night or day but to him they were I believe more joyful than otherwise for he so expressed himself before he lost the power of speech and even after that he told us by signs plain to be understood that he had no pain Some of his last words were "I shall soon be happy I shall soon join my dear Father and Mother my beautiful wife and my dear daughter Anne"[2] and the joyful way in which he expressed these feelings filled me also with a thrill of delight May we all be able to

---

[2] A note in Jevons's handwriting in the Family History papers reads: 'Misses Stokes, who for a long time kept a toy shop in Liverpool and whom I used frequently to visit. Were they descended from Stokes my grandfather's first master.' There was also a Miss Stokes who taught at the Renshaw Street Chapel Unitarian School. See G. E. Evans, *A History of Renshaw Street Chapel* (1887) p. 97.

[1] This letter does not appear to have survived. If it was in fact dated 22 November (and not 22 December) it would have been written 52 days before William Jevons's death.

[2] Anne Jevons (1796–1826), elder daughter of William Jevons. In February 1824 she married George Worthington (1787–1859), a Warrington solicitor, who later settled in Australia. They had two children, George (b. 1825) and Anne Frances (b. 1826).

meet our latter end with the same calm feeling of confidence and joy and to enable us to do so may we each in his several station* work with the same diligence as he did to fulfil his duty both to God & to Man

We are all quite as well as might be expected after the strain that has been upon us. Lucy perhaps feels the most unwell having taken a cold that seems to pervade the whole of her frame but I trust it is only temporary and that a few days care of herself will put all to rights

The funeral will be on friday* and all the grandsons that are here, except Roscoe, as well as my two brothers & myself will attend but I have not thought it right to send for you down in fact the expense to me altogether will be so great that I have thought it my duty not to incur the cost of desiring you to come down merely to attend the funeral Your sympathies and right feeling will be equally with us as if you were here to participate in the last sad pageant that can be shewn* to his earthly tenement.

You can read this note if you think fit to your Aunt and Cousins[3] to whom present my kind and affectionate regards
And I remain Dearest Stanley
    Your most aff^{te} Father & friend
      Thos Jevons

15. W. S. JEVONS TO HENRIETTA JEVONS AND T. E. JEVONS

            February 2nd 1852

Dearest Henny and Tommy

I ought to have written yesterday, but I hope you will excuse me leaving it till today.

I have not had a letter from either of you this term but I suppose you think that I ought to write to you first, as I must have more to say. I suppose you have been at school some time now, and I hope you are getting on very well. I hear that Henny is learning double bass, and I hope she likes it, though I should think she found it rather hard at first; I shall want her to give me a few lessons next holidays, that is after I have learnt my notes, which I dont quite know yet. I suppose you heard about Mr Edward's not being able to pay his debts and being turned out by Mr Booth[1] so that Tommy will have no more fights with his boys.

---

[3] Mrs Henry Roscoe, Harry and Harriet.

[1] Probably either Charles Booth (d. 1860), a Liverpool corn merchant, uncle by marriage of H. E. Roscoe and father of Charles James Booth (1840–1916) (cf. Vol. I, p. 77, n. 2) and Thomas Booth; or his brother Henry Booth (1788–1869), one of the main promoters of the Manchester and Liverpool Railway, a member of the Building Committee of the Mechanics'

I am getting on all right at college and am learning chemistry very fast so that I shall have plenty of experiments for next holidays. I suppose Lucy has come home again now, and I should think that she would not go back again with them.² Tell her that they are thinking of getting up a class of *young ladies* here, for Richard Hutton³ though of course she must not say so. I am going to a Lecture on Geology this evening, and I cannot write very much as I have to get my exercise for De Morgan⁴ done in time. The Queen is going to open Parliament tomorrow, and today they got up petitions at College for a holiday from the Latin and Greek classes tomorrow, so that I shall see it. The Queen is to go in by the grand entrance through the Victoria tower for the first time, and as it was a new thing they had to take the eight cream-coloured horses to teach them to go in properly. I went a long walk yesterday afternoon to Hyde Park and then to the New Houses of Parliament. The Exhibition looks better outside now I think as the canvass* has all been taken away off the roof and sides, and as it is to be open to the public after today I shall go very soon to see it inside now that it is empty. The Houses of Parliament look a good deal better now that the old part has been cleared away but it is very unfinished yet. The Victoria Tower and Gateway look splendid, and it would be a grand sight to see her go through it.⁵ Was it not queer for Papa to meet me in the British museum? But I was very glad that I saw him at all. What did you think of the telegraphic message.⁶ I have been learning "Probabilities", that is the chances of things happening. Thus the chance of throwing doublets at backgammon is 5 to 1 against it, while it is 17 to 19 for being able to play a six. I can or rather ought to be able to calculate the chance of anybody at whist having a particular card, or being "two by honours". De Morgan tells us that to play backgammon without calculating every chance, is like playing chess when you know nothing but the moves,

---

Institution and President of the Liverpool Institute, 1845 (Tiffen, op. cit., pp. 31, 35). The incident referred to possibly concerned a tutor in one of these households, or the owner of a small school.

² Lucy had gone to stay with Rev. and Mrs Hornblower at Nantwich shortly before her grandfather's death.

³ See below, Letter 145, n. 6, p. 416.

⁴ See Vol. I, pp. 15 and 64–5.

⁵ The new Palace of Westminster replaced the Houses of Parliament destroyed by fire in October 1834. It was designed by Sir Charles Barry (1795–1860) and completed after his death by his son Edward Middleton Barry (1830–80). An account of the formal opening of the Houses by Queen Victoria on 3 February 1852 is contained in the *Annual Register . . . of the Year 1852* (1853), Chronicle, 17.

⁶ Probably a reference to the news of Louis Napoleon Bonaparte's *coup d'état* against the second French Republic on 2 December 1851, which was received in England by electric telegraph. A cable had been laid between Dover and Calais in 1851.

and says that we ought always to do it. What a capital player he must be?, and you may expect me to beatt* you all when I come back.[7]

With best love to Lucy and Papa
I remain
Your ever affectionate Brother
William S Jevons

They have just heard that Mr Crompton is to be the new judge and are all talking about Sir Charles and Lady Crompton, and are in very good spirits. I suppose the Cromptons will be twice as grand as before, and I believe that they are going to have a grand house at the West End.[8]

16. THOMAS JEVONS TO W. S. JEVONS

Liverpool 3 May
1852

My Dear Stanley

I received a note from your Aunt[1] announcing to me in heartfelt terms your triumph in gaining one of the two Silver Medals in Chemistry[2] and I have read your own modest account of your success in your note to Lucy. I have been highly gratified by the news which called up feelings that would manifest themselves in too visible a manner to be mistaken May you dear Stanley live to turn to good account these juvenile victories and may they be the forerunners of a life of true usefulness and may its end be crowned with a never fading wreath of glory surpassing in brightness all that human institutions can reflect on the heads of its most cherished heroes or philosophers. The fame or notoriety that is acquired from effort and competition I would have you to bear in mind is only of an evanescant kind It is like the meteor light which glares for a short time & then is lost for ever. But the labor* of love which shall lead to the production of good to mankind begins not with

[7] Whatever its short-term effects on Jevons's ability at backgammon may have been, De Morgan's teaching on probabilities was to have a lasting result in Jevons's scientific work; cf. E. H. Madden, 'W. S. Jevons on Induction and Probability', in Blake, Ducasse and Madden, *Theories of Scientific Method* (Seattle, 1960), pp. 233–47, B. MacLennan, 'Jevons's Philosophy of Science,' *Manchester School*, 60 (March 1972) pp. 53–71, R. D. Collison Black, 'Jevons, Bentham and De Morgan,' *Economica*, 34 (May 1972) pp. 119–134.

[8] Charles John Crompton (1797–1865), created a justice of the Queen's Bench and knighted in 1852. He had married in 1832 Caroline Fletcher, younger sister of H. E. Roscoe's mother, and Jevons is presumably referring to the reaction to the news of his aunt and two cousins, with whom he was then living. Harry Roscoe remarked in his autobiography: '... when my uncle became a judge the family removed to a large corner house in Hyde Park Square....' (*Life and Experiences*, p. 31).

[1] Presumably Mrs Henry Roscoe.

[2] In the Easter examinations. See Vol. I, p. 54, n. 1.

the spirit of competition or conquest but with the humble effort of doing ones duty. At first it may be without attracting the attentions of the world in the least degree but as time rolls on it fills up a measure of recorded blessings the reflections of which shall burst through every shade thrown over it even in this world but which shall shine for ever with efulgent* brightness in a world to come.

You have so recently been with us that I have nothing to tell you that will be new but in fact I have been from home down in South Wales nearly all last week so that I am myself a stranger here

Mr Thom[3] began his altered service at the Chapel yesterday afternoon in which Lucy & Henny & Tommy acted each a part to their satisfaction and I dare to say that the change will be beneficial

This evening now that the two young ones are gone to bed I am all alone for Lucy has gone to her dear Rhoda and Patty to her dear Laura[4] but I turn their absence which on first thoughts was depressing to me into a blessing by seizing the occasion to commune with you my dear Stanley

Give my kindest regards to Aunt Henry and thank her for her very kind note remember me also to Harriet and Harry and thank the latter for his judicious advice to you about the examination. And believe me to remain Ever dear Stanley

Your most aff^{te} Father
Thos Jevons

17. W. S. JEVONS TO THOMAS JEVONS
[LJN, 14–15]

[9 Oval Road,
Camden Town.
May 1852]

... I am very glad that you were so pleased about the medal, as I see from yours and Lucy's letters, but I have no intention of trying very hard or injuring my health at all to get any more – that is, any more prizes, though, of course, I shall try to learn all I possibly can while I have the opportunity at college. If a person goes into an examination people are always disappointed if he does not come off one of the first, and for that reason I was rather sorry after I had gone into the chemistry examination, as I had no right then to expect anything more than one

---

[3] The Minister at Renshaw Street Chapel. See Vol. I, p. 58, n. 5.

[4] Jevons's first cousin Clara ('Patty') Roscoe [b. 1836] youngest daughter of Robert Roscoe. The family lived at Englefield Green near Windsor. See Vol. I, p. 66, n. 5. Her elder sister Laura ('Poppy') had recently married James Thornely (see below, Letter 59, p. 141).

of the last certificates. I am afraid now that you will be disappointed at my not getting anything at the college examination in June, for though I may possibly get a certificate in Greek, and *possibly* either in Latin or mathematics, I have no chance of any prize, and this is literally true as far as I can judge at present. As to the matriculation, I shall *try* to pass in the first division, and if I pass the examination at all, I shall probably try to pass the examination in honours for chemistry; but you must not expect any prizes here either. . . .

18. THOMAS JEVONS TO W. S. JEVONS

Lpool 8 June 1852

Dearest Stanley

Recurring to your last note which I am about to answer I find that it is 8 days old and all I can say as an excuse for not writing sooner is that I have been a good deal engaged with one thing or another and had not time to look for the Certificate of your birth[1] which I thought essential to send you the first time I wrote I had also some undefined feeling about money matters for Aunt Henry and even now this last named affair must be postponed but of that hereafter.

I have rummaged up the Certificate of your birth which I send you enclosed. It is a precious document which I should not like to lose. I presume you only require to exhibit it when you pass your Matriculation, but if you are required to deposit a Certificate I would particularly desire you to get a copy from Dr Williams Library Red Cross Street which you can do on paying a shilling and deposit that sending me back this original You will notice that it was entered at Dr William's Library on the 2nd Sep 1836 and is No 6127 on the register kept at that Institution.[2]

As to the money affair I will send you some by the post of next Monday night, for all I can draw this week goes to pay bills here[3] and to buy provisions for Chatham S^t and Crown Street.[4]

[1] This is among the Jevons Papers.
[2] Thomas Jevons made the following entry in the Family Book concerning the birth of his son Roscoe: 'Entered filed & Registered, according to the custom in use amongst Protestant Dissenters at the Registry of Births kept at Dr Williams' Library Red Cross Street, Cripplegate London. . . .' Jevons himself added later: 'The above and other registers of births are now in the Non Parochial Registry office – Somerset House'.
The Library was built in Red Cross Street in 1729, according to the direction of Daniel Williams (1643?–1716), nonconformist divine and benefactor. Dissenting registers of birth and baptism were kept there until the introduction of Civil Registration in 1837. The Library was moved in 1864 to Queen Square, Bloomsbury, in 1873 to Grafton Street, and finally in 1890 to its present premises in Gordon Square, in the building that was once University Hall.
[3] It would appear that Thomas Jevons was writing, as he often did, from his office.
[4] See Vol. I, pp. 6, 12 and 116.

Your sketch of the Medal awarded to you for Chemistry interested us all, but it will not less gratify us to touch the metal itself when you come home; but as for your pursuits in that recondite art you will never have a better place for practicing* in than the cellar at Chatham S^t As to the House I am planning it serves simply for a little amusement if for nothing else but I have an idea that I may perchance make a speculation in building one for sale and to make a profit but this is a deferred hope. The plan is made to carry out some original ideas that I entertain about a good planned House but I must confess that it never entered my head to make a Laboratory. I have a beautiful Library 17 feet by 17 feet with a dome like ceiling lighted by a skylight a dining room 24 by 17 feet and a drawing room 24 by 20 feet and all three connecting "en suite" as it is termed with a handsome *lobby landing* or *corridore** whichever you may call it from which all three of them can be entered separately with a handsome entrance Hall besides and a unique staircase I have excellent offices below and nine bed rooms above and what is better than all I expect that it can be built very cheaply and if you or any of your Cousins can plan a better house I will yield up the palm to him her or them!!! –

We have heard again of but not from Herbert He sailed from Natal on the 7 March for the Mauritius and the Devonian took on board two fresh Cabin passengers who would accompany Herbert all the way home to Lpool where we expect him in about a month or six weeks or at most two months.[5]

I have partly fixed on sending Tommy to Mr Greens school[6] in Hope S^t He is a friend of Mrs Richd Roscoes and was stopping a day or two at the D^{rs} at Twickenham lately

And now I have spun you a good long yarn and given you a specimen of a real good handwriting the chief merit of which is that it exercises the skill and wit of those to whom it is sent and does them as much good as a bothering Lattin* lesson or a problem in Euclid or an analysis of an unknown production of nature taken from the depths of the interior recesses of the Earth and such writing must be very praiseworthy or certainly such great Men as my Lor^d Brougham and Mr Justice Crompton would not practice* such if it were not for examples sake and so I remain

Ever dearest Stanley
Yours [   ][7]
Tho Jevons

[5] Herbert's return is described in the Journal, cf. Vol. I, p. 76.

[6] Unlike his three elder brothers, Tom Jevons did not attend the Liverpool Mechanics' Institution High School, but was sent to one of the many small private schools in Liverpool at that time. In 1855 he went to University College School, London (cf. below, Letter 67, p. 167.   [7] This word is indecipherable.

19. W. S. JEVONS TO LUCY JEVONS
[LJN, 15]

[9 Oval Road,
Camden Town.
July 1852]

... I daresay you will want to hear about the matriculation, and so I will tell you that it has all gone off very well. . . . I am not at all afraid of being plucked, and the only thing that I think will put me in the second division, if I am so, will be the history, for all the examinations were much easier than those at college. . . . I have not told you, I think, that I was invited by a student I know at college named Colvill,[1] the nephew of Dr. Sharpey,[2] with whom he lives, to go and get tea there. . . . He is a very nice old fellow, and one of the best physiologists alive. He attended Mr. Graham's class this year with all the other students, and since Easter has been working all day in the laboratory, with Dr. Williamson[3] telling him how to do the things. You must not complain of me making messes and blows – up in the cellar if an old chap of sixty begins to learn to do it. I am going to bring out something fine next holidays in the chemistry line! . . .

20. THOMAS JEVONS TO W. S. JEVONS

Lpool 17 Nov 1852

My Dear Stanley

I have two interesting letters from you which demand an answer however little time I have for the purpose But the first and most important thing I have to say is to beg you to take special care of yourself in that gorgeous follyful parapharnalia* that you are going to look at tomorrow. I have a high opinion of the character of the Duke but that does not hinder me from condemning the enormous folly of spending not one but several hundred thousand pounds for his funeral obsequies.[1] I do not approve in general of expensive funerals but think it the worst spent money that can be and in the present case it cannot add one sintilation* of fame to the history of the Dukes Life, *that* has been written in his deeds which have been in the main for his country's good.

We have not again heard anything of Herbert or his ship the Devonian. She is a slow sailer and it is supposed that having been so long in

---

[1] See Vol. I, p. 54, n. 3.   [2] See Vol. I, 82, n. 6.   [3] See Vol. I, p. 69, n. 1.
[1] Jevons describes the funeral procession of the Duke of Wellington in Vol. I, Journal entry for 15 November 1852, pp. 72–5.

warm lattitudes* her bottom has become very foul thus still more impeding her way. I am not anxious in the least, feeling perfectly confident that she will turn up before long.

You ask about the Earthquake in Chatham S,.[2] It woke me. I heard a great noise as if in the street and then I felt going up and down as if I was floating on a short chocky sea. Then I thought my blood was flowing backwards and forwards in my veins like water in a glass tube one and the other end lifted alternately up & down my pulse beat hard & rapid* & I thought I must have had strong green tea at my brothers in St James Road where we drank tea the previous evening. I heard the door bell ring as I thought but since am fully satisfied that it was the tumbler glass & bottle of water on my wash stand. I thought Tommy had got out of bed at one time & was shaking me to arouse me but he was in his right place. All these thoughts were the work of a few seconds, and hearing nothing more I again fell asleep and never heard any thing about its being an Earthquake until far on in the day It created a deal more disturbance on the Cheshire side of the River than on this for at Birkenhead many people left their rooms and some ran into the streets from fright but I have heard of no harm being done.

We cannot imagine what you allude to by the term "*great event*" at Lpool unless it be the election of Sam Holmes*[3] the bricklayer for mayor. I have in former days seen him in his shirt sleeves setting bricks with veritable trowel & mortar. But he has become rich and is now sometimes dubbed Orator Holmes He is the greatest talker I almost ever knew *about Self* in particular a vain boaster and empty headed noodle but rich selfish and unscrupulous –

We have Aunt & Uncle Hornblower stopping with us They are at times famous good company then do themselves up and have both to be nursed but in either state they make a stir in the house I assure you.

Lucy has given notice to Martha to leave and engaged Mary Bentley[4] to come in her stead –

I notice what you said about one of your philosophers going into a manufactory and not liking it. What ever you go to you will *not like* it at first. Business of every kind for underlings is hum drum. The intellect is at first very little used. You must first be drilled like a soldier and act

[2] Cf. Vol. I, p. 71.

[3] Samuel Holme (c. 1800–72), son of James Holme, a notable building contractor in the North of England. Samuel and his brother developed the firm into one of the most extensive builders and contractors for railway works in the region. He retired from the firm at an early age and entered politics as Chairman of the Liverpool Conservative Tradesman's Association; became a Councillor in 1842 and Mayor in 1852. He was also a magistrate and a founder of the Collegiate Institution. Noted for his forceful public speaking, he was described by the *Liverpool Mercury* as having 'more energy than grace in his style, which is a little too florid, and inclines to redundancy of expression'.

[4] An aunt of Anne and Charles Bolton.

according to the settled rule and it must be a long time before you can be fit to take a part in the real direction of any business. And indeed the same applies to a profession You must think of all this and make up your mind to *endure* the initiatory druggery* which is incident to every walk of life in the early stages

I can think of nothing more to say now but with every trust in your good common sense hope you will be thinking of settling down to something before very long

And remain always my dearest Stanley Your ever affectionate Father
Thos Jevons

21. THOMAS JEVONS TO W. S. JEVONS

Liverpool 9 feb* 1853

Dearest Stanley

You must not suppose from my not writing to you for so long a time that I have forgotten you but on the contrary believe that I have been more anxious about you than usual. I have you in my thoughts very frequently and it is the difficulty I experience in making up my mind what to write to you, added certainly to some few interruptions of a melancholy nature,[1] that has prevented me You are anxious like me about what you shall turn your attention to after leaving College and seem so far to be firmly fixed not to enter a profession but rather to go to business of some kind. I have no desire for you to choose one line of life more than another but only that you should select that which would yield you most happiness.

I know that your idea is, like many others before you, to amass a fortune in a short time so that you may afterwards devote your whole time to science but in this you indulge a falacy*. Fortunes cannot be amassed in a short time but only after a long and undeviating course of business, and when the whole mind & soul is devoted to the acquirement. And in the acquirement you must see that habits & tastes are formed which you thereafter follow for their own sake and your idea of a future retirement to study and science vanishes away. Knowing this fact makes me entertain the idea that it would be more desirable to choose some business which may be allied to your own tastes and knowledge and we have you know often talked about a manufacturing chymists* situation, but all you young chymists* set your minds against the humdrum work of making one or two particular articles in which at first there is no scope for the onward progress of the intellect in searching

---

[1] A reference to the death, on 1 February, of Rev. Francis Hornblower, husband of Jevons's 'Aunt Jane'. See Vol. I, p. 88.

out new wonders but only the every day toil of an office or factory, you therefore have not entertained that thought in any earnestness. In consequence of this I have been turning over with a great deal of anxiety whether I should name to you another business or manufacture which had I been differently situated myself I should probably have mentioned before viz the Iron Trade. I myself like the Iron trade very much, certainly so as a merchant, but I think I should like it ten times more as a manufacturer but there are so many difficulties in the way of your commencing this trade that I almost tremble in mentioning the subject to you The difficulty in your becoming an Iron Merchant lies in the fact that Herbert is before you and that I could not expect that you as well as he could be taken into the old concern along with my brother and Henry Jevon* & George[2] and therefore it would entail a separation of the family interests and as regards my own situation I do not know that I can recommend that. I myself bear the degradation of a sort of servitude for the good of my *whole* family, say, the whole of my own and my two brothers families, but I do not recommend any one of my sons to put up with an agency of the same kind. And my agency is so altering that I cannot teach my sons the independent business so well as if I was carrying on an independent business myself and yet I hope I may be able to make a good Iron Merchant of Herbert in time As regards yourself I have thought that you might perhaps fancy to become an Iron Master if I were to point out some of the advantages, but the disadvantages are so great that I myself would not venture to strike a balance for you

The advantages are first its suitability to your taste & knowledge 1 Mining & Geology are necessary to procure the coals & Iron-Stone 2 Chemystry* to smelt it and turn it into the Iron of commerce 3 *Mechanics*, for on the perfection of machinery in every process the success of Ironmaking belongs 4 *Engineering* you have engineering in the mines engineering in the works and engineering is a part of the profession of many of the Iron Masters who erect great works like the Britannia & Menai bridges &c &c And lastly a successful Iron Master makes more money than almost any other trade or profession

But then the difficulties & disadvantages are very great You must work and toil for several years among a class of people of rather a low

---

[2] His brother Timothy Jevons (1798–1874) and his nephews Henry Jevons (1827–1914), eldest son of Timothy Jevons and George Jevons (1818–1905), eldest son of William Jevons, Junior. Henry Jevons restarted the family iron business after the bankruptcy of 1848, under a new partnership with his cousin George (see Vol. I, p. 12.) He was a well-known citizen of Liverpool – chairman of the Chamber of Commerce and first President of the Liverpool Iron and General Trades Association. It appears from the correspondence that he acted as general adviser on family financial affairs and was of particular assistance to Jevons at the time of his brother Roscoe's death. See Vol. III, Letter 313.

description occasionally underground sometimes in the Mills & Forges and on the Furnace Banks and in the offices where the mens accounts are kept &c &c and when you have got a good knowledge of the whole mystery the greatest difficulty of all is to get a start in life. Wherever this might be it must be away from your family and this must be the case in the first instance which is an immense sacrafice* and this must continue for there are no Iron Mines in Lpool but the greatest difficulty would be in finding capital to set up for yourself. You might perhaps get a managership of Iron Works at first until you had sufficient experience to set up for yourself but it is a very hard undertaking to become the Master of hundreds of rough workmen Miners Mill men Laborers* &c &c and particularly when bad times come on and you are compelled to reduce wages to a starvation point almost

Were you to become a really great & clever Engineer & manager there would be less difficulty in getting you a first rate managership with a good salary or even a partnership with a man of capital to start for yourself but should you be an ordinary personage then probably you must put up with a managership for life[3]

These are the thoughts that have been filling my mind for a long time past about you & your prospects and with these I must close my epistle leaving all other subjects for other pens or for another time & I remain
    Ever my Dearest Stanley
      Your aff^{te} Father
        Thos Jevons

22. THOMAS JEVONS TO W. S. JEVONS

                Lpool 18 Feb 1853

My Dear Stanley
 I fully expected that my letter would set you to think deeply on the subject of your future employment but there is no necessity for so very violent an action of thought as you have entertained. A calm consideration and weighing of the subject is the best for a wise decision and an enumeration of the advantages & disadvantages in the shape of a mathematical sum on paper will help you to make up your mind with the least trouble to yourself and lead to the most stable results probably.

It appears however clearly that you give up Iron Making and I may perhaps say all sorts of employment that will take you from home to learn, and that you absolutely determine on some manufacturing employment which must be connected with chemystry* and be attainable in Lpool and this brings you so much nearer a conclusion that you may

[3] For Jevons's reactions to this letter, see Vol. I, pp. 88–9.

without letting it interfear* with your sleep or with your duties at College calmly make up your mind on the grand conclusion

There are a great many kinds of manufacture which can be learned in Lpool and some of which flourish in Lpool equally with any other situation in the world I enclose a list for you to look over

Of all that are in this list the Soap manufacture has flourished most in Lpool and as in all probability the duty will be taken off this important article at no distant day I believe that it will be a rising and an improving trade There are at present sixteen soap manufactories in Lpool – While the excise duty is levied on the article the manufacture is carried on under great disadvantages and the result of its being repealed the trade would receive an impetus beyond probably what we can possibly conceive for besides the home market for the consumption of soap there is a very large export trade in it and I should think that there was plenty of room for making money[1]

Manufacturing Chemysts* is the next in importance of the List I send you & perhaps under this name may be also classed paint & colour makers though the latter is a trade of itself

After the above comes Glass. This manufacture some years since was subject to an excise duty, like soap is at present, and was then only carried on profitably by cheating the excise. On taking the duty off the manufacture increased probably tenfold and is still a very rising trade & no cheating in it.

I do not conceive that it is absolutely necessary for you to decide any thing immediately between all these different occupations but you may think them over and if you could get to see any manufactories in London it would be all the better I should think your professors could give you a letter or letters to see some or some of your excise men could take you and a walk through one or two first rate concerns would be of infinite benefit in helping you to make up your mind

I steal time from my business to enable me to write this letter which occasions it to be written so bad which you must excuse & believe me always

    Your most affectionate Father
      & true friend
        Thos Jevons

[1] The duty on soap, dating from 1712, was repealed by Gladstone in his first Budget in 1853. The tax was then at the rate of 1½d. per pound on hard soap and 1d. per pound on soft soap, having been halved in 1833; the yield was just over £1,126,000 in 1852. This high rate of duty made the British article uncompetitive in export markets and was recognized as contributing to the public health problems of the age, as soap was priced largely beyond the reach of the poor. In addition it had resulted in illicit manufacture, fraud and smuggling from Ireland, where soap was untaxed. Liverpool was one of the principal centres of manufacture, producing about 40 million pounds of hard soap in the year ending 5 January 1852. Cf. S. Dowell, *History of Taxation and Taxes in England* (1884) IV 328–34.

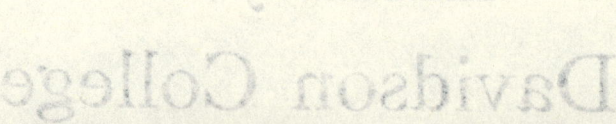

- × Manufacturing Chemists
- × Curriers
- × Wholesale Druggists
- × Dry Salters
- o Manufacturers of Earthenware & China
- × Iron Founders & Engineers
- × Oil & Colour manufacturers
- × Optical Instrument makers
- × Organ Builders
- × Iron Ship Builders
- × Soap Manufacturers
- × Sugar Refiners
- × Tanners
- × Tar & Turpentine distillers
- ☐ Glass manufacturing
- ☐ Copper works

- × Plenty of these in Lpool
- o One new & very large concern at Liscard
- ☐ These in the neighbourhood of Lpool[2]

23. THOMAS JEVONS TO W. S. JEVONS

Lpool 2 Apl 1853

Dearest Stanley

I was very glad to get your note announcing your safe arrival at your temporary home[1]

Since our visit to Prestatyn[2] I have been thinking about the management of those works and it strikes me that there is a good deal of slovenlyness* about them and want of good arrangement. The sulphur ore ought all of it to be deposited on that side of the work where all the sulphur furnaces are placed instead of which it seemed as if none of it was kept on that side of the work at all It is evidently laid down 30 or 40 or perhaps 50 yards from the spot it is wanted at which is bad economy. Then I think there was great carelessness about the salt. It is a cheap article I know but still that is no reason why it should be wasted as it certainly appeared to be by Kelly. But the worst thing I noticed was the very wasteful way in which the vitriol was used Whenever they drew it out of the great condensing vessels there seemed to me to be a

---

[2] This key is in the form given by Thomas Jevons in the original manuscript.
[1] Jevons had just returned to London after the Easter holidays. See Vol. I, p. 91.
[2] To a soda works. See Vol. I, p. 93.

loss. I dare say no one would rob them of any of it for litterally* they would burn their fingers but a good deal must be lost from the very irregular shape of their spouts and small tanks and by the modes in which they seem to pass the vitriol from one place to another and the great number of small tanks used each of which must occasion some loss There is evidently very little science or skill displayed in the arrangement and management of that work

One thought has struck me would it not be better to make the vitriol at the spot where the sulphur ore is got. There is little or no coal used in burning it and only a very small quantity to produce the steam and the weight of the nitrate of soda used is very insignificant instead then of carrying the ore in bulk down to the sea coast it would be better to carry the nitre & coal up to the ore and so carry only the vitriol down But as lime would probably be cheaper where the sulphur ore is got than it is even at Prestatyn it appears to me that probably the soda ash may be made much cheaper at the mine than any where else

I see that you cannot go so soon as you expected to the Laboratory[3] Will you let me know how soon I must send you the money –

The Great Britain[4] is just coming in with $1\frac{1}{2}$ millions of £s in Gold Dust nuggets &c and I am going down to the pier head to see her so excuse me writing any more just now

Your Ever aff^{te} Father
Thos Jevons

24. THOMAS JEVONS TO W. S. JEVONS

Liverpool 6 May 1853

Dearest Stanley

You would perhaps expect a letter of congratulation from me on the great Success[1] you have achieved at College sooner than this but a variety of engagements have prevented me writing and I have flattered myself that so many others would be sending their felicitations that you would not much miss mine or at least that you could well sustain the deprivation and at the same time not attribute the cause to any want of heartfelt joy on your reaping the Golden reward of your well earned

---

[3] The Birkbeck Laboratory. See Vol. I, p. 89, n. 2.

[4] Brunel's *Great Britain*, the first iron-hulled, screw-propelled ship, though originally built in Bristol for the North Atlantic run had begun to ply between Liverpool and Melbourne in 1852. She continued on the Australian run until 1875, when she changed hands. Damaged in a gale off Cape Horn in 1886, she reached the Falkland Islands where she remained, a condemned hulk, until 1970 when she was towed back to Bristol for restoration. Cf. L. T. C. Rolt, *Isambard Kingdom Brunel* (1957) pp. 201–16.

[1] Jevons had received the Gold Medal in the chemistry examination held on 12 April. See Vol. I, p. 94.

fame. Go on my Boy in the same thoughtful earnest and well sustained efforts in the track that your early developement* of good judgment has pointed out and I cannot doubt that added to the rewards of earthly success a prize of ineffable price will reward you in that blessed congregation in which will be gathered all that are truly worthy.

Your name appears as the recipient of honors* & prizes in most of the Daily Newspapers and you should buy one or two & lay them by as records which may turn out valuable at some future day even though it may not be until your Son or your Sons Son should rejoice his eyes with the Sight.

I have frequently had you & your prospects in my thoughts and I shall surprize* you perhaps when I tell you that a Gentleman who is a drug & colour merchant here asked me if you were open to join a person in Manchester a clever manufacturing chemist who wanted a partner with some talent & cash to extend his business. I told him that you might furnish the talent perhaps but someone else must find the cash, but that there were two other points which would at present be insuperable objections one was that you did not intend to leave Lpool and the other was that you were not of the legal age to enter into any Partnership and on that the overture closed as a matter of course. I mention it to you to shew* that there are openings likely to occur and as a good augury of the future.

I have been two days away from home and yesterday travelled 300 miles to reach home the same night. My journey was through the most splendid scenery that can be imagined From Milnthorp I went round Morecamb* Bay to Ulverston Down the district called Furness to Furness Abbey From there round the foot of Black Comb and on the Sea Coast to Broughton Bootle Ravenglass Whitehaven Workington Mary Port, Carlisle and down over the Shap fells to Penrith & Kendal & thence to Lpool What do you think of that for two days work besides actual business of which I did not a little.

I met with a Gentleman whom I knew who said he was exploring the district about Black Comb for minerals He told me that he had found Mundic[2] & Copper and was in his own mind satisfied that there were other & more valuable deposits yet to discover He has promised to inform me if any good is to come of his discoveries and to offer me to participate in any concern he may get up

We are rejoicing at having the good Doctor[3] with us again. His presence does Aunt Jane a world of good in aleviating* her pains both bodily & mental. I am happy to say that Aunt Jane is quite well enough to allow the Doctor to go out to dine at Otterspool

[2] i.e. iron pyrites.
[3] Dr Richard Roscoe, his brother-in-law.

with John Moss Esqre[4] and to go on to Woolton afterwards with Ambrose Lace[5] to stop the night.

I will now ask your excuse for naming the success of another aspirant for honors* of the scholastic kind. Your brother Tommy has had an invitation along with about 30 of his schoolfellows to a grand afternoons entertainment at Mr Greens and among all the sentiments given was one by Mr Green himself that the 3rd class lowest division was that which gave him the greatest satisfaction &c &c and this sent home Tommy who is one of that distinguished body with his countenance glowing with delight and as joyous as if he had been in the seventh heaven

The tool I write with is such as they keep in Chatham S^t where I write this letter and this must excuse the writing but the affection I bear you can be felt I trust no matter how obscurely conveyed by

Your ever attached friend & father
Thos Jevons

25. HERBERT JEVONS TO W. S. JEVONS

Lpool July 9th 1853

Dear Stanley

I am certainly deceived in the value of a Gold medal – it may bring you in some money after all. But first of all are you really to have the offer of the situation,[1] for it would be very mortifying if after a deal of anxiety of mind and just as you had determined to go, you learnt that another person had gained the place and put you out. Supposing that you are able to gain the place I dont think you would like to tie yourself to it for more than 5 years, and I for one would not wish you to go unless you could resign after 5 years time, you would then be about my present age and would be open to begin any business here or in Sydney, that you might have taken a fancy to. Do not then tie yourself for more than 5 years. There is another thing which if necessary would hinder you & that is if there are any oaths or subscribing to the 39 Articles or

---

[4] John Moss (1782–1858), then resident at the estate of Otterspool, was related through marriage to the Jevons and Roscoe families, being the son by his first wife of Thomas Moss (see below, Letter 30, n. 1, p. 56. In 1807 John Moss had founded a bank, Moss, Dales and Rogers, in partnership with his two brothers-in-law and Edward Rogers, a Liverpool merchant. His other business interests included railways: in 1826 he became deputy chairman of the Liverpool and Manchester Railway Committee and in 1831 chairman of the Liverpool and Birmingham Railway. Cf. J. Hughes, *Liverpool Banks and Bankers 1760–1837* (1906) pp. 189–200.

[5] Ambrose Lace (1793–1870) solicitor and Bailiff of Liverpool, was a second cousin of Dr Richard Roscoe and a first cousin of his wife, formerly Mary Ann Bardswell. Ambrose Lace's sister Margaret (1787–1840) had been married to Dr Roscoe's brother Edward (1785–1834), second son of William Roscoe.

[1] i.e. the situation of assistant assayer at the Sydney Mint. See below, Letter 26, p. 46, and Vol. I, pp. 96–8.

PLATE 4 William Stanley Jevons
from a photograph taken in Australia in 1858

PLATE 5 William Stanley Jevons
from a photograph taken about 1861–2

any humbug of that sort to put up with I would not have you do it. You would be very big & independant* with £500 a year for such a young chap as you, and that sum or only £300 & your situation under Government would introduce you without much difficulty into the best society, though you must not talk religion much.

Would you live in the mint, or would you be able to live where & with whom you liked & out of working hours would you be an independant* man.

Some think you would be subject to lowness of spirits at being alone among strangers at first, but lowness of spirits is like rust on Iron, which never collects when Iron is in use, so you would have daily duties to perform and have sufficient Cash to keep a little Laboratory of your own to fill up your spare time, or to buy books to read or even hire a horse to see the country with, along with another golden companion, & these things would prevent a continuance of that disagreeable affection if you were subject to it, but you are not much subject to it I think.

I should be rather disinclined to your going out, if you would be obliged to live in the mint with the other clerks & officers, for they would in all probability be Church & state & tory minded & not agreeable for your very intimate & domestic acquaintance. If you think yourself you would like to go & could live comfortably there for 5 years, then lose no time in gaining all the information about the exact situation it will be. If the place itself would be tolerably agreeable as regards time of occupation & personal liberty during the time you are not occupied in duty, there would be several collateral opportunities for enjoyment which would I should think be within your reach. You would learn sea life – catch seabirds, & sea fish, see sea sights, such as sea storms, etcetera. But do not think that papa or anyone else would wish you to go if you dont entirely wish to go on your own account. Selfishness is the first & last principle of human nature, & on it I should advise you to ask yourself two questions – should I like to go or not: if you say yes then you will be obliged to get the consent of my father: if no, then dont trouble yourself anymore about it for you have sufficient ability to earn your living either here or in Sydney: you are very young & unless you feel very much inclined to go yourself & should like to see the world a little, I would not advise you to entertain the affair. But whatever you fix, I advise you not to bind yourself for more than 5 years, for should you not like it when you are there you could then look forward to coming back in a tolerably short time, but as my father says you must know more about it, & we must talk to you first before we can say much about it.

Yours truly
Hert. Jevons

26. THOMAS JEVONS TO W. S. JEVONS

Chatham St Liverpool
10 July 1853

My Dear Stanley

I had commenced a letter to you yesterday at the office but was unable to finish it but left it there for completion another day. But on coming home last night I found your note of friday* the Subject of which is so important that it drives all other thoughts out of my head and constrains me to devote this morning the only time I have to spare to give you an answer within the time you desire to receive it.

It appears that the appointment of assistant assayer to the Mint about to be established in Sydney is almost within your grasp. The first feeling that filled my mind on hearing of this piece of news was one of exhultation* that you could be deemed worthy of such an appointment by such men as Professor Graham & Dr Williamson and all the rest of us here without exception & including your Uncle & Aunt Richard seem to participate in the same feeling and on the spurr* of the moment we seemed all to think that it is such a splendid offer that you ought not to pass it by. A more calm consideration of the whole bearing of the step and with my thoughts matured by a nights rest imposes on me the duty of laying many of the serious points resulting from such a step plainly and unreservedly before you in order that you may be able to form a better judgment as to the desirableness of accepting or refusing the appointment when actually offered for your final decision.

In the first place you seem to hint that by accepting this appointment you might almost consider it one of separation from us for the whole of life. Did I think so it would go very hard with me to advise you to accept it but I cannot doubt that it is only for a comparatively short term of years that the engagement would be made and should you decide to accept I must urge upon you as a "sine qua non" that you may have leave of absence for at least 6 mths but if possible 9 or 12 mths once in every 5 years with such a stipulation agreed upon a very large portion of the difficulty will be removed For although this is a long period of separation yet it is such as is almost dayly* resolved upon by other parents and sons in Lpool with not one hundreth* part of the safety and inducement that your case holds out. That you may look forward to revisit us from time to time if health and circumstance permitted is not a matter of any doubt or difficulty since the voyage to Sydney may now be considered as a safe one & certain to be performed within 70 days and before many years, will, I should not be surprised,* be reduced very much under that time. We have then to consider how we can bear a separation for five years. However hard it may be to me yet if it be for your benefit I must & will bear it, but as it respects your own part that of necessity must rest with yourself. That during the first year or two you would have many seasons of depression of spirits to bear with cannot be doubted and you must make up your mind to encounter them; they will be the more hard to bear because of your youth but such seasons must be indured* whatever age you might be. After awhile however and in proportion as you might gain the friendship of deserving parties those feelings would be considerably assuaged and if success attended your course when the time for your return came you would reap a joy and give to others such as can hardly before hand be conceived

The pain of separation and its continuance, and the terrible longing after home which will come upon you with an intenseness I cannot describe seems the only difficulty worth naming, for though you may meet with some trouble at first about domestic arrangements and the comforts of an immediate home those we shall be able to meet in part by introducing you to friends whom we have already settled there. I am well acquainted with Mr Tomkinson[1] who is Manager of a joint Stock Bank in Sydney He married a sister of Mr Frederick Worthington[2] who was our medical man for some years. He lived for a short time in the vale of Llangothlyn* next door to old Dr Worthington[3] and we called upon him two summers ago when we were at Llangothlyn.* Mr Tomkinson would be a good friend to you.

But your uncle Richard has a most intimate friend settled at Balmain an outskirt of Sydney with whom and with whose family he was acquainted for a great many years and once lived in his house for ten months when your uncle was settled as a Doctor at Staines near London or rather near Windsor This friends name is Rob Huntley[4] a medical man and it so happens that your Uncle has just received a very interesting letter from Dr Huntley which I enclose for your perusal

---

[1] Samuel Tomkinson (1816–1900). Served an apprenticeship with a Liverpool merchant; joined the North and South Wales Bank in 1836, later becoming a director; emigrated to Australia in 1850 to become Sydney manager of the Bank of Australasia, later moving to the Adelaide branch, probably at about this time, which would account for the fact that Jevons does not appear to have made contact with him in Sydney. He remained there until his retirement in 1887. Prominent in the political life of South Australia, he sat as a Conservative member of both houses of the Legislative Assembly and also of Adelaide City Council. Cf. obituary, the *Adelaide Advertiser* (31 August 1900).

[2] Frederick Worthington was probably a connection of the Jevons family. Thomas Jevons's sister Anne married George Worthington (see above, Letter 14, n. 2, p. 28), and his younger brother William Jevons, Junior married Fanny Worthington (1790–1871) daughter of a George Worthington, in 1817.

[3] The Jevons Family Book records that 'C. Worthington of Liverpool. Surgeon' attended the births of Roscoe, Lucy and Herbert Jevons.

[4] Robert H. Huntley, formerly a surgeon at Farrington, Berkshire, is recorded as having lived at Balmain near Sydney from 1858 to 1865; he does not appear to have practised medicine in Australia. Jevons apparently visited Huntley at least once, cf. below, Letter 56, p. 131.

This letter shewing* as it does so many of the bad feitures* of the Society of Sydney I could not on my conscience withold from you. It shews* that you may be exposed to many trials and evil influences which you might escape should your decision be to remain at home but it also shews* that there may be true friends and domestic happiness found even at that distance from these Isles I may mention that I am disposed to believe that the worst feitures* that Dr Huntley describes are rather applicable to the Gold districts and the Towns which are nearer to them than to Sydney say Melbourne Adelaide Victoria &c &c and that you may not necessarily come into immediate contact with the ruffianism he mentions This leads me to surmise whether or not there will be dwellings within the enclosure of the Mint in which the officers will be required to reside which might isolate you from the common run of society to such an extent as you might yourself desire

Should the appointment be definitely offered to you I think you should beg for a few days to consider the point and to consult your friends and you should immediately come down here because it is impossible for us to enter by letter into one hundreth* part of the numerous points that would be discussed in person or if you cannot possibly come down here then I think you must send for me to come up to Town to see you but the former is most desirable as you can then hear what all say including your Uncle & Aunt and you must remember that there is a telegraph now by which you can send me a message in a few seconds

Before concluding there is one point which I think you must make yourself sure of and that is as to whether it be a fact that besides the Salary of £100 the *under* assayer be allowed a fee on each assaye* he makes I should be disposed to think that the head assaye* master may pocket all the fees and the *under* assayer be compelled to put up with the Salary only. It will be well for you to get down in writing the actual remuneration proposed to be offered with as many of the duties and restrictions as possible because it would be a very serious thing for you to go out and be dissapointed* in the golden returns which you expect It would indeed be a bad job were you when out there [to]5 be obliged to go prospecting for instead of reaping a golden harvest.

Your Uncle tells me that Dr Huntley once resided in Lpool and was a schoolmaster here and he knew him then and after that in London when he turned to the medical profession and last of all at Staines and Mr Alport*6 was a drawing master at Burton on Trent –

Although I purpose coming up to Town with Lucy on or about the

---

5 This word is omitted in the original manuscript.

6 Henry Curzon Allport is recorded as having arrived in Sydney from London on 1 April 1839 with his wife and six children; he became agent for Colonel Edward Macarthur and died at Parramatta in December 1854, aged 66.

1 August yet as your affair is of so much importance I will not hesitate a moment in coming up at once should it seem likely that a real negotiation be entered into about your filling the situation in question I remain
Dearest Stanley
Your aff^{te} Father
Thos Jevons

27. W. S. JEVONS TO H. E. ROSCOE

13 Albert Street
Aug 28th 1853

My dear Harry

If you are to have any letter at all you must be content with a little of my ordinary run of letters at present, composed of assaying & Australian news; I have failed in an attempt to give Lucy anything else, and shall not try again with you.

I have been working very hard at assaying[1] lately often till 7 or 8 or even past, for plenty of Gold assays have been coming in, and in fact so many came in this week both from the Mint & Bank that Paul[2] could not get them done in time & did them badly then, so that there has been a regular blow-up between him & Miller[3] as well as with his own assistants. There has also been a letter from Sir J Herschel[4] and the gold assays have stopped suddenly. Fortunately Graham has been away all the time or else it would have been fearful. For I find his character just what we thought it to be.[5]

I know Miller[6] pretty well now & have been once to their place & am going again in a day or two; I think I shall like him very well. I dont know when we may get the appointments since Henry is most likely not going and they will have to find another first. I dont know how we shall have time to get the apparatus.

I have made out long lists of everything; the assay apparatus will

---

[1] This letter was written while Jevons was working in Professor Graham's assay laboratory. Cf. Vol. I, p. 97.

[2] I have been unable to discover any biographical information about Paul, who was presumably an assistant in Graham's laboratory. In an unpublished letter dated 11 December 1853, H. E. Roscoe remarked to Jevons '. . . I am sorry to hear that Paul makes such a mess of the things I wonder Graham keeps him' – Ed.

[3] William Allen Miller (1817–70), Professor of Chemistry at King's College, London, from 1845 and non-resident assayer to the Royal Mint; President of the Chemical Society, 1855–7 and 1865–7.

[4] Sir John Herschel, then Master of the Royal Mint. Cf. below, Letter 151, n. 1, p. 432.

[5] See below, Letter 66, n. 4, p. 161.

[6] Francis Boyer Miller, brother of W. A. Miller; appointed assayer to the Branch Royal Mint, Sydney, 1 July 1854, a post he is recorded as holding until 1865; lived at Double Bay, Sydney, until 1870, apparently returning to England; elected a Fellow of the Chemical Society, 4 June 1868, remaining in membership until 1889.

cost £140 to £150, the balances being nearly £40; the common chemical apparatus will be about £12, partly from Simpson & partly from Griffin, chemicals £5 to £8. Books £10 to £12, tools £6 about or altogether a little under £200.

I got your weights from OErtling[7] and they cost £1. 18. 0 but are very neat; I took them as you said to 50 Doughty Street a few days since, and hope you will get them.

I have been to an exhibition of Australian minerals in Leicester Square but almost all the specimens were exceedingly poor ones, because I suppose they have so few mines yet; there were some fine pieces of malachite however. You will have a splendid opportunity of getting minerals in Germany and I hope you will get plenty.

Graham has been sometime in Edinburgh to give evidence on a lawsuit, the chief point of which was whether a certain mineral was a coal or not. Graham, Hoffmann*[8] & 8 other chemists said it was; Frankland[9] and several others with Chapman[10] said it was not; Brande[11] Gregory,[12] Quecket*[13] Johnston[14] & almost all the chemists in England also gave evidence but Grahams side beat. Dr Miller was there too I think.[15]

I should not like to have to pay all the fees.

You must write again soon but for the present,

Believe me

Your affec. Cousin
W. S. Jevons

[7] L. Oertling, Berlin-born founder of the firm of scientific instrument makers, received an award at the Great Exhibition of 1851 for his graduated beam and rider balance.

[8] August Wilhelm von Hofmann (1818–92), Professor of Chemistry at the then Royal School of Mines (to become the Royal College of Science, 1896) since 1845, the year in which he came to England after studying under Liebig at Giessen; returning to Germany in 1865 to become Professor of Chemistry at Berlin; President of the Chemical Society, 1861–3.

[9] Edward (later Sir Edward) Frankland (1825–99), first Professor of Chemistry at Owens College, Manchester, where he was succeeded by H. E. Roscoe; Professor of Chemistry at St Bartholomew's Hospital, London, 1857–63, and 1863–5 at the Royal Institution; succeeded Hofmann at the Royal School of Mines, 1865–85; President of the Chemical Society, 1871–3.

[10] Edward John Chapman (1824–1904), mineralogist and geologist. Professor of Mineralogy at University College, London, 1849–53; Professor of Mineralogy and Geology at Toronto, Canada, 1853–95.

[11] William Thomas Brande (1788–1866) Professor of Chemistry at the Royal Institution, 1813–54; from 1852 superintendent of machinery at the Royal Mint; President of the Chemical Society, 1847–9.

[12] William Gregory (1803–58), Professor of Chemistry at Edinburgh, 1844–58; graduated from the Edinburgh Medical School, 1828; studied under Liebig at Giessen; Professor of Chemistry at Anderson's College, Glasgow, 1837; Professor of Medicine and Chemistry at King's College, Aberdeen, 1839.

[13] John Thomas Quekett (1815–61), Professor of Histology in the Royal College of Surgeons, London, 1852–61.

[14] James Finlay Weir Johnston (1796–1855), Professor of Chemistry and Mineralogy in the University of Durham since 1833; chemist to the Agricultural Society of Scotland, 1844–9.

[15] W. A. Miller did not give evidence in this suit, *Gillespie* v. *Russel*, known as 'The Torbanehill Case', heard in Edinburgh before the Lord President on 29 and 30 July and 1–4 August

28. THOMAS JEVONS TO W. S. JEVONS

Liverpool 17 Sep 1853

Dearest Stanley

I am very glad to get your letter (of the 15th) this morning notwithstanding it entails not a little thought about "things in general" as you say. It often happens that just when you are approaching the "denoumont"* of any business there is apparently a complete jumble of a vast many preparations all tending to the same end, they look like confusion worse confounded and then more quickly than you can conceive it possible all work themselves into an harmonious whole and so we hope it will be in your and in Lucy's case for I have your sister to think about just now as well as you

As to your accident it is the first that you have thought it necessary to mention. It is not one of much moment and all I can say is that it is a wonder you have not had a dozen instead of one and I therefore find an occasion of congratulating you on your being so free from accidents in such a ticklish employment Of course it will make more necessary some present to the professor and probably now would be a good time to offer it, but I think we must wait until you have gone through your probationary course at Dr Millers[1] My own ideas on the business are these that Cap. Ward[2] was much startled at the professor recommending a youth only then 17 years old, that he might well fear that after arrival out in Sydney and when getting to work with the Mint he might be troubled with an inefficient assayer and be saddled with him for a long period of time for being a Government appointment he would not have the power of dismissal. He would have all the onus of making out a case against you (as black as he could) in order to induce Government to

---

1853. A company of coalmasters, James Russel and Son, had leased a tract of ground at Torbanehill, Linlithgow, to mine coal, ironstone, iron, limestone and fireclay, but not copper or other minerals. They extracted large quantities of what was called gas-coal, which the proprietor of the lands, Mrs Elizabeth Honeyman Gillespie, declared not to be coal and therefore outside the terms of the lease. Damages were laid at £10,000. The evidence of the expert witnesses conflicted but the jury took only five minutes to deliver a verdict in favour of Russel. Detailed reports of the case appeared in *The Scotsman*, 30 July, 3 and 6 August 1853 (XXXVII 3502–4); cf. also *Chambers's Edinburgh Journal*, XX, 10 September 1853 (1854), 169–70.

[1] Although Jevons had spent the summer learning assaying in Professor Graham's private laboratory, Captain Ward then asked that he should also go for a probationary period to Professor W. A. Miller's assay office (see Vol. 1, p. 19).

[2] Edward Wohlstenholme Ward (1823–90); eldest son of Hon. John Petty Ward of the Bengal Civil Service; 2nd Lieutenant Royal Engineers, 1841; Lieutenant, 1844; Captain, 1852; Deputy Master of the Sydney Mint, 1853–69; Chief Officer of the Melbourne Mint, 1869–77; Major (Army rank) 1864; Colonel (Army rank) 1869; Major General (Army rank) 1877; K.C.M.G. 1879; died at Cannes; in 1857 he married Annie Sophia, daughter of Robert Campbell, New South Wales Treasurer; cf. below, Letter 101, p. 279.

dismiss you and as the Government would not do it without affording you the opportunity of appeal you will see that backwards and forwards he might be troubled with you for a year or two after he had got disgusted Then again he could not devine* what reason or motive Graham could have for recommending so young a person, whatever Graham said he would be hard of belief, and think that he had some hidden and private motive and would distrust to a certain extent Grahams judgment in the business It is then very natural to suppose that Graham might suggest to Cap Ward or Cap Ward might himself wish that the opinion of Dr Miller should be had in addition to Professor Grahams. I must confess that were I in Cap Wards place I would most assuredly require some confirmation from a third party of the fitness of the appointment and therefore I for one cannot be at all surprised* nor take it in the least degree in any deprecatory manner. Had the appointment been in England, less risk would be run because the removal could be easily effected but the appointment being 12,000 miles off quite alters the case and justifies the utmost precaution on Cap Wards part. I think then that it is quite right and proper that you should go to Dr Millers even though it should be for no other reason but to have his approval and to be examined by him and I doubt not that as you have acquired the highest testimony that Graham could give you will equally deserve and win Dr Millers also Go on then and do your best and the affair will come out right in the end.

18th I wrote the above at the office last night and on coming home I found a letter from Lucy which I will enclose. She seems to be getting very home sick and I doubt whether she can wait until you have settled all matters about the assayership and I fear I shall have to send Herbert over for her but I will decide nothing for a week and if by that time you can see your way clear and like the job why then I shall be glad for you to go over to fetch Lucy back but I much fear that you cannot get your liberty soon enough for Lucy's patience in which case I must send Herbert but as before stated we will wait a week at the least and then consult again about it.

I have been reading two works on Australia one called Our Antipides* by Col^n Munday*[3] and the other Twelve Years Wanderings in the Brit Colonies by J C Byrne[4] The former was recommended to me by Ashton Yates[5] the latter by Parry the Librarian[6] They are both very interesting

---

[3] Godfrey Charles Mundy, *Our Antipodes: or, Residence and Rambles in the Australasian Colonies, with a glimpse of the Gold-Fields*, 3 vols (1852).

[4] J. C. Byrne, *Twelve Years' Wanderings in the British Colonies, from 1835–1847*, 2 vols (1848).

[5] John Ashton Yates (1791–1863). See above, Letter 11, n. 5, p. 24.

[6] John Parry, schoolmaster and Librarian of the valuable collection of books possessed by the congregation of Renshaw Street Chapel.

to read and represent the Country and Sydney in particular in the most glowing colors* with one exception, and that is the Licentiousness that exists amongst a very large portion of the inhabitants at the time the books were written say 5 years since There will be enough of good and virtuous people for you to associate with and with whom your tastes & occupations will lead you to seek and choose acquaintance which reconciles me to the risk you will run for if there were not I for one could rather you abandoned the glorious prospect But you I fear not will keep steady to the right path and all risks of and temptations to vice will fly harmless by On that score I have perfect confidence in your good sense and good principles and I fear not.

You tell me you have taken up Astronomy as a subject of Study and think you can establish an Observatory at Sydney ("perhaps you had better catch your fish first") but I think you will in that new world find so much to discover in botany & mineralogy, that you will not have much time to devote to a new science the more particularly as you have already attained a proficiency in one of those sciences Botany which will give you a high starting point and your tastes will lead you to pursue that path as a recreation whilst in the other your means of livelihood is so intimately connected with the precious metals and naturally with the minerals that contain them in their crude state that you can hardly avoid the pursuit of mineralogy even against your will. As a mere recreation you may take up Astronomy superficially at any spare time you may have in a year or two or a few years to come, for the present I should recommend your learning as much as you can of the art of assaying minerals in addition to the precious metals for depend upon it there will be discoveries without end turn up in the extended search for Gold You told me once that you did not understand annalytical* Chymistry* and *that* therefore seems to me to call for your attention now I know not exactly what it means but I argue upon it from your own observation alone.

I am glad that you seem pleased with the present I intend for you If any opportunity offers I shall not fail to send it you

The emigration hence to Australia seems to be growing up strong again.[7] There are 57 large vessels now taking in passengers in Lpool of which however only eleven are going to Sydney these are however

---

[7] A wave of emigration to the Australian colonies in the 1850s reached its peak in 1852; contributory factors included the Irish potato famine, the discovery of gold in Australia in 1851 and the revelation of the colonies' agricultural wealth at the Great Exhibition. There was a comparative decrease in emigration in 1855 and 1856 owing to a general improvement in the economic situation in Britain after the 'Hungry Forties' and to an increase in employment and demand created by the Crimean War.

Contemporary emigration figures were based upon the passenger lists of ships sailing from ports in the United Kingdom and provide no indication as to the numbers intending

[of]⁸ the largest dimentions* say 1500 to 2000 Tons each For all [you] [k]now yet you may have to take your departure in some vessel to be fixed on by yourselves and the Govern^{mt} will allow you money to pay your passage instead of taking you in a *Man of War* but time will shew* this.

I do not think of any thing more to say now but that I wish you to write as often as you possibly can. Let us make the best use of present opportunities we can for in a few months we can only write to each other at longer intervals and on what may be to each other bye* gone subjects The thought that awhile hence our correspondence must be carried on at so wide a distance makes me luxuriate in writing to you now and as you see there is some selfishness at the bottom I must beg your excuse Perhaps there may be some of the garulity* of an old man in what I say but that only calls for the more necessary pardon But however distant and on whatever occasion always count on the most endearing affection and everlasting friendship of

Your only Earthly Parent
Thos Jevons

29. THOMAS GRAHAM, W. A. MILLER TO E. W. WARD
   (Copy)

University College, London
October 13, 1853.

Captain Ward R.E.

Dear Sir

The Candidate for the appointment of Non-resident Assayer to the new Mint in Australia, Mr William Stanley Jevons, whom I had formerly the pleasure to recommend to you on the general ground of superior chemical attainments has since been engaged for several months in the assaying of Gold & Silver in my Laboratory, & I am now enabled to inform you that he possesses the technical information & practical

---

permanent settlement. Estimates of emigrants to the Australian Colonies and New Zealand for the decade 1846–56 are as follows:

1846: 2,347	1852: 87,881
1847: 4,949	1853: 61,401
1848: 23,904	1854: 83,237
1849: 32,191	1855: 52,309
1850: 16,037	1856: 44,584
1851: 21,532	

Cf. *Seventeenth General Report of the Emigration Commissioners, 1857*; *Parl. Papers*, 1857 [2249] xvi 33.

⁸ A piece was torn out of the page here, apparently when the seal was removed. Missing words are bracketed.

skill which are more especially required. Mr Jevons is fully competent in my opinion to undertake at once without further preparation all the various duties of Assayer to a Mint.

I have the honor* to remain
Dear Sir
Very truly yours
Tho. Graham
Prof. of Chemistry & non-resident Assayer to the
Royal Mint.

Having had personal experience of the skill and accuracy of Mr Jevons in the assay of Bullion I have much pleasure in adding my cordial concurrence in Prof. Graham's testimony respecting his qualifications, and his fitness to undertake at once the duties of Assayer to a Mint.

Wm Allen Miller M.D.
Prof. of Chemistry, King's Coll. & non resident
Assayer to the Royal Mint –

30. THOMAS JEVONS TO W. S. JEVONS

No 1 A, Rumford Place,
Liverpool, 17 Oct 1853

Dearest Stanley

I think the whole course of my letters to you of late have been little more than a series of congratulations on your eminent success on what I may call your first start in Life. These last testimonials being joint ones from Professor Graham and Dr Miller must be most gratifying to you as they are to me they are fairly won and with your previous testimonials form the foundation of that fame & fortune which it is my pride to think awaits you through life and which it has ever been and ever will be my great delight to do all my little effort to promote

The first money you now want seems to be sufficient to purchase 2^{oz} of pure Gold to be kept as a standard for your after progress in assaying and to enable you to purchase that I enclose Bank of Engd Lpool Branch note ^v_o 26699 dated 23 May 1853 for £10 and I take this opportunity of saying that this and all the money I have already advanced & may still advance before you sail for Sydney Australia I look upon as advanced for your promotion in Life and I make it a free gift to you on one condition only which is this That in case of my death without leaving behind me sufficient means for my executors to purchase an Annuity of £150 p anm for Roscoe & without my having myself procured for him such annuity before my decease that then on the application of my executors you shall pay back to them as much of the entire money advanced by me as they may require from you towards making up a sufficient sum for purchasing the said annuity of course without your being liable for Interest for the money

My motives of action are these Roscoe is unable to take care of himself and therefore my first duty is to provide for him after my decease & Lucy and Henny will each have about £100 p an^m left them seperately* by their Mama out of Aunt Moss's bequest[1] Herbert I have supported until now, taught him bookkeeping and am still teaching him a business by which he will be easily able to maintain himself, further than this I have only Tommy to provide for He is too young yet to form any plans for but he is sensible clever and quick thoughted and if my life be spared long enough I do hope to be able to settle him in some good way of business or in a profession so that he may be able to support himself but if providence decrees a different destiny to me I must leave him a charge may I not say a delightful charge for his brothers & sisters to take care of and set up in life. And having made this exposition of my views and motives of action I trust that you will see nothing but what is just and give me your approval I must add that in my Will, after leaving an annuity of £150 a year for Roscoe during his life I leave all the rest of my property that I may die possessed of to be equally divided between all the rest of my children without any prefference* of one over another.

You ask how are you to get the money to pay for your Balances &c I answer when you have made your purchases and got a bill of any particular one send the bill to me and I will send you the cash back again with the bill that you may settle the same I have got a sum laid by which will cover it all if you are not too extravagant of which however I have no fears Any small purchases that you want to make and pay for at the time you must ask me for the cash first and you have only got to make a list and estimate of them and I will send you the cash

I enclose a nice letter from Lucy received this morning when read pass it on to Henny   I remain
Your Ever aff^{te} Father
Thos Jevons

P.S. Of course you will order the French things with Miller.[2]

[1] A great aunt of Jevons on his mother's side, being Elizabeth Griffies (1755–1838), elder sister of William Roscoe's wife Jane. She married Thomas Moss (d. 1805), a Liverpool merchant, as his second wife in 1796. Her character was both formidable and businesslike and she did much to assist the family of William Roscoe after his bankruptcy. She had no children and left a legacy to Jevons's mother.

[2] Jevons's departure for Australia was postponed because of delay in building the Sydney Mint. In February 1854 he started a two months' course at the Paris Mint. See Vol. I, p. 19.

31. E. W. WARD TO W. S. JEVONS

Royal Mint
23ᵈ January 1854

Sir

Having received the authority of the Lords Commissioners of Her Majestys Treasury to appoint you one of the assayers of the Branch Royal Mint at Sydney New South Wales at a Salary of one hundred pounds per annum, with an allowance (to be fixed by the Colony) for each assay performed for the Mint, and with permission to practice* for your own emolument so long as the government business does not suffer therefrom,

I have the honor* to notify the same to you and to inform you that your appointment will date from 1ˢᵗ July next on which day your salary will commence.

As you have expressed to me your wish to be allowed to proceed to Sydney at your own convenience I would state that I have no objection to your leaving this at any time you may feel disposed, between this and the 1ˢᵗ July next.

I am willing as soon as you inform me that your movements have been decided on, to allow you the sum of Seventy Pounds for your passage and the freight of your personal baggage; also a sum sufficient to cover the conveyance of five tons of extra baggage (which of course should comprise nothing but what you consider necessary laboratory fittings apparatus &c) on receiving an invoice of the Articles.

I have the honor* to be
Sir
Your obedient
Humble Servant
E W Ward

W. S. Jevons Esqʳ
University College
  Gower Street

32. W. S. JEVONS TO HENRIETTA JEVONS

Rue de Lille. 59. Paris
Fevrier 7ᵗʰ 1854.

Ma chere Henny

Je suis ici dans ma chambre solitaire et parce que je veux écrire à vous, et que j'ai besoin d'une exercise Française, je vais vous écrire une lettre en Français.

Vous savez qu'Oncle Timothy, Willy[1] et moi, nous arrêtâmes pendant trois jours à Londres. Nous demeurâmes à 32 Norfolk Street, ainsi bien prés de la maison ou vous étiez avec Papa, Lucy et moi. En effet nous employâmes le temps dans la même manière à peu prés qu'vous; j'allai tous les jours au Collége mais j'accompagnai Willy pour voir beaucoup des spectacles. Cependant nous n'avons pas fait de choses si jolies qu'ascendre au haut de St Pauls ou visiter l'opéra Italien.

La journée de Londres à Paris ne durait pas que pendant douze ou treize heures. Jusqu'à Boulogne elle etait fort agréable, et le débarquement et la visite des officiers des douanes à nos portmanteux nous amusions beaucoup.

Nous avons demeuré jusqu'á hier á l'Hotel Meurice dans la Rue de Rivoli. C'est une trés belle rue qui passe le grand Palais des Tuileries, la résidence de l'empereur, et nos chambres donnaient sur les Jardins des Tuileries. Vous ne pouvez pas imaginer quelle nombre y-a-t-il d'édifices grands et beaux. Par exemple, au coin opposé á cette maison – ci, il y a le Palais d'Orsay; un peu plus loin le Palais de la Legion d' Honour[2]; au bout de la rue de Lille, il y a le Palais Legislatif (House of Commons) aprés lequelle l'Hospital des Invalides. Pleusieurs de ces edifices sont aussi larges que le Buckingham Palace. C'est présque le même dans tous les quartiers de la ville, que j'ai déjâ vu.

Thursday 9th: On reading over again what I have written I think you will hardly be able to read it, between the bad writing & the bad French, so I will go on in English. Of all the things that I have seen yet, the Louvre, as it is called is by far the finest. It is a magnificent palace filled with all sorts of collections of pictures, sculpture antiquities, &c, &c, but the most celebrated I believe are the pictures by the old painters. I hope you may come to Paris sometimes, but as far as I can see there appears to be very little music in the people here. I have heard a barrel-organ or two and one band and that is about all the music except the drumming which goes on at all times of the day at the barracks opposite to my windows. It is done very cleverly & quickly on a small drum and sometimes they make regular tunes.

They never burn coal here, but only logs of wood; there is therefore no grate but the fire is on the hearth with two bars called Andirons, in a very primitive manner. They have tongs & shovel something like

---

[1] His first cousin William Edgar Jevons (1836–88) youngest son of Timothy Jevons. See below, Letter 34, p. 61.   [2] Spelt as in the original manuscript.

English ones, but *no poker*, and as the wood makes little or no smoke all the houses & buildings are white & not dark as in London or Liverpool. In fact the whole town here seems white even down to the mud in the streets which is white because white paving stones are used.

The Paris Ladies are of course rather fine as might be expected from the Fashions & every thing relating to dress coming from Paris; but perhaps you will be surprized to hear that $\frac{2}{3}$ of the women never wear any bonnets. There seems to be a natural though rather singular disposition in people here to be run over. If any man or woman is crossing a street and a carriage is coming, they are sure some way or other to meet, so[3] that the cab-man has to shout & stop, & the person to run.

I am beginning to think that all the people in Paris live in Lodgings, for I have not seen a single proper dwelling house yet with a front door. All the houses are very large and seem to be little *villages* of small houses on different floors. Each of these houses has what answers to a front door but my house here consists of only one room for[4] living & sleeping the usual way of living here.

These facts of the *natural History* of Paris people are very amusing to me who sees them but I am afraid they will be rather dull, so till I write again to you,

    I remain
    Your ever affectionate Brother
      W S Jevons.

33. THOMAS JEVONS TO W. S. JEVONS

              Lpool 15 Feb 1854

Dearest Stanley

I was delighted to receive your letter of Saturday last and particularly to find that you were so much better and apparently enjoying your sojourn in the splendid city of Paris. I believe your indisposition arose entirely from the concealed poisons in the sauces of the French Cookery and now that you have got over the first attack I trust you will not fall into the same snare again. Your description of your present bill of fare is very good I advise you to stick to fish and to such meat dishes as you know what they consist of You cannot be wrong in mutton but as for beef it is too much of it horse flesh I recommend you to get half a grilled fowl now and then and occasionally a plate of soup of some simple sort and with such fare you will not be unwell again

I am rather amused at your shiness* about calling upon De Laskis[1]

---

[3] 'to' in the original manuscript.
[4] Jevons wrote here '... of living and sleeping ...'
[1] It has not proved possible to identify De Laski.

sister. You recollect how very agreeable he made himself and how well he spoke English and I make no doubt that his sister speaks English quite as well

The Great Britain[2] arrived home yesterda[y][3] in 71 days from Melbourne a very long pass[age] as we now call it. She has brought a very large quantity of Gold say £600,000 and what is more singular 23 bags of Cotton the first ever imported from Australia. Mr S Boult[4] came home in her and I had a good long conversation with him a few hours after his arrival. He left Lpool 18 mths since for California whent* from there to Sydney thence to Melborne* and home by way of Cape Horn and the Falkland Islands He says that the ship would have arrived a fortnight earlier if her bottom had been cleaned at Sydney but it was very much fouled with weeds &c This in fact is the only drawback which Iron ships have to contend against and if you could discover some chemical substance that would cover the Iron without injuring it and which would at the same time keep off the shells & sea weeds from the bottoms of Iron vessels you would make your fortune & your fame at the same time.[5] Mr Boult said that they had given up the thoughts of having a Mint at Sydney there had been so much delay about it. He said that all the people who came out there with Government appointments were giving them up as they were not satisfied with the salaries, but when I told him that your appointment would allow of your doing business on your own account at the same time he said that was quite another thing. One of his sons (for two went out with him) arrived at home about a fortnight since and the other has gone round by way of Hong Kong so you see what great travellers they have been I dare say I shall see something more of Mr Boult soon and will tell you if I get [a]ny more information from him –

You do not say anything about a cup[el] machine I advise you to ask De Laille[6] for as he sells bone earth I should think that he would also

[2] See above, Letter 23, n. 4, p. 42.

[3] The original manuscript of this letter is in a fragile condition. The edge of the first page is frayed, leaving these words incomplete.

[4] S. Winton Boult (1809–76) was the founder in 1836 of the Liverpool Fire Office, later the Liverpool, London and Globe Insurance Co., which he made the largest fire insurance office in the world, with branches in several continents. He had travelled around the world in order to make a study of fire risks in different countries.

[5] Some solution to the problem of fouling had been found in the late eighteenth century by sheathing ships' bottoms with plate copper, which protected wooden hulls against ship-worm and made it possible to keep the bottoms sufficiently clean to prevent the ship being made slow and unhandy. Iron hulls presented new difficulties: they were found to foul rapidly but copper sheathing could not be used in the same way because the electrolytic action between copper and iron, not at first understood, caused the iron to corrode. Hulls were sometimes planked outside with wood and then sheathed with copper, care being taken to prevent contact between the two metals. Cf. C. J. Singer, *A History of Technology*, IV, *The Industrial Revolution c. 1750 to c. 1850* (Oxford, 1958) pp. 579–80, 592.

[6] The supplier of materials for the Paris Mint. See below, Letter 37, p. 70.

know something about a cupel machine As bone earth seems very difficult to get dont you think it would be better to get a little more at first say 4⊖ or 5 Cwt instead of 300[7] I suppose it will keep without deteriorating in quality

I think you will be quite right to go to Varseilles* and if you can fix on a day when the water works play that will be all the better everyone says they are a most splendid sight I should think St Clous* was also as well worth seeing It was the favorite* palace of old Napoleon

You do not say that you have yet delivered your other letter from Graham[8] which I think you ought to do at once. Graham may have written to his friend privately and mentioned you and then he will wonder why you have not called and think that you slight him.

We are all quite well at home
    I remain Dearest Stanley
      Ever your aff^{te} Father
        Thos Jevons

34. W. S. JEVONS TO H. E. ROSCOE

        59 Rue de Lille. Paris
        Friday. Febr. 17th/54[1]

My dear Harry

It seems a long time since I either wrote to or heard from you, but at last I am writing, and shall hope for a letter from you in return before long.

I came here with Uncle Timothy & Willy Jevons who went on to Marseilles where Willy is going to learn Iron Ship-building[2] under Mr Phillip* Taylor.[3] I have been here just two weeks now and have of course had enough fun in the sight seeing and enough trouble in the speaking – French, getting lodgings &c. When I was in London, Graham gave me a letter of Introduction to Péligot,[4] the Assayer at the Mint here, where I have now been for a few days at work. The French Mint has a sort of regular course for assayers and gives a diploma after

---

[7] The figures are thus written in the original mss., without any units indicated; Thomas Jevons may have meant 'three hundredweights' or '300 lbs'.

[8] One was to Peligot. See below, Letter 34.

[1] The original manuscript of this letter is incomplete.

[2] Cf. Vol. III, Letter 199, n. 2.

[3] Philip Taylor (1786–1870), civil engineer; settled in France in 1828 after being in partnership with his brother in a London chemical works and an associate of Sir Marc Brunel in the Thames Tunnel project; founded engineering works, first in Paris, then in Marseilles; in 1845 bought a shipyard near Toulon which became a large and flourishing concern: it was sold to a French company in 1855. From 1847 to 1852 he lived near Genoa where the Sardinian government had invited him to establish works, but political troubles forces him to return to Marseilles.

[4] Eugène Melchior Péligot (1811–90), Professor of Applied Chemistry in the Conservatoire des Arts et Métiers and Assayer to the Paris Mint; distinguished for having first prepared uranium, 1841.

you have passed two examinations without which you cannot practise here. I passed the first of these which consisted merely in a few questions on assaying and shall try the second which consists in practical assaying in a few weeks. The diploma of course wont be of much use but I get practise* here and see their way of working. Also they charge nothing at all except what I shall have to pay one of the under assayers for teaching me, as I have to learn all the varieties of assaying as when the gold contains platinum palladium &c &c.

I expected that as Claudet[5] originally learnt the assaying here, they would do it better here in many ways but though there is a very large establishment they do very little work and that not particularly accurately. Besides Péligot, there are four assayers, a book-keeper, and one or two assistants yet they only do 20 or 30 assays a day, with a few other things. In fact I never saw people work less, for they come about 10 or 11 and disappear about 3 or $3\frac{1}{2}$. Péligot is the same; he assays a little and seems to be going on with some bit of chemistry. My idea of Frenchmen always was that they were sharp & active, and that that was the reason the French chemists beat the English ones, but everything here seems to go on in the same easy way as the Assaying. All the museums, one of the best things in Paris, are only open for a few hours in the middle of the day.

I have rather an objection to Péligot but otherwise like the laboratory very well and expect I shall learn a good deal.

They do the work more neatly & cleanly than I ever saw done before, but then they have plenty of time. They have only twenty gas burners here while the London assayer has always from 50 to 90, & the assay balances are about 1/5 as sensitive as Œrtlings.

I should like to know whether the Germans are anything like the French.

I suppose you all speak German almost perfectly now; I *might* hope to speak French in time, but have not got on the least as yet. What I have learnt chiefly is to do things with the smallest possible quantity of speaking, and I find it quite impossible to understand anybody who speaks to me.

I am quite out in Chemical as well as all other news and shall be glad if you will tell me of anything new in Chem. I happen however to have heard of the new metal[6] which I suppose is something like platinum or palladium.

[5] Antoine François Jean Claudet (1797–1867), French glass-manufacturer who became a pioneer in photography; in 1839 became part-owner of the English patent of the daguerrotype and the following year opened a photographic studio in London; devoted his career to the development of photography on a scientific basis, inventing many instruments and techniques and publishing numerous papers; F.R.S. 1853; Chevalier de la Légion d'Honneur, 1865.

[6] Aluminium had been isolated in 1825 in an impure form by Hans Christian Oersted of Denmark and an improved preparation was made in 1827 by the German Friedrich Wöhler. Both separated it from its chloride through the action of potassium, which was expensive and

I shall be glad also to hear the particulars of the new discoveries at the Heidelberg laboratory[7] whatever they may be from their discoverer and hope you will tell me when they are published.

I have seen the Emperor twice but he always goes about very fast and you cannot see him well. One time he was with the Empress.[8] My lodgings or rather lodging, as the Paris people only fill one room, are in a street next to the Quai's and just on the opposite side of the river to the Tuileries. It is also pretty close to the Hotel des Monnaies which is on this side. Of course I think the buildings very fine here, though they are rather too much the same, and I have seen none to beat St Pauls or St Georges Hall. The best thing is that they are not *sooty* like the English ones. I had no idea of such splendid galleries as those of the Louvre before but I doubt if the collections of minerals & geological specimens of the Jardin des Plantes which are so celebrated, are as good as those of the British Museum. I dont think museums on the whole are as much public here as at London though they boast here that everything is free. Sunday is very often the only day entirely free and seems to be the general day for amusements.

There is a large barracks for gendarmes and cavalry opposite to my windows, who are continually drumming at all hours of the day and there are plenty of sentinels and large barracks everywhere, but the soldiers are *generally* very small, not much higher than me,[9] I am sure and whenever a few march into the barracks opposite I generally see the last two walking with wrong steps, that is one with the left & the other with the right & so on in other things. I think they will look rather *small* besides the Coldstream guards and the rest of the 12,000 English soldiers who are going to Turkey.[10]

---

made the process very costly. The metal attracted considerable attention but remained a laboratory curiosity. In 1854 Henri St. Claire Deville (1818–81) found that sodium could be substituted for potassium and devised a process for producing aluminium from bauxite ore found near Les Baux in southern France, thus greatly lowering the price. The 'silver made from clay' at the Paris Exhibition of 1855 drew attention to the question of its economical production. Cf. A. J. Ihde, *The Development of Modern Chemistry* (New York, 1964) p. 467.

[7] After taking his B.A. at the University of London in 1853, H. E. Roscoe had gone to Heidelberg to study at the University under Bunsen. He was accompanied by his mother and sister. He obtained his doctorate in 1854 but returned to Heidelberg the following year to continue his researches into the chemical action of light. After his appointment to the professorship at Manchester he spent the summer vacations of 1859–62 in Heidelberg continuing research with Bunsen. They became close friends.

[8] Cf. Vol. I, p. 87, n. 1.

[9] Jevons was 5 ft. 5½ in. tall. Cf. Karl Pearson, *Life, Letters and Labours of Francis Galton* (Cambridge, 1914–30) II, 150.

[10] 'The first detachments of British troops for the expedition to the Black Sea sailed for Malta in February 1854. Their numbers and the dates of their arrival were announced, without interference from the authorities, in the columns of *The Times*.' (Woodward, op. cit., p. 274.) The Crimean War began on 28 March.

35. H. E. ROSCOE TO W. S. JEVONS

Heidelberg. Feb. 21. 1854.[1]

My dear Stanley

I was overjoyed to receive your letter giving such a flourishing account of your proceedings – as I wanted to write & did not know your address – Perhaps you will not have heard of the great news which is agitating the public or rather private mind here – That Harriet is going to be married! – What do you think of that my boy – to Edward Enfield[2]– He is a delightful man – & we are all as happy as possible about it – He is older much than she is – but I think this is a particularly good thing as her character is much formed – & she will get on much better with an older man – They have been attracted to each other for a long time & I think they have both as fair a chance of being completely happy as is possible in this miserable world – we shall miss her dreadfully – & my mother & I must poke on as well as we can alone – in Wigan or some other hole – or we will come out & live upon you when you are a millionaire in Sydney –

You will have heard of poor Aunt Roscoes death – Frank & William will feel her death vy much poor fellows[3] – they were very much attached to her – she was quite a picture of a noble old lady – I had a great regard for her – It is a mercy that she had not a lingering illness –

I think you seem to be getting on splendidly – I am sure your stay in Paris will do you a world of good in every possible way – you seem to find the assaying very easy – & I suppose you can now do it as well as anyone else – I am sorry you don't find Peligot pleasant – Do you know Cahours?[4] He is at the mint is he not? At least I understood so from "Friend Bennett" Brothers[5] who honoured me with a visit the other day.

---

[1] The original manuscript of this letter is incomplete.

[2] Edward Enfield (1811–80) first cousin of Mrs Henry Roscoe, grandson of Dr William Enfield, Rector of Warrington Academy, Liverpool's first historian; one of the five wealthy moneyers of the Royal Mint (see below, Letter 58, n. 6, p. 140. Remembered for his philanthropic activities, which included chairmanship of hospital boards and a close connection with the London Domestic Mission (see Vol. 1, p. 89, n. 4. His marriage to Harriet Roscoe (b. 1835), his second wife, took place on 19 August 1854 in the house of the British *chargé d'affaires* in Berne, '. . . in a beautiful drawing Room commanding a glorious view of the snowy Alps – the English Clergyman read the service very beautifully . . .' as H. E. Roscoe described to Jevons in an unpublished letter dated 8 October 1854.

[3] Formerly Hannah Eliza Caldwell, 'Aunt Roscoe' was the widow of their uncle William Stanley Roscoe (1782–1843), eldest son of William Roscoe, whom she had married in 1818. She was the mother of Francis Roscoe (see Vol. I, p. 193, n. 6, and William Caldwell Roscoe (see below, Letter 55, n. 12, p. 123; also of Mary Ann Roscoe (1821–52) whose marriage to Richard Hutton is described in Letter 12, p. 26.

[4] Auguste André Thomas Cahours (1813–91) Warden of the Paris Mint and from 1871 Professor at the École Polytechnique; taught for many years at the École Centrale des Arts et Manufactures and carried out research into proteins and amino acids.

[5] Alfred William Bennett (1833–1902), the botanist and his elder brother Edward Trusted Bennett (1831–1908), both of whom belonged to the Society of Friends; Edward Bennett at one time edited a temperance magazine, *Crusade*; A. W. Bennett, a contemporary of

They have been in Paris & heard Dumas⁶ lecture (Have you? – you ought –) – & saw Cahours at the mint – you should go to him if he is there – He wᵈ. be sure to be polite if you mentioned Grahams name – & said where you were going – &ᶜ – & see the process of coining there which the "Friends" saw – I had a letter this evening from Phillip Worsley⁷ from Marseilles who says he was going to Paris – to stay for about a fortnight – you must find him out – he will be a nice companion for you – I inclose* a note for him which you can send by post or leave at the office of their mines in France – Edward will give me the address – He is there *now* probably. Things prosper tolerably here – I work hard but it is the old story of getting little done – I mean in the way of progress of research. I am going to make my exāmen. = be made Fiddletee & Co. before long – in about 10 days – & I hope to get through well – I & Pauli⁸ make it together. I have got several new Platinum salts – one nice crystalline sulphur salt – & I am beginning to analyse them – & I hope to get done with them in a couple of months – There are nitrogen determinations which are troublesome – I think I get on as well as any other of the students – but it is horribly slow – I had letters from Wmson⁹ & Watts¹⁰ the other day – Watts says Wmson is not doing the SO_4H &

H. E. Roscoe's at University College, London, graduated with honours in chemistry and botany in 1853; later became lecturer in botany at Bedford College and St Thomas's Hospital.

⁶ Jean Baptiste André Dumas (1800–84), outstanding French chemist of his time; studied chemistry and physiology in Switzerland; one of the founders of the École Central in Paris, 1829; assistant Professor at the Sorbonne, 1832, Professor at the École Polytechnique, 1835, as well as Professor of Organic Chemistry at the École de Médicine; obtained the chair at the Sorbonne, 1841, and also lectured at the College de France for several years, taking considerable pains with his experimental lectures. He was the first chemist in France to give practical laboratory instruction to students, among them Cahours, at the École Polytechnique from 1832 and later at his own expense in his own laboratory; achieved political distinction, becoming Minister of Agriculture and Commerce, 1849–51, and in 1868 Minister of Education and Permanent Secretary of the Academy of Sciences.

⁷ A member of a prominent Bristol Unitarian family. In an unpublished letter dated 8 October 1854 H. E. Roscoe wrote to Jevons: '... Phil Worsley after studying at Freyberg for 2 months is now in Williamson's Laboratory – wh. is *quite* full – I suppose the Taylors will give Phil some place ...' (cf. above, Letter 34, p. 61. A Philip Worsley – probably his father – was connected with the London Domestic Mission Society; in 1862 Richard, son of Robert Roscoe, married Honora Worsley (1837–79) younger daughter of Philip Worsley, who lived in London, first at Taviton Street, Gordon Square, and later at Chester Terrace (cf. below, Letter 168, p. 460. Early in 1865 Jevons corresponded with Philip Worsely in connection with research into the Worsley family history.

⁸ A friend whom H. E. Roscoe had previously mentioned in an unpublished letter to Jevons dated 11 December 1853: '... I must now go & read German & English with Pauli – who I like very much – perhaps we shall take our degrees together ...' He also wrote in his autobiography: 'Six months after I first went to Heidelberg I passed the examination for the doctorate with my friend Pauli – he died a few years afterwards of phthisis ...' See also below, Letter 38, p. 73.

⁹ A. W. Williamson (see Vol. I, p. 69, n. 1).

¹⁰ Henry Watts (1815–54) assistant Professor of Chemistry at University College, London, 1846–57, under Williamson. In 1848 he undertook the translation of Gmelin's *Handbuch der*

Al$_o^H$ determns as he ought – but has got some products of the action of SO$_4$H on Pk Cl$_5$ – Heaven only knows what they are – He is a queer man – between you & me I dont think he will ever do very much good – & I am nearly sure he cannot ever work out the high problems – which he has attempted – of Chemical affinity – a man to do anything of that sort must before everything be a most sound & deep mathematician – & that he is not & will never be – Bunsen[11] said one day to me that all these phenomena of affinity are most complicated – depending on so many conditions & actions which we can in no way estimate or control – & I believe this is very true – It is difficult to get out of Bunsen what he thinks – & one seldom comes into contact with him on these subjects. I have been lately studying the subject of the Heat of Chem: Combination – & the connection of the evolved heat in combination with that absorbed in Decomposition – It is a most difficult subject – but there is a great deal yet to be done – I have read Thomsons[12] papers – & Joule[13] – & lots of others – also one by Thomsen[14] a Dane – in Pogg: on the Formation of a Thermo Chemical system[15] – vy interesting – Thomsons papers are first rate – but *very* difficult I can't read them nearly all – as they contain so much mathematics – I mean to go hard at mathematics when I am in Paris – & perhaps here in the Summer – but there is no good man here to teach one – a horrid shame – Nothing can be done without mathematics – & I hope to make up for not attending to De Morgan as I ought to have done – Fool that I was –

Chime, the last volume of which appeared in 1872 (cf. Vol. I, p. 83, n. 3).

[11] Robert Wilhelm Eberhard Bunsen (1811–99) obtained his doctorate at Göttingen, 1830, and after a period of travel succeeded Friedrich Wöhler as professor at Cassel, 1836; professor at Marburg, 1839; succeeded Leopold Gmelin to the chair at Heidelberg in 1852, remaining there until his retirement in 1889. He made his career in the field of inorganic analysis; developed several well-known instruments, most notably the Bunsen burner (1853).

[12] William Thomson (1824–1907) later Lord Kelvin; Professor of Natural Philosophy at Glasgow, 1846–99; developed Joule's doctrine of the interconvertibility of heat and mechanical work (see n. 13 below) and was largely responsible for the acceptance of the concept of 'energy' in a precise scientific sense. Cf. Ihde, op. cit., pp. 397–9.

[13] James Prescott Joule (1818–89), physicist. Studied under John Dalton and was for many years President of the Manchester Literary and Philosophical Society; determined the mechanical equivalent of heat and established the principle of conservation of energy. Cf. Ihde, op. cit., pp. 399, 404; see also Vol. III, letter 333.

[14] Julius Thomsen (1826–1909), Danish chemist; in 1852 he began extensive measurements of the heats liberated during chemical reactions.

[15] J. Thomsen, 'Die Grundzüge eines thermo-chemischen Systems', *Annalen der Physik und Chemie*, LXXXVIII (Leipzig, 1853) 349–62; XC (Leipzig, 1853) 261–88.

36. W. S. JEVONS TO HENRIETTA JEVONS

59 Rue de Lille. Paris.
Tuesday Febr. 28th/54.

Dearest Henny

I was more pleased than you can well conceive with your letter and must not any more put off answering it. I am glad to hear that you are so busy with the cramming process, as you call it, though it seems very cruel of me to say so but I believe that you will always think with most pleasure afterwards, of the times when you were most busy and troubled. That is what I have always found in my case, and though it is such a short time ago I think with pleasure of the times when I was most busy at College. The chief way also by which I can hope to make myself comfortable for so many years in Australia will be to keep myself very much employed in business if possible, or in any other things.

Like you, I have thought and did at the time think of when we were at home and together, and had the same pleasure as you perhaps in our music, &c, but though I hope to be at home for some months more, I can hardly hope to see you for more than a very short time. This makes me almost feel as if we should never know each other again as we do at present, so much changed shall we most likely both be at the end of five or ten years. But I could never go away at all without the fixed intention of coming back again as soon as the object which makes it necessary for me to go at all has been fulfilled and I believe that you get happiness & good out of every thing in proportion to the effort it requires for you to do it.

I dont wonder at you growing fonder and fonder of music and you will have plenty of time to give to it which I think cannot be given to any pleasanter things and to very few better things, as regards usefulness. I perhaps might have been a musician but for my music mistresses, but in the present state of affairs, I dont think it looks as if I should have much to do with music.

I have now been in Paris more than three weeks, and have of course seen an immense deal. It is very amusing indeed & I have had a great deal of pleasure but still I hope to get out of it before long.

At the present time the Carnival is going on, which consists chiefly in a procession called the Boef Gras,[1] in masked or fancy balls in the evenings at the theatres, and in a general tendency of the people to have even more pleasure than usual. For you must know that Paris people seem to live for nothing but pleasure. I have had a very amusing day

---

[1] The procession of the *Boeuf Gras* takes place on the Sunday before Lent, the animals being led through the streets by butchers in costume.

today and as I can satisfy you as to seeing the emperor, I will tell you all that I have done. I went this morning to the Mint as usual thinking to do a little assaying as usual. But they did not seem to give me anything to do, and at last my master, as I may call him, said that they wanted to finish and get off as soon as possible to go to "promener," and to see the procession. So I had nothing to do and thought I might as well go and see it again. I had seen it before by torchlight on Sunday night. The procession goes for three days, Sunday, Monday, & Tuesday, through all the principal streets of Paris, and consists of a large band, & drummers, dressed up, a number of men on horseback, dressed in very handsome, dresses such as were worn a good many centuries ago, a large fat ox covered with red cloth and a triumphal car in which there is a small boy, called the king, and a number of men & girls, in different dresses with banners &c. I dont exactly understand the affair but believe it has something to do with the butchers of Paris, and as it is an ancient custom and very well managed by the military, I think very well worth seeing.

When then, this morning, I happened to go, by good luck, to meet it at the Tuileries, and seeing a crowd waiting opposite the Palace and a red velvet cloth over one of the balconies, I knew that the emperor was going to come out to see it. I have given you here a very incorrect plan of the Tuileries & the Louvre, which consist as you see of immensely long lines of building.

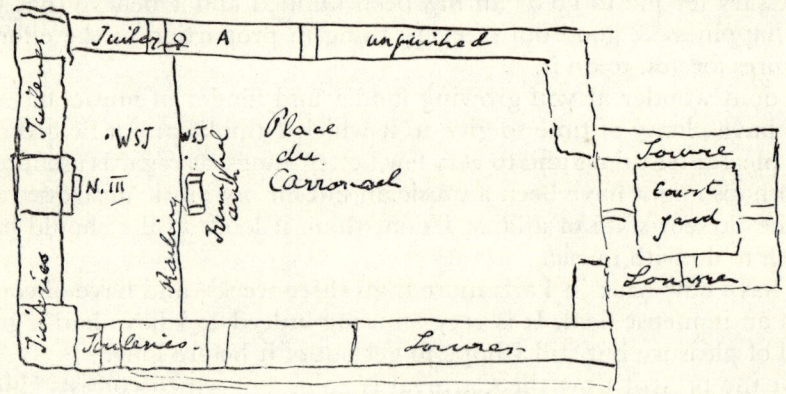

You may think how large it is when I say that the courtyard of the Louvre is I should think, nearly as large as Faulkner* Sq.[2] Well I got near the triumphal arch, as you see, the Place du Carrousel* being public, while inside the railings is the private space of the palace. The

---

[2] Falkner Square is in the Edge Hill district of Liverpool, bounded by Grove Street and Sandon Street.

procession came in at the passage *A*, and the Emperor & Empress then appeared on the centre balcony where you see N III. When the procession had all halted & gathered round the balcony, I was astonished by them opening the gates of the railing and letting a great many people in; I was pretty fortunate and got where you see the dot. I could see the Emperor pretty well though it was rather far off, and we waited there while the band played a few tunes. Lastly when the procession had all moved off they let us come close up to the Palace and of course then I could see them both very well. The Empress is quite as pretty as the prettiest of her portraits and seemed more pleased than anybody. I thought she rather liked to be cheered, and when they were going away, she came to another window, and gave sorts of small bows to the people which looked very like nodding to them. In fact I thought neither of them at all dignified, but do not like them any the less, as I think they have not had time yet to get grand. I think it was a special favour to the people to admit them within the sacred space of the Palace, and they, including myself, took advantage of it to see as much inside the Palace as possible. There was something I always thought very interesting about the Tuileries, and the building completely carries it out something like this, with very curious high roofs which I never saw before I came here.

You seem not to like the Emperor. I think that he must be a very clever man, and I admire him because he is doing the French people so much good.

Last night I was at the Academie Imperial de Musique or French Opera to hear the "Huguenots", by M^{ddle}. Curvelli.³ The scenery & acting was very splendid and the music by Meyerbeer⁴ very beautiful whenever you could get a plain air out of it, which was not very often.

This afternoon I took a walk on the Boulevards which are sorts of wide fine streets and they were crammed with people all come I suppose to '*promener*' though there was nothing to see.

I have of course seen a great many things more but if I were to tell you of any more I am afraid Miss Field⁵ would be thinking of giving an hour for reading as well as writing letters.

---

³ Probably Marie Caroline Félix Miolan (1827–95), French soprano; studied at the Paris Conservatoire 1843–7, making her debut in 1849; made her reputation on the French operatic stage and appeared successfully throughout Europe; in 1853 she married Léon Carvalho, later manager of the Théâtre-Lyric in Paris.
⁴ Giacomo Meyerbeer (1791–1864). *Les Huguenots* was first performed in Paris in February 1836.
⁵ Henrietta was at boarding school. See below, Letter 51, p. 109.

I shall try not to stop here more than three weeks more when I shall go to London for a few weeks and then home.

I remain
>Your most affectionate Brother
>W S Jevons.

37. W. S. JEVONS TO THOMAS JEVONS

>59 Rue de Lille
>March 11th 1854.

Dearest Father

I find a necessity which I had not expected to write again from here, and that necessity is *Money*.

I am pretty hard up, but hope to get off for London tomorrow at 12.0 and to get there at 10 or 11 on Saturday morning.

The fact is that I have had a *surplus* of about £13, which with the £5 of my own, was more than what I calculated that Deleuils[1] bill would be.

I went to his shop last night and he said that the whole of the things including the bone-earth[2] had gone to London. I said then that I would pay for the whole but when I had paid & got the receipt I found he had sent 138 Kilogr. of bone earth instead of 100 Kr. & the 38 Kgr. cost 76 francs; otherwise the bill was just what I expected from the one Graham had. It is a very good thing to have the additional bone-earth as you suggested, (I suppose he wanted to fill up the box) but it put me in very great doubt as to whether I had enough to pay all and get home.

On adding all probable expenses up last night I found I had just enough on condition of M^m G――'s[3] bill not being more than 170 fr. This morning however it turned out to be 204 fr. which at once made it almost impossible to get off.

This morning however I have been to the Mint & have finished all the *examinations*. The diploma & the stamp will be ready in a week or two & will be sent to Liverpool[4] and I shall then have to send them 25 francs which is all I have to pay except 10 I have given the "*garçon*". I might of course have paid all at once and would have done if I had had the money. I think then that as I pay nothing now at the Mint that

---

[1] Thomas Jevons referred to him as De Laille in Letter 33, p. 60.

[2] or bone ash, i.e. impure calcium phosphate. In the usual assay procedure 'metallic contaminants of silver and gold were converted into oxides which were absorbed by the bone ash cupel, leaving a button of the precious metal which could then be weighed' (Ihde, op. cit., p. 23).

[3] This name is indecipherable.

[4] They were not in fact sent but collected by Thomas Jevons during his visit to Paris the following year. See below, Letter 73, p. 184.

I shall have enough to get to London, by Havre & Southampton which is the cheapest & most interesting route.

2nd classe & 2nd Chambre on boat	21:00 fr.
Cabs, luggage &c	10.00
Bill of lodging to tomorrow	208
	239.00

and I have in my pocket 250.0 francs.

As soon as I get to London I shall be all right. I shall hope however that you will get this letter safe and that I shall get a little money before long directed to me *at the College* when I will go to get it

I have not time to say much more but I am all right otherwise and very glad to have finished entirely with the Mint. At this second examination this morning M Peligot & M Levol[5] 1st assayer, asked me a lot more of pretty stiff questions besides looking up the results of the assays I had done.

I am glad also that Deleuil is entirely done with now; he sent the bone-earth on the 4th March.

Your very affectionate Son
W S Jevons.

38. H. E. ROSCOE TO W. S. JEVONS

Heidelberg April 20th
1854.

My dear Stanley

I have not written to you since you were in Paris, & since we have been this long journey,[1] which has of course given us plenty to think over, & talk about. – I daresay you were glad enough to get to Old England after being among the French for so long, but it is a capital thing that you went, as you must have seen & learnt many things which you will be able to make use of in Australia. – In my journey I saw a good deal in every way of chemists & Laboratories – First I went to Giessen & saw the far famed Laboratory where so many researches have originated[2] –

---

[5] Alexandre Levol, first assayer to the Paris Mint since 1853; he had entered the Mint as assistant assayer in 1838, becoming assayer in 1847.

[1] H. E. Roscoe, accompanied by his mother, his sister and Edward Enfield, made a tour of Northern Germany in the spring of 1854. Cf. *Life and Experiences*, pp. 58–9.

[2] Justus (later Baron von) Liebig (1803–73) was Professor of Chemistry at Giessen from 1825 to 1852, when he took the chair at Munich. The laboratory which he established at Giessen, first in a disused barracks and from 1839 in a new building of his own design, was one of the earliest in Germany where practical instruction in chemistry was systematically given. It became world-famous and attracted students from many countries. Liebig's

& I introduced myself to Will[3] – Then I heard Buff[4] lecture on Galvanism – the heating powers of the circuit. – Tolerably good, but nothing particular – Then we went to Marburg where I saw Guthrie[5] & called on Kolbe[6] & saw the Laboratory. – Guthrie has been working under Kolbe at undermining Williamsons[7] Theory of the composition of Alc: Ether &c. – Kolbe says that the Carbon in Alc: is divided into two parts, & acts in different ways – & not as one radical Ethyl. – & so Guthrie takes Potassium Alcohol $\frac{KO}{Al}$ (Wmson) & puts it between the poles of a battery expecting – if it is water in w^h 1 of H is replaced by Al & the other K – that the Althyl will be evolved at the neg: pole where the Hyd: w^d be found in a water decomp – In the Expt: however he found that *no* Ethyl, but only pure Hydrogen was evolved – Therefore says he Wmsons representation is wrong – for if Ethyl replaces Hydrogen it ought to be evolved at the pole with the Hy^d. Now to say the least of it – This is a very great conclusion to draw from very slight premises – for he never examined the liquid to see what became of the Ethyl – but from the fact of the evolution of mere Hydrogen – Thinks & publishes that he has damned Wmsons Theory[8] – I think Kolbe is to blame in the matter – I dont know whether you will read this stuff, all – if you care for it I will give you more next time – So after leaving Master Guthrie we went to several places uninteresting in a Chemical but interesting in a religious pt of view as being Luthers quarters, & on to Leipsig & Dresden. At the latter Town the chief attraction is the picture Gallery w^h we diligently visited & enjoyed – There were also various collections interesting – next we went to Berlin – a splendid city – fine streets – beat ours in London – fine shops – & magnificent public

---

enthusiasm, inspiration and analytical skill were important factors in this success. Students worked on original problems and research covered a wide range of subjects. Cf. Vol. I, p. 83, n. 2.

[3] Heinrich Will (1812–90), Liebig's successor at Giessen, 1852–82.

[4] Heinrich Buff (1805–78) a former student of Liebig's; Professor of Physics at Giessen from 1839. Cf. Vol. I, p. 64, n. 2.

[5] Frederick Guthrie (1833–86) at this time studying under Kolbe at Marburg; obtained his doctorate there, 1856, the following year becoming H. E. Roscoe's assistant at Owens' College, Manchester; Professor of Chemistry at the Royal College, in the Mauritius, 1859–61; Professor of Physics at the Royal School of Mines, London, 1869; Professor of Physics at the School of Science, London, 1881.

[6] Hermann Kolbe (1818–84), Bunsen's successor to the Chair at Marburg, 1851–65.

[7] See Vol. I, p. 69, n. 1. Williamson's best known work in chemistry was on etherification and his so-called Water-Type concept. The latter was criticised by Kolbe. According to Williamson this criticism represented a complete misunderstanding of his view. See J. R. Partington, *History of Chemistry*, 4 (1964) 446–452.

[8] H. Kolbe, 'Critical Observations on Williamson's Theory of Water, Ethers, and Acids', *Quarterly Journal of the Chemical Society*, VII (1854) 111–121.

building of all sorts[9] – for accts of these I refer you to H^{tts} letters – if Lucy lets you read them – I called on old Heinrich Rose[10] in Berlin – he was very kind – a most interesting old fellow – & showed me all about his laboratory. – Among other things I asked him about a large laboratory w^h I had heard was to be built in Berlin for 100 students – he s^d it would not do & added "nein-der liebe Gott selbst muss Director segn von ein so grossem laboratorium"! This assured me not a little – I then saw Rammelsberg[11] who is at the Gewerbe Schule & has a good laboratory – but he is not much of a man – & I hear now he is not liked – Then at Munich – Liebig was unfortunately gone away – but I saw his son who showed me his laboratories & lecture room – a most splendid one – & I also saw Pettenkofer[12] with whom Pauli[13] was assistant – he was very kind & pleasant. At Berlin we saw a good deal of the military of Prussia – there was a large parade before the Prince of Prussia[14] – & we saw the artillery also – there is a garrison of 10,000 men in Berlin – I formed a high opinion of the Soldiers – far better than other German States – in a certain Hesse Weimar we saw an army w^h just comes up to the one represented in Brown Jones & Robinson[15] – the finest affair I ever saw –

We begin regular work next week – & I am trying to polish off some things this week – Bunsen is going to give me some research for the coming semestre*, tomorrow – a physical one – What I dont know – We have been busy photographing & have got some very good portraits I will send you one of my honorable* self – if you will give it a place on

[9] In his autobiography Roscoe recorded different impressions of Berlin at this time, describing it as '... not much more than an overgrown village, with detestable pavements, shabby vehicles, and medieval sanitary arrangements both as to water and sewerage ...' (*Life and Experiences*, p. 58).

[10] Heinrich Rose (1795–1864), Professor of Chemistry at Berlin from 1835; the third generation in a family of chemists; with his brother Gustav, a mineralogist at the University of Berlin, made important contributions in the fields of inorganic, analytical and mineralogical chemistry; published a large number of papers, most of which appeared in the *Annalen der Physik*, edited from 1824 by his friend J. C. Poggendorf.

[11] Karl Friedrich Rammelsberg (1813–99), a former student of Heinrich Rose; instructor at the Gewerbe-Akademie from 1850; succeeded Rose to the chair at Berlin, 1874.

[12] Max von Pettenkofer (1818–1901), biological chemist and former student of Liebig, whose most important work lay in the field of public health; appointed to the first chair of hygiene at the University of Munich, 1866; the city established an Institute of Hygiene for him, 1872; refused to accept the germ theory of disease but his theories as to the cause of typhus and cholera, though incorrect, led to improvement in the water supply and drainage systems in Munich.

[13] Cf. above, Letter 35, n. 8, p. 65.

[14] It is not clear whether this is a reference to Friedrich Wilhelm IV, King of Prussia 1840–61, or to his brother and heir Wilhelm Friedrich Ludwig, King of Prussia from 1861 and Emperor of Germany, 1871–88.

[15] Richard Doyle, *The Foreign Tour of Messrs. Brown, Jones, and Robinson, being the History of what they saw and did in Belgium, Germany, Switzerland and Italy* (1854). Doyle (1824–83) had already depicted their comic adventures in England and on the Rhine in *Punch*, for which he worked as an illustrator, 1843–50.

yr walls at Sydney – Give my love to Lucy & tell her I will acquaint Russell[16] on his return with her tender inquiries as to his moustacious*.! Give my love to Herbert from whom I shd be very glad to hear when he feels inclined – Ever yours affec

Henry E. Roscoe

Wm Stanley Jevons Esq
  Chatham Street.
    Liverpool

39. H. E. ROSCOE TO W. S. JEVONS

Heidelberg. May. 25th
1854.

My dear Stanley

Thanks for your last letter, from which I was glad to hear that you are getting so far on in your preparations. By this time I suppose you will be nearly ready, & be thinking of your voyage. The more one travels the more I find that distances which at first appear very long are in reality much less – & I have no doubt that when you are at Sydney you won't think the distance from England as far as we do – It was very kind of Graham giving you that apparatus, he seems to have behaved handsomely to you in every respect – I shall be very much obliged if you will write me a line on your voyage to let us know how you are getting on – but please direct to your own house & they will forward it to me wherever I may be, for I shall be a wanderer on the face of the Earth having no snug berth like you my boy.

Probably I shall stay with Bunsen for another session – till next March – for I have got on a piece of work which I should not like to leave directly – I dont know whether I have told you about it – I am measuring (or trying to, more properly) the action of light on bromine and organic substances – If it succeeds it will be a splendid thing, as no measurements of any kind, of light have been made – Bunsen proposed that we should make the research together so I suppose it will be published by "Bunsen & Roscoe"[1] – I am also going to translate his book on Eudiometry into English[2] – but of this I have told no one & dont

---

[16] William James Russell (1830–1909), studied at University College, London, under Graham and Williamson; demonstrator at Owens College, Manchester, under Frankland, 1851–3; became a pupil of Bunsen and obtained his doctorate at Heidelberg, 1855; succeeded H. E. Roscoe as Williamson's assistant in 1857, carrying out research into gas analysis; Professor of Natural Philosophy at Bedford College, London, 1860–70; from 1868 to 1870 lecturer in chemistry at the Medical School of St Mary's Hospital, London; held a similar post at St Bartholomew's Hospital, 1870–97; F.R.S. 1872; president of the Chemical Society, 1889–91.

[1] See below, Letters 75, 114 and 126, pp. 192, 315 and 356.

[2] (R. W. Bunsen, *Gasometrische Methoden*, Brunswick, 1857.) *Gasometry. Comprising the leading physical and chemical properties of gases*. Translated by Henry E. Roscoe (1857).

wish it yet to be known – The book is not yet finished but he hopes to get it done by the end of this semester*. – I have not yet finished my platinum salts completely – I cannot get good nitrogen determinations – but I mean to work at them during the Witsuntide* Holiday & I hope to get them then done – They are confoundedly bothering – I have taken more time & trouble about them than they are worth but I am now bound to do them & must have another try. I think Wmson is vexed with me because I told him in my last letter that I thought there w^d not be matter enough to read before the Chemical Society! –

Russell has just got out his Sulphur determination[3]. It will be a very good one – & he sends his paper to the Chem Soc immediately – nobody else in the laboratory has got out a research –

We shall be in England in September for Harriets marriage[4] – & perhaps I shall come to Liverpool to the British association[5] – I have never been at any of the meetings & Liverpool is a good place to begin at – I only wish you could stop till then, but of course that is impossible – you will be nearly at Sydney by that time – I see, by the way, that they are establishing a University at Melbourne[6] also – Salary of professors £1000 a year – I suppose you have got a letter to Smith[7] Prof: of Chem: at Sydney – you s^{hd} ask Graham for one if you have none – he will give you one no doubt – though he would not give me one to Bunsen –

The little wretch – Do you mean to take out revolvers &^{c} with you to defend yourself against any stray Russian cruiser which might pick you up on your way? – There are some Russians down somewhere about Singapore I hear, they will be coming down on Sydney & carrying off your gold if you don't look out . . .

What do you mean to be like when I see you again – a respectable middle aged old gent: worth how many millions? –

You will perhaps spare your friend a few pounds when he is hard up, out of your abundance – Next time I write will be from England most likely, as there will be no particular news till then, & I shall direct to you Royal Mint Sydney in very large & important characters – you will be then a great man there – & one must show it outside ones letters.

Give my love to Lucy & Herbert & kind remembrances to your father from your

Ever affec
Henry. E. Roscoe

W. Stanley Jevons Esq.

---

[3] W. J. Russell, 'On a New Method of Estimating Sulphur', *Quarterly Journal of the Chemical Society*, VII (1854) 212–15. See above, Letter 38, n. 16, p. 74.
[4] See above, Letter 35, n. 2, p. 64.   [5] Cf. below, Letter 46, p. 102.
[6] The University of Melbourne was founded in 1853.
[7] See Vol. I, pp. 25 and 187.

40. W. S. JEVONS TO HENRIETTA JEVONS

Chatham Street
Sunday June 4th [1854]

Dearest Henny

I have not indeed written to you yet this quarter, but the cause is not that I am too busy, but that the less I have to do the less I do even of that little. As I am beginning now to become a little busier, I therefore now begin to think of writing to you. On this principle, you may expect lots of letters from Sydney as I dont expect to have a moment to spare there.

On Thursday I had to go up to London for a day. I spent Friday there and came back by the night train so as to get here on Saturday morning. I was for two hours at the Exhibition of paintings of the Royal Academy which I think you did not see when you were in London. There were of course a great many fine paintings, but also a great many foolish & absurd ones, and a very large number of portraits which are very dull.

I shall sail about the end of this month and as you come home about the middle, I shall see you for some time more, though I shall expect to be rather bothered during that time. At present I am taking a rather larger proportion of music than would do for a continuance but you see, I shall not have any at Australia, and I shall not in all respects be sorry.

I have been playing a great deal of Spohr "Last Judgement"[1] some parts of which I am beginning to like very much and to think very beautiful. But he seems only able to be gloomy and sad[2] and not magnificent like Handel. I have also been playing some of Mozart who is always very beautiful & perfect but is not excellent in particular points like others.

Tommys examinations are going on at present, but he does not appear very anxious about them.

I suppose you have none which can be called regular examinations. They are very pleasant & exciting when you are trying for a prize with a chance of getting it, but I have altogether finished now with them.

You will see my berth on the ship, but I may tell you that it is very large, but at the stern with large beams sticking in, at all positions. It has a window looking out at the stern which makes it very pleasant. There is room to sit and read or write.

Till I see you again in two weeks
I remain
    Ever your most affec. Brother
      W. S. Jevons.

[1] Louis Spohr (1784–1859). His oratorio *Die letzten Dinge* (The Last Judgement) was performed in 1826 at the Rhenish Festival at Düsseldorf, having first been performed at Cassel.
[2] Jevons wrote 'say' in the original letter.

41. W. S. JEVONS TO H. E. ROSCOE

125 Chatham Street
Sunday June 25th/54

My dear Harry

You seem to have been thinking that I have been off for Australia some time since, without sending you a farewell letter, and a great many people, during the last few months have been telling me the same thing, when I have met them. But by the time you get this letter, you may fairly conclude that I have in reality sailed, as the ship is to go out of dock just at this time to day and will sail most likely tomorrow night.

All my possessions went on board this last week almost down to my last shirt and my last coat, so that I feel rather destitute, but not for long as I go on board myself tomorrow afternoon.

I have had enough time since last July to think about going that it ought to come pretty naturally now and as to the voyage, I expect to enjoy that very much in its way, as it is a good ship, and as I am uncommonly fortunate in my berth and my "chum".

The ship is the Oliver Lang, 1230 tons, a new clipper ship, taking about 400 passengers, chiefly for Melbourne, but of which there are only 24 in the first cabin. My berth is a rather large one at the stern with a window looking out behind and it is chosen as there is room for me to take the two assay balances in with me, so as to be sure they are safe. My "chum" is a Scotch fellow of about my own age, named John Anderson;[1] his father came from Scotland with him and seemed very anxious to see me, to be sure I suppose that I was not a runaway rascal, though I cannot say whether he seemed at all satisfied when he did see me.

My apparatus gradually accumulated till they filled 18 packing cases, besides 15 cases of acids which have already sailed from London. I think I have got almost every imaginable thing to fit out the laboratory from the best Assay balance, down to a wash hand basin and a set of blacking brushes. I have got also an assistant, Charles Bolton[2] going out with me, who has lived all his life in Mr Mosses Bank[3] here, so that he can be trusted with anything, and who will, I expect make an uncommonly good assistant.

Of course the apparatus with all the other expenses such as journeys

[1] It has proved impossible to trace any biographical details of John Anderson.
[2] Cf. Vol. I, p. 19. Charles Bolton (d. 1894) is recorded as having lived at Judge Street, Sydney, in 1857 and at an address in Paddington, Sydney, 1865–69. He left the Mint to try his luck at the gold diggings (cf. below, Letter 121, p. 340) but later returned to his former employment (cf. below, Letter 145, p. 418). Jevons recorded in his diary on 16 June 1856 that Charles Bolton was to marry Barbara Mary MacMartin on 1 July 1856; she died the following year (cf. below, Letter 107, n. 3, p. 295.
[3] Cf. above, Letter 24, n. 4, p. 44; also below, Letter 121, n. 6, p. 342.

have cost a great deal, in fact about £300 though Capt Ward has been liberal enough in allowing nearly £100 for the voyage. There will be a great deal more to pay too in fitting up the rooms at Sydney, and getting tables cupboards furnaces &c put up. I dont expect to have many assays from the Mint before next Easter, as the chief part of the machinery such as the coining presses are only going out now in the very same ship as myself and unless a little private assaying comes in, I shall have to pay all the rent, Charles wages, and his and my expenses in living for a half year without receiving anything in return but the £100 per year from the Mint. I neednt say too that for the present the money all comes from Papa.

I have had some lectures on book-keeping from Papa & Herbert,[4] and have bought a set of books, Cash-book, Day-book, Ledger & all, (the mysteries of which I dare say you dont understand yet) so as to appear a little business-like to my customers in Sydney. Capt Ward has seemed hitherto as if he did not think I knew much about the £.s.d.

I think I need not tell you that I have done nothing in chemistry for some time past now or in fact in anything else whatever except in buying & packing up, and though on the voyage and at Sydney I expect to have plenty of time for reading, I dont think it will be at all possible to keep up to the new ideas of you chemists and though I have got a pretty complete set of common chemical Apparatus & chemicals, I feel as if I should take more to Geology & botany, though I dont at all intend to stick to Science above everything else all my life.

Robert McAndrew[5] has been in Liverpool for some time, and I have seen him now & then, but he informed me a few days since that he is to sail for New York next Saturday. He is to live with an Uncle there and to go into his business in which he seems to expect to have a good place before long. I am afraid he will be awfully Yankeefied before I see him again and I have a great dislike of the Americans.

I have also seen Sam Archer[6] who is working tremendously hard at learning to doctor but keeps, as he always does to the practical part chiefly, I fancy. He attends all the hospitals & infirmaries in town, every day (Sunday included) (not all of them each day I hope) and I think is the dresser. He had the medal a little time since so you may think he is getting on.

James Jevons[7] came home from Port Natal on Saturday week, and

---

[4] Herbert had by this time been taken into the family business, having abandoned medicine and spent some time abroad.

[5] Probably a friend from University College School. See Vol. I, p. 72.

[6] See Vol. I, p. 55, n. 1.

[7] James Edward Jevons (1828–60), second son of Timothy Jevons, brother of Henry Jevons who was carrying on the family business; farmed in Natal 1850–54, where Herbert

has been away four years. I dont suppose he will go back again as he has not made his farm pay yet at all.

I remember now that I must thank you for the Photograph which is a very good one but has the usual defects of Photographs that it is not at all like you, unless the Ph.D[8] has produced a considerable change. It is now packed up to appear again at Sydney. I have had another present from Uncle Timothy of a very good desk covered with green Russia leather of a form both for travelling and using at home and which will be just the thing for the voyage. I have also had a few presents of books, including Whewells Hist. of Inductive Sci.[9] and other books from Cousin Daulbys.[10]

The meeting of the Brit. Ass. in Lpool next year will certainly be a very fine thing considering it is in such a town as Liverpool in such a building in that town. Graham, I think, told me he would come up, and I should not wonder if Papa asks him to stay here, though it will be a difficult thing to entertain little Tommy in a suitable manner.[11] I only wish I could stay till then, as much for the meeting as for the sake of seeing you again.

Graham has not given me any introduction to Sydney but has written to Dr Smith[12] about his taking the third Assayership for the Mint and about some indefinite arrangement he wants to manage between him & me which I do not quite understand. I find that Graham always works at a thing for a long time while you are grumbling from not knowing what he is doing but that he generally brings out an affair plainly & satisfactorily enough in the end.

Tomorrow is the last day for three months that I shall hear new accounts of the war and the Ministry. It seems a pity to break off just when Cronstadt is going to be taken and the Russians to retreat and perhaps Lord Aberdeen to be turned out.[13] It will be rather amusing I should think to hear, when I get there, the queer ideas people will have about the war as I suppose the news gets rather more contradictory

---

visited him in 1852. Cf. Vol. I, p. 76; also below, Letter 43, p. 89.

[8] See above, Letter 34, n. 7, p. 63.

[9] See Vol. I, p. 111. [10] See Vol. I, p. 59, n. 5.

[11] The meeting was held in the new St George's Hall. Cf. below, Letters 44 and 46, pp. 90 and 101.

[12] See above, Letter 39, n. 7, p. 75.

[13] Two naval expeditions were sent into the Baltic in 1854 and 1855 as part of the general offensive against Russia but they achieved little and did not affect the outcome of the war. Cronstadt was bombarded but not captured; the firepower of wooden ships proved ineffective against the walls of the fortress. Lord Aberdeen had little public support because of his ineffectual handling of the situation and his lack of enthusiasm for a popular war. He was forced to resign in February 1855 over the issue of his cabinet's incompetence in organising supplies for the army in the Crimea. Cf. Woodward, op. cit., pp. 274, 286.

than it is here, before it gets out there. I have now I think written enough, even for the 6 or 9 months that it must be before you hear from me again, and so I must say *good bye*.

The direction *to the Mint* will do till you get the right one and I hope to hear soon after landing in Sydney.

Give my kindest remembrances to Aunt Henry & Harriet, and for yourself, believe me

      Ever your affectionate Cousin
         W. S. Jevons

H. E. Roscoe. Esq. Ph.D.
Heidelberg.

42. W. S. JEVONS TO THOMAS JEVONS

         The "Oliver Lang".
         July 3rd 1854.[1]

Dearest Father

My last letter came up to the time when the steam tug left us in sight of Tuskar, and I am now beginning a letter in which I shall give you a short account of what has occurred since then or will occur, worth mentioning. I shall continue it every now & then and it will be always ready to send by any opportunity that there may be before getting to Sydney.

One of the chief subjects during the last week has of course been the sea sickness. To be able to write this I must of course be pretty free from it now, and the fact is that I have been among the three or four of all the cabin passengers who have not been sick. That is to say that, though I have occasionally felt sick and disagreable* enough, I have never been fairly sick, or unable to eat any meal. I am very much[2] at it as also at seeing many of the people so ill yet that they can scarcely walk, and have their beds on deck in the day. Anderson[3] is one of the worst and it does not make my cabin any more comfortable than it might be, for the present. I have kept myself well by being on deck almost every moment that I have not been in bed or eating.

I begin now to know a little more of the passengers and Captain &c, and I think it very amusing to see so many people of different sorts. Our

---

[1] It would seem questionable whether this letter was ever posted. Much of the news it contains, for example about fellow passengers, is repeated in the letter dated 11 September 1854 drafted in the Journal and included in final form below, Letter 45, p. 96. However it is useful as giving an account of the first part of the voyage and interesting to compare with Jevons's later impressions.

[2] Jevons appears to have left out a word here.

[3] Cf. above, Letter 41, p. 77.

great gun is a Mr Lane,⁴ an Irishman who has become a complete Frenchman by living in France for many years; he talks very fast & well and upon any subject, seeming to know something of everything though I dont think he is very sound at the bottom. He is a Republican and a chartist, as came out after dinner today. I always feel inclined to argue things out at length with him, and had the first good one after tea tonight on the subject of navigating balloons.

The "doctor" is evidently on his first job, but gets through his work of managing the third cabin people better than I should have thought. He is very amusing at dinner without intending it, and gives us accounts of his patients, and of his enforcing the regulations by blowing peoples candles out at night & pulling them out of bed by the legs in the morning.

The Captain I do not much like, particularly in the way he behaves to the second & third Cabin people. They have been complaining already about not having a fair proportion of the deck and I am sure the main deck is not a fit place for 300 or 400 people to air themselves, as it is not open and is always in a mess. The first mate, whom you have seen, is the best man on board as everybody would say of him at once; the rest of the mates & the crew are also, I should say, very much above the average.

The ship I believe, is considered very satisfactory, but it appears to me not to be complete in some of the last little things, as they are constantly finding things to be done in the rigging and have been busy all today getting three studding sails out.

July 5th Yesterday the 3rd Cabin men got up a petition to the Captain containing all their complaints. He seemed very much vexed by it, but called those who had signed it together and told them what they should have, and what they shouldnt so plainly that I dont think there will be much more trouble. Charles tells me that there is no end of complaining in his cabin about the eating which does not seem to be well managed except in the first cabin. We certainly have very good eating and have four meals in the day. Breakfast at $8\frac{1}{2}$, lunch at $12\frac{1}{2}$ dinner at 4, all these with several dishes of meat, fish &c, and tea at 7. The tea is the only thing complained of here, the French Irishman being very angry about that.

I must thank Lucy & Mary⁵ for the two bun loaves, and the raspberry vinegar. Partly from the sea sickness and partly from what I cant help eating at the regular meals, I have hardly tasted them yet, but they wont be long in going when I & Anderson once begin. Raspberry vinegar is very much drunk here and we shall enjoy my bottle very much now that the hot weather is beginning.

⁴ Henry Lane (d. 1873), Under Secretary for Finance and Trade, New South Wales Treasury, 1857–70.
⁵ Mary Bentley, a member of the domestic staff. See above, Letter 20, n. 4, p. 36.

Charles has been much better today and has been with me on deck a good deal. He does not seem to have any better opinion of the 2nd Cabin passengers than I have of the 1st, though his 3 chums seem as good as any of them. He seems to have been very ill but is pretty nearly over it, while Anderson seems quite sick yet.

We have just been a week sailing now, and we have I believe got on a long way though the wind has on the whole been unfavourable. This morning it was a perfect calm and the log gave $\frac{1}{2}$ a knot while soon after the steam tug left us we went at 13 knots an hour, even when pretty close up to the wind. We have in fact never had a really favourable wind yet and the Captain expects to do wonders if we can only get good winds

* * *

12 P.M. The stars, as above, indicate that as in novels something tremendous has happened and it is in reality a storm at sea. Just as I was finishing writing at 10 oclock, it began to rain violently and the wind blew through the stern window so as nearly to put the candle out. The sailors began making a row also but I thought they were only changing the tack. At last I heard the ladies in the cabin begin talking about *"being afraid"* and from this and other indications I thought something must be up.

So I went on deck in my Mackintosh and found a tremendous wind blowing with heavy rain, and the ship flying before it, with nearly all the sails loosed and flapping. The little house on deck was filled with some of the frightened passengers, (Mr Holt[6] especially being rather trembling), while the sailors of course were running about the deck & up aloft to get the sail in, some of the top ones being a good deal damaged. It was worth standing some time in the rain to see the ship cutting through the waves with the foam on each side and in a broad track behind. After a little the moon and stars came out very brightly making it a still finer sight, and for a long time there was a nearly complete lunar rainbow which is I believe a rare thing.

The captain & sailors seemed to enjoy the affair exceedingly after the danger & hard work were over, particularly when the latter were getting their grog. I believe the chief danger was that the squall took the ship on her side, when everybody was altogether unprepared and not expecting anything. The log was taken twice and gave 16 & 17 knots an hour, though the mate thinks that at the worst she was going more nearly 18 or 19.

July 6th We have of course talked over last nights affair pretty well by this. Many of the passengers did not go to sleep at all, and I lay awake

[6] See Vol. I, p. 106, n. 3.

for a long time partly from the heat I was in and partly from the awful rolling of the ship after the wind had caused a good swell. The deck was so slippy last night, that at almost every good roll numbers of the crew & passengers went tumbling about. The low bulwarks are certainly not safe in such a state of things, but I did, & always shall take care that I am not one to fall overboard. Everybody agrees that Mr Clarence Holt was in a great state of alarm and they have been joking the doctor because he rushed down below in great alarm about his medicine chest instead of thinking of himself.

Today we have had a steady N E wind, and a rate of 7 or 8 knots. It is a good specimen of the quiet dull days we shall have to pass away for the next two months and I find I take to reading considerably better than before.

I think I ought here to thank Henny and Tommy for their presents. I have been trying a little of Pope.

I cannot think what I should do all day upon a ship with very few passengers, as here my chief amusement is seeing the other passengers, 2nd & 3rd as well as 1st, and talking, I suppose you would call it *gossiping*, with a few about the rest. It is rather a curious sight, on a fine evening to see the people of all sorts & sizes, lying, sitting and walking about everywhere

July 8th The weather is now beginning to be settled and very fine, and the sunsets are very beautiful. The clouds appear to me to be in a far greater variety than I ever saw them before and there was a very beautiful rose colour in the sky opposite the sun this evening which I never saw before. The seawater became of a blackish blue colour soon after our leaving Ireland, but now it has, when you look straight down into it, a beautiful bright sky blue colour, which I should like Lucy to see. All yesterday we were in sight of a ship ahead which we overtook at about 9 at night when the moon was very bright so as to make both ships look quite a beautiful sight. We came quite close to her, when a French sailor on board spoke the vessel, which was a French ship for Lima. The band was then pulled out of bed, so they said, to play the French people off with the Marseillaise, & God save the Queen, and the emigrants giving effect to the scene, as they do on all similar occasions, by continued cheering for some time. The Captains exchanged longitudes (ours being 16°W.) which seems to be a common practise.*

The Cabin passengers are beginning now to be at sixes & sevens with each other as Herbert always describes. The Gold-digger will tease the poor doctor; the Captain likes the former but always laughs at the doctor, and blows up the Pursor* who is also quite a young fellow; and this sort of work appears to be gradually spreading among the rest. The moon-light evenings are spent now by the passengers walking about the deck, each person talking about somebody else in the same or another cabin. With the exception perhaps of Mr Day⁷ a queer old man, who has spent his time hitherto in looking out for ships with the telescope, but is now extremely anxious to catch some dolphins for which he has been fishing with my line for some time already, though there are none at all to be seen about here. We have however seen plenty of porpoises, often as big as a man, which come swimming up to the ship or jumping out two or three together.

The wind at present is a light but steady North-East one and we are going straight before it with all the studding sails out; rate about 7 knots. We have at present 22 sails set and there are 9 or 10 more not set. The ship looks very pretty indeed and the main mast in particular pleases me, like this, I intend to learn the names of all the spars sails & ropes, but it will be a very long job.

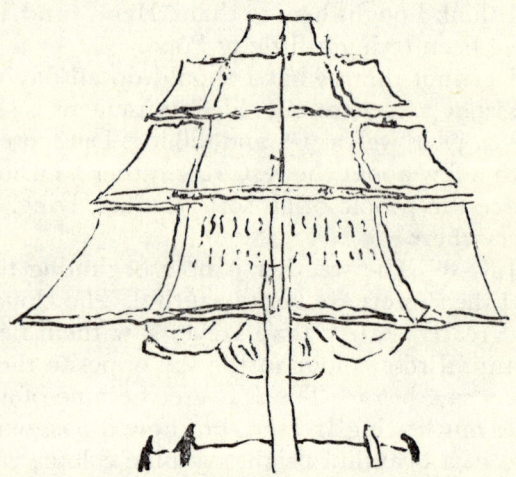

July 18th Here we are again a little past the Cape de Verd* Islands and in a dead calm and after having made but few degrees for the last week. The weather and the heat is of course the chief subject now and the latter is certainly quite as bad as I expected. Everybody talks nearly continually of their *perspiration*, and from what it is in our cabin I cant conceive how bad it must be between decks. I have often been quite ill and fainting but today for the first time have diminished my clothes to one half.

We have not been in sight of land since we left Ireland and have now no chance of seeing any till we get to Austrl^a. Though these calms are bad for the Captains temper, they bring the finest weather imaginable, rather cloudy though very hot in the day but clear and just sufficiently cool in the evenings, which we spend altogether upon deck. We have had a little amusement in the way of fishing. About a week since two very large fish called *albicores** appeared and followed us but were not caught by either lines or a harpoon. There have now been a great many flying fish seen as well as dolphins, a small one of which was caught yesterday by a line. I also saw yesterday some dolphins pursuing

---

⁷ It has proved impossible to trace any biographical details of Day.

a number of the small white flying fish, one of which I distinctly saw grabbed by a dolphin as it was entering the water again.

We have now seen the phosphorescent lights on the sea for some days

July 20th A ship being in sight ahead,[8] I must get the letter ready for sending for the chance, a very slight one, of the Captain sending a boat to her.

Yesterday morning the first *shark* appeared and created more excitement on board than anything yet. It was a much more extraordinary animal than I even expected though it was quite young & 5 or 6 feet long. It was harpooned at last and got on board. During tea another one was hooked just below the windows at the stern and it was a sight, worth anything, to see it brought on board. The first mate is a capital shot & sent the harpoon right through it at once.

There are grumblings & disagreableness* on all sides and yesterday & today they have broken out openly in our cabin. I am not surprised* at the Captain being a little out of temper at the weather but I should think it was his proper business to try and smooth everything of the sort down, which he certainly does not do.

Yesterday he commenced a row with my friend Mr Newton[9] by grumbling for half an hour at his child. This is pretty nearly all probably the result of the calm weather but I dont think a wind will be able to blow it all away at once. The second and third cabin people are more quiet for the present, having got over the difficulty of the bad arrangements about eating.

I am clear of everything and in uncommonly good spirits, between the sharks, the stars, games at draughts & cards, &c &c, and have left off wishing to be at the journeys end.

Though there is much to keep my thoughts engaged here, I have often thought of all of you at home and of the enjoyment you will have had at Dolgelly

I must now send my best love to all and remain
Ever your most Affec. Son
W. S. Jevons

PS. The writing I know is very bad, but you must excuse.

[8] Cf. below, Letter 45, p. 98.
[9] Joseph Newton (d. 1888) was appointed engineer of the machinery at the Sydney Mint on 14 May 1853. He is recorded as having lived at Carisbrook Cottage, Waverley Road, Sydney, 1858–59 and from 1865 at Woollahoa, outside Sydney.

43. THOMAS JEVONS TO W. S. JEVONS

Dolgelly 6 July 1854

Dearest Stanley,

I can hardly describe the pleasure which your several letters gave us which were written on board of the Oliver Lang during her stay in the river and down to the time when the steam tug left her a few miles south of the Tuscar.* We auguered* from these letters that you really had a fortunate set of passengers to go out with who would beguile for you the tediousness of the voyage We concluded that from the speed the Oliver Lang had already made she could not fail to make a good passage out and whether all this be true or not it has the effect upon our minds the same as if it were true and you may consider that we shall be all happiness about you until we hear from you what has been the reality of your voyage and then I hope not until then can you count upon any unhappy thoughts arising in our minds. If your news be good then will our happy thoughts continue and they from that time will take no other complexion* but such as your communications are calculated to give and therefore after the receipt of this letter there will be a community of thought and feeling not to be interrupted again for a long length of time but which I pray to God may be frought* with seeds of happiness that shall grow up stronger and stronger to an endless happiness if it should please our Heavenly Father that we should never interchange them personally on Earth.

It has been a happy thing our coming down here for no doubt the novelty of the scene has tended to inspire cheerful thoughts and the effects of the Country air and the enjoyment of the most lovely scenery has conduced to our health of body and this in spite of rather unfavorable* weather which we have had for several days.

I am greatly surprized with the scenery here it is so very different to what I expected although we are surrounded by many of the loftiest mountains in Wales which arise at our feet as it were and tower 4000 feet above our heads at the highest point which looks only like a hop step & jump from us yet we are located in one of the most lovely valleys you can imagine The whole country here is a succession of "Wood & Water Vale and Mountain" The valleys numerous & lovely the waters are exhibited in the full flowing stream of the valley, the clear and beautiful rills of the glens and in the white foam of the mountain torrents The woods are boundless in extent cloathing* the sides of every mountain stream, every declivity and broken side of the Hills and covering the mountains themselves as far up as any thing can vegetate the spaces and openings for agricultural pruposes are only just sufficient for raising food for Cattle & men, but they add beauty and give greater effect to the loveliness of the scenery. And last the rugged mountains tower aloft above all these lovely views and give a sublimity to the whole which words cannot express. We are in truth in a country more beautiful than any I have ever seen although I have traversed through almost all the loveliest spots of this paradise of a Kingdom

Cadr* Idris is the highest mountain hereabouts and its highest point is one immense rugged rock shot up perpendicularly nearly a thousand feet or more above the surrounding heights and you would think that the disturbance of nature that could tumble up such a vast monument in the midst of a thousand other supports to its base was a power which was the greatest of all in its effects upon the form of our earth and particularly when we know and see that the same power has been and still is at work on every continent we know and yet it is the saying of some philosopher that the operations of the insect race produce still greater changes on the Earths surface. The cast off shells of animals and the coral incrustations of marine insects form vaster rocks than the upheavings of explosive earthquakes. The effects of volcanic irruptions* are never I think mentioned in connection with this subject though the extent of them must be vast. Perhaps as they are the most visible of all effects upon the surface we do not give so much to the imagination in our considerations, but indeed the irruptions* cover or override each other so much the top most only being vissible* that we are too apt to conclude we see the whole and thus do not give the fullest scope to our considerations of this as a pervading cause of the highest magnitude. My own reflections lead me to conclude that the eternal flow of water is the greatest most constant and most pervading agent in producing the changes that are visible in the Earths surface It is *Gods Steam Engine* that is eternally at work grinding down the loftiest mountains and with thin debre* filling up the deepest valleys and not even sparing the depths of the Sea It is to my mind by this "Engine" that the procession of the equinoxes may be in part accounted for as the balance of the Earth is being constantly altered by its operations The prodigious effects of this great cause have never yet that I have ever heard been submitted to any calculation but I myself think that an approximate result might be obtained since the moving power is so constant and it is within our means to measure it in detail By observation and experiment and calculation it would be within our means to form some notion of the actual deposits of the mightiest rivers of the Earth, & how much water they had displaced by carrying the mountains away and placing them in the depths of the Seas. For these crude notions & speculations you may thank the journey into this wonderful world of mountains and I hope it has not tired you before you have got to the end.

And now let me advert to what may be your position about the time this letter may come to hand. I fear that Herberts opinion will be right and that it may be many months before the Mint will give you any assays to do. The Engineer who went out with you[1] says he expects to be 4 mths in putting up his machinery now[2] supposing every thing goes on pretty smoothly as all erectors are a much longer time over their work than they say they shall be you may put down 6 mths instead of four But should any part of the machinery be missing or broken it is ten to one that 4 or even 6 mths longer time must be given to replace that On the whole then I should say that you must not lose a moment in your attempt to commence assaying for the public get your Laboratory up as fast as you can and then advertize* in the papers and there will be no fear that you will get some work to do. If but very little comes in the next thing I should do would be to cause an advertizement* to be put in the Melbourne papers. The facility of sending parcels from Melbourne to Sydney is so great and the great jealousy that will exist between the different assayers in Melbourne will be such that there will I have no doubt be plenty of people who would be right glad to have an honest assaye* from an honest assayer from the Capital of the Land and this brings to mind the common saying that a prophet has no honor* in his own Country To the people of Melbourne you may appear a great assayer with the Title of Assayer to the Royal Mint but to the people of Sydney you may only appear as a very young Gentleman who has had the good fortune to secure a very good berth &c &c &c

When I first thought of coming down here my idea was that I should be convenient to the Gold mines of England and that I should revel in the prosperity of such undertakings and be able to turn the knowledge to be acquired about them here to my own benefit, but since then they are all blown up as profitable concerns and my ardour about them is all dissipated. I have scarcely thought about them since I came and the only signs I have seen of the Gold Mania[3] is a steam engine on wheels which is left on the road side at the foot of a very steep hill. It would appear that it was not worth while to put the additional horses to it

[1] Joseph Newton. See above, Letter 42, n. 9, p. 85.

[2] 'but' was deleted here in the original manuscript.

[3] '... the great days of mining in Merioneth came after 1850, when the re-discovery in the copper mines of traces of gold – which had been worked there in the days of Charles the First – brought prospectors flocking to the county. Soon there was a chain of gold mines running from north-west to south-west along the high ground north of the Mawddach, bringing fortune or ruin to a succession of mining companies (some of them presided over by John Bright) till quite recently.' – A. H. Dodd, *The Industrial Revolution in North Wales* (Cardiff, 1933), p. 168. Cf. also E. Rosalie Jones, *History of Barmouth* (Barmouth, 1909) pp. 194–205; R. I. Murchison, *Siluria. The history of the oldest known rocks containing organic remains, with a brief sketch of the distribution of gold over the earth* (1854) pp. 433–4; A. C. Ramsay, 'On the Geology of the Gold-bearing District of Merionethshire, North Wales', *Quarterly Journal of the Geological Society of London*, x (1854) 242–7.

that were necessary to draw it up this Hill and probably since the engine started from where it was built the company for which it was made may have been dissolved The engine itself I think well of. It is in fact similar to the Rail way Locomotives in many respects, but it is mounted on ordinary waggon wheels and can be drawn by horses along the common turnpike roads. Such an engine as this could be sent out from here and on its arrival in Sydney could be drawn to any locality it was required at, and put to work in a couple of days after it got there. I have seen a drawing of this engine in an advertizement* in the Mining Journal frequently, but in the Journal I send you along with this letter I do not see it.[4]

I hope Charles Bolton has arrived safely with you and in good health You can tell him that his sister Ann is along with us in this beautiful country and that she would enjoy it more than she does if she could only get the people to talk English but that very few do here and the reply we mostly get from the country people is dein sasenec or "No Saxon" The Welsh call the English Saxons themselves Britons But I dont think that they can honestly sing the national ballad Britons never shall be slaves for as we walk along the roads every soul almost man woman and child doff their hats to us Saxons which is said to be a mark of a subject nation.

In a letter I have received from my Brother[5] today I learn that H^y Wood[6] has offered James Jevons a situation in his Chain and Anchor Works at Saltney near Chester but he does not say that James has decided to accept it as yet but I should think he will do as his Father and Mother wish him so much not to go abroad again We shall see in a few days and I shall mention the result in my next. I fear that James will not do much good in business.[7]

I write and post this letter at Dolgelly as much out of curiosity as any thing since I believe that when I get back to Lpool I shall be able to write again and post a letter to you that shall come to your hands

---

[4] It seems most likely that Thomas Jevons was referring here to the 'Patent Portable Steam Engine on Wheels' manufactured by Messrs. Medwin and Hall, Blackfriars Road, London. In fact only two illustrated advertisements for this machine appeared in the *Mining Journal* during 1854; the second included a list of engines sold during that year, one of which was supplied to 'Sir A. Webster, Bart., Dolgelly, Wales.' Sir August Webster had discovered gold in the bed of the River Mawddach during the summer of 1852. Cf. *The Mining Journal, Railway and Commercial Gazette*, 13 May 1854, no. 977 (XXIV); 17 June 1854, no. 982; Ramsay, op. cit., p. 247.

[5] Timothy Jevons.

[6] A first cousin of Thomas and Timothy Jevons, being the son of their mother's brother George Wood; before her marriage to William Jevons their mother had been Ann Wood (1767–1846) of the Lye, Staffordshire. Henry Wood was married to Harriet, sister of Timothy Jevons's wife Catharine.

[7] See above, Letter 41, n. 7, p. 78. James Jevons did emigrate again and died near Sittewaka, Ceylon, at the age of 32. See below, Letter 149, p. 424.

before this can do but no doubt this letter will keep well enough for all it may be worth It will however serve to convey to you whenever it reaches your hands the assurances which I hereby give you of the enduring love and friendship of

      Your affectionate Father
       Thomas Jevons

44. THOMAS JEVONS TO W. S. JEVONS

            Chatham S^t
            1 Sep 1854

Dearest Stanley

  I could not take up my pen on a more appropriate day than this to address an epistle to you. It is your birth day and I trust that you are wending your way fast towards that goal which is to be for better or for worse for you for many years to come. I wish you many happy returns of the day to be spent in the distant land of your adoption & after that may I live to see you returned to my fond embrace with all your honors* thick upon you. Looking upon the map and trying to guess your position on this day I set you down as not very far from the Cape of Good Hope I hope you are somewhat to the Eastward of the Cape making your way with a good steady trade wind at a slapping pace of at least 300 miles a day towards the land of promise where it is my prayer that this letter may meet you soon after your arrival in safety and in health.

  As you may suppose I take more than a common interest in any scrap of news that comes from Sydney in the hopes of turning anything I may meet with if possible to some account for you but I have nothing special that I can report to you. From the market reports that I have seen and from advertizements* for the sale and letting of houses I flatter myself that you would not find it so very difficult to obtain a place as we have heretofore anticipated. I have however seen a paragraph in a paper about the dies for your Sydney coinage which makes me fear that it may be a long time before you get to work for the mint. The paragraph I saw states that Mr Wyon[1] is now engaged on the Dies for the new Sydney Sovreigns* and we know from long experience that these Die sinkers and especially Government ones are a tremendous time over their jobs. This being the case I see no help for it but that you must use your best efforts to get employment from the public and the necessity for this is greatly strengthened by what Cap Ward told you He in fact urged you

---

[1] James Wyon, resident engraver at the Royal Mint, 1851–60; a member of the renowned family of engravers brought to the Mint from Birmingham in 1811. Cf. G. Duveen and H. G. Stride, *The History of the Gold Sovereign* (1962) pp. 77–95; Craig, op. cit., pp. 276, 294–9, 321.

to get out and begin on your own account as soon as you could which proves that he thought it might be a very long time before the mint would be ready to help you. If it does not prove that it proves something that may operate equally prejudicial perhaps. It is just possible that he wishes the assayers to be well established in their private business before the time comes for the Government to fix the amount of fee in order that the Government may have a good excuse for fixing a lower fee than otherwise they ought to do There is no question but that they will take private practice into account when they come to settle the fee & therefore it is absolutely necessary for you to have some private practice or otherwise you will be cut off with a half remuneration. How to get this practice whether by advertizing* or otherwise you must decide for yourself and on consultation with your friends of whose value you will have found the benefit before this letter comes to your hands.

Before your embarkation I had thought that I would send you the Mining Journal weekly but it contains such a quantity of stuff that is not worth your reading that when it comes to the point I decide against it. Instead however whenever I see any article that I think will be of use or interest you I will cut them out and enclose them. I enclose four paragraphs which I have cut out of the Mining Journal of the 26 Augt which may interest you The one headed "New Light" I myself communicated to the Journal having received it from a correspondent of ours a M^r W E Coffin of Boston for whom we have purchased 2 barrels of the Benzole spoken of, which he is going to use himself. I dare say we shall hear more about this invention before long.[2] If you thought well of it you might send such a paragraph as that or indeed all of them to the Sydney Herald. Enclosing them in a note addressed to the Editor signed by yourself Of course not to have your own note put into the paper but only the paragraphs. By furnishing the Editor from time to time with food for his paper like this you make him your friend and Editors of papers have a great deal of power in their hands, which they can use for the evil or the good of any public character in the State and you as assayer to the mint are unquestionably a public officer. But it strikes me that probably you have a news room in Sydney where the

[2] The article to which Thomas Jevons refers described a method of lighting for domestic or public use, patented by C. P. Drake, a Boston electrician, using gas evaporated from benzole (distilled from coal tar). It was said to produce '... a superior light to that of coal – gas, being clearer and softer; the flame being of fuller volume, and burning with greater steadiness, while the expense is about the same . . .' It had the additional advantage of being simple to operate. The article appeared between two others, entitled 'Electric Gas' and 'Indurated Stone', which may also have been enclosed with the letter, although the cuttings are no longer amongst the Jevons Papers. There was widespread interest in developing methods of lighting deriving from various oils distilled from coal as an alternative to coal gas, which had been used in major cities since early in the century. Cf. *Mining Journal* . . . 26 August 1854, no. 992 (XXIV) 572; Singer, op. cit., pp. 102–6.

Mining Journal is taken as mining is one of the great elements of the success of your Country and if so then you can see the whole paper and I need in future only point out any paragraph that may strike me. But even if there is a news room or a Club room to which you might resort on subscribing to its funds perhaps the subscription will be too high for you at first and in that case you would not subscribe until you can afford it nor until you have leisure to bestow on desultory reading I will therefore continue to send you such paragraphs as I think worth your reading.

My last letter to you if I recollect right was written and posted from Dolgelly where we were enjoying ourselves greatly but written before I had visited any of the Gold mines in that district, but before I left I visited several of them and the matter of fact inspection tended to damp considerably any remaining expectations that the serch* for Gold in England will ever become an extensive or remunerating employment. I saw the Dolfrwynog mine which seems to have been the best conducted and one of the most promising of them. It was not at work for want of sufficient water power. We have had a very dry summer and a great deal of the water power of the Country is suspended from the same cause so there was nothing particular in that. The workmen however put on what little water there was and turned the amalgamators and crushers for a short time without putting any fresh feed in, just to shew* us the operation. The Mill employed at Dolfrwnog* is not Burdens* nor is it Parkes* but one partaking of a little of both, put up by the engineer of the works. They have fixed basins, with a shaft revolving inside them which shaft has four arms upon it and these arms as they run round push before them four round balls which are quite loose and all of the same size and these of course grind the mineral to powder. There is a constant supply of water into the basins along with the ore and the agitation which the balls give to the mixture washes it gradually through sives* or gauzes of very fine texture From the gauzes it runs down a small pipe & is let out at the bottom of a receiver in which is contained mercury. The mixture cannot escape without rising through the mercury and it is supposed that the mercury seizes upon the larger portion of the Gold. The tailings which flow over the top of the small vessel with mercury at the bottom, are washed over & over again and strained &c &c[3]

They have unquestionably obtained Gold regularly at this place but I believe it is very doubtful whether it does not cost as much as it is

---

[3] Berdan's and Perkes's machines appear to have been amongst the most widely known of the various types of crushing equipment then available. The previous April the *Mining Journal* had carried an account of 'The Berdan Gold Machine Company – A company has just been formed for working the patent taken out by Mr. Berdan for his machine for pulverising, washing and amalgamating gold ore. The machine, it is well known, has been at work for four months at the Windsor Iron-Works, in the City-road, and is now in operation in the new establishment, Lett's Wharf, Commercial Road, near Waterloo Bridge . . . as also at the

worth. The shares which two or three months since could hardly be had at all have fallen gradually in the market from £4 or £5 each to only 12^s/6 each which certainly proves that the public have no confidence in the undertaking. The mineral which is worked for this mine is

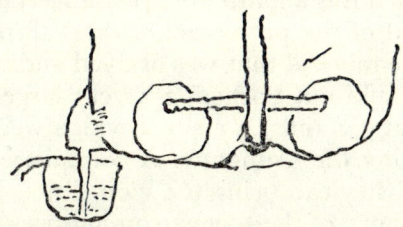

got out of pits and seems to have no other metal in it. Occasionally they meet with some quartz in the mine which has Gold visible in its structure but such specimens are like Angels visits few and far between

I visited the Cwmhesien* Mine which is within a mile of the other but is a totally different affair. At this mine they have got a couple of Burdans machines but after trying them for weeks they have failed in securing any gold worth mentioning. I believe that there is a fair quantity of gold in the ore obtained at this mine, but it is mixed with so many other metals and mineral substances that they are altogether foiled in their attempts to separate the Gold. As a last resort they are now grinding their mineral to a dry powder and are going to have it smelted and if that fails they will abandon it as a Gold mine

There are a great number of mineral veins at the Cwmhesian mine principally Lead veins. The largest which comes to the surface is certainly a most splendid vein but it has all sorts of metals mixed in it, Lead, Copper, Tin, Antimony, probably Cobalt, Sulphur or mundic Arsenic &c &c &c and it has baffled every one that has had to do with the mine as yet even those who worked it for Lead only before Gold was discovered in it. The Company is in a state of insolvency and the shares can be had for 2/6 each as many as you like – I saw several other mines

---

Cwmhesian Mines, which may be said to be the first opportunity of practically testing its merits . . .' – 1 April 1854, no. 971 (XXIV) 209. In March, the *Mining Journal* published a report of 'the new experimental gold reduction establishment of Mr. Samuel Perkes, Upper Thames Street . . . the progress made, and still making, promises the most successful and satisfactory results . . . Quantities of mineral, up to a ton a day, are at present reduced and amalgamated in what may be termed a model machine, three feet diameter, with six crushing rollers, weighing 400 pounds each, and set in motion by a force equal to about 2-horse power of the steam engine which works it, and which has now been working satisfactorily upwards of two months . . . Among the novelties introduced by Mr. Perkes, with a view scientifically to produce the best results, is a mechanical mercury strainer, superseding the crude method of squeezing the amalgamated mercury through leather by hand . . .' 18 March 1854, no. 967 (XXIV) 176. A large illustration of 'Samuel Perkes's Gold Reduction and Amalgamating Machine' appeared on the front page of the *Mining Journal*, 13 May 1854, no. 977 (XXIV).

in the same district but not one was at work and on the whole it seems to me that the Gold mania is at present defunct.

As regards the Poltimore Mine they are now turning their attention to Copper only of which they have sold a small quantity but whether it will pay any dividends is a matter of great uncertainty. It is generally believed that several of the promoters of the Poltimore mine actually put the gold into the mineral that was assayed and so got the shares up in price when they sold out pocketing a very large sum. They sold a great many shares at £2 and £3 a share which were given to them as free shares for starting the Company. A committee of investigation is now sitting to try if they can bring the swindlers to book, but I should think there is no chance of the money coming back. The present price of the Poltimore shares is 4/- each at which some were sold last week. The average of what mine cost is about 26/- each so that I am a large loser by the swindle. I should add that it is thought that nearly all the experiments at Burdans machines Windsor Ironworks were tampered with.[4] With respect to the South Poltimore mine in which I took 100 shares at £1 each the Committee have returned 17/6 a share they were prudent enough not to proceed far in the undertaking until they saw what success attended the first Poltimore On receiving back this money I invested it in a Lead Mine in France called the Pontgibaud Silver Lead Mining & Smelting C° in which I hold 8 Shares, now worth £16 p Share so you see having been bitten a little by the mining mania I cannot altogether and of a sudden give it up.

We are to have the meeting of the British Association in Lpool in about three weeks from this time and I bethought myself that Professor Graham would be sure to attend so I sent him an invitation to make my house his home I have this morning received his reply from his brothers in Yorkshire where he is staying written in a very friendly manner but stating that he should only be one or two nights away both between Lpool and Manchester in consequence of which he could not at this time conveniently accept my kind invitation, but he will be sure to call to see us.

---

[4] Manufacturers of the various types of crushing equipment carried out trials with specimens from different gold mines, the results of which were published in the *Mining Journal* by way of advertisement for both machines and mines. For example, the paper had reported in March, 'In consequence of the removal of Berdan's machine from the Windsor Iron-Works to extensive premises on the banks of the Thames, the experiments during the week have been suspended; but the greatest exertions are making, under the auspices of an influential company, to get the machines into operation, and it is confidently expected one will be in working order by the end of next week . . .' Then followed figures giving the weight and description of specimens, the mines from which they came and the amount of gold extracted per ton. The report then referred to experiments being carried out with Perkes's machines: 'Some important trials, amongst others, have been made upon fresh samples from the Britannia Mine, which have produced very favourable results, and we understand the proprietors are determined to arrange for one of Mr. Perkes's largest size machines . . .', 11 March 1854, no. 968 (xxiv) 160.

On the occasion of the meeting of the British Association we are to have a public opening of our Grand St Georges Hall and Lpool is all on the tip toe of expectation as to the effect. The Hall is beyond all dispute exteriorly* one of the finest buildings in Europe and those who have seen the interior speak very highly of that, but time will show what will be its real merits. We shall probably go to one of the performances for I should say that three days are given to grand musical performances previous to the meeting of the learned bodies We are to have Oratorios in the mornings and grand Concerts in the evening for which the first talent of the land are engaged There is quite a furor* to secure tickets already and as the hall is a vastly spacious place there must be a large profit which is to be given to the charities[5]

We are having a most magnificent harvest in this country which puts every one in spirits. Bread the Staff of Life is falling in price very considerably and the poor will soon again be well fed and trade be prosperous in spite of the War. But in respect of these public topics I think I had better refer you to the newspapers which will give you everything more in detail than I can do in a letter however closely written I shall post a Mercury for you which will give you as much local news as you will like and as for the general politics probably your Sydney papers will extract as much from the London Journals as will be at all interesting.

I hope Charles Bolton has borne the voyage out pretty well and is enjoying good health in which case I have no doubt you find a great deal of comfort in his services. I am sorry to say that his Aunt Mary Bentley has been suffering very much for some time past with a gathered thumb arising from a cut while scraping potatoes It got so bad and gave her so much pain all up her arm that we were obliged to send for the Doctor. He had to cut into her thumb several times and once or twice as deep as the bone before the matter could all be let out but since then it has gradually been recovering and she is all right now in her general health though she cannot yet use her right hand and will not be able probably for some time to come. Ann Bolton is quite well and not over worked in consequence of Mary's illness as we had an assistant in Marys place all the time

Although I have intended to leave domestic matters for Lucy yet

---

[5] St George's Hall, the first of the palatial town halls which symbolised the North of England's prosperity, was designed by Harvey Lonsdale Elmes (1813–47) and begun in 1838. It has been called the finest neo-classical building in Europe. St George's Hall contains the Law Courts, made necessary when Liverpool became an Assize Town in 1835, and was the first civic building in a block which includes the Brown Library and Museum (1860), the Walker Art Gallery (1876) and the Picton Reference Library (1879). The Hall was inaugurated by a musical festival which began on 19 September 1854, although the courtrooms had been in use for the previous three years. Cf. Chandler, *Liverpool*, pp. 213–14; *Annual Register*, 1855, Chronicle, 156–7. See also below, Letters 46 and 59, pp. 103 and 142.

as I am somewhat on that tack I may as well tell you that Shaw, the stiff and prim waiter, is going to be married She has given us a months notice and then "off to the wedding"

And now Dearest Stanley having spun you a good long yarn I must *bring the end to a close* I need not say how anxious I shall become to hear from you about the time when a letter may be expected and your first letters will be read and re read many times over pray write as full and particular as you possibly can we shall want to know *every thing* down to the most minute particulars

Before I close let me put in a word about your calling on Mr Huntley[6] at the Gass* works I wrote to him to prepare him to receive you and as your uncle the Doctor[7] lived so many years with him at Staines there can be no doubt that he will greet you like an old friend And now goodby* until next Mail when again you shall hear if all be well from
     Your ever aff^{te} Father & friend
      Thomas Jevons

45. W. S. JEVONS TO THOMAS JEVONS
 [LJN, 40–45]

The Ship "Oliver Lang",
11th September 1854.[1]

Dearest Father

As we are now in pretty nearly the last week of the voyage to Melbourne, it is high time to be beginning some sort of an account of it, to let you know how pleasantly it has been passed by myself, or how unpleasantly by others. . . . In the Tropics it was certainly often extremely hot, but we felt it less than I expected, and the delightfully cool evenings made up for the days. For two or three days near the Tropics we had rather curiously in the middle of a dead calm a very large but low swell, which shook the ship about in a most uneasy and uncomfortable manner – it must have been caused by a storm just before. I can remember perfectly some of the splendidly fine days we had in the Tropics when we were lying on the deck under the awning all day, reading, playing draughts, or cards, etc., after tea, watching the sun set and the moon rise, and then sitting out in the night till late. Sometimes the sun went down quite alone without a cloud all over the sky. More often there were clouds of all variety of shapes. One time the sky all round was covered with bright fiery-coloured clouds, which, being

---

[6] See above, Letter 26, n. 4, p. 47.
[7] i.e. Richard Roscoe.
[1] This letter is a shortened version of the draft appearing in the Journal, Vol. I, pp. 101–13.

of a scattered shape, looked exactly like ridges of flames; another time there were splendid mountainous masses of cloud about the sun, with others of different shapes and colours about the sky. Besides the clouds, there were the tints of the sky, which were very beautiful, chiefly singular greens, every variety of reds and oranges, and, after the sun set, a very beautiful rose or pink tint. Not to tire you as we were tired with too much fine weather, I must come to the gales. We saw a little of the sort on the 22d of August, but on the 24th at 10 P.M. began the strongest. Though the captain had fully expected it, he had, according to his usual custom, kept all sail out. One topsail was reefed by the men very slowly, but they as good as refused to reef the two others, though ready hauled up, and accordingly they were both soon torn; three of the stay sails had been split at the first, and the three jibs were torn completely to shreds. These, with one royal, made nine sails more or less injured. The next day a different gale came on at 10 A.M., and we ran all day before the wind with only the mainsail and foresail set, looking more like a wreck than anything. A very heavy sea, of course, rose, and the large waves rolling in astern, and leaving by the head, looked very grand, and more like rather distant mountains and valleys than anything else.

On 4th September and the night before we had another tremendous gale, during which five or six more of the principal sails were more or less torn, including the mainsail and foresail. About this time, too, we had plenty of hail and snow, and water often froze on the deck.

Since then we have only had one other gale worth mentioning, on the 9th, but the captain had taken in sail before it began, and we ran quite safely and without injury through it with close-reefed topsails. Studding sail booms have been carried away without number from time to time, and two of them by dipping into the waves and snapping off with the force of the ship's motion. I always said that the ship could not be rigged well in such a short time as it was, and it is quite proved now by many things which are defective. Most of the iron-work is of the most horrible iron, and this is the chief cause of the loss of so many sails, as well as of the falling of two of the topsail yards, though luckily not down to the deck.

We have, of course, had the usual succession of fishes and birds to amuse us. We wondered for a long time at the porpoises, until at last some dolphins were seen, a small one of which was caught by a line. In the Tropics we saw thousands of the small white flying fish, sometimes chased by porpoises, and at length a shark appeared with his two pilot fish. He swam round the vessel for some time, but was caught, with some difficulty. Several others were caught from time to time, but the best sport was with the last one – he appeared in the middle of some Cape pigeons he was trying to catch, but soon came up to the ship. The hook with a large piece of pork was put over the stern, and we saw him slowly turn over twice and take it in his mouth. He was not, however, hooked till the third bite, when he was hauled straight up and dragged away to be cut up. He was about five or six feet long, and had a pigeon in his stomach, swallowed whole.

We have had Cape pigeons following the ship now for nearly a month. They are very pretty black and white birds, of the shape of a pigeon, and fly about the stern in great numbers. Among them are nearly always several albatrosses. We have seen none of these of a white all over, and most are of a dull black, but they are magnificent birds, floating about in the air with the greatest ease, and without even moving their wings, which I have scarcely ever seen them flap. I have had very poor luck with my lines. We had some very pleasant meetings with ships till the bad weather began, since which we have not seen one. On the 23d of July the *Fletcher*, from London to New Zealand, came up to us, and ran a race for several days, falling back at last. There were often two or three in view at the same time, but there was no chance of sending a letter back.[2]

To come now to the first cabin passengers, it is no easy matter to know how to tell you about the continual quarrels. They have affected me very little, as I have been on friendly terms with almost everybody, but even considering that we are all Australian emigrants, and that most are only second cabin passengers turned into the first cabin, I could scarcely have conceived that so much jealousy and hatred, as well as petty quarrelling, could have been crammed into such a small place as this cabin during three months. . . . I kept clear of everything, till finding that Mr. Lane[3] was not the one in fault, and that he was a gentleman well worth knowing, I became more intimate with him. Mr. Lane is from Cork, but has lived twenty years in different parts of France, so as to have taken completely the appearance of a Frenchman. He has been lately professor of literature (English, I suppose) in the College of Amiens. He is therefore a very well educated man, and knows a great many of the first men of France. I have had a great many very pleasant talks with him, but he has rather extraordinary political opinions, being a regular republican, engaged a little in the revolutions at Paris, as well as the Irish Rebellion. He is going to Sydney to see his father,[4] and I shall therefore probably see something more of him. Mr. Newton[5] is the one I care most for after him. He is a working engineer, at one time an engine-driver, but a very superior man. He has been engaged making

---

[2] This passage does not appear in the Journal draft. Cf. Vol. I, p. 105, n. 1.
[3] See above, Letter 42, n. 4, p. 81.
[4] Possibly Samuel Lane, from Cork, recorded as having lived in Sydney in 1841.
[5] See above, Letter 42, n. 9, p. 85.

the mint machinery, and is sent out to see it put up. After that he will remain there on his own account, but will probably be employed by the mint. As he is such a sensible, pleasant man, I shall try to get him to let me lodgings in the house he is going to take for his wife and family, and I should then, I expect, be comfortable enough. I should even, if possible, like to have my laboratory in the same house, but I cannot tell how it can be settled till it comes to the fact.

About John Anderson, my chum, I need only say that he is as good a fellow in every way as I could wish to know, but he is going to a farm near Sydney, and I shall not see very much of him. Mr. Day,[6] a retired old grocer and butter dealer from Shoreditch, London, is one of the kindest old men I ever knew. He has told me so many tales about all he has seen and done in London that I think I could write his Life. He is a great cribbage player, and I have had some very pleasant games to help over the long evenings, reading being impossible. Mr. Day is going to Melbourne, as well as Mr. Grylls,[7] a young solicitor, and a sporting gentleman. Mr. Clarence (*alias* Joseph) Holt is a very amusing sort of man, but not from his acting, which is all tragedy. He is in a state of the greatest fear during the gales, standing in one corner of the cabin and asking everybody who passes what they think of the danger. The second cabin passengers are, on the whole, a very disagreeable set, though Charles Bolton's chums are amongst the best of them. The third cabin and intermediate passengers, on the contrary, are the best behaved in the ship. I have read very little, a thing nearly impossible on a ship, but have spent the time chiefly watching the weather and such things, talking, and playing draughts and cards. In the fine weather, especially in the Tropics, this was all very pleasant, but since the stormy weather and long nights began it has got more tiresome. Twenty-four hours of some of the gales we had is enough to tire anybody out, from the motion of the vessel, noise, and wet; and I can give you no idea of what scenes there sometimes were at dinner, when, with a sudden lurch, hams, fowls, loaves, and cheeses, would roll off the table; water, soup, gravy, etc., would spill over you; and the knives and forks would fly into the corners of the cabin.

Off Port Phillip Heads,
22d September 1854.

At last we are in sight of land, and lying several miles outside the harbour, with the pilot on board, and all anxious to get in, but without a breath of wind to take us in. We were expecting land all yesterday,

---

[6] See above, Letter 42, n. 7, p. 84.
[7] It has proved impossible to trace any biographical details of Grylls; but cf. below, Letter 52, p. 112.

and at seven o'clock in the evening the revolving light on Cape Otway was seen right ahead of us. The first land or mark of any sort that we had seen since we lost sight of Cape Clear. We hove to ten or fifteen miles from it, in order not to reach the Heads too early in the morning, and you may imagine what a pleasure it was to feel yourself near land, the Heads being then just in sight. The pilot came on board at eight o'clock, but the breeze had gone down entirely, and we therefore did not attempt to enter. At six o'clock P.M. a light breeze sprang up, which brought us just within the harbour, where we are anchored close to two lighthouses on Shortlands Bluff. The air now has a very distinct and pleasant smell of the land, and the water is of a dull green instead of its usual deep blue. We shall start to-morrow morning for Melbourne, which is still forty miles off. The coast on the western side of the entrance is very like that near Liverpool in appearance, with a small hill exactly like Dinas Dinlle, near Carnarvon; on the other side it is more uneven and rocky, with a range of hills in the distance. With the telescope I can see very plainly the scrubby dark-coloured trees and the dull green hills just above the beach. The day is very fine and warm, and I should like nothing better than a walk among the rocks and trees. There are splendid pieces of branched red sea-weed floating on the water, which show me what to expect. Since I wrote last we have had some more stormy weather, particularly a very heavy gale on the night of the 14th, and a very sudden and violent squall on the 18th. One day a shoal of large grampuses passed us, which looked very singular with their great round snouts slowly rolling out of the sides of the waves. On the 14th and 16th we had fine displays of the aurora australis, which were much finer than anything I have seen of the sort in England.

Melbourne,
Sunday, 24th September 1854.

Here we are, anchored a mile or two from Melbourne,[8] and near enough to the shore for us to examine by the telescope the manner of life in Australia. The appearance of the houses in Richmond and Williamstown, which we see, is very strange and ugly, and tents are very common. The land round Melbourne is flat and not very inviting, but there are ranges of hills all round in the distance very similar in appearance to the Carnarvonshire mountains. I shall very probably go on shore to-morrow, and I have rather luckily made out Caldwell, Train, and Company's[9] name on a large building at the water's edge. . . .

[8] Cf. Vol. I, p. 108.
[9] Cf. below, Letter 53, n. 6, p. 116.

46. THOMAS JEVONS TO W. S. JEVONS

Liverpool
30th Sep 1854

Dearest Stanley

The news that is uppermost in our minds at home is that we have heard of the Oliver Lang being spoken not very far from the Island of Assension* on the 5th August We of course instantly turned to the map and have made our calculations and have come to the conclusion that your Ship had performed well so far. I consider Assension* rather more than 1/3rd the distance in measurement of space but more than half the distance in point of time and what is more I believe that the most dangerous and troublesome part of the voyage is from England down to the Line. On the 5 August you had been at sea just 40 days and I strongly believe that 35 days more would bring you to Melbourne and when there you would consider yourself almost as good as at the end of your voyage With the Ship almost to yourself and a supply of fresh provisions the passage from Melbourne to your future home would be like a holiday trip the only drawback being the thoughts connected with your fitting up when once fairly landed at Sydney But the landing over and your place of business and residence decided upon then for a while you would be so full of active employment in putting your things to rights that I doubt not you would be in a comparative state of happiness provided only that you had your health. And on this point let me say a few words. If you have not your health what is Sydney or riches or England or any place in this world worth. Health is the *first* of all considerations. When in fair health we little think of the real value of it but when it is gone then how very much we lament that we had not taken more care of it Now there are periods of life and of position when it cannot be denied that we are bound in duty to take more than ordinary care of ourselves and our constitutions In so thorough a change of climate and occupation and even of diet as you will be undergoing on your settling in N.S.W. it behoves you to be more than ordinarily on your guard about your health and as symptoms of complaints may be different in your new abode to what they are in England you should the sooner seek the aid of a medical man if you feel at all poorly and unequal to your work. But one thing I must guard you against most emphatically dont permit your extreme absorption of employment in setting up your laboratory cause you to neglect your health. You may be so absorbed in your work that the premonitory symptoms of a complaint may be over looked by you and then a complaint come on and gain head before you take any steps to meet it and remove it and then perhaps you would have to submit to severe measures to remove it and lose much more time than you had gained by your intense application that may have brought on a complaint. No, my dear Stanley make it a rule never under any circumstances to be broken until you have been acclimated by a residence of two or three years in N.S.W. to make the preservation of your health the very first consideration In wet or in dry seasons in the hours for your recriations* and for your meals never give way particularly as to the regularity of your meals I would lose a hundred experiments rather than put off those points that are essential to the preservation of a high tone of health Preserve yourself in a good state of health and your mind will be equal to achieve nay to command success but allow your health to be ever so slightly undermined and then your success in life becomes a matter of doubt You may think all this unnecessary but I nevertheless should not think I was doing my duty unless I had inflicted it upon you and if ever so slight an effect is produced on your conduct by what I have said I shall feel abundantly repaid –

We have had a splendid meeting of the Brit Association in LPool the last week. I met Graham in St Georges Hall one evening and introduced myself. What a little gim crack of a fellow he looks but there is mind in his head and feitures* that cannot be mistaken I invited him to come and see me to dinner and again to breakfast but he would not come and I did not see him again at all He called in Chatham S^t and left his card and that was all He had a young lady with him in the Hall, it was at the general Suorre* I met him, and the Lady seemed as if she was his sister though much younger than him. I went into the chemical Class or Section once just to take a peep at Dr Miller who was in the Chair and I was fortunate enough to see him What a sharp keen looking eye he has and evidently a first rate man I saw an immense number of the learnedly great men and heard many of them speak or lecture and on the whole never remember spending a week with so much of intellectual enjoyment as the last. I shall post a newspaper to you which will give you a better account of all the business that was done than I could report to you One set of experiments only I will mention those of Monsieur Fecault*[1] who discovered the pendulum experiment for proving to your eyesight the diurnal rotation of the Earth He shewed* the same results now by the rapid revolution of a sphere hung so that it could keep its position though the Earth on which it is placed turns round Again he shewed* that a sphere put into rapid motion and hung on a universal joint something in the manner of the card and needle of a compas* will always place itself or its poles in the position of the poles of the Earth, if

[1] Jean Bernard Léon Foucault (1819–68) French physicist, inventor of the gyroscope. In 1851 he verified the earth's rotation by means of apparatus known as the 'Foucault Pendulum', a heavy iron ball suspended on a wire 200 feet long, which swings through all points of the compass in one day. In 1855 he was awarded the Royal Society's Copley Medal for this demonstration.

spun round in the direction of the Sun and if spun round in the opposite direction it will shift its own pole to the opposite direction like a thing that has life Another most remarkable experiment he shewed* us he took the sphere or top for it is something like a humming top spun it round and then stuck one only of its poles on the top of a stand where by its own revolution it supported itself in air and performed a series of revolutions around the stand that supported only one end I will try to make a diagram of this instrument[2] for you but it must necessarily be a very imperfect one as I only saw the instrument from a distance as I sat in the Hall where these experiments were shewn* There is one other affair I will just mention and that is a *photograph of the moon*. It was taken or rather many of them were taken by means of a large & powerful telescope on a small glass plate which takes what I may call a most excellent copy of the moons surface. This small photograph was put into an improved magic lantern lighted with the electric light and we had a drawing of the moons surface before us *drawn by herself* of about 30 feet diameter a most wonderful work indeed

The meeting of the Association has been distinguished by the opening of our St Georges Hall in which building the whole of the Sections were held and all at the same time The Great Hall is pronounced by everyone as the finest room in Europe. Indeed I cannot imagine anything that can surpass it The Philarmonic* Hall is a poor mean low looking place compared with St Georges Hall and even the lighting up of the Philarmonic* which we used to boast of very much before is put quite into the shade by the most splendid shandaliers* of the St Georges Hall heightened as the light is by reflection from the polished granite columns and polished variagated* marble fronts of the Gallery sides The vaulted ceiling is seen to perfection by Gass* light and is the most glorious arch I have ever seen I will try to enclose a drawing of it.[3]

2 Oct, We have glorious news from the Crimea today The Allied Armies of France & England have taken the Strong hold of Sebastopol[4] I will send you the Lpool Albion of this day to tell you all we know about it.

I do not know whether you have been informed that Eliza's[5] marriage with Mr Barham is definitely fixed at last It is to come off so early as

[2] The diagrams and account of the experiment were contained in a separate sheet enclosed with the letter. See below, p. 104.

[3] He does not appear to have done so.

[4] The report proved to be false (cf. below, Letter 79, p. 204). The allied armies had sailed from Varna at the end of August to attack Sebastopol and six days after landing near the fortress fought a battle at the River Alma (20 September) in which Sebastopol heights were gained and the Russians forced to retreat. The allied commanders could not agree to press home this victory and lost the chance of taking the fortress. Cf Woodward, op. cit., pp. 275–280.

[5] Jevons's cousin Eliza (b. 1832) second of the three daughters of Timothy Jevons. See below, Letter 70, p. 176.

next thursday* the 5th Inst Lucy is one of the bridesmaids and is very busy indeed about it so much so that she has not time to write to you by this mail She desired me to tell you that she sends her very best love and will write you a long letter by the next mail I remain Dearest Stanley

Your Ever Aff^{te} Father
Thomas Jevons

1 Experiment of M Fecault* to prove the diurnal motion of the earth – *a* a top.

If you put the top *a* upon a pedestal* when the top is at rest and both together upon a table or stand if you move the stand round you move also the pedestal* and top round. But if you give a very rapid circular motion to the top so rapid that the top may be said to be asleep & you then move the stand or table round the pedestal* & top will not move round with the table but will keep themselves in exactly the same position. In other words the tendency of the top while asleep to keep its position is more strong than the friction of the pedestal* on the surface of the table. Now if you fix a finger or pointer upon the pedestal,* it will always point while the top is in motion in one certain direction whilst the table on which it stands and the floor of the room also go round with the diurnal motion of the earth If then the end of the pointer points to a graduated scale fixed against the wall of the room you can see how fast the room turns round –

2 If you take the top while asleep and fix one end of its axis on the top of a stand like *c* it will support itself as represented and at the same time go round and round the stand, thus shewing* the motion of the earth round the Sun and the diurnal motion at the same time and supporting itself as it were in air

3 Put the top into a metal ring as at *d* then put it to sleep by spinning it and put the metal ring & top onto a pedestal* the axle of the top will arrange itself in the direction of the poles of the earth provided the top be spun round in the direction of the Sun. If you take the top out and spin it in an opposite direction then the axle of the top will arrange itself in the opposite direction. I have made a mistake in drawing the two figures *e* & *f* but I think they will serve to enable you to form an opinion of what is intended "*a word to the wise*" The Conclusion to draw from these experiments is that if the top be spun with extreme rapidity and placed on a universal joint, as free to act as the card of a compas,* it will assume of itself the position of the heavenly bodies and in fact it does represent the various motions of the planets in their orbits

I have caught all this only from a distant view of the apparatus in the lecture in St Georges Hall with 1500 people all around me and therefore you must only take it as a smattering of the facts of the case but all the *motions* I have represented I SAW with my own eyes as clearly as I ever saw any thing though I could only catch a general idea of the form of the top and its axles and ring

I should mention that M Fecault* had a small piece of frame work with multiplying wheels which he used to set the top in rapid motion He did not tell us now many revolutions a minute but I should guess a thousand or two

The top or sphere seemed to me about 2½ or 3 Inch in diameter and about 1¼ Inch to 1½ Inch thick & of solid brass

Sep 1854

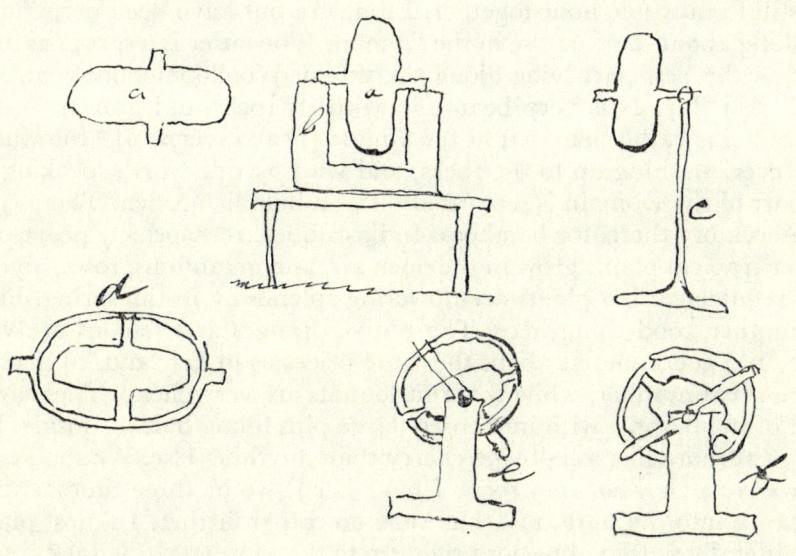

47. W. S. JEVONS TO LUCY JEVONS
[LJN, 45–6]

Sydney,
16th October 1854.

... The passage from Melbourne was a very long and tedious one for the distance, and we were for five or six days continually expecting to be at Port Jackson the next day. At last we got up one morning with the port in sight, and I was quite disappointed to see nothing but bare perpendicular rocks and barren hills. I could not understand all I had heard about the beauty of Port Jackson till we got quite into it. Then I thought it really the most beautiful place I had ever seen. You must imagine an ornamental lake something like the Prince's Park,[1] one of a very large size, with a continual succession of bays, creeks, points, and islands. The banks are everywhere old rocks overgrown with bushes and trees – with very neat gentlemen's houses here and there – and when you get to the shore, the rocks under water are covered with sea-weeds and oysters and other shells. Altogether it is the most beautiful bit of scenery I ever saw, the different views of bays and points being endless in number. When I got into the town I was glad to find it looked such a pleasant old place, most of the streets being something like those of an old English town, though the verandahs round many of the houses give it a curious appearance. In the day-time I have not been able to sit still for a whole hour together, I am sure but have been perpetually walking about town or else in the Domain. The latter is a sort of natural park – the best part lying along the side of Woolloomoolloo (can you spell it?) Bay. It is very beautiful, with its rocks and gum-trees, the shore being rather like that at the Dingle [near Liverpool],[2] the water, however, washing up to the rocks, and with no tide worth speaking of. A part of the Domain is separated off as a botanic garden. There is no conservatory there, for bamboos, India-rubber trees, prickly pears, and other tropical plants grow in the open air, and geraniums, roses, and all the regular garden plants are flowering splendidly in the spring. Fruit is another good thing here. The native oranges and lemons are very fine, and good ones at about the same prices as in England, so that we eat a great number, while the fruit loquats are very cheap. These are a sort of small apple with immensely large pips filling half the inside, but they eat more like a half-ripe cherry than anything else. We shall have peaches and grapes very soon. I have been two or three times a short distance into the bush, but shall soon go rather farther. In most places it is literally nothing but bush right up to the shores near Sydney, and if you walk a few yards into it you see a most extraordinary variety of flowers and flowering shrubs. I was quite astonished the first time Mr. Newton[3] and I went a walk; almost every flower we met was a very pretty one, but quite different from the last, till we picked, I should think, thirty or forty different flowers in the course of half an hour. You may imagine what a collection I shall have. . . .

[1] Prince's Park, Liverpool. The Park had been given to the borough of Liverpool by Richard Vaughan Yates. James Martineau built himself a house in Prince's Park.
[2] Cf. below, Letter 51, n. 3, p. 110. The words 'near Liverpool' were presumably inserted by Mrs Jevons in the LJ text and did not form part of the original manuscript.
[3] The Mint engineer.

48. W. S. JEVONS TO THOMAS JEVONS
[LJN, 47–8]

[16th October 1854]

... It was fortunate that before I left England I had never expected the mint to be ready till about Easter, for otherwise I should certainly have been disappointed to hear that the building had hardly been begun (only six weeks since), that rents were enormously high, and that there was very little other assaying to do....

As to the cottage,[1] I think we could hardly have made a better assay office with all the planning and considering we had together. The laboratory room, which has been a kitchen, has no ceiling, but is open to the roof as well as along over the ceiling of the other room. This will make it cool and airy, but the ceiling of the small room, being floored above, makes a store-room for everything I shall have to put in it. I think I can manage to put up the cupel and melting furnaces without disturbing the chimney and fireplace much, and the other fittings-up and furniture will not be so expensive as you would imagine. As to domestic arrangements, I am going to buy a small sofa-bed to sleep in, in my private room, while Charles will sleep somewhere about the laboratory or loft. We shall probably cook for ourselves entirely, and I have calculated that we shall live so cheaply in this way that the whole expenses and rent will not be so much as continuing in lodgings. You will probably say that we shall be uncomfortable living by ourselves in this way, but it must be done, as I have not money otherwise, and it is not thought at all an extraordinary thing here.

There are some disadvantages about this cottage certainly; it is an old tumble-down place with lots of cobwebs and rats, and Mr. Korff[2] has the lease for about a year more only, so that I may then be turned out, though, as he says, he will most likely have it again, and let it to me again. I shall therefore make the least possible alteration or improvements, and there would be less trouble in moving than perhaps you would imagine....

---

[1] The cottage at Charlotte Place, Church Hill, Sydney. See Vol. I, p. 20.

[2] This reference to 'Mr. Korff' as the landlord of the cottage is not supplemented by any biographical information in LJ, and it has not proved possible to find any further details about him.

49. W. S. JEVONS TO THOMAS JEVONS
[LJN, 48]

12th November 1854.

... The fittings I have done in the laboratory since I wrote are (besides the cupel furnace, which is put up in the corner) building the melting furnace, making the laboratory table, the work-bench and some other things, setting the balance in order, and getting the gasfittings done. I daresay you will wonder that I have done so little, and I am myself astonished that work should take so long and be so tiring. The melting furnace I built with Mr. Miller's[1] help, and though at first our brick-work looked rather crooked and loose, it has turned out much better than I expected. The draught is excellent, and will be better when everything is finished, and the furnace is very convenient to work at. It is bound together with sheet-iron corners and iron hoops; next it I have put up again the old oven, which may be useful. The greater part of the chimney is stopped up with sheet-iron. The gasmen have been at work now for two or three days, and everything is done but joining on the service pipe to the fittings inside, which will be done to-morrow morning.... By the end of this next week I hope to be really in working order, which it is high time that I was....

50. FRAGMENT OF A LETTER FROM W. S. JEVONS TO LUCY JEVONS
[Nov./Dec. 1854]

between themselves who was to assay them, but Mr Miller has been very busy the last two or three days calling here & there, even on Solomon,[1] evidently trying to make sure of them coming to him. I was taking a walk, this evening & met Mr Miller coming from Solomon's house; he immediately began explaining a great deal about these assays and why he had been calling. I walked a little way with him and just as I was coming in again I met Solomon who had come to see me. He told me the whole story over again from a diametrically opposite point of view, and ended by saying he would have the assays done a second time by me if I would do them at a lower price. It is of course impossible to reduce the price for anybody as it would endanger our price at the Mint so that I shall not get them at all.

Mr Miller has in fact *opposed me* which from what he has always

---

[1] See above, Letter 27, n. 6, p. 49.
[1] A bullion broker. Cf. below, Letter 53, p. 115.

professed, I did not think he would ever have done. Here again I ought to know whether we shall have the fixed salary from the mint for if so it is no use troubling myself about private work for the 2 or 3 months more, but if we dont I shall push on a bit more & see if I cannot look after the assays as well as Mr Miller.

I may be some time before I can write again and I hope I may have something more certain to tell you. I am in perfect health & very good spirits considering but I wish I was done with these troublesome men of business.

With best love to all
   I remain
      Ever Your affec. Brother
        W. S. Jevons.

PS. I dare say you will think this an awfully dry letter to write to a sister but my head is full of the things just at present & I cannot help.

51. W. S. JEVONS TO HENRIETTA JEVONS

         8 Church Hill. Sydney.
         Sunday. Dec. 17th 1854

My dearest Henny

It seems an immense time now since I said goodbye to you at Chatham Street, and I can hardly believe now that this is my first Australian letter to you. You have told me to think particularly of you on a Sunday evening, and that you would do the same; you I suppose happy with the rest of the girls at school thinking how near Christmas is and what a little time separates you from home. I cannot think the same, but I can feel how near I can be to you and the rest at home in thoughts. It must be a long time before I can have a chance of seeing you again but still I must say that in everything that I do, I have the object in view to return home again as soon as it is possible and right.

The top of Church Hill is a "Holy Land" like that of Hope Street and contains two churches,[1] one not finished, a Scotch Church and a Catholic chapel; I sometimes take a little walk up there in an evening and listen to the organ of the Catholic chapel, which is really an excellent one. It makes me wish I had my own one here; I dont know what may happen to it now I am away but I hope to see it again some time. I may possibly meet with an harmonium here pretty cheap in a year to two and that will do better than nothing.

    [1] 'church' in the original manuscript.

Sydney is in my opinion a quiet pleasant old place. A large proportion of the houses are small one stories* cottages with large verandahs,[2] and there are very few houses at all without some sort of verandah to cool oneself in when it is very hot. My cottage however is without one and stands in a dirty old yard full of bottles broken bottles & lumber; but after six oclock in the evening the gate is shut and we have it all to ourselves which is better than having the street before you. To make up for the dreariness of the place itself, it is very easy to get to some beautiful walks about the harbour near the botanical gardens. It is very like indeed to Miss Yates Dingle[3] in style, there being a small bay with rocks at each side and the gardens gradually sloping up from the water at the end.

I must give you a short account of some of my best walks. One Saturday I set off for Botany Bay and had a beautiful walk over the sandhills & swamps between here & there. Once I came to a place where the tall thick bushes covered with magnificent red flowers the handsomest near Sydney, were so thick, that I had to walk a long way before I could find an opening through.

Near Botany I met the alarming appearance of a snake about a yard and a half long but he quietly moved out of the way. On the shores of Botany bay which is a wide & open and not unlike the upper part of the Mersey though not so large, there are plenty of trees though not very elegant ones, but there is nothing so remarkable & beautiful about it as Port Jackson.

A still pleasanter excursion was to the Entrance of the port and the sea coast. Here there are immensely high perpendicular cliffs with here and there a sort of ravine filled up with tall thick bush. In one of these I found a small wild geranium quite a contrast to the large stiff Australian flowers, and which reminded me of English flowers.

Dec 30th I have unfortunately not touched this letter since the last date and I have now time only to say a few words. *Christmas has passed*, but in any letter I forgot to mention the name so different has this been to any former one. The name has seemed to me quite hollow and I cannot imagine you sitting down to the regular good old dinner, with good cheerful fires, frosty out of doors, with the prospect of skating perhaps. While here what green bushes has[4] been put up are withered

---

[2] Jevons appears to have written 'verandal' here.

[3] Anna Maria Yates (1787–1866) and Jane Ellen Yates (1794–1877) were the two surviving daughters of Rev. John Yates (1755–1826) whose family lived for many years at The Dingle, Toxteth Park, at that time near Liverpool, now one of the inner suburbs of the city. The Misses Yates devoted their lives to charity and good works. Cf. Samuel Ashton Thompson Yates, *Memorials of the Family of the Rev. Jhon Yates*, (privately printed, 1890). See above, Letter 11, n. 5, p. 24.

[4] Jevons first wrote 'holly' here but substituted 'green bushes'.

up by the heat and there seems to be nothing by which you can recognise the day again.

But goodbye, I hope I shall sometime see another English Christmas. Give my best remembrances to Ann[5] if you are at home; she will think I have forgotten her.[6] And with best love to yourself I remain
    Ever your affectionate brother
        W. S. Jevons.

52. W. S. JEVONS TO F. B. EDMONDS[1]
        Nº8 Church Hill. Sydney
        Jan 26th 1855.[2]

My dear Edmonds

I am quite in doubt whether this letter will reach you for time has gone on so far that you may have vanished entirely from University College & Fitzroy Square too. In spite of it however and after having just finished a long letter to Graham (Prof. I should have said) and having written during the week no less than three to various relations in Liverpool, I shall sit up tonight till I have finished this one too, for the very chance of your getting it.

You see I have not quite forgotten you though I have put off writing rather long and I am not indeed likely to forget College affairs so soon, as it was to me a very pleasant time & I should not mind being there yet. Still I *am* here without any doubt & I had perhaps better tell you first how I got here.

Our ship was a first rate clipper, new St John built,[3] 1272 ton, emigrant ship with *nearly* 600 *souls* (as they say) on board about 16 first Cabin, 50 second Cabin 50 crew cooks &c & the rest third Cabin. I always used to think what would become of these 600 souls if the ship was on fire or going down, as the boat wouldn't hold half the number and they would kill or drown each other in the scramble. However the case never occurred and we were never in any danger and I must say that on

---

[5] Presumably Anne Bolton.
[6] 'here' in the original manuscript.
[1] See Vol. I, p. 54, n. 3.
 It has not proved possible to establish any biographical facts about Frederick B. Edmonds; he appears to have been a son of Thomas Rowe Edmonds (1803–89), actuary of the Legal and General Assurance Society from 1832 to 1866 and author of *Practical moral and political economy* (1828) and *An Inquiry into the Principles of Population* (1832).
[2] The original manuscript of this letter is in the Mitchell Library, Sydney.
[3] Clippers, introduced by the Americans and designed for speed, proved ideal for use as emigrant ships, and were hired and bought by Liverpool shipowners anxious to take full advantage of the Australian emigration boom. Some owners, including James Baines of the Black Ball Line, placed orders for new vessels in shipyards in Boston and Nova Scotia. Cf. C. Jones, *British Merchant Shipping* (1923) pp. 25–33.

the whole a sea voyage is a very pleasant way of spending three months.

Our Captain was a young man whose chief object was apparently to make himself disagreable* to everybody, kicking up rows with the sailors & officers, neglecting or abusing the second & third Cabin passengers and among the first Cabin ditto appearing to raise rather than stop quarrelling & shutting himself up in the ladies cabin with an emigrating milliner who first took a passage in the third Cabin but afterwards appeared as a lady in the first, & who was married to him a short time after we arrived & (I am glad to say) has gone back. Most of our cabin passengers were of the same sort including the celebrated Mr Clarence Holt of the Royal Lyceum Theatre London & his wife Mrs May Holt. Also a very respectable old grocer from London & a very pleasant old man who I used to play cribbage with at a tremendous rate. Also M^r & Mrs Grylls he, a lawyer, the son of a banker in or somewhere near *Penzance*. A Mr Lane an Irishman who had lived 20 years in France lately as a Professor, who had been in the French Revolutions and was a regular Republican, though somewhat scientific & a very pleasant man for a voyage.

(He & the captain has [sic] some tremendous & almost fatal quarrels) He landed at Melbourne but was to have come on here but as he has not come I shouldnt wonder if he has joined the diggers insurrection and got put out of the way at Ballarat.[4]

We sailed the ordinary course & with ordinary winds past Madeira, the Canaries & Cape de Verds* but without sighting any of them. We then, about Lat 10° N., got into a most extraordinary succession of calms but some of the days then were the best of the voyage. The sea sometimes would be as smooth as glass, barrels &c floating out to the side & showing that we were not moving one inch forwards. We would generally be lying on the deck under an awning playing draughts or cards, or reading (nearly an impossibility at sea). Occasionally a shark would show himself to give us a little amusement; in a minute then the shark hook would be over the stern with a large piece of salt pork; he would generally swim straight up to it, swallow it at once be hauled on deck in two minutes & half cut up in 5 minutes more. They are magnificent fish and it is first rate to see them turn over & swallow the hook.

With these & other amusements we passed several weeks of calms when we got on but little. We sailed SSW to within 600 miles of Rio Janeiro* then to Tristian* d'Acunha. After this we fell in with some very different amusements viz. good strong gales for 3 or 4 days together till you were quite tired of holding to the back of your chair & getting no dinner as it was a difficult thing to eat with everything rolling about the table. The sea looked splendid sometimes; in the gales we

[4] Cf. below, Letter 55, n. 2, p. 122.

were generally running before the wind with 2 or 3 sails up (the rest in general blown away as our Captain let the wind save him the trouble of taking them in) the immense waves rolling in astern & looking as if they were going to roll over everything.

At last we came in sight of Cape Otway the first point of land seen, and in a day or two were at Melbourne. There I went ashore one day and saw a little of the town. I was quite surprized* to see such splendid shops & stores but the streets were chiefly rows of wooden & iron houses. Our voyage out to Melbourne was in 86 days; a long passage on account of the calms we had had. After 10 days sail round the coast here which was the pleasantest part of the passage we anchored here on the 100th day.

I do not intend to trouble you with any account of the bother of getting lodgings finding a suitable place for a laboratory, carting my boxes of apparatus but will simply say that I am living in a small two roomed cottage at the back of 8 Church Hill. The smaller room forms my parlour, bed room, office, study, balance room & anything else you like; the balances on a cedar wood table along one side, my library of 170 vols. in a cedar wood bookcase, a table, 2 chairs sofa bedstead &c &c. The other room is the laboratory, formed out of an old kitchen. I wish you could see it. With the exception of the gasfitting & such things, I & my assistant did everything ourselves and were 4 or 5 weeks working making tables shelves, building furnaces &c &c. All the apparatus is complete & works well and within the last three months I have had a few assays to do for the public as well as 57 assays for the Mint. We are paid 6^س 6^d an assay. The Mint however is not much more than half built yet and it will be some months yet before it will be got to work. Till that of course we shall have very little work and I only hope we may have enough to pay expenses after it begins. Just fancy living here with a rent of £104 a year, & a salary of £100, & yourself & assistant consequently to keep on – £4 a year. What do you think of £2 per week for 2 rooms; many other things here are dear in the same proportion.

I do not find it possible at present to read much or be very scientific, but I have mounted a barometer, registering thermometer &c &c, & observe the weather which I think is peculiar & interesting here. The heat & the shape of the coast cause a strong sea breeze, but after a hot wind from the interior or a very hot day, very sudden squalls from the south called "Brickfielders" or "Southerly Busters" spring up & blow the dust about in Sydney in a ferocious manner. The air sometimes becomes regularly stifling hot in an afternoon here, & once the thermometer was up to 100° in the shade. Today is a very hot day & the temp. indoors is 80°.

Sydney on the whole is a pleasant & cheerful place. The Harbour is not large but is everywhere very deep, and with beautiful little bays & coves on every side between the sandstone ridges. The rocky sides are covered with bush & altogether it looks like a large ornamental lake. The bathing in it is beautiful but I prefer going to the railed off baths, as there are plenty of sharks. Of course boating & yachting is the great thing in the Harbour, and as today happened to be the Anniversary of the foundation of the Colony, there has been a general holyday* & a grand Regatta. I was invited to see it from Dawes Battery the house of the Master of the Mint, which stands on a point with a capital view. We also had a first rate lunch with plenty of champagne & the best eating I have had in Australia.

In the chief race, one yacht upset, and another broke their topmast. Another yacht also had upset previously besides a few rowing boats, in fact it seems quite a common thing here with the gusty winds and excites no surprize.*

It is fine fun taking excursions into the bush but I have not been far yet. There is no mistake about the bush & within a few miles of Sydney I have several times been overhead in it & not able to move a step forward. Altogether I shall be very well content to live a few years in this place particularly if assaying prospers.

The war news which we get from time to time is as interesting as if we were in England. I remember you thought the war would be chiefly of advantage for trying experiments on screw steamers, large guns &c &c; I hope you are nearly satisfied as to the results. From what they say about getting ready new ships, boats, guns ammunition &c, I should think they must intend to drive the Czar away altogether. I hope he wont come in this direction.

Having now written a quite long enough letter, I will conclude.

   Believe me ever
        Yours very truly
        W. S. Jevons.

PS Remember me to Colville[5] when you see him as well as Whittaker if he is still alive at College, & any others there may be. I shall probably write to Colville soon, but I thought he was not likely to be moving away so soon. As I expect a letter from you in time, direct to

    8 Charlotte Place
    Church Hill
    New South Wales.

but after Midsummer you had better direct to the "Royal Mint" Sydney as I might possibly be moved from here.

    [5] See Vol. I, p. 54, n. 3.

53. THOMAS JEVONS TO W. S. JEVONS

Liverpool 31 Jany 1855

My Dear Stanley

I begin this letter a few days before it will be posted in order that I may be able to fill you up a bumper if I may be able.

We are now in possession of your letters by the Great Britain and by the Calcutta or Overland Mail.[1] The latest dated one is that in which you communicated the fact that you considered your Laboratory finished[2] and waited only for the first customer to bring you your first job and that you expected the bullion broker Salomans* would be the man and that he would appear the following day. I trust you would not be disappointed in that or any other of your well grounded expectations

Your letters give us a most clear and full account of your operations and I will at once and in short say that all your arrangements seem to me excellent the work well carried out and your decisions in which judgment between two different courses was necessary were characterized by true wisdom and you will reap your reward.

I am not surprized* at your receiving visits from such fellows as Jones[3] pretending to a knowledge of our family and under that plea begging of you what you might be disposed to give. If this only were his object it might be innocent enough, but under the plea of begging many a rogue gains admission to premises for a far worse purpose and this consideration leads me to make the only improvement in your premises that I can suggest. I would advise you to put up a counter in your lobby which should bar the entrance of every stranger beyond a few feet from your outer door. I have not the sketch of your office before me now because your letters are gone up to London for the Doctor and your Aunt Henry to read but I will make a sketch of what I mean and enclose it before I post this letter.[4]

Returning to your history of your expedition, shall I call it, we seem to be short of two letters from you to make the history complete. Your first letter ended by telling us of your being anchored in the Oliver Lang about one mile from the shore of Melbourne and that you could see through a Glass the name of Caldwell Train & Co on a warehouse on the Quay. The next letter received by us tells us of your landing in Sydney and being met on the deck of the ship by Mr Miller & Sergeant Tricket.*[5]

---

[1] See below, Letter 57, n. 1, p. 133.
[2] See above, Letter 49, p. 108.
[3] The letter in which this incident must have been mentioned is not among the Jevons Papers.
[4] This sketch is not among the Jevons Papers.
[5] Joseph Trickett (d. 1878) formerly of the Royal Engineers; served in Gibraltar before emigrating to Australia in 1853, where he superintended the building of the Sydney Mint;

Not a sylable* have we had from you to inform us of your landing at Melbourne and what you saw there but we happen to know that you did land for George Train[6] in a letter to Hen[y] Jevons[7] says that you had called upon him and delivered my introductory note He is pleased to call you a "fine young lad" and that he had invited you to dine with him and expected you but that the sudden sailing of the Oliver Lang prevented you from filling your engagement.[8] This is all we know of your doings at Melbourne, and think it just possible that you may have written us an account of your stay there but that your letter has misscarried*. The other hiatus in your epistles is the non communication to us of the arrival out of Captain Ward. You tell us of an interview which you and Miller had with him about raising your Salary or making you some extra allowance[9] but you had not previously told us of his arrival out. It is a matter of no consequence whether you told us or not and I only mention the circumstance to account to you for the loss of a letter if you ever have written a letter containing that fact to us.

Your account of your financial prospects has given all of us, and me in particular, the greatest satisfaction. Before the receipt of your late letters I had been under some concern about you on this point, and I had rather reproached myself for not having before hand put your mind at rest in case you might be anxious on the subject. I had resolved before the receipt of your letters and to put your mind quite at ease, to inform you, that in case of need, you might draw upon me to the extent of £100 in addition to the sum I had previously given you authority to draw for. So that besides the hard cash you took with you I should be prepared to accept and pay your drafts to the extent altogether of £200 and in case you meet with any unforeseen drawbacks which should still render it necessary for you to draw for this sum I shall be prepared to meet your drafts and I authorise you to draw accordingly. With the position you hold in Sydney I dont apprehend you will find the slightest difficulty

---

appointed Superintendent of the Coining Department, 23 June 1853, a post he is recorded as holding in 1865. He lived at Double Bay almost continually from 1858 to 1870, his house being next to that of F. B. Miller; he died in London. There does not appear to be any record of his becoming Colonial Architect; cf. below, Letter 76, p. 196.

[6] George Francis Train (1829–1904). Born in Boston, Mass., where he became a clerk in the shipping house of a relative, Enoch Train & Co.; went to Liverpool in 1850 to manage a branch of the firm and in 1853 to Melbourne, where he established business as a merchant and importer in partnership with Captain Caldwell of the same firm, although it is uncertain whether or not they severed their connection with Enoch Train & Co.; acted as agent for the Liverpool White Star Line and James Baines & Co.'s Black Ball Line, both prominent in the Australian emigration trade. Train left Melbourne in 1855; published a series of letters entitled *The Merchant Abroad* ... (1857); he died in New York. Cf. Clive Turnbull, *Bonanza: the story of George Francis Train* (Melbourne, 1946).

[7] See above, Letter 21, n. 2, p. 38.
[8] Cf. Vol. I, p. 108.
[9] Cf. below, Letter 54, p. 120.

in cashing your draft at any one of the Banks in George S^t indeed so far from any difficulty experienced I think they would be quite glad to get your drafts offered to them. I will add for your satisfaction that now that I am again associated with my Brother in my old business[10] I am much more at ease on money matters than I was during the time I was with Guest & Co and although the Iron trade is just now very much depressed and sinking yet for an additional £*100* it will not put me to the least inconvenience and therefore *in case of need* do not have any scruples about it.

I have been thinking that if you come to melt down much Gold dust and assaye* the ingots whether it would be desirable for you to have a stamp with which you could impress the surface of the ingots with your name and the fineness of the Gold thus

> 22 CARAT FINE
> W S JEVONS

If you think well of this idea send me a sketch of what you wish done and I will have one made[11] It can be done well in Sheffield where they make such stamps to impress on bars of Steel and you can probably see such impressions in the shop or store of any one who sells steel in Sydney. I apprehend the die can be put into a press such as you saw at work in the Stamp Office London or possibly your heavy hammer would be sufficient as a screw press would cost a good deal. If there is any die sinker in Sydney you may perhaps think it worth your while to get a stamp made under your own eye without waiting for one from England. I believe Mr Piper[12] who keeps a store some where in Sydney is a Sheffield man and has a firm at Sheffield we are very anxious that you should become acquainted with M^r & Mrs Piper and therefore if you thought well of it you might call upon him and ask him if he could procure you the die from his correspondents in Sheffield. I sent you an introduction to Mr Piper some time since from Mr John Hutton.[13] He and his wife were to sail from London for Sydney on the 24th of this month and may be expected out at Sydney about the time this letter comes to your hands

There is a Mr Grundy[14] lately gone out to Sydney and settled as a Civil Engineer and has had a good deal of employment in making

[10] Cf. Vol. I, p. 12.
[11] Cf. below, Letter 79, p. 204.
[12] Probably Frederick Piper, a partner in the firm of Levicks and Piper, recorded as carrying on business at 141 Pitt Street, Sydney, 1857–63.
[13] Cf. Vol. I, p. 11.
[14] Francis Henry Grundy, civil engineer and surveyor, recorded as having carried on business in Sydney, 1857–78; he appears also to have been manager of the Mining Co., Sydney, 1873.

Roads. He is the Brother of Mrs Swinton* Boult and the Son of the Revd Mr Grundy the Unitarian Minister for a great many years settled in Manchester Mr Grundy was the Minister who opened Renshaw St Chapel for us I should think his Son would be an excellent acquaintance for you But perhaps I need not mention all the Unitarians I hear of as being out at Sydney for you will soon know them all when you come to attend the Chapel which I trust you have done ere this. By way of enlivening my letter a little I will just relate this anecdote about Revd Mr Grundy He preached a series of Lectures in Manchester to prove the non existence of the Devil and the populace gave him the soubriquet of Kill Devil Grundy.[15]

1 Feb^y

The Doctor seems highly gratified with your letters He sends his best Love to you and Mrs Richard joins. They have sent your letters to your Aunt Henry who, they say, is copying extracts from them to send to Harry who is still at Heidelberg.

I have just thought about the propriety of your Insuring your property from *Fire* The premium would no doubt be very high and had you some accumulated money with you it might not be worth while to insure but when you consider that you cannot in case of your being burnt out apply to me for the needful to set you up again under 4 to 6 months and possibly longer dont you think that for the first year or two of your domicile in Sydney you had better insure all your effects in which case should you be burned out you can draw funds at once to replace your stock and apparatus &c

We have intensely cold weather here for the last fortnight the thermometer ranging from 22 to 28 with a strong East wind most of the time which extracts the heat rapidly from our bodies and almost dries us all up I dont think they have more severe weather in the Crimea barring their rain and snow The only persons who rejoice in it are the skaiters* of whom Tommy is now a distinguished individual I bought him a splendid pair of skaits* which cost £1 which are rather above his caliber* at present but will be appropriate enough in a year or two and may save me buying a second pair then which I probably should have had to do had I bought for him a mere childs pair now.

I have had a call today from a Mr P. M. Crane formerly an Iron Master near Neath but now secretary of the Irish Peat Company who manufacture Paraffine*, Reeces Patent Oil and other oils, Naptha

[15] Rev. John Grundy (1782–1843) Minister of Cross Street Chapel, Manchester, until 1824; minister of Paradise Street Chapel, Liverpool, 1824–35. His preaching was controversial and caused considerable religious ferment. Rev. Grundy of Cross Street Chapel conducted the afternoon service on the opening of Renshaw Street Chapel on Sunday, 20 October 1811, delivering 'an eloquent discourse'. See Evans, op. cit., p. 9.

Sulphate of Ammonia and Charcoal for Agricultural and Deoderizing purposes all distilled from the peat got from the Bog of Athy in Ireland. I recollect seeing in the Chrystal* Palace specimens of these, with other products from this peat The oil proves to be of the same property or quality as some patent Mineral Oil distilled from Coal at Glasgow which particular coal is said to be formed from peat compressed in the bowels of the earth I think this one of the most curious facts of our time to prove by so close an analogy the identity of one particular description of coal of a formation perhaps millions of years old with the living substance, so to say, of which it is formed in immense abundance on the surface of the earth in our day. If I can spare a few days next summer I will go over and see these works Mr Crane says that their bog is 36 feet thick and there is any quantity of acres of it.[16]

My determination to give you a bumper has I fear driven me to put a good deal of matter into this letter that may be neither interesting or useful and inflicted upon you a waste of time in its perusal but it has given me great pleasure in merely trying to arouse some pleasurable sensations about things at home and I hope therefore that you will excuse my dulness* for my own sake I remain Dearest Stanley
   Your ever aff^{te} Father & friend
     Thomas Jevons

[16] The Irish Peat Company established a large factory at Kilberry, near Athy, in 1849 to work a process patented that year by a London chemist, Rees Reece, for obtaining products from peat. The company operated under the guidance of Sir Robert Kane, Director of the Museum of Irish Industry, and Dr William Sullivan, a chemical officer of the museum, who later undertook extensive experiments to examine the scientific process involved and to assess whether this process might form the basis of a large-scale manufacturing industry. There was considerable interest in processes for converting peat into valuable commercial products, on the Continent as well as in Britain: peat products were exhibited at the Great Exhibition of 1851 (cf. *The Art Journal Illustrated Catalogue of the Industry of All Nations, 1851*, 'The Science of the Exhibition', II). The turf-distillation factory at Kilberry was the first of its kind in the world; £10,000 was invested in plant and buildings. Despite this promising start, however, the company failed and the factory was closed down during the 1860s. Cf. T. Johnson, 'The Irish Peat Question', H. Ryan, 'Reports upon the Irish Peat Industries', *Economic Proceedings of the Royal Dublin Society*, I (Dublin, 1899–1909) 1–72, 371–420, 465–546; *Report by the Director of the Museum of Irish Industry on the nature and products of the process of the destructive distillation of peat, considered specially with reference to its employment as a branch of manufacturing industry*, Parl. Papers, 1851 [1393] 1 669.

P. M. Crane was awarded a patent for products from peat on 27 July 1855. No further information about him has come to light.

54. W. S. JEVONS TO E. W. WARD

8 Church Hill. Sydney
Jan 31st 1855.[1]

Copy of letter to Capt Ward in answer to his proposal of a fixed salary.[2]

Sir

I have considered the proposal which you made personally to me yesterday of a new arrangement of my salary & position as assayer to the Sydney Branch of the Royal Mint, and I understand the terms to be as follows.

Firstly, that I am to receive £500 a year as a fixed salary dating from January 1st of the present year, with the temporary increase of £175 a year at present allowed to those holding a salary of £500 from the Colonial Government.

Secondly, that all my apparatus & materials for assaying are to be purchased from me at a fair valuation, the lease of my present laboratory & other liabilities connected with it being taken off my hands by the government, and the expense I have been at in fitting up my rooms made good to me, for instance the gas & water fittings.

Thirdly, that I am to become a regular officer of the Royal Mint, relinquishing all private work, and performing the assays for the Mint in a laboratory provided for me, everything being found, and all expenses borne by the Mint.

In reply I have to say, that I am quite satisfied with the amount & conditions of the salary, but I would at the same time ask your attention to the following considerations.

For nearly the whole of the last 18 months, I have been employed in choosing & purchasing my apparatus & managing its transfer here & fitting up in my laboratory here, having received during the time up to Dec 31st 1854 only £50 and having actually paid during the time £352 (as per account inclosed*), the whole of which with the exception of the price you would give for my apparatus, will be entirely lost to me upon this change of agreement, to say nothing of the trouble inconvenience & risk which I have had to bear.

That if I had been appointed originally on the present proposed terms (and I suppose that £500 would have been the least salary offered to me in that case) I should have incurred none whatever of the expenses above mentioned but would have on the contrary received £250 salary with the temporary increase of £87.10.

While agreeing then to the other terms of the proposals you have

---

[1] The original manuscript of this letter is in the Mitchell Library, Sydney.
[2] This note, possibly added later to the letter, appears to be in Jevons's own handwriting.

made, may I not justly make it a condition of my accepting the fixed salary, that I am to be paid in full both the expenses and the arrears of salary, viz.

	£
Whole expenses in England & Sydney	352..6
Arrears of salary	337..10
	689..16
Subtract	
Salary already received £50. 0	
Money paid me for freight £27.10	77..10
	612..6

Of course, the expenses I have incurred will be subject to your judgement & approval as to being reasonable & necessary in the circumstances in which I was placed.

&c   &c

55. H. E. ROSCOE TO W. S. JEVONS

Heidelberg. 12th.March 1855.

My dear Stanley

I have been extremely interested in the accounts you sent home of your doings, & which Lucy kindly sent to my mother who copied the letters for me – You seem to be getting on very well indeed, & I hope now you are on the right road my boy! Take care of your health however – & keep well whatever you do – I am glad you find Miller a nice man & one with whom you can make friends – that is a great matter – If you come to amicable arrangements about business &c it is so much better than driving any sort of opposition. By this time I suppose the Mint is getting on, & you will be more busy, I hope you will write to me before long, & direct to your house & then it can be forwarded to me wherever I have the luck or misfortune to be settled. You must feel very pleasantly independant* when you retire into your own small dwelling – You will get a regular old bachelor like me –

Since I last wrote in November[1] a great deal has happened both publicly & privately here, & with you too there seems to have been a pretty state

---

[1] Possibly a reference to his letter dated 8 October 1854 (unpublished). If he wrote in November the letter is not among the Jevons Papers.

of things – However the rising seems to be put down[2] – & was nothing dangerous – The colony is I fancy by far not yet ready for selfgovernment, which of course in time it must have. In Europe here the chief attention is of course drawn to this unfortunate Crimean Expedition in which our whole army, & what is more our military position amongst European states, has been totally ruined.[3] It is a horrible affair, & I try not to think much about it– You will hear however so much better from letters from England & in the papers what is going on that I will not further dwell upon politics.

I have been to London since I wrote last, I was away for about a month & enjoyed seeing all my friends amazingly, after 18 months absence. – I read a paper at the Chemical Society[4] on the absorption of Chlorine in water, a small affair which I worked at whilst the light research was going on. Williamson, Watts,[5] Graham, Sharpey &c were all very glad to see me & kind – but there seemed no prospect of any place turning up, & now the war will make it still more difficult to get anything to do. Harriet seems extremely happy in her new sphere of life, & is very much beloved by all her new relations.[6] Her house is a most beautiful one, & Edward is everything that could be wished – My mother has lodgings quite near – in which she has the furniture we had at Oval Road, & Henrietta Fletcher[7] is come to stay with her. Still she finds living alone in lodgings naturally dull & disagreable* & I must get back as soon as possible to make a home for her. Frank[8] was very well – he lives with the Oslers[9] at Ham & seems to like it, he is still at the office at Austen

---

[2] Probably a reference to the armed rebellion of miners on the Ballarat goldfields in December 1854 in protest against the Victoria Government's system of licensing at the diggings; about thirty miners and five soldiers were killed. The goldfields laws were reformed in 1855. Cf. G. Blainey, *The Rush That Never Ended* (Melbourne, 1963) pp. 46–56.

[3] Since the failure to take Sebastopol the previous autumn (cf. above, Letter 46, p. 103) two battles had been fought – Balaclava (October 1854) and Inkerman (November 1854) – neither of which had seriously weakened the Russian defences nor caused the French and British armies to be dislodged from their positions. An exceptionally severe winter halted further offensives until spring. The immense hardship and enormous losses through sickness suffered by the British troops during the winter outraged public opinion and brought down Aberdeen's government (cf. above, Letter 41, p. 79). A commission of enquiry into the condition of the army and supply services, set up by Palmerston, went to the Crimea in March 1855, Cf. Woodward, op. cit., pp. 274–86; also C. Woodham-Smith, *The Reason Why* (1953).

[4] H. E. Roscoe, 'On the Absorption of Chlorine in Water', *Quarterly Journal of the Chemical Society*, VII (1856) 14–27.

[5] See above, Letter 35, n. 10, p. 65.

[6] See above, Letter 35, n. 2, p. 64.

[7] Mrs Henry Roscoe was a daughter of Thomas Fletcher (1767–1850), Liverpool merchant and banker; Henrietta may have been her niece, a daughter of her brother Francis Fletcher (b. 1799).

[8] Francis James Roscoe (1830–78). See Vol. I, p. 193, n. 6.

[9] Timothy Smith Osler and his wife Henrietta, a first cousin of Jevons and H. E. Roscoe. See Vol. I, p. 73, n. 1.

Friars & does not know I think what he is to do ultimately. Arthur[10] is on the loose somewhere – he disappeared in the autumn & no one knew where he was for some months when he suddenly turned up looking very seedy – Thomas[11] is feeding cattle in Ireland – an intellectual occupation! William[12] as you will hear is going to be married to a Miss Somebody at Derby Mrs John Huttons sister, I am very glad of it & I only hope she is worthy of him. Saint William appears again to have got into a fix in that "narrow & straight road which leadeth" &c & is in difficulties about vulgar money – & wants the poor Dr to stump up[13] – which he very reasonably refuses. & then Jane R[14] is just married to Mr Ho-r-r-r-r ace R. r r r r r r os osss coe St John,[15] & we have now the priviledge* & honour of counting that interesting individual amongst our cousins. I had a very fine discription* of the speech which Uncle Tom made on the occassion* from my mother who was present & who at Jane's desire at last pulled Uncle T down into his chair to stop him – of course he went rambling on all about nothing & would be going on still if it had not been for my mothers timely interference – He began all about the length of their attachment &c & got quite maudling,* & then went off at a tangent about the animals at the Zoological Garden – how the lions had died – & the swan had died – (& the people could not imagine what the deuce he was going to say) when at last he wound up with, "in fact the only animals left are the pair of turtle doves"! He is a most rum old cock – I think, with all due deference to an Uncle – that he must be rather cracked!! Now I will tell you what I can

[10] Probably Arthur Roscoe (b. 1825), second son of William Stanley Roscoe, elder brother of Francis James Roscoe and Thomas Roscoe. He later settledin New Zealand. Cf. below, Letter 143, p. 405.

[11] Thomas Stamford Roscoe (b. 1826) third son of William Stanley Roscoe. Cf. below, Letter 143, p. 405.

[12] William Caldwell Roscoe (1823–59), eldest son of William Stanley Roscoe. He married Emily Sophia Malin (1830–86) on 8 May 1855 (cf. below, Letter 60, p. 145). She was the youngest daughter of William Malin of Derby, another of whose daughters, Eliza, had married John Hutton as his first wife in 1847. William Caldwell Roscoe took his B.A. at University College, London, in 1843 and was called to the Bar in 1850, becoming Marshall to Mr Justice Crompton in 1852. His early death of typhoid fever cut short a literary career; his *Poems and Essays* were edited posthumously by R. H. Hutton and published in two volumes with a memoir in 1860. Cf. Mrs Russell Barrington, *Life of Walter Bagehot* (1914) pp. 179–80.

[13] Presumably a further reference to William Caldwell Roscoe, whose father had died in 1843 and who would possibly have received financial assistance from his uncle Dr Richard Roscoe.

[14] Jane, third daughter of Thomas Roscoe (1791–1871) William Roscoe's fifth son. She was authoress of: *Audubon, the naturalist, in the New World* (1856); *Englishwomen and the Age* (1860); *Masaniello of Naples. The record of a nine days' revolution* (1865); and *The Court of Anna Carofa; an historical narrative* (1872).

[15] Horace Stebbing Roscoe St John (1832–88) journalist, youngest son of James Augustus St John (1801–75) author and traveller. For many years he was the leader-writer on political topics for the *Daily Telegraph* and frequently a special correspondent for *The Times*; he was also author of *A Life of Christopher Columbus* (1850); *History of the British Conquests in India* (1852); and *The Indian Archipelago; its history and present state* (1853).

about my work – I have at last I am happy to say succeeded – & have I believe got hold of the law of the Chemical action of light. It is a very remarkable thing – & will I think be of great importance & certainly is extremely interesting – You must know that I have been working for nearly a year upon it – & up to within 6 weeks of the present time had not got out any regular action, & I was as you may imagine in something like despair. I act upon a mixture of equal vols: of dyCl & H with light & I used to determine the amount of decomposition by estimating the quantity of free Chlorine w^h remained undecomposed. This was a very tiresome & troublesome process & although I made a great number of expts I could get no regular action – Now however the apparatus is altered & instead of measuring the action by an analysis, I measure it by the rising of water in a tube connected with the Insolated apparatus, & this rise shows exactly the amount of HCl formed in any given time – water is of course present in the part of the apparatus w^h is exposed to light – In this way I can make a great number of observations every day – & I have proved

1. That the action is proportional to the time of exposure.
2. That it is proportional to the amount of light.

It remains to make more extended & accurate observations when the weather improves & the light is more constant. Then there are some very curious facts relating to the action of the light on the mixture – The action does not begin at once – a certain time is necessary before the light begins to decompose the gases. The Chlorine must first enter into an allotropic condition before it is decomposed by the light – (like cane sugar in fermentation) & then the action attains a maximum & progresses regularly. This allotropic condition seems to be constant, for if the light be shut off & after some time again admitted, the maximum of action is attained almost immediately – The action of coloured rays upon Chlorine will be very interesting, the redrays will probably not be able to induce this allotropic condition, but when that has been brought about by other light the redrays will probably continue the action. All this & thousands of other things are yet to be done – so you can have some idea of the amount of work before me. It is really an important subject & opens an entirely new field of chemical inquiry. I expect that the apparatus or one similar will become a regular meteorological instrument whose changes will be just as often observed as those of the Barometer or magnetic needle.[16]

You must set one up in Sydney before long I will send you the apparatus

---

[16] Bunsen developed the actinometer, an instrument to measure the amount of light absorbed by a system undergoing photochemical change, with Roscoe. Its application was extended to the measurement of direct solar radiation.

if you will undertake to observe.[17] It will however be some time before the subject is in a sufficient state of devellopement* for that. Bunsens new laboratory[18] is to be ready for the summer semestre* – & it will be very perfect. We have now just begun the vacation but of course I stay here & go on with my work. I work in a dark room all day alternately observing the rise of water in the tube & peeping through a hole in the shutter to see the reflection of the sky in a mirror placed at 45° outside! We have had a very cold winter & in England it has been colder than since the year 1814. We are now going through the miseries of a third winter, & snow & rain fall regularly every day. I am however in hopes that before long we shall enjoy a little spring weather which is in perfection here when it once begins. Poor little Tommy Graham has lately been very ill – Williamson has been lecturing for him – My mother met Graham the other day at the Brodericks & she says he enquired after you & was very much interested to hear how you got on – He looked more like a Chimpanzee than ever – she says – such a mouth from ear to ear! poor little man – I begin to look down on our present English Chemists – they are really very unscientific when compared with the German standard – Bunsens particularly – & they do not keep up with the March of Science here either – for instance in Electricity & Galvanism – who in England knows anything of the laws which are all both mathematically & experimentally proved by Germans. I will write to you again before long & give you some German ideas on these points perhaps. You ought to learn German. – Do write soon & often to me – I am always interested in everything you do – How I wish I could come over & see all those fine plants & scenery.

     Ever my dear Stanley
     Your very affec.
     Henry. E. Roscoe

56. THOMAS JEVONS TO W. S. JEVONS

Chatham St Sunday 18 Mar 18545[1]

Dearest Stanley

Last evening we had the happiness to receive your long looked for letters one to Henny begun 8 Nov another to Herbert dated

---

[17] Jevons developed his own actinometer; cf. below, Letters 66 and 107, pp. 161 and 297; Letter 110, p. 306; Letter 122, p. 344.

[18] H. E. Roscoe described the original laboratory at Heidelberg as '. . . a quaint one; it had been an old monastery. The high-roofed refectory had been fitted up with working benches, whilst the chapel became the store-room . . . Before his appointment Bunsen had stipulated with the Government of the Grand-Duchy of Baden that new laboratories should be built for him and these were shortly completed, and the old monastery pulled down to make way for a new physical institute and a zoological museum . . .' (*Life and Experiences*, pp. 47, 51).

[1] Thomas Jevons appears to have made this correction himself. Jevons, when listing his

30 Dec^(r2) and an open letter to be forwarded to Harry. From these we gather the pleasing thought that after you had completed your fittings up, you had enjoyed a week or two of rest, during which you were enabled to take some walks about the neighbourhood of Sydney, and as it appears to us, must have gained a little strength after the fatigues of your hard work for the first two months of your residence in Sydney. A small quantity of assaying seems to have come to you just enough to shew* that you were noticed by one or two parties not connected with the Mint. Though not enough to pay for bread & cheese, from these however I trust you derived some comfort and the hope that a little time would bring all to rights. The week or so after came your 51 assays from the Mint which seems to have set you to work outrageously and I recapitulate all this to give effect to what I am now going to state, viz that your too hard and too anxious working at those 51 assays must have brought on those boils again. When working in the way I can imagine you did do, you no doubt neglected proper food, proper rest, and proper attention to all bodily warnings, and you reduced your strength and induced that poverty of blood which ended in those ulcerations called boils. Being the first real money making job that you had, one may easily pardon your eager anxiety to do it well, and soon, but I do trust that in future you will never let money making or any other pursuit interfear* with your health. I am most gratified to hear that they have fixed your remuneration at 6/6 p^r assaye.* If you will recollect our highest anticipations before you left England did not exceed 7/6, whilst we had made up our minds to be satisfied with 5/– p^r assay let us hope then that it is the happy medium between the extremes, not so low but that it may enable you to lay by a little for the future, and not so high as to lead to remark by the public that you are paid too highly and so lead to its being cut down. I notice that you think it will be May before the Mint will begin to coin but as the melting department would be at work much earlier than that I trust you would have some assaying from that department. The Mint authorities indeed ought not to send out any bars or ingots of Gold from the melting department without being assayed first and the rate of fineness stamped upon them by authority for otherwise dishonest dealers might sell ingots of Gold melted at the Mint and put a spurious value upon them. It is worth your while, and Millers, in conjunction with you, to look to this point and if the Mint does not get their ingots assayed to petition or memorialize the Mint Board to order that no ingots be melted without being

---

father's letters in the Journal, incorrectly dated this 18 May 1855 and numbered it '27' whereas it should have been placed twenty-third. Cf. Vol. I, p. 120.

[2] These letters are not among the Jevons papers nor have they been published in LJ.

assayed before delivery from the Mint. We have received your *old* Sydney Herrald* and found out your advertizement.* What a large paper it is and how full of advertizements* of all sorts I notice that there are a great many ports to which vessels seem to run regularly and from this I should think Sydney would become a great trading and commercial town. You did not, by the by, tell us whether your 51 specimens of Gold dust & nuggetts* came all from N S W or generally from all the Colonies of Australia. If from N S W only there would appear to be plenty of scope for "prospecting" and lots of assays will come to you in time.

As to the prospects of the Mint it is curious how the public opinion about it is changed by the consideration that it may become beneficial to individuals. I understand that your Coinage will be made a legal tender in all Her Majesties Colonies. If this be so it is almost as good as saying a legal tender all the world over, for there is hardly any portion of the Globe where we have not got a Colony. As respects England it will be a matter of no moment or not of much moment their not being made a legal tender here, there are advantages in its not being a legal tender. Suppose Gold to be worth more in England than the standard value of £3. 17. 10½ p oz³ your Sydney Sovreigns* could be legally sold at a higher price, or melted, whilst the London Mint Coin could not, and thus your Coin would really be sought after. And none the less so if Gold should fall below the Mint standard because your coins would be immediately bought up for exportation. Our English Mint coins will always be laboring* under a disadvantage from the severe restrictions to which the Law subjects them whilst your Sydney Coin being entirely free will monopolize nearly all the trafic* in Gold which is carried on to such an enormous extent from & to this Country, so my dear Stanley you see how important a personage you are your assayings are to govern the dealings of millions of pounds sterling in the transactions of millions of peoples. Make no mistakes and Sydney Sovreigns* will rule the roost the World around.⁴

We had a visit a few days since from a Mʳ Lyons a cousin of Ann Boltons and consequently of Charles'. He was one of the company of eight persons who found the great nuggett* of 98 lbs weight and which was made a shew* of at Melbourne⁵ He has come home quite rich

---

³ The price on the Australian goldfields was barely £3 per ounce. The Branch Mint was established in Sydney largely for the purpose of raising the price immediately obtainable for local gold. Cf. Craig, op. cit., p. 386.

⁴ Sovereigns coined at the Sydney Mint did in fact become legal tender throughout the British Empire in 1868. For details of the process by which this came about, see Craig, op. cit., p. 387.

⁵ 'Most of the alluvial gold in Victoria was in small pieces . . . In some ground, however, great lumps of alluvial gold lay buried . . . at the White Horse Gully in Bendigo in 1852 diggers found one foot under the ground a quartz-encrusted nugget which they sold for

worth about £4000 He says he will get married and then I suppose he will want to go out again but that he does not speak of yet. He shewed* us a small nugget weighing $\frac{1}{2}$ lb of great purity I suppose from its great weight in the hands. Tommy tried to deceive me with it by putting it along with the Poltimore specimens[6] on the chimney piece, but I found it out the moment I felt its weight though I had not heard of Mr Lyons being in the house

We had a meeting to day in the Chapel after the morning Service about the monument to your Grand Papa Roscoe. Our considerations about it have been brought into harmony by the proposal of a bust, and Mr Davis the Sculptor[7] had prepared, in a wood pattern, a representation of what it would appear to be when put up in the place we had thought of for it, when, I am happy to say, that it gave perfect satisfaction as far as a model in would* painted could do. He was ordered to proceed with his work and so in due time we shall have it erected.[8] I shall urge on the committee to have a drawing of it Lythographed or a wood engraving of it and then I can send you a copy.

To return to your own prospects and comfort, for considerations of that kind very often dwell upon my mind I have been thinking that if you get on pretty well in your gains you will soon begin to think that your present Cottage is too small and the confinement night & day in so confined a place particularly with all your apparatus about you, will not be good for your health, and the rent too will be considered too high for a continuance, you will therefore be thinking of a change. If you have saved any money by the time this letter reaches you it may not be unwise in you to entertain thoughts upon the subject and to be on the lookout for a suitable place. Now my thoughts on the subject are these, I would buy a plot of ground, unbuilt on, and would put up a Corrugated Iron Cottage upon the back part of it, and then sell off the front again for building upon, or if you could afford it keep it for a garden. There seem to me to be plenty of building lots round Wynyard Square which might answer, as they seem as near to the Banks or nearer generally than Church Hill. In the map you have sent I notice three or four building lots in Margaret S^t opposite Wynyard Sqre, a most excellent

---

£2,100. Nearby another beautiful specimen was bought by the Victorian parliament at the fabulous price of £4.17s. an ounce and presented to the Queen' (Blainey, op. cit., pp. 44-5).

[6] Cf. Letters 44 and 59, pp. 94 and 142.

[7] Possibly Edward Davis (1813-78), a native of Carmarthen, who produced a number of busts, including one of William Rathbone, and exhibited two others at the Liverpool Academy.

[8] The life-sized bust, with inscription, was erected in 1856. It is now in Ullet Road Church, opened in 1899 to replace Renshaw Street Chapel which was demolished to make way for Central Hall, Liverpool. This bust is not included in the selection of portraits, etc., of Roscoe listed by Chandler, *William Roscoe of Liverpool*, pp. 158-9.

situation. Then at the other end of Wynyard Sqre in York S^t, there are two or three lots right facing Wynyard S^t, and which lots can be seen out of George Street, and the lots both in Margaret S^t and in George Street go through to back Streets. Now my idea is this that one of these lots of land might be bought for £400 to £500 – and the party who owns it would take payment for it at the rate of £100 down on signing the contract and £100 every 6 mths afterwards until the whole is paid, giving you possession on payment of the first £*100*.*

Then as soon as you had bought it, and let me know, I would send you out a house of such dimentions* as you should direct, in fact to your own drawings, only you must make the drawings on a larger scale than you generally send us. Now supposing you can get the land for £*500*, the interest of that at 5 p cent is only £25 p an^n for the whole plot. Then suppose the Iron house costs in England £*250* and as Iron is now getting very cheap you can have a good large house in the rough for that sum. Then perhaps the freight out and fitting up in Sydney might cost £*150* perhaps by the time it got out you might raise a portion of this yourself, but if not I think I could allow you to draw a bill upon me for it in two or three sums a month apart. In a word you may contrive I think to put up a house or say a 4 or 6 room Cottage of Corrugated Iron all on the ground floor for perhaps £*800* in the best part of Sydney and thus lye[9] at a rent of £*40* a year or if you can raise the whole money yourself at no rent at all instead of paying £2 a week for a miserable back premises. One of my motives for thinking of this is the almost utter impossibility of you and Charles standing for any lengthened period the confinement which your present place will occasion. I suppose that you can never both leave at the same time and as Charles must go out perhaps often to do your marketings, to deliver notes, to go to the Mint and the Banks with the assays you will be the worst off, but with a room or two in addition you may have a servant as well as Charles and her room or kitchen might be within hearing of the Laboratory so that if absolutely necessary you might both be away or it might be contrived that if both were out a party coming might ring a bell and the servant would answer and take any message for you at the door. These are such thoughts as come up in my mind and I write them crudely off whether for good or otherwise. Understand that what I am talking about is my

---

* Any one of the Banks for whom you assaye* would advance you the whole money on the land beyond £100 and would allow you to pay it out by assaying for them. But you can get Mr Huntley[10] to enquire for you. Or the Fire & Life would lend you as much as you might want and you can ask Mr Grundy[11] to get the information for you.[12]

[9] He may have intended to write 'live' here.
[10] Cf. above, Letter 26, p. 47.
[11] See above, Letter 53, n. 14, p. 117.
[12] This note was added in the margin of the fifth page of the letter.

willingness to help you with a loan of a few hundred pounds at Interest if such a loan will enable you to secure a good situation for your business at a cheap rent, but I do not recommend you to think of such a move as this unless your business is so far established as to warrant you in the certainty that you will have a surpluss* over your every day expenses which is sure to enable you to clear off any engagements you may contract and so to make the Cottage and land your own absolutely in the end.

20 March I mentioned in the former part of this letter that we had received an old Sydney Herald we have since received a new one dated 30 Decr I have been looking all through it and find it a very interesting paper This particular paper seems to be a special one published expressly for the English Mail and contains a great deal of information. I notice in it a general account of the different Gold districts from which the 51 specimens you assayed were collected The extent of the districts all added together is immense, they say covering an Area of 200,000 square miles. If this be so you may depend upon it that you will become grey in the service before it is all worked out and assayed. I see no mention, in the published account, of the services of the Assayer perhaps that will come in time. Then there is another interesting account in the paper of the Flower Shew* and the prizes awarded to the successful exhibitors. You do not say whether you went to this exhibition, which as a botanist I should have thought you would have done, but probably you were in the very midst of the assaying for the Paris Exhibition[13] and could not go. I notice that there were many new plants not named and never figured which must be curious to see, one of them strikes me to mention from its name the Rafflesiana Nepenthes If this is anything like the Rafflesia Arnoldi[14] it must be a very curious plant indeed.

In this paper there seems to be no end of Houses and Cottages and lots of land to be sold by Auction or private treaty. I observe some in Macquarie S^t opposite the domain, I should think a very excellent situation being both Town & Country, but until you are well established you must stick to the neighbourhood of the Banks who will undoubtedly be your best customers. To be near the Mint you need not care for, since they are bound to you and cannot go to any one else, and it is only the consideration of the trouble to a messenger going backwards & forwards which is not of much consequence; but I have said enough on this subject before so will drop it.

---

[13] Cf. below, Letter 71, p. 179.

[14] A rare tropical plant with very large flowers, which smells like putrid meat; the 'Rafflesiana Nepenthes' was probably a species of pitcher plant, growing in boggy ground in tropical areas.

As far as we can judge from your letters you have not been to call upon any of the parties you had letters of Introduction to except Mr Huntley whom you have not named a second time. I see Mr Grundy is Surveyor to the Liverpool & London Fire & Life Insurance Comp^y's Branch at Sydney. You had a letter to him from his brother in law Mr Swinton* Boult. I am sure Mr Grundy would be very glad to see you, and being a public man & professional, it must be to your Interest to be acquainted with him. Then you seem not to have called on your namesake the Revd Mr Stanley[15] nor I suppose have gone to the Unitarian Chapel. You have no doubt wanted rest on the Sunday so far but your great labors* being surmounted I trust that we shall hear of your going about amongst your friends and getting into regular ways of life like all other conspicuous people, for conspicuous you soon will become I feel sure.

Herbert has bought you to day the thermometers and Murchisons *Siluria*[16] I have been looking over the Siluria this evening, what a splendid work it is, and I can fancy that it will be very useful to you occasionally when talking with any one about the geological feitures* of N.S.W. to be able to point out analogous stratifications in the Old World. This though leads me to the enquiry what public Libraries there are that you can have access to. No doubt there are circulating Libraries as in most Towns, but I should think in Sydney there must be some great public or Government Library open to all or at the least there must be a Library attached to the College[17] and probably you may have access to it when you have time to devote to reading and can leave your Laboratory without fear which time I trust may be before long. You had some very valuable letters from Graham[18] and other professors in London to some of the professors at the College which you do not say that you have yet delivered but I think you ought most undoubtedly to deliver those letters and get acquainted with the individuals they are addressed to, for you do not know what advantage it may be of to you. Let me beg of you if you have not already delivered those letters not to delay a day longer but at once make your calls. In fact you are slighting them not to do so, and in all probability you have been mentioned to

---

[15] Rev. George Heape Stanley (1818–91), son of a Manchester merchant; emigrated in 1853 and became the first Unitarian minister in Australia; Minister of Macquarie Street Unitarian Chapel, Sydney, 1863–5. He may also have been a schoolmaster as he is recorded as having lived at Paddington House School, Point Piper Road, Paddington, Sydney, 1865–75, and at Morven Collegiate School, Cooper Street, Woollahoa, 1882–5; he died at Coogee.

[16] R. I. Murchison, *Siluria. The history of the oldest known rocks containing organic remains, with a brief sketch of the distribution of Gold ovdr the Earth* (1854). Cf. Vol. III, Letter 279.

[17] Jevons would probably have had access to the Library of New South Wales, Macquarie Street, Sydney, founded in 1826 and the University of Sydney Library, founded in 1852.

[18] Cf. above, Letter 39, p. 75; Letter 41, p. 79.

them in private letters, and they may be wondering why you do not call and they may put it down perhaps to a wrong cause, so that on every consideration you should deliver those letters and the sooner the better. March 21. This is the day of Humiliation and Prayer by *Command*[19] and as we Unitarians dont pray by Command of any human authority Herbert and Tommy and Fred Jevons[20] are gone an excursion through Chester to Delamere Forrest* where I trust they will enjoy themselves and return all safe and well at night.

We expect two Miss Malins on a visit this evening to stay with us about a week They are coming to purchase wedding things and furniture &c and I suppose we shall see a good deal of Wm Caldwell while they are here[21] They are going to live at a place called Machyntlleth about half way between Dollegelly* & Aberystwith* where they have a slate quarry I wish them all happiness and prosperity.

Herbert will send your Siluria and the thermometers by the *Startled Fawn* a Black Ball clipper to sail about the 15 April from this direct for Sydney. When you ask for any thing again it will be as well to name all that you think you may want for a small parcel costs as much as a box we cannot get any thing taken under 10/6 and the square box or case we sent you lately by the ship with the queer name only cost the same, I mean the Willhem something.

Goodbye! May peace and prosperity attend you is the prayer of
 Dearest Stanley
  Your ever aff^{te} father & friend
   Thomas Jevons

57. THOMAS JEVONS TO W. S. JEVONS

Liverpool 1 April 1855

Dearest Stanley

The Overland Mail is in to day and with it a mail from Sydney but we have no letter from you. We have to hope that you have sent a letter but that you have omitted to put upon it *via Marseilles* and that it will come when the heavy portion of the mail comes in, which instead of being despatched from Alexandria to Marseilles and so by Rail to Calais and then to Dover and thence by rail to London is sent by the Steam Boat all the way from Alexandria to Southampton and by this route they are four or five days longer on the way. It costs considerably

---

[19] A Royal Proclamation had commanded that 21 March 1855 be observed throughout the nation as a 'day of solemn fast, humiliation and prayer' for peace.

[20] Jevons's first cousin Frederick (1834–1916), fourth son of Timothy Jevons. In November 1865 he married Sarah Acland Taylor, elder sister of Jevons's future wife. See below, Letter 139, n. 17, p. 391.

[21] Cf. above, Letter 55, n. 12, p. 123.

more postage to come across France but we would always gladly pay the difference to get your letters four days sooner to hand. And in fact it may be of great consequence for the mail that will carry this letter to you leaves here on the 4th whilst it is ten to one we dont get your letter via Southampton before the 5th Inst, thus you see that if you had sent your letter via Marseilles I could have answered any enquiries in this letter. In writing via Marseilles it is as well to write on thin paper as the French single postage only goes to ¼ oz while our English & Colonial single postage covers ½ oz Our mails to N S W are all at sixes & sevens just at present but I see our Government have given notice in Parliament that they are going to reorganise a Steam mail conveyance direct to Australia and the sooner the better say I![1]

I see that a paragraph is going the round of the papers stating that Graham has been appointed Master of the Mint in London a place I should think worth £2000 a year.[2] Who knows but some day you may follow such a leader. I have cut the paragraph out of the paper and shall enclose it for you. If you have not written to Graham this will be a good opportunity for you to do it to congratulate him upon his appointment. Of course he will have to give up being assayer to the Mint and would it not be a good thing for Harry Roscoe if he could get that appointment. I have heard nothing about who succeeds to the assayership.[3]

I have cut out of the paper another slip which states that some fossil

---

[1] The Australian and New Zealand colonies were the last settlements to receive regular mails from Britain. Mail was carried by private ships until 1844 when Parliament authorised the Post Office to take control of the postal arrangements for these colonies and a regular mail service, subsidised by the British Government, was begun. It proved unsuccessful and was discontinued after 1848 by which time the colonists were demanding a steam service, which the gold rush of 1851 made vital. The Peninsular and Oriental Steamship Co. (P & O) ran a steamship service to Australia every alternate month, by extending its mail line from Singapore. During the Crimean War steamships were withdrawn from the Australian route for military use and sailing packets took over: the Admiralty contracted with the two leading Liverpool lines, James Baines's Black Ball and Pilkington and Wilson's White Star. P & O eventually resumed the Australian mail service after the war.

During the 1830s mail from India via Alexandria which missed the packet for the sea route via Gibraltar, was sent overland through France. A postal convention of 1839 recognised this carriage, which was regarded as an expensive express service for urgent mail: the rate was 1s. per half ounce via Gibraltar, 2s. 8d. per quarter ounce via Marseilles. By 1860, however, most of the heavy Indian and Australian mails were sent by the overland route. Cf. H. Robinson, *Carrying British Mails Overseas* (1964), pp. 164–5, 184–97.

[2] Thomas Graham succeeded Sir John Herschel as Master of the Royal Mint in April 1856, at a salary of £1500. He held the post until his death in September 1869. Cf. Craig, op. cit., pp. 323–7.

[3] i.e. as consultant assayer: a resident assayer was attached to the assay department, a post held by H. W. Field, 1850–71. Thomas Graham and W. A. Miller were appointed as non-resident assayers at the instigation of Sir John Herschel in 1851, to provide an additional and independent check.

After Graham's appointment as Master, Miller continued to act as consultant assayer until his death in 1870. In a review of the Mint administration commenced after Graham's death in 1869, C. W. Fremantle and C. Rivers Wilson recommended the abolition of the

fish eleven feet long have been found in the Coal strata on the coast south of Sydney[4] I dare say you will see or hear something of this wonder of the antediluvian world Fossil *Ichtheosaurus** we have in abundance but I never heard of fossil fish of so gigantic a size as 11 f^t.

In the last long letter I wrote you I told you I thought this was the day of little things and I am going to prove it to you by sending you half a dozen 1^d lead pencils which are 14 Inches long and full of Lead all through them, and I will put in the same box two excellent yard measures which cost only 1^d each, they are made of wood and fold or shut up so as to be only 4½ Inches long when closed, and are really very respectable concerns though they will not stand much hard work

We went to see Miss Cushman[5] act Meg Merriless* on friday* last. She acted most splendidly to a cram full house, and this day Sunday we had the pleasure of seeing her with your friend D^r and Mrs Muspratt[6] at our chapel to hear Mr Channing[7] preach, though I dont know but that she might have been at our chapel even if only Mr Thom[8] had been there for she is a Unitarian and I have seen her at Renshaw Street several times before It is said that Miss Cushman is going to be married and I have heard of her having taken a house in London which may be a sort of confirmation of the report or otherwise her having taken a

---

office of consultant assayer as being extravagantly expensive. The work of the non-resident assayers was accordingly taken over by salaried staff of the Mint in December 1870. Cf. Craig, op. cit., pp. 323–8; Fremantle and Wilson, *Memorandum on the Mint, Parl. Papers* 1870 (7) xli; Vol. III, Letters 322 and 323.

[4] In the *Quarterly Journal of the Geological Society of London*, XI (1855) 408, there is the following passage in a notice of W. B. Clarke's 'Notes on the Geology of New South Wales': 'Mr Clarke also refers to the existence of fossil fish (of which he has sent 'rubbings') in the upper rocks of Sydney. They have some resemblance to Permian fish'.

The newspaper cutting is no longer with the manuscript of this letter, but it seems probable that it referred to these discoveries by Clarke. For biographical details of W. B. Clarke, see below, Letter 107, n. 11, p. 298.

[5] Charlotte Saunders Cushman (1816–76), one of America's most notable actresses, outstanding in tragic or character parts, particularly that of Meg Merrilies in a dramatisation of Scott's *Guy Mannering*. She was well known to English audiences, making her first appearance in London in 1845. She returned to America in 1849 and toured there until 1852, when she announced her retirement from the stage, but she continued to act intermittently until her death.

[6] James Sheridan Muspratt (1821–71) a Liverpool chemist, son of James Muspratt (1793–1886) who founded the alkali industry in Lancashire and also in 1848 the Liverpool College of Chemistry, a private institution for the training of chemists. In 1848 J. S. Muspratt married Susan Phillips Cushman (1822–59), sister of Charlotte and herself formerly an actress.

[7] William Henry Channing (1810–84) American divine, nephew of William Ellery Channing (cf. Vol. I, p. 99, n. 4). Minister of Renshaw Street Chapel from June 1854 until November 1857, during the absence abroad of Rev. J. H. Thom; then succeeded James Martineau at Hope Street Chapel. An ardent advocate of the abolition of slavery, he opposed the Fugitive Slave Law (cf. below, Letter 62, p. 151). Channing returned to the United States at the outbreak of the Civil War, but afterwards settled in England and died in London.

[8] See Vol. I, pp. 58, n. 5.

house has given rise to the report.⁹ For the last week we have had two Miss Malins on a visit with us and W^m C Roscoe has been every day to see his dear Emily They have been buying furniture and wedding dresses &c &c and William C and Emily are to be married early next month¹⁰ They have made it a busy house for us but they leave tomorrow.

I see by the Mining Journal that several of the Gold mines in the neighbourhood of Dolgelly are going on with their works as if they had not lost all hope of success in the end. They say that in working a little further into the quartz veins the Gold becomes more visible but it is in very minute particles and it is yet a doubtful point whether it will pay to extract One communicant says *"we have not yet tried the alluvial deposit for nuggets"* so that you see there are some floating notions that nuggets may yet be met with in the quiet and beautiful vales of Cambria.¹¹

April 3rd – We have to day heard of a person who is going out to Sydney with the hope of getting employment in your mint and he offers to take any parcel we may have to send to you so we shall pack up the Siluria and the other little things and send them by him He is a person who has been employed at the mint in London but in what department has not been named to us it is your Aunt Henry who has informed us of the opportunity.

Apl 4th Since I have begun this letter my thoughts have been turned several times to the absence of a letter from you by the Overland Mail and considering that in your last received letter you stated that you had been attacked with boils again which were so bad that if you had not had the Paris specimens to assaye* you should have taken to your bed I have rather a mistrust arising that you may really have been ill and that you have missed that Mail on purpose. Now I beg you never to allow a mail to go away without a line if it be litterally* only a small note that you can *write in three minutes* to tell us that you have no time to write more by the said mail The sight of your hand writing will have a wonderful solace to all fears that may arise and recollect that we have no other Correspondents in Sydney that we can hear from about you there is no side way by which we can get any information all must come

---

⁹ She lived in England until 1857 when she returned to New York. She did not marry.
¹⁰ Cf. above, Letter 55, n. 12, p. 123.
¹¹ '. . . At the Dolfrwynog Gold Mine they are proceeding rapidly with the erection of their 80-horse steam-engine and crushing pans, which it is expected will be in full operation by July next . . . Mr. Harris is testing the commercial value of the gold lode at the Great Cambrian Mine. We hear the lode is improving in width and richness . . . Capt. George Williams has discovered *visible* gold in a vein of lead at a place called Garn, about 4 miles north-west of Dolgelly . . . I think I am again further warranted in saying Merionethshire is the richest district in Her Majesty's dominions for gold &c.; and, from the quantity of gold now *visible* in the quartz lodes, believe they are as rich as Australian or Californian. As to the alluvial soils, I do not think any person has tried them. – J. Harris: Dolgelly, March 28'. *Mining Journal* . . . 31 March 1855, no. 1023 (xxv).

direct from yourself. Ch^s Bolton has written once or twice only to his family here but he probably only writes while you are writing and if you miss writing he misses also so you see that we are dependent upon yourself alone for every information about your health and proceedings – The heavy portion of the India & Australian mail is not expected to arrive in Southampton before 9th Inst and consequently we cannot know whether there be in it any letter from you before the 10th or 11th being a long suspense from the 1st

In my last letter I dwelt at some length on the desirability of your preparing to leave your present quarters and getting a permanent place for yourself and I suggested your buying a piece of land in Wynyard Square and I offered to send you out an Iron house to put upon it and to lend you some money if that were necessary to enable you to carry out such a skeme* I now confirm what I said in that letter I trust the letter will get safe to hand consequently there is no need for me to go more at large into the subject now. If you think the scheme will do you must advise me that you have made a contract for the land send a plan of it and a plan of such an Iron Cottage as you would like and I will send it out to you charging you Interest on the money it will cost until you can pay me back again.

The last letter we have had from you was the one you wrote just after you had completed the 51 assayes* for the Paris specimens so you will perceive that up to the time I close this letter our information is very scanty and very old At this moment I do not know whether you have seen any of the parties you had letters to (except Huntley) nor whether you have even been to Chapel nor done any thing else but just work at your Labratory* and nothing else but I hope the next letters which we are very anxious to receive will be written more at your ease and tell us more about your new acquaintances and particularly if you have formed any acquaintance with any of the Professors of the College[12] for it is among such men as them that you will meet with kindred spirits to your own and such as those by giving you countenance will contribute to your success as an assayer for the public

I believe you will have other letters by this conveyance which will give you all the domestic news and therefore you must excuse me entering on that vein and believe me dearest Stanley

Your ever aff^{te} Father & faithful friend

Thomas Jevons

---

[12] There were only three professors at Sydney University: Rev. John Woolley, M.A., Principal and Professor of Classics; Morris Birkbeck Pell, Professor of Mathematics and Natural Philosophy; and John Smith, M.A., Professor of Chemistry and Experimental Physics, with whom Jevons became friendly (cf. Vol. I, pp. 25, 132).

58. THOMAS JEVONS TO W. S. JEVONS

Liverpool
18 April 55

My Dear Stanley

I begin a letter to you not knowing before hand that I have anything to say, but believing that you are glad to receive any sort of a letter from home I shall endeavour to spin out a yarn of some sort. I should not have allowed the South Carolina to sail without a letter had I had time but I was particularly engaged at the office which indeed I yet am in consequence of Henry Jevons[1] absence on a Journey to America and in the evening I was also engaged one night at a concert and another night at the play not so much for my own gratification as to accommodate others but nevertheless it consumed the time which I might have devoted to you and so I hope you will excuse my not writing by the last letter bag and take this as my amende.

On conning over some thing to say I may as well tell you of something that relates to my own inventive powers. Some three or four years since I had a model made for an Iron Coaster for carrying our Iron from Wales to Liverpool which I had made to be built without any Iron ribs at all.[2] I contended that the ribs and outside plating of an Iron built ship could never act in perfect unison together and in fact that they were not of much assistance to each other. I made up my mind that if the weight of Iron which is usually consumed in or appropriated to the ribs were applied in increasing the thickness of the outside plate that the ship would be actually stronger. I now learn that the person whom I employed to make the model has actually built two ships on my plan one of which has made a very successful run out to the East Indies and the second has only just been launched under circumstances that had brought my attention to her and caused me to find out the fact of the Construction being after a plan of my own This second vessel on being launched stuck fast when she was about two thirds out of the building yards and one third upon it. In fact she stuck upon the corner of a stone sea wall and as the tide went down her stern rested on the bed of the river and her head cocked up in proportion The next tide her stern was lifted up again only to be let down again the third tide. They got her off in a curious way. They got two or three steam tugs to pull at her in a straight direction first but that was no go! At last they pulled her side ways in one direction then they pulled her sideways in the opposite direction and they found that in one tide they got her about one foot forward so after working her a few feet forward in that way they

---

[1] See above, Letter 21, n. 2, p. 38.
[2] Cf. Vol. I, pp. 3–4.

managed at last to make her go off. I was interested to learn what damage she had sustained and learned that £20 would cure all on which I made further enquiry to know how she was built when to my surprize* I found that the engineer who had made my model was the engineer to this ship and that he had built her entirely on my plan without ribs You thus see that though I may not bring many or any of my plans and inventions to any successful result myself yet I am I trust of some use in suggesting to others plans and schemes which their more fortunate circumstances enable them to carry out to a successful issue. I hope you will excuse this little bit of egotism which I should not have given you but only that I sat down to write without a word to say and this incident by accident came into my mind and a capital one it [is][3] you will perhaps say to serve the purpose of a man at fault to fill up a letter. I shall perhaps learn something more about these vessels by and by when if I do and it turns out in their favor* I may perhaps return to the subject and be able to tell you more about them

We have told you of Henry Jevons having gone to America on our business affairs We have to day had his first letter after visiting the first batch of our customers in Boston. I am happy to say that he has sent us home a good lot of orders although he had been only one day and a half which he could devote ashore to business. The Iron trade has been very much depressed for six months or more, but it seems now as if the worst was got over for we have had two rather better packets before this, but the one that has arrived today is more like those which used to come in the best days of the trade so it puts one in good spirits.[4] During the slack time of the trade I have been turning my thoughts to business in new quarters and we have engaged a young Italian exile to come for a few hours each day to write foreign letters for us. I write the letters in English first and he translates them and already we have despatched letters in German French and Italian It is very interesting to me at first but what the result may be we have yet to learn. I do not think that much good can arise until one of us has been a journey to look up customers if any are to be obtained in France in Italy and in Germany and there is some chance that I myself may go a journey with this view

[3] Omitted in the original manuscript.
[4] Cf. S. G. Checkland's comment: 'There appears to have been a strong disposition to confine attention to problems of selling, rather than to think about new products and new processes. The iron masters were subject to very great vicissitudes of trade, so that, in improving times the urgent task was to get the works into full operation, while in bad times, with excess capacity, there was neither the incentive nor the means for improvement in plant . . . It was part of the game that iron masters must accept losses in depression, to be made up in good times. This meant that, as prices began to recover, the producer sought to hold back output until a remunerative price was obtained . . . the iron master had to enter upon the expansion with as few old orders on his books as possible, for new orders at higher prices were his aim. . . .' *The Rise of Industrial Society in England 1815–1885* (1964) pp. 154–5.

which will give me great delight not only at the thought that I may be extending our business relations but that I may visit countries which I have had a longing desire to see for a large portion of my Life – If I go I may perhaps take Lucy with me and for two reasons one is that perhaps I am now too old to go alone to so distant a place from home and the other is that it will be a grand opportunity to let Lucy see something of the wonderful works of art and nature that are to be met in that Classic Land of Italy in particular and at a moderate expense too for my own personal expenses being on the firms account would be paid by the firm and Lucys expenses only come out of my private resources But all this Castle building may yet turn out to be only like an inflated bubble which may burst and leave no trace behind. We shall see!

In looking over the "Bills of Entry" which I do every day to see what parts of the world our English Iron is exported to I never fail to look at the exports to Sydney and there occasionally I see a little Iron entered and I bethink myself how I should like to instil into some of your Iron dealers or Iron mongers or blacksmiths or engineers what excellent Iron the firm of Jevons & Co can and do supply and how much it would be to their advantage to send us some orders over to be executed by us should the nuggets be sent along with the orders If you become very intimate with any of such people you can just tell them what capital Iron Merch^{ts} we are and then they may send us an order or two on trial but the Cash must be provided on this side as we have not capital enough to give such a credit as to wait returns after the Iron has been received out Though notwithstanding this you know I have been boasting of lending you money to enable you to build a house for yourself. However that would be one solitary sum or transaction whilst dealing in Iron is a succession of transactions and each of which may come to more than one small Iron Cottage

Following out this course of thought I will tell you of another branch of business which your copper assaye* has suggested. Of course as some copper ore was brought to you to have your opinion whether the same could be brought to England without the fear of spontaneous combustion it follows as a matter of course that Copper Ore is one of the products of your favored* Land. Now you being so exact an assayer can one would suppose tell the value of Copper ore better than any other person then it occurs to one to ask why with such a knowledge at your finger ends you cannot buy up such lots of Copper ore as are offered for sale *at half their full value* and so send them on your own account to England to be sold for your profit you might by such means as these make a vast deal more profit than ever you can do by assaying only

I must acknowledge that is rather early in your sojourn in N S W to put such thoughts as these into your head and in the case of almost any other person but yourself I might be doing a very great disservice but you are so steady that I trust you will not be carried away by such a flight as this. But there is this point that might arise out of my suggestion. You might put some[one]⁵ else up to the business on the condition that they constituted you their sole assayer for all the copper ore they might buy and if I might recommend anyone to you to whom to mention it I think Mr Grundy would be the man. Being an Engineer and Surveyor he would have a good knowledge about the cost of working for the ore and bringing it to market and being connected with the Lpool Fire & Life Office I think he would have facilities for raising the funds to pay for the ore and so make a good thing out of it My idea is that he should buy the ore at the mine where he would get it dog cheap and undertake the carriage of it himself to the port of shipment and you would take care that he was not deceived about the quantity of real Copper in the ore. Excuse this sudden escapade upon the business. Let the thought mature awhile in your brain and if it does not fructify there why then cast it off as useless and believe only that it has served the purpose of filling another page of this dessultory* epistle –

Lucy has had a long letter from your Aunt Henry this morning who mentions you with great feeling and I think it very likely that she will write to you by the young man who takes out our small parcel with the Siluria As I understand now Mr Enfield who married Harriet was in the Mint in London⁶ and this young man was under him and he thinks that having such an introduction he thinks he can get employment in the Mint at Sydney. But should he fail in that the young man has several near relations who live about 100 miles only from Sydney and who are doing very well and so he considers that he has two strings to his bow and goes out with every confidence of success

Since writing the above I have cut out of an old mining Journal some account of the Sales of Copper Ore⁷ just to enlighten your darkness a little on that subject.

It is now getting late and I can write no more tonight and as this letter must be posted early tomorrow the 20 April I am compelled to close it without filling the sheet which I hope you will excuse I remain
    Your ever affectionate Father & friend
                    Thomas Jevons

⁵ Omitted in the original manuscript.

⁶ Edward Enfield had been one of the five Fellows of the Company of Moneyers, abolished in 1851 as a result of the recommendations of the Royal Commission on the Mint, 1848. He had served with the Company for 23 years. Cf. Craig, op. cit., pp. 315–20; Letter 35, n. 2, p. 64.

⁷ The *Mining Journal* published weekly, quarterly and annual figures of the scales of copper and other ores. Thomas Jevons may have been referring to the annual statistics of the copper trade for the period from 30 June 1853–30 June 1854, *Mining Journal*, 22 July 1854, no. 987 (XXIV). The figures for the period 1854–5 were not published until 14 July 1855.

59. THOMAS JEVONS TO W. S. JEVONS

Liverpool 3 May 1855

My dear Stanley,

I think we have the advantage of you in finding opportunities for writing for here am I sitting down to write another letter to you without having received one from you to afford me food to make another good full letter. To enable you to understand the latest position which we have any account of from you I must mention that you had just got an invitation from M^r say Captn Ward to visit him at the Battery[1] and you added "you thought you should go". I have answered in previous letters every thing received from you that required an answer up to that point and not having heard from you since I am left to the necessity of writing about any thing that turns up promiscuously in my own thoughts, which kind of writing seems indeed to form the staple of most of my letters to you.

The first information I can give you is that we have had your Aunt Robert[2] from Englefield staying with us for a week. She is as you know a very quiet personage, gives no trouble & is quite satisfied with every thing "en famile"* as they say Though very busy at our Office all the time I yet made a point of shewing her as much attention as possible I took her to the Docks to see a Ship's Cabin and an Emigrant vessel and to the Philarmonic* Hall to a Concert &c &c and I think she left us to return to Englefield much gratified with her reception. She had been staying for several weeks with her daughter Mrs James Thornely (Poppy[3] as you know) at their new house at Knotty Ash before she came to us but she went about very little there it was nursing all day Poppys two young ones that filled her time up there I have not yet seen Ja^s Thornelys new House at Knotty Ash. They tell me it is a much better house and better situation than his old one at Lea Brook but still it is a long way to Knotty Ash and I for one shall not go often there to see them

Now that your Aunt Robert is gone we have got your Cousin Mary Katherine*[4] stopping with us They are painting and pointing their house at St James Road all over and so your Aunt & Uncle Timothy

---

[1] Dawes Battery, Sydney Harbour, Captain Ward's residence.

[2] The widow of Robert Roscoe, whom she married in 1819. Formerly Martha Walker (b. 1798) she was the daughter of a London tailor at whose home he had lodged. Cf. Vol. I, p. 66, n. 5.

[3] Jevons's first cousin Laura ('Poppy') Roscoe. Born in 1828, she married James Thornely (1822–98), solicitor and member of the prominent Liverpool family, in March 1852. They had four sons and four daughters. In July 1885 their second son Thomas (b. 1855) married Mabel Martha (b. 1859), only daughter of Thomas Bolton Ogden, one of Jevons's school companions in the boarding house at Gower Street (cf. above, Letter 6, p. 14).

[4] Mary Catherine Jevons (1827–1908) eldest daughter of Timothy Jevons.

are gone to pay visits to H^y Wood[5] to Mrs Newtons and to Henry Jevons house while he is away in America and M C has come here. I think I told you in a former letter that Kate Newton was engaged to be married to Mr Mead King. The affair came off at the Birkenhead Unitarian Chapel the day before yesterday so I suppose Kate King is a Happy Queen now, though not yet 20 years old

There is no change in our domestic affairs to tell you of, but on Saturday next Lucy is to go down to Derby to be ready to act as Brides maid to Emily Malin who on the 7th or 8th Inst is to be married to your Cousin Wm Caldwell Roscoe[6]

The Organ in St Georges Hall[7] was publicly opened the other day with a Concert of Organ Music alone played by a Mr Best.[8] I perhaps ought to say that it was privately opened for there was no one admitted but those who had tickets given them by the Town Counsel.* The place was cram full to excess but as I have no friends in the Counsel and made no effort to get Tickets I was not there. The papers say that the Concert passed off extremely well and that the Organ is the most splendid one in the world. Altogether Hall & Organ there is nothing anywhere else to compare with it.

As yours is a Country for trying new things I enclose an account of a wonderful pea which I cut out of a newspaper thinking that it might be useful You might send it to the Sydney Herrald* which would make the knowledge of this pea[9] public in Sydney. I dare say however that there is a specimen of it alive in your Botanic Garden[10] or if there is not after it is known I dare say the curator of your Garden would write to China for one. I dare say you have plenty of China men at Sydney and they would know how to make the paste or if you have no China men at Sydney there are some at Melbourne and the Sydney Herald would spread the news about this pea into that quarter and so I make you a present of all the fame and fortune that this wonderful pea is likely to yield

I wonder how Copper Mining gets on in your part of the world with me it gets on very poorly at the Poltimore. We have had an Annual meeting and instead of a dividend they have made a call but it is only of 1/-p Share and principally with the view of making the shareholders

---

[5] Henry Wood. See above, Letter 43, n. 6, p. 89.

[6] See above, Letter 55, n. 12, p. 123.

[7] Cf. above, Letter 44, p. 95; also Letter 11, n. 3, p. 23

[8] William Thomas Best (1826–97) organist and musician. After various appointments in Liverpool and London he was organist to Liverpool Corporation, 1855–94.

[9] The cutting is no longer with the letter and cannot be identified. It is possible that it may have been a traveller's tale concerning the soya bean, then mainly confined to China.

[10] The Sydney Botanic Gardens, the oldest in Australia, were established in 1816; covering 66 acres, they are situated at Farm Cove on the site of the earliest farm in the colony, now in the heart of the city.

register themselves or give up their shares The Committee seem to think that it will yet turn out a paying mine though they have been swindled out of nearly all their capital

I think I told you before that I am trying to open a connection for the sale of our Iron in France and Italy one of our French correspondents told us that he could not understand our £ s d and wished us to quote our prices in francs Instead of doing this I have quoted our prices in £'s and decimals of a £ and thus probably I am the very first man to begin the decimal system of accounts[11] in England. It has pleased me so much that I contemplate asking our Yankee customers if they would like to have our moneytary* affairs carried on in the decimal form and if they will I for one would instantly begin it but I doubt very much whether my Brother[12] would agree but it will rapidly now come on, and it being known that a single individual has introduced it I think that others will follow like a flock of sheep

Poor Tommy is laid up with the mumps which he has caught from Mr Greens son at School[13] We have had Mr Higginson[14] to him who says he must take care and avoid catching cold and then in a few days it will go away, but Tommy cuts a pretty figure with the lower portion of his face swelled twice as big as it ought to be. Herbert is pretty hard worked at the Office every day, now Henry is away, as he takes the chief part of Henrys department I think however that it does Herbert no harm but on the contrary a great deal of good as it has convinced him that his services are valuable and what is more he now knows something of the value of our business and how we are enabled to get a living by it. Herberts grown much stouter than he used to be though he takes a good deal of medicine so I believe. Henny is the most cheerful companion you can imagine She is up to take very early lessons with Mr Hermann two or three days a week and her progress in music is very rapid as she practises 3 hours a day. She plays splendidly and whenever you ask her jumps up in an instant and flourishes away like a first rate professor Of Lucy I can only say that she is my right hand I could not carry on without her or at least very badly She was not very strong a while back, but is a good deal better now. Changes will come in the health of young people I dare say you will experience this and if you do as you are as it were alone I hope you will not fail to call in a medical man so that you run no risk of anything serious. You know the old proverb a stitch in time saves nine so you be sure and send for the Doctor to stop the first rent

---

[11] Cf. below, Letter 63, p. 155.
[12] Timothy Jevons. See Vol. I, p. 12.
[13] Tom Jevons was still at school in Liverpool. Cf. Letters 18 and 67, pp. 34 and 167.
[14] The family doctor. See Vol. I, p. 60, n. 3.

And now dear Stanley I have to tell you that after several trials to get back some of the overcharge made by J^{as} Baines & Co for your passage I at last made a formal claim in a letter I wrote them dated 30 April of which I hand you a copy enclosed. it is addressed to Mr Mackay[15] one of the partners whom I know best This letter has brought me the return of £5 which I have acknowledged as p copy of my note enclosed and I hope now that you will give them credit for some degree of honorable* feeling and in future support the Black Ball Line as being conducted by an honorable company I hold the £5 at your credit and it will go to that extent in payment of such things as you may order us to purchase for you I have bought and paid for the Siluria and the two thermometers which together cost £1.15/- so that absorbs some portion of the £5

I have been attending with the Committee today for the final approval of the Bust of Roscoe for the monument in our Chapel[16] and I think it an admirable production. When the marble bust is finished I will try to get a Photograph of it for you I dare say I can send it in a letter without injury.

There is a vessel to sail from here with the funny name of "Startled Fawn" belonging to Hamilton Fletcher.[17] She sails on the 9th Inst and Herbert talks of writing by her She is an Iron built ship and will probably get out nearly if not quite as soon as the Oliver Lang

I have no time to say more now but only to reiterate the expression of my boundless affection

Your ever faithful friend & aff^{te} Father
Thomas Jevons

60. THOMAS JEVONS TO W. S. JEVONS

p Startled Fawn

Liverpool 9th May 1855

Dearest Stanley

I think I ought not to let this vessel, the Startled Fawn, go direct from Lpool to Sydney without her bearing a letter to you though it may be the fourth or fifth letter I have written since I received one from you. In consequence of the lack of information from you I have nothing to answer and can only fill up a letter with a little tittle tattle and whether that be acceptable to you or not I have no means of knowing. But before

---

[15] Probably Donald Mackay (d. 1880), a Boston shipbuilder, who built several ships for James Baines & Co. Cf. below, Letter 60, n. 3, p. 146.

[16] Cf. above, Letter 56, p. 128.

[17] A Liverpool shipowner who was possibly related to Mrs Henry Roscoe.

going further I must repeat what I have told you in several of my last letters that our latest news from you is the letter in which you said you had got an invitation to the Battery to meet a large party invited by Capt Ward a sort of house warming I suppose from him. A knowledge that this is the last letter which we have received from you up to this moment seems necessary to be communicated to you least* you should be dissapointed* in the contents of our letters. As far as your progress at Sydney goes we cannot make any allusions beyond the circumstances that have come to our knowledge and now to go on with my letter –

Lucy is away at Derby at your Cousin W C Roscoes wedding. It came off yesterday and Henny has a note from Lucy this morning saying that it went off admirably the sun shone splendidly (for England) all the day and the bride & bridegroom started on their journey in the highest spirits. Patty from Englefield[1] was one of the bridesmaids and Lucy is bringing her to Lpool to spend some time with us. But Patty & Lucy are coming home by way of *Llangothlyn** to look for some lodgings for us for the holidays When we were at Llangollen some three years since we liked it so much that we think we will go there again and if Lucy can meet with a suitable place she will engage it for a month or six weeks in the holidays. Tommy has got the mumps, and they linger long upon him, he has been confined to the house for more than a week but they seem to be going away now and I trust he will be none the worse for it when he has got entirely quit of them. I dont think Tommy is quite so strong in constitution as the rest of you for whenever he has anything the matter it always takes longer to cure. His flesh is softer and his nerves are less strong and he is of a more delicate nature altogether. Still he may outlive many a sturdier being for all that. Henry Jevons is still away on a Journey in America he is doing a good deal of business for us. Our name stands very high with all the Iron dealers in that part of the world and we are getting orders now when all the other Iron dealers are scarcely getting any orders at all. The Iron trade has gone through a state of great depression for the last year or two, with difficulties of all sorts to contend against and such times prove the sterling character of men of business and I think I am justified in concluding from the fact that we alone have had good orders by the last four or five packets that have arrived that we have come through the ordeal with flying colours

I am engaged more particularly of late in trying to open a business in France & Italy. It cannot be brought on rapidly without a journey there which I cannot at present take but I have opened a few accounts by letter writing only having obtained the names of a few Iron dealers there when I was agent for Guest & Co. I purpose going into France &

[1] See above, Letter 16, n. 4, p. 32.

Italy if all be well after we come back from Llangollen and then I shall see if we can make a business in that quarter of the world or not

I cut out a paragraph about Electricity the other day from the Mining Journal[2] thinking it might be of service so I enclose it

We had a vessel arrived here yesterday from Melbourne she has brought a great many packages of Gold dust a large quantity of Wool and Tallow and a very large and miscellaneous assortment of English merchandize* returned! God help the owners! She was sent out by James Baines & Co[3] and I should guess that some of the returned goods belong to them The name of the vessel is the Constance It is James Baines & Co who are loading the Startled Fawn which I hope may have a good run out and expect she will as she is an Iron Ship. I told you in a former letter that J^s Baines & Co had returned £5 on account of your passage money and so on that account I am disposed to cry them up I have placed the £5 at your credit and it does to pay for the Siluria and the two thermometers and leaves £3.10/- still at your credit to pay for anything else you may order

I can find nothing more to say now but you may rely on my writing again by the first opportunity whether I hear from you or not remaining
    Dearest Stanley
        Your ever aff^{te} Father
            Thomas Jevons

61. W. S. JEVONS TO LUCY JEVONS
[LJN, 50-51]

Annangrove Cottage, Sydney,
28th May 1855.

... I am now at my new, and I hope final, lodgings here, and I have been here three weeks already. I have been living, of course, in a more comfortable and civilised way, but the chief comfort is, that I now have regular and moderately hard work every day in town, after disposing of which, I come out here to spend the evening quietly either in my own room or the parlour (for we have regained the long-lost distinctions

---

[2] Probably the account of the second of a course of lectures on electricity delivered by Dr John Tindall at the Royal Institution on Tuesday, 24 April 1855, which was published in the *Mining Journal*, 28 April 1855, no. 1027 (xxv) 269.

[3] The firm founded by James Baines (1823–89) of Liverpool; clerk in a shipbroker's office; established a line of ships to make rapid passage from Liverpool to Australia, called the Black Ball Line, 1851. His fleet of 30 fast sailing vessels was chartered to convey troops to India, 1857; Queen Victoria and Prince Albert inspected the *James Baines*, considered to have been the finest and fastest of his ships, before she sailed to Calcutta, 1857. The general introduction of steam later reduced Baines's business. Cf. Jones, op. cit., pp. 30–31.

of parlour, drawing-room, sitting, bedroom, kitchen, etc.) My little room will be much more comfortable when I have got a few more things for furniture. If I get the first payment of my salary towards the end of this week I shall probably buy a bookcase with glass doors to keep my books and other things clean and out of the way. Possibly I may even spend £30 in getting an harmonium, as I wish very much to have a little music; but this may seem very extravagant. My life is now as active as it was idle a little time since. I get up about eight, off to town at nine, getting to the office by ten o'clock. The assays there, if an easy *batch*, are finished by four or five o'clock, and I start off back for dinner. The distance to my office is quite four miles, and I walk on an average six miles out of the eight; still, though quite fresh to it, I do not find it too much, and am often ready in the evenings to cut firewood, etc. In fact, I am in most excellent health, and this place is a deal better than Sidney for health. The road is one continuous line from here to Church Hill – viz., along the Parramatta Road, Parramatta Street, and George Street, and a more disagreeable road it is impossible to conceive – dusty or muddy, straight, and going through the hills by cuttings. It is crowded in the daytime with herds of cattle and sheep, bullock teams, drags going up the country, mail coaches, omnibuses, diggers on horseback, etc.; in fact, it is something like what the roads must have been in England before the time of the railways. . . .

62. THOMAS JEVONS TO W. S. JEVONS

p Donald Mackay

Liverpool Sunday Even^g
3 June 1855

Dearest Stanley

We are in possession of your letter by the James Baines up to March 13 That vessel delivered her mail at our P O on the 21 May after the most extraordinary passage on record for a sailing vessel. I hope the Donald Mackay will at least equal the James Baines which she deserves to do as she is if anything a finer ship and larger

The principle* topic of your letter by the James Baines is about the proposed change in your position & standing at the Mint viz making you a public servant at a fixed Salary instead of your doing your work by contract as I may say e c* for £100 a year fixed Salary and a payment of 6/6 for each assaye.* Before you can get this letter the affair will have been fixed either for better or for worse and any thing that I can say will not alter it immediately nevertheless I will tell you what occurs to my mind on the business which may be a hint to you how to act should any other change be desired at a future period

In the first place it appears to me that it is the altered price of Gold that has lead* to the change. As Gold is below the standard value in Sydney Capt Ward thinks that everybody will bring their Gold to the Mint to be coined & consequently that your fee of 6/6 an assaye* would bring you in a very large income indeed so large that he fears he would be considered to have made a bad bargain with you and so before the thing is tried at all he recalls his own acts and wishes to put you & Miller upon a fixed salary of £500 p an^m. I think this is any thing but just right or honest in Capt Ward He tempted you & Miller to go from your own family and home and Country to the extreme end of the Globe by a tempting offer of a Salary & pay that should bring you in or be calculated to bring you in about £600 p an^m and beyond that you were to have as much more as you could get by private assaying for your own exclusive benefit. Having thus tempted you out and got you into his power and finding that there is a chance that your estimated pay from the mint will reach more than was expected he turns round upon you and now resolves to cut you down to only £500 a year and to strip you of all your fees for assaying which I think is most shameful In point of fact he wants you to take the Salary and the fees to go to the Mint

Before the Mint was at work and in the unsettled position in which you were placed I am not surprized* that you should yield so easily to his proposition and under all the same circumstances I should no doubt have done the same and it may be for your happiness that you have placed yourself so much in the hands and in the power of Cap Ward now you are in Australia but I will say this that had we foreseen that they would have cut you down in your prospects in the way they have done I should never have urged you to accept the appointment When a man expatriates himself it is generally with the view of making a rapid fortune and returning to enjoy it at no very distant day in his own Country again and that was why you went out and it is a fraud upon you to blight that prospect so completely as Cap Ward seems to have done. Now having been circumvented by him as I believe most unfairly and you at the time having yielded from compulsion as it were I think you may fairly seize any opportunity that offers to regain your position and to turn the tables on Cap Ward when you happen to have him in your power which may not be long first Now there may come a time when the assays will come in very fast and numerous then I think you may claim extra remuneration if you do them all. At £500 a year you are bound to work from 10 oclock until 4 but not faster than very ordinary work I think you should do no more assays in that than would cover your salary reckoning it at £500 p an^m which in fact would not be more than five assayes* p day Now that would I have no doubt leave the Mint very greatly in arrear and Cap Ward would be urging you on to greater exertions In that case you would have a just right to say Pay us better and then we will work longer hours and I have no doubt you would soon get the better of him. I am quite aware that something fixed and certain is very desirable in your particular case for a year or two and until you feel so entirely master of your situation as not to dread the consequences of a blow up and therefore if I had been with you I should have counselled some modifycation* of the original agreement Your actual agreement stood thus £100 p an^m and 6/6 for every assay now the fairest way of adjusting any outrageous inequality that might arise from such a way of paying you would be not to upset it altogether which makes the inequality as bad against you as Capt Ward feared it would turn out in your favor* but it would have been much more fair to say that we will lessen our assay price just in the same proportion that you increase the Salary portion for instance give us £200 a year and we will take: 5/6 p assay or £300 a year and 4/6 p assay: or £400 a year and 3/6 p assaye* or £500 p an^m and 2/6 p assaye* and at this point I would have advised you to make a stand. No doubt the mint will charge 6/6 for every assaye* you do and if they get you to work for the £500 p an^m as hard as you did for the assayes* for the Paris exhibition the Mint will make a fortune out of you. Now there are two or three ways for going to work. If you are required to work after 4 oclock ask and demand a fee for every assaye* you do after that hour, and then I will be bound that you can double your Salary if there be assayes* enough brought to the mint to enable you to do so and at times there certainly will be more assays brought than you can do leisurely between 10 and 4 If Cap Ward will not agree to pay you a full fee for assays done after mint hours then let him agree to pay £500 a year and 2/6 every assaye* and then you will undertake to do all that comes in even if you work until 12 at night Of course I do not mean that you would work always until late but there may be times when there may come in an extraordinary press of assays and in such cases to clear them off well you ought to be paid well Considering that you were tempted abroad by an offer of a Salary and fees that would bring you in about £600 p an^m with liberty to practice* for yourself by which you were lead* to hope you might get £500 or £600 more I think you will be perfectly justified in using every art and device to make your situation produce you that Sum at the least and should the mint have a very large trade I would strike for an advance of pay equivalent to the advantages held out to you before you accepted the appointment. I am rather surprized* that Mr Miller seems to have yielded so easily but I account for it by the fact that he has a wife to provide for as well as himself and the risk to run is therefore doubly weighty for him to bare* – The necessity for his securing a living is certainly much greater than yours and this may account for his eagerness to secure what little private assaying there was to be got hold of. And this thought reminds me that Capt Ward will have a great advantage over you in dispossessing you of your apparatus, because though he may pay you what it has cost if you should leave the Mint you cannot replace the whole of the things under 6 mths at the least

These are the thoughts that come into my mind in hearing of the change that was proposed at the date of your last letters say early in March and having unburthened my mind of them I must leave what I have said whether it be for your peace of mind or not

I am sorry to learn that you seemed to suffer from the effects of the long drought and the restricted sorts of food that it had occasioned but your meditated trip to Paramatta* would I hope put all to rights again Whenever you experience lassitude continued for any length of time or indeed any kind of depressing illness or weakness a journey is decidedly the best and surest remedy. You breathe a different air your faculties are enlivened by new scenes and new persons your frame is put into a different and more multifarious action and you become a new man at least I have ever found that to be the case with me and it is natural to suppose that you are somewhat of the same temperament and therefore I advize* for you as many journeys as you can possibly compass particularly if you are in any way low or poorly. There are plenty of short sea excursions from Sydney which ought to be cheaper than land and they make the change greater and as you are a proved good sailor perhaps you may venture on the broad ocean at times when a sufficient stimulus called you to do so.

I think I told you that H^y Jevons has been a Journey to America He returned home about $\frac{1}{2}$ past 11 last night. He has been absent rather more than three months & his Journey has been a most successful one He is very popular with the Yankees and has sent home lots of orders which have kept us all at home quite hard worked to execute them He has brought quite a heap of orders with him nearly amounting to 1000 Tons which is a splendid lot and puts us all in good spirits previous to his going out we had been rather slack at the office but as soon as we began to receive letters from him it set us a going famously and Herbert and I have been kept hard at work ever since early and late and scarcely having time for dinner in fact Herbert has gone without his dinner frequently which is a thing I have not approved of Now Henry is back again we shall not be quite so hard worked since we shall have his help and shall be quite satisfied if we have about half the quantity of orders to work at so you see we shall have less work and more to do it for the benefit of us all.

Our minister Mr Channing¹ has been starring it for two or three weeks in London preaching very frequently and speaking at numerous meetings of different Unitarian bodies and he seems to have given great delight to his hearers. We have given him an invitation to continue our minister for 2 years after his present agreement is terminated but he has accepted it for only one year leaving it uncertain whether he can stop longer in England He says he thinks one part of his mission on Earth is to help to abolish Slavery in his native land America and he thinks that in a year or so from this time his services there on such a mission will be most effective and the moment he is convinced that that time is come he shall think it is duty to go and he hopes the Congregation will pack him off by the first packet after news comes that he will be wanted. You probably understand what the Fugitive Slave Law is viz a Law passed by the General Government of America to enable parties to go into any free state to recover Slave[s] who have escaped from a slave state The working of this Law has been most galling to the free States as in fact it makes the free States accessory to Slavery so the free state of Massachusetts is passing a Law in the State Legislature to negative the fugitive Slave Law and the contest seems likely to lead to very important results and I suppose it is in view of this that Mr Channing contemplates being called home so soon. The question of Slavery is the most onerous one for America and is not at all unlikely to bring about a severance of the Union the North from the South and if that were to happen then undoubtedly at the same time there would be a separation of the East from the West and the wonderful progress of that great family of the Earth would be stayed never to advance again with the same rapidity and momentum.²

We are beginning to get over our War troubles at last as you will no doubt see by the Sydney Paper if you do not get those which we send you Only think of our driving the Russians out of that sealed water the Sea of Azof, it is like getting into the very heart of their Kingdom *by the back door* and it will not be long before we enter at the front door you may depend. My old friend Ja^s Naesmyth*³ is making some guns that

---

¹ See above, Letter 57, n. 7, p. 134.

² The Fugitive Slave Act had been passed by Congress in 1793 to provide for the rendition of fugitive slaves. The Act was amended in 1850, abolishing slavery in the District of Columbia but providing that a master had only to claim a Negro as his slave before the proper federal agent: if the agent ruled the claimant to be the master, the Negro was handed over without right of trial or evidence. Heavy fines and prison sentences were imposed for any laxity or obstruction in administering the law. The Act created much bitterness in the non-slave states; it was repealed in June 1864.

³ James Nasmyth (1808–90), popularly remembered for his association with the invention of the steam hammer, patented in 1842. Thomas Jevons had been responsible for introducing Nasmyth to his future partner Holbrook Gaskell (1813–1909) in 1836. The firm of Nasmyth, Gaskell & Company was established in that year for the manufacture of engines and machine

will throw a Shell of ½ Ton weight a distance of 5 miles with what an unexpected and awful crack such a shell will descend there will be no getting out of the way of it and Cronstadt[4] itself must succumb to the terrors of such a hughe* fiery Monster

I dont think I have written to you since we received your letter that told us you had had a long visit from Professor Smith of Sydney College.[5] I am very glad to hear that you are becoming acquainted with one of the more valuable class of Society. I would encourage the acquaintance of all such and make them your real friends if worthy of your trust in other respects As to the Revd Mr Stanley you perhaps are rather too much expecting from him. If as you say he has got a Chapel full of friends he cannot find time to devote very much attention to each individual and it may be said to be quite as much your duty to find him out and dance attendance on him as for him to dance attendance on you It is certainly a most extraordinary thing that Unitarianism which here can hardly hold its head above water should be so triumphant in your land of promise and all I can remark upon the fact is that I suppose that when folks wend their way to a "new home" they leave all their prejudices behind them

4 June We have had the Great Organ of the St Georges Hall publicly opened since I wrote last to you, but I was so much engrossed with my business every day that I was too tired to go to the opening and so I missed it altogether I have not heard so much talk about it as one might expect from which I conclude that there was nothing so particularly striking about the playing of Dr Wesley[6] who was the great Gun at the opening Indeed I did hear someone say that his playing was "heavy"

Reverting again to your own affairs let me note what you say about your picking up a mangy dog in the streets and taking it home to make a pet of it. There was danger in such an act but I hope you have succeeded in curing it and that he will be a comfort to you But whether that result take place or not it may be said of you for doing such a deed what was once said of your grandmother Jevons or like it viz that the spirit of your mangy dog will never rise up against you in judgment at the last day

As I have a world of business before me today I believe I must break

---

tools at the Bridgwater Foundry built at Patricroft. The partnership was dissolved in 1850; Nasmyth retired in 1856. Cf. R. Dickinson, 'James Nasmyth and the Liverpool Iron Trade', *Transactions of the Historic Society of Lancashire and Cheshire*, 108 (1957) 83–104.

[4] See above, Letter 41, n. 13, p. 79.

[5] See Vol. I, p. 25.

[6] Samuel Sebastian Wesley (1810–76) cathedral organist and composer, professor of the organ at the Royal Academy of Music; chief adviser to the Liverpool Corporation in the construction of the huge organ in St George's Hall.

off but shall write again next and indeed every mail when I am able and so reiterating ever the best wishes of the kindest of parents I remain
Your most aff^{te} Father
Thomas Jevons

63. THOMAS JEVONS TO W. S. JEVONS

Llangollen 17th June 1855

Dearest Stanley

You see above where we are, just come up to this beautiful spot to enjoy the holidays and I only wish that you could be one amongst us But that not being possible the next best wish is that you could enjoy such a lovely green group of hills and vales as surround this farm called Pengwern but that not being possible any more than the other at least until someone can invent a means of making an artificial atmosphere I am reduced to the necessity of wishing you the utmost happiness that it may be in your power to attain under the suns that shine so resplendently over your nether world We were once in these Lodgings before for a week at Easter once but I do not think that you were with us then. Still you must know something of the Vale of Llangollen so famed for its young and beautiful Jenny Jones the Maid of Llangollen celebrated in Song, and famed for the no less remarkable dames The Lady Elizabeth Butler and the Hble I Ponsonby[1] at one time as famous in the highest fashionable Circles in London as the lowly but beautiful Jenny was famous in this renowned valley The two elderly dames as you will recollect had a surfeit of leading the ton and so they left it under a vow to devote the remainder of their lives to a homely country life to do all the good they could to their neighbours and so they lived to be octogenerians in the abode they had chosen not many hundred yards from the spot in which I am writing and they have left a name behind them that will never be forgotten and a character which is held in reverence by the people around as if they had been veritable angels on earth a wonderful contrast to the glitter they had cast around them in the ambitious days of their youth and womanhood.

The most conspicuous objects in this neighbourhood are Castle Dinas Bran in English Crow Castle an old Roman Fortress that crowns a remarkable Sugar Loaf Hill now of course in Ruins and the Vale Crusis*

---

[1] Lady Eleanor Butler (1745?–1829), sister of the seventeenth Earl of Ormonde, and Sarah Ponsonby (1755?–1831) who was related to the Earl of Bessborough; they renounced the world to live in complete seclusion in a cottage at Plasnewydd in the vale of Llangollen, becoming a considerable attraction for tourists, including distinguished foreign visitors.

Abbey celebrated in Verse by your Uncle William Stanley Roscoe in those beautiful lines beginning

> Vale of the Cross the Shepherds tell
> Tis sweet within thy woods to dwell &c &c²

and we shall visit both these places before we leave although it will not be the first time by many that I have seen and admired them in days of yore

18 June Now I dare say you will like to know who is here with me though perhaps you might easily guess that Lucy & Henny & Tommy were of the party in which you would be quite right but as to Herbert though I asked him to come and spend Sunday with us I could get no answer at all, but after a good deal of pressing he said dont bother me I know I can come if I like! but he did not come. My intention is that he and I shall as they say "ride & tie" while we have these country lodgings me one week and him the next and so on alternately until the end of our lease of six weeks.

Our Lodgings are not in the town of Llangollen but at a farm house about a mile out of Town in a secluded vale called Pengwerne.* It is like the valley in which Johnson placed his Rasselass³ surrounded entirely by lofty hills covered with grass or trees with only two other farm houses within the baron or circumference of the parish and consequently it is one of the most secluded spots you ever saw or can imagine and here we are vegetating on pure butter and milk from our Landlords cows on eggs from his hens and on rashers of ham from a neighbours pig to say nothing of the mutton from his mountain sheep or the veal from his calf all of which we have tasted and can pronounce most excellent. We are quite happy both indoors and out and when we want to see a little of the world around us we ascend one of the surrounding hills and then we have a view of surpassing beauty and extent We were on the top of one of these Hills yesterday afternoon from which we could see the whole of Pengwerne* and the whole line of the Vale of Llangollen the vale Crusis* the town of Ruabon the vale Royal of England with Boston Castle and the Pecforton* Hills and on probably to Chester & Lpool had we had a telescope with us. Then on the other side of us a world of Mountain tops which add beauty to the beautiful and particularly as the afternoon was most favorable* the clouds flying rapidly across the blue and sun lit sky shed their rapidly passing shadows along the sides of the mountains and giving a variety which was wonderful

---

² These are the first two lines of a poem entitled 'On Visiting Vale Crucis', which is included in the volume of poems by the Roscoe family entitled *Poems for Youth, by a Family Circle* (1820–1). See Vol. I, p. 5. William Stanley Roscoe (see above, Letter 35, n. 3, p. 64) published a volume of collected *Poems* in 1834.

³ Samuel Johnson, *The History of Rasselass, Prince of Abissinia* (1759).

and yet lovely to contemplate we could with difficulty withdraw ourselves from the lovely scene and retire to the calm of our secluded retreat.

Strolling out late last evening not a hundred years from the house who should start into view but two genteelly dressed Ladies one of whom to my very great surprize addressed me by name and expressed the greatest delight that she had met some one whom she knew. It turned out to be Miss Lawthwaite formerly a great friend of your Aunt Jane and a friend of hers with her and they had lost their way having strolled a long way round from Llangollen and got round into Pengwerne* from which they could not get out again without a guide We shook hands heartily passed a few rapid words that momentarily sprung up and then she hurried away in the direction I pointed out but too glad that she found that her home was within the distance of a single mile though in Pengwerne* there is no more appearance of a Town than there is in the moon –

I told you that there were only three houses in Pengwerne* but in one of them a friend has come to lodge just simply because Lucy has come here It is Mrs Wills formerly Miss Kimberly M^r & Mrs Wills were staying at New Brighton where Lucy went to see them As Mr Wills was obliged to return to his business in Birmingham Mrs Wills did not like to be left all alone and as Lucy was coming here she resolved that she would leave New Brighton and follow Lucy if possible so she got Lucy to write about Lodgings for her and Mrs Wills with her two young children and servant maid are our next door neighbours. The mention of Mrs Wills servant reminds me that I have forgotten to mention that Ann Bolton is come with us here and she seems as happy as the day is long laughing & talking and telling wonders to the simple farmer and his wife and their Girl & boy servants which four compose the household when no strangers are here and so now you have the whole paraphernalia* of our population and I shall say no more on that point.

I think I have told you before that I was interesting myself a little about the Decimal System of Accounts and Coinage Mr Browns[4] motion about it in the house of Commons was carried but not until it was stripped of all its operative effects and it may be said to have been a dead letter affair In consequence I have written a long letter to him proposing to him that he should no longer wait for the countenance and concurrence of Government but that he should institute a great League to consist of 100,000 persons or firms and that when the whole number

---

[4] William Brown (1784–1864), Member of Parliament for South Lancashire, 1846–59; he is best known in Liverpool for his gift of the Free Public Library and Derby Museum, opened in 1860. He especially favoured the idea of decimal currency and was author of a pamphlet entitled *Decimal Coinage. A Letter from W. Brown, Esq., M.P., to Francis Shand, Esq., Chairman of Liverpool Chamber of Commerce* (1854).

proposed had been made up and joined that then they should all adopt the Decimal System of Accounts voluntarily and without waiting for the action of Government I only posted my letter last night from this place so I do not know what sort of an impression my proposition will make[5]

If you do not know what the decimal scheme is it is simply this to divide the £ into one thousand parts to be called Mills* instead of into 960 parts called farthings – The following few lines will shew* you the workings of the new scheme at a glance

£	mills*	£	£
£1. 0. 0	1.000	£0. 0. 9	£0.038
0. 15. 0	.750	0. 0. 6	0.025
0. 10. 0	.500	0. 0. 4	0.017
1. 0	.050	0. 0. 2½	0.010
		0. 0. 1	0.004

It is impossible to change every sum or coin into an exact equivalent in decimals but the differences are so small as really to be no obstacle in the practical working of the system and the moment that the Government would consent to coin a piece to be called [a][6] Mill* then the whole discrepancy would be no longer in existence. I shall let you know from time to time how the work proceeds as I do not suppose it will be frequently mentioned in the papers.

We are again without letters from you for a longer time than I like owing to the irregularity of the passages of the sailing vessels. The last letter we have is that mentioning about your proposed change from out

---

[5] A cutting containing the proposed resolutions on Decimal Coinage was attached to a letter previously received by Thomas Jevons from William Brown, which is reproduced below (p. 157): 'That, in the opinion of this house, the initiation of the Decimal system of Coinage, by the issue of the Florin, has been eminently successful and satisfactory: That a further extension of such system will be of great public advantage:

'That an humble Address be presented to Her Majesty, praying that Her Majesty will be graciously pleased to complete the decimal scale with the Pound and the Florin, as suggested by two Commissions and a Committee of the House of Commons, by authorising the issue of Silver Coins to represent the value of the one hundredth part of a pound, and Copper Coins to represent the one thousandth part of a pound, to be called Cents and Mils respectively, or to bear such other names as to Her Majesty may seem advisable.'

These resolutions led to the appointment of a further Royal Commission, which sat from May 1856 until April 1859 and in its Final Report opposed the introduction of a decimal coinage, largely because of the influence of Lord Overstone. In later years the issue of decimal coinage became involved with proposals for an international currency – a question in which Jevons was much interested: cf. his paper 'On the Condition of the Gold Coinage of the United Kingdom, with reference to the question of International Currency' (1868), *Investigations*, pp. 244–96, and the correspondence in connection with it reprinted in Vol. III, especially Letter 302. For a full account of the history of decimal coinage in England, see N. Davey, 'The Decimal Coinage Controversy in England' (unpublished Ph.D. thesis, University of London, 1957,) and on Lord Overstone's part in the controversy see D. P. O'Brien, *The Correspondence of Lord Overstone* (Cambridge, 1971) 152–9.

[6] The edge of the page is torn here.

door assayer to an indoor officer of the Mint and my last letter to you was an indignant one at the conduct of the authorities, who I am disposed to think are taking advantage of you, but if you like the change better than the old agreement I have no reason to complain. With reference to hearing more regularly, I am glad to see that the Government are about treating for the East India Steam Pkt C⁰ to run a boat regularly between Sydney & Galle[7] to meet the overland mail and if that is carried out we shall have a mail regularly every fortnight which is delightful to think of and who knows under such circumstances that I may not run over and take a peep at you.

I have just asked Lucy what she has got to say to you and she says give him my very best love and tell him that I will write next mail Thommy* says my dearest love and tell him I think I shall find some fossils here and if I do I will send them to him Henny says ah well I dont know I dont know if I have anything in particular! The fact is that Henny is deep in a Novel which she has been reading at for the whole of two days almost and she cannot spare a thought for any thing or any body else So now dearest Stanley excuse me saying more and believe me ever

Your most aff^{te} Father
Thomas Jevons

I hope Herbert will post some papers to you from Lpool as we have none here to send

64. WILLIAM BROWN TO THOMAS JEVONS[1]

Fenton's Hotel
London 24 May 1855

My Dear Sir

I thank you for your letter of yesterday – You are probably aware that the Coinage is a prerogative of the Crown & our Association determined that I should introduce the enclosed resolutions into the House – I will submit your views to them with the draft of the Bill, but from the temper & position of our present Ministers I am sure it would be lost time to try to introduce any Bill this Session – If we can get the principle established, & the Coins as Books of instruction, it will be a step in advance –

Mr Arbuthnot,[2] one of the principal clerks at the Treasury, has drawn

[7] See above, Letter 57, n. 1, p. 133.
[1] The original manuscript of this letter was sent to W. S. Jevons by Thomas Jevons as an enclosure with Letter 63 above.
[2] George Arbuthnot (1802–65), Treasury official from 1820 to death, Auditor of the Civil List, 1850 to death; private secretary to Peel and Sir Charles Wood.

the skeleton of a Bill differing from yours, but adopting as you have done, the Pound as the unit –

I think when you read the debate in Parliament which will take place on the 12th June you will see that we are doing all we can to make progress – There are so many conflicting opinions it is difficult to reconcile them, although all have the same object in view –

Yours truly
Wm Brown

65. W. S. JEVONS TO HENRIETTA JEVONS
[LJN, 51–2]

Annangrove Cottage, Sydney.
1st July 1855.

... I will now tell you a little about the house I am living in here. It is a low neatly-built Australian-shaped house; the little dining-room is comfortable, and looks on to the road; the drawing-room is a fine room of three windows, comfortably and handsomely furnished, and which would be admired as a good room anywhere. My little room is awkwardly shaped and placed, but being now furnished according to my own ideas of comfort, convenience, and elegance, I am thoroughly satisfied with it. At one end is the harmonium, always open and ready for an occasional tune; the bookcase is a really handsome one, with glass doors, standing on a chiffonier containing a large drawer and fine cupboard to hold large books, and other things.

It is easier to plan than to perform things, but, of course, when the work of the mint becomes easy and regular I shall begin to think of long walks, collecting Australian plants, etc. Returning to home matters, however pleasant life here may become, one does not look upon it for one moment but as temporary. Everybody talks of home, even, it is said, those who have been *born here*; but whatever other people do, home, you may depend upon it, *I* shall come in due time. These thoughts occur to me now more especially because last Wednesday or Thursday was the first anniversary of the day on which I left home. If other years pass as quickly as this seems to have done, and they will no doubt pass quicker, the time will not seem so far distant.

... By the by, very fortunately, the day before yesterday I found a delightful way to the town through woods and dales instead of along a dusty road. I start off in the wood at our back door, and walk through close tall gum-trees and over picturesque rocks for a full mile, when I come to a stream, an inlet of the harbour; this is crossed by a bridge formed of a large gum-tree which has been blown down and fallen across it, a long row of bullocks' *skulls* being laid in the mud as stepping-stones on one side: the view here along the stream is also quite pretty, at least to Australian eyes. Then another mile through bush land and trees brings me within a few hundred years of the omnibus stand at the end of the town. . . .[1]

66. W. S. JEVONS TO H. E. ROSCOE

Annangrove Cottage.
Sydney. July 11th 1855.

My dear Harry

Among a number of other pleasant letters from home by the last mail I found one from you which was very interesting, particularly as to your own movements in chemistry. I must really congratulate you on being at work upon such a first rate subject as the chemical action of light and two or three simple laws & facts about this well established are in my opinion worth any number of new complicated organic compounds. I do not understand what sort of an action it can be, as in the combination of Cl & H we should have heat i.e force liberated but from the gradual action of the suns rays it looks as if there was absorption of force from them. It hardly seems like the action of a *light* in exploding mixed gases. The preparatory action of the light on the mixture is very curious but quite conceivable; it must consist in a resolution of complex atoms of the separate gases into simple atoms or vice-versâ. I object however to having any more of these allatropic* substances in chemistry as they are a great bore, and I hope you will discover as few of them as possible.

Through the whole of science there is nothing that I should like to follow up more, & spend my whole life in than the *atomic theory* & theoretical chemistry, but my road seems to lie another way. Lately however a sublime idea (as I think it) occurred to me for the foundation of an atomic system, which would altogether beat Williamsons ideas; it is to suppose that the ultimate atoms of bodies (small spheres perfectly elastic & *similar* whatever element they form) are subject only to the force of *gravitation* which is thus made quite universal. Two spheres under the influence of each others attraction would approach & revolve (like double stars) round each other forming a compound atom of the first degree of complexity. Instead of two we may have any larger number, as in compound stars, of atoms revolving round the common centre of gravity, thus producing the different elements & explaining

[1] This passage recurs in Letter 72, p. 181. It is possible that when compiling LJ Mrs Jevons combined extracts from the two letters without indicating the separate dates.

the curious relations of the equivalents. Next, two of these compound atoms may revolve round each other, as wholes, like the planets *accompanied by their satellites* revolve round the sun, and these atoms of the second degree of complexity may combine (i.e revolve round each other) & form atoms of the third degree & so on.

You will easily see that this system would admit of an almost infinite number of combinations or compounds, while the variations of the speed of revolution and of the actual free motion of gaseous atoms, would correspond to the quantities of combined & sensible heat, and the increase of the orbits of atoms by increased speed would give the *dilatation* by heat. In solids the centre of gravities of the compound atoms being fixed at certain distances & positions with respect to each other, the planes of the orbits may be supposed parallel to each other and the faces of the primitive form. The orbits may then be affected variously in shape & size explaining unequal dilatability of crystals, and probably all sorts of *polar* forces. Of course atoms must come against each other sometimes, which is rather awkward, and I have got no idea of what would then take place in solids & liquids. In gases I believe two compound atoms meeting would appear to pass *through each other*, something like two *ghosts* each coming out at the other side of exactly the same form, but probably composed of different ultimate atoms which had been *exchanged* in contact. The mechanical properties, *diffusion*, dilatation specific heat &c &c of gases I am almost sure could be easily worked out mathematically on the supposition of these atoms freely *scampering* about each other in all directions under nothing but the force of gravitation. This is enough of my theory which I only tell you because it is tiresome to think of things without having a soul here to communicate them to.[1]

So you are going to invent a meteorological instrument upon your research on light, to measure the force of the chemical rays in the solar spectrum. I shall be only too glad to have any such instrument to observe with here as it is just the subject I am upon. I am setting up as complete a meteorological observatory as I can manage of the ordinary instruments. I can however only take two observations a day 9 am & 9 PM, with maxima & minima and am deficient on a great many points, such as the direction & force of the wind which I have no means of obtaining accurately & can hardly even guess at from the sheltered

---

[1] The idea of the force of gravitation explaining other phenomena beyond the motion of the planets was not a new one. C. L. Berthollet (1748–1822), in his *Researches into the Laws of Chemical Affinity* (Paris, 1801) (Engl. translation Farrell, Baltimore, 1804), thought that the forces responsible for chemical combination were gravitational in origin, and assigned differences between astronomical and chemical attractions to the different scale of distances at which they acted. However, it had been recognised for some time before 1855 that the chemical phenomena which Jevons is here discussing would require explanation in terms of repulsive as well as attractive forces.

position of the house. What I attend too* most is the *clouds*. The ordinary names for them (Howard's)² sound very well, but I believe them not to be altogether correct & philosophical so that I want to propose some alterations. I want to get too an idea of the causes of the forms of clouds, of the precipitation of rain & such like things.

I have also begun a little about solar & terrestrial radiation; at Church Hill I carried out some sets of observations of a radiating thermometer, throughout the 24 hours, so as to obtain curves of the variations which were curious. There seems to be no good instrument for the force of the suns rays at all but I have ordered out one called an Actinometer³ which seems a very clumsy affair. There really seems to be no means of measuring *terrestrial radiation*.

So Graham is *Master of the Mint* a grand title and the summit of his ambition I should think. It is an appointment which must give satisfaction everywhere & to everybody I should think. He will manage the Mint better than Sir John, for he must be more business like & practical & more acquainted with everything bearing on such things as coining & assaying.⁴

Capt Ward has hinted to us that as the first *pyx* of our sovreigns* is going home we might write to him and explain whatever we wished about the *assay* of them. I shall certainly do so for this, as well as in a friendly point of view to congratulate him.

What will the college do.

You are talking as usual about having no prospect of a good position, but it is impossible to see what you will get till some fine morning it turns up unexpectedly like my affair did. There is no chance of my remaining many years as an assayer and I dont know what I shall do then; I shall be more afloat than you ten times.

You will perhaps have heard something about my affairs, but I may

---

² Luke Howard (1772–1864), manufacturing chemist in London; made observations on the clouds from 1802 and first adopted the terms cirrus, cumulus, stratus and nimbus for rain cloud; from 1806 he kept a meteorological register; F.R.S. 1821. He published two important works, *The Climate of London*, 2 vols (1818–20); *Essay on the modification of clouds* (1830).

³ The results of Jevons's researches in this field were contained in his paper 'On a Sungauge or New Actinometer', published in the *Sydney Magazine*, August 1857. See below, Letter 107, n. 8, p. 297.

⁴ Thomas Graham took up the appointment on 27 April 1856. Neither of these two prominent scientists appears to have been regarded as a successful Master of the Mint. Craig says of Herschel: 'His rule at the Mint does not appear to have been happy' (op. cit., p. 323); of Graham: 'Graham's administration caused some unease' (p. 326). He adds 'The Treasury's comment on the mastership of the Mint in the light of the last twenty years' experience [i.e. 1851–69, from Herschel's succession until Graham's death] was that great scientific attainments "were not essential to the successful administration of the Department which depended rather upon an active and intelligent control and the application of well-trained experience in matters of business"' (p. 327).

as well tell you directly. Capt Ward as[5] obtained for both of us a fixed salary of £500, buying all our apparatus &c &c, and we are now on the same terms as any of the other Officers of the Mint. We shall soon have laboratories in the Mint. I live out here very comfortably with M^r & Mrs Miller having a little sitting room & bedroom and everything in fact as well as I could wish it. It is 4 miles from Sydney, therefore regularly in the country & surrounded by woods, but upon a turnpike road on which omnibusses* run continually to Sydney. By these we go a greater or less part of the distance, have a good days work in town at our offices, from about 10 to 5 oclock & then return to dinner. Bolton the assistant I brought out has also a salary of £150. Expenses however are very heavy here and we spend pounds like in England you spend shillings. Prices of all provisions have been undergoing one continual rise ever since we arrived and are now frightfully high. (price of bread risen 8^d to 1^s)

I have bought a *harmonium* here which stands in my room and is in my opinion an instrument on the whole equal to an organ of a much greater price & size. It is a first rate thing having a bit of music even in Australian wilds.

The Mint has now been at work about 2 months and moderately satisfactorily. The gold coined amounts to something above £50,000, and the Sovreigns* are passable though not equal to English coin in execution. I am more particularly acquainted with the standard of assay, of course, and we have not been without our difficulties in this, for Capt Ward brought out some pieces of Gold assayed at home and some of the English Trial plate &c with which we dont quite agree. We are all uncertain however whether after all we had not better trust to our own assay as we cannot conceive it wrong on any point. Yesterday & today as well as several times before, there have been frightful *mudges* in the assays, I mean they are wrongly placed so that we bring our results in different order, but Mr Miller & I are now quite convinced that the fault lies at the Mint not with us and if anything is said we shall kick up a jolly row; a fellow must stand on his own bottom here, in fact I am getting quite *colonial* (an expressive term not to be understood in England) which means being up to everything & everybody. You will be surprised what tricks we shall play you honest Englishmen, after living a few years among the thieves & convicts of N.S.W. This is not all joking either, for in living here, you necessarily become acquainted with numbers of convicts, particularly in the gold trade, who you know are no better than they were before but more cautious.

What a state the war news has got into; the taking of Sebastopol seems really no longer probable at least as they are now going on, and I

[5] Jevons appears to have omitted a word here.

dont think they will risk an expedition anywhere else considering the failure of this. How strange it is that there seems to be no person fit to make a minister in England, & no General to command.[6]

Having exhausted all my subjects I must conclude this letter. I hope you will write often to me as you are my only scientific correspondent, and I shall be glad if you will let me a little into the news of the chemical world, especially as to your own proceedings.

Remember me kindly to Aunt Henry when you have opportunity I often think of Oval Road, as of a very pleasant part of my life as yet.
    Believe me
      Ever your affec. Cousin
        W. S. Jevons.

67. THOMAS JEVONS TO W. S. JEVONS

p Biobio

Liverpool 14th July 1855

Dearest Stanley

A ship going direct ought to carry a letter and although I have only a very short time to devote to it yet I will fill that time up by stringing a few thoughts together. This is Saturday and in the afternoon I am going back to Lucy at Llangollen after having been all the week away from her. This has been the case ever since we had those Lodgings except for the first ten days. I have come away every monday* morning and returned every Saturday evening but I am now going to finish out my Lease at Llangollen stopping an entire fortnight all at once and as the regular mail will leave England before I return I shall endeavour to write you a letter from that quiet beautiful spot

I was at Birmingham on thursday* and called to see Roscoe[1] whom I found in excellent health and exhibiting signs of great pleasure at seeing me, and also at hearing me speak of you and the rest, but he is unable from his malady to make any reply in words. I do really believe however that he is improving in some respects, there is more thoughtfulness in the expression of his countenance and such an evident delight in the tenor of what I said to him that I could draw no other conclusion but that he is better than I have seen him for a very long time

The object of my visit to Birmingham was to attend the quarterly meeting of Iron Masters.[2] We see the whole of them assembled together

---

[6] An assault by the British and French on Sebastopol had failed in mid-June, with severe losses. Lord Raglan, the British commander, had died shortly afterwards. Palmerston had become Prime Minister in February; for the composition of his Cabinet see Woodward, op. cit., p. 665.

[1] See Vol. I, p. 8.   [2] See Vol. I, p. 120, n. 3.

and get information about the trade which we cannot get so well in any other way besides we frequently make our purchases of Iron at those meetings and settle matters which are better done in person than by letter. I both bought Iron and entered into arrangements for future business quite to my satisfaction and the meeting to me was a very cheerful and successful one

I dont know whether I ever told you that I bought a few shares about a year ago in a Silver Lead Mine in France called the Pontgibaud Mines under the management of John Taylor & Son of London I bought 10 Shares at £16 and £17 each and I have just got a dividend of £1 p Share the first dividend the concern has made. I am in hopes that it will turn out a good investment The ore is rich in Silver, at least some of the veins are, and they smelt it on the spot having a Coal mine on the same property and I dont see what is to prevent them making very large returns. You will recollect going to Newton Keats & Cos Lead works in Flintshire and seeing them turn out a splendid plate of Silver now if the Pontgibaud Mines C⁰ can raise the ore and the Coal on the spot and produce such plates of Silver as we saw in Flintshire I feel sure that it must become, when fully developed, a most splendid paying Concern. I have not yet seen the report of the Committee but expect a copy soon and if that seems to bear out the good impression I have of the undertaking I will invest a little more money in it as soon as I have any to spare. So you see notwithstanding my failure in the Poltimore Gold Mine I am not deterred from a new adventure in mining property but in a little more prudent way[3]

We are terribly busy at our old house[4] painting and papering it almost all over and to day we are getting out the old kitchen grate and putting in a most beautiful compact little range that beats any thing I have ever seen before.

[3] Cf. above, Letter 44, p. 94.   [4] Chatham Street, Liverpool.

There is a very small fire in the centre an oven on one side a roaster on the other and a boiler at back and this small affair will cook for 20 people at once The flame from the fire divides itself into three flues, one portion goes straight forward under the boiler B, another portion goes over the top of the roaster R down the side farthest from the fire, then under the bottom, and then up at the back and then touching the side or end of the boiler. Then the third portion of the flame goes round the oven O in the same way. H is the hot hearth which covers the top of the fire and of both oven and roaster and it has openings in it such as I have marked which have movable plates fitted in so that if you want to boil a kettle very rapidly take off the movable cover and your kettle is immediately over the top of your flame There is a small door over the grate bars ☐☐☐☐ it is a close door, when you shut this door the fire burns like a furnace, when you open it the fire burns very gently, when shut all the draft comes right through the coals when open you admit cold air over the top of the coals which immediately allays the strength of the fire. If you want to fry a bit bacon or cook a steak or chop you take off the movable cover over the top of the fire and then your Grid Iron is right over the fire The movable plate exactly over the fire consists of one plate within another so that you can uncover more or less of the fire in fact that plate is a large square one with a smaller round one in the middle and you[5] can either lift off the whole square or only the small round plate in the middle of the sqre The hot plate when the fire is in full force will make water boil on any part of it but the principal working part is of course direct over the top of the fire, in my sketch I have made the boiler project too much onto the hot plate it in fact only projects about 4 Inches leaving plenty of room for any kind of pot or pan you want to get right over the top of the fire I will try, on another paper to shew* you the flews* thinking that you may not understand the description very well

Llangollen Sunday 15th July Finding that the Biobio does not sail until tuesday* I have brought this letter over with me to this place to shew* Lucy and to add any thing more that I might think of. Lucy who knows nothing of the new kitchen range than what she has read and seen in this letter is quite delighted with it and says she thinks she shall turn Cook in order to enjoy the delights of such a beautiful cooking apparatus And here I might mention that that they have christened it by the name "*Kitchener*". It is a Kitchener that I have bought and described on the other side. In case you should be puzzled to know the difference between the Oven and the roaster I might mention that they are exactly the same in every particular except this that when in use a current of air is allowed to pass through the roaster whilst the oven as

[5] He included a small sketch here.

the name implies is entirely closed against the external atmosphere At the bottom of the door of the roaster there is a small apperture* with a register covering by which you can let in as much air as is necessary, about as much as will go through a half Inch pipe is enough, a corresponding outlet is made for the heated air and steam of the meat being roasted, at the top of the roaster and into the flew,* of course well guarded to prevent any of the smoke or sulfurous* matter from descending from the flue into the roaster, this exit apperture* is a small one also but can be adjusted by a damper to let out the gasses* faster or slower at pleasure so that you perceive that the meat which is being roasted in the inside of the roaster is surrounded with a changeable atmosphere just the same as it would be if turning round on a spit before the fire grate. The atmospheric air introduced through the small apperture* at the foot of the door becomes quite heated before it ascends as high as the meat which is placed on a Grid Iron shelf in the very centre of the roaster and there is a dripping pan under it just like as if it were before the fire, but the meat lies quietly on the grid iron as it is surrounded on all sides by air as hot as it can well be made. I might add that by means of the different dampers you can throw the whole of the heat & flame of the fire through one flue alone to the exclusion of the other two or you can work only two together or all three so that there is great power of forcing any one department to "ripen its produce" sooner than the others if necessary to do so. The last point I will mention is that none of the smoke or sulphur of the fire is admitted into the kitchen it all goes straight into the flues and is carried off into the chimney by the draft even when you lift off one of the appertures* in the hot plate it does not allow the smoke to come up for the air of the kitchen goes down it and then into the flues and all its effect is to check a little the draft* through the heated coals of the fire grate.

I think I answered your letter which told me of your being about to remove your lodgings and to live with Miller in Mr Grundys house on Paramatta Road[6] and the nice little sketch of the house which it contained. I lent the sketch for Mr Grundys Sister Mrs Boult to see, and through Mrs Boult in some way your Aunt Henry has heard of the sketch and having manifested a very strong desire to see the plan on your account Mrs Boult has sent it to her and they have kept it amongst them for a good while now, and I fear that I shall lose it. With reference to the plan the only thing I see wanting in it is a scale by which we could tell the size of each room without the scale we are left to mere conjecture and my plan was to estimate your lobby as 6^{ft} 6^{in} wide and so apportion all the rooms accordingly. And this reminds me that I have not mentioned any thing about the size of my Kitchener and indeed have not

[6] i.e. Annangrove Cottage.

drawn it to any scale at all, but I know that it is exactly 5 feet across the front which is the exact opening of the fire place in our kitchen and therefore it fills it up beautifully.

The country here looks lovely beyond compare We had a very severe winter which lingered on to an unusually late period and people began to think that we should have no summer but for the last month or six weeks we have had the most glorious weather for the country that could be desired copious and warm rains at first and since then dry and sunny days and every thing seemed to shoot into life just like magic. I declare that from week to week as I came through the country I could see everything on the fields at least 3 Inches taller than the week before In fact we have the promise of the most splendid harvest that has been garnered for many a year in old England (and Wales) They are busy every were* just now with the Hay, but the corn begins to change colour and instead of being a very late corn Harvest as was at first expected it gives promise of being ready very soon for the sickle. Fruit too of all kinds is most abundant and perhaps I shall surprize you not a little when I tell you that we had to day a desert* of wild strawberrys* which Tommy gathered in the edge* rows about this place. Though small in size they were very tasty and fully ripe and with a little sugar to them by no means to be despized*. I never saw a whole dish of wild strawberrys* in this country before though I have gathered here and there a few, but in France they are sold in considerable quantities in the markets and are valuable as being later than the cultivated plant. I have seen them in Paris two or three times as large as those we have gathered here

The time having now come for my determining something about Tommy I have made up my mind that he shall go to the London University and I will give Mr Green[7] notice when he returns to school that he shall remain only three months longer with him If your Aunt Henry should by that time have settled her plans and be willing to take Tommy I should be most glad to let him go to her but if she cannot take him we are thinking of writing to Rich Hutton to ask him to speak to Dr Carpenter[8] or some other person on whom we could depend to take him and *do* for him.

I shall be anxious to hear from you with an account of your final arrangements with the Government of N S W and with the starting of

---

[7] See above, Letter 59, n. 13, p. 143.

[8] William Benjamin Carpenter (1813–85) physiologist and naturalist, eldest son of Dr Russell Lant Carpenter (1780–1840), Unitarian divine. He was Professor of Medical Jurisprudence at University College, London, 1849–56 and subsequently Registrar, 1856–79, making an important contribution to the development of the University. An active Unitarian, he was at this time (1851–9) principal of University Hall, a post in which Richard Hutton had been his predecessor for a short time (cf. Vol. I, p. 80).

the Mint I hope you will send us a paper with the full account in it You may have sent us numerous papers but up to the present time we have only received three papers at the most When we get the paper that will announce the opening & working of the Mint and the Staff of the Mint all set out in order I shall eagerly look for your name and it strikes me to mention that as you and Miller are officers of the Mint you ought to have a *uniform* You must petition Government to furnish you with a red Coat and Sash and Epaulets* and a cocked Hat and feathers so that you may support the dignity of your Capt Ward and strike with astonishment all the beholders as you strutt* along the streets either going to or returning from the Mint Then as it is Gold which you will have to deal with your Uniform ought to be covered alover* with Gold Lace The uniforms of the officers of the Army ought to be nothing in comparison with yours who are an officer of the *Mint* and you ought to shine like a new sovereign just coined.

Monday 16th July – at Llangollen. We have a wet day to day which interfears* with the hay harvest but it is capital for the growing crops. To give you a proof of the extraordinary growth of vegetation I cut out of a hedge the other day a sapling from a briar or wild rose tree that was at least ten feet long all of this summers growth at the top it had branched off into some half dozen branches and each of these had shot out tender shoots which were about eight to ten inches long and covered with beautiful leaflets. I think in all my experience I never saw in England a more extraordinary growth for one Season It seems to me to be equal to the growth of the Corn Stalks of the Southern States of America but it was only a briar.

In this district of country there are some very ancient Yew Trees Lucy has made a drawing of one which I have not seen but there are several in a churchyard a few miles off that are larger and probably older than the one she has figured But a day or two since I went to look at an old stump of a Yew which though growing is made into a gate post It is cut down or has been blown down to a mere stump about ten feet high but crowned with a round green ball at top[9] It is decayed and holow* in some parts of it and we got out of the inside some pieces which might be called touch wood but they exhibited with great perfection the lines of growth of the tree The tree is about 4 or $4\frac{1}{2}$ feet in diameter at three feet from the ground and by measurement of the yearly lines we made out that the tree was 460 years old. It is strange that having been cut or broken down to so short a length and being hollow and decayed yet the ball at the top was one entire mass of foliage with young shoots of green yew spikes or leaves all round and apparently as healthy & vigorous as possible. I cut off a beautiful sprig which I wore

[9] A small sketch of the tree is given here.

in my buttonhole in honor* of the tree for the remainder of the day. I should mention that if the decayed pieces of the yew are swollen which I think not at all unlikely and that the sound part would shew* the lines of growth much closer together, that in that case the age of the tree must be calculated far more than I have named supposing the decayed wood to have swollen to double its original thickness then the age of the tree would appear to be nearly a thousand years I enclose a small piece or two of the decayed part of the tree and shall be glad to know if you think that this wood is or is not swelled from its living state

We have some neighbours come to live at the next farm house whom we would rather not have seen It is M^r & Mrs Husson. Mrs Husson was a Miss Tate, then she married a Mr Beal who died and Mrs Beal was a teacher of music and Henny went to her for a considerable time, but the last half year and since Mrs Beal has married again we have taken Henny away from Mrs Beal or Husson and put her to Mr Herman at which Mrs Husson was very indignant at Lpool and now she has come to confront us in our retreat which is not pleasant but I dare say we shall get over it The only other neighbour we have is Mr Freme of Lpool who has bought Pengwerne Hall a regular old farm House with some portions of it having pretentions to have been part of a monastery or something of that sort and he has got a considerable estate with it of which he farms a good deal himself I am executor to his Uncle John[10] so I know a good deal about Mr Freme but there is not much in him that I like still I make a merit of necessity and as I have no other acquaintance within reach I make the most of him which I suppose I may call true philosophy

And now I hope all this rigmarole will not tire you all out entirely but that bit by bit you may be able to get through it and if like a barn door fowl you can only pick a grain of wheat out of a bushel of straw I hope I may consider that I have not written this lengthy epistle in vain

You will gather from what I have said that we are all well and as one or two more of us are writing I need add nothing about the minutiae of domestic affairs but assuring you of the increasing love & affection I bear to you only heightened if possible by long absence in person and almost interminable distance in space

I remain Your aff^{te} Father & faithful friend
Thomas Jevons

---

[10] Probably John Rowden Freme, an influential member of Renshaw Street Chapel in its early days. He subscribed £500 towards its foundation and, like William Roscoe, was one of the original trustees. Cf. Evans, op. cit., pp. 8, 114.

68. W. S. JEVONS TO THOMAS JEVONS
[LJN, 52-3]

Annangrove Cottage, Sydney.
16th July 1855.

... The first good news as to money matters is Captain Ward's proposal of a fixed salary. To know that I have really accepted and received the salary of £675 would, of course, remove all your anxiety about my money affairs, for I have been getting very low in pocket. I have now, however, the pleasure of repaying instead of borrowing money, and am sending £180, which is as much of the £200 granted for back salary as I can well spare now. Before the end of the year I shall no doubt be able to send some more, particularly if we receive soon the £200 owing us for apparatus. I must say the money has given me very little satisfaction, except that of sending it home. Whether in the bank or in your pocket I find £100 like a very disagreeable weight upon the mind, so I shall be very glad when it is off my hands, though I hope safe in yours. I don't know whether I shall feel the same with respect to money always, but if so it is rather depressing. ...

We are not altogether without amusements here, and I have been several times lately to the theatre to see Brooke[1] act. I like a play now as well as anybody, but it involves a long solitary walk at night, which suggests revolvers and convict highwaymen.

I am telling you now, however, very little of the assaying. Even now, when so little gold is coming in, we are very hard worked; and if we had any large quantity of coinage we should require additional assistants. It is the common remark at the mint that the assayers are the hardest worked of any. We have also not been altogether free from anxiety about these sovereigns, but I have no doubt they will be all right. They are now getting quite commonly into circulation. ...

69. THOMAS JEVONS TO W. S. JEVONS

p^r James Baines   Liverpool 1 Augt 1855

Dearest Stanley

My two last letters to you were by the Biobio direct to Sydney and the Shalimar which took out the last regular mail. Since those letters

---

[1] Gustavus Vaughan Brooke (1818–66) an actor of Irish origin, who had little success on the London stage and made his career mostly in the provinces. He was at this time touring Australia where he made successful appearances in the principal cities; he had previously toured the United States. He was drowned in a shipwreck in the Bay of Biscay on his way to Australia for the second time.

were despatched your letter of the 22 April by the Red Jacket has come to hand. This letter is the most cheerful of any we have had from you since you first landed and has given us all the greatest pleasure You seem to be luxuriating in the thoughts of all the pleasures you anticipate from your change of residence and I dont wonder at it. You certainly must have suffered from being couped* up in such a small hot, stifling, room as that at Church Hill filled as it was with all your delectible* acids alkalies & ingredients of all sorts with a raging furnace and gass* lights heating the place to a temperature like that as described of the regions below. But you are out of it now and far off into the country where I trust you will soon get up your health and strength and so drive off that affection you have been troubled with of late which I firmly believe arises from weakness occasioned altogether from *over work* of body and mind. The anxieties you have gone through since you first received the proposition to take upon you the office of assayer to the Mint at Sydney have been sufficiently great of themselves to bear but when we add to them the immense labor* and pains you have indured* to work out the affair from first to last I am perfectly astonished that you have borne it all so well as you have done and I think we have all occasion to be grateful to our heavenly protector that you have not been cast down but on the contrary are now in a fair way to attain the fullest health and happiness that your constitution is capable of enabling you to enjoy.

You are very facetious in your letter now before me comparing the progress of the erection of your Mint with that made in the Seige of Sebastopol but bad as your Mint has been you have all out beaten the great operators in the Crimea That they will succeed in taking the town and Harbour of Sebastopol I make no manner of doubt but it will be a tough job yet. I have thought several times of sending you some plans of the Crimea and Sebastopol, but have not been moved sufficiently strong to do [so]¹ thinking that the print sellers of Sydney may very likely have them in their windows almost as much as we have them here. I have bought several plans one after another but the interest in them is a good deal abated since the works before the place are become so intricate that no plans can give us any adequate idea of them

Reading in one of our newspapers the other day I met with an account of a newly invented press for printing colours. It is the invention of a Yankee rejoicing in the euphoneous* name of Babcock.² It seems to me to be a clever machine and as I was very much pleased with the account

---
¹ Omitted in the original manuscript.
² George Herman Babcock (1832–93) American inventor and engineer. He was engaged upon daguerrotype and newspaper work until 1854, then invented the first polychromatic printing press in collaboration with his father, a well-known mechanic and inventor.

I cut it out and enclose it for your perusal and if you have a mind to enclose it to the Editor of the Sydney Herald I dare say he will be glad to insert it in his paper And this reminds me to suggest to you whether you could not turn to some account some of the different series o observations you have been marking out for yourself to take and register at your retreat at Amangrove* Cottage. If the Herald or any of the other papers have no corner for the record of such observations it is perhaps because there has been no one to furnish them and I suggest to you that you should offer for a fair remunerative consideration to furnish the same regularly at such stated periods as may be agreed upon. You know what these communications may comprize* much better than me but in fact you name many of them in your letter such as observations of the Thermometer & Barometer the Wind and Lightening* Conductor the rain gauge to which I might add the moisture and dryness of the atmosphere the tide table &c &c. I do not know how such communications are valued in money but every little will help and if they would give only 10^s/- a week for them that would be better than nothing but it is possible that a daily paper might give double that sum particularly if accompanied occasionally with some extended remarks

3rd August The days are slipping away and I have not been able to do any thing more towards finishing your letter but in fact I seem quite drained out and cannot trump up any news to tell you of. We are getting pretty comfortably settled at home again with our house burnished up and a splendid new carpet on our drawing room floor and all the pictures rearranged by Lucy most tastefully and most critically it would do your heart good if you could be here to see it but that cannot be and perhaps I am doing you no good by conjuring up thoughts of your old home in your memory thoughts which cannot for a long time to come be reduced to a reality either by you or me but we will live in hope that some day the time will arrive when you may be released and once more rejoice us with your presence But enough of this and I hope what I have said will not tend to make you melancholy You know we have all our duties to perform and our greatest happiness consists in performing them well and I feel sure that I can trust you to bear up manfully against your longing after home as I myself do my best to bear up against the privation which I have to bear in your absence so let us both rest happy in the thought that we are bearing our lot in life bravely and that we shall one day be rewarded to our hearts content.

I am sorry to tell you that the Poltimore Copper and *Gold* mining Comp^y is come to a very untimely end and with the loss to me of every penny I put into it if not worse. I enclose you a slip from the Northern Daily Times which contains the report of a meeting held here yesterday and which will tell you all that I know about it I do not send you the paper for I fear you do not get them as we certainly do not get all you send to us The paper which you say you send by the Red Jacket we have not received and in fact up to this time we have only received *two* newspapers from you

4 Aug at the Office – Turning over some papers this morning I find a letter from Graham dated July 1853³ which shews* that it is now 2 years since you were engaged in the Mint business. I think [that]⁴ the Govern^t or Captain Ward have used you very ill but of course they have it to say that you have been assaying for the public or might have been all the time. I think if the Mint does well *which I have no doubt it will do* you and Miller should never let Cap Ward rest until he gives you a fee for every assaye* beyond the £500 p an^m – I don^t think you should *strike* for it but I think you should *teaze** the Cap into it and don^t do too much for your £500, work slow and put on your hat at 4 oclock but if he will consent to give you 2/6 p assaye* as an additional fee or 2/- or if he will allow you to assaye* for the public giving you half profits for it in addition to your Salary that would answer and you & Mr Miller be equally interested any way that will increase your gains to nearly what was held out to you to induce you to go out to Sydney They certainly held out the hopes of your making £1000 p an^m and they ought to be made to make that up in one way or another

I have nothing more to say by this conveyance but remain
    Your ever aff^{te} Father
      Thomas Jevons

70. THOMAS JEVONS TO W. S. JEVONS
              Liverpool 26 Aug 1855

Dearest Stanley

I am going to start tomorrow on a long talked of journey to Paris Switzerland and Italy on which I expect to be away between two and three months and therefore it is that I sit down to write to you now which otherwise I should not have done just yet because I have written to you three or four letters recently¹ and all since I received one from you and that is above a month since and your letter is dated so far back as the 22 April. Since its receipt however we have had one recognition of you which you will be gratified to hear of we have received the Sydney

---

³ This letter is not among the Jevons Papers.
⁴ The page is torn here.

¹ Only one of these – the letter of 1 August 1855, Letter 69 above – is among the Jevons Papers.

Almanac[2] which you have sent and Ann[3] has received a box of insects They were brought here a few days since by a Mrs Heathcote whom I did not see and I cannot find that she communicated much news about you or at any rate recent news as she had been in England some time before she got to Lpool She only stopped a very little time in our house as she was in a hurry to go somewhere but promised to call again and this is all the account I had I thank you very much dear Stanley for this remembrance and can assure you that I was not long before I had looked into every page of the book, though a mere almanack* to gather every bit of information about your new country that I could gather from it. Sydney seems a very important place even if we allow for a sort of tact which they seem to have of making the most of every object & subject that they can turn into a Company or establishment or board Counsel* or Committee or Government &c &c No doubt many of the associated bodies enumerated in the Almanac are really useful bodies and do honor* to the country and to the individuals that compose the Committees and some day I make no doubt I shall see your name figure as one among them but perhaps you will answer to this as the Song says "There is time enough for that say I". The box of Insects you sent for Ann or which Charles sent for we do not know which sent it is a most interesting present We admire the Grasshopper a good deal but it is the Locusts that interest us most. A flight of such animals (I will call them) of many miles in extent and so dense as to cause darkness on the land must on alighting in any country destroy every thing that the Husbandman has labored* to produce and in fact must breed a famine in the land. That such an effect does take place in some countries is true because it is recorded in Scripture and we know something of it from the experience of James Jevons[4] at Natal and indeed Herbert saw a flight of Locusts come over James Jevons farm while he was on a visit there, but I trust that this devouring Insect does not swarm in such clouds in your adopted country as I have never heard much said against them. Indeed from what Herbert says your Locusts are rather a genteel sort for they are neither so large nor so ugly looking and consequently not so voratious* as the African Locusts. If I am at home when Mrs Heathcote calls again I shall question her more about these insects and the book and yourself and Charles than any of the others have done you may depend.

I think I have told you in a former letter something about our journey

[2] *Ford's Australian Almanac for the year 1851 (−54)* (Sydney, 1851–3); continued as *Waugh and Cox's Australian Almanac for the year 1855(−56)* (Sydney, 1855–6); continued as *J. Cox & Co's Australian Almanac for 1857* (Sydney, 1857); continued as *Waugh's Australian Almanac for 1858 (−62)* (Sydney, 1858–62); further continued as *The Australian Almanac for the year 1863 (−68, 70)* (Sydney 1863–70). Cf. below, Letter 128, n. 8, p. 363.

[3] Anne Bolton. [4] See above, Letter 41, n. 7, p. 78.

but I will repeat it by way of duplicate. Our party as far as Paris will consist of your Aunt Timothy[5] Mary Catherine[6] and Frederick[7] & Lucy and myself We shall stay a week or ten days in Paris from which place your Aunt Timothy & Fred return Home but me and Lucy and Mary Catherine go on via Strasburgh* into Switzerland cross the Alps by the Splugen Pass into North Italy and we hope to visit Genoa Venice Leghorn Rome and Naples and all the principle* Towns on the route generally visited by travellers (Dont you wish you could go with us) It is a journey I have long fostered in my mind both on business account and likewise for the instruction and enjoyment I cannot fail to reap from it the only draw back is the great sum of money that it will cost but I trust that it will be amply returned to us and that we shall never have Cause to regret the expenditure. When at the Paris Exhibition I shall look out for the 51 specimens of Gold from N S W and I shall glote* upon them as being assayed by you and perhaps forgive Cap Ward that he has not paid you for your trouble nor even for the silver & lead and acid consumed in the assaying to say nothing of the gass* & water &c &c &c

Our Queen you know has been in Paris for a week or rather she is there *now* but is to leave there tomorrow and during her stay there Paris has been *too* full or say *two* full, that is double filled, but I must leave you to gather all news about her visit from the papers only saying that it is perhaps the most wonderful exhibition of popularity, of welcome, of splendour and of gorgeousness of reception that the world ever saw[8] she will have left a week about before we get there so I hope she has cleared some room for us lowly as we are

When I am in Paris I mean if possible to get you a specimen of the new metal Aluminium as it is said that some medals are to be struck off with this metal and if they are and not outrageously dear I will buy one for you but *dont expect it until you see it*. Instead of the metal itself I send you enclosed a description of the way to make it and perhaps you will be able to send me a specimen of it of your own making before I am able to send you one

Lucy had a great escape going to Englefield The train got off the rails and the engine after knocking down a wooden bridge ran up the side of or rather into an embankment smashing itself very much and the tender and next carriage or two were overthrown and broken and many of the passengers hurt but none seriously. Lucys carriage though next

[5] See above, Letter 12, n. 3, p. 26
[6] See above, Letter 59, n. 4, p. 141.
[7] See above, Letter 56, n. 20, p. 132.
[8] Queen Victoria was on a state visit to the Emperor Napoleon III, who had been entertained at Windsor a few months earlier. The exchange of visits and accompanying jubilations celebrated the *rapprochement* of England and France, now allies in the Crimean War.

to one that was upset yet kept upright & Lucy was not hurt at all She was thrown upon an elderly Lady who sat opposite to her and that I suppose saved her. Lucy had a small bottle of wine with her which was a most fortunate thing for she and the old Lady were wonderfully revived by it, without the help of the *Dozen* Doctors who were soon on the spot to pick up a job but who had to go away again rather chap fallen. I suppose you will be smashing away on the Sydney & Paramatta* Railway before long.[9] They ought to bring that R R smack down past the mint so as to serve to take you every day to your Country Lodgings or to Amand* Cottage as you call it, it ought to be Almond Grove Cottage which would be a sweeter name, but whats in a name as Juliet says you may be as contented and happy in a cottage if you have a happy disposition no matter what the name may be which I hope you will have found out before this line meets your eye

You will be sorry to hear that Mrs Swayne Mary Bentleys niece is seriously ill. She has had an abscess in her thigh and that being stopped it has turned to dropsy and I fear it may be said to be only a matter of time for her departure, for a cure is I fear out of the question The doctors have said that they can do nothing more for her but recommend generous living and she being without the means and her relatives also I send her every day a dinner from my own table She is a person whose industry and patience I have long wondered at and admired and I have a real pleasure in selecting the most delicate parts of the joint for her comfort and support from day to day

We have told you of Dick Roscoe being at Laces office.[10] His time is just up there and Mr Lace has offered him £100 a year to remain longer and so Dick has accepted it You know of course that he lives with his Sister Poppy or Mrs James Thornely as I should call her now as she is the mother of two children and by the by I should tell you that Henry Jevons has got a second daughter[11] and Eliza Mrs Barham[12] has got a Son & heir and so the world is you see being peopled fast enough by different branches of our family.

I called over the water this afternoon to see your Aunt William and Annie[13] Your Aunt looks but indifferent well Annie was not at home.

[9] The railway was completed in September 1855.
[10] Jevons's cousin Richard Roscoe (1833–92) third son of Robert Roscoe of Englefield Green; also educated at University College School, he was admitted a solicitor in 1857 and became a partner in the London firm of Shaen and Roscoe (now Shaen, Roscoe and Bracewell). Ambrose Lace, a Liverpool solicitor, was distantly related both to himself and to Jevons. See above, Letter 24, n. 5, p. 44.
[11] Henry Jevons had married Susanna Thornely (1830–1915) in 1853; they had six sons and six daughters, the second of whom was Elizabeth (1855–1921).
[12] Cf. above, Letter 46, p. 103.
[13] The wife and daughter of Thomas Jevon's brother William Jevons, Junior; see above, Letter 12, n. 5, p. 26.

Your Uncle & Aunt and Annie are going down to Brighton again to spend all next winter for Annies sake but I fear she will never be strong enough to spend a winter in these northern regions and they must either migrate hence every winter or leave Lpool altogether which is a melancholy thing to think of on account of the Cause.

Well now havnt* I spun you a good long yarn just before my departure I have done it to make up for any deficiency in letter writing during my journey but if I am unable to write you may rest satisfied that the scenes I shall go through will not drive the thought of you away from my mind but the more intensely they may affect me the more shall I think of you and my heart will yearn to my far distant Son with the strongest desire that he could enjoy with me in reality the wonderful works of God that will be before me and which can be enjoyed the more in the company of those we best love

   Your ever aff^{te} Father & faithful friend
       Thomas Jevons

71. THOMAS JEVONS TO HENRIETTA JEVONS

         à Paris rue de Lille 59
          2nd Sepr 1855

My Dearest Henny

I hope you will pardon me for not writing before to you but as business with me has been the great moving cause of my journey I have felt it a duty to devote my first actions and first letters to it but this being Sunday I have no call to business and can therefore with every freedom sit down and converse a little with you my Dearest Henny.

I dare say Lucy will have written to you many particulars of our Journey so that I will only just run rapidly over the few stages. On coming up to London I had some agreeable companions in my carriage one of whom shewed me a diamond worth £7000 what a splendid jewel it was. The owner was going to Paris to try to sell it to the Emperor but whether he has effected his sale or not I do not know for I have not met him since I came to Paris. Your Aunt & Cousin Mary Catherine and Lucy joined me on the day appointed in London say last Wednesday and on Thursday we went down to New Haven a small port about 3 miles from Brighton and took the packet for Dieppe where we arrived by half past four. The sea was as calm as we could wish, the day splendid we had an excellent Lunch on board about noon and when we arrived at Dieppe we found the *Table dhote* ready spread and for the first day in France we enjoyed a regular French dinner

A French Dinner is so different to ours that I will try shortly to describe it. The most important dishes are put on the table as in England but no one touches them, but they are there only that you may see some of the things that are for dinner in their turn. The dinner begins with the waiters bringing every one a small dish of soup*. Then as soon as you have eaten that, they bring you a small bit of boiled meat with Sauce covering it, and you either take that or not as you like and besides the sauce there are potatoes on the table and they hand round other vegetables to eat with the meat. After the boiled meat they bring you a small plate of fish In Dieppe this was excellent and the sauce to it also. After the fish they brought you a bit of chicken with sauce also – Then a bit of duck with some green pea sauce Then a plate of calves head ached [sic] with sauce Then a delightful plate of pudding then a bit of Lobster and then cheese and by that time I felt as if I had had enough but we had a little fruit which was all about the table and we helped ourselves to that and then we had a bottle of Bordeaux wine and a bottle of Seltzer Water to wash it all down and thus we made our first dinner at a Table d'Hôte in Dieppe We have dined since even more grandly than that at Rouen and as soon as I finish this letter we shall hurry out to some Table d'Hôte at Paris where we shall probably be treated more magnificently still –

We got to Rouen the same evening and found good accommodation at the first Inn we called at. Rouen is an extraordinary old Town It has two very Grand Cathedrals and a remarkable church about 2 or 3 miles out of the Town on the top of a high Hill overlooking Rouen and the plain in which it is placed and the river as it winds through the plain with its beautiful islands that studd* it like gems of emeralds. This church the true & faithful Catholicks* of all parts are subscribing to redecorate and it is in the inside one mass of Gold or rather Gilded ornaments and golden stars on a deep blue ground except one end which is deep green and Gold. The windows are all stained glass and the whole is so gorgeous that it puts religion entirely out of your head and you rather think that you are in the Theatre with a gorgeous glittering scene before you made as fine as the eyes can bear to look upon It has one good effect however for as soon as you get out of this bedizzened temple of mans device a temple of nature opens itself to your astonished gaze lovely beyond all description and truly elevating your thoughts to him who has given to us this glorious earth to live in and filled it with a boundless harvest of all that is needful and good and this is heightened by the contrast with the puerile work of man which he is exhausting all his art to lure the weak to admire & *subscribe to.*

We left Rouen at 2 oclock yesterday afternoon and arrived in Paris at 5. The road runs in the same direction as the river Seine which we

* The dishes are taken off the table and cut up and carved by the Landlord at a side table.

have in view a large portion of the way. It is truly a rich valley the entire way studded by many Towns and Chateaux and the hills which receede* at some short distance from the river are covered with viniards* and orchards; and the whole way you are filled with delight at the beautiful prospects which continues [sic] even more beautiful as you approach the great metropolis of this Kingdom.

As soon as we could get our baggage passed at the Station we got into a Car and drove direct to Stanleys old Lodgings where we have found rooms that are satisfactory and not dear but the only thing we did not expect was that they do not cook dinner here so we shall have to go to a Table d'Hote somewhere every day to dine.

We went and heard High Mass at Le Madelaine* for about an hour This building in the inside is very much like our St Georges Hall though not so large after that we have been to the Statue Gallery and the Museums at the Louvre which has rather tired us and so we have come back home to rest a little before we sally forth to hunt for a dinner

We have only seen the outside of the Chrystal* Palace[1] as yet for they say it is very crowded on a Sunday so we shall begin that probably tomorrow We have not yet heard anything of Fred but have been hunting after him at various places I am desirous he could come as early as he can that I may have time to look out for business Well now I think I have told you about the one hundredth part only of what we have seen and done and must leave the ninety & nine for Lucy to relate but I must reserve to myself to say, if I *can* tell, what is the depth of the affection I have for and shall ever hold to

   My ever cherished daughter
    Your most aff^{te} Father
     Thomas Jevons
Love to Tommy & Herbert

72. W. S. JEVONS TO HENRIETTA JEVONS

September 9th 1855.
Petersham. Sydney.

Dearest Antipodal Sister,

For you see I return the complimentary manner in which you address me, – your letter received some time since with the others gave me the greatest possible pleasure, and I never remember to have received a nicer one from you. I do not much like writing letters and am never

---

[1] The Paris Exposition of 1855 was housed in the 'Palais de l'Industrie' on the Champs Elysées, a structure of glass and wrought iron encased in classical façades of white stone, larger than the Crystal Palace. It was the intention of the Emperor Napoleon III to present a brilliant spectacle that would surpass the Great Exhibition of 1851.

satisfied with them when done, but this quiet Sunday evening I must have a little chat with you whether I write anything worth reading or not.

One thing which naturally occurs to be mentioned is my birth-day, which passed over here like any other day, but of course it occasioned reflections which are natural on that day. Time indeed is passing on fast enough and already I have left home more than a year. They always seem to me precious years that are passed away from home and I hope that what one gets here will turn out worth the expenditure.

Time also will be changing you and I dont know whether I shall be glad or sorry when I see you again for you to be so much older, and so much improved as you will be. On this point your letter was particularly satisfactory to me and I have no doubt that what you express a wish to do, you will not fail to do.

I am no doubt generally supposed to have come out here on a money making errand, and it is certainly my intention to pick up here as much of the precious metal as I can conveniently get, but I think it would be very short-sighted[1] policy in me or in any other of my age or older.

To spend every moment in money-getting and lay by every farthing you get is to impoverish your own means even so far as money-getting is in question; for a little time and money judiciously expended in other things is like manure to a field, and enables you afterwards to reap ever so much more.

It is a great thing is *Progress* and I have adopted that idea as the foundation of my whole philosophical system. It is progress alone which in my opinion constitutes all human happiness and all men however good or bad can only obtain happiness by being progressive. It is like the barometer in which you must regard only the risings and fallings the stationary points being of little consequence. Take the best of men and if one day he feels that he has stood still and is not better than yesterday, he will be unhappy compared with the worst of men who had made one step in advance. As a sort of illustration, it has always appeared to my mind an impossibility to conceive what *happiness in Heaven* can be like, for as when you reach there, you must be at the top of the tree, or at least all exertion must cease, there can be no furthur* real progress which is not at all an inviting idea.

This theory of mine also explains the unanswered question of "Is the World any happier than it was", with all its steam engines electric telegraphs, great guns &c &c. It is simply this; the happiness is in the *acquisition* not the *possession* and that age which produces the *greatest proportion* of improvement and progresses most is the happiest.

You must excuse such a long sermon about such a dry subject, and I must say I do not see its connexion with the rest of my letter.

[1] Jevons wrote 'sighed' here.

See however if it is not true, for instance in your music in which I have no doubt you are progressing as fast as ever you did.

I stick to music just as much as ever, in fact it seems necessary to me, and I should never get on without it. I am altering my style a little, playing quicker sacred pieces as well as opera airs &c. I am beginning to think psalm tunes rather *heavy* and *slow*. I may almost say that now I go to the play or opera *often* and I enjoy the music and acting very well. I think it neither a waste of time or money so long as the play is the real object. The theatres here take a much higher place than they do for instance in Liverpool, and supply the place of the Philharmonic and such things. I have seen Miss Hayes[2] twice, the first in Sonnambula,[3] where as I have before said it was altogether splendid and since in an English Opera, the "Bohemian Girl"[4]; She did it as well as before, but the performance otherwise was much inferior. I am looking forward to some amusement from seeing it announced that "those celebrated *artistes* M^r & Mrs *Clarance* Holt[5] will shortly appear". I saw them soon after they arrived displaying themselves in George Street in state, in order to create a *sensation* but they will find themselves much mistaken as the Sydney people know what's what.

I am amused at my father mentioning in his letter, my "mangy old dog" as he calls it; however the[6] dog is quite well and gives us an immense deal of entertainment. He is named "Crucible", and is one of the handsomest dogs in Sydney though very simple-minded. He generally comes a part of the way to town with me in the morning then runs off and amuses himself during the day in the villages, bathing &c.

By the bye,* very fortunately, the day before yesterday I found a delightful way to the town through woods and dales instead of along a dusty road. I start off in the wood at our back door and *walk* through close tall gumtrees and over picturesque rocks for a full mile when I come to a stream, an inlet of the harbour; this is crossed by a bridge formed of a large gum tree which has been blown down and fallen across it, a long row of *bullocks skulls* being laid in the mud as stepping stones on one side; the view here along the stream is also quite pretty, at least to Australian eyes. Then another mile through bush-land and trees brings me within[7] a few hundred yards of the omnibus stand at the end of the town.[8]

---

[2] Catherine Hayes (1825–61), a popular Irish soprano; after studying in Dublin, Paris and Milan she made her début at Marseilles in 1845; she toured Europe before appearing in London in 1849; she left shortly afterwards for a tour of America, India, Australia and Polynesia, returning to England in 1857.
[3] Bellini: *La Sonnambula* (1831).   [4] Balfe: *The Bohemian Girl* (1843).
[5] See Vol. I, p. 106, n. 3.   [6] Jevons wrote 'he'.   [7] Jevons wrote 'with'.
[8] There is a pencilled sketch map, now too faint for legible reproduction, at this point in the letter.

Sept 17th. Yesterday (Sunday) and the day before, we had what is very unusual here, rainy weather, but it is what you may call real rain and none of your drizlling* dirty English weather. $4\frac{1}{2}$ inches deep fell in three days which it would take you about two months to get together in England. On Saturday I had to walk right through it into town which I resolutely accomplished in my waterproof carrying a bundle of dry clothes to change immediately on arrival, and the same coming home. Umbrella's are not popular in Australia, and in rainy weather almost everybody appears completely and ingeniously enveloped in waterproof clothes and the abundance of oilskin and water give the streets quite a *fishy* appearance.

Today the weather is beautiful again, and you can hardly imagine how pleasant the air is here generally, particularly in the winter half of the year, which is the best in this part of the world.

My dog "Crucible" ran away a week or two since and we now call him all sort of names for his faithlessness. I discovered his new abode, but the people refused to give him up and I have not taken any more trouble to get him for I only found him myself. Mrs Miller's dog "Flask" also ran away and as there was only left "Billy" the bull-dog and "Bobby" the lap dog (a little white haired animal) Mr Miller brought home another fierce little animal to act as watch. Billy seldom barks or gives notice when people come about, for it would spoil his game, and he reserves himself patiently for a tremendous spring at them with the hope of having a good bite. The new little dog is the bark and wakes[9] us at night. There are a great many little chicks now out, and some young ducks expected but I take little interest in these.

Today has been a whole holyday,* which every other Monday is with each of us, but I have done little but take a walk through the wood to Johnstones Bay, cut a little fire wood, read &c.

Have you ever heard of the celebrated Lola Montez.[10] She has been acting here, and a little time since I went to see her out of curiosity. I was altogether astonished to see what a beautiful woman she was, and she acted a part of her own life. However she has proved herself to the Sydney people as bad as ever for being in debt several £1000 she wanted to run off to Melbourne; but Mr Brown[11] the bailiff came on board the steamer just as she was starting to take her up. What do you think Lola Montez did but go to bed immediately and Mr Brown after trying all

---

[9] Jevons wrote 'wake'.

[10] The stage name of Marie Dolores Eliza Rosanna Gilbert (1818–61), adventuress and 'Spanish' dancer; gained international notoriety through her association with King Ludwig I of Bavaria, with whom she was exiled in 1848; danced and acted in America, 1851–3, then in Australia; she spent the rest of her life in America.

[11] Probably Thomas Brown, principal Sheriff's bailiff, Sydney, 1847; Supreme Court bailiff, Sydney, 1851–65.

sorts of ways found himself baulked everywhere and had to go back without her as the steamer had already got some distance out to sea.

I am sure I have written you enough for some time now, and this page must be the last.

Remember me particularly to Ann and dont let her think I forget her; also to Mary Bentley, Ann Salisbury[12] and anybody else.

With best love to all I am as ever
Your affec Brother
W. S. Jevons

73. THOMAS JEVONS TO W. S. JEVONS

Rue du* Lille 59
Paris 9 Sep 1855

Dearest Stanley

Behold where I am at this moment domiciled and have been for the last week. I am accompanied by Lucy & your Cousin Mary Catherine and what will perhaps astonish you more by your Aunt Tim^y and Fred. The last named have taken advantage of our coming through Paris in order that they may see the great Exhibition as well as ourselves they however will return to England whilst my self and Lucy & Mary Catherine will proceed onward through Switzerland and into Italy where we are looking forward to spend about two months. But I ought to explain that I am led to take this Journey in the hopes of extending our connections in Business and it is at the expense of the firm that I go whilst Timothy and me pay for our daughters out of our own pockets. To see all the sights of Paris in a week including the exhibition you will know to be impossible so we only glance over the chief objects of attraction. The Exhibition in some things excels the London Chrystal* Palace Exhibition though as a whole it might be pronounced secondary to it. In paintings it is far beyond us. The tapestry and china are also very superior and likewise the furniture But what has surprized* me most of all is the perfection of the Machinery which is exhibited, and from all the principle* States in Europe except Russia. The discovery of Railroads and steam boats seems to have set every nation to work to learn the art of making these invaluable and now almost universal machines of Locomotion and all of them having had our example to follow have made vast strides in the art of constructing them and this has led them to cultivate the manufacture and workmanship of Iron generally in which they seem to have great success. I made a particular point of going to the quarter where the productions of N S W are exhibited

[12] The Jevons children's nurse.

hoping to see your specimens of Gold but I failed in that as the Gold specimens were lodged in some more secure place which I could not find out I shall have another try if I possibly can before I leave

I admire the *wood* of N S W extremely It seems to me to beat all other Countries quite outright Those woods which particularly struck me are the Beef Wood, Forest Oak, Blackwood, the Myalaccasia, and the *Tree Fern,* the latter a great curiosity. The shew* of wood is very large and numerous from all parts of the world Canada Brazil, West indies,* East Indies and from most States in Europe and though they have no doubt all done their best yet to my judgment N S W bears off the palms –

In all the turmoil of this place I have not forgotten your Mint affairs. I called there yesterday and saw Mr Levol,[1] with two or three who seemed to be under him In the place where we first saw him there was a melting pot almost close to the door on the left hand side, it seemed to have been just emptied as the lid was off and it was of a cherry red heat inside. We made ourselves known who we were, for you must be informed that Mary Katherine* went with me as interpreter, and what we came for and when they comprehended us they said your things they thought were sent away to some other place but they would have a search. So while they searched they put Mary & me into another room or office it is the room where there hangs on the wall a specimen of a Gold Coin a 40 fc piece of an old french King with the weight written upon it[2] I dare say you will know the room from this description Mr Levol soon came to us again saying that the things were not at the Mint but that he would get them and bring them to our Lodgings which he did in the evening viz the deploman* and a steel die. The deploma* I will inclose* in this letter and the die I will take the first opportunity of sending by hand or in a parcel but I will give you an impression of the die below that you may feel quite convinced that it is in my possession I inquired for Mr Peligo*[3] but he had gone into the country

Now I did not stop at this success but asked Mr Levol where I could get a specimen of Aluminium which after a good deal of trouble I was enabled to obtain from Mr Rousseau[4] rue de l'ecole de Medecine I could not obtain it as a medal but have got a small square lump for which I paid 24 f^{cs} and as the price is 3 f^{cs} p^r Gram so you will see that

---

[1] Cf. above, Letter 37, n. 5, p. 71.
[2] In the original manuscript there is a small drawing to illustrate the coin.
[3] See above, Letter 34, n. 4, p. 61.
[4] Emile-Pierre André Joseph Rousseau (b. 1815), chemical manufacturer; received medals at the Great Exhibition, 1851, and the Paris Exhibition, 1855; before founding the firm in 1843 he had been apothecary to the Faculté de Médécine, lecturer in chemistry at the École Centrale des Arts et Manufactures and Professor of Chemistry at the École d'Enseignment Supérieur de la Ville. Cf. *Annuaire des Notables Commerçants de la Ville de Paris* (1861), p. 157.

I have got 8 Grammes I will take the first opportunity I can of getting it rolled out and will send you half of it

Since writing the above I have taken an impression of the die and find it a very bad one indeed in fact it is no go!

I am now off to Varseilles!!* and tomorrow morning at 6 oclock to Strasburg*

Your aff^{te} Father
Thomas Jevons

dear Stanley

I am writing you a letter which I shall send by the next opportunity dear love to you. I often think of you in these lodgings – LAJ.[5]

74. THOMAS JEVONS TO HERBERT JEVONS

Faido Canton Tessin
25 Sep 1855

My Dear Herbert

I have concluded that you would read all the letters I have sent home to whomsoever addressed, and therefore have not made any particular point of addressing one to you; but now I will do so because I have got a subject to write about which however it may carry me away in enthusiastic feelings arising from the sublimity of the sights I have seen yet it is quite sure that no expressions that can be used can come up to the reality of the impressions these sights are capable of raising We have passed the Summit of the Pass of St Gothard and are got so far as the town above named on our way to the Italian plains But I will begin and give you a succinct account of our last two days journeying and write it as soberly as I possibly can –

We started yesterday morning at 5 30 by the Steam Boat from Lucern* to Fluellin* a distance of about 30 miles. At Lucern* the scenery is extremely beautiful but of a softened expression because the lofter* mountain region is more distant but as we proceed along the Lake we approach every mile nearer and nearer the grande* mountains which vastly increases the interest you cannot help feeling in the absorbing views. But to give you a sort of tangible description which will bring what I wish to describe to you more accurately to your vision I must refer you to the two pictures in our drawing room one of Lugano the other of Como and then you must conceive that the upper end of Lucern* Lake is grander than those views represent in as much as the

---

[5] Lucy Jevons wrote this across the left-hand side of the first page of the letter.

mountains about Lucern* rise to the height where perpetual snow abides. Many spots at the upper end of the Lake are memorable from their having been the site of the glorious deeds of William Tell.

There was a scene on the Steam boat which I think worth mentioning as shewing* some insight into the character of one class at least of the Swiss people. A party of Soldiers five in number were passengers to their homes on furlow.* These men inspired by the delight of revisiting their homes struck up a Swiss air or two they all joining and singing different parts The effect seemed to excite them more and more and for at least half an hour they poured out a succession of national airs which were listened to very attentively by most of the passengers. They sung with great feeling & correctness and the time & place and occasion added greatly to its effect.

On the arrival of the boat at Fluellin* we had no difficulty in hiring a carriage and horses to take us all the way from Fluellin over the Pass and down to Belinzona* for the round sum of 100 francs allowing us to stop at as many places on the way as we like so we soon had our Luggage strapped on behind a regular travelling chariot and putting down the top entirely we started for the Pass

For the first hours drive we go through a rich and beautiful valley the road being lined on each side with Walnut Trees in full bearing. Gradually afterwards the sides of the valley draw closer and the mountain sides that are visible are higher & become clothed with fir trees chiefly. This kind of scenery deepens more and more as you progress until at length it resembles the pictures which I have seen of Norwegian scenery and again I will refer you to a palpable representation by desiring you to look at the engraving of Norwegian scenery in our bookcase and you will see there scenes which we actually realized yesterday

But on proceeding higher up the Pass we get beyond the region of firs to what I might aptly name the region of the everlasting Rocks. The valley itself has become here little else than the bed of a torrent and the granite rocks rise on each side to a height of some 6 or 8000 feet and for a considerable distance on one side we had what may be called a perpendicular wall of rock of 1500 to 2000 feet high

We reached a village called Hopital* last evening where we slept and which is placed at an elevation of 4000 feet from the Sea which is nearly the same as if we were to sleep at the top of Snowdon We found it very cold and the Ladys* had a stove lighted in their rooms

The rise from Lucern* to Hopital* through all this craggy defile is 2000 feet and for a very large portion of the way it is effected by means of zig zags the road being supported on one side by a wall not very unlike our dock walls and the other side against the rock or bank of the Hill. The road in this upper region is in fact a series of raised terraces made expressly to ease the ascent or rather to make it passable at all by carriages and I should not be far out if I said we had passed up & down above 100 turns as sharp or nearly so as "right about face" and yet with all these aids the rise of the road is hardly ever less than 1 foot in eight as far as I could calculate.

Now I will try to give you some idea of one or two of these zig zags* Starting at a in this sketch and following the line I have drawn rising 1 in 8 every inch of the way you will be perhaps *50 yards* more forward in your journey as the crow flies and probably 200 feet higher in elevation or perhaps 150 feet higher When at b you look down to see where you have passed you see every one of those turns & zigzags below you There are some of the turns far more singular than the above but they would look so very curious on paper that you would hardly believe them to be a true representation

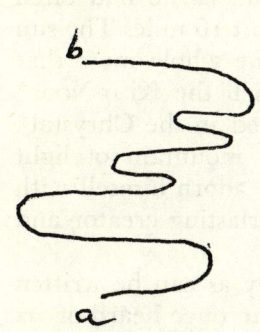

At Hopital* you are about half way up and here and here only on this Pass road is there a little level drive of about a mile or so and some little meadow land is seen We had pretty good entertainment for the night with three other travellers who staid* there also One was Sir Wm Young Bart[1] a youth of about 16 or 17 with his tutor The Revd Mr Stillingfleet[2] and the other was a rather pompous Irishman one of the Guinnesses of Dublin whom the young Baronet facetiously dubbed the Stout Gen^m meaning the Gent^m who makes "Stout" or porter.

The rise from Hopital* to the summit of the pass is more steep, more zig zag, more rocky, and more desolate. We have here to ascend 2500 feet in a much less space than the 2000 below Hopital,* and consequently the torrent by our side all the way is one succession of waterfalls nearly all the way thus heightening the sublimity of the scene more than I can describe. Well when you are at the top you would think you would see something quite different to what you have passed over for so many hours of uphill work but here you would be mistaken The mountains on each side of you seem to rise quite as high about you as they appeared to do when you were 4,500 feet lower down in elevation you see a little more of the snow about the summits than you could below but they are

[1] Possibly William Mackworth Young (1840–1924), not himself a baronet but younger brother of Sir George Young (1837–1930) of Formosa Place, Cookham, Berkshire, who had succeeded as third Baronet in 1848. W. M. Young became a Scholar of Eton and King's College, Cambridge, and entered the Indian Civil Service in 1862; Governor of the Punjab, 1897; knighted the same year.

[2] Possibly Rev. H. J. W. Stillingfleet, curate, Chaplain to the Union, Wantage, Berkshire, 1852–3. Cf. *The Clergy List for 1852, 1853* (1852, 1853) pp. 252, 254.

equally as inaccessible which shews* more than any thing else the enormous altitude of the crowning summits

About half way up the latter portion of the ascent the Mountains or rather Rocks I should say open on one side and display a desolate sort of a valley which however afforded us a spectacle which I shall never forget for it opened to us a clear and pretty comprehensive view of the glassier* of St Paul. This Glassier* our driver told us he had often been to and its extent was 4 hours in width or about 16 miles The sun shone upon it with resplendent brightness and the whole mass that was in sight reminded me more of the effect which the Ki o Noor* diamond had when I saw it raised up from its bed in the Chrystal* Palace. It, that is the whole Glassier* was one mountain of light litterally* a Jewel which no earthly potentate can adorn himself with and which can alone befit the sacredness of its everlasting creator and possessor

At the Summit level of the Pass I saw as plainly as can be written that curious fact in geology which I have more than once heard of viz the attrition of rocks by the passage of other rocks over or through them by some extraneous force which is supposed to be the passage or descent of icebergs in the under surface of which granite rocks are enclosed The whole surface of the summit level of this Pass, the width and length of which I cannot guess at with any accuracy it may be one or it may be 2 miles wide by [a][3] mile long, is all rubbed & rounded like the grannite* stones of a well worne* thoroughfare, but many of the rocks exhibit besides, scratches along their sides as if a still harder rock had been pushed forcibly along its side with an effect like the chissel* of a planing machine on a piece of Iron.

As I have before stated at the Summit of the Pass you see nothing but enormous mountains all around you for the way by which you have gained the summit by a short turn soon hides the valley or ravine through which you have gained the summit and the descent is begun by entering a defile of a tortuous course which continues for a considerable distance so that it is a very long time before you get any long view before you but when you do get out of this defile you find yourself at the summit of a vast alpine valley above the region of pines even and stretching for many miles before you and you can see your road descending by zig zags innumerable before to enable you to reach the habitable parts below. To enter into a more particular description of the descent would be to give you the history over again of the ascent the chief difference being this that the character of the scenery on the descent is of a more mild nature more wood when you get low enough for it more grassey* spots and in the distance the great valley of the Levantine open before

[3] Omitted in the original manuscript.

you for the extent of many miles laid out like a map and the roofs of its cottages and villages displayed to you as if you were looking over the wooden houses of a childs toy.

Before we got down to the habitable parts we met with the remains of an avelaunch* of Snow which had slid down and filled up the bed of the river close by the road, the torrent however soon making a way through it and dividing it into two halves I stopped the Carriage and soon was upon the surface of one of the sides which I jumped and danced upon for a short time. It was much softer than I expected as it gave way to the feet an inch or two at each step, but to be still more convinced that it was actually snow I was standing upon and had before me I took a taste of it and found no mistake!

I will not further describe the descent than to say that it filled us with as much wonder and delight as the ascent had done that we enjoyed uninterrupted beautiful weather and arrived safely at Faido where I began this letter. But to shew* you how very thankful we ought to be for such extraordinary good fortune as we have had in respect of the weather a Lady & her family who arrived at Faido about 3 hours after us told us that she had been envelloped* in clouds nearly all the way and had seen scarcely anything –

Lugano, 26 Sep 1855 We have come from Faido through Bellinzona to this place today. Nearly the whole distance has been through one great valley called the Levantile* Valley It consists of a cultivateable portion at the bottom with a river flowing through it and bounded on each side by very lofty mountains generally wooded to their summits This valley seems almost interminable for no sooner do you pass a bend of it thinking to see the end than you find another reach of the same valley quite as long as the last and so on until you almost wish for a change though the beauty of the ride surpasses any thing I can call to mind in either England Scotland Ireland or Wales North or South

The valley of the Levantine, or perhaps more commonly called Ticino, for this is the name of the river which flows through it terminates at Lake Maggiore into which the Ticino flows. We followed it until we got within two or three miles of the lake when we turn out of it and ascend a considerable mountain called Mount Cenere* in order to gain the Lugano district but in ascending this hill we had as good a view of Lake Maggiore as we wish preferring in every respect to put up for a night or so at this place.

We arrived here too late to take any walk out and can only judge of what we have seen on our approach. The Country around seems to be extremely rich growing all sorts of crops that you can name almost and generally two crops growing together on the same ground the later one to ripen after the first crop is gathered. Indian Corn seems a favorite* crop as we see plenty of it growing everywhere and scarcely a cottage but has the cobs of it hung out in the front of their windows to harden by the sun. I have seen crops of some kinds that I never saw before such as Millet, Buckwheat, Meillio which I understand is Bird seed and one or two others which we could not make out at all as the names given by our driver could not be found in the dictionary.

We have informed you that our intention is to make our way to Venice but we do not intend to go there without telegraphing first to know how the cholera is in that town but the office was closed before we had prepared our message and we must stop for that formality until tomorrow but I do not wish to keep this letter a day longer from you and therefore one of us will write from here after we have got an answer from Venice to let you know with certainty our next course

Give my Dearest Love to Henny & Tommy. My kindest and aff^{te} remembrances to St James Road and Parliament S^t and accept for yourself Dearest Herbert the sincere love and enduring friendship of
Your affectionate Father
Thomas Jevons

Lucy's best love & hopes you wont be tired of hearing twice over about some things, though she cannot pretend to the full, true & particular accounts that Papa enters into – my love to dear Henny & Tommy[4] –

75. H. E. ROSCOE TO W. S. JEVONS

25. Fulham Place. Harrow Road
London. Oct. 15th 1855.

My dear Stanley

I fear that before this reaches your abode you will have quite given up hopes (or fears) of hearing again from me – be sure however that I am far from having either forgotten you or I hope you me. – The fact is that all the summer I have been tremendously busy – but the best thing I can do is to give you an account of my doings instead of making useless apologies. – Before I begin I will only say how very glad we were to hear of your change of plan & increase of salary, which I think is much more satisfactory than the original mode of proceeding. –

Now for an account of my own doings – When I last wrote from Heidelberg I was busy with my research on the Chemical action of light. – I worked away like a trooper all spring & summer till the middle of August, & got some very interesting & important results (of which more anon), I then left Heidelberg for Paris where I arrived just whilst the

---
[4] Lucy Jevons added this pencilled note at the end of the letter.

Queen was there,[1] & saw all the grand doings there & wandered about the grand streets & the Exhibitions with several of my German friends & in fact had a very jolly time of it – As however you will have seen from the papers all the accounts of these grand doings I will not inflict any of my descriptions upon you, I will only say that I never saw such a piece of work or such a row in my life – The Duke's Funeral (do you remember?)[2] was nothing to the crush & crowd & soldiers – whose names were legion. – I then returned to the "home of the free & brave" accompanied by a German friend who I am afraid did not feel such sensations of enthusiasm &c &c as such a barbarian ought to have done on stepping on Albions shore I should have said that at the end of July Williamson wrote to me stating that he had been elected to Grahams Chair & asking me to assist him with the lectures – Now as nothing better seemed likely to turn up & as the £60 which he offered me for the winter although not much still was better than "a poke in the eye with a burnt stick" I settled to be with him again till March. – So I came to London & settled about our first paper which Watts[3] was to put in the Chemical Journal,[4] & looked out for a house for my mother & myself to lay our heads in – After fruitless attempts on this latter point I trundled down to Liverpool & met my mother at the Booths.[5] There I concocted an account of our experiment to read before the British Association at Glasgow, & after spending a few days on my way with the Cromptons at Grasmere I (accompanied by Charles Crompton)[6] went on to Glasgow. There I fell in with Andrews,[7] Miller, & Playfair[8] & was elected one of the Secretaries of the Chemical Section; in this way I got to know all the Chemists & people there, & enjoyed myself amazingly. – We lived in the same Hotel with Playfair, Miller & Andrews whom I got to know quite intimately. – I read my paper, or rather gave an account of our experiments, but it is very difficult to describe in 10 minutes, work which has taken up nearly two years[9]! & so I fear I did not make myself very clearly understood. – Now I shall

---

[1] Cf. above, Letter 70, p. 175. [2] See Vol. I, p. 73.
[3] See above, Letter 35, n. 10, p. 65. Watts was editor of the Chemical Society's *Journal*, 1850–84.
[4] R. W. Bunsen, H. E. Roscoe, 'Photochemical Researches', *Quarterly Journal of the Chemical Society*, VIII (1856) 193–211. The paper was first published in German, 'Photochemische Untersuchungen', in Poggendorf's *Annalen der Physik und Chemie*, XCVI (Leipzig, 1855) 373–94.
[5] See Vol. I, p. 77 n. 2; also above, Letter 15, n. 1, p. 29.
[6] Charles Crompton (1833–90), eldest son of Sir Charles, who was at Tainity College, Cambridge, at this time. Cf. above, Letter 15, n. 8, p. 31
[7] Thomas Andrews (1813–85) Professor of Chemistry and Vice President, Queen's College, Belfast, 1849–79; President of the British Association, 1876; famous for his researches concerning ozone and for formulating the concept of critical temperature, i.e. that a given gas will not liquefy above a certain temperature, regardless of the amount of pressure applied.
[8] See Vol. I, p. 85 n. 2.
[9] See above, Letter 39, p. 74.

inflict upon you a short account of these expts, which as you know, Bunsen has made with me. First of all, we examined the action of the light upon Chlorine water & Iodine & Bromine – solution in presence of organic (hydrogenous) substances. We however found no constant action, or simple relation between the amount decomposed & time of action &c. Then we found that the Hydrochloric acid (or other substances) formed during the decomposition greatly retards the decomposing action of the light – so that the amount decomposed in the second unit of time is not so large as that in the first & so on. The difficulty now to overcome was that of getting rid of this Hydrochloric acid, & as this cannot be done in the case of liquids we had to give up our first method. We next used the mixture of equal vols of Cl & H which is obtained by the electrolytic decomposition of Hydrochloric acid – & in order to get rid of the H Cl which is formed by the action of the light, we simply allowed water (saturated with the gas) to be present, this immediately absorbed the H Cl & the diminution of the gaseous volume ensuing from this absorption we use as a measure of the Chemical action. As soon as this disturbing influence of the H Cl is removed we obtain beautifully regular results – & arrive directly at 2 laws. 1. The chemical action is proportional to the time of exposure (with constant source of light). 2. It is also proportional to the Intensity or amounts of light (with equal times.) – These results were very interesting. – Now just when we had got thus far I one Sunday got hold of a number of Poggendorfs Annalen in which to my horror I found a paper on the same subject by a man in Munich[10] – who had obtained very similar results. We soon saw however that this man had got the wrong pig by the ear & we made all his experiments over again & the results of these expts is given in our first paper which I inclose* for your edification – He has made a great fool of himself as you will see – Then our further results are not yet published but Bunsen is collecting them & arranging them for the press, but it is doubtful whether they will be printed this winter[11] or whether he will wait till I can come again & go on with them in the Summer which I intend & hope to do. –

The people in Glasgow were much interested with my results & I got a grant of £20 to continue the expts. – We had a most successful

[10] W. C. Wittwer, 'Ueber die Einwirkung des Lichts auf Chlorwasser', *Annalen der Physik und Chemie*, XCIV (Leipzig, 1855) 597–612.

Bunsen and Roscoe remarked in the introduction to their paper in the *Quarterly Journal of the Chemical Society* (see n. 4 above), 'Although these our first experiments were not carried on with a view to publication . . . we nevertheless are obliged to make known these results, in consequence of the subsequent publication of a research on the same subject by Dr. Wittwer . . .' (p. 193).

[11] The papers resulting from this joint research were published in Poggendorf's *Annalen* and the Royal Society's *Philosophical Transactions*; see below, Letters 114 and 126, pp. 315 and 356.

meeting, Leibig, Frémy[12] & Peligot being there & almost all the English Chemists, & our section was always crowded & we had lots of papers although not many of very great interest.

So we are settled now comfortably for the winter in a small snug little house, & I am working away with Williamson at his lectures – This is a very different sort of work from that which I have latterly been doing in Heidelberg & I cannot say that I am enchanted with it. What is to be done next heaven only knows – at least I hope it does, as Williamson says – I wish to get a small Hospital to lecture at – but I don't see any chance – however patience – What a lucky fellow you are making how much? £700 a year – Can I believe it? – This has been a very egotistical letter & I expect to get one equally so from you – Liebig is here staying at Tommy Grahams where I met him last night quite alone! So it was very pleasant. My mother says it is so funny to see me hob & nob with the three greatest Chemists in Europe, Bunsen Liebig & Graham! – Do you find any alteration from Tommy being made Master of the Mint? A good thing for Science to get hold of some places of that sort: – I will add some more when I get the papers.

Oct. 25th. So you see my boy it has been some time until the papers did turn up, & meantime I have received your welcome letter from Herbert.[13] I am delighted to hear that you keep up your interest in scientific matters – & I hope & believe that you will do something good in your time – ie when you are a man of fortune & can keep 2 or 3 of us poor devils to work for you! – However joking apart – it is a very good idea of yours of making meterological observations & whenever you have a sufficient number to give any results send them to me & I will see about getting them published[14] I know so little about measurement of radiant heat that I cannot tell whether there is any accurate method for measuring solar radiation or terrestrial – but I shd think that with Melloni's[15] Thermo-battery & a galvanometer (wh had been previously graduated by a tangent-galvanometer) there would be no difficulty in obtaining accurate measure of the sun's direct rays of heat. But I doubt if this has ever been tried. If one could manage this it would

---

[12] Edmond Frémy (1814–94) of the École Polytechnique in Paris; in 1854 he carried out experiments which were an attempt to isolate the gas fluorine.

[13] Almost certainly Letter 66, above, p. 159.

[14] 'On the Cirrous Form of Cloud', *London ... Philosophical Magazine*, XIV (July 1857) 22–35; 'On the Forms of Clouds', *London ... Philosophical Magazine*, XV (April 1858) 241–55. Cf. J. A. La Nauze, 'Jevons in Sydney', *Political Economy in Australia* (Melbourne, 1949) pp. 41–2. See below, Letter 94, n. 7, p. 244.

[15] Macedonio Melloni (1798–1854), Italian physicist, whose most important work was in the field of radiant heat; he determined the properties of various substances in transmitting heat. He published the first volume of a projected work on heat, *La thermochrose ou la coloration calorifique démontrée par un grand nombre d'expériences, et considerées sous ses divers rapports avec la science de la chaleur rayonnante* (Naples, 1850).

be a very good thing. It is only the difference between the temps: of the two ends of the sets of bars which is measured, so that if one were kept shaded & the other in the direct rays, currents of hot or cold air would have no effect on the deviations of the needle. – If I have time in a few weeks I will look up the subjects & let you know what I can grab up about it – I will get hold of Melloni's book "La Thermochose"* if possible.

I forgot to tell you that I spoke of you to Miller & he was very glad to hear that you were with his brother & doing so well & so comfortable – My brother in law Edward Enfield will inclose* some notes for some men whom he knows in your Mint – They were under him & he wants you to know them. – You talk of bread being from 8^d to 1^s as so very dear – Why we consider that cheap! Everything here is tremendously dear – War prices – & now we seem to be getting into hot water with America.[16] Who knows where it may end – However "never say die"! Sebastopol is gone that is something.[17]

    Ever my dear Stanley yours vy affecnly
        Henry E. Roscoe.

N B. My mother sends her love & wants to know if you have heard or seen anything of her pictures[18] & if you can sell them for a good round sum.

I forgot to add that since writing the first sheet I have heard from Bunsen who says that our other experiments are rather too imperfect to publish without making some more to fill up gaps – so the paper must be postponed till after next summer – This is in some respects rather a bore – But it is better to do the thing at once completely & well – so you will not get our second paper for some time.

I hope to get to Heidelberg in April to stay till August – in that time I can get through some work.

[16] Probably a reference to the anger aroused in America by the enlistment of American citizens in the British army. In December 1854 Parliament had authorized the formation of a foreign legion to provide reinforcements for the Crimea; recruiting agents in the United States received the support of British officials. Recruiting was stopped after strong protests by the Americans. Cf. Woodward, op. cit., pp. 306–7.
[17] The fortress had finally been captured on 9 September.
[18] Mrs Henry Roscoe was a talented artist; after her husband's death she had helped to support her children by teaching watercolour painting at a girls' school near Liverpool. Cf. below, Letter 94, p. 251.

76. W. S. JEVONS TO THOMAS JEVONS

Annangrove Cottage
Sydney.
October 29th 1855.[1]

My dearest Father,

Your letters to me lately have been numerous, and I have had[2] great pleasure in being kept so well aware of what is going on at home.

I am afraid that my accounts, in return will be considered but poorly written but surely they come often enough though you complain of not getting them, as well as newspapers. I have sent many more than 2 newspapers, sometimes 2 at a time, Heralds, Empires, & Illustrated's; also Map of Sydney, Almanac, &c, &c, which I do not remember being acknowledged.

At last I have got the package per Aunt Henry and am even better pleased than I expected; my room looks gayer for the "valances" which are long since up, Tommys present is in daily use for meter. obs., the books will be read & therm^{rs} used in due time. I only hope the pictures will sell as easily as the rest of the things are disposed of.

I often think myself niggardly for not sending more things home, but it is from the want of things to send. I remembered some time since that I had promised Cousin Dalby's*[3] some Australian shells; I went to the only shop in Sydney for such things and they *very colonially*, tried to pass off upon me some of the commonest possible shells, & being disgusted I gave it up. For collecting I have not a moment of time; I should like them to know the reasons of my not having fulfilled my promise.

To pass to other affairs, the Mint is going on at a rattling pace, 14,000 oz last weeks receipts of gold. This causes somewhat hard work and stirs us all up. *We* are pretty well prepared for it and cannot very well complain, everything we asked for having been allowed. We have each of us had a boy as additional assistant who takes a deal of the drudgery off me & Charles.

My days work now is

 8.15 get up.
 8.45 get breakfast
 9.0 observations, & off to town in omnibus (all the way from the door for 6^d)
 9.45 get to laboratory & commence weighing hard
 12.30 weighing finished
 1.30 5 minutes for lunch.

[1] The original manuscript of this letter is in the Mitchell Library, Sydney.
[2] Jevons wrote 'have' twice here.
[3] See Vol. I, p. 59, n. 5.

4.30 assays finished & weighed up.
5.0 reports made out
5.15 home by omnibus.
6.0 dinner.
8.0 tea, play harmonium
9.0 observations. read newspapers &c till go to bed.

The work of assaying is not like other peoples work; it is hard drive-ahead work all day, and for every half minute lost, you are in mortal fear of not getting done by time for dinner.

It is not much to the credit of Capt W or the other head men of the Mint that the work still continues irregular and assays are wanted in a hurry because the other departments are behindhand in their work; I really believe the assay department has never caused a delay or disappointment yet.

There are rumours of changes; Mr Trickett after building & finishing the Mint does not like the coining work, or manage it particularly well. It is possible he may be very soon made Colonial Architect when somebody else will have to be coiner; no doubt this will not affect us. The accountants work too is said not to be in the best order, and some change may possibly occur there, but these are things only known since yesterday when Trickett was spending the day here.

In a few days my lease of N°. 8 Church Hill will end, and I hope everything connected with the old arrangement will be cleared off. I have this evening begun a long bill for the apparatus amounting to £223, which having been already approved will be at once paid. £15 I have already received for fittings, and the rooms have been put into order & repaired by the Mint to be given up to Mr Korff.

I can then also send in a bill for more than £50 for rent and altogether I shall have in my hands in a week or two about £370. so that money begins to mount up. £170 I still owe, leaving £200 for gains during first year in Australia besides about £100 more of property. I think then there is no cause for dissatisfaction and I look forward to going quietly on freer from much of the trouble I have had.

The weather now is splendid; of moderate temperature and sufficient dryness while a fresh sea breeze, and considerable *cloudiness*, keep off the suns heat from being too much felt.

Yesterday morning I took the second or third walk in the country in this direction. Going across some open ground opposite the house I was surprized* to come just across the railway to a hill, named Norwood whence there was a splendid view all round. In fact the finest view I have seen in Australia something in the way that you get such beautiful views from the hills near London. Botany Bay is the most striking part and I will try and give you a sort of outline of it as seen from there. I only wish I could sketch so as to let you see what we look like here. The sketch I find makes the bay look 2 or 3 times too near, but you must imagine it about 5 miles off with a plain lying between crowded with short trees & bush, with however houses here and there; Norwood is one of the newly made towns of which there are no end continually appearing near Sydney; an auction sale of allotments took place there today. Next Norwood is a similar new town called Sydenham with a railway station, and there are dozens more along the railway. To the back of our house the wood is laid out into another town *Leichhardt* town.[4]

Oct 30th

I have not much more to say. Today I gave up the key of Church Hill with considerable satisfaction the lease terminating on Nov. 2nd. Mr Korff seems a very nice man and I am likely to close with him without any trouble. Mr Miller is at loggerheads with his landlord Mr. Lunn, who is a cantankerous old man very hard to deal with when he is vexed. The Mint is repairing our offices for us free of expense, & mine being an old place was easily made as good as when I entered. I dont think the Mint would have done it but that Mr Trickett began to repair by mistake & without orders, and then he & Capt W thought it best to go through it.

We get lots of European news now but I find it a very hard job to get through it all. One's interest in the War is somewhat lessened, but I think politics, particularly in England are getting more & more interesting. It is very disgusting to see that some of the newspapers are writing now all for peace, after crying up war so fiercely for so long. I hope however the English will stick to it and make the Russians really knock under.

Of all things however that are disgusting, I think the Americans are the worst. According to all accounts they are going-a-head into all absurdities imaginable and it is well known that they are completely Russian. They must be about the only people whose progress (which we hear so much about) is backwards. They are something like our neighbours the Victorians who are always going-a-head, & who are very much despised on that account in N.S.W.

Royal Mint. Oct 31st.

Nothing new. I have just received another Illustrated London News. You can easily understand how acceptable they are to myself as well as everybody else who sees them.

[4] The right-hand portion of the remainder of this page is taken up by a sketch.

Work is getting a little slack again this week; when I have time it is very pleasant to go and have a look at the sovreigns* spinning out of the presses. The coining presses however are very liable to get out of order and give a great deal of trouble. The rollers also are very difficult to adjust so as to roll to the right weight and are not so true as they should be.

We are saved a deal of trouble here by being supplied with many things that we should otherwise have to make.

Distilled water is the chief thing, we get any quantity by a small condensing pipe connected with the boiler. You have merely to turn the tap and distilled water runs out in any quantity without furthur* trouble at the rate of about 6 quart bottles the hour.

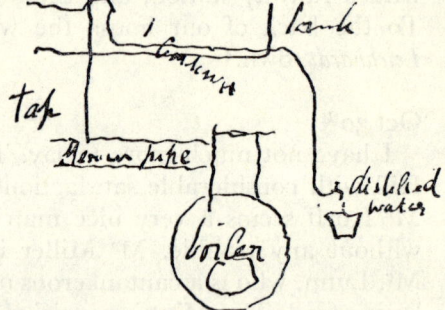

You mention in your last letter[5] that you think I might send Meteorological Reports to some paper. It is just the thing I have thought of myself, intending at first to put them in the Empire if they would have them in opposition to some very stupid ones there are in the Sydney M.H.

Many thinks have occurred to put it off, as it would require me to devote a deal of time & trouble, quite continuously, more than I have ever given as yet.

When much work comes as at present it of course turns your thoughts off. I may put them in a new Illustrated Paper that will perhaps be published soon.[6]

Want of time & subject makes me think I had better finish and take it to the post at once, but not till I have sent my best love to all others at home as well as yourself.

I remain

Your same affec. Son
W. S. Jevons.

C. B. has been much better in health for some time past; he lives very comfortably[7] about two miles from the Mint in the same direction as me something.

[5] Letter, 69 above, p. 170.

[6] Jevons's first weekly 'Meteorological Report' for the *Empire* newspaper did not appear until 3 September 1856, and he published nothing earlier than this. Jevons contributed more elaborate monthly meteorological reports to the *Sydney Magazing of Science and Art* from its inception in June 1857; this may perhaps have been the 'new Illustrated Paper' to which he here refers. Cf. La Nauze, op. cit., pp. 38–41.

[7] Jevons wrote 'comfortable' here.

He has lately bought a first rate wood turning lathe from Mr Severn of the Mint, which I dare say he will make good use of. Of course Charles is well pleased with having a boy under him upon whom he can put a great deal of his own work.

77. THOMAS JEVONS TO W. S. JEVONS

Rome 29th Oct 1855

My Dearest Stanley

If any one had suggested a year or two since that I should ever set my feet in the Eternal City I should have replyied* that it was not within the bounds of probability and yet here I am the day & year above written And what is no less remarkable here to* has followed me your letter of the 1 June which has added greatly to the pleasure and delight I am constantly receiving on this grand tour at the climacteric of my years. I am not sure that I have addressed any letter to you since I started on this journey say on the 28 Aug last just two mths since but no doubt some of us have mentioned By the By I recollect I wrote to you from Paris & sent you a piece of Aluminium so I need not recapitulate any thing prior to that but for your information I will just give you a list of the places we have passed through any thing beyond which would seem almost an impossibility. We left Paris for Strasbourg & then went to Basle, Zurick,* Lucerne, Fleuellen* and then *across the Alps by the St Gothard* Pass the Grandest ride conceivable then Lugano & Como and from Como we went as direct a road as we could to Venice where we staid* 8 or 10 days We went from Venice back to Verona thence to Mantua Bolognia* and Florence where we staid* five days. From Florence to Pisa to see the leaning Tower and to Leghorn whence we embarked for Civitta Vecchia* and took the diligence for this City – you will perceive that we saw the two Lakes of which we have beautiful paintings of [sic] in our drawing room viz Como & Lugano The latter is the finer Lake of the two and I think I like it better than any other we saw.

In the pass of St Gothard the most striking feiture* of all is that for miles you are bound in by rocks which reach perpendicularly (to appearance) above your head to the enormous height of 1500 to 2000 feet I only noticed one opening all the way up, but through it we had a good view of the Glassier* of St Paul the most Glorious and majestic sight in Nature This Glacier is said to be several hundred miles across at the time we saw it the Sun was shining brilliantly upon it and it appeared like one Great Mountain of Light a real "*Ki o Noor*"*

Venice is a most remarkable city called the city of Palaces for there are more than 200 of them. Its great peculiarity is that you approach all its principle* buildings except St Marks and its Piazza by water, the city being crossed in all directions by Canals to the number of 400. You soon get accustomed to call your Gondola instead of your coach and you would not change back again for any consideration

Verona is an interesting Town having many Roman remains among the rest a Colloceum* which will seat 25,000 people and every seat is perfect. Florence has the finest Collections of Paintings we have met with and Pisa will ever stand famous as long as her beautiful Tower hangs or rather overhangs its foundations by just fourteen feet

As for Rome The Eternal City where are to be seen buildings of to day and those which date thirty centuries back as well as all intermediate stages to describe it in a letter is a folly Yet I have been guilty of that in a letter to my brother and I think my best plan is to ask him to send that letter to you for your edification and of course you can return it again if my brother desires it.

There is a diversity in their notation of time here which is curious The common people begin their day at 6 oclock in the evening and they count the hours successively up to 24 If you ask them what time they dine they tell you at eighteen oclock and what time they sup they say two oclock meaning our 8 oclock in the evening But while this prevails with the Com^n people I find that many of the Church clocks never strike more than 6, two clocks of this kind are within hearing of these lodgings and I have seen one very large church clock dial on which only the six hours are noted so that these would indicate that these particular churches divide the day into four equal periods of six hours each. I have not as yet heard any explanation of this peculiar diversity in the notations of the hours of the day.

They have a perfect system of Decimal Coinage and money of account established here which when you once understand renders all calculations extremely easy The money of acc^t is the *Scudi* which was originally I feel certain the old Spanish dollar and its present value which is about 4/6^d indicates as much The Scudo is divided into Pauls and Biocchi, ten Biocchi make one Paul ten Pauls make one Scudo They have a beautiful Gold coinage of which I have seen

>first a one Scudo piece
>2nd a 25.0 Paul piece or 2½ Scudi
>3rd a 50 Paul piece or 5 Scudi

which latter coin is a little larger than a Napoleon and a little smaller than a Sovreign* The Silver coinage consists of a 3.a 2 and a 1 Paul piece with floods of ½ paul pieces. It is in a wretched c[onditio]n[1] all

---

[1] The page is torn in several places.

the imprint being worn or hammered out s[o] that any one so disposed may make as many such coins as he chooses without troubling either the Mint or the assayers in the least The Copper Coinage is in good order and consists of a 1 a 2 and a 5 Biocchi piece respectively.

We were at Gibsons² Studio yesterday and saw a new Venus he has sculptured for Mr Preston of Liverpool³ This Statue he has colored* to resemble life, a new practice which he alone is introducing. It is a most exquisite production of his chissel* but it will be long & long before the public will make up their minds whether the new prac[tice] of painting his statues is an improvement or not I am my[self] rather disposed in its favor* –

I must now turn to your letter and congratulate you on the altered position in which you find yourself and express my fervent hopes that health and happiness may long continue to be your lot though I can never forget that they have bamboozled you out of the golden harvest they held out to lure you from your native land. However you may perhaps have your triumph yet. The Mint will answer beyond expectation in my opinion and when that is manifest will be your time for demanding an extra fee and enforcing it by every means in your power. I notice the sketch of the room that Capt Ward is going to allott* you and all I can say is that I fear you will be stifled in it. It is absolutely unworthy of a national concern to push you into such a stove.⁴

I see that you purpose sending me back the money which I invested in your outfit I shall receive it from you with grateful and thankful feelings, but if you see any opportunity of investing it for me in some safe undertaking by which it would be doubled or trebled in a year or two I should be very glad for you to do so we can make very little profit out of money at home and shall be glad of any better means of gaining good returns

      My Ever best love be with you
         Your affectionate Father
            Thomas Jevons

P.S. Since writing the enclosed I have found out that the day of 24 hours is called the Ave Maria day and that it does not follow a fixed

---

² John Gibson, R.A. (1790–1866), the Rome sculptor. In 1827 a bust by him of William Roscoe was presented to the Liverpool Royal Institution.

³ Robert Berthon Preston (1820–60), principal partner in a Liverpool firm of mechanical engineers, Fawcett, Preston & Co.; a patron of art, he made a collection of modern and antique works. Gibson, who believed that the ancient Greeks coloured their sculpture, executed the 'Tinted Venus' expressly for Preston, 1850–5. The six-foot marble statue, in classical style, tinted with wax colours, caused a sensation when it was first exhibited. It has recently been acquired by the Walker Art Gallery, Liverpool.

⁴ He then wrote 'of a place' but crossed it out.

mean time but is regulated by the Cannon* Law The day sometimes begins at 6 sometimes at 7 and sometimes as late as 9 Oclock at night so that the Ave Maria day must be sometimes considerably more than 24 hours long at other times as much shorter I have not been able to get any satisfactory explanation of the six hours division of the day further than that it is used by the clergy All tradesmen and other higher classes of the Town use the 12 hour rotation as the rest of Europe does.

We do not expect to reach home before the beginning of Decem^r so that if you have no letter from me of a date between this period and that you will know the cause viz that travelling in a strange land prevents me writing

Again Yours aff^{tely} Thos. J.^{5}

78. W. S. JEVONS TO HERBERT JEVONS
[LJP, 54–5]

Petersham N^r Sydney. N S W.
November 29th 1855

My dearest Herbert,

To-day I received the letters per "Lightening"* and found them more than usually interesting on account of the letters from the Continental Travellers.

What a pleasure it must be to Lucy & Papa. Fred too it seems was going to Paris, & if he likes it as well as Willy & I did, it will do. The longer it is off, the more I think of that visit of mine to Paris, particularly that now so much is happening there. The fact too of their lodging in the same house 13(?) Rue de lille [sic] is pleasant as they would start off each day from the same point of view. And a fine view it was too to walk just onto the Quay by the Palais d'Orsay.

I hope my time will come soon to travel a little more than I have, and I will go somewhere when I leave here. In which of the four quarters of the globe my travels will be, I have as yet no idea at all; rather a wide choice from this point of view.

Papa's last letter before leaving was very kind, but I hope to hear furthur* from them on the journey before long

As to my own affairs I have little to say since my last long letter, with the exception of the fact of sending £170 more to my Father. This I believe fully covers what I owe him; When I left it amounted to £323 to which must be added £15 for freight and a few pounds for books clothes &c that you have sent since.

^{5} See Vol. I, p. 22.

I have left about £180 which I have put in the Oriental Bank, besides £56 due on the 31st.

The Mint goes on swimmingly now, 20,000 oz being an ordinary weeks receipt. Nevertheless I cannot say we are overworked, for we get to do the assays very quickly and often do not work longer than from 10 to 3. Still when you add in everything that I have to do, it does not turn out to be a very easy life.

On the whole however I may say that we are getting on at Petersham better than we ever did before and there is nothing like an active life to be pleasant.

My health is very good, in fact better than it was a month ago when I felt a little queerish, probably on account of the Spring season, but it was nothing I thought worth mentioning then.

These few nights I am very busily engaged copying out a Register of the weather kept on board "Maid of Judah" from London by the Captain. It was the ship Mr Trickett came out in *two voyages ago*. I am copying the whole for Trickett as well as parts for myself. The obser^s are every 2 hours but were made in a rough sailor-like manner. Still they are worth having. At the same time we are having thunder showers here, and the splendid thunder clouds cause me a deal of trouble in obser^n & description &c.

There is no doubt I believe now that Trickett is going to leave the Mint in order to be Colonial Architect a much better position. His successor is quite undecided upon as yet as far as we know, but the change will not affect us I think.

A little time since I was at a very jolly thing viz. a moonlight concert in the Domain. It struck my fancy as the most enjoyable way of hearing music from the place & manner being completely natural. The Domain is a sort of natural park and you walk about it or lie on the grass in the moonlight just as you like. I shall write again probably to one of you soon but tonight I have not time to say more.

I do not know how long this ship the Eliza will take to get to England, but if the mails are delayed & irregular, whose fault can it be but the Liverpool people's whose ships carry them. I never can forgive that "Oliver Lang"; the Capt I hear could not get another ship: no wonder.

With best love to all who may be at home.
    I am
      Ever your affec. Brother
        W. S. Jevons.

79. W. S. JEVONS TO HERBERT JEVONS

Petersham. N.S.W.
December 17th/55[1]

Dearest Herbert

Never have we had such a mail before as that by the Red Jacket last Tuesday, bringing the news of the Fall of Sebastopol. The first indication of it which we had on getting near town was the Telegraph flagpoles decorated with flags (it was just a year since that they were similarly decorated for the false news of the Taking, after the Alma[2]). Soon a number of small boys appeared rushing along with the supplement just published for sale, and when we got into town it was in a state of complete excitement.

The *banks*, according to the custom here which is rather curious, immediately shut up & proclaimed what they called a "bank holyday",* and everybody felt inclined to take their pleasure over the news.

At the Mint I found a most imposing letter from you, directed, stamped, sealed, & marked all over; I immediately thought of the aluminium *or* the diploma, which my father had mentioned before, but what was my pleasure when I found them both, with a letter from Lucy[3] into the bargain.

I showed the aluminium to most of the officers in the Mint and those who understood it were very much pleased and surprized. Capt Ward was more pleased with the diploma which I showed him also. He seems to think the *Stamp* may be of real use, in case he issues any *standard bars* with the mint stamp and then with my stamp they would be better received if ever they got on the Continent; the mistake of the name will be of no real consequence as the stamp is equally authentic. However I think our name of Jevons will be the ruin of us some day, & do what you like some letter of it is sure to be put wrong. The aluminium is certainly extraordinary stuff and its discovery is undoubtedly a great one. It is however by no means an ornamental metal, the lustre seeming to be much inferior to silver, & something like platinum or perhaps zinc. I think it is already proposed to make balances of it.

I shall be glad to have Papas account of the Paris visit so as to know what he did at the Exhibition, Mint &c.

Lucy's letter finished at Basle is very kind & contains a deal for its length, though perhaps I could not expect much accounts [sic] from them on the journey. I am in expectation of the new slippers which it will be a pleasure to wear

---

[1] The original manuscript of this letter, which is incomplete, is in the Mitchell Library, Sydney.

[2] See above, Letter 46, n. 4, p. 103.   [3] These letters are not among the Jevons Papers.

December 21st

Christmas is now very near, but beyond one or two days with no assays to do and a rather better dinner than usual, it is of little matter to us here. In fact we miss here a deal of your English pleasures and the year is very dull & monotonous because the seasons are so nearly the same all the way round. In the autumn it is rather rainy; in the winter rather cold of a night, sometimes near freezing but fine pleasant weather; spring is not marked as a season that I can see but that it is less hot than summer. The appearance of the country never changes all the year round, unless perhaps, as at present, continued showery weather freshens it & gives a green appearance to the grass otherwise of a light yellow brown colour. The garden also supplies vegetables all the year round.

With respect to colonial news, we have been very much amused & interested in the proceedings of the Legislative Council in its last few days of existence. They had appointed select committee's to enquire into a number of the Government Departments & works. They trumped up charges against Commissioners, contractors directors & everybody connected with these and there is no doubt, picked out the evidence in a shameful manner all on one side. Most of the reports of these committee's were adopted by the Council and sent to the Governor,[4] when he answered them in pretty plain terms that he would not do anything they directed and in fact blew them up awfully. They were awfully savage in return and proposed a vote of censure on him which was only lost by a minority of 17 to 22 so that but for the Government officers & nominees, it would have been passed.

A day or two since he came in great military state and dissolved them and in a few months we shall have the new Parliament. It is to be hoped the Governor will be more moderate with the new *lower house* whatever they do, or there will be a jolly row.[5] The affair is very discreditable I

[4] Sir William Thomas Denison (1804–71), formerly of the Royal Engineers; Lieutenant-Governor of Van Diemen's Land (Tasmania), 1846–54; Governor of New South Wales and Governor-General of the Australian Colonies, 1854–60; Governor of Madras, 1860–6; a skilled engineer, he became president of the Sydney Philosophical Society, before which he delivered a number of papers. Cf. below, Letter 94, p. 249.

[5] The political scene in the Australian colonies was very confused at this period. The Australian Colonies' Government Act, 1850, had given to the five colonies then existing the power to frame their own constitutions. The controlling Legislative Councils, two-thirds elective and one-third nominated by the Crown, were therefore temporary bodies engaged in devising new forms of government, made particularly necessary by the acceleration of economic and social changes as a result of the gold discoveries. Two important constitutional issues in New South Wales were the extent of the British Government's control over the colony's affairs and the attempts of the landed interests to preserve their supremacy. The New South Wales Constitution Act, 1855, proclaimed by the Governor on 24 November, granted responsible government, i.e. local self-government, in which the Governor was to act on the advice of ministers chosen from, and responsible to, the Legislature. A provisional council controlled the colony until the Constitution became effective. Denison, an able administrator,

think to the whole council, for why did they not appoint honest men for the committees or what need had they to adopt their reports when evidently full of lies. Capt Ward made several speeches, chiefly in defence of the great contractor here, Mr Randle.⁶

I cannot say now that our work is very heavy, for having got everything to work very regularly & surely, I only do a *single assay* on each lot of gold, trusting it for being correct, while always before we have done *two assays* so as to compare them, except with *standard assays* in which we can instantly detect an error. It works however very well, as I have not had a *repetition* since I began, i.e. a disagreement between Miller & me, caused by my error. Very lately large quantities of gold have been coming in and we have several times had more than 30 ingot assays; representing perhaps twice as many ingots of gold, for the number of assays on the gold is quite reduced to a minimum. Yesterday we had as many as 22 standard assays at a time, the largest number yet, with only *4 ingots*; today nothing but 8 ingots, this week being an easier one. The Melbourne people still refuse our sovreigns,* out of jealousy of us.⁷ I cannot help thinking they are quite Yankeelike there. They are said to have received the news about Sebastopol with no signs of pleasure like what were showed here and in the other colonies. In fact they are going just the same road as the Americans and I am sure it is a road straight downwards.

I have to tell you I have at last got a first rate little dog that I hope will stick to me. He is a little white bull-terrier puppy and the cleverest fellow for his age that ever was. It is good fun taking strolls in the bush

---

provided an important lead during the transition period. The new Parliament was to consist of an elected Legislative Assembly and a nominated Legislative Council: the election of the former took place in March and April 1856; the ministers of the Legislative Council took office in May. The select committees to which Jevons refers were appointed at the instigation of the Governor, to examine the Surveyor-General's department and public works, including railways. Cf. *The Cambridge History of the British Empire*, VII, Part I: *Australia* (Cambridge, 1933), pp. 258–9, 272–95. See also below, Letter 94, p. 247.

⁶ William Randle, railway contractor and director of a number of railway companies around Sydney and Melbourne; the son of a railway contractor, he worked in the construction of narrow-gauge lines in England for twelve years before emigrating to Sydney, where he arrived in July 1852; employed by the Sydney Railway Company until 1855; constructed about forty miles of railway line between Sydney and Parramatta, and Parramatta and Liverpool. Randle appeared before the Select Committee on Roads and Railways, 1854, and gave evidence regarding the quality of bricks and cement used in the city sewerage works before the Select Committee on the City Commissioners' Department. There appears to have been some suggestion of improper practices; the Committee's Report described Randle as being '... so unscrupulous in his interpretation of his contract ... that ... he is a man in whom no confidence can be placed ...'. Cf. *Report of the Select Committee on the City Commissioners' Department, Notes and Proceedings of the Legislative Council of New South Wales* (1855) III. Randle is recorded as having lived in Sydney, 1852–9, and in Melbourne, 1860–8, when he appears to have moved to Queensland.

⁷ See above, Letter 56, n. 4, p. 127.

& wood, which I do several times a week, more or less. Last Sunday I walked with M^r O'Connel,* Mr Millers brother in law, to a small town called Canterbury on the Cooks river (named after Capt Cook) running into Botany bay.

We looked out for snakes, but only saw two at a distance which got away, but I hope to get some worth keeping for you. The other night we caught a large *centipede* in the pantry, one of the most awful looking animals I ever saw; he is about 5 inches long, and the bite is very bad & venomous though not fatal. A few weeks since a child was killed in Petersham by the bite of a small *death-adder*.

I am very much obliged to you for all the newspapers which I get pretty regularly. The last

80. W. S. JEVONS TO THOMAS JEVONS
[LJN, 55–7]

Petersham, N.S.W.,
18th January 1856.

... I know that at any time you will be glad to have a letter from me, and so, without any particular prospect of a mail, I am going to write you a few pages. I have been much occupied the last twenty-four hours with an incident that occurred to me last night, and which I shall not easily forget. On going upstairs to bed about 10.30 P.M., with a candle, I had got but a short distance into the room when I saw a long irregular black thing lying on the floor. I was puzzled at first to think what it was, but a very few moments of examination were required to decide the question, for it was without doubt a black snake, and still further to convince me, the thing began to move and to hiss! To tell the truth, I then went out of the room quite as fast as I came in (as people say), and, to have him in safe keeping, shut the door. On returning with Mr. O'Connell, provided with sticks, etc., for his destruction, we could see nothing of him, but ultimately discovered him hidden in a corner under the bed, from which being displaced, Mr. O'Connell soon killed him with a few good knocks, but not before he had made a great display of his wide-opened mouth and forked tongue. The fellow was then found to be over a yard long, but though he be no wonder himself, everybody acknowledges it to be *the* most singular fact they remember of a snake getting into a house, for besides crossing the yard, he had to go up several stone steps into the lobby, and then up long, steep, and rather awkward stairs into the room. Everybody says, too, that he is a regularly poisonous rascal. It is well, however, that it was as it was, for if he had simply moved under the bed before I came in, I should have probably gone to bed with him under me – a very disagreeable thought. I have thus been giving you an account of the affair as lengthily as if I had been talking to you, and I do not know what for, unless for my own satisfaction and amusement, but I hope not to your alarm. It is singular that this is the first snake of any size that any of us have met this summer, and in all probability I may go to bed every day of my life and not meet a second.

... Though often rather tired when assaying in the midst of hot winds and the present awfully close weather, I am very jolly and well. Last Monday I went a long walk through the bush and *swamps* to the shores of Botany Bay, but it is rather an uninteresting place, except for its associations, and I got back without anything worth relating. ...

Sunday, 27th January. – In many of your letters, some months since, you noticed my having been to a *déjeûner* at Dawes Battery last year, and seemed to take pleasure in it. The same thing came off yesterday again, being a general holiday for the anniversary of the foundation of the colony; but as Captain Ward, of course, knows ten times as many people as he did then, it was on a much more extensive scale. It was most excessively formal; but I found it easy to get on without being noticed for any peculiarity among the number of people, and I was somewhat pleased to have an opportunity of observing the Australian aristocracy. That you may understand the occasion of the whole affair, you must know that the Sydney people, liking holidays, make the anniversary day a good excuse for one, and the whole town turns out in a way unknown in England, unless it be a Good Friday or a Fast-Day. The chief attraction is the regatta, the principal one of the year, and the points at Fort Macquarie and Dawes Battery are crowded with people, as well as all other places within sight. Captain Ward's house, on the top of the point, has the best view of the whole; and from the pictures you have of the harbour you can imagine what a really beautiful scene it is to see it covered with different yachts and sailing boats, innumerable row boats, many of the large coasting steamers strolling about with bands, and full of visitors, and all the shipping and flag-poles fully decorated with flags. Any one arriving from sea on a regatta day must indeed think Sydney a fine place. ...

81. W. S. JEVONS TO LUCY JEVONS
[LJN, 58–61]

14th February 1856.

... A sad day indeed has this been to me, for the mail, *per Mermaid*, this morning brought me numerous letters, in which the one intelligence was the death of a father such as ours was, far away from our common home, and that home still farther off from me. Your letter (of 12th November),[1] I may truly say, has been a very great comfort to me, written with so much feeling and love, which I know could never be away from you; but also in so collected and thoughtful a manner, as could hardly be expected after such a sudden and heavy loss, and in such desolate circumstances. I thank you for it, particularly for portions of it assuring me that my conduct and progress (such as it is) were to the last a great satisfaction, nay, a great pleasure, to him. This forms my chief consolation now, and will through life leave a bright mark of joy upon his memory. This great loss must of course alter for all of us very much our motives, duties, and plans. For myself I feel as if I had very suddenly and almost unexpectedly lost an object which for a long time has been more and more a motive urging me to exertion, namely, to please him whom God has just taken from us, and thus partially to repay the affection which he has always shown to all of us in such perfection and constancy; the same must be the case with each of us, particularly with you whose part it has been so long to care and manage for him, and whom he speaks of in one of his letters to me as acting as his 'right hand'.[2] But you will stop me instantly and say that, though he is no longer bodily present with us, we must act on, in such a way as would give him pleasure still; and, besides this, that we still remain bound by the affections of brothers and sisters. Nevertheless, one feels that the loss of our last parent is like the removal of a rest upon which we stood, and that now one enters the problem of life in a wider, freer, but perhaps less cheerful sense. Such at least it is with me; but a little thought and habit will no doubt bring things back to a more regular and proper course. . . . You have mentioned his pleasure in reading my last letters received in Rome. I wonder what those letters were? I am afraid my letters there were not so long and good as I have since tried to make them; and it is sorrowful to think that my letters will still keep arriving at Chatham Street for six months, and he no longer there to read them. You mention some small gold coins which he was keeping for me; they will be kept as carefully as a small present I received in a similar way through Uncle Dick from my mother. As to any other things, I had better leave it altogether in your hands. The drawings of parts of Pisa will be a very thoughtful present of yours.

As to the journey, it really seems as if the pain were diminished by knowing that his life was terminated in the midst of such really deep pleasure, almost happiness, which I can well believe he took in great and interesting sights, and as his letters and descriptions plainly show. From all accounts, and my own knowledge, this journey has for some

---

[1] This letter is not among the Jevons Papers.   [2] See above, Letter 59, p. 143.

time been a favourite design and object of his life; and as all pleasure and good is to be got only by exertion, and as exertion must be accompanied by risk, thus alone has arisen the occasion of his death. Also, if I understand rightly his object in combining business with travelling, the present state of affairs with America is near upon the point of proving his foresight. He seems to have been excellently attended in his short illness, and you were fortunate in finding such a kind man as Dr. Lambe.[3] ... As for myself, I take it and bear it, I hope, as I ought. Beyond half a day (Mr. Miller taking a box of assays off my hands) it will not interrupt my usual business, and the people at the mint will know or observe little more than the simple fact. But it will be long before the current of my thoughts in private can be turned from constantly dwelling on you and the others now forming my much-changed home. Thus have I given you with much more freedom than perhaps I should on any less occasion all my thoughts for the first few hours after getting the letters, and the time spent in writing this in the dead and quiet of the night, which seems the pleasantest of the day; for never before did I feel more inclined to be and think alone, unless indeed I could be in Liverpool; and it is the first time I have been able to consider things calmly and fully, and without the confusion of thoughts that one has at first.

Monday Evening, 18*th February*. – Though my thoughts have been almost throughout the day ever upon you and the one sad subject, the work and other occupations of the day are now done and laid aside, and I sit down for a quiet *think* and a quiet write. It is my way of bearing such a loss without *anybody* near to sympathise with me. Last night was the most beautiful night conceivable, or that in fact I think I have ever seen. A cloudless sky, bright moonlight casting shadows among the trees, and air so warm and yet so pleasant that I sat out late at night, and felt no feeling of chill. But the beauty of the weather only reminded me the more of Italy, which this country is said to resemble most in climate, and the very hot wind we had to-day is like the sirocco. Thus I shall often be reminded while here, even by the weather, of the place and beauties amid which our father died; and you no doubt too will similarly feel anything reminding you of the scenes you saw when accompanying him there. I must say I think of these things with feelings scarcely to be called painful, so happy is it to be able to know that at the last his life was *full* of pleasure and satisfaction: when one thinks of it thus one could hardly wish it otherwise, for the very taking of such a long journey shows conclusively that his mind was quite at ease as

[3] Inquiries in both Britain and Italy have failed to establish definitely any further biographical details concerning this Dr Lambe. He could possibly have been George Lambe (1766?–1862), who had a distinguished career in the Army Medical Service in India, becoming Physician-General of Bengal in 1849, a position from which he retired in 1852.

to money matters, and free from other anxieties, except that indeed of getting back safe for his children's sake; and as to this he was saved from pain by the shortness of his illness. Under this view, you can, no more than I am sure that I should, feel regret about this journey, or look back upon it with anything like pain.

Dearest Lucy, you tell me 'never to forget that home will not have passed away because the head has gone'. These words I shall remember, for they are intended to remind me that your love and the others, as well as affections, perhaps, that we shall now more than ever feel the value of, remain. Yes, home will always remain, and in conception will have the same good, indeed heavenly, influence over us in all places; but how can we hope always to 'think of it as of old?' for we must all feel that Providence often separates those who love each other best, and that a family must often be broken up for its mutual advantage. I set not my hopes, then, in living again in a settled home, for we do not know how our lots may next be cast. In this *I* particularly, have been well instructed, for, for three years I lived the greater part away, and then when I would not willingly have gone again, the offer of this affair made it evident that on all accounts I must, and so I left for longer than ever, but is it not sure that *he* felt much more sorrow in sending me than I perhaps in going? In all probability then, we must be contented with two things: 1st, we must treasure up the remembrances of home as it was long ago 'of old', and this I am sure will remain with me, more than with most men, the happiest recollection of my life; 2d, we must still keep up a sort of ideal *home* formed of the mutual affections of brothers and sisters, though distantly separated, and surrounded by the kindness of other relations and friends, and this *home* must take the place for the younger ones, who most require it, of that more actual and complete one that they have lost. Even as to this, who can deny that it will even have a sort of completeness in feeling, for how can we ever think of each other and not of our father as well as our mother who died while yet *I* as well as the little ones stood in need of her love and care, which was supplied in feeling much in the way I speak of; and, as we know, chiefly through yourself?

Dearest Lucy, when I think of these things I begin to feel as if I had a right to lament his death more than any of you, for I have been away more, and was away during the last year. Hence I almost think I must be actually less acquainted with him than I should otherwise have been, and it is after such a loss that we best learn the value of that loss. But you would never think or believe at any time that because I less knew and saw him, and was far away on my own affairs towards his end, I any the less knew his value, feel his loss, and now feel sorrow at his death. . . .

82. W. S. JEVONS TO HENRIETTA JEVONS
[LJP, 61-3]

Petersham near Sydney N.S.W.
February 15th 1856

My dearest Henny

So far away as I am from all to whom I can feel true & deep love or friendship, there is great difficulty in knowing how to receive & bear such unhappy intelligence as the death of a father, but the course I think that is most reasonable & consistent, is to pursue my business & ordinary occupations during the day,[1] much as usual though mournfully, and at night when everybody else is still, to give myself up to my thoughts & feelings, and to use the only means of claiming & imparting sympathy, by writing freely to each of you.

This is the occasion of the great, it might seem, unnecessary length to which my letters are extending, but after being so long from home, one finds them act as a great *relief & comfort*. What a pleasure it is to know that he received & read some letters of mine in Rome, and how I could wish that those letters had been expressions of all the love I bore for him, & which, unlike the rest of you, I had no means of showing since I left but by letters or by actions that would prove it.

One finds a trace of selfish feeling in these which are the first few thoughts that struck *me*, & would I dare say most others also for themselves. I feel quite conscious that I should be more pleased by knowing that I had pleased him, myself than that the same amount of pleasure had been given by others whom I ought in unselfishness to love & esteem before myself. This however is no more than takes place with all our thoughts & motives which never seem to spring from a perfectly pure source. But for the happiness of one to be necessary for the peace of another, is nothing but *sympathy* between them which we must look upon as the *true good*, & sympathy you know is only what is meant by *love*.

I do not know whether you will easily follow all this and I give them merely as thoughts which naturally come across me.

One of the things I said in my letters, and which was repeated again from home, was a sort of wish that *home* should remain the same as it was when I left it, so that my idea of it then should remain continually true, but how far otherwise has it turned out in less than a year & a half. True it was not a positive hope, for every one is aware of the uncertainty of life, if he have it not continually before his eyes, and as to Papa we know that he had already lived many years for which we have so much

---

[1] 'during to the day' in the original manuscript.

cause to be thankful. Therefore I was not unprepared for letters such as yours & the others, and I cannot doubt that in parting from me, he strongly felt the possibility almost probability that he should never see me more on earth. That parting day, when I think of it, brings tears into my eyes more quickly than any other circumstance, and not now alone but each time that it has come into my mind since I left, I have felt the manner of that parting to be most touching. A whole afternoon, my last one I believe in England, he staid* at home *with me & near me*, disregarding his usual business & most unmistakably showing the great difficulty he felt in allowing me to go so far away and for such a length of time. And when before hand one is sure of a father's love is it not the highest proof & trial of its nature that it can thus allow its object to remove & stay at such a distance & with such a possibility, at his age, of never being together again. That parting will always form my last personal recollection of his love & goodness and you can imagine that a book which he gave me that day, his own library copy of our grandfather Roscoe's life,[2] and which he must have set the greatest value on, will have with me now an accumulated value, & shall always remain my own, though before I felt as if it properly belonged to the house and not me alone.

Dearest Henny, for I am afraid I am writing in too distant a manner, and am not enough filled with others sorrow, I will address this letter more fondly to yourself. I am glad you are now just of an age to comprehend & distinguish as well as instinctively to feel Papas goodness, love, & worth, & though your sorrow may thus be all the deeper & more lasting, it will be full of meaning & understanding. In this way the death of a father may well be made to form one of the greatest & deepest lessons of our lives. The ordinary course of affairs (in which let us hope that pleasure always predominates) is disturbed, the question of life seems forcibly laid open to us and one then perceives, if ever, its inexplicable nature, its incompleteness. This course of thought it is which leads us most irresistably to believe in a future life to come, for this life being unfinished, the object unattained, we cannot but look forward to a future existence in a more perfect state, certainly in an incomparably happier one.

February 19th
Tonight I am very tired, for the last five days which have passed since I got the letters I am now answering, have been no easy ones, and have seemed twice the length. How long & full of grief must the first few days have been to you & Tommy waiting till Lucy & Herbert returned, & still more so to Lucy & Mary watching disconsolately for Herbert's

[2] See Vol. I, p. 61.

or Willy's[3] arrival at Pisa, or to Herbert obliged to travel hurriedly on such a sad duty.

Last Sunday I hit upon an employment which I though particularly fitted for all my circumstances. It was to collect together all my fathers letters that I possessed, arrange them in order & commence carefully reading them.[4] Thus I obtained a fresh & connected view of all his goodness to me and had also brought up to my mind, many little events connected with others as well as myself, which it was generally a pleasure to remember. I dare say I have more of his letters than any one of you, certainly than you yourself, & sometime perhaps we may have the pleasure of looking over them together. Another little thing too I possess of inestimable value now, Papas' Photograph which he himself got done & gave me shortly before I left. I am not sure that Lucy had not one too, at all events I hope so.

And now, Dearest Henny, I will close this letter, but you in reading it, three months hence, must remember it was written in the first few days of sorrow, and be accordingly indulgent. May we not still look forward, each to a happy contented life wherever we may be, & therefore each of us to sympathetic pleasure with the other. Here is the proper place to ask you to remember me with the truest & warmest love to Tommy. I often think of him and of the loss which he has peculiarly sustained but let it only cause him to form a stronger determination to grow up & get on in the way that Papa would have continually taught him had he been still alive, both by example & advice, namely to be *good* and *honourable* as well as to strive to make himself of *use* & *value* in the world.

Remember me also most kindly to Ann Bolton. She will feel his loss as much as any of us almost for she must have known him well and loved & respected him much too. Mary Bentley & Ann Salisbury I could not forget for they have always been true to us and now that Papa is gone will have even more affection for his remaining children that they have seen grow up.

As for Yourself Dearest Henny, I have no need to assure you that I am now, as ever
Your loving Brother
W. S. Jevons.

[3] Their cousin William Edgar Jevons, who was probably still at Marseilles. See above, Letter 34, p. 61.
[4] For Jevons's summary of his father's letters, see Vol. I, p. 115.

83. W. S. JEVONS TO HERBERT JEVONS

Sydney, N.S.W.
4 March 1856

Dearest Herbert,

This morning I started for the Mint with far more eagerness than usual, for I knew the Marco Polo's mail had at last arrived and that I should have the wished for news of home arrangements.

One letter I found on my balance table, but the news it contained was so satisfactory and the prospect of a continued happy home so pleasing, that ten times the amount of most letters would not have given me the same delight.

My father's death remains with me, and ever will, the same mournful, but scarcely painful subject; certainly it is a pain to feel that he no longer hears of me with love or pleasure, and for you at home it must be a far sharper pain to visibly lose him from his place. Still one feels that his life was complete & happily ended, and his death, was more the natural termination of it, which was soon to be expected, rather than any cutting short of it, to be particularly regretted. There is a feeling too which has often occurred to me strongly viz that the remembrance of the dead, ought not to be at all allowed to check the cheerful & free action of the living, but rather to prove the necessity of making the most use of the present time. Therefore it is that I do not spend more time or writing in sorrowful thoughts but proceed to you & my present affairs. The journey from which you had just returned with Lucy, must have been an excessively severe one to all, and I was really glad to hear you had got home well. So soon after it too it was not to be expected that Lucy should write again to me, though I may hope for some more letters soon.

I feel sorry not to be more acquainted with the circumstances of my fathers money matters, as now when I am away from you all, I can form no judgement at all about things. From the way he spoke, about the annuity for Roscoe I supposed his property could not be near so large as it seems from your letter to be, and from the particulars you give me of Uncle T's & Henry's proposal, you will all be most comfortably off. I should guess that you would none of you quite spend the sums you name. I find that the *money I spent in London* for the three years, was about £100 per year so that £150 for Tommy will well cover everything. *You* will I dare say spend less even than him, living quietly at home, indeed my expenses here now, in lodgings & with Australian prices, must be under £200 per year. Lucy & Henny with all that they can desire, & Roscoe with more than his comfortable living costs, I think we may indeed be glad to be so well off in outward circumstances and to have an Uncle & relations to be so liberal & kind.

For myself, I acknowledge I am excellently well off and shall soon be likely to save a considerable sum of money, but in spite of this I think I may point out to you how much more certain & satisfactory your own circumstances have just lately become. I believe you take considerable pleasure in the principles of trade &c, at all events it is a thing very well capable of being interesting; You find yourself in better health, I hope, almost every day, & with Lucy & Henny at home & Tommy to take care of, life may easily be cheerful; finally you have the promise of, & naturally fall into a partnership in a first rate business in which you will soon make more money than I shall in all Australia, or by cutting about to the furthest ends of the world. To speak plainly about myself, a salary of £675 is a fine thing and I am happy to think that it has not only saved my Father much trouble and anxiety, but even been an unmixed pleasure to him: also to think that I am independent and able to help others rather than need help and that I am now saving a sum of money which will always be a great help. In short I am glad to find myself here, and glad *to have come to Australia*, still the *furthest* thought in my mind is that of spending in Australia any time that could be called a *considerable portion of my life*. I wish to land back in England (D.V.) the only country that I have any esteem for, still young and able to turn my attention to whatever is best suited. In this way I hope to return with a good deal more than I left it, but let me stop longer (say 10 years) and I verily believe I should not be worth carrying back, unless I were worth a fortune. By that time I should have regularly *stuck in the mud* as regards all science or any other knowledge or experience, and should have gained only "colonial experience" & money. ("Colonial Experience" is a term not to be understood outside of the colonies where it is alone to be gained).

Hence in due time I hope (D.V. again) to land in England and while I have great pleasure in hearing that you intend keeping up a home in Liverpool for yours, Lucy's but particularly Henny's and Tommy's sakes, may I not almost hope some time to join you there & again, though under much altered circumstances revive one's ideas of home.

Thus you see though it may not be very wise, I cannot help dwelling on the thought of home in some form or other. I can well imagine as you will be perhaps by the time you get this letter, Chatham Street given up to Henry and changed for some pleasant little house, possibly in the country, where *you* yourself will live exactly as usual though in better health from country air, Lucy will paint, housekeep &c, but will still, I cannot help thinking, be receiving a double number of those interminably kind invitations to stay at places in all the Counties in England, all of them *too kind* to be refused (perhaps I only judge of invitations by my own liking of them, very small yet) Henny will continue no doubt playing better every day as I understand she always has been, & Tommy will spend a few pleasant months in it every now & then, just as I used to do, only leaving again with a satisfactory feeling that it is what, in the nature of things, he ought to & must do.

If there were one more circumstance about it I should wish to be, I would have the *home* (in a fairy manner) find itself placed in some beautiful situation on the shores of Port Jackson, or on the Waverley Hills with a fine wide view of the Pacific Ocean; and then what few pleasures I have now, would be increased by what I should derive from it.

One feels a reluctance just at present in talking of mere enjoyments, though I have explained how I think they are not incompatible with feelings of sorrow. At any rate I have a real enjoyment before me. M^r OConnell, Mr Millers brother in law, not obtaining any work in Sydney, is going to the diggings, & wanted a companion on the road. I said I should be most happy to go, if I could have the time, and it wanted but one suggestion more that I could ask for a holyday* and the thing appeared possible. This morning, I stuffed a deal of boldness into me and asked for 2 weeks holyday,* on the excuse of the work being very light at present. Though one of the lightest worked, I am still the first in the Mint to ask a holyday,* but Capt Ward, very kindly gave it, & a Memor^n to the effect, is signed & all right. We start next Saturday or Sunday, & tramp it all the way up (about 150 miles) to some fine new diggings Yorkey's Creek, Ophir, to which there is quite a rush, being the first new discovery for a long time. We shall be 7 or 8 days walking up, then I shall spend a few days looking about me, & return by the mail in time to commence work within the fortnight. It will be a fine opportunity to see a little Australian life, and I have the greatest desire possible to see some Australian scenery and gold digging into the bargain. With a knapsack or bundle containing shawl or blanket, waterproof, two or three pieces of clothing, a few provisions, &c, and myself with *aneroid barometer*, two or three little thermometers, & a few other things, we shall set off walking from Parramatta (going there by rail). We shall get along I dare say 20 miles a day, chiefly in mornings & evenings, camping out at night, in some retired bushy place, with a good fire, & spending the middle of the day leisurely. I shall take what meteorological observations I can particularly among the mountains. If you have a map of New S Wales, you can trace the route, from Parramatta, through Penrith, & the Blue Mountains, to Bathurst near which are Ophir & some of the other chief diggings. The camping out is very nice & healthy in a climate like the Australian, unless indeed it is rainy

weather, and then I shall have plenty of money & can go to the Inns.[1]
Having no more time to write, tonight
Believe me, with love to all the others
Ever your affec. Brother
W. S. Jevons.

P S. Please to forward the enclosed letter to Harry Roscoe wherever he may be. I will write again after coming down with an account but do not expect it too soon.

84. W. S. JEVONS TO HERBERT JEVONS

Petersham near Sydney N.S.W.
April 6th 1856[1]

My dear Herbert

You will remember that in my last letter received no doubt long before you have this, I said I was going a tour to the *Diggings*. The tour too I did go and it lasted two weeks, and was most agreable* and amusing; having been now fully two weeks returned, it is time I thought of writing you some account of it, and I therefore devote this Sunday evening to the job. Latest news from England is now 110 or 115 days old, and this with other things has almost tended to take ones thoughts, temporarily only, off home and it is therefore with great pleasure that I turn to any employment that will bring them back upon it and that will enable one in some way to share one's enjoyment with those at home. I will proceed direct on the journey, for all other things I can better write about another night after some of the mails have come in.

I was to go you know with M^r OConnell, the brother in law of Mr Miller, and as he was going to walk up to the diggings, I undertook the same. As we intended camping it out regularly at night, we provided ourselves accordingly, and the chief things we took were 2 loaves 2 or 3 meatpies, biscuits & other provisions, including especially 1 lb tea & sugar, 2 tin cups, a clean shirt each, pair of stockings &c and a few other things. My share of the provisions and my other things I rolled up inside a large old shawl of Lucy's which served most capitally to sleep in, and the whole pack, I then carried over my shoulders by straps. Lightness of course is the first consideration, and even the few things we did take were soon left behind.

---

[1] For a full account of this trip, see Vol. I, Jevons's 'Diary of a Journey to the Gold Diggings at Sofala, March 9th – March 23rd 1856', Appendix, p. 213.
[1] The original manuscript of this letter, which is incomplete, is in the Mitchell Library, Sydney.

We started for Parramatta by the first train on Sunday morning, so that the first 12 miles were travelled with as much ease as is possible anywhere in the world; I often wished the other miles could be done as easily. I will not delay in describing Parramatta, furthur* than that it is a pretty little town, nicely situated, but not of much importance, in a business point of view, & likely to be of much less soon, for when the railway is extended & takes the place of the roads, no one will think of stopping at or going into Parramatta, which is a mile from the station.[2]

Here we got on the Penrith road, the first chief stage of the *Great Western Road of New South Wales*. This requires little to describe it; a wide track cleared through continuous & perfectly uniform woods of gum tree running straight a-head over hill & dale, for about 20 miles, the country on a general level, but as it would be described, *undulated* with gentle ranges of hills running chiefly parallel to the coast. The view is generally limited to the other side of the road, and there being nothing that I know of, of any interest along it, a more monotonous walk you could hardly pick out. I must confess our first days performance was nothing to boast of, for on account of frequent stoppages &c we found the sun setting before we were much over half the distance. Before you laugh at this in England, take into account the difference of climate, and the heat of the sun by which M^r OConnell was extraordinarily affected, and also the weight, perhaps 20 lbs that we had each to carry. However just beyond a creek of the name of Toongabbee, on which is a small village, we turned off into the wood in search of our first nights camping ground. When tired you are but little particular, and so long as you are near some water, & out of sight of the road, room to light your fire, & stretch out your legs is easily found.

Once for all I will describe the proceedure* of "*camping out*" though it is a way in which thousands of *carriers*, diggers, shepherds, travellers &c are continually living in Australia. The fire is most indispensable & also most easily made, by collecting the old sticks & dead wood in the bush, within a few yards circumference, & setting fire to it, when it burns at once with extraordinary quickness & heat. On this the tin pots are set full of water to be boiled for tea; of the water one may say, "Get water, clean if you can, but get water"; it is sometimes fresh spring water, but it is sometimes only thin mud. Tea making is the process in its greatest simplicity; ebullition having commenced tea & brown sugar are added by the fingers in proper proportions according to taste, and the pot stirred & withdrawn to cool ready to drink. In large parties you may see the tea made in one large pot, from which each person's own tin can be filled but any way tea is the universal drink, so long as spirits are unobtainable and is usually taken to all the three meals of the day.

[2] See Vol. I, p. 135, n. 2.

After finishing tea we at once followed our strongest inclinations and lay down *to go to bed*. The shawl, and my *traps* as a pillow constituted the bed, and I was soon asleep though not to sleep a very easy night. Do not think I was uneasy at the gloominess of the wood with its tall bare trees just discernable in the blackness against the sky, or the stillness & silence only broken by croakings of frogs, and the most unmelodious cries of different Australian birds.

We were both awake at day-break, and after manufacturing tea as before, & eating breakfast, were ready and eager to proceed. This day we went the second half of the distance to Penrith; the road needs not one word of furthur* description; it was like yesterdays road. A few miles on this side [of]³ Penrith, a small town is passed named St Marys, South Creek, consisting of a few dozen small wood or brick verandah cottages, scattered along the road for about a mile on cleared allotments of land. A few of these are the *stores* or shops which supply the neighbourhood, and an astonishing number of inns & public houses, accomodate* travellers and the drunkards of the place. Penrith, when we reached it, we found just such another place, only much larger, so that many of the buildings were of a proportionately greater size & importance.

In reaching the top of the last of the *undulations* we caught sight of country beyond of more interesting features. This was a singular flat plain, of a narrow long shape, quite distinct from the bushy hilly land we were passing over, and still better bounded on the other side, at a distance of 2 miles by one continuous steep rocky hill, entirely covered by a thick forest of trees. The plain though very rich, was almost treeless, except such as had been planted; large portions were covered by Indian corn & other crops, & the remainder was no doubt grazed. Through the length of it, which is parallel to the coast, runs the first considerable river I had seen in Australia, viz the Nepeān, a slow full stream, one or two hundred yards wide. Over it was a neat & certainly very good bridge of wood just opened, and accounted a wonderful piece of work here. The banks of the river surprized* me; they were very steep & high, & composed of *pure alluvial soil*, which from a section I saw at the side of the road must have been something like 15 feet deep. Passing the river you enter the principal part of the plains, named *Emu plains*. The road wandered through them and very boldly faced right up to the unbroken line of Steep hill, in which no opening or road was visible. We approached it less confidently, and being tired & the sun declining we determined upon camping at once.

The country was here picturesque & varied and any spot would

---

³ This word is omitted in the original manuscript.

have served us as a resting place, but *water* again must be sought. Turning off the road just at the foot of the hill, we followed down a hollow, & found ourselves in a most beautiful secluded little gully in the bottom of which were clear pools of water: the trees were prettily grouped, instead of being monotonously crowded together, and between them were flowering bushes, most of them odoriferous. I will not waste more words in saying that here we passed a most pleasant night, and that I got up quite refreshed & pleasant, & none the worse although the dew had been sufficient to wet everything about us.

I felt quite sorry to leave this beautiful little place which afforded us the pleasantest nights lodging I think that we had, Inns included. Getting onto the road again we set off with the usual intention of doing a long days work, but were then quite ignorant of the level of the country we were going into. This was the most remarkable piece of the whole road, for it was a continued incline upwards for some miles, the first portion being entirely cut out of the side of a narrow deep gully, which ran straight into the Hill, named Lapstone Hill, in a westward direction. The scenery in parts was very wild & mountainous, but was somewhat obscured by the morning mists hanging among the trees.

The goodness of the roadway here surprized us, for it seemed quite a finished piece of work & by no means new; this was difficult to understand until, the *convicts* came into our minds, whom we always hear of being sent "to labour on the roads". It must have required no small amount of labour too to make a road through such a piece of country, and you know that it is said that the commencement of this mountainous land for a long time formed the westward boundary of the Colony.

On proceeding furthur,* always upwards, we seemed to leave behind all the fine scenery and to be doomed again to a road nearly as bad as the Penrith road.

85. W. S. JEVONS TO T. E. JEVONS
[LJN, 63–5]

2d May 1856.

... I daresay you will hardly think how much I am interested in your proceedings in London. It is from the great wish I have that you should, in the best meaning of the word, be successful, and obtain all the possible good from the new course of life you are beginning. Being the youngest, you were the one of us about whom my father had the *fondest hopes;* and, now he is gone, all the rest of us look forward just the same to seeing those hopes fulfilled. Moreover, I feel a great interest in a younger brother going through exactly the same sort of life which I remember myself with so much pleasure, and you must therefore write me now and then a good long letter about everything you are doing at school, everything you see in London, and what you are intending to do.

People, at all events many people, do not like to be beaten, *i.e.* surpassed, but this feeling may in some circumstances be overcome by better feelings. Therefore it is that I hope after you have been in London a year or two, that you will leave me nothing to speak of, as to prizes and the like; but whatever you do I do not doubt you will do it with the best of motives, *i.e.* to gain real good and worth, and not in the least for show or the *name of the thing*. Stick to the real solid desire of improving yourself, and in some way or other, more or less direct, rendering yourself useful, and then you need not care a straw about other persons' opinion of you. It is the most comfortable thing in the world to know yourself to be better than people think you, and it gives you the truest ease of mind; and this I have no doubt is worth all the pleasure one can have in being considered *a clever fellow*, or *a very jolly fellow*, or even *a very good fellow*, which are the commonest ways in which a *fellow's* worth is measured and expressed in society. In short, do not look to others' approbation merely. . . . I did not think you would have taken so high a place as to classes. But do not think too much of the place you have got in the school. In this (as I believe in most other things), the *rate of rise* or improvement is far more to be considered than the *point actually attained*. I was rather surprised, and, I must own agreeably, to find you say 'All the masters mentioned Stanley, Mr. Key[1] himself included', and I shall take an interest in all you tell me about the old school. How do you like old Mr. Travers?[2] I think he liked me better than any, and he was rather grieved at not giving me his first prize, but he gave me first mention, and a place equal with the first boy, instead. London is a fine place, and while you are in it make the best of it. You will do no harm in going to plenty of exhibitions, all sorts of sights and the like; and they are no loss of time or money, provided they do not interfere directly with your lessons. I remember I used to think the Queen opening Parliament, etc., the best fun possible, and used to try how often I could manage to see her.[3]

When you are a little older I think you will find it very well worth while to take walks through London just as you would through a pretty country. The portions of London are as distinct in appearance and character as the nations of Europe, and they are large enough to take

---

[1] See above, Letter 2, n. 2, p. 5

[2] Newenham Travers, a teacher at University College School, 1850–61; assistant Master from 1855.

[3] See above, Letter 15, p. 30; also Vol. I, p. 70.

long excursions among them. I will leave all *cautions* to Lucy, who is great at them.

Living as you are with Aunt Richard, and among company, I am afraid you will grow too fond of parties and suchlike, but my real honest opinion of them is that they are of very little good; and, though you have no occasion to be like me, you would hardly think how much time is lost by going out one night here and another there. Of home, where you will be, I suppose, when you get this, I cannot say much, as nothing was settled even at the latest dates I have heard news of. I daresay you, most of you, think me a lucky fellow, for a good sum of money goes a long way, but how I should like to be among things again, something like the 'lags' (convicts) of Botany Bay in former days must have wished to be at their old practices. However, I amuse myself as I best can, and always with a view to my *term expiring*. . . .

86. W. S. JEVONS TO HENRIETTA JEVONS
[LJP, 65]

Sydney.
May 3rd 1856.

My dearest Henny

Though I have lessons and no end of other things to do tonight, the answering of your last letter, (the one from a place with a Welch* name)[1] is so inviting an employment, that against all proper rules I will do it first, the others after if there be time!

You said you wished to write an interesting letter, and it was interesting. Between us two there seems to be an extraordinary similarity of feelings & thoughts which does not by any means always exist between persons who love & respect each other equally well, or even between brothers or sisters.

People are usually essentially different by nature as well as education (see Friends in Council I. 114[2]) and this we must always take into account. Where two are found nearly alike, love is no doubt more *easy* and *unrestricted*, but do not suppose I would even hint that it is therefore less *true or lasting* in other cases, for I do not see any reason to think so, nor do I find it to be the case.

These remarks are rather abstract but are suggested by our always having "two or three exclusive subjects to write about" and your last letter was occupied by a scarcely larger variety of matter. Music is one of those subjects and it happens that just lately I have been in a rather

[1] This letter is not among the Jevons Papers.
[2] Sir Arthur Helps, *Friends in Council: a series of readings and discourse thereon*, 2 vols (1847).

musical *humour*, or more properly *rage*, occasioned perhaps by going to several of Anna Bishops[3] farewell concerts: She is a singer of the first class and a splendid actress, but she is also such a nice *truly English* woman, & chooses such excellent *first class* music of all sorts, that it is a real pleasure to hear her. I have heard her sing ballads ("Home sweet home" in particular) sacred music, & operas. One night she & "all the available talent in Sydney" performed parts of the "Creation" "Elijah" & "Messiah"; being better acquainted with music & older than when I heard the splendid performances at Liverpool or London, is the reason, I suppose, that this evening gave me more pleasure than any before; also the Song "Angels ever bright & fair" sung by her then, was the most exquisite bit of singing I ever heard.

The last time I heard her was in Norma which was of course fine; but afterwards she came down from heaven (among the scenery) and, dressed as the Goddess of Liberty, sang the Marseilleise* Hymns. This was very well received & *encored*, but imagine the state of the theatre when she suddenly & unexpectedly appeared dressed as "Brittania"* and in the most splendid manner sang "Rule Brittannia"* followed by "God Save the Queen." Everybody was amazingly delighted as all must be who like England as well as me. She also makes such a good dignified goddess that what might be ridiculous with others made a really fine scene. So well did this and the Sacred night succeed that they were *repeated* in a great hurry before she left Sydney. It cannot be denied therefore that good music is appreciated in Sydney which is certainly a point on the favourable side.

I now give you a list of what music I have and am now playing. X is put to those I find difficult or cannot properly manage.

1. Opera's.	Sonnambula	Masses, 3 by Mozart.
	Norma	X Oratorio, The Creation
	Lucrez. Borgia	Selection of small sacred pieces
	X Huguenots	for Harmonium
	X Don Giovanni	Sacred pieces, about 6
	X Figaro	various.
	Der Freyschutz*	(of which "Cujus animus" from
X Overtures, 7, of different operas.		Rossini's Stabat Mater is very beautiful)

When I say I can play a thing, I must always be understood to mean

---

[3] Ann Rivière (1810–84), English soprano of French descent; studied in London, 1824–31, when she married Henry Bishop and took the professional name of Madame Anna Bishop; after 1839, when she eloped to the Continent with Boscha the harpist, she mostly travelled: she sang in Naples 1844–6; in 1847 she went to the United States and in 1855 to Australia, returning to New York via South America; she spent most of the rest of her life in the United States.

in *my own way:* I never *pretend* or *intend* to play to please other people; people dont usually read books to please others, & I do not see why they should always be supposed to *read* or play music to please others. I regard a fine piece of music like a fine poem, or essay or philosophical work, that is as a thing to be studied understood & remembered. In this point of view playing music though it may *bore* others is still as good an employment of time *to a certain extent* as reading.

You advise me to look into *thorough base** &c. I should like, even intend too, but I dont know when I shall find the time, as it is a wide subject.

You are perhaps surprized* to hear me speak of *lessons* in the first line of this letter; know then that regularly twice a week I go to learn French & German (one time each) & hope in time to be well up in them. I have only had four lessons as yet (terms £8.8 per quarter). French I find myself already pretty well advanced with, and German I find easier & pleasanter than I thought as I remember something of what I learnt one year at Univ. Coll. School. As I depend chiefly on my work at home of course, it takes up a deal of time, and these letters to you, Tommy, Lucy &c grievously interfere with it. If this was all I should not care, but there are the Meterologics which now & then take a good deal of work, Scientific works to be read, and I am getting quite Poetical withal, reading Byron & what not!!!

Thank God, the work is very easy at the Mint at present more like a *continued whole holyday** than anything, with a good salary into the bargain.

Besides Music, (how I should like a few evenings with you to hear your execution (which I am sure must be splendid by this time), receive suggestions as to my improvement & practise with you singing) your letter is filled by a somewhat *grave and extensive* religious question. In this I am more than ever convinced of our similarity of natures for they are just such thoughts as have occurred to me before now, and as I have often heard my Father express, & admired in him. They are *liberal* and *charitable*, but though I like them myself I am still sure that the more *concentrated* & *defined* opinions, that Lucy for instance or many more even among Unitarians only, have, may produce the same amount of ultimate, good, & happiness of mind. My opinions go in the same direction but rather furthur* than yours. All the religions & religious opinions on the earth, I regard only as so many different exteriors, one may say Costumes, thrown over a few simple & eternal truths or principles which are more what would be commonly called "*moral truths*". The exterior religion has varied with different times & people, from the most barbarous (examples it is is unnecessary to name) in which the inward meaning was often quite lost sight of or misrepresented, down to the most simple & truth-like which I have no hesitation in saying, is, among creeds, the Unitarian.

I will venture even to say that a man who has a really serious mind, such as would reflect on the nature of the world, & on the way in which we are temporarily placed in it with the evident design of seeking the purest & greatest possible pleasure, is sure to gain certain principles or feelings, such as a trust in the course of things (i e Providence) a persuasion that we have all duties to perform to each other, without which *society* could not be endurable, and also something of the nature of *sympathy with the feelings of others,* out of which arises *love* &c, and that these are the essence of all true *religion*. The man may even be said to be *religious* though he never heard of God by any name, and had never been used to put his feelings into the form of any creed or set opinions. God is but the *embodiment* of the first & greatest principle of the world, viz, *universal good, order* tending towards good, *design*, all coming under the comprehensive term Providence, & *Christ* I conceive to be an example of a *Perfect Man*, and of the relation which such a character must bear to God.

Having commenced reflecting on such subjects you will probably not stop till you have settled your opinions on some foundation, but I cannot quite agree with you that it is *necessary* or even profitable for everyone to spend much time studying or discussing religious points provided that by their *good moral conduct* they give evidence of possessing, more or less, the natural *religious principles* which I have mentioned. People evidently refer to these feelings or principles when they say a man is *unprincipled,* than which you can hardly use a more *condemnatory* term

For myself, I have not thought half so much about religion lately as a year or two ago, for possessing I believe a consciousness of those principles as much as most, I feel rather like one who having made up his mind what is to be done, without more talking or deliberation, pulls off his coat and sets to it. Fortunately for me I am face to face with a well paying work, & having no better opportunities to look forward to or wish for, and nothing particular to look back upon with regret, I am in a happy *quiescent* state of mind, which I never experienced so much before. Perhaps Herbert, who is often very matter of fact, would say this was all from having a comforting monthly supply of the *needful* (£.s.d.) but I should not like to believe it entirely so, and should not like to leave New South Wales, richer only in gold. Sooner or later *must* come the time for again travelling across the world (by a longer or shorter route) & reaching, I hope, my old home But what there will be for me to do there I have not the slightest idea, & time only will disclose.

In your letter I found a small pocket pin-cushion which pleased me more than most would expect, for besides the fact that it was made by you, my old one was worn out and a new one *needed,* an assayer often wanting pins in his little *dodges.*

May 20th. It is necessary now that I should finish up this letter. I have lately begun reading Spencer's Treatise on Music in *Weales Series,*[4] but find it *excessively dull* as well as rather difficult. But I must try and get on with it In playing Operas I am much bothered with the mixture of *triple & common* time, and I cannot conceive how to play the following

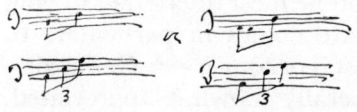 and I generally play them

(I have only written these with respect to *time* not notes)

Am I not wrong. How stupidly contrived the *notation* of music is, is it not. I should improve it I think if I had much to do with it.

I hope you will be pleased with the miniature photograph of Papa, that I am sending you, and I shall be anxious to know that everything arrives safe.

There is no need to send any *loves* as I find I have actually written a letter to each. As to yourself, our love is too deep & real to require any forms or expressions so believe me as ever

Your affec. Brother
W. S. Jevons.

87. H. E. ROSCOE TO W. S. JEVONS

Heidelberg. May. 10th
1856.

My dear Stanley

I was really ashamed when I received your acceptable letter[1] the other day to think that I had not written to you for so long; not since the death of your poor Father which I am sure you must have felt even more at such a distance than those who were with him at the last. It must be a comfort however to you to hear how bravely Lucy bore up against her sad troubles, & how she is now resting & enjoying the company of her friends in London – I hope that this change in your family circle will not induce you to give up your situation sooner than you

---

[4] Charles Child Spencer, *A Rudimentary and Practical Treatise on Music,* 2 vols (1850). John Weale (1791–1862), London bookseller, published *Weale's Rudimentary Series* in four parts (1849–50).

[1] Possibly the letter mentioned in the postscript to Letter 83, p. 218; it is not among the Jevons Papers.

otherwise would. Do not think of coming home at present unless something certain offers itself. It seems rather uncharitable advice, but I believe it is right. I know how unpleasant uncertainty as to ones future is! You are now making money, & doing good work in your meteorological researches – don't give it up in a hurry – Although you may be sure my boy that I should be delight'd to see you in England again, still you ought to stop some years out there still – I must now make the most of my time & paper & relate what I think will be most interesting to you, of Chemistry in General, & of my private doings in particular. In General then. Chemistry is going ahead fast – of course – & Gerhardt – Williamsons views are becoming more generally known & appreciated. Gerhardt has not done anything new lately, but has been busy writing his book[2] – Williamson for the last two years has been in love & has also not published much – Since August last he has been very busy – first getting married[3] & setting a house in order, then getting his lectures ready, & attending to the laboratory & his own researches – His lectures were on the whole very successful, but I had an immense deal of work to do – For you heard I suppose that I was to assist him in the preparation of the first courses for the large sum of £60 for six months – We had many new & striking experiments, & in the arrangement of a new Museum[4] & making apparatus & preparations I can assure you that I had enough to do. After the lectures were over in April I came over here to continue our research on the chemical action of light, & am now hard at work. Hofmann[5] has lately been resuming his scientific researches – & in conjunction with Cahours[6] he has published some very important results. This will put Williamsons dander up & before long I doubt not that we shall have some good researches from him. Of Graham I do not hear much but I should think that he makes a very good master.[7] The Chemical World has lately been disgusted by the appointment of R. D. Thomson[8] to the Examinership at the University of London

---

[2] See Vol. I, p. 87, n. 2. Gerhardt was Professor of Chemistry at Strasbourg, 1855–6; the book to which H. E. Roscoe referred was probably *Traité de Chimie organique*: 4 Tom. 1853–6).

[3] In 1855 Williamson married Emma Catherine, third daughter of Thomas Hewitt Key; they had a son and a daughter.

[4] '... The effective development of the study of geology and mineralogy [at University College, London] belongs ... to that general revival which begins about the year 1855, and at that date also the gift of collections made by Murchison and Greenough laid the foundation of the geological museum ...' (Bellot, op. cit., pp. 269–70).

[5] See above, Letter 27, n. 8, p. 50

[6] See above, Letter 35, n. 4, p. 64. A. Cahours, A. W. Hofmann, 'Note on a new Class of Alcohols', *London ... Philosophical Magazine*, XII (October 1856) 309–14.

[7] i.e. of the Royal Mint.

[8] Robert Dundas Thomson (1810–64), eldest son of James Thomson (1768–1855) editor of the *Encyclopaedia Britannica*; M.D. Glasgow, 1831; deputy Professor of Chemistry there, 1841–52; F.R.S. 1854; he was lecturer in chemistry at St Thomas's Hospital and Medical Officer of Health for Marylebone, 1856.

vacated by Tommy. Thomson never published anything – nor has even written a book – in fact may be (& probably is) perfectly ignorant of the progress of modern Chemistry. Williamson ought to have applied – Miller did I believe & even he is a better man than Thomson.

What I am to do, heaven only knows – I suppose something will turn up before long, & I must get on by private teaching I suppose until something is vacant – I should have applied for the professorship of Practical Chemistry at Kings College vacant by Bowman's[9] death, but I was not orthodox which they make a necessity – So Bloxam[10] got it – What humbug that is! –

I forget whether I sent you a copy of our first paper published in the October number of the Chemical Journal – However I will send you another along with the second paper which I hope will appear in the next October number –[11]

You heard that I was in Glasgow at the Association – I enjoyed myself very much & made very many acquaintances – in my own line – which is useful.[12] Then I came direct to London & worked away at the lectures without intermission.

I was asked to give a Friday Evening at the Royal Institution, on the results of our experiment, & I did give one on the 4th April.[13] Of course it is very difficult to give such a lecture & such a subject to an audience of ladies – & I fear that many did not understand what I was talking about.

The line of research which seems chalked out for me is physical chemistry – determinative research. There is certainly much to be done in the land lying between these two Sciences – but whether I can manage to do anything remains to be seen. It is very difficult. I think that Williamson is perhaps a little vexed that I do not follow in his line, & I of course cannot expect so much help from him as if I was more one of his school – but we shall see how it will go –

I have a glorious prospect – though a very uncertain one – for the Summer vacation – Bunsen wants me to go with him to Italy & Sicily to visit the volcanic districts & make all sorts of observations & collect material for future work – on Etna, Vesuvius & the Liparic Islands – Whether I shall think it right to go remains to be seen – I have many reasons for doubting – but I will write to you when it is fixed – & if I go will send you a copious account of our doings –

[9] John Eddowes Bowman (1819–54), Professor of Practical Chemistry, King's College, London, 1851–4.
[10] Charles Loudon Bloxam (1831–87), Professor of Practical Chemistry at King's College, London, 1856–70, and of Chemistry, 1870–87.
[11] See Letters 75 and 114, pp. 191 and 315. [12] See above, Letter 75, p. 190.
[13] An account of this paper, 'On the Measurement of the Chemical Action of Light', appears in the London ... Philosophical Magazine, xi (1856) 482–4.

I expect my mother here for the Summer months – & Harriet & Edward come through on their way to Switzerland. I saw Lucy, & Henny before I left they both seemed very well. Tommy is a capital fellow – he will get on in life I think – he likes his schools uncommon – Tom Booth[14] is going to Cambridge – having been one year at University College – Frank[15] is well, still in the city – William has got a baby[16] – & he says it is so ugly that he never believed in Original Sin before he saw it but that now he does! – Richard Hutton is well. & John Thornley[17] also – Harry (long)[18] in Norwich – rather down because his lady love is just married to some one else – Don't you marry a native my boy, & bring back some black piccaninies* I would not come to see you then –

I will write again before long
Ever my dear Stanley

      Yours affecly
      Henry E. Roscoe

W. Stanley Jevons Esq
Royal Mint
Sydney.

88. W. S. JEVONS TO HERBERT JEVONS

Sydney, N.S.W.
May 20th 1856

My dear Herbert,

Your letters lately have taken the form of short notes and you have deferred writing longer accounts till things were more determined upon, which is perhaps as well.

In consequence I will also defer any longer letter to you till I know more of the particulars of our affairs; though I cannot help saying a few words by this mail.

You did not seem to put your faith in the "Royal Charter" or the Auxiliary Screw principle, with rather a want of your usual sagacity. I look upon this Auxiliary method as a great and new principle and I have no hesitation in saying that it is *the thing* and will supersede as to general advantage both regular steamers, and common sailing ships. On

---

[14] H. E. Roscoe's first cousin, the son of his mother's sister Emily (formerly Fletcher) and Charles Booth, and brother of the statistician Charles Booth (1840–1961). See Vol. I, p. 77, n. 2.

[15] See Vol. I, p. 193, n. 6.

[16] William Caldwell Roscoe had three children: Elizabeth Mary (b. 21 February 1856); William Malin (b. 6 August 1857); and Margaret Henrietta (b. 26 November 1858).

[17] Presumably a member of the Liverpool family, possibly a brother of James Thornely.

[18] Possibly another of their cousins, Henry Roscoe (1830–99) eldest son of Robert Roscoe.

the "Oliver Lang" when we used to be lying for weeks in calms about the tropics I often thought what a small engine & screw would do for us. Talking of the Oliver Lang, very lately I got tea at Mr Newtons quarters in the Mint with Mr Wilber our old first mate,[1] and two more sensible & agreable* men you might go far enough to get tea with again, though but mechanics & sailors. We heard accounts of the fate of Capt Manning which satisfied even our grudges against the man, viz, that J. B. & Co[2] sent out a Captain to take his place by the steam tug, and that when he arrived in dock all his property was seized; also that he was afterwards obliged to take a mate's place.[3]

J B & Co's day is over, and their "sun's going down – " &c & G. B & Co will take their place and bring us our mails with rather more regularity.[4]

You ask me to send you more papers, so I will try & get todays paper to send as it is full of information about Sydney and our Mint at the top of all.

On the 14th of this month it completed the first anniversary of its active existence. It is only a short time since we received the first Report from England (by Graham as Master of the Mint) on coin we issued here June & July 1855. You know that specimens (called a pyx) are picked out by chance and sent home to be weighed and assayed, as a check on us.

The mean assay in England of 32 coins was *916.69*, true standard you know being 916.67. This extreme accuracy to the $\frac{1}{50,000}$ we do not think of claiming credit for, as assaying cannot be expected to go beyond $\frac{1}{10,000}$, (i e 000.1)[5] even in a mean result. But what will people think when the next pyx report from home is found to turn out about 916.4 or $\frac{27}{100,000}$ wrong. The fact is that about July 1855 Capt W who had been till then trusting entirely to our assay reports, bethought himself of some standard assay gold, and some of the celebrated *Assay trial plate*[6] of the English Mint which he had with him.

---

[1] See Vol. I, p. 107.
[2] James Baines & Co. See above, Letter 60, n. 3, p. 146.
[3] For Jevons's criticisms of Captain Manning's conduct during the voyage see Vol. I, pp. 103–7.
[4] Probably Gibbs, Bright & Co. of Bristol and Liverpool, who put the *Great Britain* on the Australia run. Cf. above, Letter 23, n. 4, p. 42.
[5] As written in the original manuscript.
[6] New gold trial plates were made for the Royal Mint in 1828 to replace the plate of 1688, which had been virtually used up. See Vol. III, Letter 322.

Our assay upon these did not agree for we found the former something like 916.0 instead of 916.7. It was altogether evident that we did not agree with the English Mint report, so that our first coin issued might be expected to assay in England 917.0 or more and Capt W altered the proportion of alloy accordingly. But under Grahams management our first issue appears to be exactly standard, hence our later ones must be considerably under.

The cause of these extraordinary discrepancies, it is impossible to understand being hid in the mysteries of assaying and Mint management. I should think it must be caused by a reform in the management by Graham, but any way our report having proved correct, we are perfectly clear of course.[7]

These particulars I thought would interest you but you had perhaps better not let them go furthur.*

You told me I had better invest what money I save in shares or other things. I have chosen in preference Government Debentures, and about a week since bought £300 at $95\frac{1}{2}$. The interest is 5 per cent payable by *coupons* and the principal is payable in 20 years. They are most imposing looking documents on parchment with 40 small coupons round the sides for the payment of interest halfyearly. They feel like a solid provision for life, and have a most secure and comfortable app^{ce}.

One advantage is that they are payable also in London, therefore I can take them home without any losses by *exchange* &c. I hope I may keep them for the full 20 years.

I was rather surprized though it must be confessed agreably* to hear that £400 would remain to me of my Fathers property, besides I suppose the £100 due when I am of age.

You ask me if the former sum could remain in the Iron business to form I suppose a part of your capital. Even for my own interest I should be very glad that it should, with the other £100 too if you like, for you see I can only get about $5\frac{1}{2}$ p. c. interest here. But it will be, I suppose, a private loan from me to you and not to Jevons & Co at all, so that I shall have nothing to do with this *limited liability* bother,[8] of which I have seen so much in the papers.

It occurs to me that now my money account will have to be with you instead of my father, and that you had not any of my money to pay for the things you sent in "Canopus" and the whole expenses of the parcel, but you will I suppose in September receive & hold the £100 for me out

---

[7] For an account of Mint policy in regard to stating the fineness of gold, see Craig, op. cit., pp. 307–8.

[8] Probably a reference to the Limited Liability Act which had received the Royal Assent in August 1855 (18 & 19 Vict. c. 133); it was repealed after a few months and incorporated in the Joint Stock Companies Act 1856, the first of the modern Companies Acts. Cf. L. C. B. Gower, *The Principles of Modern Company Law* (1969), pp. 40–50.

of which you must repay yourself for all expenses on my account. I will write more about these things when I hear more from you. I hope you will not be disgusted by my writing on picture note paper; I thought you might be interested in these views of the three principal Australian towns.[9] They all look indeed equally disgusting but from my letter to Tommy[10] you will see what pretty walks there are about Sydney.

       I am
      Your Affec. Brother
       W. S. Jevons.

89. W. S. JEVONS TO HERBERT JEVONS

           Sydney. N.S.W.
           July 4th 1856.[1]

My dearest Herbert

Today and not before I received the long and anxiously expected parcel per Canopus, 178 days out!! and I will leave you to imagine the satisfaction with which I engaged a barrow man at the Circular Wharf at the first price he demanded to wheel it up to the Mint, where my first business was of course to open it & examine its contents.

I write now with little more purpose than to thank you for all your trouble and kindness about it. The Compass & sextant are *precisely* what I wanted, and packed up so carefully as they were, were of course quite uninjured. The Compass is quite as good & expensive as I have any need of, and as far as I can judge, for I have no knowledge of these instruments yet, the pocket sextant is quite a superior instrument; its perfection & completeness is quite surprising and I have had some trouble to find out the use of all the parts.

I have to thank you also for your care about the little things belonging to Papa and need say nothing as to the value with which I regard them as you will fully understand it

You send also four books of which three are singularly *à propos* as I am at present reading on "*Music*", have been fond lately of Statistics, and have wanted several times to refer to "Vestiges"[2] which I read some time since, and approve of greatly on the whole. (Hiawatha[3] I cannot make out)

---

 [9] Jevons wrote this letter on three sheets of writing paper, each of which was headed by an illustration, entitled as follows: 'Church Street, Sydney'; 'Melbourne from Collingwood'; 'Adelaide from Hindley Street'.
 [10] This letter is not among the Jevons Papers.
 [1] The original manuscript of this letter is in the Mitchell Library, Sydney.
 [2] Probably Robert Chambers' *Vestiges of Creation* (1844). Chambers (1802–71), joint founder of the publishing firm, wrote and published the work anonymously.
 [3] Henry Wadsworth Longfellow, *The Song of Hiawatha* (1855).

I miss only my French assay stamp which I understood was to be sent;[4] whether it never reached England or was accidentally forgotten in sending the box I do not know. It is however of little importance, and chiefly an affair of curiosity, as I have my "diploma" and should never want to stamp gold in all probability.

I feel almost inclined to *complain* that your letters are not fuller, for they have to me a sort of *substantial* interest different from that that ones sisters letters can afford. Believe me that no amount of writing will be thrown away if the pleasure it will give me in reading is any consideration. You mention something about signing a trust-deed; does it mean a partnership, and that you are now a partner in Jevons & C⁰ along with Henry. If so I congratulate you on having such a sure and straightforward business to enter upon. The American Dispute no doubt gave Liverpool merchants some anxiety but what fear is there of a War when we read in the same paper of an English review of some 250–300 steam war vessels and of the admirable navy of the United States consisting of 31 fine vessels of all classes, of which several no doubt are steamers, and which are scattered pretty equally all over the globe.[5]

The news of Peace[6] was received very joyfully here, and Monday is to be a holyday* and a general illumination. The Public Buildings are all going to illuminate and the Mint will I expect present a distinguished appce on the occasion. I have had a glimpse of the design which is something as follows.

Among other things I may mention that today for the first time I

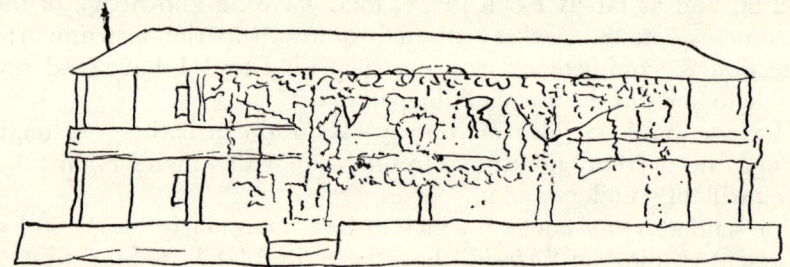

[4] See above, Letter 73, p. 184.
[5] The dispute Jevons refers to was probably that concerning the enlistment of American citizens in the British army during the Crimean War (see above, Letter 75, n. 16, p. 194). The political differences between the two countries during the period immediately preceding the Civil War inevitably caused fears of disruption in international trade: 'It was the cotton trade which dominated the Anglo-American nexus, at least down to mid-century, or perhaps to the Civil War. America increasingly attracted attention, with traders closely studying the political kaleidoscope with one eye, and with the other watching eagerly for an opportunity to adopt new methods of transport to both North and South America . . .' Checkland, op. cit., p. 110.
[6] The treaty of Paris ending the Crimean War had been signed on 30 March 1856. The news was received in Australia in June.

received the half yearly dividend of £7.10s on my debentures. I hope by the end of the year to add £300 more to them, besides which I shall have about £500 I suppose (including Mrs Moss money?)⁷ in your hands, and yielding the same interest of 5 p.c.

You will have heard of the *total loss* of the Shomberg. We have had much discussion about it here, and my opinion is that the Captain was entirely to blame; with a south west wind he should never have come near the coast there at all till reaching Basss Straits; this you will find in the Australian Sailing Directory.⁸ At his trial he got off by the uncertainty of the evidence about trifles.

I have written a long letter to Willy Jevons which perhaps he will let you read as it contains a short account of my trips to the Diggings & to Newcastle &c. I have written also to Lucy.⁹ I am immensely *busy* at present with all sorts of affairs both at home and at the Mint. For the present Good bye.

Ever your affectionate Brother
W. S. Jevons.

90. W. S. JEVONS TO THE EDITOR OF THE *SYDNEY MORNING HERALD*

"*The Railway Discussion*"[1]

Sir,

There seems to have arisen lately, in Sydney, a great Railway Discussion, carried on by means of papers read to the Philosophical Society, newspaper letters, &c. The one side are gaining themselves odium as the opponents of railway communication and such improvements in general, while the opposite, and it must be acknowledged, the most numerous body, are merely attacked by abstract arguments from the principles of

---

[7] See above, Letter 30, n. 1, p. 56.

[8] *The Australia Directory, Vol. 1, containing directions for the Southern shores of Australia from Cape Leeuwin to Port Stephens* (Admiralty Hydrographic Office, 1830).

[9] Probably the letter of 3 July 1856 (LJN, 66); nor is the letter to his cousin William Edgar Jevons among the Jevons Papers.

[1] On 9 May 1856 the Governor-General, Sir William Denison, read a paper entitled 'Development of the Railway System in England, with suggestions as to its application to the Colony of New South Wales' before the Sydney Philosophical Society. From the entries in Jevons's diary for 1856, it is evident that this gave a specific focus to the general interest in political economy which he had been developing for some months, and that he began to compose a letter on the subject on 1 June 1856 (Cf. Vol. IV, Part III).

This letter, and Letter 98 (p. 262) can be considered as Jevons's first published contributions to economic discussion, and the prelude to the articles on Land and Railway Policy which he wrote for the *Empire* in 1857 (reprinted in Vol. IV, Part II). Neither this letter, nor Letter 98, is included in the bibliography of Jevons's Australian writings appended to J. A. La Nauze's article 'Jevons in Sydney' (op. cit., pp. 39–44).

political economy, or are warned against expending the public revenue recklessly and unjustly, or incurring the burden of a public debt.

Professor Pell's[2] arguments are founded upon one simple proposition, viz:—"that the pecuniary return from the traffic on a railway is the true measure of its usefulness and value to the whole community," provided that the fares and tolls be adjusted to the correct rate at which the returns attain a maximum. A railway indeed, which shall confer all the benefits so lavishly attributed to it, of enormously increasing the public revenue by indirect taxation on additional population, of increasing it by the sale of Government waste lands, hitherto worthless, or of benefiting the whole public in a hundred undefined ways, must necessarily be a dividend-paying concern. If the advantages of the railway be so immense, surely persons availing themselves of it should be capable of paying the fair cost of carriage; so that the difference is seen to be chiefly one of *terms*. No Government would construct a railway unless convinced that its advantages to the community would be equivalent to its cost; no private company could be found to undertake it without a reasonable prospect of dividends. On our view of the question, the two cases are identical.

It may be urged, however, that, though the railway might be made to pay its current expenses and interest on capital, by exacting high tolls, it is better to reduce the latter with a view to the indirect benefit, and then make up the deficiency by general taxation. Professor Pell, however, argues clearly and at some length that the method of taxation by tolls and fares is the justest, or in fact the only just way of raising the money, because everybody throughout the community is thus made to contribute to the expenses of the railway in the exact proportion that he receives benefit from it. It is evident that the whole weight of the toll does not fall on the farmer, for instance, bringing his produce to market, any more than the duty on spirits falls entirely on the importer. In both cases the charge is fairly divided among all who use the respective articles, or have any transactions with them. Arguments apart, the injustice of constructing and maintaining at the public expense, a railway to any part of the colony, for instance, Goulburn, which will enable the settlers of that district to undersell all others, at whose cost equally it is carried on, is self-evident.

And we thus arrive at the unavoidable conclusion that no railway should ever be undertaken but with the probability of its being self-maintaining, within a reasonable period after its completion.

---

[2] See above, Letter 57, n. 12, p. 136. On 11 July 1856 Pell had read a paper to the Sydney Philosophical Society, entitled 'On the Application of Certain Principles of Political Economy to the Question of Railways'. The text of this paper appears in the *Sydney Magazine of Science and Art*, 1 (1857) 124–8.

It is altogether another matter, and a question more of individual opinion and judgment, whether railways are profitable national investments in a colony like New South Wales; at the present day the majority will carry the point, and no doubt a vast majority will be found to decide in the affirmative, as we hope, without in the least infringing any of the principles deducible from the science of economy as advanced above.

I am, Sir, yours, &c., HONESTAS.

Sydney, July 19th, 1856.

91. W. S. JEVONS TO LUCY JEVONS
     [LJN, 67–9]

Monday, 22d September 1856.

... A letter from you had been long looked for, and two or three mails in succession had arrived without a sign of one, – a disappointment which I now find is owing to the irregularity of the mail ships, since I to-day received the expected letter 113 days old. The pleasure of such kind, long, and interesting letters, too, from each of you, was almost more than I had hoped for; and after reading and considering them, I have felt that there is a deeper meaning in them, especially yours and the one of Henny's, than almost any letters I have had before. The reason soon suggests itself to me – viz., that while my father lived he was properly the subject of all our most serious thoughts, and the one in whom to confide them; now, however, that this centre is removed, we are all in all to each other; and our common love resumes a degree of immediate importance and interest which it did not need to have before, though perhaps it was equally strong. If you knew (as perhaps you may imagine) how entirely the letters I write home are the only way in which I express my feelings, being as I am completely among strangers, and without one I care to confide them to, you would understand the necessity I feel to answer such as these, and the real encouragement they give me. If it is quite true that I have often, especially of late, felt a certain degree of real loneliness, I do not mean want of society, since that is what I never did or shall want, but the feeling of an accumulation of private and personal thoughts and objects which come at last to weigh too heavily. Perhaps I am not quite right in being so exclusive, and caring so little for other people's society: it began no doubt in a habit or infirmity of what is called bashfulness, and though that operates still, I do not think it is the whole cause and reason of my character in this respect. If I were, on the whole, like other people, I should no doubt resemble them in this also, and I cannot help feeling that the real difference there is between me and others in many respects, and which I can mention without any fear of egotism, is *partly* the reason of my caring little for the society of the generality of people. My life always was, and is now more especially, a laborious one, and I have always looked more to the future than to the enjoyment of the present; what that future, or the end itself may be, God only knows, but I am convinced that if only moderately good, it will fully justify me for somewhat in appearance disregarding most other people, and prove me not in the least *selfish*, as perhaps some might think me. I give you these thoughts simply because they are what are uppermost. While my father lived they did not arise so distinctly, and were chiefly absorbed in a plain feeling of duty to him. Now one's objects and views are more one's own, regulated only by general ideas of what is right, or modified by the remaining love and interest among ourselves. My father's death has with me, as with the rest of you, never taken the form of *regret*; it was no loss or unhappiness to him for he died with as much pleasure, of the truest as well as of a more material kind, surrounding him as almost ever happens on this earth; it is with each of *us* that the loss occurs, felt on my part in a manner that I tried to express in my first letter. For yourself, dear Lucy, it must be a satisfaction for you to consider, both how plainly marked and unmistakable your *part* has been, and how completely and lovingly you have always performed it to its utmost extent, viz. that of attending and supporting my father while he lived, and also of taking care of all the rest of us more or less, as I may say. Now more than ever it seems to me that you are necessary to us, not only in directly bringing up Henny and Tommy, but in keeping the whole of us together, in a manner that is sure to produce better feelings in each, and, as far as I am concerned, to prevent that feeling of loneliness and *objectlessness* of life that I have alluded to before, and which I so fear. . . .

92. W. S. JEVONS TO HERBERT JEVONS
    [LJN, 69–70]

Monday, 22d September 1856.

. . . The mint goes on steadily, but without much work. Our sovereigns, you will probably know, have obtained a very good character in England; I see no possible objection, therefore, to their sending us out some proper *dies*, and making our coinage imperial, and therefore current in England and everywhere.[1]

[1] See above, Letter 56, n. 4, p. 127.

Assaying goes on all right, and I am comfortable enough in my private office and laboratory. I am generally engaged more or less with attempted improvements or some little experiments, but it is no easy thing to introduce substantial and practicable improvements in a thing like the gold assay process, that so many have tried their hands at.

Sydney was rather alarmed last week to hear of the capture of an immense shark in the harbour. I went to see it, and there is no mistake about the fact; it is twelve or thirteen feet long, and nine feet in circumference, and with an immense mouth about eighteen inches across, so you may imagine what a really alarming fact it must be for those who are fond of bathing about the harbour. It is said to have been long known to boatmen under the name of 'Big Ben', and I have myself seen sharks' fins appearing above the water in Darling Harbour.

A short time since I went a walk on Sunday morning on a bush road past Cook's River, and was surprised to meet a large black snake, nearly five feet long, as deadly a sort as the devil. I had no idea of attacking it with a short walking-stick, and could not kill it with big stones before it escaped into some scrub. Unpleasant sort of acquaintances these sharks and snakes.

I am kept pretty busily engaged at home now by my meteorological observations. I have lately commenced sending a weekly report to the *Empire*,[2] and I send you two papers containing my reports. Mr. Parkes[3] has given them a very good place in the paper, and printed them exceedingly well, but this confounded Government service prevents me

---

[2] See above, Letter 76, n. 6, p. 198; also below, Letter 94, p. 244.

Jevons's Australian Diaries reveal the sequence of events leading to the publication of this first meteorological report. In the entry for 6 December 1855 he wrote: 'Made out a specimen of Meteorological Report for the Empire from Dec 1st–7th'. The matter is next mentioned in the entry for 1 August 1856: 'Received a note from Mr Parkes of the "Empire" newspaper in answer to mine of Dec 11th '55 offering to publish my meteorological reports. Very much puzzled to know what to do'. Unfortunately no letters of this immediate period are available to throw light on the reasons for his indecision and it is not mentioned in the letters of the following months. Remarks made in the letter to his father of 29 October 1855 suggest that he was simply reluctant to turn what had hitherto been a pleasure into a regular commitment (above, p. 198); his position as a government servant also created difficulties. He had made up his mind by 7 August 1856 when he recorded: 'In evening wrote letter to Mr Parkes agreeing to send a weekly Meteor Report'; the letter was posted two days later. The entry for 27 August 1856 shows that he 'Wrote out a form for Meteorological Report to Empire in evening'. This was published on 3 September. On 7 September he wrote in the diary: 'In evening finished & copied out Report for Empire being in a slightly different form from first report'.

[3] Henry (later Sir Henry) Parkes (1815–96), one of Australia's leading politicians, five times Prime Minister of New South Wales, 1872–91. The son of a poor Warwickshire farmer, he emigrated in 1839, tried various trades and educated himself; he became bankrupt in 1858 when the *Empire* closed (see below, Letter 121, p. 341) and again in 1870; his political ability and impressive oratory gained him dominance over the confused political scene in New South Wales, 1854–91; he supported free trade, land selection and increased European migration, encouraged the development of education and worked for the Federation of the Australian colonies.

either asking or receiving any money any other way, and I therefore do it more for fun. It takes about two hours a week to calculate and make it out, but this is little more than I should do for my own satisfaction. I am engaged now too in copying out, correcting, and calculating my two daily observations for the last twenty months, which I had allowed to accumulate; it is a work of some forty or fifty thousand figures, independent of continual calculations, *drawing of means*, and other work. I am beginning, however, to get some results out to repay me.[4] . . .

93. W. S. JEVONS TO HENRIETTA JEVONS
[LJP, 70–71]

Petersham near Sydney. N.S.W.
October 1st 1856.

My dearest little Henny

Your letter of May 14th[1] was very interesting to me, and though I had not time to answer it with Lucy's & Herbert's, I take the next opportunity, as I have much to say. You will perhaps be surprized at my saying *much*, as my last letters were quite reasonably long enough, but the longer I am in Australia the more I feel the want of writing home occasionally to those who are more to me than anybody else.

Your letter rather struck me in two or three things that you said, and has caused me some reflection.

You say you never knew me properly before the last letters which you had received from me. This makes me sorrowful in remembering how much I have been away from home, and how little opportunity there has in this account been, for our knowing each other better. But it reminds me also of what has often occurred less forcibly to me before, being that nobody at all does really know me and that either from a habit of reserve[2] or some other perhaps more satisfactory reason, I have never opened myself to any one as 9 out of 10 would have done. This as you will allow is really a *heavy thought,* and one that requires the exercise of the truest and longest patience. I have enough ado indeed to find out what I am myself exactly and to persuade myself that it is what is right, and to this end I have often entered into sorts of long mental discussions as to what the word (of all the most disagreable*) '*selfish*' really means. Generally, however, they terminate much about

---

[4] It seems likely that this work formed the basis for his article 'Some Data concerning the Climate of Australia and New Zealand', *Waugh's Australian Almanac for the Year 1859*, pp. 47–98 (La Nauze, op. cit., p. 44). See below, Letters 94, p. 245.

[1] This letter is not among the Jevons Papers.

[2] See above, Letter 6, p. 15.

where they began, and I have lately begun to accept the wish to be *unselfish* as tantamount to the fact.

While thus becoming gradually satisfied in my own mind, I cannot help knowing that no similar process of mind will go on in other people & convince them of the same fact. Words, indeed, would not be sufficient to prove it, and I could not possibly say what I am writing now except only to be read by you and the rest at home. Acts are, I believe, the only way to show it and for this a life-time is only sufficient as we know in many cases, insufficient. So far does this feeling go with me, indeed, that I almost believe my only fear of death would be the dying misunderstood, and I confess I should certainly feel more or less regret in dying at a time when as we may say, the "working plans" of life are first being drawn out and not a stone of the edifice laid to show where it was going to be built.

I have said enough I dare say to puzzle you, but these are thoughts ordinary to me, and as you say of yourself do not think I am in any alarming state of mind.

It has often struck me and more & more by degrees that you & I are very like each other, and were or so to speak, cast out of very similar moulds. I think you also and others must have perceived it. It adds no doubt an element of *friendship* to my love to you as a sister, but you will understand me properly when I say that it is apart from and does not *increase my love* upon which Lucy has even a greater claim than yourself. One proof is that we both like Music in an exactly similar manner; a new one I find in your account of your own thoughts on the subject of religion. You say you are perplexed by all the minute & conflicting differences of opinion on this subject, and I can understand it because I went through something like it. With me however they have long since dissolved away and seem almost to be things of the past. At the bottom however I found several lumps of insoluble true substance, meaning by this a few fundamental principles of *truth* and *goodness* which are sufficient for any man, & are the only guides I have followed. You might perhaps expect me to describe more fully my own opinions and I should be glad to do so, but my wish is rather that you should form your opinion in an entirely independent & unprejudiced manner. I may positively say that I hardly care if you form the same exact opinions as myself; your mind may be in some way slightly different, or you may be more influenced by those whose views of religion are more *personal*. I look solely to what is commonly expressed by "principle", viz a sort of truthfulness & honesty of purpose, joined to a real regard for the good of others as well as oneself, which forms the essence of a good character, and may take the form of almost any opinions whatever. As is commonly said of ordinary religion, most people act better than they profess; where do you hear people damn each other but in their prayers and their creeds, or in what is there less real *charity* a true consideration for every one in general, than in Churches and *ordinary* religion. I do not speak of Unitarians who I believe are mostly superior to any forms of opinion, and possessing that "principle" I have named above, as much or more than other people, exercise it with true charity and unconstrained by the ordinary and far less sublime religious ideas. This is the reason that Unitarianism as a creed makes no head at all; they do not profess to teach people any creed and therefore do not exhibit the bigoted zeal of other sects which seems to succeed so well. In general they only teach others to be good & principled, a thing too indefinite and uninviting for most minds. At least this is my view of Unitarianism, and only thus far would I call myself a Unitarian.

This letter may appear to you a little gloomy. So it seems to me and as it comes naturally I shall not try to make it the least otherwise. I have felt indeed for some weeks some degree of a slight melancholy of which I do not know the cause. I do not think it arises from anything disagreable* for I never got on better with work of all sorts than I think I have lately, but it seems to be a tendency to take everything in a serious point of view. If there is any other cause it is the thought that I have only been 2 years in the colony and that 3 similar ones must probably be passed before I could follow with satisfaction to myself or others my strongest desires. Everything I do or think has reference to my being again in England sooner or later & for better or worse, and this not only in order to see & be with you & the rest again, but because I think it is the only place where I could be what I should wish. You did not overestimate the chances of a man in my position marrying & staying here. An income of £700, a light & not uninteresting business, a pretty country & cheerful town, a few not unpleasant acquaintances plenty of employment scientific, musical or otherwise and finally a house of one's own and a home here is what few I flatter myself would resist & give up, but if you ever thought seriously of such a thing, all I can say is that you did not count rightly upon me. The strongest inducement to such a life as that, supposing such were to occur as you may imagine would be insufficient to change my views such as they are, though I cannot help feeling that such a determination, throws any prospect of quiet and settled happiness a long way into the future. My life has never yet been an easy though a happy one; I have always worked & thought of the future instead of enjoying the present; the feeling too that it probably always will be so is perhaps the reason of my present tone of mind joined as it is with a suspicion that life may not always be so easy & successful as at the present & past, and that to go again to London in search of new employment & new ends, is in fact voluntarily entering again the Battle of Life after having once found a quiet and secure shelter. It seems however natural and unavoidable and therefore must be so.

Oct. 10th After writing for a long time at this new chapter of my book, intended for your edification,³ you cannot expect much letter writing, you will perhaps think the less the better. So Good Night.

And with best love to all the rest to whom I will presently write plenty more letters,
    Believe me
     Your same loving Brother
      W. S. Jevons

94. W. S. JEVONS TO H. E. ROSCOE

        Petersham near Sydney N.S.W.
        October 21st 1856.
My dear Doctor

I have had a feeling upon me for a long time that a letter has been long owing from me in answer to one or two very interesting & kind ones from you.¹ I should be sorry for you to imagine that the feeling was at all a heavy one; on the contrary I have often thought with pleasure how much I should have to say upon my own affairs as well as your own, so far as I have information of them, but a letter is a thing one is apt to put off, and then when a Mail is advertised, I find so much that I must say to two or three brothers and sisters who make great demands upon me, that your claim is deferred till about 1. 0 AM of the day the Mail leaves when I naturally give it up & going to bed, defer it in similar manner till the next opportunity.

It is now a year since you sent me your papers on the Photochemical research,² for which I have never before thanked you. I read them carefully as well as a short notice in the Phil. Mag. of your lecture at the R.I.³ Of all the things that are gratifying to a scientific man, to deliver a Friday evening lecture must, I think, be the most gratifying, in a room too that will always be celebrated on account of Davy and Faraday.⁴ I congratulate you, too, on having hit upon such a substantial and useful, still interesting and almost untouched subject of Photochemical action. You will be in fact laying the foundations of a new branch of Science,

---

 ³ This is probably a reference to the book on music which he was writing and sending home to Henrietta, chapter by chapter. It has not survived. See Vol. I, p. 32.
 ¹ The only letter relevant to this among the Jevons Papers is Letter 87, p. 227.
 ² See above, Letter 75, p. 192.   ³ See above, Letter 87, p. 229.
 ⁴ For Jevons's account of one of Faraday's Friday Evening Lectures at the Royal Institution, see Vol. I, p. 81.

about which Photographers and others who are continually engaged with its effects, have as little real knowledge or understanding as the old alchemists had of chemistry in general a hundred years or so back. You give it rather unmercifully to poor Dr Wittwer,[5] and almost excite one's pity towards him, but perhaps it is well to make an example now & then of Scientific criminals. I shall be happy to hear of your proceeding furthur* with the subject but I can well conceive what a laborious affair it must be. You say you have rather changed your politics in a scientific point of view, and have adopted Physico-chemical determinations rather than Organic Ethyls & Methyls as your sphere. It is undoubtedly somewhat a desertion of Williamson and his *anhydrous acids* but a very excusable one when you had the fortune to meet with such a man as Bunsen.

I myself am an awful deserter, having given up all ideas of engaging in chemistry again; indeed I doubt if I shall ever be able to call myself a scientific man, for although I am yet deep in more than one scientific subject, I find myself gradually spending more and more time over other more general subjects for which I believe I am equally well or even better suited. I am pretty sure too that a Scientific education is one of the best things possible for any man, and worth any amount of Latin and Greek. It tends to give your opinions and thoughts a sort of *certainty, force,* and *clearness* which forms an excellent foundation for other sorts of knowledge less precisely determined and established, provided you do not allow your mind to become completely formed to Science.

I am, however, awfully deep in Meteorology at present. I cant say exactly why, but I began it nearly two years since and having invested something like £60 or £70 in apparatus, feel bound as well as well-inclined to follow it up while I am in Australia. I have lately commenced sending a weekly Meteorological Report to the "Empire" daily paper; I enclose you one of my reports as a specimen, but it happens to be a week when there was little to say in the Remarks.[6] I do it chiefly for pleasure (the pleasure of appearing in print??) as there is a stupid rule that Government officers cannot receive private remuneration; never you be a Government fellow if you can help. My *forte*, I consider, is in the *clouds*, and I think that if I followed out the subject properly I could soon publish a deal that is new about them,[7] and perhaps give

---

[5] See above, Letter 75, n. 10, p. 192.

[6] A cutting of Jevons's Meteorological Report for 19–25 October 1856 is enclosed with the letter.

[7] Two articles were published in the *London . . . Philosophical Magazine* in July 1857 and April 1858 (see above, Letter 75, p. 193). The latter article was an abbreviation of a long paper Jevons read before the Sydney Philosophical Society on 9 December 1857, 'On Clouds: their various forms and producing causes' published in the *Sydney Magazine of Science and Art* (January 1858) 163–76 (La Nauze, op. cit., pp. 41–2). Jevons's views aroused some controversy: see below, Letters 118 and 122, pp. 329 and 345.

them a fair scientific position. The formation of *cirrous** or fibrous cloud is quite unexplained as yet, or attributed only to absurd electrical ideas; I consider that I have discovered and nearly proved that it [is][8] produced by the *interfiltration* of portions of air of different temperatures and moistness & consequently of different density. If the denser portion[9] happens by any chance to be *top* it filters down into the down portion by virtue of its gravity, passing into it in the shape of *minute threads* and causing precipitation of *cloud* according to Huttons Theory.[10] If however the denser portion is lowest, but the two portions are caused to mix mechanically at their surfaces, *stratous** or *sheetlike* cloud only is produced. This theory allows fully for all the various & beautiful forms assumed by the *cirrus* and it explains also why *Cirrostratus* should be such a common form of cloud

I have had a long job lately *reducing* & calculating out nearly 2 years 2 daily observations, but one is rewarded by getting out the results and putting them in the form of curves. I am just going to carry out a new idea too, which is to register the wind & app^{ce} of sky *graphically*, in fact draw a plan of the atmosphere every day, like for instance this plan of yesterdays sky. One of the prettiest meteorological facts I ever observed occurred yesterday. The day before there was a W N W *hot-gale*, one of those awful winds of which you have perhaps heard. The next day there was however a pleasant NE sea breeze (as marked), still I observed passing over Sydney at an *immense* height, the smoke of a *bush fire* only a few miles furthur* inland This proved that the hot westerly wind was still blowing within a few miles of the coast, and illustrated the theory of the sea breeze beautifully; it is the first time I ever saw smoke (which is no bad Meteorological indicator) get into any upper current of air.[11]

I have taken observations on *ozone* for nearly a month now, having got a set of Schönbeins[12] test papers. The results in England seem but little certain, but I am very much pleased to have ascertained in such a short time one distinct fact viz that these W or N W hot land winds give o or 1° or 2° only, and the strong "Southerly bursters"* or gales

---

[8] Omitted in the orginal manuscript.   [9] Jevons wrote 'portions'.

[10] James Hutton (1726–97), Scottish geologist; devoted himself to scientific pursuits after abandoning medicine; his 'Theory of Rain' was published in *Transactions of the Royal Society of Edinburgh*, III (1794) but his work was little recognised until the publication of John Playfair's *Illustrations of the Huttonian Theory* (1802).

[11] Jevons describes a 'hot-wind' day in Sydney in his article 'Meteorological Observations in Australia', *Sydney Magazine of Science and Art* (January–February 1859) 161–7 (La Nauze, op. cit., pp. 43–4). Most of the right-hand side of this page of the letter is devoted to the sketch reproduced overleaf.

[12] Christian Friedrich Schönbein (1799–1868), Professor of Chemistry and Physics at Basel; in 1839 he revealed a new form of oxygen by recognising ozone to be a definite chemical substance.

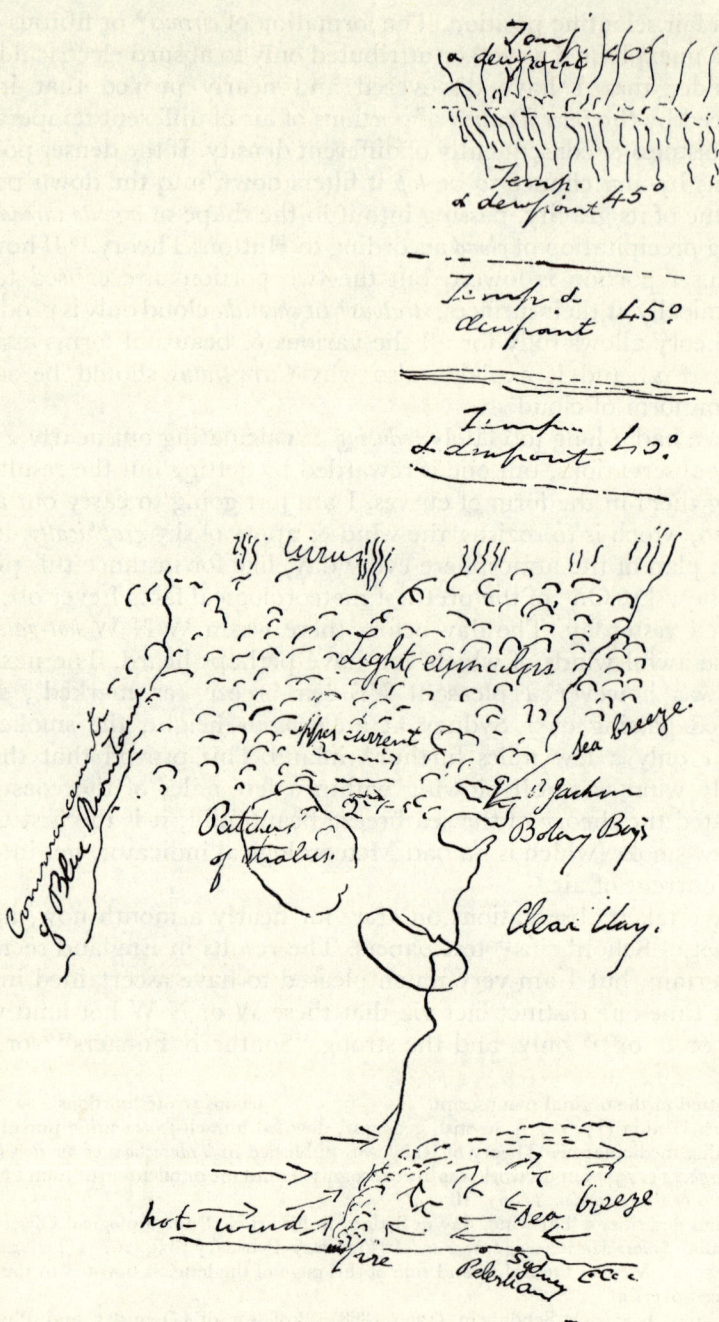

which follow them and are off the sea give generally 10° or nearly so. I think these observations will have some interest when I have got about a year of them but the above fact is distinct enough to make me almost sure of it already.

But dont imagine I am altogether taken up by Meteorology. We get on quietly and regularly at the Mint; there is very little to do and my necessary work would not occupy more than 2 or 3 hours, if I liked, just at present, but of course we attend nearly the full office hours and employ ourselves as well as we can. I have lately been writing a rather long paper on Mint Gold assaying from a "Methodical" point of view; i.e. it is about the employment of *comparative determination*, and the means of eliminating slight errors in the process &c &c, but I do not think anything will come of it just now, as it is awfully dull & stupid.[13] Our receipts now are only 3 or 4000 oz per week or about £15,000 which is very miserable. I have long since formed an opinion however that it is no use coining gold here to be exported and recoined in London. Gold here is necessarily an article of export and I do not see what need there is to coin it here unless indeed our Australian Sovreigns* were current in England. The whole of the English Coin in N.S.W. has been sent home already and replaced by ours; the same will take place with Victoria as soon as they are obliged to proclaim our Sovreigns* legal (never done as yet!!) and after that every Sovreign* we coin will be *exported*.

Our Mint now has the Gold Escort business, that is the armed escort from the Diggings deliver the gold at the Mint.[14]

Politics here are in a very singular state; Responsible Government was Inaugurated as they grandly express it about six months[15] ago ever since which unfortunate event the colony has been perpetually in the agonies of Ministerial Crisisesss.* The new Responsible Ministers have resigned or been kicked out two or three times already, three elections have taken place in Sydney within about 8 months and our new Parliament has debated for weeks together without passing a bill. It is all carried on nearly next door to us at the Mint and we sometimes turn into the gallery of an evening to have a bit of fun and hear the Ministerial and Opposition benches abusing each other. People here however are so very orderly & quiet that they seem to do quite as well without a government; even the third contested election in the year cannot excite them to a breach of the Peace. This is all very absurd no doubt but I am afraid that there is something more serious in it. The opposition consists in fact of a lot of clever but blackguardly *pure democrats* with Parkes,

---

[13] See below, Letter 122, p. 345.
[14] See Vol. I, p. 152.
[15] 'month' in the original manuscript.

the editor of the Empire, Dr Lang[16] (of whom you may have heard) and the members for Sydney, altogether called the "*bunch*", at their head. The respectable party had the first chance of forming a government and had a small majority, but they have all along made such a mess of it, that the other party gains at nearly every step, although their own ministers were, to be sure, kicked out in no time because they appointed as Attorney General and Minister of Justice one of the most notoriously bad men in the colony. It will of course be the ruin of the country for democracy to gain, and we should all turn into dirty Americans (which God forbid) I dont see any way of getting out of the scrape but by dissolving our new Parliament and electing a fresh one altogether. A nice Inauguration of Responsible Government and a new Constitution this.

Within 6 or 8 months I hope that we shall be living in a house of our own in a beautiful situation on the Harbour. Mr Miller with whom I live, is building himself a house at Double Bay which is just commenced and will be finished by that time It is in a most beautiful situation on the flat shore (water frontage) at the head of the bay with a pretty view of the Harbour, and a

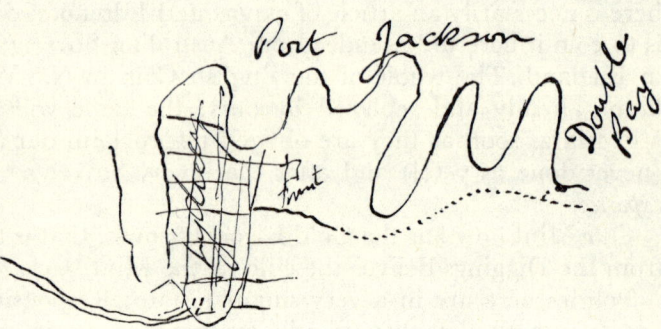

pleasant 2½ mile walk to town Boating & bathing can of course be had in perfection, but the latter is somewhat checked by the recollection that a true shark 13 feet long was fished up out of the Harbour a few weeks since (pleasant!!).

Oct. 28th In order fully to carry out my determination of being quite ready with a letter for you this mail I am going to finish this tonight, three days before the vessel goes!! I will let you a little into our private Mint matters; whatever you do, take care not to be a Government Servant. It is true we have very little to do, and get £675 per annum and a comfortable little private laboratory but still the Government service seems to me a d——d thing at least according to Capt W^s interpretation. His theory is that for £.s.d. received you give your

---

[16] Dr John Dunmore Lang (1799–1878) emigrated to Sydney in 1822 after graduating from the University of Glasgow, to become the first Presbyterian minister in Sydney. He had an active political career in the colony, with wide interests particularly in education and immigration, which he believed was the solution to Britain's industrial problems; he travelled frequently to Britain and the United States.

whole services to the Government, and my opinion of him is that he has long since given his *soul* as well as his body away to it. What do you think of this; having tempted & partially obliged Miller & me to sell him our apparatus &c (for myself I was glad of the change) he is now *forcing* us to teach as many of the Mint clerks to assay as he likes to send into our laboratories. I am quite at a loss to know his reason, but it is a most evident injustice to make us teach them to carry on the routine work of the offices, after we have sacrificed so much in coming out here and have overcome all the difficulties of starting the coinage right. It is against all custom, too, to make people teach their profession for nothing, except in this confounded Government service. Also, to teach clerks who have had no particular education and not a scientific idea in their heads previously, to carry on the process by mere rule & practise,* is directly contrary to the new system at home, of only appointing properly educated scientific people to such places. What would Graham think of these doings, as he owes his position to Science.

Capt Ward, in fact, is little more than a military man, very determined & arbitrary as well as businesslike, and very clever in a sort of a way. But I cannot perceive that he has any degree of general knowledge, or ability and he carries his business transactions to the verge of honour, because he always does everything for the Government, and he has, as I said before, given his soul to the Government in a manner nearly equivalent to giving it to the Devil himself. In his behaviour he is generally civil and attentive but very distant and I dont think there is a soul likes him. The old Governor General is very much the same sort of a man being also a Captain of R.E. but he is really scientific and a better man I think in several respects. He and Capt W. with Dr Smith, too, have started a Phil. Soc. to which I & some others of the Mint belong,[17] but on the whole it is a decided failure as yet and one feels too much under the thumb of the RE's and as if the public were graciously permitted to sit at a distance and hear them talk, which is not the right thing in a Scientific Society where all should be on an equal footing. I must except however a paper by Dr Smith on the Sydney Water & its action on lead which was a very interesting one.[18] He discovered that all Sydney was being poisoned by lead pipes (myself a most serious case, too,) but that all lead whether in solution or not could be removed

---

[17] The Sydney Philosophical Society, a revival of an earlier one, was inaugurated in May 1856 with the Governor General, Sir William Denison, as President. He took an active part in the Society's affairs, reading papers on such subjects as the 'Development of the Railway System in England' and 'The Moon's Rotation'. Jevons had been elected a member, with many others, at the meeting of 13 June 1856. Cf. La Nauze, op. cit., p. 28.

[18] Professor Smith read his paper 'On the action of Sydney Water upon Lead' before the Society on 13 August 1856. Cf. *Journal and Proceedings of the Royal Society of New South Wales* (1881), xv 6.

perfectly by sand filtration, similarly to what I have since observed in the Phil. Mag about sand-filtration in London. (Paper by Witt of Gov. School Chem.)[19]

The other morning I invented a Self-calculating Dry & wet bulb Hygrometer which would, undoubtedly give the Dewpoint according to Glaisher's[20] method of calculating it, at inspection after a couple of screw adjustments. It might however be rather troublesome and somewhat too complicated for common use and I will not say anything more about it till I have more considered it. Such a hygrometer is decidedly the greatest desideratum in Meteor. at present.

In the Phil. Mag. too I read a beautiful lecture by Dr Tyndall[21] of R.I. on *Slaty cleavage* agreeing in a most gratifying manner with my own former opinions, that it is produced by mere pressure, and without any electrical *humbug*. He must be a very clever man; at all events he is hard working, from the number of magnetical & other researches I see of his.

I might do a deal more at Meteorology & such things only that my Music takes up such an awful deal of my time. I have got, as perhaps you know, a moderately good harmonium on which I play for an hour or two per day an indiscriminate mixture of Operas & Oratorias,* Sacred or Profane, beautiful or sublime musical compositions in much of my usual style of execution. It does not seem to injure anybody else, nor myself either, so I play away by myself to my hearts content, and say as people always say of music "its no harm". I likewise attend most of the Concerts in Sydney, and it is my firm belief that if I were in London I should go to some concert or theatre every night for three months. The last Philharmonic Soc's concert was a very good one as we had Miska Hauser[22] a first rate violin player whose playing I was delighted with. I was also somewhat pleased to see a fair assemblage of the ladies of Australia, most of them young. Opinions are very much divided here upon their charms and the question was lately the subject of a law suit (Lutwyche v. Fairfax, of the S^y Morning Herald)[23] the

---

[19] Henry M. Witt, 'On the Variations in the Chemical Composition of the Thames Water, during the year between May 1855 and May 1856', *London . . . Philosophical Magazine*, XII (August 1856) 114–24. Witt was Assistant Chemist to the Government School of Applied Science at this time.

[20] See Vol. III, Letter 506.

[21] John Tyndall (1820–93), Professor of Natural Philosophy at the Royal Institution, 1853–87; scientific adviser to Trinity House and the Board of Trade, 1866–83. His paper, 'Comparative View of the Cleavage of Crystals and Slate Rocks', was published in the *London . . . Philosophical Magazine*, XII (July 1856) 35–48; it had been delivered at the Royal Institution on 6 June 1856.

[22] Miska Hauser (1822–87), Hungarian violinist and composer; from 1853 to 1858 he made a tour of California, South America and Australia.

[23] This action for libel was heard before the Supreme Court in Sydney on 26 August 1856. On 3 May 1856 the *Sydney Morning Herald* published a list of men to whom seats in the Upper

former having been charged with writing letters to the *Morning Chronicle*, calculated to injure their reputation. For my own part I thought them in general very pretty, but not being acquainted with any one of them, I cannot speak of their inward qualities. Their behaviour in public is usually decorous and on the occasion referred to I noticed only one slight breach of etiquette, which was that a very handsome girl apparently fell dead in love with me, truly at first sight, or at all events expressed it in a series of the most determined & gratifying nods from the opposite side of the Concert room. How do the German ladies behave if there are any, for I dont for the moment remember ever seeing one?

By the bye* I am learning German and take 1 hours lesson per week & ditto for French. I have arrived at last at the point that I can translate a page of Schiller in the course of the evening, but to remember the meaning of German crackjaw words is one of the hardest jobs I have met with in the course of my experience. What an astonishing deal you must know by this time if you have learnt them all. It costs me £32 a year but I think I will try two years of it and see how I get on then.

Time, Space, Matter, & Mind are all failing me which being, according to Whewell, our simplest ideas, my letter must indeed be near its close. The last indeed, viz your Patience must have been sorely tried by two sheets of such writing as this. You must understand I mean it all the same whether it is legible again or not. I just remember one of Aunt Henry's Water-colour Drawings,[24] which have been rather long upon the Sydney Market. At present I can only say they were not sold when last I heard but I will endeavour to ascertain their ultimate fate from the auctioneer in time to inform you. Remember me most kindly to Aunt H; it would be impossible for me to forget the comfortable & happy days I passed at your house at Oval Road, though everything connected with London & Liverpool seems now just as distantly and completely removed from me, as is the prospect which I always hold to and enjoy of sometime revisiting & living in them again. Remember

---

House of the Legislative Council had been offered. Two days later the following letter to the Editor, signed 'An Australian', appeared in the paper: '. . . In the list of the Legislative Council is the name of a gentleman who is said to have been the correspondent of the London *Morning Chronicle*. It would be desirable that one of the letters should be re-published in your journal that the colonists may see the character given of our wives and daughters . . .' Alfred James Peter Lutwyche, a barrister, later Solicitor-General of New South Wales and formerly correspondent of the *Morning Chronicle*, interpreted this as a reference to himself. He sued the proprietor of the *Sydney Morning Herald*, John Fairfax, for damages of £3000. The jury found the defendant not guilty, awarding the plaintiff damages of 40s. A detailed report of the case appeared in the *Sydney Morning Herald*, 27 August 1856.

[24] See above, Letter 75, p. 194.

me also to any old college friend you might meet, for instance Colville, and who might also happen to remember me.

For yourself I need not furthur* assure you that I am
Your truly affec Cousin
W S Jevons.

95. W. S. JEVONS TO LUCY JEVONS
[LJN, 71–5]

1st *January* 1857.

... I started about five o'clock on Christmas Eve by the Parramatta Railway, and reaching Parramatta in about three-quarters of an hour, took the coach for Windsor. This was a very old omnibus, and as I was inside and it soon became dark, I cannot describe the beauties, if any, of the country through which we passed. I may mention, however, to give you people a delicious idea of it, that we passed through the largest orangery of the colony, of many acres extent. After travelling twenty miles in four hours we found ourselves at the door of an inn in Windsor about 10.30 P.M. I never experienced, nor never will again, such a high temperature on Christmas Eve – four fellows in a small attic – thick mosquito curtains – evening of a very hot day – windows wide open, but no perceptible effect. However, I arose on Christmas Day quite *solid*, and walked all morning about the cultivated plains and banks of the River Hawkesbury near Windsor. The country is fine in an agricultural sense, but not over picturesque. I sought for a dinner later on in Windsor, and while eating it thought how much amused you would have been to see me eating my Christmas turkey and passable plum pudding with a fat old landlord and his growing-up family, including a rather showy young lady, and two or three more travellers, at one end of a long table in the deserted ball-room of the hotel. Dinner done, however, I soon quitted Windsor with no pleasant reminiscences, for as a rule I detest all Australian towns. ... Passing through ordinary woody country, I reached Richmond towards evening. The prettiest of towns in New South Wales, so they say, but with no pretension to beauty but a few pretty cottages with exotic-looking gardens and green creepers. In passing on a few miles further I crossed the River Hawkesbury by Richmond Point, and put up at an inn on the opposite bank in a lonely situation. The river is a broad deep fine stream, the Thames of New South Wales, but bordered by very tall steep alluvial banks, which the river is said to overflow in times of flood, occurring every few years. It was bordered by gardens and orchards, though rather too bare of trees, but the bushy hills surrounding the plains on all sides, and especially the ranges of bushy mountains in the distance, which I hoped to explore on the morrow, rendered the scene very beautiful when aided by a true Australian evening, delicious cool airs, and a calm clear sky, succeeding the dry winds and powerful sun of the day. Tea of *damper* and remains of Christmas goose; large solitary bedroom. So ended my third Christmas Day in Australia.

Next morning I started walking through the mists soon after six in the morning, and by eight o'clock entered a most beautiful, open, and very hilly country. It was considerably cultivated, and every half mile or so was a log cottage, of which the inhabitants were very friendly, and gave me all the directions and supplies of drinkables that they could. It was not, however, till I found an old bushman that I could get any information of a track across the mountains in the direction I wished to go. He directed me to go back the way I had come a considerable distance, and then cross the Grose river at *Ben Carver's*, and with the magical name of Ben Carver I with infinite trouble sought out my way at last and reached the Grose. Here I found the bed of a mountain torrent which drains the Blue Mountains, but its banks had the chief attractions, for I was botanising, and I found here several remarkable flowering shrubs, which I have seen no trace of elsewhere, and also blackberries or brambles, and a single delicate and truly modest violet, the only one exactly like those at home that I have seen. There was also a small geranium, and the common sarsaparilla plant. As I had twelve miles before me to the next town, I started again without much delay and proceeded about five miles without much worth relating. The country was not here mountainous, but only hilly, woody land rising from the River Nepean, to which I afterwards found I was close, but as I was approaching some steep long ranges, I detected with my meteorologic eye a fine specimen of thunder-cloud rising up from behind them as being peculiar; low rumbling thunder soon confirmed my worst fears, and I gave myself up for a drenching. However, I had seen at intervals cleared spaces and railings, and I now came in sight of a well-established little farm and cottage, where I even applied for shelter, and was well received by an old woman. While the storm was brewing – and it was a rare one, with long forked flashes of lightening extending across the greater part of the sky, and sudden stormy squalls of warm air, though it was worse to the northward near Richmond – the old woman made some tea, and set out dinner for me, herself, and little boy, the viands being as usual the remains of the Christmas goose and pudding. I evidently shocked the religious feeling of the old lady by drinking my tea, the usual accompaniment of an Australian bush dinner, before she had said grace, which we hardly think of doing in New South

Wales, though I was probably more really thankful for that cup of tea than for any other I ever drank.

The dinner done, my prospect was not improved. The storm, instead of passing over in a definite small body, seemed extending everywhere. The whole sky was covered by dark heavy masses of cloud, which seemed determined to catch me wherever I went, and I looked forward with no pleasure to the six miles yet to be walked. Soon losing the path the old woman pointed out, I trusted to my senses to reach the top of the nearest range, upon the point of which I fortunately discovered the track, and at the same time gained a fine view of the plains and winding river, which, although a second heavy shower came on, I was longing for you to sketch. Then I set off as hard as circumstances would allow me to walk, following up the path, which was the faintest track imaginable, even covered by bushes, in pushing by which the rain-drops continually drenched my legs and knees. But do you know that I have a secret satisfaction in walking any number of miles through these uninhabited, monotonous, but rugged, bushy, or thickly-wooded mountains? They are not picturesque, for the only other things seen are other similar ranges separated by long gullies, but they are wild and natural, and except a faint path, and a tree cut down or *barked* here and there, there are no traces of man. The old large gum-trees too have often a very picturesque appearance, or rather a desolate wild-look – shattered by lightning, burned by the bush fires, or when blown over, sometimes falling into each other's arms, or with broken branches of large size supported in the most fantastic ways.

After a long weary walk the path became more distinct, then began to widen into a good road, and after passing a few deserted huts, a tent or two, and such-like signs of life, I reached the broad main road from Penrith to Hartley, close to Springwood Inn, but nearer to a small eating-house at which I got some tea. On going away, the old woman addressed to me the question: 'Is it jewellery, or what is it?' which it struck me at last referred to my old botanical collecting box. I enlightened her on that point, but remained much disgusted, when I remembered similar remarks of the innkeeper at Windsor, which I had not understood at the time. *The assayer of Her Majesty's Australian Mint to be taken for a wandering dealer in false jewellery!* I had indeed hoped that my appearance, though in a now very dirty light suit of clothes and a cabbage-tree hat, would have saved me from such a fate. I made, however, the rather complimentary reflection that tourists, especially pedestrians and scientific ones, are unknown objects in Australia as yet.

A few miles down the road brought me to the old Pilgrim Inn, a very good house for such a place, just as 'the shades of evening,' etc., and as the rain was beginning to come down again. A hot cobbler of brandy and a comfortable early bed soon set me up again, although I had been out more than twelve hours, and walked somewhere near thirty miles under such circumstances.[1] . . .

96. W. S. JEVONS TO HENRIETTA JEVONS
[LJP, 76–7]

Petersham near Sydney N.S.W.
Sunday. Jan 4th 1857.[1]

My dearest Henny

In face of the reproaches of my French & German Master, (for he comes tomorrow & I have not prepared a scrap of lessons) I sit down to write a letter I have long contemplated in answer to your last long one. This latter, I was long afraid was lost since I received several of later date from Lucy or Herbert before I got it, but when it came it excited a very strong interest in me.

This is chiefly, I believe, because most of the feelings & opinions, which you express, are precisely what I have felt lately myself and which are even now animating me in everything I do. If I had spoken myself I could not have said more plainly that "at present to acquire knowledge (my) (& general education and improvement) is (your) business"; it is precisely what I am occupied in, every hour & minute of my life here. As to *Money*, though I have a very considerable salary (fixed at £630 now) and am altogether in comfortable circumstances here, I should not hesitate to throw it all up, if I thought that thereby I should gain any advantage as to the point in question, but you will perceive as well as me, that besides having given my father great satisfaction by the position I obtained so soon, I am now laying by money that will very much smooth my way afterwards, and give me the greatest possible facilities even as regards education. Within three years, all being well, I *will* throw up all that I have here, both with the hope of seeing you all again and with the intention of following more freely my own views, but not without the fear of meeting a far less easy or perhaps successful life than I have hitherto enjoyed. I say this because we Australians gain an idea by degrees, that England is a wretched old place where people are always wandering about in search of employment and often dying of starvation, and I really think it will require no small courage

[1] For a complete and more detailed account of this trip, see Vol, I. p. 134.
[1] The original manuscript of this letter is complete.

on the part of a fellow with a good salary here, to leave it and throw himself back into such a world of hungry people as there are in London or Liverpool. But I see no reason why I should not now inform you and the others at home of another step, and a rather long one too, which I intend to take before reaching home. Within a year I have been three trips about the colony of N.S.W.[2] which to me are full of amusement and instruction, though to most others I believe they would be unendurable, but in these I am merely stretching my wings for a much longer flight round the globe. How many times round I shall go or by what path I have not in the least decided. I mean, in short, after leaving here for good, to travel at discretion and not to terminate my wanderings at home until I have fulfilled the purposes I have in view, equally as I am doing now in another way. Though in this I may run some dangers, may spend some hundreds of pounds, and spend something under another precious year (spend it, too, away from home) you at least will approve of it since it accords with your principles, and I shall have full time to learn what Lucy & Herbert think.

I am at present even more engaged than ever in various ways; my duties (self imposed) of *Meteorological Reporter to the Empire daily Journal*, I find quite onerous, and I am now I believe the sole acting meteorologist in Sydney, the other one having forged £700 & cut![3] I have just lately been making up my Meteorological Accounts for the last year, for you must know that I keep quite a series of *books* which I have to attend to daily, weekly, monthly & yearly, and they take a large portion of my time, but I intend after a bit rather to drop than increase my Meteor. work not however ceasing altogether. Ones subjects may be changed from time to time provided it be done consistently and with a uniform ultimate object. I have lately started again at Botany though I feel it is almost one thing too much, but I do it with almost a greater pleasure than anything else, because it was my first *subject* and one which I remember my Mother always favouring.[4] I have preserved a few plants out of our wood, as well as some which I gathered up the country and am reestablishing my old Herbarium in better style.

My music is much the same as ever, and I have not bought any new lately; I have been playing Mozarts Last Requiem a good deal and do not hesitate to declare it the finest music ever written. Indeed I can point out what I am sure is the finest *bar* of music ever written, viz. It is

---

[2] These had been to the gold diggings at Sofala in March 1856 (see Vol. I, Appendix, p. 213; to the River Hunter and Maitland in May 1856 (see his account in Vol. I, pp. 123–30; and to the Richmond district at Christmas 1856 (see Vol. I, p. 134). The following April Jevons made his fourth trip, to the Illawarra district (see below, Letter 101, p. 280).

[3] Cf. below, Letter 99, p. 269.

[4] See Vol. I, p. 6.

so simple perfect, sublime, & beautiful in every way that I am never tired of playing it.⁵ I advise you to buy the Requiem and work well at it till you understand it (it may not suit the piano quite so well as the harmonium). With me to play music is *reading* it like one would read *poetry* or anything else; it is a simple pleasure to myself and independent of show or the pleasing of anyone else. One consolation I have too is that one can understand and appreciate music pretty well without necessarily playing it brilliantly or even perfectly; otherwise I should be wasting a great deal of time. I agree, too, that if you like, you should cultivate singing more than the piano, for as it is the essence of music only that we require, the instrument by which it is produced is a secondary consideration, and nothing can be better than a good voice when it can be had (it does not however, unite all the effects of harmony etc).

Jan. 6th. This afternoon, I espied some new editions of Oratorios in a window, and to my great joy obtained "Elijah" & "Israel in Egypt" both of which I have long wished for; from what I have seen of them this evening they will be enough to satisfy my musical appetite for months. "O rest in the Lord" in the former one, I take to be one of the finest pieces of *Melody* ever written, that is the whole force & meaning of it is contained in one simple series of notes, independent of any harmonical additions or of any particular rhythmical effects &c.

I wish you would try to write some music of whatever sort, & when you have done it, send it me; I often try to extemporise* a little and have once or twice hit upon a good air, I think, but I generally forget them immediately afterwards and have not time like you to go at it properly or to learn the rules &c of Composition.

Last night I indulged, i e went to the theatre to hear Brooke⁶ & Mr & Mrs Robert Heir. The last lady is from Liverpool (formerly Miss Fanny Cathcart)⁷ and I patronise* her on this account as well as

⁵ The specific bar here quoted by Jevons comes from immediately after the opening choral paragraph of the first movement of Mozart's *Requiem* (K. 626), and is in the major key immediately following a move to the minor.

₉ See above, Letter 68, n. 1, p. 170.

⁷ Fanny Cathcart (1833–80), leading Australian actress of her day, renowned particularly for Shakesperian and high comedy roles; daughter of a provincial theatrical manager, she had been discovered by Brooke in Liverpool and went with his company to Australia in 1855; in July that year she married Robert James Heir (d. 1868?) a young Englishman with the company, who became manager of the Theatre Royal, Melbourne, 1858–9. She partially

because her acting and her face are both a credit to my native town. I saw her comfortably & easily smothered in Othello and who do you think I sat next there but one of those that you have so much confidence in, a Unitarian Minister M\(^r\) Stanley.[8] He made some sort of excuse about it being such a good *study of elocution*, and he had come with a large volume of Shakespeare under his arm; I was rather floored because I am in the habit of excusing myself for not going oftener to chapel on account of the Distance of Petersham, yet he always sees me at the Philharmonics, Philos. Societie's &c.

You speak much in your letter about Unitarianism, and if I am to answer it and speak openly of such a subject, I must confess that I am never at all troubled by such religious differences as you refer to. My own views are so liberal and simple that the whole vast mass of different sects, including even the most of Unitarians, vanishes in the distance, and appearing only as a small object upon any religious horizon, draws a correspondingly small share of attention from me, and though a curious, interesting & certainly very complicated construction when closely examined, it is not to me of any importance compared with the other broad & vital questions which lie around. If I may call myself a Unitarian, it is for this one reason, that of all sects, I believe, they alone are *charitably* disposed towards others, and instead of blackguarding, quarreling* & fighting with them, would rather make common cause with them, as having all both the same subject & object in view. If I gave any creed for my own belief, I should give it from the Bible and say that I have Faith, Hope, & Charity, but most of charity, and it is to me a horrible thing to consider how completely the whole system of Christianity, I may say, is opposed to this sentiment as well as to the general tenour* of Christ's teaching. My charity indeed goes this far, that I think it as absurd to say that anyone will be unhappy after this life, as to say that 2 & 2 make 5. To define what you mean by *God* and then to say he created anybody to be *damned* is a simple contradiction in terms.

Jan. 9\(^{th}\). The Royal Charter mail leaves tomorrow, so I will send this letter by her, and then write again to the others Per "Oneida".

There is one thing that I cannot leave unanswered in your letter though perhaps I cannot answer it to your satisfaction. You consider *my* idea of God to be *little better* than *Abstract Good*, and to be therefore quite opposed to your own idea of Him as a personal Being and Father. You have hit the point very correctly, and I must confess that my only idea of God is as a general Principle a purpose of

---

retired from the stage in 1864 but continued to act intermittently in New Zealand and the United States as well as Australia until 1877; she died in Melbourne.

[8] See above, Letter 56, n. 15, p. 131.

97. W. S. JEVONS TO HERBERT JEVONS

Sydney. N S W.
January 18th 1857.[1]

My dearest Herbert,

I begin a letter to you this Sunday evening not for any particular purpose, but to render you a general account of things here, and because you tell me not to shorten my correspondence.

I must first of all thank you for the two books "Felice Orsini"[2] and "English Traits"[3] received by post which are perhaps the next best substitute for a long letter, and do not cost in reaching here, more than I should have to pay the bookseller. The *Tiptree* having only just arrived (!!!) I have not read much of Emerson's book; I do not at all like his style, but though an American he seems to understand properly what a Great People the English are.[4] It has been a frequent thought of mine lately that England is now the Genius of the World, from which all great improvements and advances proceed and that instead of losing her position in the World, she is becoming more the Centre & Leader of it everyday. The Americans go for nothing, for though they are *naturally* powerful and *might* have superseded England, they have already degenerated and lost all moral power. The "Punches" too which you have sent are very excellent and the Saturday Review seems a good sort of a thing.[5]

I must have made a mistake about your being a partner in the Firm of Jevons & Cº but I hope to hear soon of its being a fact. You have indeed told me very little about family affairs for a long time but you explain it by saying that they have been quite stationary. I suppose that Nov 8th having passed when my Father's Money would be released from the firm, something would be done immediately. You told me in one letter that £100 would come to me on my 21st birth day but though that is now

---

[1] The original manuscript of this letter is in the Mitchell Library, Sydney.

[2] Felice Orsini, *The Austrian Dungeons in Italy. A narrative of fifteen months' imprisonment and final escape from the fortress of S. Giorgio.* Translated from the unpublished manuscript by J. M. White (1856). Jevons mentions in his diary reading *Austrian Dungeons in Italy* in December 1856. Cf. below, Letter 143, n. 13, p. 408.

[3] Ralph Waldo Emerson, *English Traits* (Boston, 1856).

[4] In his diary entry for 24 January 1857 Jevons commented: '... his style is exceedingly forcible & clear but becomes sometimes affected and too authoritative. It is nearly always exaggerated and would not carry much conviction to those who did not believe what he says beforehand. He has however accurately hit the solid character and real greatness of the English people and I could have but little more to say in their favour myself...'

[5] The *Saturday Review*, owned by Beresford Hope (1820–87) and edited by J. D. Cook (1808–68), had commenced publication in 1855. It was the first weekly journal which did not rely on news as a principal feature, and many distinguished Victorians were numbered among its contributors. Cf. Leslie Stephen, *Life of Sir James Fitzjames Stephen* (1895); Merle M. Bevington, *The Saturday Review, 1855–1868* (New York, 1941).

long past, you have not mentioned anything furthur* about it. There are no doubt also many things else in which I have necessarily a great interest, but which I know nothing at all about, and as it is from you alone that I am likely to hear such things, I shall be really very desirous of learning more about them from some of your next letters. I have a very nice little letter from Tommy[6] with a long and good account of his school affairs in which he seems much interested. He tells me he is only 15 years old, and it seems to me almost a pity that he could not have a longer schooling, but of course as I am so far away I can form no opinion of what is proper or necessary under the circumstances. I should like Tommy to feel that everything depends in reality upon himself, although circumstances may cut his education a year shorter, and chance may partly settle his business. If he wished to show what stuff he is made of, neither of these things will in the end materially keep him back. He must make the best use of the excellent teaching he is now getting in London, which I have no doubt he does do, and after that he will find plenty of leisure time to go on with what things he feels best suited for.

January 22nd

I think I told you in one letter that we were in fear of having our salaries cut down when the estimates were voted by the Legislative Assembly. Miller & I attended in the gallery on the occasion, in some degree of trepidation, but the debate took a very favourable turn and we heard ourselves styled by the fiercest leaders of the opposition, as "highly skilled men", "men whom it would be impossible to replace", "gentlemen of the highest scientific attainment" (from Parkes, whom I favour with my reports) and they finally voted the whole estimate in a lump. 25 per cent has been taken off the *temporary increase* of every salary and the remainder made permanent so that my salary is now fixed at £630, but in nearly every other Government department, furthur* reductions have been made in the most arbitrary manner.

A short time since I predicted that the receipt of gold at the Mint would diminish because New South Wales is saturated with our coin, even in spite of Capt Wards assurance that we should have plenty. It turns out that instead of having 15,000 or 20,000 oz per week of Melbourne gold, as we had at this time last year, no gold comes at all from Port Phillip and our receipts are usually about 2,000, even as low one week as 438. We are not much concerned because a Gold duty bill is just being passed here, and when the duty is the same as at Port Phillip, it is expected that the Victorians will proclaim out coin legal, and we shall then have to replace the whole English there, which must be

[6] This letter is not among the Jevons Papers.

several millions. This will keep us at full work for a year or two, and it is not impossible as suggested by Graham himself that our coin might be rendered legal in England ultimately.

This is partly because our coin has turned out so satisfactorily especially as regards *assay* or fineness, that it is much superior to the English coinage itself. I will just give you Grahams reports upon our *pyx* pieces sent home.

	Coined during	N° of pieces	Mean Assay Report.
The standard fineness you know is $\frac{11}{12}$ of ·916667	June–July 1855	32	·91669
	July–Sept 1855	15	·91668
	„ „ Half sovs	6	·91670
	Oct–Dec. 1855	114	·91674
	Jan. March 1856	101	·91667
	half sos	38	·91659

Our work now is exceedingly light, generally only between 5 & 10 assays per day. I should not wonder if several days of each week I am not occupied over the assays more than ½ hour per day; but I nearly always attend the full 6 hours, and fill up the time by preparations for larger numbers, or various things of my own.

The last few days I have been working very hard to finish a paper on a Meteorological subject, viz the Cirrus or *feathery cloud*.[7] Not only do I give the first reasonable explanation viz a *filtering* of portions of air into each other, that has ever been offered but I extend it to explain the whole origin of *thunderstorms* and many other things. I am sending it Per Oneida to Graham, to see what he & London think of it. Whether my anticipations will be fulfilled I cannot tell and I must wait about 6 months before I can hear anything more.

It is writing and copying out this paper which has taken up all my time lately, prevented me finishing this letter till the last moment, or writing at all to Lucy as I intended.

Things in general are the same as ever here. I am always quite well as are most people, but often feel an intolerable feeling of weakness and lassitude, occasioned by the hot close weather we sometimes have preceding thunderstorms. You have heard before of our new house at Double Bay (it is as good as partly mine since I have lent Miller £200 to build it). It will be finished in about a month and within two months I hope that we may be settled in it. There we shall have North East

---

[7] Probably 'On the Cirrous Form of Cloud', *London . . . Philosophical Magazine* (July 1857), 22–35 (La Nauze, op. cit., p. 41). Jevons noted in his diary on 9 July 1857: 'Received . . . a note from Graham acknowledging the receipt of my paper on Cirrous Cloud, calling it "extremely interesting" and promising to publish it. . . .'

sea breezes and sea bathing which are just the things for freshening me up.

Last week there was a very grand cricket match here between Sydney & Melbourne, Capt Ward being the principal player & bowler of the Sydneyites; it was in the Domain which from its natural beauty and splendid position and the immense number of orderly people in it presented one of the most beautiful spectacles I ever saw. To show you how the Sydney people take holydays,* I will tell you that Sydney proper contains 60,000 inhabitants, that of these 8 or 10,000 were at the cricket match at one time the first day, 15,000 the second day, a large proportion of these spending the whole day there after 12.0, and many thousands the third day when it was finished in a few hours, the Sydney beating awfully.⁸ Thus nearly 1/4 of the population was at the match at one time and the business of the town was quite interrupted. I take this to be a sign, not of laziness, but that the people are so well today as to be able to spare more holydays* and really to enjoy themselves more than the people of other countries.

It is just possible I may start Saturday on a trip with Hunt⁹ of the Mint & Some others to Wollongong a beautiful place on the coast, but I am not sure.

Give my best love to Lucy, Henny, Tommy & believe me to remain
Ever Your affec. Brother
W. S. Jevons.

98. W. S. JEVONS TO THE EDITOR OF THE *EMPIRE*

[10 February 1857]

THE WESTERN LINE OF RAILWAY, AND THE GENERAL POLICY OF GOVERNMENT RAILWAY EXTENSION

Sir-

A short time ago a paragraph appeared in the papers, containing the information from the railway surveyors, employed upon the projected western line, that they had discovered a practicable route as far as Hartley. The line leaving Parramatta, it seems, is to cross the comparatively level county of Cumberland, towards a point in the Nepean River, between Castlereagh and Richmond.

---

⁸ Jevons appears to have left out a word here.
⁹ Robert Hunt (1830–92). Born in London, he was appointed chief clerk of the bullion office of the Sydney Mint in July 1853 and arrived in New South Wales in 1854; served in the melting and refining departments until 1870, when he was transferred to the Mint in Melbourne; 1876–7, acting-Deputy-Master of the Sydney Mint in the prolonged absence of General Sir Edward Ward; Deputy Master from January 1878 until his death; C.M.G. 1888.

Thus far no great difficulty is encountered, excepting the ranges of hills immediately around Parramatta, and branch lines to Penrith on the one hand, and to Richmond and Windsor on the other, might, perhaps, prove profitable by collecting the whole traffic of the rich plains of the Hawkesbury and the Nepean Rivers.

But proceeding towards Bathurst, the main line must first cross the channel of these rivers by a bridge, which will be a larger work, I suppose, than any yet executed in the colony, and afterwards make its way (say the surveyors) up the valley of the Grose River, into the heart of the Blue Mountains. Then cutting through the summit of the range by a tunnel only two and a quarter miles in length, somewhere about Blackheath, and dashing through a second slight rocky obstacle of a few hundred yards in thickness, some outlying rocks of Mount Victoria no doubt, it successfully reaches the beautiful valleys in which Hartley stands.

Now, without regarding the few miles of tunnelling through solid sandstone rock, a difficulty which any one can appreciate, though he have never been within a thousand miles of the spot, and of which the cost might no doubt be accurately calculated out by an engineer, at so much per yard at current wages, what I wish to point out is the absurdity or rather the utter madness of supposing that anything of the nature of a railway can be carried through or across the Blue Mountains, in the present condition of the colony, either by the above route, by that proposed by "An Australian Mountaineer," in the *Herald* of last Saturday, or in any other direction.

"Mountaineer's" own account of the facilities of the route by which he proposes to avoid the Blue Mountain difficulty altogether, is well worth quoting, since it renders any further objections to his plan unnecessary.

"In the next place, the $2\frac{1}{2}$ miles' tunnel is saved, as by running up the Cox River we run clear of the Blue Mountains, with the exception of their lower slopes, of which here and there a point reach the bank of the river. It may be found necessary to cross the river two or three times wherever a bulky range comes close to the river; so that a bridge across the river would be less expensive than to cut through the range, as there is no place where the ranges come close to the river on both sides, but flats and ranges run on alternate sides, and by crossing over wherever a bridge would be the least expense, we should shorten the line considerably. As regards the range that divides the basin of the Cox from that of the Fish River, I have very little doubt that by applying horse-power to a twenty miles length, that is to say, ten miles on each side, it is probable that we may get over it without a tunnel, by taking the range in a slanting direction, and winding through the most favourable openings."

At such a description of the route from a person apparently exactly acquainted with the localities, and with the chance that here and in some awkward little corners the ranges might not distribute themselves quite so conveniently as he supposes, the boldest railway engineer might well shake his head, and the mightiest railway contractor would undoubtedly hesitate to send in his tender, if he had had a few months' experience of Sydney prices and wages. And as, too, on looking at the map, we see that the Cox River takes a great roundabout and leads us far from the Windsor and Penrith Districts we must surely acknowledge that this line, if the most practicable, is at least sufficiently impracticable.

With respect to the Surveyor's route, it happens that last Boxing day I visited the Grose River, a few miles above its junction with the Hawkesbury.[1] I discovered the nearly dry bed of a mountain torrent enclosed between high alluvial or rocky banks. Even here appearances were unpromising for a railway, but, with the exact nature of the higher parts of its course, I must confess myself unacquainted, except by maps, for the reason that within a few miles distance, the river entered the gorges of those pricipitously* steep and thickly wooded sandstone ranges, peculiar to the Blue Mountains, which both shut out the view, and are impassable to any but an experienced bush-man. It was powerfully suggested to me, however, that these ranges would here and there run down on both sides close to the water, in the way especially guarded against in his plan by "Mountaineer." On this point the public have not yet any certain information.

But now, I ask, on what engineering plan are we to ascend these precipitous gullies? Are we to lay lines in the bed of a mountain-torrent or to affix them to the sides of mountain ridges, winding about like a turnpike road; or shall we adopt the mixed plan of "Mountaineer," "by crossing over wherever a bridge would be the cheapest plan," which, indeed, has evident advantages? I merely venture to suggest that those who recommend the route should point out how the line can possibly be constructed.

Anyone ascending Lapstone Hill for the first time must be surprised, after reaching the top, to find a road usually nearly level or gently inclined upwards, until reaching Mount Victoria, where a steep descent takes place: does not the nature of the country suggest that the only feasible plan is that which proposes to cross the mountains on this line, by a wooden or iron tramway laid down on the road, either just as it stands at present, or slightly modified according to circumstances? A steam railway might be made as far as Penrith or Emu, and inclined planes constructed and small stationary engines employed to raise the wagons up the steep inclines of Lapstone Hill and Mount Victoria at a

[1] Cf. Vol. I, pp. 134–54.

comparatively small cost; but would it not be well to postpone altogether the idea of extending the line beyond Hartley for the present? Here the road divides into two or more branches, and the country, chiefly founded on hard slate rocks, presents serious difficulties to any railed line, although the roads, from their harder bottom, are not so much dreaded by carriers. Supposing some sort of line carried over the Blue Mountains to Hartley, might not a sort of depot be established in this well-suited place, where the teams from the interior might load and unload?

Though fully constructed railways be not possible to any great extent in New South Wales, it may yet be well to survey the country through which they may possibly run at some future period, in order that any advances which may be made shall lie in the right general direction. But in the case of the Western line, I maintain that there is no prospective possibility of a full locomotive railway being taken to Bathurst, and that we should, therefore, content ourselves with such inferior substitutes as appear practicable, choosing our line without any regard to the future employment of steam upon it. I would beg here, Mr. Editor, the favour of a somewhat extended space in your columns for a few remarks on the general question of railway extension in New South Wales. A few months ago there was a great discussion on it, in both the *Empire* and *Herald*, but the confusion of ideas seemed only to become worse the more they were agitated. Still I am sorry that the question was left incomplete, and that both the public and that greater public of Mr. Donaldson's,[2] the Legislative Assembly, have become silent, and allowed the Government to proceed without any definite policy being determined upon.

I have still in my memory that extraordinary declaration of the Governor-General's, that a railway need not necessarily be capable of paying any profits, since indirect benefits to the population may repay its cost.[3] This I maintain to be completely false in principle, for the reason that the money returns of the railway, though not the object of its construction, as in private concerns, furnish, when the fares are adjusted to the *maximum paying rates*, an exact *measure* of the benefits conferred, direct or indirect. It may not be always necessary or desirable to exact the highest paying rates, as is at present the case with the

[2] (Sir) Stuart Alexander Donaldson (1815–67); emigrated to Sydney, 1834; partner in the mercantile firm of Donaldson & Co., 1836–56; returned to the Legislative Assembly as member for Sydney Hamlets, 1856; in April that year called upon to form the first ministry under the provisions of the New South Wales Constitution Act, 1855; first minister and Colonial Secretary, June–August 1856; Colonial Treasurer under the Watson–Parker ministry, October 1856–September 1857; appointed commissioner for railways, 1857; returned to England, 1859; knighted 1860. Cf. above, Letter 79, n. 5, p. 205.

[3] Cf. above, Letter 90, n. 1, p. 235. Jevons here reproduces the argument which he had attributed to Pell in his earlier letter. For comment on the view of railway economy developed by Jevons in 1856–57, see Vol. IV, Part II.

Post Office, but if a sufficient number of persons do not find it to their advantage, on any arrangement, to afford fares of sufficient amount to repay the cost of the railway, it evidently proves that the latter actually does not repay its cost by benefits, direct or indirect, to these or any other persons.

The error of those maintaining the opposite opinion arises from neglecting to consider that any benefit bestowed upon any part of the country, or the world either, will be sure to re-act upon those actually using the railway. It is the full use of the railway which can alone produce any return, and it will be stimulated, whoever is supposed ultimately to receive the benefit, or if it be not thus stimulated to a compensatory amount, it proves that it is a dead loss; that money has been invested and is not making an equivalent return.

When starting thus upon principles of economy radically false, it becomes doubly necessary to watch the steps of those who are charged with executive power, and entertain such opinions. This, the Legislative Assembly, in whom the duty certainly lies, does not appear to be doing: on the contrary it seems to me that the well-known members of the Opposition, so apt at knocking off some petty constable or messenger, or reducing by a few pounds the salary of some deserving public officer, cannot extend their minds to grasp anything above a hundred thousand pounds; much less can they conceive the amount of such a sum as £3,000,000, proposed to be immediately guaranteed for railway extension in his Excellency's minute. Witness the large sums voted for deficiency in the revenue, for railway surveys, for immigration, &c., amounting to about two thirds of a million, with scarcely more discussion than must often have occurred over some attempted reduction of £50 of expenditure.

The Opposition are fond of taunting members of Government with introducing no grand measures, such as had been promised; they have at all events allowed one great measure to be introduced by the thin end of the wedge, and to be passed almost unnoticed – viz., a very fair commencement has been made of a National Debt.

Now, though a debt which has been incurred by productive expenditure is very different from the unproductive debts of Great Britain and other countries, it behoves us carefully to preserve this difference, and to spend not a pound upon public works which will not be probably paying 5 per cent interest in value, within a reasonable number of years, say five years to come.

What lines of railway are likely to pay this, among those proposed, or whether any at all will do so, it is not for me to judge; I only say let the paying principle be maintained in these things.

The Parramatta Railway has not yet succeeded in a monetary sense, much less the Liverpool extension. It is true that the goods traffic has not yet fallen into this channel, so that this line as yet affords no criterion – but it is an evident fallacy to suppose, as I have heard advanced, that as the lines are extended north, west, and south, better results may be expected. More traffic will no doubt pass between Parramatta and Sydney, but what of those branches of the line upon which only a portion of the traffic will travel although the expenses of the line will be much the same? For, of course, considerably less than half the traffic terminating in Sydney will travel on either the western or southern branch, and as to overland communication with Melbourne, the railway can surely not compete for a long time to come with the present regular and swift steam service.

It is customary in projecting railways to draw largely upon the traffic that the line is said to create of itself, and in the case of Australia in particular we are apt to carry on in our minds a short-proportion sum by which we deduce from the population of New South Wales a few years ago, and that at present, its probable population a few years to come.

Now are we quite correct or safe in either of these assumptions? Is it likely that traffic will be created in the bushy wilds of Australia as it was through the open, fertile, and closely populated counties of Great Britain? There were millions of persons already located and carrying on immense manufactures and transactions, only cramped by the want of better intercommunication than turnpike roads and canals. There were only needed inventive minds who could show how the abundant supplies of coal, iron, and water, could be combined, so as to produce cheap and effective locomotion.

If the example of America be once more adduced, in which cheap and long lines of railway have led civilization out into the midst of primeval forests, truly, so it is said, creating traffic, can we here hope to run lines on the same method, through the rugged wilds and mountainous tracts of New South Wales, or have we a large population continually shifting more westward as that of the United Stated is known to do.

In the States, too, the lines of railway are, I believe, projected and executed by private speculators, Yankee men of business, of well-known foresight and cuteness. Does the general success of Government works in this colony or any other country whatever, warrant us in supposing the same economy and foresight will be employed, or the same success attend the Government railway undertakings at present in question.

Again, with respect to emigration, to which, with the exception of the ordinary growth of population by births, we must, of course, wholly look for our expected increase of traffic, it is almost certain that the prodigious stream of emigrants which has of late been flowing from Great Britain, cannot continue at the same rate, even if a complete reaction does not follow. Rapid emigration commenced from Great Britain about the year 1817, from causes chiefly internal to that country itself; it was accelerated, as far as Australia was concerned, by the diggings in 1851, since which time the progress of New South Wales, and of Victoria more especially, has been most rapid. But the diggings, though their yield of metal may not decrease as yet, will never again bear such an attractive name as they have hitherto done, nor can we, in conscience, expect such a stroke of fortune to be repeated for Australia, since she must have enjoyed within five or six years the most extraordinary discovery of sudden wealth known in history.

Therefore, I say, let not the legislators of New South Wales speculate too easily upon what Australia may become, or upon what traffic may arise in its, as yet, uninhabited tract of bush. Let them not enter into any monetary engagements not sanctioned by that cautious foresight and intelligence best exhibited in the counting-house of the merchant. In such large matters, let them not lose the check of a sure monetary repayment; but above all, not a step must be taken under such a principle as that which supposes this check to be superfluous, and *insolvent railways* to be a public benefit.

Lastly, I hope that in these remarks I may not be thought to forget the motto, "Advance Australia", to oppose, even by my feeble voice, but, I hope, more powerful reasons, any means of *bona fide* progress of which New South Wales can avail itself, or to be in any way or degree a "croaker." Unproductive expenditure and a public debt will only burden and retard this colony, will drive away from its shores those emigrants who come here to be free from the burdensome taxes of England; it may perhaps involve it in difficulties. Any progress made, and we are always making progress, should be on safe and sound foundation.

I am, Sir, your obedient servant,

O.

99. W. S. JEVONS TO THE EDITOR OF THE *EMPIRE*

METEOROLOGY AND THE *HERALD*

Sir – Observing in the *Herald* of to-day a rather strange editorial note, in which the readers of that journal are presented with a meteorological report (interesting and good of itself, though very curtailed), taken at a place called Goonoo Goonoo, I cannot avoid congratulating them on the appearance, once more, of some such valuable and necessary information in their columns. At the same time they had better have omitted the following sentence, – "The meteorological observations kept at the South Head have been given up, as our readers are aware, because of Mr. Peacock having bolted from the colony, and now no register is kept that we are aware of."

It seems to me that –

1st. It was far from creditable to the proprietors of such a well-to-do journal to allow a series of observations – continued regularly, I believe, for 20 or 25 years – to lapse, and the instruments employed to be sold up by the Sheriff, "because of Mr. Peacock having bolted from the colony." Some qualified person might surely have been found and induced to continue them even at the expense of the money payments which I understand Mr. Peacock received; especially, too, as Mr. Scott,[1] with his Government observations, would have taken such a burden off their hands by the end of the present year. The *Herald's* anxiety too for the progress of the science of meteorology comes rather late in the day, I think, when Sir William Denison's twelve meteorological stations are on the eve of being established.[2]

2nd. I can hardly credit the assertion of the editor of the Herald, of being quite unaware that any other register was being kept, for having taken such a series of observationsa at Petersh'm for more than two years, I have for about the last six months made out a regular weekly report, which the *Empire* has been kind enough to publish sufficiently conspicuously in its Tuesday or Wednesday's issue. Surely the *Herald* people's habits of attention and memory must have been sadly deficient as regards their contemporary's production, the *Empire*, published within a few yards of them, if they have really missed these reports; but on the contrary supposition, surely we may be astonished that the acrimony and rivalry, almost excusable in political matters, should be carried by them into a subject of scientific or general interest.

If the conductors of the *Herald*, not possessing such source of information themselves, had not sufficient virtue to direct their readers where to find it they should at least not ignore its existence altogether.

I am myself happy to be the means of connecting the *Herald's* old set of observations with those which will be shortly commenced by the Government, thus preventing a break in a long serious* of years which would have been most unfortunate, and as far as we know irrecoverable.

    I remain, Sir,
        yours obediently,
          O.

February 25, 1857.

[1] i.e. Rev. William Scott, Colonial Astronomer. See below, Letter 118, n. 1, p. 329.
[2] The Sydney Observatory, which is still in use, was built on Flagstaff Hill, 1856–8.

100. W. S. JEVONS TO HERBERT JEVONS
[LJP, 81–4]

Double Bay. near Sydney. N.S.W.
March 9th 1857.[1]

My dear Herbert.

I am very happy to be able to write by this mail from our new home, for I have a very pleasant account to give you of it. Our house having been finished for a short time we bid good bye last Monday to the dry monotonous country of Petersham and the frightful dusty Parramatta Road, and I am now completely settled in my new apartments.

You will remember me telling you that the intended situation of the house was changed from Rose to Double Bay and though the name is less flowery and enticing, and we are now just within the confines of civilization, we have every reason to be glad of it otherwise, for Rose Bay is not within walking distance of Sydney and therefore altogether inconvenient. The situation here is most delightful. You must imagine to yourself a small circular bay of blue waters, bounded on either side by rocky ridges, either covered by the original bush, or ornamented by handsome houses or pretty Australian villas. The view out of the Bay to the North extends across the Harbour to the jutting heads of the North shore which terminates in a perpendicular cliff, the *Middle Head*, and beyond which we have just a distant glimpse of the North Harbour. On the south side of the Bay is a circular white-sandy beach rising with a moderate inclination to a few feet above high water mark whence a narrow alluvial plain or flat of fertile sandy land extends into the country about a mile and a half between the steep & bushy sandstone ridges which form the country here.

Just on the edge of the beach and of this flat our house is built; on our left hand is a pretty little villa in which the old father of Mr Daniel Cooper[2] the owner of the whole neighbourhood lives; to the front of course is the view of the Bay and Harbour, and on every other side is as yet the original bush, which is uncleared except within a few feet of the house. It is here real picturesque bush rising about ten feet

---

[1] The original manuscript of this letter is incomplete.

[2] Daniel (later Sir Daniel) Cooper (1821–1901) merchant and philanthropist. Born in Lancashire, the second son of Thomas Cooper, merchant, he emigrated with his parents but returned to London in 1835 to complete his education at University College School; after abandoning a legal career and gaining commercial experience, he returned to Sydney in 1843 to a partnership in the family mercantile business, which passed into his control in 1852; owned extensive property in and around Sydney; also held large stations in the western districts; a director of the Sydney Railway Co., President of the Bank of New South Wales, 1855–61, an elected member of the Legislative Council, 1849–51 and 1855, and Speaker of the first Legislative Assembly, 1856–60; in 1861 he returned to England where he furthered the colony's interests, and died in London.

high with a large variety of the peculiar narrow leaved shrubs of N.S.W. and a thick undergrowth of ferns and grass trees.

The house is a very comfortable, suitable but unassuming one. (of which I again give you a plan as you may forget it) and it is of course doubly agreable* since it is our own. My parlour is 12 feet 6 inches by 10 feet and quite large enough therefore for my purposes particularly as it has no fire place and the bed room though small does very well since the two form but one when the middle door is open. I have spent about £12 or £15 furnishing them and with the furniture I had before, they are very comfortable. I have a very pretty coloured new carpet, a sort of escritoire side table with small drawers and a little mahogany *what-not* for my music books. Below I give a panoramic sketch of the sides of my parlour which with the addition of plenty of imagination will give you some idea of it perhaps. Just outside my window is the thermometer case a wooden erection of singular appearance designed to shelter the thermometer from the sun by sides formed of three separate boards.

The weather now is very close and hot and while I write the thermometer is at 88°.

As you see there are four doors to the two rooms but besides the convenience of exit this gives me plenty of ventilation, than which nothing is more necessary and pleasant here. I think however that we shall not be deficient in this here, for except when other winds are blowing a sea breeze sets in nearly everyday but has been lately particularly fresh. Most people at home do not know what a sea-breeze is I expect, but they would soon understand it here. It sets in a little before noon from the N E, or nearly directly up the Bay, increases till about sunset and drops off again about 9 PM. We scarcely felt it at the Petersham house, where however we had the more truly Australian climate which my observations here will not so well represent. It seems to render the readings of the thermometer very equable as the following numbers show (at 9 am & 9 pm)

March 2.	67.9°
	69 9
3	72 6
	72 7
4	70 2
	70 9
5	73 7
	67 9
6	72 9
	73 4
7	74 3
	73 4
8	75 9
	76 7
9. No sea breeze	82 8

With respect to business (which seldom enters our thoughts now, since we have none) this house is about 2 miles from the Mint, but as the road passes over several ridges, forming the Bays of Rushcutter, Wooloomooloo,* etc, the walk is by no means easy taking 40 m. in and 35 out. Several mornings lately, I have been drenched with perspiration in going in, from the closeness of the air, to an extent that would surprise you, but in cooler weather the walk will be very agreable* I expect.

This place, too, is like a perpetual watering-place for nothing could be better adapted than³ this beach for bathing. I have bathed the last four mornings between 6 and 7 a.m. and it is very delightful. Being within a few yards of the water, one can almost turn into it out of bed, and twice I have turned back again into bed after it which is still more delightful. The only drawback are some weeds which a little spoil the clearness of the water. By-the-bye* I was nearly forgetting the sharks of which there are undoubtedly many in the Harbour since their fins are often seen above water, and a large monster of 14 feet length and a ton weight or so was lately caught. But some how or other no accidents occur though hundreds of people bathe even off the most exposed rocks about the Harbour. They keep I suppose in the deep waters, and are never known to come [to]⁴ a shallow bay like ours. Lucy therefore may be quite at her ease whether as to sharks or any other dangers, which do not exist.

The country about here is very different from the usual Australian bush, consisting of low *scrub*, or thick bushy shrubs instead of the eternal gum trees woods which cover all the rest of the country. The strip of

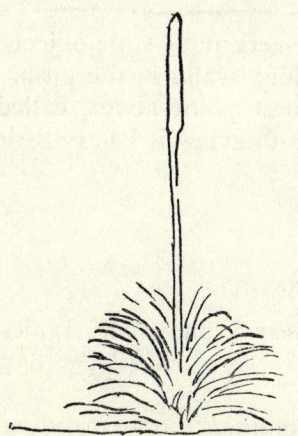

land 2 or 3 miles from the coast consists of nothing but⁵ long ranges of hills covered by drifted sand with the scrub growing on it, and with multitudes of grass trees which give a most peculiar app^ce to the vegetation. These are as in the drawing and are about 6 or 8 feet in height the flower and stalk being not unlike an enormous bullrush, springing from hard spiny grass. I anticipate many delightful walks about this country and I have moreover got a little research in hand concerning certain *ancient raised sea-cliffs* which I have discovered round the Harbour, as well as the *alluvial flats* which are connected with them. They struck me first near Petersham where I found parallel lines of rocks in the middle of the bush & proved them to be always at the level of about 40 feet above the sea. I send you a

³ Jevons wrote 'that' here.   ⁴ Omitted in the original manuscript.
⁵ Jevons wrote 'of' here.

supposed section of Camperdown creek. At the head of the flat of Rushcutters bay I find them again very perpendicular and as I think at the same height. Yesterday in a walk I took with OConnel* I discovered unmistakeable* signs of a second higher series of cliffs perhaps 120 or 150 feet above the sea, of which a portion is to be seen disinctly at the North shore on a projecting Head though not so distinctly as in the figure. The question is a very interesting one being connected with the curious subject of the formation of Australia and I do not know that these cliffs have ever been noticed before, being indeed seldom very noticeable objects. It is a pleasant subject too from leading me long walks in the bush.

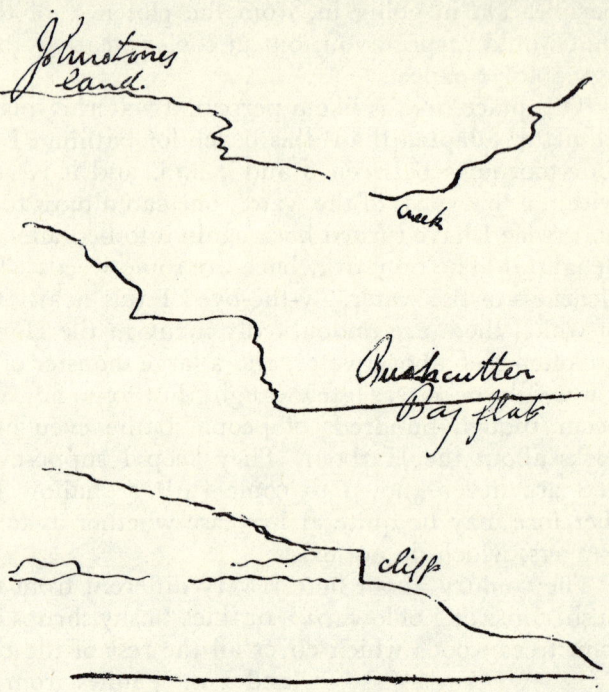

In our walk yesterday we got to the highest point about, called Belle-vue Hill a name for once appropriate, as the view is I have little hesitation in saying, the finest I ever saw

101. W. S. JEVONS TO HENRIETTA JEVONS

Double Bay near Sydney. N.S. Wales.
April 4th 1857.

My dearest Henny

Tonight, though it is rather late, I must commence my correspondence for the next mail of the 10th. as I have much to say to several of you, and you can form no idea of all my other pressing business! I am no longer an assayer, but in name (dont be frightened) for really the assaying is the very least considerable of all my duties, and between my meteorological work, music, reading etc down to my monthly letter writing, I feel that if time went five times as slow as it does, I could not get through it as I should like.

To tell the truth, your last letter¹ has not a little occupied me since I received it, and to unburden my mind as soon as possible of what lies consequently accumulated on it I begin your answer first.

It was written in that seriously thoughtful way that I so much like in your letters, and which perhaps leads me to answer them with so much pleasure in the same kind, but forgive me if I say I was almost sorry to hear your own account of yourself. You describe yourself as "poor in spirit", "in great danger of falling into frivolous ways" etc and the principal cause you seem to say is balls, parties, and such-like truly frivolous things. I have always as you know, had a prepossession against such things, which was not however from my own judgement but grew up naturally with me, but now my judgement comes almost to confirm my prejudice, and I feel inclined to say Damn them altogether if they are the least likely to change you from what I thought you were, judging by your former letters. I have all my life, as I find on looking back, been in search of some one that I could call *my real friend*. You understand already I dare say what I mean; I do not want one to love, for I have many that I love already, nor one to think a *good fellow*, and to talk and chat with, for any one will do for that on a push, but one who besides being loved and liked, is somewhat of the same character, feelings, & purposes as myself and who could consequently understand & receive my confidence as nobody else could in matters which go beyond the depth of common things.

Such I am altogether hopeless of finding here; I have looked round the mint with the most negative results; it would be absurd to continue the search in New South Wales. Even when I was [at]² the London University, and had a pick of 200 or 300, there were but 1 or 2 that looked likely. To one of them I wrote from Sydney and received a most disheartening reply chiefly about rowing boats and pulling. In your few last letters in short lay my only chance, and to write to you thus will show you how much I should value such a friend even at the distance of 13,000 miles or so.

I cannot say I am quite unacquainted with the state you describe yourself to be in. I felt it, I think, during the holydays* which I used to spend at home between the terms at College when having no fixed & necessary occupation and not finding it possible to settle steadily to lessons, & not being inclined to give myself up entirely to amusements I used to get into a very lazy good for nothing way of which ill-humour etc were the consequences. Here my life is regular & cheerful. I have light

---

¹ This letter is not among the Jevons Papers.
² Omitted in the original manuscript.

but very necessary duties in town every day which takes me a good walk in and out and the consequence is that I am always in health and spirits and nearly always disposed for work.

In your case, the want of energy, for such it is, probably arises for your being now for the first time in your life, left with a great deal of time on your hands and with nothing but ordinary occupations to employ it. It is but lately you left school where of course you were not your own Mistress, and then you spent some time in London and in circumstances where there was much novelty and much to keep you going.

Now you have to depend upon your own industry and energy and I hope that you will succeed. Probably even before you get this you will find yourself more accustomed to the change & more the master of yourself. The fact is I often wonder how ladies do manage to spend such dull lives as theirs must be in general; most of them without occupation or purpose. Even with respect to Lucy it has often seemed a mystery to me how she can keep herself busily employed at home year after year, (and she numbers some years now you know) without more change than an occasional.[3] Perhaps it is that her rather frequent *gaddings*, as she fancies I think them, act as a medicine, but at all events you had better learn the secret from her and apply it in your case.

I shall not think of giving you any advice as to what to occupy yourself with; let it depend entirely on yourself but it must be something in which you either have or can *get up* a strong interest. But you should never read or learn *passively*, that is just receiving the facts and thoughts of others; there should always be an equal original action on your own part which consists in never receiving anything but what you *agree in* from the conviction of your own thought and in never being afraid of venturing original ideas or objections of your own. Try English composition upon any subject you are interested in; this was for a long time a thing I could never accomplish, but now I think I have made a start in it. To write one short article upon any subject is as satisfactory and I dare say as useful as to read half a dozen books upon it. One good kind of exercise in writing is the epistolatory* and I do not care how many of such exercises you compose and address to me. I must say that your letters already are such as few girls (young ladies who have finished their education I should say!) would write

One thing in your letter I entirely disagree with and that is *your desire to leave yourself alone and work for others*. To work for others is no doubt a good wish, but in either your case or mine I believe it to be *bad economy*, to do it immediately. To work tooth & nail for many years upon yourself alone and with all appearance of doing it selfishly, may

---

[3] Jevons appears to have left out a word here.

be in reality the best means of rendering yourself capable of benefiting others to an extent altogether surpassing what you might have done by working for a longer period with undeveloped strength. To teach charity children is a very good thing; but to teach yourself for many years to come, may yet leave many years to teach charity children, and render you able to teach the world besides, and this is a better thing. You must consider this.

I rather object to your feeling "how much ones life and character are influenced by the people and events passing around you. For instance Mr Channing's[4] etc etc". On the contrary I would have you never be influenced by any one; agree only on the conviction of your own thoughts, as I said before, and from the natural diversity of the human mind, you will seldom find anyone with whom you can thoroughly agree. If you follow any mans opinions it should surely not be without using your own reason & judgement and in this case it can hardly possibly happen that you should coincide in all opinions with him. I occasionally meet with a writer, Sir J. Herschel[5] on physical subjects for instance, whose thoughts I can follow without disagreement, but I find it extremely rare, and seldom agree to more than half of any one book.

I do not know what you mean by saying that you have a leaning towards the Catholics, and that you should like uncommonly to go to Confession fast etc. Mrs Miller here may be called a complete bigot against the Catholics, and when hearing them abused right & left I feel inclined to say they are not all bad but sometimes good. I must say however that whether considered as a spiritual religion or a practical system Roman Catholicism is very disgusting and only better than irreligion. The good in it chiefly exists independently and almost in opposition to its principles, as indeed in some other religions.

You should stick well to your music whether singing or the pianoforte and likewise read a little about it. I have not time just now to go on with any more chapters of my book,[6] nor anything in my head to write about it just now, but I have not quite forgotten it. I play, if any thing, more than ever, as I find it always a recreation. As I have got a large quantity of music including about 10 oratorias* 20 operas, 7 or 8 masses besides dances, psalm tunes, etc etc, I could not play the whole of it many times in the year if I went through it all in succession, so that I am necessarily imperfect in nearly all, but as I play for my own edification & amusement I do not care for this and shall improve in the whole by degrees. My last acquired piece is a very beautiful one viz *A te O Cara* from Il* Puritani set for the piano but it unfortunately contains

---

[4] See above, Letter 57, n. 7, p. 134.
[5] See below, Letter 151, n. 1, p. 432.
[6] See above, Letter 93, p. 243.

some vast flourishes for which both the range of my fingers & of the octaves of the harmonium are quite inadequate.

I am sorry to say that Brooke has acted for *most positively the last time*, and left Sydney till he comes back again. I have spent some of the pleasantest evenings at his representations of Shakespeares that I ever remember and it has given me a liking and understanding both of Shakespeare and a good theatre which I never had before. I saw, Othello, *A Winters Tale*, Taming a Shrew, Much ado about Nothing, Macbeth, Tempest besides *Virginius*,[7] Serious family[8] etc by other writers. The Winters Tale was very well represented and was exceedingly interesting and amusing, and the rest were all more or less so. But the Tempest was the one which chiefly astonished & pleased me. It was exceedingly well brought out, in fact nearly as well as it could be done in any but the best theatres of England, as to scenery & management, but the subordinate actors were bad. The play is both the most comical, and at the same time the [most] highly imaginative and poetical that I had any idea of. Take the first opportunity to see some of Shakespeare acted.

We have now an Opera House opened with some good singers but I have not yet been.[9]

I cannot well describe to you how comfortable I find myself here in most respects. My rooms are perfectly adopted to my wishes barring a few physical imperfections. As I sit here writing about 10 30 PM. with the French Window open and the uncleared bush & blue sky in front of me, there is no sound to disturb my thoughts but the occasional short wash of the water on the beach, and the extremely faint but continual and uniform roar of the distant ocean breakers on the coast. This low roaring sound is very peculiar & not unpleasant; I used to hear it in the quiet of the night even at Petersham and here it is very distinct.

The walk into town is a convenient distance and along a most picturesque road winding over the hills and across the flats of the bays bordering the Harbour. When reaching the Mint too my employments are of the highest description, the assay work though it must be performed punctually and exactly being nothing in quantity. Hence I

---

[7] A tragedy by James Sheridan Knowles (1784–1862), first produced in 1820.

[8] Morris Barnett, *The Serious Family. A comedy in three acts* (1849).

[9] The Prince of Wales Opera House, under the patronage of the Governor-General, opened on Saturday, 4 April 1857, with a performance of Bellini's *Norma*.

The large, elaborate Prince of Wales Theatre, off Castlereagh Street, Sydney, had opened in March 1855 at a cost of £30,000 and with a capacity of over 3000. Sydney already possessed the Royal Victoria Theatre and it became clear that the city was unable to support both. It was therefore decided to convert the Prince of Wales Theatre into 'a spacious Music Hall, where ... the works of the greatest masters might be rendered in the full perfection of musical science ...', to compare with those in Britain, which would attract the best European artists. Cf. The *Empire*, 11 and 13 March 1855; 18 August 1856; 4 and 6 April 1857.

spend most of my time writing or reading the Newspapers for instance, and seldom find it lie upon my hands There is very little however to excite or interest us here and Sydney is at present in a very quiescent state. There is not the least intelligence stirring, and the Newspapers are chiefly occupied (in a convict colony) with the endless account of murders, garrotte robberies, tickets of leave, Bank failures, and fashionable Swindlers in England. We are almost ashamed here of our Mother land.

Sydney is a little compact town of a convenient size for extensive gossip, and you never heard such stories and scandals as occasionally go the round. One gets to know by sight & more by account and name, almost every principal person in the town, and their origin whether convict or otherwise, and I think I could name every shop in the town successively.

The raciest bit of gossip which has delighted our ears for some time is that when M^r & Mrs Miller were seeing the "Tempest" recently (I was unfortunately away) Robert Campbell[10] Esq M.P. ex-Colonial Treasurer, and one of the first men of the Colony had a regular fight in the dress boxes with a distant relation of his about a family quarrel, the other man having seized him by the hair of his head. They were separated with some difficulty and the affair was ventilated for several hours at the Police Court, Mr Campbell having been summoned by the other man but getting off rather the best in the end. But the best of it is that Capt Ward, our respected Chief, with whose name in connection with a certain rich Miss Campbell gossip has long been busy, was in the box with them, had the pleasant duty of separating & protecting his intended father in law, and of afterwards being chief witness at the examinations. Didnt this amuse his subordinate officers as well as the rest of the public no doubt?

Our supplies of gold continue very small and our receipts will be considerably less than they were last year. In fact unless some change takes place by which we can receive the Melbourne Gold besides that raised in New South Wales, I do not think the Mint will be continued here more than a year or two. It will very likely be moved to Melbourne in the end, but will probably last here as long as I shall wish to stay.[11]

[10] Robert Campbell (1804–59) second son of Robert Campbell (1769–1846), merchant, pastoralist and politician; born in Sydney and educated in England, 1810–19, Campbell became a partner in the family business, 1827; became leader of a campaign to end transportation to New South Wales, 1829; elected to the Legislative Council, 1851; resigned 1856 and was elected to the Legislative Assembly, becoming Colonial Treasurer, an office he held almost continually until his death. Cf. above, Letter 28, n. 2, p. 51.

[11] A second branch of the Royal Mint, at Melbourne, was authorised in August 1869 and officially opened in June 1872; a third branch was opened at Perth in June 1899. The Sydney Mint was not closed until December 1926, by which time it had become clear that Australia could not support three mints economically. Cf. Craig, op. cit., pp. 388–9.

My determination not to waste more time than I can avoid here increases in strength as that time gradually passes. As you say I think *a work will come for me to do* and I do not regard money making as any fit work at all. At my time of life it may be very useful to save money, but it is not necessary and on the contrary it may be better to *invest* it in oneself, even if it were only in the end to be enabled to gain more money. I do not mean to say I shall get home penniless because I have already saved £700 and am rapidly saving more, but because I shall not hesitate to spend a portion of this in travelling or otherwise, if I think proper For I do not go home to lead a lazy life, and therefore, excepting unforeseen accidents, I can work for my living there and all the better for what I may have invested upon myself. Do you see.

I have been much occupied lately with a new Subject viz, Political Economy, which seems mostly to suit my exact method of thought. It is difficult to conceive what it is but by learning it and you might very well look into it a little. I think we used to have "Smiths Wealth of Nations", which is an excellent though rather old book upon it. The last two or three days I have been working at a letter to the Empire on some questions of Economy here; I delivered it yesterday at 5 PM at the Office and Lo! it appears this morning in $2\frac{1}{2}$ columns of large type. (signed O.)[12] I will perhaps post a copy of the Paper. You dont know how pleasant it is to appear in type.

Good Friday is within a day or two, & as I think I can scrape together a holyday* or two, I was intending to go to the Illawarra district[13] which is very beautiful and singular country, but I am afraid I must postpone this trip. At the worst I shall get in some coach or other and wander about for a day or two as in my last trip at Christmas to the R Hawkesbury Windsor etc. By next mail I intend writing to Tommy. I shall write some more letters for this mail, if I have time; otherwise my other sister and brothers must remain contented with the brief notice that I am still their living & loving Brother. For yourself Dearest Henny, I have only to say I hope you will return me equal measure, that is to say a letter of equal length breadth, but believe me through all and for ever

    Your loving though distant Brother
        W S Jevons.

[12] Entries in Jevons's diaries for this period provide further evidence of his being 'much occupied . . . with a new subject, viz., Political Economy'. Relevant extracts from the diaries are reproduced in Volume IV, Part III.

Jevons's diary entry for 28 March 1857 reads: 'Wrote & sent letter to Empire with view of shutting up writers about Protective Humbug'. The letter was actually published in the *Empire* on 30 March 1857 and is reproduced below (p. 281). Jevons was replying to William B. Allen, Secretary of the Protective League, whose letter on protection had been published in the paper on 28 March 1857.

[13] For Jevons's account of this trip in the Journal, see Vol. I, pp. 159–78.

102. W. S. JEVONS TO THE EDITOR OF THE *EMPIRE*

Mr. Editor,

By your favour, I beg to submit to your readers, that they need not for the future occupy themselves, except for amusement, with any articles headed "Protection".

All will agree, Mr. Editor, that you acted only fairly and rightly in allowing all to have their say, even on such an exploded subject as Protection, but it now remains for the public to express its opinion and decision. Unless, then, some one with abundant leisure time will undertake the thankless task of looking into these articles and thoroughly confuting their sophistry, the public may very easily give their opinion by maintaining perfect silence on the subject from the present date.

I have myself spent a deal of time this morning in trying to get through W. B. Allen's letter in the *Empire*, in which by industriously leaving out all considerations of capital invested in woollen manufacturing, viz. in the building used as a manufactory or the expensive machinery, engines, etc., imported from England, as well as the current expenses of fuel for the engine and a hundred other things, and by assuming the only cost to the colony of 72,800 yards of tweed to be the wool consumed and £15 per annum per man, "for imports in medicine, tea, sugar, &c., &c.," he proves as he very likely might in this way, that the gain on 10,400 suits of woollen clothes made by colonial tailors, from the abovementioned 72,800 yards of tweed, would be £11,629. 3s. 7d.!!!

The Secretary of the Protection League's triumphant conclusion is "This is your saving from your tailors and shows every two tailors you employ save as much as every five shepherds produce".

I lapse into silence myself after the expression of hope that W. B. A. will for the future devote himself to some occupation more remunerative to himself and the public also, for whose good he is so solicitous, or that before appearing again in print he will come prepared with the conclusive results of experiments upon his own productive powers in the various occupations of shepherd, storekeeper, agricultural labourer, and wool weaver or slubber, etc.

Yours and W. B. A.'s obedient servant,

O

Sydney, March 28th. [1857]

103. W. S. JEVONS TO THE EDITOR OF THE *EMPIRE*

Sir,

On the adoption of wise regulations with regard to the sale or distribution of the unoccupied lands of the colony, and of a right policy in the formation of railways or other means of access to the various parts of the territory, must chiefly depend the progress of the wealth of New South Wales, and consequently, no doubt, the general improvement and increased happiness of its inhabitants.

A short consideration of the real condition of a colony will, I believe, convince any one of ordinary comprehension and unbiassed mind, of the truth of this remark. For the sole cause which induces persons to leave the civilized and generally happy society of Europe to undergo all the labour of raising similar comforts and means of advancement on the other side of the globe, is the expectation that here he may obtain abundance of unowned land which by the application of a moderate amount of labour will give large and almost spontaneous returns of corn, wool, or mineral wealth, the whole or nearly the whole of which will form a clear profit to the labourer. In short, the country is unowned by hereditary landlords who, as in old countries, can demand a high rent for its advantages, so that the natural fruitfulness of the soil is a free gift which the first comer may obtain at the mere solicitation of a little labour.

His produce will either directly supply his wants in abundance or may be very advantageously shipped and exchanged in Europe for those productions of simple labour and skill, to the manufacture of which he could not of course profitably turn his attention here, since with respect to these he enjoys no more or even less advantages than if he were in Europe.

A certain number of persons will of course be engaged in carrying on the necessary operations of exchange, or commerce, and a further portion of the population must be employed in building or supplying those productions which cannot be easily imported; but all these persons must be induced to remain in their occupations by wages or profits correspondingly high to those they might obtain as farmers, shepherds, or gold-diggers.

The commercial and partial manufacturing interests, thus created and of necessity existing, are, however, entirely secondary in importance to the agricultural, pastoral, or mining interests, which are evidently the original source of the wealth and general prosperity of all colonists.

How we may feel surprised, then, that so little attention is paid to the large questions of economy affecting these main interests, and that so little wisdom or consistency has been exhibited in their management hitherto, as in this letter I shall attempt to show. With this purpose I shall, to the best of my knowledge, define the present, *de facto*, schemes of Land Distribution and Railway Extension in New South Wales, without respect to persons or parties, and by briefly discussing their principles try to prove that, as I believe, they are in theory separately incorrect and inconsistent when compared together.

As regards Lands, it may be stated that –

1st. The waste Crown lands of this colony are regarded as an immense and valuable national estate or property, the sale of portions of which from time to time will, for the present generation at least, furnish a considerable portion of the general revenue.

2nd. To carry out this principle, and ensure an economical expenditure of this great natural fund, a high minimum price is placed upon all lands whatever, the purchase to be made at public auction with immediate payment in cash.

3rd. The Government undertakes the arrangement for the selection and surveys of the best lands to be offered for sale.

The present Railway policy, as far as definable, I understand to be the following:-

1st. New South Wales being a large, wild, and in many parts, a very rugged tract of country, in which water-carriage is non-existent, and locomotion by ordinary methods very difficult, railways, even of expensive construction, will be in reality the most economical kind of roads; and the formation of great trunk lines through every part of the colony will render large tracts of fertile land accessible, will draw all parts nearer to Sydney, and thus bring the produce to the market of the world, and will, therefore, not only increase the profits of all present colonists, but, by force of these advantages, will attract an increased stream of immigrants.

2nd. But as from the small and widely spread population, the difficult nature of the country, and the high price of labour, the formation of these railways would not be a successful undertaking, commercially speaking, or, at least, not sufficiently so to attract private enterprise; the Government must undertake the entire construction and management of these lines, as it always does of several much smaller public works.

3rd. And if (a fact which few, I think, can now doubt) these railways cannot be made to pay their whole expenses, including interest on first cost, by means of tolls, their expenses must be defrayed by a general taxation on all members of the colony, in consideration of the *indirect benefit* which all will receive from them, in the cheapening of food, the increase of business, &c.

I shall examine these two questions, supposing, of course, that the above statement is correct, from three different points of view.

1st. Pecuniary return to the revenue.
2nd. Immediate *indirect* action on the prosperity of the country.
3rd. Prospective indirect action from increased immigration, &c.

It is evident, however, that the third depends more or less upon the second, since immigrants or capital can only be attracted, or the increase of population and the development of the country stimulated, by immediate benefit offered in one way or another.

Now we find that the sale of lands contributes a consideration sum, say £200,000 per annum, to the general revenue of this colony, a direct advantage easily appreciated. A certain proportion of this, impossible to be estimated, would be received every year from the sale of lands, even if no minimum price were imposed beyond the *natural price* or exchangeable value of the fertility of the lands in the market of the colony.

The establishment of an uniform upset price upon all Government lands is of the nature of a monopoly, and has the effect of artificially raising the value of all lands by its precise amount; for this price must be paid for the very worst lands that are to be occupied, and the natural advantages of the most fertile, or otherwise valuable lands, will therefore be competed for at auction till an addition is made to the upset price, about equal no doubt to the above-mentioned natural market price. I therefore regard any sum of money raised by the operation of the minimum price as of the nature of a tax upon the act of occupying land (equivalent to a tax of one shilling per annum per acre for ever), but raised in a manner the most injurious conceivable, viz., by demanding a large sum in cash from the farmer or other person requiring land at the moment when he requires all his capital to commence cultivation or other improvements effectively.

Nor will the effects of the tax fall merely on the purchasers of the land; their capital being diminished, and the cultivation or employment of lands altogether retarded, the wages of labour will not rise as high as they otherwise would. Other profits also will be correspondently diminished, and all this for the sake of a portion of the revenue which it is one of the chief duties of the Government to raise in a manner as equitable and as little injurious as possible from all classes of the community.

The immediate indirect effect of the minimum price is therefore injurious, and as no one will, I think, be found to maintain that a price of land artificially raised here by law can have any prospective effect but that of discouraging immigration and the general increase of the colony, the present Land Regulations can only be recommended from the first point of view, viz., on account of the revenue raised.

The waste but fertile lands of a colony are an inexhaustible store of wealth; but this is to be obtained only by the application of labour, and to lay a tax on the act of occupation and cultivation instead of on the large and continually increasing stream of profits following the act of occupation, is surely a mistake too egregious to be misapprehended by any, when separated out from the other considerations usually mixed up with it. The distribution of the public lands is no loss to the colony, is no deduction from its store of wealth. It is on the contrary the very means of its enrichment and gain.

I turn now to the question of Railway Extension.

No one can possibly suppose that if railways be made through all parts of the colony at a cost of three to five millions of pounds sterling, as proposed, the present population can make them pay, or that the real cost of the conveyance of their produce will be in the least reduced below what it is under the present team and dray, and mail-cart system. We must look then to the general increase and improvement of the country from the immediate indirect benefits, or from an increased number of immigrants, attracted hither by the advantages of railway communication, to make us any return on such a vast outlay, or even to enable us to discharge the debt conveniently.

But if a railway, making no pecuniary return, do not give some tangible indirect benefits, I do not see what there is, except the mere name of "railway communication," to attract immigrants and cause the development of the country. Yet it happens, as may, I believe, be satisfactorily shown, and as was argued some time ago by Professor Pell of the Sydney University, that in the case of railways, the *indirect benefits* are an illegitimate consideration, and that in undertaking vast works, which admit of and in other countries invariably yield a monetary return as a condition of their construction, the principle of *indirect benefits* will lead to delusive and dangerous results. The argument in as brief and simple terms as I can put it, is the following:- That if any considerable amount of indirect benefits be conferred in any manner, that a corresponding amount of traffic must have run on the line. A railway is made to be used and by use only is beneficial, and it is evident that if no traffic or an inconsiderable amount run on the line, it is as if the latter never existed.

Furthermore, in the payment of tolls, undoubtedly the only equitable method of taxation for the support of the railway, a fair and voluntary exchange is made of a certain sum of money for the conveyance of certain articles or persons, and if the advantages of their conveyance, whether to persons actually travelling or conveying articles, or to any other persons whatever throughout the world, exceed the sum paid for tolls, the production and conveyance of articles, as well as personal travelling, will be stimulated, and increased returns will be received from the same or higher tolls. This *stimulation*, or if the advantages derived fall below the price remanded, the *retardation* will, I believe, take place with mathematical exactness, as in the theory of other commercial operations, a fair time only being allowed for things to reach the point of equilibrium, and then I conceive that the monetary returns of a railway, with properly adjusted tolls, will exactly *measure* or represent the benefits of whatever kind conferred.

For instance a railway paying $2\frac{1}{2}$ per cent. dividends confers an equivalent value of indirect benefits, but if the colony pays 5 per cent. for the money borrowed and spent in its construction, I maintain that the difference of $2\frac{1}{2}$ per cent. is a total loss to the community, at least if continued beyond the first two or three years.

My conclusion is that in constructing railways we should look entirely (or at all events almost entirely), to a direct pecuniary return, not so much as a profit, but as a proof that the investment is remunerative in its indirect effects, and through these on the future development of the country by immigration, &c.

The Government, I believe, avowedly looks to indirect benefits, and indeed I do not see how any one, with the means of judging we now have, can propose an outlay of £3,000,000 in this colony with any hope of a return in the shape of interest. I cannot then avoid the conclusion that the present policy of railway extension is radically and entirely incorrect, and not calculated to advance the colony in any way but to involve it in large profitless expenditure, from which will surely spring an unproductive national debt.

The present land regulations we have already shown are incorrect in theory because they raise a revenue at the expense of those interests which it is important chiefly to promote. We now discover our policy to be not only incorrect in each case but inconsistent and contrary when the two are compared together. We indeed pursue at present a most clumsy and absurd method of promoting the prosperity of the colony, ignoring the indirect benefits of the distribution and occupation of lands when on these chiefly depends the welfare of all, and, on the other hand, going about to invest immense sums of money to obtain indirect benefits which are merely delusive, and do not exist but when money is employed *remuneratively* in the commercial sense of the term.

Such broad subjects cannot be further developed in a single letter, but I cannot close without briefly alluding to a few arguments upon which silence would probably be thought to be intentional.

The upset price of land is said to be useful in checking injurious speculation, and the monopoly of lands by rich capitalists; it certainly must effect this to some extent, but only in the same proportion that it checks all sales and transactions with land whatever, from the larger sums of money involved in them. All land being artificially raised in value by £1, the capitalist is still able to overbid the poor man, and obtain a monopoly of the best lands, upon which he will then demand, and sooner or later obtain, a profit proportional to the larger capital sunk. Besides, I do not know that speculation is so objectionable as is supposed; it is at all events to the advantage of the speculator to choose the best land, sub-divide it conveniently, make the best approaches and other improvements, and dispose of it again as soon as possible, and this will probably be done with an amount of dispatch and success unknown to any governmental action throughout the world. To suppose that any rich man would buy up hundreds of square miles of land, and hold them without any attempt to make a profit, is a mere chimera, and a stupid, ignorant one. The richer the man the more careful he usually is that every pound shall be usefully invested, and capital even when employed in land speculation will be advantageous rather than the opposite to the whole community. Freedom for all commercial transactions is the spirit of improved legislation, and I see no reason why it should not be applied to lands.

The Government regulations are also said to tend to concentrate population. Against this, I hold that each man is the best judge, whether he will gain most in his own case by settling near a road or a town, or far off; and as the interests of a number of individuals make up the public interest, any interference of Government will be again injurious.

To accomplish any change of the Land regulations with a due regard to vested interests – that is, to those who have bought land on the faith of the upset price of £1 being always maintained – is, of course, the great difficulty; but one that is well worth while to attempt to overcome.

The results of this letter are of a very negative character, only detecting faults in the schemes of other persons. The great length to which it has already extended, prevents me from entering at all into the *affirmative* side of the question which may, however, form the subject of some future letter.

Hoping that the above may not be altogether uninteresting or useless,
    I am, Sir, your obedient servant,
            O.

Sydney, April 7th, 1857.

104. W. S. JEVONS TO LUCY JEVONS
[LJN, 87–8]

Double Bay, Sydney,
16th June 1857.

... Another month is past and gone, and I find myself quietly settling down in my little study about 10 P.M. after spending rather a lazy evening, to employ the remaining couple of hours in a delightful duty. Life is chequered here as elsewhere. One is sometimes cheerful and pleased and contented with everything round you; sometimes a little dull and lonely; sometimes confident and hopeful of oneself; at other times less confident, if not disgusted and desponding. At present I must say there is nothing at all to disappoint or make me unhappy in the least, yet my hopes are so high that I cannot help feeling that they must be in the end disappointed. But in whatever mood I may be, there is one thing sure to please and make me happy, and that is my sisters' letters.

... I am thought here as well as at home remarkable, if not foolish, for avoiding people's company, or at all events extending my friendship to a very limited circle. Do not believe that I have really one whit the less love in me, though it may seem rather thickly covered up. To prove this to you I will tell you that I have lately arrived at the opinion that there is no foundation for any religion but in the feelings of the human heart. For some six or seven years past I have been chiefly engaged in learning science and taking the very evident views of things, and the consequence has been to show me *greatness* and wonderful *order or design* in nature, but no *feeling* or actual *good*; on the contrary, we find *evil* or *pain* prevailing everywhere almost equally with pleasure. It is in the human mind (made as we know after the image of God), but particularly in the feelings of love and friendship that I can find any indications of positive *good*. *Evil* is inseparable from *nature*, and no writer has ever explained satisfactorily why evil should exist at all. I can no more understand why it is to be found in material nature; but I discover in man certain properties and feelings which enable him in thought to triumph over evil, and form a conception or rather an expectation of a state free from it, and approaching, therefore, to perfection. How different are my opinions from those of many who call themselves Christian, yet are always talking of the original sin of man or their essentially sinful nature. I admit their weakness and the unhappiness thereby caused, yet place my faith in the fact I find to afford the possibility of perfection or superiority to evil, *i.e.* the sympathetic nature of the mind. It is perhaps well, at all events no harm, to talk thus seriously to those we can so well trust and love as a sister; but this is no reason why I should make a letter into a sermon or religious discussion, therefore to lighter and more cheerful subjects!...

105. W. S. JEVONS TO HENRIETTA JEVONS
[LJP, 88–9]

Double Bay near Sydney N.S.W.
June 17th 1857.

My dearest little Henny,

If little yet you be, I cannot let a mail go without a word for you in answer to your own interesting letter. I have to thank you two[1] for the present of a pin-cushion, which though a trifle, I find an indispensable trifle and I was reduced to carry a most shabby one in my waistcoat pocket. I am in great straights for a small *pen-wiper*; a very small one, per post, of the newest & most improved construction would be most acceptable.

I must thank you as well as Lucy for the box which is sent but not yet received; it is a pleasure which I am particularly looking forward to enjoying. I am glad, too, to think that you will have received the parcel per "Great Britain" before this letter, and that you will find therein, one or two pieces to appease your intense musical appetite for a few days, because I suppose you are so accomplished that you will play them right off two or three times and then want some more. The "Chant du Soir" to tell you the truth is what I bought but could make nothing of. "O te, O Cara," was for a long time my favorite* piece, though I could never get over some of the elevated, rocky, regions about the middle of it without great difficulty. I now send the piece to its proper destination, *a te, O Cara*, but still have a copy of it in a simple form in my opera book of "Il* Puritani".[2] Mendelsohns* songs are simple & nice particularly the *first & last one*. "My diligence in the Music line" which you speak of has been by no means exemplary of late. I merely take an occasional whiff of it every day just as a man takes his cigar of an evening to fill up a few moments and to soothe or divert him. It would require the most intimate acquaintance with the Doctrine of Chances to calculate, which of 500 psalm tunes, 500 opera airs, 500 Oratorio airs or choruses & 500 dances & miscellaneous pieces etc. (take numbers less exaggerated if you like) I shall be likely to play on any given occasion, but it would require very little knowledge to determine that the chance of my knowing any one of them perfect is

---

[1] Presumably Lucy as well as Henrietta.   [2] Bellini, *I Puritani di Scozia* (1835).

Nil. When I return, a time that I am by no means disinclined to look forward to, you will no doubt be able to accompany me with your voice, but the converse proposition will require demonstration to establish its truth.

So say you have looked in the Proceedings of the Phil. Soc. of Sydney for my name, & found it not, tacitly assuming therefore that it should be there. For myself I do not see the necessity, but to relieve your disappointment have appended my name, in all its native ugliness, to a monthly report in the Proceedings of the Societies, where it will appear not once but twelve times every year. If this is insufficient, pray inform me³

How did you like Mozarts Requiem. I have never heard it performed but in particular moods admire it above everything. It is melancholy, grand, & singular. I have given up the theatres etc, etc, for the last few months as the Opera Co^y did not succeed and there is nothing worth hearing.⁴

Your description of the comfort of your home is cheering. Most of the furniture, paintings, books, etc I know of course as well as yourself; the house itself I have been in and the whole neighbourhood, views etc I can never forget, and by combining them all, I can form a pretty good picture of my English home. I often think of the old Park Hill Road house⁵ in all its diminished dignity; have you ever been in it again? By the bye* there was a small shilling novel I read a short time since, the "Batcher* of the Albany",⁶ which is chiefly concerned with the very respectable & comfortable family of the *"Spreads"* in Abercrombey square, (Liverpool). It pleased me immensely, not only because it is excellently & very amusingly written but because it seemed to [be]⁷

---

³ Cf. *Journal and Proceedings of the Royal Society of New South Wales* (1881). A pamphlet containing a list of office-bearers and members of the Sydney Philosophical Society in 1857, including Jevons's name, together with a list of papers read before the Society in 1856 and 1857, is amongst the Jevons Papers.

⁴ See above, Letter 101, p. 278. Jevons mentions two visits to the opera in his diary: on 27 April 1857 he saw '... Lucia di Lammermoor, and an act of Ernani. Many parts of the former were very fine & musical, especially the last scene, and there was much good singing.' On 2 May he records having seen 'Don Pasquale and a scene of Lucia di Lammermoor'. His opinion of musical life in Sydney is borne out by his diary entry for 15 June 1857: 'In evening to S. of A. [School of Arts] to a most wretched performance of Handel's Judas ...'

⁵ The Jevons family had lived at Park Hill Road, Toxteth Park, Liverpool, from 1835 until the bankruptcy of 1848 forced Thomas Jevons to sell this house and move to a smaller one at Chatham Street. See Vol. I, p. 12.

⁶ Marmion Savage, *The Bachelor of the Albany* (1848). In his diary entry for 16 May 1857 Jevons commented about this book: '*The Bachelor of the Albany* is a man who tries to keep clear of all social responsibilities and duties and the *morale* of the tale enforces the fact that this is impossible practically speaking, with a social being such as man. It is indeed my habit more or less to keep myself clear from society and its requirements, and I am therefore somewhat interested in the book....'

⁷ Omitted in the original manuscript.

not at all a bad picture of our own way of life, or rather as we should have lived if money had been as plentiful as with the "Spreads." Get it and read it, if you have not done so already.

You wish me to lecture & direct you what to read and learn. I wish I were with you so that I could do it, and assist you over the difficulties of mathematics. The application of Algebra to Geometry is I can remember, very disagreable* & difficult to understand. For my own part I have never had the courage to open the many mathematical books I have with me, but what do you think I would do if I had opportunity over again, attend College & De Morgans Mathematical lectures. The utility of Mathematics is[8] one of the most incomprehensible things about it, but though I was never bright or successful in his class, in spite of working hard, I feel the greatest benefit from it. Mathematics are like the *Calisthenic* exercises of the mind*, & make it vigourous* and correct in form and action, but it depends of course on other circumstances how you apply & use your mind as well as your body. To go figuring about with your arms or legs is not the object of Calisthenics.* I think therefore you cannot waste time or trouble spent over mathematics; the more the better for the present at all events. You speak of a New Ladies College in Liverpool[9] which must be a great advantage; tell me about it.

You speak of reading Macauley's* History.[10] History must no doubt be an excellent & useful subject but my only feelings as to it are those of despair; for I never can remember a thing, & therefore am not a fit adviser for you. I am sending you a little "Handbook of Natural Phenomena".[11] What there is of it is very good, though not always perfectly correct. I do not mean you to enter on the study of Meteorology, for it is a most troublesome, extensive, & to most an uninteresting subject. I have however involved myself in it to an awful extent and must go on with it I suppose while I am here. It is a most complicated

---

[8] Jevons wrote 'of' here.
[9] A Ladies' College was established in April 1856 by the Directors of the Mechanics' Institution, Liverpool. A school for girls had been founded earlier by the Directors and opened in 1844 in Blackburne House, Liverpool. It appears that the Ladies' College occupied rooms in the girls' school until 1858, when expansion of the school made it necessary to transfer all the adult classes except those for music to the newly established Queen's College, which was housed in the boys' school building (see Vol. I, p. 198, n. 2). The opening of the Ladies' College was greeted with enthusiasm; in the first session there were fifteen classes with 165 students. Numbers declined however and in the following year there is mention of only three or four classes. The College continued until 1867, after which date its classes ceased to be advertised in the Directors' Prospectus. Cf. Tiffen, op. cit., pp. 103–5.
[10] Thomas Babington Macaulay (1st Baron Macaulay), *History of England*, 5 vols (1849–61).
[11] Jevons is probably referring to *Natural Phenomena* (1850), a pocket-sized volume published by the Society for the Promotion of Christian Knowledge; it contains thirty short chapters, with illustrations, on such subjects as rainbows, aurora borealis, coral reefs, glaciers, volcanoes, etc.

subject requiring a knowledge more or less of heat light chemistry electricity etc, etc, and is therefore a sort of difficult *scientific exercise*, rather than a science itself.

But the subject I have been most of all concerned in for the last six months is Political Economy. You will not know what it means or is unless you have read about it, but to those who interest themselves in it, *it*, on the other hand, is *deeply* interesting. Among other books upon it, I have read a small one by Harriet Martineau[12] and it occurred to me why you might not be as good as H Martineau any day. Among the old books you will find Dr Smiths "Wealth of Nations" which is the best work though rather old. You send me some notes of a lecture by Mr Channing on "Labour"[13] which is not a little interesting to me & closely connected with my subjects. He takes his view from a very different point from mine, and by no means a practical one. He objects to persons working for pay or wages. Does he expect that, practically speaking, people will ever work without wages? He appears to object, too, to luxuries & refinements, and blames the rich for the poverty of others, in which I only partially agree. The lecture is however very clearly & nicely reported on your part. "Time is short" and this necessarily shortens my letter.

I am
Ever Your affec. brother
W S Jevons.

106. UNDATED FRAGMENT OF A LETTER FROM W. S. JEVONS TO T. E. JEVONS
[LJP, 89–90]

[July 1857]

... must plainly tell you it is not an unmixed good. You should consider a contented and cheerful enjoyment of present social and other pleasures as a luxury not to be much indulged in. It is often said that contentment is the chief essential to a happy life; I dare say this may be true in some respects but I am very sure that it is far from being a correct maxim of life. A cat sitting and purring by the fireside seems to me a representation of this kind of happy life, but with this exception

---

[12] Harriet Martineau (1802–76), elder sister of James Martineau; journalist, traveller, prolific writer of works on religion, economics, politics and social questions. The work to which Jevons refers was probably part of her *Illustrations of Political Economy*, 9 vols (1834), a series of illustrative stories, first published in monthly numbers.

[13] Possibly William Ellery Channing, *Lectures on the elevation of the labouring portion of the Community* (Boston, 1840).

that the cat can really manage to be quite contented, while if a man tries to be the same he will always encounter a succession of petty little things always enough to disturb his contentment. A man therefore should not aim at this kind of contentment at all; he should always look to something in the future and the higher he looks the better provided it be not so high, that the impossibility of his attaining the point disgusts him. It is true the life of such a one must be made up in some sort of discontent; the few things already done, or the short distance already passed over appears disgusting, the present rate of travelling does not seem to promise anything more satisfactory and when any position is at last attained it turns out to be only like a mountain top from which a higher mountain is each time visible. Such a life of disappointment may seem hardly a very desirable one, but I have a lurking suspicion that the sum total of a persons enjoyment is generally equal to what we should call in mathematics a "constant quantity". The small discontents of the one probably balance from their great number, the one large continuous discontent of the other.

This is, I am afraid, a gloomy view of life, but I recommend it to your attention. You will also perhaps think it advice given in such very general terms as to be nearly incomprehensible & incapable of reduction to practise. But you know it is so long since I saw you and at your age[1] changes are proportionally so rapid, that I am quite at a loss to know how to give you any particular advice. This I must leave to Lucy and Herbert; Henny acknowledges herself in need of advice which is certainly the next best thing to not needing it at all. Your school time is not yet terminated and you ought to feel it a privilege to remain longer, which is not to be lightly thrown away. Afterwards you will have to enter some sort of employment and all that I can say is – do not be contented with that employment alone. Be discontented with it, but at the same time consider that to stick to it well for a time or even for ever may be really the way to help you to something better in the same or another line.

It may seem rather curious, & liable to misconstruction, what I am going to say, but I think it will harm neither you nor myself. It is with respect to the quality *cleverness* which is generally thought so much of. At school & college I used to think I was rather deficient in it; though I got a fair show of prizes &c, it was at the expense of a vast deal of trouble, and other people seemed to do as much, or more than I, with half the trouble. Now however I begin to think I am rather more clever than I expected, yet I can never think but that other people could do just as much as I do if they only took the trouble. Be convinced on your part that if you only take the trouble to try you will find yourself

[1] 'ages' in the original manuscript.

as clever as almost any people you may meet; but mind you whatever cleverness you have will be a very useless or even injurious article unless it is well worn and at the same time worn in the right use. It is also very essential that you should keep it continually in use. If you only work hard now and then, you will never work well, and will have reason to be discontented. Talents are things which become rusty by being laid up, so that when you have need of them again you are disgusted to find them not ready to your hand, and are very likely inclined to put them by again for a little longer . . .

107. W. S. JEVONS TO HENRIETTA JEVONS

Double Bay near Sydney N.S.W.
July 16th 1857.

My dearest Henny,

I have put off commencing my monthly correspondence till the last night and am afraid I shall send but a poor answer to your last letter,[1] which was interesting and cheering though dated from such a singular place as a church yard with a tombstone for your desk. I fear my memory is scarcely retentive enough to enable me to follow you in all your wanderings and visits to near relations, but I am glad to think how Lucy must have enjoyed the pleasure, now no longer open to her, of entering a new tract of country, previously unsketched and unexplored by her, viz the S W of England.

I must, first of all, thank you for the box of things which was safely received a week or two ago. I could not exaggerate the pleasure which such presents give me, and not only is it prolonged as I gradually dispose the things about me and bring them into use, but ever afterwards I am reminded of everything that can give me the greatest pleasure each time that I look round my walls, or open a drawer, or play a tune. Lucy's pictures were as acceptable as ever, more acceptable I could not say. The Thames at Ham has been much admired and is now in a frame over my Harmonium. The *Dee* and its sands is also a pretty picture but of course more interesting to myself than others, since it reminds me of days long ago when I used to play about the sand banks & wade across the pools and fancy myself getting into dangerous quick-sands. Uncle Dicks[2] photograph is most excellent and you no doubt anticipated the value I should set upon it. Yet it is almost too well done and I cannot help thinking there are traces in it of the few years that have passed since I saw him. It is hung in a gorgeous golden frame, which is almost too large & heavy. It is only last night that I completed the

---

[1] This letter is not among the Jevons Papers.   [2] Dr Richard Roscoe.

arrangement of my pictures, quite to my satisfaction, and in the accompanying plan of my walls.

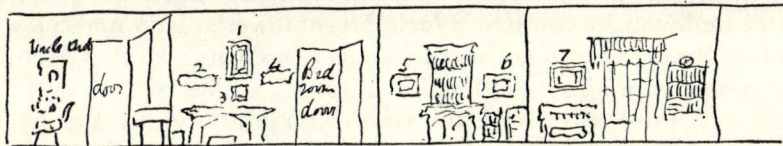

1. Sketch of rocks & bush
2. River Dee
3. Photograph of Pisa
4. Sketch from Bryn Rhedyn.
5. Rocks & shore scene.
6. Hilbre Island.
7. Thames at Ham.

I really have not space to say all I would about the other things, books, slippers, metronome which I presume is your own peculiar present, dried plants, chimney ornaments, assay stamp, &c &c. Lucy can be only pleased when she hears that Charles Bolton got all the jam & damson cheese for Mrs B.'s cough, and she is truly in want of anything that will do her good.[3] The plum pudding I also consigned to him with the understanding that I should go to dinner with him when it was cooked, next Saturday being appointed for the occasion. The cheeses which Herbert sent were in perfect condition. One I gave to Mrs Miller, half to C B. and the remaining half has been pronounced excellent both by myself and those of the Mint officers who happened to drop in while I was at lunch. I am still in expectation of Lucys larger pictures for which I must find room some where. Dr John Taulers book[4] is certainly very pious but I have not quite read it through as yet. Its very Mediaeval appearance has excited unpleasant misgivings in the minds of Mr & Mrs Miller, who evidently consider Lucy, if not yourself also, is, like Elizabeth Spread (in the Bacher* of the Albany), on the high road to Rome.

Your last letter was not less interesting because it contained much about Music and your difficulties in it. I am not much surprized at your not liking the Requiem first time, for its beauties are as you express it, *hidden*. I have played most of it through as well as I can, the last day

---

[3] Charles Bolton's wife died just over a month later, of tuberculosis (Jevons's diary entry for 24 August 1857).

[4] Johann Tauler (c. 1300–1361). *The history and life of the Rev. Doctor John Tauler of Strasbourg; with twenty-five of his sermons (temp. 1340)*. Translated from the German, with additional notices of Tauler's life and times, by Susanna Winkworth . . . and a preface by the Rev. Charles Kingsley (1857).

or two, and still think it though difficult, out of the way, and perhaps unpleasing in some moods, yet the most grand, expressive but melancholy music I know. I dare say you will soon have a similar opinion. It used to be favourite music of Uncle Hornblower's. I do not know the Hymn of Praise, but do not on the whole agree with you that Mendelssohns music contains "hidden beauties",[5] at least not so much as Mozarts. I think Mendelssohn strikes you at once. By the bye* I never knew what good music was till a short time ago when I began practising Beethoven's Fidelio, which I had had some time without being able to play or understand. It contains the most exquisite music and some parts are positively magical. A *mass* by him is also very beautiful.[6]

Your letter as you say is full of complaints about your own want or loss of opportunities of getting forward in music or other things. Your complaints cannot displease me half as much as your confidence pleases me, and believe me that the pure love of a thing or pursuit which leads to real application and interest in it, together with a little system of setting to work and a few opportunities of instruction &c, are all that is necessary for success. All these I am sure you have and though from "girls having no fixed occupation when they leave school", and from your *coming out* into Society &c &c, you are no doubt unsettled & disheartened, I have no doubt you will soon get into regular train again and do no one knows what.

You speak very sensibly about religious opinions, and I quite agree with you that "men cannot be too liberal in their opinions of one anothers religion". Creeds, dogmas, all opinions in short, I have for the present at least, thrown clean over board, and I have therefore attained a point from which I can regard those who still hold them with perfect impartiality. I judge of a religion by the abstract morality it contains, and by its effects on the character, condition & happiness of men. If I find a Catholic more sincere, trustful and moral, and therefore in general more happy (not that it is so) than a Churchman, I prefer the former, for in my eyes their particular opinions are equally absurd, and do not admit of any comparison or preference. I must confess myself however, still afloat and on the lookout for an anchoring ground of which when obtained I will send you the bearings.

To give you a short account of my own affairs during the last month, I must say I am generally busy but from the dawdling habits produced

---

[5] Mendelssohn's symphony-cantata *Lobgesang* (Hymn of Praise) was dedicated to Frederick Augustus, King of Saxony, and first performed at the June festival in Leipzig in 1840, held to commemorate the invention of printing. The first performance in England took place in Birmingham the following September.

[6] Beethoven's Mass in D Major, op. 23 (*Missa Solemnis*), first performed in Vienna in May 1824.

by having much time on my hands, do not effect so much as I have time for. After much trouble I have made up a table of my two years observations which appears in this months magazine⁷ (I send two numbers, one for H E Roscoe). Having been asked by both Dr Smith & Capt W, I made up a paper on the sunguage* being the paper which I sent to H E R, improved & extended. Dr Smith read it but I was there, and as no one attempted any discussion on it, I got through the evening with the greatest equanimity.⁸ I send you the account of the proceedings that you may at last look through it and not miss my name. I exhibited some grand diagrams. I felt a little flattered today when Mr Parkes sent me up proof slips of my paper and of an article on Public Lands,⁹ to be corrected, saying that he was *perhaps* going to reprint them for the Mail number for England. The Public lands of N.S.W. may not much interest you at home, but are as you may imagine of great importance to the colony. You will see at all events in what an independent manner I settle the Affairs of the nation. I am at present engaged in a more lengthy affair which will perhaps soon appear but which this letter tonight is seriously interrupting.¹⁰ I performed an unwonted feat last

⁷ In June 1857 Jevons had published his first monthly Meteorological Report for James Waugh's *Sydney Magazine of Science and Art*. 'These contained elaborate data for every day of the month. Continued until June, 1858. There were two yearly summaries, in the numbers for July 1857, and July 1858.' (La Nauze, op. cit., p. 41).

⁸ Jevons wrote in his diary entry for 29 January 1857: 'Working at my new Actinometer or sun guage* which is an instrument on the principle of the cryophon to measure the heat received on any surface by the amount of water evaporated & condensed(?) in a separate tube.' His paper 'On a new Sun-gauge' was read before the Sydney Philosophical Society on 8 July 1857 (*Journal and Proceedings of the Royal Society of New South Wales* (1881) xv 7). It was published under the title 'On a sun-gauge, or new Actinometer', *Sydney Magazine of Science and Art* (August 1857) 58–62. La Nauze comments: '... Diagrams and tables. Elaborate descriptions of the new instrument, and account of the theory of sun-gauges. Previously printed, without diagrams, in *Empire*, 14 July 1857' (op. cit., p. 41). Jevons had earlier sent a short paper on this subject to H. E. Roscoe: in an unpublished letter of 15 May 1857, he wrote to him: '... You offered in one of your letters, to get any results of my work here, that were worth it, published in the proper manner in London, and as I think the idea of a Sun guage* is original as well as practicable I send you the enclosed short paper upon it for the above purpose. I am pretty conscious that the paper is neither very lucid or concise, that the instrument is rough and inaccurate and that I have not enough entered into the subject to show how it is to be improved. With respect to the two last things, my excuse is the difficulty of carrying on any experiments with all the disadvantages of isolation, and the inconveniences of a colony, but especially the want of a working instrument maker, to blow the glass and make the vacuums. But I hope that the evident theoretical simplicity and accuracy of the principle of this sun guage* in measuring & recording radiant heat will make the paper worth publishing, in your opinion, in spite of its defects.' The paper was published in the *London ... Philosophical Magazine* xiv (November 1857) 351–6. Jevons wrote in his diary on 28 January 1858: 'At the Library was gratified to find my paper on Sun guage* duly published by H.E.R. in the Philosophical Magazine with a note from the Editor concerning Pouillet's researches.'

⁹ 'The Public Lands of New South Wales', *Empire* (24 June 1857). The article was reprinted in the Summary for England on 17 July 1857. See Vol. IV, Part II. Cf. La Nauze, op. cit., pp. 40–41.

¹⁰ This is presumably a reference to his analysis of towns, on which he had begun work the previous year and which formed the basis of his spare-time survey of Sydney. He undertook

monday* in spending the day *over the water* taking a bush walk with the old Revd Mr Clarke,¹¹ the geologist, afterwards dining with him, & Mrs Clarke, and two Miss Clarkes. The latter, let me tell you, were girls of rather more than your own age and of most favourable & reasonable appearance. But besides that I am far from being orthodox as you may well believe, I may say I intend never to fall in love or marry anybody till she will bear comparison with my sisters (as I remember my father saying of my mother) and you may rest perfectly satisfied of my remaining single as long as I am in N.S.W. Nevertheless I heard the younger Miss C. playing the March in Norma and Suoni la tromba in Il* Puritani in a manner and with a choice implying a fair liking of music.

Mint. July 17th Tell Herbert that I am obliged to him for the account of money affairs and am perfectly satisfied that he should arrange my money just as he thinks proper. All I wanted was just a rough guess as to what I might count upon. I shall probably write to him next month, hoping however that he will in the mean time have found some way "to bring himself to write" more lengthy letters to Sydney.

I am posting you plenty of papers which contain all the little news which keeps us alive here. It is worth your while to read the accounts of the floods in the Hunter River¹² district which in such a quiet well conducted climate as England may appear very extraordinary. You will see from my monthly report that about 4 inches of rain fell, the most of it in 12 hours. Mr Clarke thinks it was a Cyclone storm or hurricane, which it certainly resembles in many points; at any rate it is the worst storm I have seen here as yet.

---

this in 1858 and apparently intended to publish it in instalments. The results of this survey are contained in a manuscript which is in the possession of the Mitchell Library, Sydney, and which has been given the title *Social Survey of Australian Cities*, 1858 (M.S. no. B864). Jevons published only one article on the basis of this survey, 'The Social Cesspools of Sydney. No. 1. The Rocks', *Sydney Morning Herald* (7 October 1858). The greater part of the manuscript was published in November and December 1929 in the *Sydney Morning Herald*. Cf. La Nauze, op. cit., pp. 33–7, 42–3. See Vol. I, pp. 28–9.

¹¹ William Branwhite Clarke (1798–1878), Anglican clergyman, who had studied geology under Sedgwick while at Cambridge; emigrated to New South Wales, 1839; rector of parishes in Sydney, 1840–71; kept meteorological records at his homes in Parramatta and North Shore, 1839–57; discovered gold in the Blue Mountains, 1841; carried out a geological survey of the colony, 1851–3; his claim to be the scientific discoverer of Australian gold was disputed but the New South Wales government granted him £3000 in 1861 for his part in the investigation of gold resources. His most important contribution to Australian geology was his work on the New South Wales coal deposits, for which the Geological Society of London awarded him the Murchison medal, 1877; F.R.S. 1876. Published numerous papers in Britain and Australia; also *Researches in the Southern Gold Fields of New South Wales* (1860); *Remarks on the Sedimentary Formations of New South Wales* (1867). In 1832 he married Maria Moreton Stather; they had a son and three daughters. See also Vol. I, p. 163, n. 1.

¹² For Jevons's account of a visit to the Hunter River District, see Vol. I, pp. 123–30.

Having taken up what time remained by writing a note to Ann Bolton I cannot add more for yourself. You or Lucy can I suppose take it

I think I wrote a long letter to Lucy last mail; she may depend on my repeating it by the next steamer.

With Love to Tommy also, whether he be in Liverpool or London
>Believe me
>>Ever your affec Brother
>>>W. S. Jevons.

108. W. S. JEVONS TO LUCY JEVONS
[LJN, 90–94]
Sunday Evening, 23d August 1857.

... It is not long since the last mail left with letters from me, and it is some weeks more before the mail will close. But a letter need not always contain the latest intelligence, and I know that anything I may feel inclined from time to time to write seriously to you will be read with more or less interest. I have always, indeed, much that I could say to you, and this evening more than ever; and though my reflections be upon a very painful subject, that is no reason, so far as I can see, that they should be untold. ... Not to alarm you about myself personally, I will tell you at once that an awful shipwreck occurred the other night within a few miles of this, which, besides exciting a great sensation all over Sydney, has more particularly affected the circle of the mint from sympathy with one of the members. I have often mentioned to you Mr. Hunt[1] of the mint. I have always been inclined strongly to like him ... As to age, he is a few months older than I am, but was appointed from the Government School of Mines in London, just the same as I was from the University College, London. Rather more than a year ago he received the news of his father's death in Paris, and his mother having been dead for some time, he had few relations left except two sisters of the ages of eighteen and twenty, who were then, I believe, in school at Bordeaux. After remaining there a short time it was arranged that they should come out to him here by the ship *Dunbar*, and in the shipping intelligence by the last mail their names were duly inserted in the list of passengers. In Sydney, Hunt had long expected them with pleasure. Very lately he had been busy choosing a small house on the North Shore, furnishing it, and even engaging servants, and was only waiting for the telegraph to announce the arrival of the ship. He was

[1] See above, Letter 97, n. 9, p. 262.

continually coming into my room, which commands a good view of the flagstaff, and when disappointed by the flags, always discovering that the ship was in reality not quite due yet. Last Thursday night a storm began, with heavy rain, black clouds, and very strong gales from the east. The next morning he was unusually watchful of the telegraph signals, but who has not known hundreds of people uneasy in such cases? Towards the middle of the day the rumour, however, crept rapidly through the mint that there was a large wreck somewhere outside the Heads. This was doubtless unpleasant intelligence, but no one saw any reason to believe it was the *Dunbar*, and the shipping list, when appealed to, contained a number of ships much more likely to arrive than the *Dunbar*.

That afternoon I was detained unusually late by assays, and had no time to go out to the South Head, where close beneath the lighthouse the wreck was said to have occurred. But at daybreak the next morning (yesterday) I got up and started with O'Connel for the Heads. After a five-mile walk through mud and rain we reached the lighthouse, and soon made our way to a low part of the cliffs, where a small number of persons, some from Sydney, by cabs and horses, the rest from the neighbourhood, were already collected. The place is called the *Gap*, being a partial break in the great line of cliffs opposite the part of the harbour called Watson's Bay, which, indeed, is produced by the same break. Here the cliffs fell to the height of less than 100 feet, and beneath there was a slight recess where a flat shelf of rocks, just a little above the sea level, ran out to a short distance. On looking down with the rest nothing was at first sight apparent but the huge waves of the Pacific Ocean, regularly rolling in, and each time entirely covering the lower rocks with a boiling sea of pure white foam, or now and then striking the projecting shelf, with a loud bursting noise, and throwing out a dense misty spray almost as high as the cliffs upon which we stood. But soon there was evidence of the wreck: small fragments of wood mingled with the sea-weed; portions of spars, or pieces of large timber, already quite rounded off by grinding on the rocks; bits of clothing, some apparently of silk, also long pieces of sheeting or bedding torn into shreds, and other clothing apparently tied up in bundles, were now and then seen. All these things were carried up on the top of one wave, lodged on the shelf of rock and exposed to view for a few moments till the succeeding wave enveloped them again in foam, and thus invisibly removed them. But as you will anticipate, there was now and then mingled with them objects of yet more fearful appearances. . . . But to leave descriptions perhaps of needless horror, we then walked along the cliff a few hundred yards to where the hull, or main part at least, of the vessel was yet supposed to lie, marked only by one or two fragments of spars yet attached by the rigging, or by loose rope ends now and then appearing at the surface. The ship appears to have run full on to the cliff almost below the lighthouse, some time during Thursday night, and to have gone to pieces and sunk almost immediately, unknown to any one on land, and possibly, we may hope, almost without the consciousness of any on board. The fragments of it had drifted with the wind and waves into the mouth of the harbour, and there gave the first indication of the wreck to a coasting steamer entering the following morning. A few articles such as I have described were retained in the Gap by an eddy, and would there be out of reach till the waves subsided. You will now comprehend the utter destruction of the ship and all on board, and the mystery which for a whole day surrounded its very name. The papers of the morning in question announced, however, that a mail bag marked No. 2 *Dunbar* had been found, with other evidence which left no doubt about it, and then followed the mournful list, in which the Misses Hunt of course appeared as passengers. The sensation in Sydney this day was really extraordinary, and arises partly from the fact that almost every person in the town has passed a voyage at sea, and entered the very Heads which this ship has been the first, as far as they know, to strike. . . . The excitement was curiously increased when a second edition of the papers announced the suspicion that one man, if not more, was yet alive in the crevices of the great cliffs, a thing which all thought so perfectly impossible that few, I expect, had ever troubled themselves to look carefully. An hour or two later a further edition announced that by ropes the man had been hoisted 200 feet up the cliffs, such as I have before drawn and described to you, and was alive and well. More I cannot tell you till the account of this man is published to-morrow; but I have told enough for you to imagine the effect upon our feelings here. A slight anxiety was, once out of a hundred times, converted into a horrible certainty. Hunt's sisters must have perished in the most frightful of circumstances the night before. . . . It is impossible to conceive the full intensity of the disappointment and sorrow.

6th September. – Hunt stayed away from the mint until last Monday, having been busy in searching all the time for some relic or trace of his sisters. . . . When I just saw him on Monday his look struck me very painfully, and he seemed very much altered. You can easily conceive that I feel the more for him as I have two sisters, who, although I have brothers also and many other relations, are quite as much to me as his sisters could have been to him; and the thought has not suggested itself to me now for the first time, that there are less terrible and unfrequent events that can separate people for ever than the shipwreck just described. There is no reason to fail in enjoying life because it may be taken away, or to avoid friendships because they may be broken; on the contrary, in my creed love is the most tangible form of immortality, and we can scarcely imagine its being in any way affected by death. . .[2]

109. FRAGMENT OF A LETTER FROM W. S. JEVONS TO HENRIETTA JEVONS
[LJP, 94]

Sept 7th [1857]

Late last night, as I was sitting quietly writing, I heard two loud guns booming over the waters of the Harbour, and instantly thought with pleasure of the letters I was sure to receive this morning, by the mail then just arrived. Your letter,[1] my dear Henny, is indeed most pleasing, and in many parts contains the very words & thoughts that I might myself have written. "I made several attempts like you, to find a friend among my schoolfellows but I always found I became more a friend to them than they to me. I have long since left off expecting more than mere companionship from them, and for a long time past I have looked to you as my best friend and told you in letters all my plans and views in life." I can only add to the above the qualification, that having many habits or characteristics, which render me by no means an agreable* companion to those who are not real friends, (perhaps it may be my own fault that I do not take the trouble or spare the time to make myself agreable),* I am in general without either friends or companions. No doubt I appear to most people strangely unsociable and uncompromising, and even where I do invest persons with the rather imaginary attributes of friendship, I seldom seem to give the satisfaction that I am delighted myself to derive from them. But I have always two consolatory reflections left, — first, – neither agreableness* nor even friendship, (of ordinary composition) are real objects in life but merely means. In general they are the means of very trifling, present happiness, and those who seek for happiness of other kinds, or seek not for happiness at all (if any) are not necessarily obliged to adopt the means of sociableness, and although the latter might be of much advantage and in neglecting it they may commit an error of judgement of considerable magnitude, their fault at all events cannot be as great as if they had the means and used it not to any proper end. Agreableness* or sociability is often down right selfishness in a very specious and deceptive form.

[2] This letter was based on an account of the wreck contained in Jevons's diary entries for 21–23 August 1857.   [1] This letter is not among the Jevons Papers.

Secondly, I always congratulate myself that if my friends are very few in number, (considerably less than half-a-dozen) they are at all events choice and true. And as it is the natural effect of a woman's character to soften and subdue the sentiments of men, so it is Lucy and and you who chiefly command my whole feelings of friendship.

But to go to subjects on which I can write with less uneasiness, being less perhaps in the wrong, I must say that your letter is on many other points most pleasing. Your reading books "passively" is undoubtedly a fault in my estimation; the exercise of one's own thought is half the value of the reading, although it may doubtless be profitable to some people merely to learn and collect facts. Your illustration of the analogy of passive reading to receiving accounts from foreign lands which you cannot or will not yourself visit is very good. To take an extreme instance, a person might read twenty metaphysical books on the definition and nature of an *"idea"* and yet never take the trouble to enquire or observe in his own mind how an idea appears to be derived & formed, although his very employment in reading, is in receiving & comparing innumerable ideas. In travelling, handbooks or accounts of the country may be very valuable or even indispensable in gaining a correct knowledge of it, but the vivid idea which remains will always have been derived from the glimpse, however slight, of the real country, and will be long remembered when the books and their authors are entirely forgotten. So in reading, even when the books are on abstract or far-removed subjects, it is far more the glimpses which, as it were, the mind takes of the things presented in words by the author, than the actual ideas & thoughts which that author himself conceived, that are transferred to the readers mind, and profitably remembered there.

With respect to English composition, I can both understand your dread of such a formidable undertaking and at the same time offer you some encouragement. But a year or two ago, since my living here, I can remember both my wish and despair of ever being able to write easily. But now I have become such a confirmed scribbler that I am half ashamed & sorry for my new acquisition. During yesterday (Sunday) & parts of the two previous evenings, would you believe that I wrote two long Meteorological reports, one article on Meteorology for the Empire and [a][2] great part of another letter for the same on Railways,[3] besides doing a deal of very tedious & long meteorol^{al} work. As you observe, Parkes puts my letters often in large type, once reprinted an article, and has lately increased the type of all my reports, and an editor should be a good judge of what will take. But otherwise I should feel less

---

[2] Omitted in the original manuscript.
[3] Probably the article 'Railway Economy', published in the *Empire* (29 December 1857), signed 'An Exact Thinker'. See Vol. IV, Part II.

assured about the quality than the quantity of productions that flow from my old silver penholder, (which by-the-bye* is nearly worn out). My letters home increase progressively every monthly mail, and God help the readers of them if I stay much longer in Australia.

I have today received a note from Graham to say that my paper is published in the Phil. Mag.[4] He says that it "reads very well in print", and in former notes he called it "quite conclusive" and interesting. This is very moderate praise, but I am of opinion that in this life, where mistakes, failures, disappointing chances, or down right misfortunes seem chiefly to prevail, any success however moderate should be considered matter of congratulation, without cavilling at quantity or degree. I do not know whether you will have seen it.

Sept 9th. I have since received a large parcel of the paper on *Cirrous* *Cloud*, and will post some to you in case you should not otherwise receive any. Will you see that one is given to Willy Jevons if in Liverpool, also to anybody else who may have sufficient interest in me. *One to Uncle William Jevons.* I also post a paper to W.E.J.[5] Will you believe that I am this month posting so many things that I have had to make a list of them and to mark down the people they were intended for, to prevent mistakes. The little sketch of your bedroom was highly interesting to me and I can easily think it is comfortable and well arranged. It seems quite intellectually fitted out with desks book cases, collections of ferns, chess boards, and a telescope to view a comet that never came. Excuse me writing more now, and with very best love to Tommy believe me to be

Ever your affectionate Brother
W. S. Jevons.

110. H. E. ROSCOE TO W. S. JEVONS

25 Fulham Place
Paddington. London.
September 27.
1857.

My dear Stanley

What do you think of me as Professor! You must make your mind up to it for so it is – I am elected to be Franklands[1] successor at Owens' College Manchester, and in a fortnight must begin my lectures &

---

[4] This was his paper 'On the Cirrous Form of Cloud', *London . . . Philosophical Magazine* (July 1857), 22–35. His diary entry for 8 September 1857 reads: 'Received by post 24 copies of paper on Cirrous form of cloud which Graham says *reads well*'.

[5] William Edgar Jevons, referred to above as 'Willy', who may still have been at Marseilles. Cf. above, Letter 34, p. 61.   [1] See above, Letter 27, n. 9, p. 50.

laboratory instruction. It will be a great change living in Manchester & very hard work for the first two years – but it is a very good position & I have a capital laboratory – perhaps the best in England – & also a tolerable allowance of money & a good chance of making a good deal by consulting practice.[2]

The choice lay at last between myself & an old Manchester Chemist by name Dr Angus Smith,[3] a man very much respected there & a good man, although he has not done much scientific work. Russell[4] & Guthrie[5] & several others tried for it but were not consulted by the Trustees.

Scott[6] is no longer Principal – & Greenwood[7] has been appointed to that office. I know none of my colleagues[8] – but I daresay I shall get on well enough with them – though they may not like so young a man coming in amongst them! However here goes! We shall see how I succeed & I do not mean to spare pains – I have so much to do now, in preparing or rather considering the general arrangement of my course, & getting up an introductory lecture which I must give, & going on with my London duties that I cannot write more now – but will give you any spare hour I may get hold of when fairly into the work at Manchester.

I must thank you for your last welcome long letter – glad to hear you

[2] H. E. Roscoe held the Chair at Owens College until 1886. He resigned upon being elected Member of Parliament for the Southern Division of Manchester in the autumn of 1885.

[3] Robert Angus Smith (1817–84). Born and educated in Glasgow, he studied under Liebig at Giessen, where he obtained his doctorate in 1841; the following year became assistant to Lyon Playfair, Professor of Chemistry at Manchester Royal Institution; F.R.S. 1857; President of the Manchester Literary and Philosophical Society, 1864–6; inspector-general of alkali works for the United Kingdom under the Alkali Act, 1863; 1876–84 joint inspector under the Rivers Pollution Act, 1876; edited *The Life and Works of Thomas Graham* (Glasgow, 1884).

[4] See above, Letter 38, n. 16, p. 74.

[5] See above, Letter 38, n. 5, p. 72.

[6] Rev. Alexander John Scott (1805–66), Professor of English Language and Literature at University College, London, 1848–51; first Principal of Owens College, Manchester, 1851–7. After his resignation as Principal, he retained the Chairs of Comparative Grammar, English Language and Literature, and Logic and Mental and Moral Philosophy until his death. See Vol. I, p. 41.

[7] Joseph Gouge Greenwood (1821–94). Served as assistant Classics Master at University College School and for a time as substitute for Henry Malden; Principal of Owens College, Manchester, 1857–89; Professor of Greek, 1851–85, and of Latin, 1851–69. He was one of the authors of a pamphlet submitted to the Council of Owens College in 1875 advocating its transformation into an independent University, a transformation which his efforts had done much to make possible. H. E. Roscoe wrote of Greenwood's appointment: '. . . He was exactly the man for the post. A scholar and classic, he had wide sympathies, and even understood that if the college was to succeed it must be on modern lines . . .' (*Life and Experiences*, p. 104).

[8] In addition to Scott and Greenwood there were only three other professors at Owens College at this date – Archibald Sandeman (Mathematics and Natural Philosophy); W. C. Williamson (National History); and Richard Copley Christie (Jurisprudence and Law, History, and Political Economy). Cf. Thompson, op. cit., pp. 626–7.

are well – happy – & employed. Go on with all your scientific work. I liked your paper on clouds much. The other you sent was good – but the subject wanted more working at (Sun-measurer) – I sent it to Francis[9] for the Phil. Mag. You better work one thing out *well* than 50 badly or imperfectly.

Read Pouillets experiments on the Sun's heat – Poggendorfs Annalen Vol. 45 for 1838.[10] – Get "Müllers Lehrbuch der Kosmischen Physik" Vieweg Braunschwig* 1856.[11] & if you dont know it yet *Learn German*

Ever yours very affely

Henry. E. Roscoe

W. S. Jevons Esqr –

III. W. S. JEVONS TO HENRIETTA AND LUCY JEVONS
[LJP, 94–7]

Double Bay ^{nr} Sydney. N. SW
Nov. 17th 1857.[1]

My dearest Sisters

I have just received, this evening two letters, one from each of you, besides a very pleasing little one from Tommy.[2] I will not say that they are the most interesting or important letters I have ever had, or that I do not remember more interesting ones from you both, but there is something in them something in my own state of feelings, which has filled [me][3] with most serious and overwhelming thoughts. I have [a] second nature within me hidden to the world, yet directing all my behaviour towards the world. Towards you this second nature tends strongly to disclose itself, to throw off every covering of reserve or false modesty. My letters lately have all exhibited this tendency; I have always felt that a word, a single word would explain so much to you, and would relieve [me][4] of a great load of loneliness, which I have for a long time borne.

I cannot, I really believe, exaggerate to you the intensity of the

[9] William Francis, one of the five editors of the *London, Edinburgh and Dublin Philosophical Magazine and Journal of Science*; partner in the firm of Taylor and Francis, Red Lion Court, Fleet Street, E.C., printers and publishers to the University of London.

[10] H. Pouillet, 'Ueber die Sonnenwärme, das Strahlungs – und Absorptionsvermögen der atmosphärischen Luft, und die Temperatur des Weltraums', *Annalen der Physik und Chemie*, XLV (Leipzig, 1838) 25–57.

[11] J. Mueller, *Lehrbuch der Physik und Meteorologie*, 3 vols (Brunswick, 1856–8), III, *Lehrbuch der kosmischen physik*.

[1] The original manuscript of this letter is incomplete.

[2] These letters are not among the Jevons Papers.

[3] A small portion of the page was torn out on removal of the seal, leaving gaps in the wording denoted by square brackets.

[4] Omitted in the original manuscript.

feelings of my second nature. They are a reality, I rise up with them, before me, and go to bed with them still upon my mind and never take any ordinary enjoyment but as a relaxation from their pursuit. Indeed, I really believe that if I were about to die, which I always look upon as a possible contingency and a most probable contingency within the years to which I look forward I should not much care except that *myself* would die before ever it had appeared, unknown, unthought of, and without benefit, except to the peace of my own thoughts.

But now it occurs to me strongly, as it has before occurred partially, that there is no reason why I should be unknown to you. If I am over-confident, foolish or vain, it will not make me worse to confess it to you; the truth & sincerity of what I say will be tried in the saying, and in the perfect loneliness of my second nature, for it never knew a friend nor th[e] shadow of an acquaintance, I begin to consider it qu[ite] a privelege* to have two sisters, whom I dare to consider such friends.

But I must come to the point and tell you while I yet have courage, what are these inmost thoughts. I remember them as long ago as my first living in London, or even before. They have grown ever since, and every day become developed in more fulness* and distinctness. I consulted them when I came out here, although I was then greatly influenced by my fathers wishes, and I have consulted them in the determination that I have come to, to leave Sydney within a moderate time, to be numbered in months rather than years. My whole second nature consists of one wish, or one *intention, viz* to be a *powerful good* in the world. To be *good*, to live with good intentions towards others is open to all. To be unselfish as they term it; to be a pleasant companion, or an agreable* fellow in the ordinary range of society; to marry a wife & make her comfortable, & so on, are all different ways of being *good*. But they seem to me to be very circumscribed, & rather indulgent ways of doing it. To be *powerfully good*, that is to be good, not towards one or a dozen, or a hundred but towards a nation or the world, is what now absorbs me. But this assumes the possession of the *power*. To be as powerfully good as I could wish does not fall to the lot of one in a million; how slight indeed is the chance that my powers fall within the same narrow chance!

My thoughts on this point shall be equally open to you, for I see no harm in speaking of oneself sincerely to those who will likewise listen to it sincerely. I used not to consider myself clever, in fact I am almost sure I was not formerly above the average. As many boys as not could understand a thing as sharply as myself, but owing partly to my dislike of society, I have always given my attention so entirely to learning that I begin almost to hope that the result is appearing. You will easily understand that it is highly important for me to determine what my *mind* is, since it is the most important of the elements of the *power* I mean, and I really believe my conclusions are pretty impartial. I have scarcely a spark of imagination & no spark of wit. I have but a poor memory, and consequently can retain only a small portion of learning at any one time which great numbers of other persons possess. But I am not so much a store house of goods, as I am a machine for making those goods. Give me a few facts or materials, and I can write them up into a smoothly arranged & finished fabric of theory, or can turn them out in a shape which is something new. My mind is of the most regular structure and I have such a strong disposition to classify things as is sometimes almost painful. I also think that if in anything I have a chance of aquiring* the power, it is that I have some *originality*, and can strike out new things. This consists not so much in quickness of forming new thoughts or opinions but in seizing upon one or two of them and developing them into something symmetrical. It is like a kaleidoscope; just put a bent pin in, or any little bit of rubbish, and a perfectly new and symmetrical pattern will be produced.

I should not like, myself to estimate the comparative worth of different kinds of mind, but after forming the conclusions stated above, the following passage from one of Sir J. Herschels, Essays was not unpleasing. "As a conquering, contriving, adorning, and imaginative being, the vestiges left by man are innumerable and imperishable; but as a reflective and reasoning one, how few do we find which will bear examination and justify his *claim*!"[5] The field for reflection and reasoning then is not filled; there is yet an infinite extent of new country to explore and bring to use.

I know it is said that "knowledge is power" and I think the faculty of producing or discovering knowledge must be power of a higher degree, but I am quite aware that in the sense in which I desire power, other qualities may be desirable if not necessary. One of these is *personal power* the employment of manners language, persuasion to accomplish an end, and of these I am quite sure I possess *Nil*. I do not blame myself much for their absence; it is owing to a great extent to my animal constitution, but I acknowledge that I have done and am doing nothing to make the animal bend to the mental constitution. There is here doubtless a great deficiency.

[5] J. F. W. Herschel, *Essays from the Edinburgh and Quarterly Reviews: with addresses and other pieces* (1857) p. 145.

112. W. S. JEVONS TO LUCY JEVONS
[LJN, 97-9]

11th January 1858.

... To come to my own affairs, life here is very quiet, not one evening in the month do I spend anywhere but in my own little study, to which I am becoming really attached. Fancy a little French-windowed room close to the 'sad sea waves'. A square centre table, covered by a neat walnut-marked oilcloth, from which an inkstand with a sort of little dock full of pens, pencils, paper-knives (most of them mementos), a couple of large observation books, a pile of two or three books in process of reading, and a miscellaneous collection of papers in process of writing, are never absent. Close at my back and right side is a neat and well-made escritoire and side-table, whose five drawers are filled by collections of almost everything that I ever scribbled (one drawer being indeed a secret and almost sacred repository by means of a Hobbes'* lock),[1] while the top of the table is loaded by a travelling-desk, a large atlas, a portfolio of your drawings and other precious things, as well as other books, etc., of less immediate use; at one side of the room is a large glazed bookcase crammed with my more valuable books (the two lowest rows particularly please me), the surplus finding a place either on a home-made series of cedar shelves fixed to another part of the wall, or hiding in various drawers or cupboards; the large chiffonier cupboard below the bookcase is now partly appropriated to photographic apparatus, while the mahogany camera, fixed on its three-legged stand, serves to fill, in a very knowing way, an adjoining nook which was always before distressing to me. Barometers or other instruments are either suspended or recline in the other corners and nooks of the room. Now, too, it is quite a picture gallery, and indeed you need not come here to see the pictures, for they are all your own presents, or sent through you. There are two or three scenes near West Kirby, Wales, etc., two or three which look like the Thames, one beautifully painted scene with bush and trees which you say you copied in Italy, but which pleases me amazingly; and lastly, but most particularly of all, a photograph of Pisa, and a wonderful photograph of Uncle Dick. My room is completed by the harmonium and a small neat music-stand filled with music. I have lately added a superb and most convenient music-holder of my own design and manufacture. But you

---

[1] Alfred Charles Hobbs (1812-91), American lock expert and manufacturer, mechanical engineer; in 1851 travelled to the Great Exhibition where he attracted attention by picking some of the best Chubb's locks; he afterwards formed a partnership, Hobbs, Ashley & Co. of Cheapside, for the manufacture of locks; he returned to the United States in 1860.

must not think that, however much my life here is in most respects to my liking, I have any thoughts of prolonging my stay here beyond the shortest decent limits. I feel as if I could give up everything that I now enjoy, and enter in London, a life of labour, trouble and small gains, if it would be more likely in other ways to bring me nearer my desired end. I have explained to you before what I seek, and in seeking it one must not be too nice about ordinary common sense, prudence and so forth. I cannot stay here much longer, or my best years will be gone; I shall have suffered in mind from the want of other minds to communicate with, and in body I shall be unfitted to live again in a cold climate. I wish, too, to see a little of the world before I again settle in civilised old England, where there are no holidays; indeed, I contemplate travelling for at least a year in some quarter of the globe, and if I only stop a year longer at the mint I shall be about twenty-five years old before I can fairly start again in London. If I said, therefore, that I had determined to make this my last year at the mint I should not be far wrong. It is a serious step to take, I will allow, but none except yourself, or Henny and myself, can understand it or judge it; but whenever I am occupied in planning and projecting, one thing always occurs to me now, and that is the *Dunbar*.[2] It is perfectly right to lay out one's life before one, to invest a large capital in it, as it were, even with the hope of very distant and uncertain returns; this indeed is the only way of using life with true economy and effect. But always remember that you cannot effect an insurance upon such capital; it is life itself, and life and every hope and every return, except the inner return of a peaceful mind, may any day suffer a sudden shipwreck. I have just begun to read *Jane Eyre* for the first time; I am only half through it, and will not yet express any opinion on it, but one passage struck me so much that I must copy it out for you, chap. vi. p. 55: 'I hold another creed, which no one ever taught me, and which I seldom mention, but in which I delight, and to which I cling, for it extends hope to all, it makes eternity a rest – a mighty home, not a terror and abyss. Besides, with this creed I can so clearly distinguish between the criminal and his crime; I can so sincerely forgive the first, while I abhor the last; with this creed revenge never worries my heart, degradation never too deeply disgusts me, injustice never crushes me too low, I live in calm, looking to the end.'[3] I never before saw my creed written out, but here it is. This is what Helen Burns says, the schoolgirl who soon dies of consumption, but I suppose it is the creed of Charlotte Bronte, who wrote it, and, if so, it is enough to give me an interest in her.[4] I recommend this to you. . . .

---

[2] Cf. above, Letter 108, p. 299.   [3] Charlotte Brontë, *Jane Eyre*, 4th edition (1857).
[4] Jevons quoted several passages from Mrs. Gaskell's *Life of Charlotte Brontë* in an undated entry in the Journal, probably written at about this time. See Vol. I, p. 178.

113. W. S. JEVONS TO HENRIETTA JEVONS

Jan 24th 1858.
Double Bay. Sydney.

My dearest Henny

Nothing calls me to write this evening but the simple desire to communicate a few thoughts & feelings to one who will so fully understand them. It may indeed seem strange of me to *complain* of anything. I have here a free cheerful home, the pleasantest little study in the world in a sea-side spot that would delight English eyes; I have a good situation, plenty of money, a little laboratory in town at my own disposal, light congenial work, plenty of pursuits to follow up both at home & at the Mint, & plenty of time to follow them. What can I have to complain of then, or what more to desire? It is that I have not here anyone that can be to me a real friend. You perhaps know what a real friend should be; most people do not. Or rather I should say that the friends which most people require are found on everyside; I cannot find one here at all.

From one week's end to another, I am full of thoughts reflections, hopes, shames, but as they come up to the surface one by one, I have nothing to do but to shove them down again. I have not time to write them out and I have no one to tell them to.[1] Where is the use of expressing serious thoughts to persons who cannot respond to them, or hopes, fears, or intentions to those who will think them absurd. This is my condition; I have everything I can want for a happy life except a *mind* to answer mine.

I have been stirred into a state of unusual agitation, almost boiling over sometimes, by reading two novels by Charlotte Bronte (Currer Bell).[2] They are "Jane Eyre", and "Shirley". I scarcely know what there is about them so much to attract one, but perhaps it is that she was herself a quiet retired *thinker*, to whose original & truthful thoughts few I dare say would respond in common life and society, but who possessed the power of writing them so that all might & would read them and some might understand them. I would give anything to know such a person as Charlotte Bronte. From what I can see in her books I think her religion and mine are all of one kind and differ only that from habit or necessity she retains the use of a few fixed phrases with which I dispense. The sentence which I copied into my last letter to Lucy shows that she perfectly understood the force of what I found

---

[1] Jevons wrote 'too' here.
[2] The Brontë sisters published a volume of poems in 1846 under the pseudonyms Currer Ellis and Acton Bell. Charlotte Brontë used the name 'Currer Bell' for the publication of *Jane Eyre* (1847). When novels by the other sisters were also ascribed to this author, Charlotte had to give up her anonymity in order to prove that this was not the case. *Shirley* was published in 1849.

all my Faith upon. It is a faith in Humanity; in the fact that man was created for happiness. In nature we find an inexplicable mixture of evil. Pain and death may always come to our bodies, and, say what they will, nature cannot therefore be perfect. It is in the mind and nature of man that we find a provision against this. By a thought, a hope, a wish, an intention, or even the remembrance of a thought, or hope, he can rise superior to evils.

But I must not lose myself in depths which to me are yet dark and doubtful. But when instead of enquiring the foundation of my Faith, I enquire whether I have any and what it is, I find such a solid definite object, extending through every part of my mind, & forming apparently its whole framework that I scarcely care whether it be well founded or not. It is a solid fact. Now such a sort of faith appears to me to be indicated in Miss Bronte's books. In her there is no trace of *conventional religion*. Jane Eyre displays through her life a high degree of morality, and in many cases resists the most tempting pleasures and involves herself in toil & trouble in obedience to indefinite but unmistakeable* *principles*. Such *principle* is not what is usually acquired by reading chapters in the Bible or by going to Church. It is of the nature of my internal, unmistakeable* but apparently baseless Faith. My principles indeed have never been severely tested but I believe they would lead me to reject the most present & tangible pleasures for the most distant and abstract good.

But to pass to less heavy subjects, Miss Bronte describes in Jane Eyre, the inmost construction & motives of a mind as I have never seen them described in any other case. The same is true of Mr Rochester and in a greater or less degree of all the other characters. One thing, too, which distinguishes her most virtuous heros* and heroines, is that there is nothing angelic about them. She displays firm moral principles & good original minds as few others have done, but she always adds the imperfections of spirit or temper which go to make up the human character.

I said that I was greatly in need of a *friend*. There is another want I also experience and of which these books of Miss Bronte have reminded me. I would give anything to find a person *better than myself*. Whom I could respect, admire, and look up to. I really cannot say (what a shocking absence of all conventional humility) that I meet such here. At home I must do; when near such a person I should feel as if I were sailing with the tide. With him (or her) what I think well of in myself would go for nothing. My faults only would stand out.

As I make no question that you wish me home, I daresay you will not be displeased to find that I am not absolutely contented with this place. The result of the most earnest & impartial reflection on the subject comes out more & more plainly to the effect that I must not linger here. When I leave here all of a sudden, & still more when I am unexpectedly³ turn up in England, everybody will ask why I leave a good position & comfortable circumstances here and cast myself adrift again. But no matter; it is sufficient that I have reasons within myself, or that I am not contented to be an assayer of gold all my days, or to rust in a distant colony & different climate till my mind & body are equally unfitted for the society & air of England. *We* know reasons why it should not be. While taking such a step I am not thoughtless as to the consequences; it may be long before I am so comfortably circumstanced again, or it may be never. Still I feel, so to speak, that a hard struggle through the bush toward the right point will be better than miles of smooth walking along good roads away from it. God grant however that I may meet smooth roads instead of bush in England, figuratively as well as literally. But you would scarcely believe what a change in my thoughts the turn of the year has made. Before I thought of myself as a naturalised Australian. Now I am an English Exile waiting for the approaching opportunity to return. Already I look upon my study & my laboratory with the fond eye of one about to leave them, and already I have ceased to undertake any extensive alterations. This is all because what was before counted in years is now counted in months. Within twelve months I hope to make a start; within about two years (D.V.) to see you again. My remaining time here seems so short that I am already putting on a greater pressure of steam to get through the necessary work. But it does not do to dwell too⁴ much on the future, which is always uncertain, though we ought undoubtedly to plan it out beforehand and attempt to conform to that plan; now to more immediate subjects.

Music is ever to me the same; a part of my soul; but I have not played so much lately, because it robs me of time, and when I am buried in Mendessohn* Mozart or Haydn the clock fingers go round so fast, that the evening seems half to vanish and my work consequently remains tangibly undone. I find myself a little capricious in music, and poor old Handel might well be in the dumps at present if he looked only to my favour. Mendelsohn* is all the go, and I play little except his "St Paul" and "Elijah". These oratorios I regard as quite equal to any of Handels excepting the Messiah & Israel in Egypt *in some respects*. Considering too that Mendelsohn* wrote music of all kinds, & all of the most beautiful kind while Handel wrote oratorios only,⁵ one cannot

³ Jevons altered this sentence. He began another word after 'unexpectedly' but crossed it out.
⁴ 'to' in the manuscript.
⁵ Handel's other works were comparatively little known and seldom performed in England or Australia at this period.

but think Mendelsohn* the greater musician. I have an uncomfortable conviction that Handel is rather overestimated in England at present. Mozart as I said in my lectures to you, is the musician *par excellence*; he stands alone as the writer of *pure music* of universal style & universal character. Handel is the writer *par excellence*, of *oratorios*. Mendelsohn* is equal to the last, & next below the former. Surely he must hold the second place. Then come a crowd of others; Beethoven Haydn, Weber, Rossini, Spohr etc etc in a very slowly descending line; it is unnecessary to judge between them because they are all different in style & subject.

Does it not surprise you to consider that a great part of the finest music is a thing of the present day. Mendelsohn* is only a few years dead;[6] I remember reading of his death in the paper. Rossini & Spohr are still alive. In some moods there is nothing I like better than the gloomiest strains from the "Last Judgement" of the one, or the "Stabat Mater" of the other.

But to return, the "St Paul" of Mendelsohn* is a fine thing when you get fairly into it. It is perhaps rather slow and heavy, but grand & massive in some parts and extremely pathetic in others. There are also some surprising oratorial parts. Such as "Now we are Ambassadors".

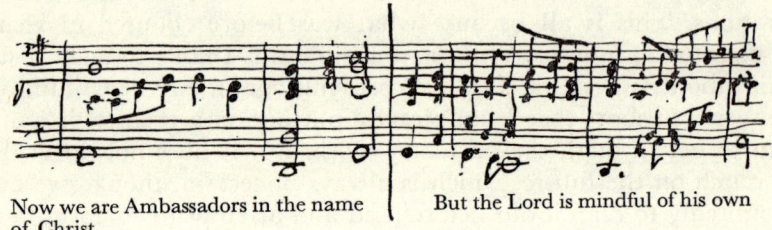

Now we are Ambassadors in the name of Christ. | But the Lord is mindful of his own

The air "But the Lord" is only to be compared with "O Rest in the Lord" in Elijah.

Mint. Febr. 10th. I hope you will like the enclosed photographs which I have been working at very hard lately. I send also my last paper on clouds,[7] though I dare say it will not much interest you.
    I remain, with best love
      Your ever affec. Brother.
            W S Jevons.

It strikes me that it is some time since you last wrote.

[6] Felix Mendelssohn (1809–47).   [7] See above, Letter 94, n. 7, p. 244.

114. H. E. ROSCOE TO W. S. JEVONS

Owens College Manchester
Feb. 1. 1858.

My dear Stanley

I was much interested in & obliged for your last long letter which I ought to have answered before this.

Your graphic description of that awful wreck was very interesting[1] – & I am always glad to hear of your Scientific pursuits & studies – You will soon be the great Scientific Don of the Antipodes!

At last I am able to send you a copy of the 2 first papers printed by the Royal Society in the Phil. Trans. a third I shall send you in the course of a few weeks.[2]

I always forget when I wrote to you last – it was I rather think since I came down here – at all events since my appointment – I have had, as you may imagine, enough to do here – What with my regular course of lectures (3 per week) the laboratory analytical class, the preparation of specimens, of which Frankland left a miserable lot, and two evening courses which I have lately begun. Then I have also to go on with my own researches, keep a German assistant going[3] – & work up the light experiments which I made last Summer, for Bunsens editing. Then what with visiting & making new acquaintances here, a matter of necessity when one first comes into a place – I have my time pretty fully occupied. During the Christmas holidays – of a fortnight – we went to London, staying chiefly with Harriet & Edward – & enjoying returning to old haunts & seeing our friends faces not a little – I called on friend Tommy – & he gave me some of your papers on Cirrous* Clouds – which I keep in my possession – awaiting orders from you. He (Tommy Graham) is very busy making experiments on the Diffusion of Gases – the law of w^h. (inverse square roots of densities) has been impugned by Bunsen in the book on Gasometry w^h. I translated.[4] Graham says that

---

[1] Jevons recorded having posted a letter to Harry Roscoe in his diary entry for 10 September 1857; this letter is not among the Jevons Papers.

[2] R. W. Bunsen and H. E. Roscoe, 'Photochemical Researches: Part I. Measurement of the chemical action of light. Part II. Phenomena of photochemical induction. Part III. Optical and chemical extinction of the chemical rays', *Philosophical Transactions* (1857), 355–402, 601–20. See below, Letter 126, p. 356.

[3] Wilhelm Dittman (1833–92). Born near Darmstadt, he had been an assistant in Bunsen's laboratory at Heidelberg; came to England to assist H. E. Roscoe in the private laboratory he established in London with the aid of friends in 1856; Dittman continued to act as his private assistant at Owens College; succeeded Guthrie as demonstrator in the department of chemistry, 1859–61; he became chief assistant in the chemical laboratory at Edinburgh University, 1861–9, later returning to Owens College as assistant lecturer, 1873–4; Professor of Chemistry at Anderson's University, Glasgow, 1874–86; naturalised in England, 1881; F.R.S. 1882.

[4] See above, Letter 39, p. 74. The law of diffusion of gases, which Graham had discovered experimentally about 1830, is still accepted as valid. Cf. Dampier, *A History of Science* (1968 ed.) p. 229.

B is quite wrong & that the law is still true – as however the expts are not yet finished much less published, I am rather inclined to side with Bunsen – whose methods are always precise & delicate – & in whose work I have great confidence.

Have you seen the 2nd vol: of Grahams book – edited by Watts?[5] – if not, get it – The appendix is particularly good & does Watts great credit – all the newest results in physical chemistry is[6] introduced most clearly & completely. Then if you want to read an interesting & most masterly book get the first vol of Buckles History of Civilization in England[7] – Although he may not be correct in all points, it is most clever – & *the* book of the age – Holding Science & Scientific method so high – & applying them to the study of History – There will soon be a revolution in public opinion regarding Science – it will – I hope in our time too – come to be considered as the true basis of knowledge – & looked upon in a very different light from what it has been or still is – There is certainly that one comfort about being of a Scientific turn – that one feels that one is ahead of the crowd – helping – however feebly – the coach forward – & this will soon be acknowledged on all hands – This book of Buckles' is a symptom of the coming time. So everyone interested in the welfare of science should read it.

I have an impression that there was something in your last letter which I should reply to – but I have unfortunately lost the letter & forgotten what the exact thing was – In future I will write as soon as I hear from you & then this cannot happen again.

The numbers in my classes are not as large as I could wish – the whole College has been going down as regards numbers – but I hope by hard work to raise the numbers in the Chemical Dept: – I have now, as many as Frankland had last year – & I have accomplished what he was unable to do – viz. get together an evening class. He had only about 4 or 5 applicants & did not lecture at all – & I have now 20 entered & have had some 50 or 60 present at various times. I believe that with good management we may succeed in establishing a very numerously attended series of evening lectures in the course of next winter. We have every facility & appliance for having a good Chemical School here – & I shall try to make it – but it will doubtless be uphill work.[8]

[5] Thomas Graham, *Elements of Chemistry* (assisted by H. Watts), second edition, entirely revised and enlarged 2 vols (1847).
[6] He first wrote 'knowledge' instead of 'results'.
[7] Henry Thomas Buckle, *History of Civilization in England*, 2 vols (1857).
[8] He wrote of his appointment in his autobiography: '... There were in the college at the time about thirty-five students, of whom fifteen were working in the laboratory, which had been fitted up by my predecessor Frankland.... Public opinion in Manchester at that time did not appreciate the value of the higher education, and it was not understood that science could be made an efficient instrument of education, and that such an education was absolutely necessary for an industrial career. To make a school of chemistry worthy of the great

Williamson in London has only 5 or 6 private students – & 16 Excisemen! Now I have already 12 working in the laboratory, and although some of them are very young, yet they are attentive & work – and one has better and more pliant material to work with than when one has to lick a great rawboned exciseman into shape! –

Now I must conclude – & hope that I shall soon hear again from you.

What are your plans – of remaining – or returning – I should be so glad to see you in England again but I cannot advise your leaving £680 per annum for £0.0.0 the largest sum you will make here – unless you get some offer of a place & *then* come if only ¼ your present salary. My mother will add a few lines in acknowledgement of your kind present. Ever my dear Stanley yours affcly

H. E. Roscoe.

115. W. S. JEVONS TO HENRIETTA JEVONS
[LJP, 99–102]

Sydney. N.S.W.
February 28th 1858.[1]

My dear little Henny,

Only on one condition can I allow myself to neglect every serious task tonight – that I spend the leisure time in writing home. The mail arrived a few days since *several weeks behind her time*, but I had awaited the expected pleasure with a sort of calm resignation, quite distinct from indifference, which previous experience of disappointments has long since taught me. When I got a letter & opening it found a sheet or two from each of you, a real pleasure indeed seemed to be before me.

To express my true feelings on hearing from those I fully know and love, I must say, that I have lived so long away from home, have acted & thought so independent of others whether near or far from me, that it does not seem, so to speak, a self evident proposition, that I have sisters, brothers, and even other persons, to whom I am by nature & by every tie of feeling closely drawn & related. When as long as you remember, certain sisters, & brothers or other persons have been your constant companions, they become a condition of your existence; a

---

manufacturing district of South Lancashire was my ambition, and after thirty years of work I think it must be admitted that this was, to some extent at least, realised, for there were, I believe, few engaged in that district in any large way of business in which chemistry plays a part who did not show their appreciation of the value of scientific education by sending their sons or their managers to learn chemistry at Owens College.' (*Life and Experiences*, pp. 102–3).

[1] The original manuscript of this letter is incomplete.

necessary fact. It can scarcely occur to you that they might be away or not exist at all and if it does the things would appear almost as difficult or impossible to conceive as that 2 & 2 make 5.

Now I have grown out of this. Without reserve I say that home is not now a condition of my existence. I am independent or even isolated, little accustomed to meet persons with whom I can freely say my thoughts; this it is that seems my ordinary position. I am accustomed if not reconciled to it; the pleasure of free or affectionate mental intercourse is a negative condition of my life. When I receive a letter from home it therefore causes me a slight surprise it is an unexpected treat, and if the time had passed without it taking place I might not have strongly noticed it. But then there comes a feeling peculiarly sweet; it is that I am privileged in possessing those friendly minds which I might not have possessed. I am not utterly isolated & self-dependent, and whatever I might have felt to be painful in that contingency, I have an opposite pleasure in knowing the reality.

I do not wish to enquire whether happiness of the highest, truest, intensest & most legitimate kind may not be possible in the state of isolation; I rather think it may, and that those who by any cause are thus placed, have only one out of many paths to pleasure closed against them; many modes of spending life with proper effect & purpose may yet be open, just as a blind person employs his touch smell & other means of sense to replace his sight. A person born blind cannot be said to suffer any painful loss at all. But you must understand clearly that I allow friendship (or rather sociality) to be perhaps the most ready and easy way to happiness. I recognise the pleasure of doing a kindness or good to others or in other ways[2] performing the part of a friend; perhaps I may remember the feeling as experienced on a few occasions. Yet I do not object to confess that my chief pleasures are not thus derived; that I do not think they ought to be, and that I would purposely avoid spending too much in seeking the pleasures of affection & sociality. Affections which exist and which you have once recognised, are like unalterable laws which cannot be broken; it is a *pleasing duty* to neglect other calls that these natural & inevitable but delightful calls should first be fulfilled. This being accomplished, there are as I have said many ways in which ones time and opportunity may be converted into happiness, and not like a sweet beverage be left to ferment & turn sour for want of being used. A few of these *modes* are 1. the pursuit of some physical science, in which the pleasure of exercising reason is gratified each time that a great striking, beautiful, or even an insignificant fact is vanquished, while there is added the savour of contemplating & wondering at things *that are, because they are*, and of

[2] Jevons wrote 'way' here.

discovering things which *always were*, but unseen by man. 2. *The pursuit of some mental science*, in which the mind is pleased, amused or, so to speak, *tickled* by the sense of obscurity, vagueness & danger in which it works. When a psycological* fact is once believed to be established the very slightness & unpalpable nature of its foundation, and the length & sublety* of the building process are pleasing reflections, just as in the completion of a lofty *card-house* which a breath might have knocked down. 3. *Philanthropy* in which the mental part of our nature recognises the important, & practically useful character as well as the high moral position of the occupation, adding at the same time a little of the satisfaction which the pursuit of a physical or mental science might afford, while the *sympathetic* part of us usually (though not altogether necessarily) throws in a spice of livelier feeling. 4. *Some Aesthetic art*, (either music, painting, sculpture, poetry, pure literature &c) yielding a pure & simple delight of which the source is unseen, & inexplicable (as if a continual gift of God) although the supply is abundant, & never failing. 5. *Travelling* in which the pleasure of a mere rapid succession of novel ideas & sensation, (and where the ideas were not quite novel but anticipated from previous account, the pleasure of realization & verification is in no way less) is joined to a partial exercise of the reasoning & aesthetic faculties. 6. A *practical pursuit* whether it be to farm land, to dig a mine, to carry on a successful business, or to produce good & cheap manufactures; in these I think, much satisfaction, besides that of an *avaricious kind*, is derived from merely conquering nature & carrying the point you had proposed.

However my dear Henny, I began this letter with small thoughts of reading you such a lecture as the above, & so I abruptly drop it. I will not even stay to explain anything I have said liable to misconception, or to dwell furthur* on the exact psycological* or moral relations of the undoubtedly great pleasure which your[3] last letter afforded, lest I should again indulge unconsciously in a parenthesis of 4 or 5 pages.

You say that I seemed from my last letters not so much occupied with *music*. This can scarcely have been the case for Music is always to me the same, a condition of my existence, a part of me. I believe I could live a *life of Music*. If our physical nature did not interfere, I can almost conceive it possible that a man might play music *ad infinitum* and still never tire. Have you ever felt when much pleased & interested by several different things in the same day, as if you would like to have a separate existence for each, something in the way that in *vingt'un* you can divide a pair of similar cards & play two or more separate hands.

[3] 'you' in the original manuscript.

Now I think that nothing less than a life time would quite satisfy my musical thirst while I find with concern that a single hour per day out of the 24, considerably interferes with other affairs equally or more important. Music thus ought to be a rare but still legitimate & occasional delight.

I greatly envy you with your music master & lessons, & new pieces & concerts & other grand opportunities. Here I come to a stand surprised & pleased if I hear a (supposed) young lady strumming in a second floor room in a Sydney Street. Of the ladies of my acquaintance, none play except in such a detestable way that, (although by no means fastidious & in fact quite loving those large barrel organs at home) I immediately decamp, on hearing them commence. The Philharmonic concerts, with their questionably performed overtures & symphonies have now ceased because the Concert room has, in the most Gothic manner, been converted into an auction room.[4] Of musical (as well as dramatic) 'stars' the Sydney sky from horizon to zenith has been *quite clear* for at least six month.* You can understand then the dull & miserable thing that it is to ramble through the beauties of all the chief oratorios &c & yet be beyond the reach of all those grand performances I hear of in London & Liverpool. If one of the Exeter Hall oratorios (at 3^s) took place here and the price were raised to £10 I feel pretty nearly sure I should go.[5]

About two weeks ago I fell upon Beethoven's 'Mount of Olives' and 'Pastoral Symphony', and instantly buying them at the price demanded, have since played scarcely anything else. Many pieces in the first I have mastered, I really think, better than anything before; most of the latter is beyond my power altogether and I can only here & there catch an air. Of the Mount of olives* I can only say that it contains some things of the beauty or sublimity of which I had before formed no conception. It is like gaining a new insight into a thing. My two favourite passages I copy out;[6] they are the simplest parts of the whole, but surpassingly beautiful or striking. Beethoven's music seems to me characterized by being *"full of soul"*; every note seems to be a thought

[4] The first Sydney Philharmonic Society was founded in 1854, under the patronage of the Governor-General, and gave performances at the Concert Hall in the Royal Hotel Sydney until it terminated in 1858 in the manner here described by Jevons. A further society was formed in 1885. Cf. R. B. Barton, G. M. Thompson, *A Short History of the Sydney Philharmonic Society* (Sydney, 1903), pp. 1–2.

[5] Jevons's last mention in the diary of attending a musical performance in Sydney was in the entry for 14 August 1857, when he recorded having paid ten shillings for a "Ticket for oratoria of St. Marys Cathedral". Regular diary entries ceased after the end of October 1857.

[6] A small fragment of music sheet containing these passages is enclosed with the letter. Of the two extracts, probably quoted from the original Novello octavo edition of Beethoven's *Christ on the Mount of Olives* (op. 85), which Jevons copied on to this sheet, one comes near the close of movement no. 6, for solo and chorus, and has the tempo indication *Allegro molto*. The second, shorter, extract is from the orchestral introduction to the duet, no. 8.

or at least a part of an expression, while the whole seems to be an *inspiration* rather than an exertion of mere musical knowledge, art, or talent. Of all other composers, Weber seems to me most nearly to resemble him in this; Haydn, Mendelsohn,* Spohr follow next in this respect. Mozart & Handel though perhaps greater than any in the whole, are distinguished especially the latter by the preponderance of the musical art, *pure* or combined with the dramatic.

These thoughts & criticisms I give quite freely although I know I have no foundation or opportunity of judging, and I wish you would do the same of what you play. I was pleased to hear of your lessons from Mr Hermann, and his present of a fourth lesson showed that your liking for music or something in you excited his interest. I have Il Trovatore and know the air of the piece (there is 'Balen' & 'Sorriso' & some other gibberish in the name)[7] he gave you. I like it tolerably but am puzzled with regard to Verdis' music in general. I do not like to condemn it outright, as I might be suspected of doing so because other people do the same. His music is undoubtedly *original* & *striking* but seems to me to want in simplicity & absence of art and elaboration. His last, La Traviata, is downright trash, I am sure.

In speaking of your own and my health you say you think the *physical frame may overpower the mind*; the very same thought before now has occurred to me, though I accepted it with equal hesitation. In good health one has a pleasure in mere existense;* might not a state of weak or uncertain health drive one to other sources of pleasure.

I am glad you found Political Economy tolerable. The "Wealth of Nations" is perhaps one of the driest on the subject. You will perceive that *Economy*, scientifically[8] speaking, is a very contracted science; it is in fact a sort of vague mathematics which calculates the causes and effects of man's industry, and shows how it may best be applied. There are a multitude of allied branches of knowledge connected with man's condition; the relation of these to political economy is analogous to the connection of mechanics, astronomy, optics, sound, heat, and every other branch more or less of physical science, with pure mathematics. I have an idea, which I do not object to mention to you, that my insight into the foundations and nature of the knowledge of man is deeper than that of most men or writers. In fact, I think that it is my mission to apply myself to such subjects, and it is my intention to do so. You are desirous of engaging in the practically useful; you may feel

---

[7] Count di Luna's aria from Act 2, 'Il balen del suo sorriso' ('In the light of her sweet glances').

[8] The original manuscript ends here. The text is continued according to the version in LJ, pp. 101–2.

assured that to extend and perfect the abstract or the detailed and practical knowledge of man and society is perhaps the most useful and necessary work in which any one can now engage. There are plenty of people engaged with physical science, and practical science and arts may be left to look after themselves, but thoroughly to understand the principles of society appears to me now the most cogent business. The Association for the Advancement of Social Science[9] is a great step certainly, but it seems to me as yet scarcely founded on a sufficiently wide basis; I do not think also that it should be confined so much to *details and practical* suggestions.

116. H. E. ROSCOE TO W. S. JEVONS

Owens College
Manchester
March. 20. 1858.

My Dear Stanley

Many thanks for the kind congratulations in your letter received a few days ago.[1] I am glad to say, & I am sure you will be glad to hear that I like my place here very much I have plenty to do & hope in time to succeed in making this the school of Chemistry in the North, but I find much to improve & to begin with it will be uphill work.

I have now 13 in the laboratory, 11 in my long course of lectures, and 25 in a short evening course which I am giving, and besides I have a class of 30 working men once a week on Physical Geography at a working mans' college which we have lately established here & which is flourishing grandly, as we have 250 students.[2]

I do not know what you mean about changing your objects in &

---

[9] The National Association for the Promotion of Social Science, founded in 1857 and sponsored by Lord Brougham, was an attempt to bring together all those concerned with the social problems of the age. It was organised on the model of the British Association, and subdivided into Departments. Annual congresses were held in the principal cities of the British Isles with the *Transactions* published as a volume. The Association became for a time an important pressure group in matters of social reform, but as various social interests began to set up their own bodies its influence declined and financial difficulties arose; the Association went out of existence in 1886.

Jevons became a member of the Association during his Manchester years and his article 'On Industrial Partnerships' (*Methods*, pp. 122–55) was originally presented as a public lecture under the auspices of the N.A.P.S.S. in 1870. Cf. B. Rodgers, 'The Social Science Association, 1857–1886', *Manchester School*, xx (September 1952) 283–310.

[1] This letter is not among the Jevons Papers.

[2] A working man's college had been inaugurated in Manchester the previous January, at the Mechanics' Institution. H. E. Roscoe was a member of the management committee. His physical geography lectures were held on Friday evenings between 8.30 and 9.30. For a full account of this and similar developments in Manchester, see Thompson, op. cit., pp. 220–36.

mode of life. – I daresay that you find it difficult to do much in experimental science in the bush as you say, but I hope you don't think of giving it up entirely. – What do you intend to make of political economy & statistics? I should like to know what view you have – as you seem to have some – about your future line of occupation. My own feeling is that it is very dangerous to change from one line of occupation & thought to another – & think you ought to consider well before you make any change in your places – particularly a change so great as from an Assayer & cultivator of physical science to a political economist. You will excuse me thus freely expressing my opinion in a letter just as I should if you were talking to me, but I do feel that there is nothing in life like sticking to one thing, & you have made a capital beginning in one line & should take care not to get off that without getting on to another equally good & going on as smoothly & quickly as you are now.

As you are interested in meteorological observations I am forwarding to you a solid glass sphere to form part of an apparatus constructed by a friend of mine for measuring the duration & amount of the direct solar radiation at any given spot by burning a line on a wooden hemisphere in the centre of which the glass lens is placed – Thus

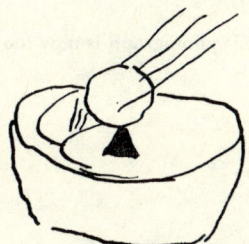

a regular line being drawn by the rays in the focus being a line in the wood. Owing to the alteration of the suns declination the several lines come each day lower & thus a complete register of the sun shine for half a year is kept. I thought that it might interest you to have an instrument as it would also interest us to see how much more direct sunlight the Australian climate than we do.[3]

By rights the instrument should be set up either on the longest or shortest day so that the lines commence either above or below. However you will see the details in the paper of Campbell's[4] which I inclose*

[3] Roscoe appears to have left out a word here.
[4] John Francis Campbell (1822–85) of Islay; educated at Eton and Edinburgh University; held various court and government posts, traveller, writer on highland folklore, geology, and meteorology; invented the sunshine recorder for indicating the varying intensity of the sun's rays. In his *Thermography* (1883) p. 189, Campbell refers to the paper mentioned here by Roscoe as 'published by the Meteorological Society in 1857'. See *Report of the Council of the British Meteorological Society* (May 1857), 18.

in the box together with some other papers which may amuse & perhaps interest you – and several of your own paper on Cirrous.*

The drawing inclosed* is a photograph of one of Campbells spheres upon which the path of the sun is marked.⁵

I should be very much obliged if you have a chance of securing any good Australian minerals to do so for me. I am always on the look out for minerals particularly well crystalized* ones & I fancy that Australia has many besides Burra-burra & nuggets. I am of course meaning that you should buy any for me – & then I will transmit the money per post.

The original print of this photograph is now too faint for reproduction.

The other day I got the number of the Empire & was astonished to see that you have such an intensely hot Summer. We had a very hot time of it in Heidelberg last July & August but I don't think the temp rose as high as 100° in the shade.

⁵ The photograph, which is now too faded to allow reproduction, was pasted to a separate sheet of paper, on which the following notes, not in the handwriting of Roscoe, appear:
'J. F. Campbell, Jany. 1858. – Photograph of the inside of a registering sundial at Campden Hill, Kensington. – The figures indicate the hours. –The white lines were burned by a spherical lens, on black paint, covering a portland cement bowl, during a period of six months, from June to December 1857. The dark spaces in the white lines indicate sone imterruption of the sun's rays.'
The instrument itself did not reach Jevons in Australia; see below, Letter 122, p. 343.

You must excuse this rambling & most uninteresting letter, I will write more & it is to be hoped more brightly before long
  Believe me dear Stanley

W. Stanley Jevons Esqr.

Yours very affecly
Henry. E. Roscoe.

117. W. S. JEVONS TO HENRIETTA JEVONS
   [LJP, 102–3]

June 9th 1858.
Double Bay. Sydney.
(Royal Mint)

My dearest Henny
  I scarcely know how to express the satisfaction which your occasional letters give. I have described to you before my wish for that almost ideal thing a *true friend*, by which I do not mean one who is friendly & useful, one who is amusing and beneficial as a companion or even one who bears under all circumstances the most sincere & deep love. I mean one whose mind locks together with my own; whose ultimate purpose in life being identical with my own, every slight action & every momentary thought & motive almost must be comprehensible to me & obtain my sympathy, even as I may feel sure that my own actions & motives will be regarded by that friend. If I say then that every letter from you assures me that I know of such a friend, it will express as shortly as possible what I feel towards you. I have before noticed how much similarity there is between us in some things but I could scarcely have believed that there could be such coincidence between the disposition of mind, the spring of motives & the general views of two separate persons. In all except a few particulars I might mistake many of your letters, as my own allowing only two or three years difference. Your thoughts have been my thoughts, your doubts, my doubts.
  The subject of your latest letter is extremely interesting to me. I take it to be your misgivings on the subject of a revealed Christian Religion. It has often occurred to me that such doubts must strike a mind of your character sooner or later and though I believe I have not done anything to suggest them, you see I am right. I sympathise with every word you say; your bewilderment in finding that you have no longer a post to cling to, and that all around are bottomless waters, with nothing but floating straws to catch at. Perhaps you feel that you touch a bottom now & then, and that if the fixed creed or the firm inward faith of Christianity is lost, you have at all events found a rock in *Deism* or *Natural Religion*. But then your[1] mind will be so excited &

[1] 'you' in the original manuscript.

full of the fears of doubt that whether Deism prove eventually solid or not, it will seem to slip away, and you will almost prefer a fatiguing swim upon the open waters of doubt to such a treacherous support. Justice goodness, duty will prove intangible shadows, mere form without sound reason; even human affection and the dearest love will at last fail, and loosing* that most strong and sustaining of all human feelings, you will fear momentarily that you are sinking into the truly bottomless pit of Atheism – the absence of love for God or Man.

This is somewhat the course of my past feelings; they were never so strong as seriously to destroy my peace of mind. In fact I never gave myself up to pure thought but was always more or less engaged with solid objects that could not melt away. Do not misunderstand me when I say that I am in some respects an Atheist. I cannot say that I have the Love of God because no image that I can form of him answers the conditions & withstands the assaults of reason. On the other hand do not be surprised when I say that I almost Deify the Love of *Man*. I seem to be forming by degrees, a creed so singular, so original (as far as I know) & perhaps after all so unreasonable that I do not recognise it although I know that its elements really exist within me. Philosophers say that Nature is perfect; one vast harmonious design of which each fragment shows in itself a beneficent purpose comprehensible in many cases to man. But yet whatever the ultimate object of this vast machine, it certainly does not work uninterruptedly & with results free from evil. The teeth of a large animal are purposely designed to seize & mangle a smaller one. A thunderstorm though serving some purposes of the harmonious design may strike a man dead, or the falling branch of a tree may half crush him, & he may lie in pain for many hours only to die at last. I cannot understand how *pain & evil* are consistant* with perfection. The belief in a Future life, free from all evil but very partially explains this difficulty, & to mention that doctrine is to add fresh impossibilities[2] – the coexistence of time & eternity, of material & immaterial life.

There is but one thing that I can through every thing retain – The love of one human mind towards another. I do not say that this love does in general remove all imperfections of Nature with respect to men. A man may hate his species, and the picture of such a man dying in the midst of pain and execution, is a thing of unmitigated horror which I cannot reconcile with any views. But in the worst of circumstances human love may add a ray of delight. I can conceive but do not really suppose it to occur, that a man dying in the most horrible way may be filled with pleasant feeling by merely remembering that hundreds of thousands of men, in no way conscious of or caring for his condition,

[2] Jevons wrote 'impossibities' here.

are enjoying themselves. Human love then is capable of approximating indefinitely to a mastery over the evils of Nature, or in short to Perfection.

I have now written you off a few remarks on my own state of opinions, but do not wish you in any way to regard them. Trust yourself to your own sound & sincere reflections, and as long as you love your fellow-men, you will never be without some sort of faith.

I am much amused at what you so profanely wrote at the top of the page of some Scripture books. "Christian Mythology" is a most appropriate name for what all religious sects even down to Unitarians accept as sacred truth. I do not in the least blame those who place their faith in these Myths. In some cases, indeed, so called religion is a horrid & inhumane thing, so incredible that one cannot suspect any one, (unless a fanatic) of sincerely believing it. According to some small sects all other sects including some two or three hundred million heathen savages are all to be dammed in Hell everlastingly. A man that believes or professes to believe such has nothing so wicked about him as his religion. The best thing about him is probably his *good nature*, his sympathy with any man who is in pain for half an hour; such things constitute that mans real *faith* if he have any.

With other persons Christianity is the most humane & pure faith in a rather poetical, allegorical or personified form. This adds a distinctness & intensity which those whose faith is spread over the wide waters of unrestricted speculation, may envy. This, too, may suit particular minds, & though I do not intimately know Lucy's opinions I have no doubt she is a devout Christian, and one whose faith, if less grounded in reason, is more intense, & perhaps more delightful than ours.

I never distinctly learned my Father's opinions either, but I have no doubt they were very free; I may take this opportunity of saying that he was the most humane of all men, and that my opinions just described I think were insensibly derived from him.

When you say you are puzzled how to employ yourself I always wish I were with you. Besides giving you books to read & learn, I can assure you that if you shared half my work you would have enough to do. *If ever* we live together again, I shall hope every evening to see you sitting opposite me writing, correcting, copying, checking, calculating & enabling me to get on as fast again with the work I am sure to have in hand. For Lucy I shall have plenty of diagrams, maps etc to draw which I manage very badly myself. Social science is the wide subject before me, and I have even had for many years the idea of a work on "Towns & Cities," to analyse their constitution, and causes, the relative character of their parts, & the relative character of particular cities[3] & thus

[3] See above, Letter 107, n. 10, p. 297.

eventually lead to such knowledge of their nature & shall ensure their improvement, as any Scientific knowledge is eventually reduced to practise. If you are not afraid of work & look favourably upon my proposal turn your attention to social subjects, read such things as you come across but especially reflect upon them, and get into the habit of regular & unmistakeable* *work*. It is not a charming prospect to devote oneself to unceasing *work & drudgery* but it is a fate I should not shrink from. I feel sure too that you desire above all things to *work* at something useful, but you feel a natural difficulty in setting to it, or even finding anything to do. A year or so and you will require no leading; you will be thinking, acting, and writing for yourself, with many subjects before you and only regreting* that necessary things will interfere to take up your precious time.

Your essay, though certainly very short, is greatly approved of. You seem to me to handle your subjects very firmly and give each point a fair if a very brief consideration, not running off at tangent like most beginners and writing all about one point while the others are all flying off in every direction. That is what always used to and always does bother me.

I am glad to hear that music progresses with you. I envy you going to Mendelsohns* nights & great concerts, but hope that I may yet go to some with you. I think in that case that there will not be two other such sincere musicians in the room as you & I. There has been no addition to my musical library since my last letter nor do I intend to buy much more. Come what will, it is a pleasure to think[4] that I can send you a compact little library of all the best classical music, including even operas. It is probable that I shall have no time in England to keep up my music and you will then be performer for the family. Indeed I should not care for playing myself if there were others to play for me, a treat which I could not here enjoy. Beethoven's Engedi still has my highest admiration, & there is even a chance of hearing it performed here because the Melbourne & Sydney Philharmonic Societies (who do not always attain what they *love*) are joining to have a grand go here, in short a festival of three days, in the grand new hall of the University: & I know the former society can play the Engedi.

I think there are no characters one loves so much as Great Musical Composers. Mozart, Beethoven and Mendelsohn* seem to be the intimate friends & benefactors of all who hear their music; what a privilege thus to delight millions of people for ages to come! Those three poor Germans will be known when Victoria is forgotten, & London perhaps will be distinguished as the place where the Messiah was first

[4] 'thing' in the original manuscript.

performed.⁵ But it is an interesting question with me whether musical writings will have the everlasting character of poetry or whether it will become antique & be superseded. Davids Psalms, Homers Iliad, Shakespeares plays, and Miltons Paradise Lost will be read as long as there are readers. Will the Requie, the Messiah, the Engedi, & Elijah or St Paul be played, & perhaps rearranged for instruments of improved construction. Very probably it is so and the last century, scarcely yet terminated is a grand musical epoch that may never recur with such original beauty & grandeur.

Let me hear from you often & long.

Forgive an abrupt conclusion.

From your loving Brother
W. S. Jevons.

118. W. S. JEVONS TO THE EDITOR OF THE *SYDNEY MAGAZINE OF SCIENCE AND ART*

REV. MR. SCOTT'S[1] CRITICISMS

Sir – Any one may see how Mr. Scott (in page 264 of your last *Magazine*) misrepresents the contents of my Paper "On Clouds," by looking over that rather lengthy paper (pages 163 to 176) or merely reading the brief conclusions (page 176).

I never enunciated, as a *new theory*, the non-agency of electricity. What I did was, to propose theories concerning the forms and causes of clouds, and to attempt to shew that they are the simple effects of heat and motion upon bodies of air containing moisture. Then, I finally argue, "that is unnecessary to suppose that electricity possesses any active agency in the production or modification of clouds." This may certainly be termed a theory – but it is a *negative theory*, which fifty persons might prove upon fifty different grounds. An electrician might assert, for instance, that electricity is incapable of the effects observed; another person, that the mechanical power of lightning is inconsiderable, and so on. To prove the negative proposition, "A is not B", it is sufficient to prove that A is C, D, E, &c., of which one or more is not B. Kamtz may use the argument C, Schubler the argument D, Sir John

---

⁵ Handel's *Messiah* was first performed in Dublin, at the Music Hall, Fishamble Street, on 13 April 1742. The first performance in England took place on 23 March 1743 at Covent Garden.

[1] William Scott (1825–1917). The son of a banker, he was born in Devon and educated at Blundell's School and Cambridge, where he then lectured in mathematics, 1848; ordained 1850; Government Astronomer of New South Wales, 1856–62; headmaster of Cook's River Collegiate School, 1862–5; Warden of St. Paul's College, Sydney University, 1865–78; retired from the church in 1882. For some years he was secretary (1867–74) and treasurer of the Royal Society, formerly the Sydney Philosophical Society.

Herschel the argument E, and I may still attempt to use the argument F, without being liable to the charge of plagiarism which Mr. Scott would fix upon me. This simple point of logic could not have escaped that gentleman.

But if Mr. Scott acknowledges to a misapprehension of this point, I have yet to ask him, why he omits the very last nine words of my paper ("a conclusion which is, on general grounds, highly probable"), while quoting the eighteen words immediately preceding? or, why he has entirely overlooked my quotation from Sir John Herschel's Essays (paragraph 81 of my paper), while searching out, himself, no less than three sentences from German and other authorities, with the purpose of proving that "Mr. Jevon's is no new theory." If Mr. Scott had not omitted my last nine words, and the sentence of Sir J. Herschel, it would have instantly shown that I had carefully guarded myself against any charge of plagiarism arising from a misapprehension of the point above explained. As it is, the more authorities Mr. Scott can produce as to the non-agency of electricity, the more he confirms my theories as to the formation of clouds, which form one ground for asserting that negative theory.

Hoping that Mr. Scott may, in future, better succeed in "provoking" profitable and friendly discussion.

I am, Sir, your obedient Servant,
W. S. JEVONS.

Double Bay, June 23rd, 1858.

With regard to Mr. Scott's remarks on "Geology and Genesis,"[2] I may draw his attention to a paper lately read before the Royal Society upon the "Geological History of the Alluvial Land of Egypt", by L. Horner, Esq., V.P.R.S. (also, see *Saturday Review*, February 20th 1858). It appears that, in boring into the alluvial flood deposits, a small piece of pottery was brought up from the depth of 39 feet, which Mr. Horner shows to be a record of the existence of man 13,375 years before A.D. 1858, and that man must, even then, have been in a state of partial civilisation. The "abundant negative evidence" of man's existence in earlier periods than that assigned in the Biblical account, is quite unavailing against this fragment of positive evidence, confirmed

---

[2] Jevons appears to have been engaged here in a further controversy with the Rev. Mr Scott concerning geological theory, centred on the Rev. George Wight's *Geology and Genesis: A Reconciliation of the two Records* (1857). Although Jevons's own list of his early writings does not bear out La Nauze's inference that Jevons wrote the review of this book which appeared in the *Empire*, 12 March 1858, it is true that he did come to the defence of the review in this letter to the *Sydney Magazine of Science and Art*, II (1858) 17–18. Jevons did not record having read *Geology and Genesis* in the diaries but his Australian entries are erratic after October 1857 and do not extend beyond February 1858.

as it is by Chevalier Bunsen's opinion previously expressed, "that the first epoch of the history of the human race demand at least a period of 20,000 years before our era, as a fair starting point in the earth's history".

If Mr. Scott asks whether "a difference of opinion really exists among geologists of any note in the present age", with regard to fossil human bones proving him to have been contemporaneous with icthyosauric and other primaeval monsters, I think I may answer him in the negative. There is internal evidence in man's perfect structure that he is the latest and highest object of Creation. But when a fragment of evidence turns up, in a deposit, scarcely to be termed geological, yet proving that his history already extends over a period that the mind can scarcely grasp, what a grand idea does it communicate of the previous geological ages, or still more of the periods elapsing between the several creative acts as mentioned in Genesis. If a soil deposit, 39 feet deep, in a narrow valley indicate 13,000 years, what shall we say of the sandstone formation, of which this Australian continent is chiefly composed, to be measured as it is only by thousands of miles in length and thousands of feet in thickness. There is but one analogy I know of to impress such immensities of time – the periods of man's history, long as they are now known to be, bear no more proportion to the periods of geological or cosmical history than distances upon the earth, or within the earth's orbit, bear to the distances of the remotest stars and nebulae. In short, they are inappreciable.

W.S.J.

119. W. S. JEVONS TO LUCY JEVONS
[LJN, 103–4]

9th July 1858.

... My monthly despatches will this time be comprised within a small space, for the mail has not arrived, and I have consequently no letters to answer. Life here is as quiet as usual. There is nothing in the least striking to tell you of. If often occurs to me, is it well to live thus undisturbed? Will the future be better than the present to one who makes no present sacrifices? Granting that a given position is good, may it not be wisely relinquished if a happier one may be attained, even after much trouble? What man of sense that had a hundred acres of land would dig a single acre, and sowing it with potatoes, rest contented that he is not likely to starve, and owes no man anything? Will he not pinch himself and go through years of toil that his whole estate may be rendered a productive farm? It is just so with me. I have plenty of potatoes to live on, and might lie down in sunshine if I wanted nothing else. But may I not fairly believe that I have other capabilities, that my soil will bear other and better products if properly tilled? and am I to neglect this for the sake of the trouble? You already know so well what are my intentions that I need answer none of my own questions, but you will understand that self-proposed arguments, such as the above, are now and then necessary when transitory misgivings arise. It requires no little courage to do as I propose, and I am not naturally by any means courageous. To abandon a good income of potatoes will be thought madness by all those potato-growing friends who have no idea that corn, milk, and fruit might be raised off the same ground with a little extra trouble. . . . I do not know whether I have before explained why I desire at once to leave Sydney. It is because I believe my education is but now continuing, and that by staying here it is checked, and irretrievably deferred. I have gained many advantages by my residence at the Antipodes. If I could again be left to decide, quite unbiassed by the opinion of my father and others, whether I would accept the assayership, it is perhaps more likely than not that I should do so. But I feel sure that a few additional years' savings (surplus of potato crops) are far outbalanced by the irremediable injury to future fruits of greater value. I have done something here, but a change of life from easy to hard and busy, from Sydney to London, a better knowledge of the world both physical and human, the mixture with enlightened men and great objects, the abandonment of a pleasant but scarcely profitable seclusion from all society, and thus a diligent use of the advantages of London, are what I seek. Yet I fear these things will not increase my potato crop! . . . I am at present very busily occupied with meteorology. I left off my regular observations at the end of last month, and am now working out all the results and arranging all information I have concerning the climate of Australia, so as to publish it if I like.[1] I shall then have pretty nearly finished with meteorology. I don't think more than a month more will be necessary for this. I have then plenty to do with assaying, photography, botany, and preparations for my travels, to occupy five months more, so that I expect the time will pass very quickly. . . . In working up the climate of Australia I have read a great many books of voyages and expeditions,[2] and take quite a romantic view of wild primeval forests and cannibal blacks. *Robinson Crusoe*, *The Swiss Family Robinson*, and *Masterman Ready* I used to think amusing

[1] See below, Letter 121, p. 340.
[2] These included Sir Thomas Mitchell's *Journal of an expedition into the interior of tropical Australia, in search of a route to the Gulf of Carpentaria* (1848), which he read during January and February 1856; also *Humboldt's Travels* and *Mutiny on the Bounty*, according to the diaries of 1856 and 1857.

but childish fiction, yet the true incidents which happen in Australia or the 'Islands' (by which we here denote Polynesia), are quite as singular and interesting, minus a little of the *couleur de rose*. England must be a very prosy conventional place, where there is no square yard that 'the foot of white man has not crossed', and where the aboriginals were exterminated some 2000 years ago....

120. W. S. JEVONS TO HENRIETTA JEVONS

Double Bay. Sydney.
4 August 1858

My dearest Henny

It is not as a duty, not as a leisurely occupation, not as a light amusement that I begin this letter tonight. It is as a delightful relief from the almost tiresome companionship of my own ceaseless thoughts. I have reflected, calculated, resolved, & set to work; but very soon, the reflections & resolution come all over again into my mind so that nothing is done. I have indeed much to look forward to, much to reflect upon, but having once decided on the future, it would be better to dispense with thoughts which only interrupt action.

It is ever to me a source of satisfaction that whenever I reflect most deeply, I can confess myself exceedingly happy. It may be wrong to say so, because it is almost equivalent to ignoring faults which ought to cause dissatisfaction. Confident that my general motives and intentions will bear as close examination as those of most men, I should be glad of some one to accuse me of my faults and to show how little my actions accord with my motives.

August 6th I can hardly trust myself to write to night for my thoughts are not of the most cheerful character; but yet I can do nothing else. For two long months I have waited, and to day I got the expected letters. If I were truthfully to tell you how much I desire long interesting letters both from you and Lucy and were nevertheless to say that on this occasion I was not disappointed, the two statements would be incompatible. The letters which I love to get are those which best lay bare the soul, and show that it is accordant with my own. I may be wrong to expect it of any one. It may be what a brother cannot expect of a sister But if so my doom in life will wear even a blacker hue than I had thought. I confess I think you are one whose views nearly coincide, so far as they are formed with my own. From my experience of life as yet, I have no hopes of finding others. It is true that you were very young when I left; I judge only by a few letters; but how much therefore do I value letters which will give me furthur* insight.

I do not know whether to say now that I am happy or miserable. I have lately reflected more than usual on my present & future position, and such reflections do not promote lightness of spirits though they may give a sort of heavy calmness. The mind never does perhaps never should remain always in the same dead level. It is proper there should be a circle of thoughts & moods, that every side of the picture may be contemplated. Sometimes everything seems favourable past labours appear successful, and future tastes of easy accomplishment. Let a week or two pass, and it looks very different; you wonder at your own folly & want of discernment. Past labours, you fear, will only subject you to ridicule; future labour then is useless & is better spared. But, thank God, no phase of mind has yet presented a picture at which my resolution failed; when in good spirits I have rejoiced that the accomplishment of my wishes is in the distance; when less sanguine I have felt that good intentions unaccomplished may not be unrewarded.

Concerning my intended movements, how can I consider them? Are they self-indulgence or a sacrifice? I have often thought how many ways there are of attaining happiness and how curiously my footsteps seem picked so as to avoid them all but the most prolonged & weary. I am fond of Physical science and I believe not unsuccessful in it; but I must give it up. I am fond of music and would gladly study it thoroughly and with constant pleasure devote a life to it. Yet I hope it will never take up so much of my time as it even now does. I have seen people here marry upon $\frac{1}{3}$ part of my income, and have almost envied them a pretty quiet little cottage and a pretty quiet little wife. Dont think it foolish of me to say that the idea of myself under such circumstances was highly pleasing. Nor would its realization be a matter of much difficulty if I were only a reasonable person.

Among other things less imaginary, the *Overland Route* presents itself. A few months here, and a few on the way would appear nothing if I felt I was hastening home to England. That would be self indulgence indeed. At present it seems anything but self indulgence to interpose a year of solitary travelling. Unless the pleasure of moving about and seeing the world drives away home-sickness, which at present I scarcely expect, it will be a sacrifice. To be at home again is a pleasure which at present I cannot realize. Past recollections scarcely serve to form anticipations. The thing itself is so essentially changed, and on my part all thoughts & habits have grown up almost in ignorance or independence of the comforts & solid advantages of home. At present the seas seem too wide, the mountains too high & rugged, man's contrivances too imperfect, men themselves too wicked & heartless, external fortune too fickle, and my internal frame too delicate & feeble, that my voyage should be successfully prosecuted even to a temporary haven.

In previous letters which I hope have been seen by no one but yourself and Lucy, I have told you even too openly what my views are. To a certain extent a man has not freedom; there are obligations to parents, brothers, sisters, friends, which perhaps even nothing can dissolve. In theory at all events, it is my wish to discharge such obligations; perhaps from my nature & temper I have not done so properly. But beyond this it must be allowed that every one has the time, abilities and possessions at his own disposal. All this would I devote to one single comprehensive purpose – to effect in the most direct and suitable manner, the greatest possible amount of good in the world. How it can best be done I do not pretend to say. Internal capabilities and external opportunities must show the mode; the *will* must develope* itself into a *way*. At present it seems to me that quiet diligent study is the way. There are various classes of men & minds, ranging from the most theoretical to the most practical. A great mathematician, metaphysician, or the discoverer of any remote & abstract principle is a great good to all succeeding generations; few perhaps know it, and none actually feel the benefit, for it is widely diffused. At the other extremity are to be placed, mechanical men, inventors of every kind, and all those public men who carry on the constant thread of business. I might prefer to be a practical man; to see the effect plainly following the cause; to have those about me acknowledging the usefulness of each production or effort.

But say what people like, *disposition* is a certain fact. Habits are a thing difficult to alter but inward character, united to bodily constitution is almost immutable. Now as you know my character is very strongly & unfortunately marked in certain respects. I do not, perhaps cannot, bear a bold front. What I am is not written in my appearance & manner. I feel no personal influence even with a child. It is only by the gentle immaterial influence of mind, motive or opinion that I effect anything. Perhaps you will tell me that to overcome such a great obstacle to usefulness should be my first purpose. Demosthenes the greatest of orators we know had to overcome an obstacle before he could speak plain. But the parallel cannot be maintained. My obstacle is of the most deep-seated nature; it could scarcely be eradicated, therefore it would always tend to grow up again. It would be an obstacle always to be opposed. How much better then to use ones efforts in a direction where no such obstacle exists. And such a direction I think I can almost point out.

It seems to me that *Man* is a subject as little understood now as the *Heavens* (Astronomy) were by the Ancients. Within the last hundred years, sciences almost innumerable have sprung up, but mostly devoted to physical Nature. Comparatively few have perceived that Human

Nature may also be the subject of a science. It is indeed a many-sided subject. Religion, metaphysics, ethics, jurisprudence political economy, politics, & even, medicine, art, poetry and many other studies all have man for the subject. But the social condition of man as influenced by the many internal & external circumstances is perhaps an indefinite but a wide & rich field for future research. Do not think from what I have said above that I consider my unfortunate disposition to include every fault, and that I therefore think it the easiest way never to oppose any of these faults. By no means

---

The fearful irregularity of the mails & other unfortunate circumstances have put a stop to all *correspondence* properly so called. I cannot expect *answers* but I do hope for letters. Lately I waited for two months and thought it long. Remember that after a few months more, it will be useless for you to write to me any more. I shall be without any *direction*; I shall be homeless, and for a whole year I shall have little chance even of hearing of home.

I have carefully considered what few words I have from Lucy & you, with a view to learning what is of so much interest to me – what you are doing and thinking. To know that you are happy would I hope under all circumstances be a pleasure to me, independently of everything else. But there is happiness of many kinds. Some happiness is like a *passing playful smile*. It is produced without effort and itself it yields nothing, but leaves emptiness behind. Should I wish to see you thus passingly happy? I neither wish it nor fear it, for I know you can recognise beneath an exterior that has few inviting points, whose face has a grave & wearied look, that happiness which will not pass away. It arises out of vigourous,* consistent & long-continued efforts, directed by good intentions. Opportunities & capabilities vary, but happiness may be sought by all according to their circumstances and will assuredly be found. The playful smile misleads many or perhaps most; they forget the empty and annoyed look which that face will sooner or later wear. I should not fear as to which kind of happiness you would on reflection, choose, and I hope nothing may prevent such reflections having place in your mind.

But I am lead* now to consider what way of life is best to attain such happiness & work out such purposes as I have here alluded to. Is solitude or society best? I have little hesitation in saying that continual intimate acquaintance with great numbers of persons is quite inconsistent with serious reflection & the pursuit of serious purposes. I allude only to persons of your or my age; I need not here enquire concerning others. I have seen it stated in books & can understand myself that continual intercourse with others must deprive the mind of its characteristic points, especially those *buds of truth* which are yet small, unperceived things, so lightly attached as to be easily rubbed away. The mind must vegetate undisturbed before these buds can become developed into branches, firm & useful. Yet I would not shut a person up in a cellar any more than the plant. Both require air, and sun, and suitable nourishment

Now I very much fear that a gay unsettled life is just what would rub off from your mind many buds of truth of which I have caught a glimpse. In plain words I do not like to hear of too much visiting. My experience of life has not shown me that much is to be learnt from others, or that there is much incitement in ordinary friendship to anything beyond ordinary friendship. It is the playful passing smile. In common life the best of people even do not wear their souls outside; at the best they behave decently & kindly towards you. If therefore you form your ideas of the way of spending life from what you see around you, you cannot be above *commonplace*. If you possess any points of peculiar value, I fear that constant familiar contact with others will soon wear them away. No one can rise above the common level if he do not cherish within him an almost secret soul to animate & guide him. Partial solitude is necessary to earnest thoughts. I might give many instances to prove this; I will only notice one which is closely applicable viz. *Charlotte Bronte*, who had few or no friends except her sisters & lived in a quiet retired home.[1]

I do not deny that a gay life & wide acquaintanceship has many advantages. You gain a knowledge of the diversities of human character. In this respect I am in danger of being deficient. By plenty of visiting you will become a very agreable,* well behaved, model young-lady. I shall be charmed to see you singing, dancing, dressing, chatting to the admiration of a room full of people; but these, as I have said are things of passing charm. I hope there will be many a serious thought beneath the trivial words & smiles which you must wear in ordinary life.

I dare say that Lucy rather fears the peculiar & earnest disposition which seems to belong to our family. It upset Roscoe's health; it has injured Herberts health & somewhat unsettled him. If I may speak to you of Lucy, I should say that it has less affected her, because her mind equally earnest is of somewhat different mould; instead of doubting & enquiring, it learns & believes; it is in the attitude of *Faith*. For myself I have a body which has never failed me yet, and my mind has never felt the least oppression; I hope that I can rightly balance the outward everyday routine of work against the inward will. However much I may sometimes be perplexed as to the grounds of duty and the

---

[1] See the comment on the subject of 'visiting' quoted by Jevons from Mrs Gaskell's *Life of Charlotte Brontë* in an undated Journal entry, Vol. I, p. 178.

nature of life, I always see my way far enough for another day's journey. I feel sure from the open happy disposition which you possess more than any of your elders that your thoughts & course if serious will not be gloomy.

I have a little to say upon another point, viz *money* which commands the comforts & conveniences of life. To give up a good salary here with only the chance of getting a poor one in England has slightly distressed me when I remembered that Lucy & you are accustomed to a very comfortable home, & a fair share of pleasures. I cannot think it likely that for a long time at least we shall have money at our command to obtain equal comforts & pleasures. In your present round of visits, too, you will see a very agreable* easy side of life, & perhaps acquire expensive habits which may prove incompatible with our keeping house, supposing that I only succeeded in getting a small income. For myself I care not a *rap* for money; but I am aware how precious it might become, and how seriously its absence might interfere with prospects of happiness.

August 9th Excuse the preceding long lecture, and do not think that I am not happy. My spirits are becoming rather variable now that such a great change approaches, & when I feel most gloomily disposed I begin a letter to you. I am much afraid that in your round of visiting which has to be continued for a year & a half more, your music will be sadly neglected.

I am *fonder* of music than ever. I have chiefly worshipped Mendelssohn* of late, and consider him the most alluring & delightful of composers though not the most profound, or grand. His works too are so diversified. I suppose you know some or all of his "Songs without words." If not I shall in a few months be sending them to you with all my musical library. They are the most delightful pianoforte music ever written; the melodies are simple but beautiful & the running accompaniments which add the chief charm are most ingenious & surprising.

The following two[2] are my chief favourites

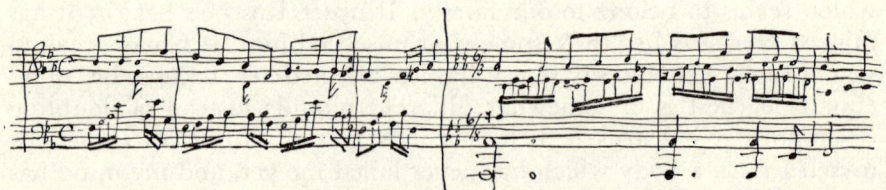

I have also been playing Mendelsohn's* hymn. 'Come let us Sing'[3] a good deal. One or two pieces in it are very beautiful. This evening I

---

[2] Jevons wrote 'too' here. The passages he quotes are from Mendelssohn's *Songs without Words*, book 6, op. 67, No. 31 in E flat (1843) and book 3, op. 38, No. 18 in A flat, 'Duetto' (1836).   [3] Mendelssohn's Psalm 95, op. 46 (1839).

repeated one of my most cheerful programmes You may judge of it by the following list.

1. Waltz (a most beautiful one ending with a long descending trill; you must know it)   Beethoven.
2. Waltz. 'Le Desir'.   – do –
3. Waltz. Duke of Reichstadt's   Strauss.[4]
4. Waltz's, 3 or 4 more ordinary ones   Beethoven.[5]
5. 'Ah Perdona'   Mozart.[6]
6. La Marseillaise.
7. Mourir pour la Patrie.
8. Serenade, the beautiful, from Don Pasquale.[7]
9. Weber's *Last Waltz*.[8]

The last piece is I suppose the most intensely expressive & beautiful piece ever written. The first part of it expresses the "last long lingering look." The second part is more full of agitated feeling, & you will see is an exact representation of *sobbing*. The third part has a more subdued & patient tone but the effect of repeating the first part at the end, with more slowness and impressiveness is unparalleled.

And now, Dear Henny, good bye. I'll warrant that all your spare time for the next month wont be sufficient for reading this over three times.

    I am
        Your affectionate Brother
            W S J.

121. W. S. JEVONS TO LUCY JEVONS

            S. R. Mint.
            Sept 10th/58.

My dearest Lucy

I commence a letter without much hope that it will be either long or interesting. The mail of course is not in, so that I have nothing requiring answer, and I already begin to experience that unstable condition of mind which usually precedes a great change. Three months and a half yet remain, a short period indeed, but the move

[4] By Johann Strauss the Elder (1833).
[5] None of the waltzes known to have been composed by Beethoven answer the descriptions given here by Jevons. However, there is a set of six waltzes of doubtful authenticity, the first of which, 'Sehnsuchtwalzer', might well be translated 'Le Desir'.
[6] 'Ah perdona al primo affeto', a duet from Mozart's *La Clemenza di Tito* (K. 621, No. 7).
[7] Arrangement of the Serenata 'Com'è gentil' from Act 3 of Donizetti's *Don Pasquale*.
[8] Probably Weber's *Auffordung zum Tanz*, op. 65 (1819). This work was well known in England with the title word mistranslated as 'waltz'.

seems already to have commenced because Bolton is on the point of leaving the Mint. In short Sydney is in a partial *gold fever*, a new diggings having been discovered some 600 or 700 miles to the North at a place called Port Curtis and most of those who have not a certain employment are moving in that direction. Now Boltons place has never been very secure and Capt Ward is very fond of saying he wont need him long. A short time since he distinctly said he would only keep him to the end of the year. Everyone seemed to think therefore that Bolton had better embrace the present opportunity which is just what he himself would most like to do. He has often spoken of going to the diggings and perhaps a little excitement & open air life would be by no means a bad thing.[1] I do not think that the hope of any very extravagant gains enters into many peoples heads.

He goes with Maurice OConnell, Mrs Miller's brother, who has been chiefly out of employment for a long time, and has lived with us. He has been my only companion almost in all excursions & walks so that I may say that I lose in them two of my chief friends. They will form a very suitable couple of diggers ready for every turn, provided only that Bolton does not overwork himself at first. I think he would soon become accustomed to heavy work. The place will be very hot, being just within the tropics, so that in the summer the sun will be vertical at noon, but Bolton does not feel the heat in Sydney at all, although occasionally it is as great as anything you are likely to experience elsewhere. In tropical parts it is more continued & equable.

I am of course very sorry to lose Charles as an assistant but it is only for a few months. Supposing that the diggings turn out well my first trip will be direct there. The journey is only a sea-voyage of a week, and a walk of 30 miles. I shall there see a little real wild life & have splendid subjects for photography. Imagine a photograph of a real diggings in active operation.[2]

Since last writing I have not been much engaged upon anything whatever, but have commenced the photograph season, as you will see by the enclosed pictures. I hope you see some signs of improvement.

I have finished an essay of about 60 or 70 pages, on the Climate of Australia, which I shall have published free in the Sydney Almanack* at the end of this year.[3] This will conclude all my writings for the

---

[1] After the death of Charles Bolton's wife, Jevons commented 'His has been a life of wearisome & generally thankless toil . . .' (diary entry for 25 August 1857). There is among the Jevons papers a letter dated Christmas Day 1858 from Charles Bolton, written in pencil on pages taken from a notebook, in which he describes life and conditions at the goldfields.

[2] See Vol. I, Plate 3, facing p. 15.

[3] In his list of 'Work to be done' during the year in the diary for 1858, Jevons included 'Work on Climate of Australia'. On 30 January he made the following entry: 'I have great thoughts at present of undertaking a small work on "the Climate of NSW & Australia from data original or Compiled" to be published as soon as possible after I have terminated my

present. I am quite silenced too by the bankruptcy of the "Empire" newspaper, which happened suddenly a few weeks ago.[4]

I scarcely know what to think of my home prospects. Pleasure, you may depend I feel at the prospect of seeing you and Henny & Tommy again, perhaps in a home of our own, but how many serious considerations are intermixed. It is quite natural I think that I should not always feel very light-hearted. The sensation of self-distrust, approaching to despondency, is one to which many people are liable & myself among them. It may be a good quality rather than otherwise, but it is not a pleasant one. I can remember feeling almost in the same manner with regard to coming out here. I can only hope that I shall have as little trouble on the next occasion. Herbert mentions that Uncle T & H. J.[5] regard my intended changes as the "greatest folly"; I am afraid they must think our family, one and all, as most obstinate stupid people always running against their own interests. You have shown yourself just as bad as the rest of us I suspect as regards Tommy's education, and your opposition to his entering the office (Of course he remains for his B.A. In a few months I shall be sending my money home to the care of Uncle Timothy, £100 to be for Tommy's use when necessary) If we all live long enough perhaps there may yet be reason to acknowledge that we did not act so very wrong in following our own ideas.

Charles Bolton is now no longer engaged by the Mint, and will only come for a day or two to teach the new assistant. I am rather glad he should leave a short time before me so that I may see him quite on his own footing before I go away altogether, and if his first spec. does not answer help him to another. Perhaps you had better write a note to Ann Bolton & tell her about his affairs, with my best remembrances. Charles is not writing himself.

The change seems very sudden for me, and disappoints me of many excursions to which I looked forward this summer. I shall now have to go almost by myself. But a few short months more and I shall be missed

---

series of observations next July. I think I could render it a work of considerable interest, by introducing plenty of various information & occasional discussions . . .' On 1 February he wrote: 'In evening began "Climate of Australia"'. Entries in this diary were discontinued after 4 February 1858 and not resumed until 1860.

This presumably formed the basis of his article 'Some Data Concerning the Climate of Australia and New Zealand' (Waugh's *Australian Almanac for the Year 1859*, pp. 47–98), which La Nauze describes as an 'extensive discussion in seven chapters, including many statistics from Jevons' own observations and the collation of explorers' journals, newspaper reports, etc. Shows his constant searching for 'laws', and his interest in weather cycles . . .' (op. cit., p. 44).

[4] In August 1858. It was revived after Jevons's departure under the management of Samuel Bennett (1815–78), superintendent of a printing office, who bought the paper in 1858. La Nauze, op. cit., p. 39.

[5] Timothy Jevons and his son Henry.

from the Mint myself and shall no longer be an assayer. I have always felt Charles to be somewhat of a charge upon me, although I was glad to see how much more independent, & healthy, and cheerful he has lived here than in the old Dale Street Bank.[6] He has had his own house, his servant-maid, & for a time his wife. When Herbert talked of coming to N. Z. I thought that he might give him work but if the new diggings turn out well I hope the difficulty will be solved.

Last Sunday I went to Middle Harbour with OConnell who considers it as beautiful as the Lakes of Killarney with the exception of the want of very high land. We did not go very far as the weather looked suspicious and I failed in what photographs I tried. You cannot imagine the beauty of the wild flowers this spring; we saw great masses of flowering *creepers* such as the *clematis* quite covering small trees. A great many bushes too are in flower. The *rock-lily*, a magnificent kind of *orchis* is also bearing long spikes of white flowers; we have planted a number in a kind of rockery at Double Bay of which I send a photograph. It does not show it well but you see the dark leaves of the lily, the flowers behind. At each side is a *young* tree fern and at the right hand side some small *stag-horn ferns*. We found in Middle Harbour the finest mass of stag-horn fern I ever saw, about four feet wide growing on the edge of a rock. We brought about half of it home in the boat.[7] These are vegetable beauties which you homebirds have only a chance of seeing carefully doctored up in some English Conservatory

But now I must finish. I am sending a newspaper to Tommy at College and if I can finish a letter for him to night I will send it by the supplementary mail to Melbourne. My best love to Henny.
     Believe me your
      Affectionate Brother.
       W. S. Jevons.

122. W. S. JEVONS TO H. E. ROSCOE

Sydney. Oct 9th 1858.[1]

My dear Doctor,

I address you by a dignified & safe title, feeling great compunctions as to whether the more natural & familiar address of 'My dear Harry'

---

[6] Before going to Australia, Charles Bolton had been employed by Moss's Bank, which had been opened at 4, Exchange Buildings, Liverpool and was moved in September 1811 to a new building in Dale Street. It occupied these premises until 1864, when it became a joint-stock bank and the building was reconstructed (Hughes, op. cit., pp. 192-5). See above, Letter 24, n. 4, p. 44.

[7] Here Jevons began a small sketch of this plant, on the left hand side of the page, but crossed it out.

[1] Jevons pasted an oval-shaped portion of a small photograph at the head of this letter and wrote beside it: 'North Head of P. Jackson looking outwards'.

is fitting towards a professor. We still, I am glad to say, enjoy here the pleasure of writing letters, but the arrival of a Royal Mail is a most unlooked for and unlikely event. For two months we have now been without letters & almost without news from England and you may easily imagine how unsatisfactory is this state of suspense. A person could never be thoroughly comfortable here unless he were to take a stake & perhaps a wife in this country & disconnect himself more or less with home affairs.

I received two letters from you sometime since which were quite a boon, but you became again silent. I have to thank you most warmly for the Sun-instrument of Mr Campbell's,[2] just as if it had been received. But it seems unfortunately to have missed; Herbert left it with the ship agents in Liverpool, but as he had several times done before, did not obtain a bill of lading. I went down to the ship on its arrival here but they knew nothing of it, and so I fear it is lost, especially as Herbert is not now in Liverpool to enquire after it. This is very vexing.

I am now fully prepared & very impatient to leave the Mint. Though some of my English friends may think this step rash & foolish, & though you will perhaps shake your head & wish that 'something certain' should turn up first, yet I am sure you will not misjudge me. To explain all my motives is more than I could profess to do, or think necessary, but my main argument in favour of leaving is this – Every year I spend here is so much cash in pocket, but curtails by so much the time yet open to me for improvement and for qualifying myself for any position I may desire. My actions now will influence me for life, and a few hundred pounds weigh very light in the balance of my mind against the satisfactory employment of the many future years I look forward to. I have heard that prosperity tries a man's metal even more than adversity. His elasticity yields to the seducing ease & pleasant inaction of the former while the hard blows of the latter unless they actually break the spring must call into play an equivalent reacting force. But of all enervating employments perhaps a well paid Government post is the worst, and adding to this the isolation of colonial life, the many difficulties in the way of study, and the few other pleasures which present themselves, and you have the sum of what I object to in my residence here.

I have learned to detest the Government Service. It might perhaps be better under another Head than Capt W. but I expect it is the same everywhere. The hours of work are short, & our employment light & accomodating.* I do not complain of this; but you know I am not naturally lazy and am always eagerly employed in some pursuit. Now this is what the Gov^t Service does not admit of; whatever other fruits

[2] See above, Letter 116, p. 323.

my labours here may have borne I have at all events earned the dislike of Capt W. who is the very model of the military official & skilled diplomatist. Although he is supposed to have a scientific reputation, I have scarcely exchanged half a dozen words with him on any scientific subject and lately he has even begun to obstruct me in the management of the assays Miller & I are both too independent for him, and some terrible rows would I think ensue if I had not now the *nonchalance* of one about to move to other scenes. If on the contrary I were about to settle here, I should shape myself very differently & devote my time to cultivating flowers & to catching fish in the Harbour.

But how glorious are the prospects before me; come what will afterwards I have time & money at my disposal to travel & see the world. How happy I shall feel when I am again on the Blue ocean; there are some who do not know its pleasures, poor wretches. And then to travel hundreds of miles over the wild interior of Australia, to visit the tropical Fitzroy river, to cross the strange internal watercourses of Australia, to see Ballaarat* & Bendigo, & every place of interest in Victoria. Of my furthur* travels I will not speak as I cannot be sure where they will lie.

I am at present pretty busily employed in finishing up various subjects, I am commencing too the photographic season, and send you rather a poor specimen of my art. My photographs never attain perfection as you see but then I always work out of doors in a tent, which is far more difficult than working in a comfortable dark room with all the conveniences of a laboratory. It is almost impossible too to produce good prints in my small dirty assay office, but I shall preserve the negative plates to print in England.

As it will be very interesting to test the value of my sungauge by observations in various parts of the world I am trying to construct reliable ones & to determine their average results in Sydney. My mode of observation will be to expose the sungauge on a cloudless day and to divide the observed reading by the line of the sun's elevation either observed roughly by a pocket sextant & art. horizon, or calculated from the Nau. Alm. (I have bought a first rate compensating gold watch to give the time accurately). I have finished a small & very convenient little instrument only about 8 inches long which gives about a millimetre per minute as the result, but the vacuum is not quite perfect nor have I been able to produce any perfect vacuum. I find no difficulty now in hermetically sealing the tube but however long & carefully I boil the water the air is never quite expelled as it should be. Perhaps after all I must put the matter into the hands of Flavelles the instrument sellers, who say they can make it but Heaven knows only whether they will do it properly & how many pounds they will charge. They have seen the length of my purse already. It seems to me that the absolute perpendicular intensity of the sun's rays can vary but little in different climates.

I have carried on with success my improved manipulations in the assay process by which 16 numbered 'Comets' or less are boiled together in one flask instead of being treated in separate small flasks. The increased facility of the process is evident; it is what they were always trying to accomplish at Graham's & Miller's but could not do.³ I shall probably write a short paper on the subject of Mint Assaying including my improvements which I will get you to send to some practical chemical journal.⁴ By the bye* it rejoiced my heart to see my last paper on Clouds in the fore most part of the Phil. Mag.⁵ for which I have a high respect. As yet I do not know that any notice has been taken of my views, but I am convinced in my own mind that I have lead* the way to a rational mode of treating atmospheric subjects; I have a perfect belief in the theory of the Cirrus, and have no doubt that my views of the cumulostratus, thundercloud, & even of the electricity of the latter will prove correct. I am quite reconciled to the expectation that every thing which I have said will be attributed to some previous writer or adopted by some subsequent one, so that I shall be quite shorn of all credit. The Revᵈ W Scott,⁶ colonial astronomer & meteorologist, proclaimed mine as 'no new theory' here in our Scientific Mag. but in the succeeding number I gave him a smarting answer.⁷

I am becoming quite accustomed to the pen as a weapon of offence & defence, indeed I suffer under such a rage for writing that I am scarcely to be trusted with a pen in my hand. I often write a newspaper

---

³ Jevons had been experimenting with this process for some time: he wrote in his diary on 23 October 1857, 'Occupied during this week at Mint chiefly with the new mode of boiling the assays, the comets being numbered & put 16 or a less number together in a large flask. The first few days the correction was very variable and gave some trouble, and one comet being defective had to be repeated but nothing in the least to be called a failure occurred from the first.' See above, Letter 94, p. 247.

⁴ This probably formed the basis of 'Gold Assay', one of a number of articles which he contributed to Henry Watts' *Dictionary of Chemistry* between January and August 1861.

⁵ i.e. his article 'On the Forms of Clouds', *London . . . . Philosophical Magazine* (April 1858), xv, 241–55.

⁶ See above, Letter 118, n. 1, p. 329.

⁷ See above, Letters 118 and 94 n. 7, pp. 329 and 244. To this 'smarting answer' Scott replied temperately in a letter dated 7 July, 1858, *Sydney Magazine of Science and Art*, II, 35.

In his paper read before the Sydney Philosophical Society in December 1857 and published in the *Sydney Magazine of Science and Art* in January 1858, Jevons concluded that '. . . the forms assumed by clouds . . . are solely determined by simple dynamical causes . . . [and] . . . it is unnecessary to suppose that electricity possesses any active agency in the production or modification of clouds . . .' (quoted, La Nauze, op. cit., pp. 41–2). This drew a response in the May number of the magazine from Rev. Scott, who had read a paper 'On the Meteorology of New South Wales' to the Philosophical Society on 14 October 1857. He commented that Jevons's view that electricity did not affect cloud forms was 'no new theory', to which Jevons replied in his letter the following month (above, p. 329).

article and am then on thorns for ever so long after for fear of a libel action. But alas! my organ the 'Empire' has passed away in bankruptcy and I am now reduced to that milk & water affair the 'Herald' which too has not yet learned to appreciate me, and sticks to small type, on the back pages, whereas Parkes always gave me large type next after the leading article, & usually reprinted me for the monthly summaries.

I send you the monthly summary of the Herald which is certainly a wonderful publication for a single day; the number of copies sold too is something enormous. You will find in it every scrap of colonial news; I draw your attention especially to the New Diggings discovered at the Fitzroy River, Port Curtis on the NE coast (lat 23°) The sudden rush of diggers was preposterous and many thousands are either there or on their way, while it is yet doubtful whether there is any gold to get or any food to eat in the wild new tropical country. The worst is that my assistant Bolton who accompanied me from Liverpool went with another of my friends among the first. I advised him to it on a general calculation of probabilities before the gold fever attained any height; but still they may do something & if not they have money to carry them back. If gold is not found in plenty there will be one or two thousand penniless & destitute men in an[8] uninhabited country. Supposing the diggings to be satisfactory I shall start for them in about 3 months & a rare trip it will be. Gold digging photographing, botanising, geologising, & living a wild free life in a tent amid tropical scenery. I shall be able, too, to use my Sungauge under a vertical Sun. This 'rush' is said almost to equal the great rushes of 1851 & 2. It was a strange thing to see the crowd of gold diggers, each with his one or two mates, and a 'swag' of tent, blankets, cradle, prospecting pan, etc. Carts & horses, boats, stores etc are also shipped with wonderful rapidity, and even government has sent 12 policemen, a few officials & a hospital in the shape of an iron hut. We have received & assayed small quantities of the gold at the Mint. You would scarcely believe what a general move a gold fever creates; several working men have gone even from Double Bay leaving their 'grass widows' & families to vegetate in their absence. Every person has his list of acquaintance & neighbours who are on the move.

Very lately I called at the commission agents place where Aunt H's drawings are left; the proceeds are as yet represented by $£\sqrt{} - 1$.

I often think with pleasure of your agreable* position in England and of the opportunities you had in Germany. Indeed if there is any man I envy it is a professor. Still when I knew you in London, you devoted all your prospects to a pursuit of which the primary results are never very

[8] 'a' in the original manuscript.

brilliant & often long deferred. Even well off as you now are,[9] you may perhaps be considered to have better luck than many Scientific men. Do not blame me therefore, for abandoning a good salary because it interferes with other desirable things, even if I starve in consequence, as is not improbable.

The first year of your lectures would not perhaps leave you much time for original research, but I suppose it will afterwards be almost your chief employment. I shall consider it a great pleasure to talk chemical subjects over with you at some future time but I am now you know no chemist. Manchester will be a bad place I should expect for sun experiments.

There is naturally much that I shall regret to leave here such as[10] A pretty suburban residence with water frontage & a boat which renders an excursion to some part of the Harbour an almost irresistible counter attraction to the Unitarian Chapel on a Sunday Morning. It is a fine

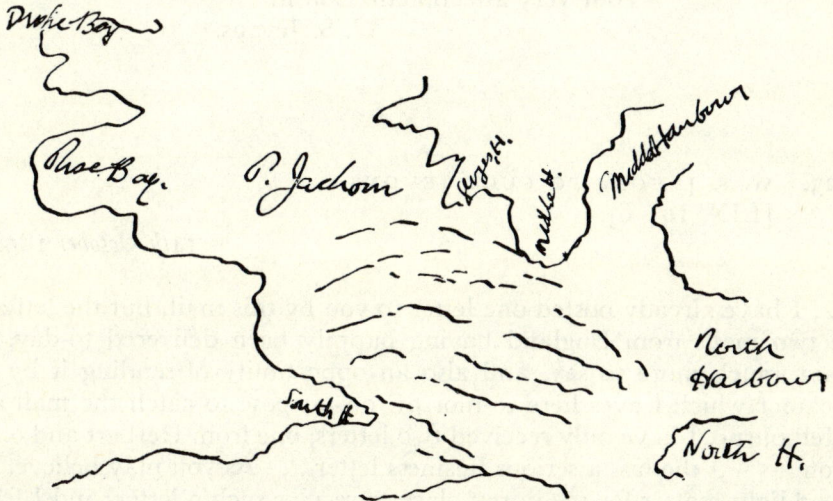

thing too in calm weather to go round Middle Head where the extremely long & incessant swell of the Southern Oceans rolls slowly in but breaks grandly with a loud roar, and a vast burst of spray upon the projecting rocks. My last excursion was to North Harbour where I had a very pleasant day with the engineer of the Mint, my shipmate in the 'Oliver Lang'.[11] Middle Harbour is a very picturesque uninhabited place branching into a number of bays surrounded by high rocky slopes clothed in dark bush, but in the moist gullies choked up by

[9] Jevons first wrote, 'Even if you are well off now'.
[10] Jevons added these two words without altering the next sentence.
[11] i.e. Joseph Newton.

a beautiful vegetation. It is said somewhat to resemble the Lakes of Killarney on a small scale. So great is the length of the shores that hundreds of pic-nic excursions might be accomodated* with private delightful dells at the same time. I have not yet succeeded in getting photographs of it.[12]

For the present I bid you good bye. I look to you for a few letters before I leave here because afterwards I shall receive none. Indeed after getting this letter you must quickly write a last one or none at all. I may not be here at all after the end of February. I shall take care to let you know my progress, and though I make no rash promises I will see what I can do towards forwarding a series of specimens from the gold fields. There are no facilities for collecting here, beyond picking things up and putting them in your pocket, and gold diggers are a jealous race.

Give my kindest remembrances to my Aunt. To yourself I remain
Your very affectionate Cousin
W. S. Jevons.

123. W. S. JEVONS TO LUCY JEVONS
[LJN, 104–6]

14th October 1858.

... I have already posted one letter to you by this mail, but the letters of two mails from England having happily been delivered to-day, I have much more to say, and also an opportunity of sending it by a steamer which leaves here to-morrow on purpose to catch the mail at Melbourne. I have only received two letters, one from Herbert and one from ———,[1] the last a serious business letter ... As you may believe, it is no light matter for me in my place to receive such a letter, and I feel at the moment as if I had more upon my shoulders than ever before, even than in that dreadful week which passed a sentence of transportation upon me. It is one of those things which strike you with the chill of money, and which sums up all that is desirable, good, and necessary, in fact life itself, into a total income of £ s. d. Show that you can provide this cold metallic coin, and virtue, worth, enlightenment may be followed as ornaments and accomplishments. Pleasure is

---

[12] For Jevons's significance as a photographer, see Vol. I, p. 31. Two albums containing photographs taken while he was in Australia are among the Jevons Papers.

[1] Probably his cousin Henry Jevons, who appears to have looked after family financial affairs (see above, Letter 21, n. 2, p. 38). He was still living at the time of the publication of LJ, which may account for Mrs Jevons's unwillingness to name the person in question.

measured simply as the expenditure of so much money, and he who lives at £1000 per annum is in the world's eye five times as happy as he who spends but £200. Is a man thus posted up in his cash-book? Is everything thus 'closed with golden bars, and opened but with golden keys?' . . . But I am very glad, while about to take a step which I can never retrace, that the most chilling view of things should be presented to me. Nothing could have come more in the nick of time than this letter, for only a day or two since I was hesitating whether to wait for the mail before giving notice of my intended resignation. Now I scarcely waver in my resolution, but I act with the greatest reluctance and heaviness of spirits. . . . I may find out my mistake some day, perhaps I may drawl away a wretched existence sometime, but I declare that in my present state of mind I am ready to throw myself into the battle of life for mortal combat, and to strip myself of everything for the purpose of paying debts of affection while I can, and then of providing as far as possible for a successful issue. I verily believe I do not, and will not, spare myself, but it must be a cause of increasing regret if I inflict anything upon others. . . . As to the college I do not now decide, but I am sure that another year's regular hard study, especially at my increased age, will be invaluable, and its loss would be regretted to the end of my life. I am often now much vexed at my want of knowledge which I should in another year obtain, and have already been impeded by it. It has occurred to me that in returning to England I may seem to disregard the opinions and wishes of my father, who certainly influenced me to come here, but I do not think it is so. Could he have foreseen things as they are, I believe he would not have sent me here – he could not have been aware, as I was both reserved and but little conscious of it myself, of my entire devotion to serious views and studies, and he had also a somewhat exaggerated idea of my prospects here. They have been better than could reasonably have been expected, but my father seemed in his letters slightly disappointed. It is not true, also, that he wished me to stay here. On the contrary, he distinctly said that he could not bear to let me go if, after some years, he did not hope to see me again. And now that he is gone, is the bond which connects me with home entirely dissolved? and are the circumstances entirely changed which in his opinion rendered a return judicious? But I am quite certain that if at the time I had stated my wish for further study and a different start in life, he would have immediately agreed. Am I wrong, then, in carrying out such views at present, or is it much worse to refuse a good salary after four or five years' benefit from it, than from the first? . . . I feel the cold weight of the decision I am making as I never felt it before, although it was always a serious subject. . . .

124. W. S. JEVONS TO THE EDITOR OF THE
SYDNEY MORNING HERALD

[29 October 1858]

CANOONA DIGGINGS[1] IN A SCIENTIFIC ASPECT

Sir,

It is surprising that so little information has been hitherto published as to the physical features of the so-called diggings on the Fitzroy River. Having received a very minute and trustworthy account of the locality from a person who was there, and prospected in the neighbourhood of Canoona, together with a small series of mineralogical specimens from the place itself, I will attempt partially to supply the deficiency. At the same time, it is open for the many competent persons who must have a personal acquaintance with the diggings to correct any errors into which I may fall.

The wide and very flat alluvial lands of the Fitzroy are broken about 35 or 40 miles from Rockhampton, by steep, stony, barren ranges, or *tiers* of serpentine rock. These, with their spurs and branches, are so numerous, intricate, and perfectly similar in aspect, that it is almost impossible for a person to find his way back to a place from which he has travelled a few miles. Many diggers, it is to be feared, will loose [*sic*] themselves while prospecting, and die a solitary and miserable death. The diggings of Canoona lie in a small valley, or rather a wide flat-bottomed gulf, enclosed on three sides by serpentine ridges of some elevation; the upper or north end is not, however, quite closed, since two narrow gorges or crevices there divide the range. The bottom of the valley is separated into two very distinct parts, the lower of which is a real alluvial flat composed of black clay and earth, in which a scanty supply of water is found by sinking numerous wells, while the upper part is covered by small *rises*, or hillocks, which appear to be formed of disintegrated rock and other *debris*. It is among this that the gold was found.

The following is a list and description of the principal specimens:-

1. Massive serpentine rock, of the usual characteristics; the ranges are entirely formed of this.
2. Fragment of a very hard *chert* boulder found lying on the surface; this consists of serpentine rock, altered by an infusion of quartz, in the form of chalcedony.
3. Soft white stone of less gravity than water, and of the nature of *meerschaum*; this would probably be termed *tufa*.

[1] Thousands of prospectors had rushed to a goldfield in Queensland known variously as Canoona, Port Curtis, Fitzroy and Rockhampton in the spring of 1858; the 'rush' proved to be a disaster. Cf. above, Letter 121 and Blainey, op. cit., p. p. 84.

4. Compact pure white mineral, the same as No. 3, only very much indurated and altered by heat.
5. White opalescent mineral, harder than glass, but of a very much fractured and contracted form; the same substance as Nos. 3 and 4, still more altered. Diggers call this *burnt quartz*.
6. Portion of a mass of disintegrated or decomposed serpentine rock from around and among which the Canoona gold was almost entirely taken.
7. Highly vesicular volcanic scoria, from the surface of the ground.
8. A peculiar black, soapy, magnesian clay, forming the flat of Canoona.

All these substances, with the exception of No. 7, and the quartz in No. 2, are magnesian minerals, derived from, or closely related to serpentine; but it is evident that, at the locality in question, a disturbance of an igneous or volcanic nature has taken place. Thus specimen 2 was formed, and thus the very distinct series of minerals (3 to 5) were produced. In the valley of Canoona there seems to exist no vestige of the quartz and slate rocks with which gold is nearly always associated. On the contrary, small nuggets and coarse grains, of a peculiar character and covered by a black crust, are found in considerable quantity, close together and within a few feet of the surface, in the midst of these serpentinous minerals. The surrounding parts of the same valley, and even the alluvial flat below, appear to have contained mere traces only of gold, while diligent and repeated prospecting in the neighbourhood round (and we may be sure that spots of similar aspect to Canoona would be tried first) has failed in disclosing even the colour of gold.

The sudden and disastrous rush to the Fitzroy, unprecedented as it is even in Australia, seems to ahve been occasioned, in reality, by a *bone fide* discovery of gold equally unprecedented, in a scientific point of view, viz., a considerable and solitary mass of gold among serpentine rocks. The origin of the gold is at present a mystery, which it is very desirable that a competent geologist should attempt to clear up upon the spot. Considering all these remarkable circumstances, it is quite evident that we are not justified in arguing the existence of a great and paying gold-field in the far north, because any analogy between the present discovery and the great discoveries of Louisa Creek, Ballaarat,* &c., &c., is, as yet, non-existent. And I believe it was the common opinion of the many experienced diggers who visited Canoona, that it was unlike any gold field they ever saw, and was, in fact, not a gold country at all. The Rev. W. B. Clarke in asserting that gold would be discovered north of Moreton Bay, doubtless argued this from the existence of silurian rocks in contact with igneous rocks. His opinion may still hold good, as regards the long mountain tract, stretching north to Cape York, but is quite inapplicable to Canoona, where the rocks are so different.

One result of the scientific consideration of this question is, perhaps, to exonerate all parties of any considerable blame in causing the Fitzroy rush, and the great pecuniary loss attending it, amounting, probably, to £250,000, at least. A considerable discovery of gold did take place, and at the moment there were many reasonable inducements to suppose that a large gold-field might exist in the north. Yet statements were made as to the wide extent of auriferous country, which now fail to be realized, and while operating much on the public mind, must have been made quite at random.

It may also be well to guard your readers against attaching too much weight to scientific geological predictions. The prediction of Sir R. Murchison, that gold-fields would be found in the Australian cordillers, will be for ever famous, but has been realized to an extent, it must be particularly remarked, altogether beyond anything he could have expected. There is a certain probability, perhaps a certainty, that in particular rocks more or less gold will be found; but it is the quantity and mode in which the gold is found that determines the commercial part of the question. As regards this, the geologist is as much in the dark as the rest of his fellow men; he knows what will be his luck as little as the gambler, who is about to throw the dice. While it would be folly to spend any capital in searching for gold (and the same is the case with coal, and some other minerals), in formations where the geologist states that it never has, and, perhaps, cannot be found, it is also folly to risk much upon his legitimate counter-assertion, that gold will probably be found in such and such a place, and large nuggets may be found. It is evident that we deal only with scientific probabilities, of very moderate amount, and that fortune is, really, the goddess to whom the prospector should address his supplications.

W. S. J.

125. W. S. JEVONS TO LUCY JEVONS
[LJN, 106–9]

Sydney, 8th *November* 1858.

... The weather has been too changeable here of late to admit of successful excursions, but I am still stiff in my limbs from the last, which was an out and out one. Mr. Hunt of the mint agreed to go photographing with me, and accordingly we started about 2 P.M. last Saturday in company with Mr. MacCutcheon (mint clerk and my successor) for Middle Harbour, intending to camp it out all night and photograph in the calm clear air of early morning. Hunt's boat is a beautiful light skiff or wager boat named the *Terror*, and accounted the third or fourth best boat in the harbour. Still, with Hunt's good management it is very safe, and it soon carried us, with a very large amount of luggage, round Middle Head. Here our photographic zeal was so incited by the bold water-worn cliffs that we decided on landing my lighter apparatus, and taking them off, as the phrase is. The sky being very cloudy, and the cliffs looking away from the sun, this was not easily done, nor, after spending an hour and a half over four trials, did we get at all a perfect photograph. When Hunt and I had again packed up we were surprised to see the boat drifting away with no one apparently in her; MacCutcheon, who had engaged to keep her afloat away from the swell on the rocks, having lain down in the bottom of the boat and gone to dreamland. Shouting was of no avail, and after some twenty minutes we were much relieved to see an arm appear above the gunwale, and then a fellow looking about as if he did not know where he was. We now proceeded through the panoramic scenery of Middle Harbour, passing a succession of small coves with white sandy beaches, rocky headlands, picturesquely covered with trees, evergreen shrubs, and staghorn ferns, and better than all, little shady dells, where a gentle stream trickles down among moss and lichen-covered stones, between which grew luxuriantly the most beautiful shrubs, creepers, ferns, and orchids, again over-arched by noble old gum-trees. The photographer cannot leave these alluring little scenes without a pang of disappointment, and yet if he attempt them he will find that he cannot convey to the plate an impress of one-tenth part of their beauty. As we were now bent on taking the Willoughby Falls, we went at once up Waterfall Bay, at the head of which the falls are. Before we got there the sun was set, and the place was examined more with an eye to the comfortable lodgings it could afford than to its picturesqueness. At the falls there was plenty of water, but no sleeping-place. One overhanging rock near at hand, which would have done nicely, was already engaged by some occupant, of whom blankets, tin pots, candles, firewood, and matches were too plain a sign. As he was probably a black man, or, still worse, a drunken white man, and would probably arrive home some time in the night, we cleared away in the boat to the other side of the narrow bay, where we at last selected a small flat space of land upon a point, and just above the sea water. Fresh water we had brought with us from the falls, so we at once set to work in that co-operative busy manner which only those who are intensely and personally interested in the result employ, to erect the tent before dark, and cook the meal, for which we had so good an appetite. In a very short time we had a large sail forming a one-sided tent sloping towards a rock; at one side of this was our fire, lighted against an ancient log of wood blackened in some bush fire, or perhaps by a previous camping party. Water was soon boiled, and tea made, mutton chops were soon fried on forked sticks, and a quite elaborate meal was laid beneath the hut on the ground, well covered with oilskins and blankets. It was now dark, but candles and a lantern were forthcoming, which swung suspended from the tent pole and illumined our camp. Thus within our tent was civilised comfort, but stretching out your head, you looked around on a beautiful and perfectly natural scene of placid clear blue waters; on rocky shores sculptured by nature, and variously decked with shells and bright-coloured sea-weeds; on high, bold, rocky slopes, forming a succession of picturesque headlands, and including in every angle small rustic dells, the interior beauties of which were present to the mind, but not the eye; and on the sky above. All was now wrapped in darkness, so that sea and land and sky were nearly indistinguishable, but the impressions of beauty all seem to me present to the mind, even when thus veiled over; sounds, too, which are unnoticed but in the dead of night, are then strangely suggestive of pleasant images, the gush of water at the waterfall, the roar of the great Pacific waves upon the coast not far distant, now diminishing, but again bursting out as the large seventh wave recurs, the rustle of the tree-tops, exposed to the motion of the upper air, the wash of the rippled water near at hand, the flickering crackle of the camp fire re-echoed from a neighbouring rock, and the various cries of animals, not wanting here, but less harmonious than elsewhere, – all these suggest through one sense, the beauty or power which another sense usually informs us of by day. I confess to sleeping with difficulty on the ground; I am not naturally sleepy, and a little excitement of my thoughts drives sleep away more than the want of a mattress, to which the sharp intolerable buzz of a persecuting crowd of mosquitoes, every now and then attacking you with their acutely-poisoned little daggers, strongly contributes. At last I could stand the tent no longer, but rising and making up the fire, now half out, and wrapping myself in my shawl (a bequest from you), I ascended to the top of the overhanging rock, and on that hard, but aerial bed, I watched the stars until I slept. Daylight was not unwelcome, but it came half obscured in doubtful-looking clouds. We exerted ourselves early, however, commencing with a refreshing bathe in the deep clear water into which the boat with a single push floated. Then leaving MacCutcheon to prepare breakfast, Hunt and I proceeded to the waterfall, dragging up our apparatus by main force. By half-past six we took the first plate, but rain at the moment began to fall. After breakfast, however, at which we each consumed four eggs, the weather cleared up in some degree, and we made repeated trials on the same subject, until satisfied that a more satisfactory result could not be obtained. Hunt has since printed and mounted one of his plates, producing a really beautiful picture, and certainly the best he has taken. My plate is smaller, and has a slight defect, but otherwise ought to turn out even better. Our excursion was now in fact ended, for the day was hot, and the wind from the north-west, and the clouds wild and threatening, indicating unmistakably a 'southerly burster,' or squall, during the day, which would prevent us rounding Middle Head, unless we did it quickly. With little delay, therefore, we rowed home to Double Bay, reaching there by 1.30 P.M. Hunt and MacCutcheon then went homewards in his boat to the north shore. Before quite reaching it, however, the thunderstorm burst with a tremendous squall from the south, tremendous torrents of rain, and large hailstones; they were instantly drenched, but otherwise all right; I congratulated myself on the prudence which had brought us home just in time. The afternoon was fine, but a second white or cloudless squall followed in the evening: this storm was one of the most violent I have ever seen here, only lasting about half-an-hour; the rain which fell was, I think, an inch in depth, or nearly one-twentieth part of what falls in England during a whole year. . . .

126. H. E. ROSCOE TO W. S. JEVONS

Manchester
Nov. 14 1858.

My dear Stanley

I will write a line to you tonight in the hopes that it will reach you before you leave Sydney in February – as after that I shall not know where to direct to you for your year of wandering.

I chiefly write to tell you, what I hope you will take for granted, that I expect when you return to England you will come to stay with me for one of the first visits you make. You will I am sure be interested to see my laboratory & I daresay you will have interest enough left in Physical Science in spite of your taking to the Mathematics of Society to like to have a talk about such matters.

I think you are doing quite right to spend a year in seeing the world as you have come to the conclusion to leave Sydney altogether, & I hope you will have a prosperous journey – I do not know anything I should more like than to go to India for some few months. Of course you will go there – I should go to Delhi if I were you. Pray write to me from some of the extraordinary places you visit & let me know how you get along –

As for news about home & myself – I think I have not much to communicate – We are now settled down to our winters work here – & the laboratory is pretty full – having 18 students – During the Summer vacation I was again at Heidelberg working at the never ending light research – & got out very good & interesting results which will be published early in next year in the Phil: Trans:[1]

I was obliged to you for the specimens of rocks you sent me some time ago – as well as for the black sand which I have not yet analysed – when you come across granite or any other *plutonic* rock in your wanderings – I wish you would bring a small sample of each – from the middle of the rock – for me with the name, locality &c. on a bit of paper with the stone – Of course I mean when you get into a plutonic district – when you come upon masses of the rock. Bunsen has, as you know, got a grand theory about the composition of all plutonic formations – & I should like to send him a few specimens of rocks from some portion of the Earth which he has not yet examined – The great point to bear in mind is that it must be a fair average sample of the total rock – not for instance a piece in which large crystals of any one mineral predominate.

I hope your book on the climate of Australia[2] has got on well – I think it is a very interesting subject.

I was in London last week & saw Graham; he is very well & busy – he gave me an Aluminium medal which he has been striking for experiment –

I hope you will excuse this short note – hardly fit to go round the globe – but nevertheless it will assure

you that I am ever yours affely.
Henry. E. Roscoe

W. Stanley Jevons Eqre.
    Sydney.

127. W. S. JEVONS TO LUCY JEVONS
[LJN, 110–11]

9th December 1858.

... Another month is gone, and in a very few weeks I shall no longer belong to Sydney. The change is one of some magnitude, but seems to

[1] R. W. Bunsen and H. E. Roscoe, 'Photochemical Researches – Part IV. Comparative and absolute measurement of the chemical rays. Chemical action of diffuse daylight. Chemical action of direct sunlight. Photochemical action of the sun compared with that of a terrestrial source of light. Chemical action of the constituent parts of solar light', *Philosophical Transactions* [1859], vol. 149, 879–926.

[2] See above, Letter 121, n. 3, p. 340.

steal upon one very quietly. Perhaps it is in consequence of my slightly-increased years that I feel very cool under all circumstances. . . . It would now be one of the greatest disappointments possible to me, if circumstances prevented my immediate return home; but this has nearly happened.

I will tell you that I might have a fair prospect of an income from £1000 to £2000 a year in Melbourne. Mr. H——,[1] a chemist, whom I knew here, has lately moved there, and in a few months established a gold-melting and assaying business which already pays nearly £2000. He much wants a partner, however, and proposed to Mr. Miller to join him. Miller got two weeks' leave of absence, and went to Melbourne to see how the truth stands. He returned yesterday very well satisfied with everything, but I do not think he will finally decide on leaving a fixed salary. H—— is equally willing to take me, but told Miller that it must be for a permanency. This was my salvation. . . . I had almost made up my mind, that I could not refuse such a chance of making money if I could hold it for say two or three years. But a *permanency*, or even the nine years' partnership, which H—— would require, is *altogether out of the question*. I would almost as soon hang myself at once, as the surest way of procuring a permanent settlement. . . . I have thrown over the Melbourne idea almost entirely, and with no small relief to my spirits. It would indeed have been difficult to reconcile myself to a sudden change of plans which would defer for several years *everything which of my own inclination I desire*. I have no love of money, no love of an easy life, and no love of an ordinary consequential position, all which I might easily attain in these colonies. What I do, concerns myself alone, unless it is positively injurious to others. . . . Now I have no fear that any of you will ever reproach me with this, but, to be on the safe side, I would freely engage that so far as my present or future possessions go, any necessary or reasonable assistance shall be yours, in short everything that I have should be yours, rather than that I should act selfishly. But I cannot believe that any of you would ever wish me to sacrifice everything that I hold dear *after* my love for yourselves. It is rather a grave business to refuse an almost certain fortune, such as I should doubtless obtain either here or especially in Melbourne, but so

---

[1] Probably Charles J. Hodgson, assayer and secretary of the Fitzroy Iron and Coal Co; he carried on business at George Street, Sydney, and lived at Stanley Street; the Sydney Street Directory, 1858-9, lists him as an assayer, of 307 George Street; he is listed as a member of the New South Wales Philosophical Society, 1857-8. Jevons appears to have been on friendly terms with Hodgson for some time: he noted in his diary on 6 January 1856, 'Called at Hodgsons to show him my Aluminium'. An unpublished letter dated 28 October 1862 to Jevons from his brother Herbert indicates that Hodgson died in 1861 and that his assaying business in Melbourne, which had declined owing to the banks' policy of employing their own assayers, was carried on by his son.

it must be, and upon my own shoulders will be the consequences. Life has run smoothly with me as yet, but I am quite aware that it may not always be so, and I hope that you also look upon it in this light. ...

128. W. S. JEVONS TO HENRIETTA JEVONS
[LJP, 113–8]

Double Bay. Sydney N.S.W.
Jan 30th 1859.

My dearest Henny

Yesterday I returned from my trip to the Braidwood diggings,[1] and for a few days I enjoy the comforts of a quasi-home. You might perhaps be interested by an account of what I have done & seen in this primitive country but I prefer, in the first place at all events, writing some sort of answer to an interesting and pleasing letter from you which met me here.[2] I did some time since write you a very serious and rather uncommon letter, and you may depend upon it that what I said, I also meant to say. But I am glad to find that it was not misunderstood by you and that in fact you agree with me as far as could be expected concerning the comparative values of an agreable* and a useful life. It could never be supposed that in the course of a rather gay, stirring life such as you have been lately spending, there would always be opportunities for serious work or even reflections; these things are not always right and necessary. In some leisure interval you probably wrote a letter which reached me when I happened to be in a very serious & not very cheerful state of mind, and accordingly I addressed you somewhat of a sermon which as it did not, I hope, cause you much trouble, would not do harm, although it was not strictly deserved & necessary on your part. The letter, however, which I now have from you, shows that you have turned what I said to the best possible account and renders me almost satisfied to be deprived of your letters for the next nine months.

I can perceive that your views of the proper uses of life coincide satisfactorily with my own, and we enjoy a common understanding upon that basis, which is a considerable privilage.* But in conducting yourself upon that basis of conduct you have not I think sufficient patience & confidence which leads to a certain degree of wavering & inconstancy, and the consequent dissatisfaction of your own heart, "the battling" as you term it, "of your two natures within you". Do you not perceive that a girl of 18 years or even a man of 22 or 23 years, can really do little or nothing in the world; it is only an extraordinary

[1] See Vol I, p. 24.
[2] This letter is not among the Jevons Papers.

precocity of intellect, very rare and scarcely to be desired which can enable them to do it. It is quite sufficient if after a life of 40 to 70 years a person can look back and say that he has done something – not so much as he would have liked to do, but perhaps nearly as much as his innate nature & circumstances enabled him to do. Suppose that this has proved to be very little; suppose that ill-health, blindness or some other cause has nearly disabled him; that he has always remained poor, unfortunate, or as some people sometimes really are, *unlucky* in every step; that he has followed throughout as many do, a favourite idea, dogma or theory, which he when too late perceives to be false, & the reverse of beneficial. Much regret will doubtless be mixed up with his reminiscences, but he will still, I feel sure, be rewarded with the peaceful conscience of one who has done his best.

Now, if as I believe, you are really desirous of a useful life, I recommend you to defer all reckoning up of what you have done until either death suddenly calls you away and threatens instantly to close your account, or until a full old age invites to legitimate retirement and ease. Your life may end in a day, a month, a year, or not for fifty years, but as you are utterly deprived of the knowledge when it may end, it is perfectly clear that you must act as if the average length of life would be your lot. If two men enter life with coincident views and determinations, but one die off while the other lives to see every wish fulfilled, the one is not less praiseworthy than the other. Perhaps if we could regard their world from another point of view altogether we might say that the earlier death was the happier, and that a promise given was as good as a promise fulfilled. How unreasonable then at your age or mine is all impatience to have any absolute result, to see a stroke of the work struck, or a nail driven home. Sufficient that you are considering its magnitude and importance; that you are looking about & seeing what results others achieve; that you fix your attention on the greatest works hitherto achieved, and wonder how they were done; that you steadily and patiently exercise every smallest member of your mind and body, uncertain upon which muscles or upon which faculties the strain will fall; or that you collect and learn to handle skilfully the tools which you feel sure will be of vital use. Be in no hurry to stand upon the actual work; almost draw back from it, that your preparations may become all the more complete. Take it coolly and confidently and leave the result as I have said for years far in the future.

Perhaps you not only agree to what I say above, but will has anticipated it. In that case I think you do not duly appreciate the comparative importance of *preparation and performance*, or perhaps as I may illustrate it, of *Capital* and *labour*. You desire to begin and hammer away at once, instead of spending years in acquiring strength and skill and then striking a few blows of immensely greater effect than your unskilled ones however numerous, could be. We enter here into one of those deeply laid & simple propositions of Economy which I hope some day to work out into a symmetrical & extensive manner hitherto unattempted even by Mills[3] or Adam Smith. It comprehends the whole question of Education and the employment of Capital in Industry, and will define the proper relation of *preparation & performance*. I will illustrate this by a simple instance.

Suppose a man in early years to be as struck with the value of railways as to determine to devote his life their construction, and suppose him to live for sixty years. Suppose him to have moderate money means at his disposal. Should he buy a spade and a barrow, and set to work at once digging away at a railway cutting? Or would he do better to abandon for some years all care about rails, sleepers, embankments and locomotives, and learn nothing but mathematics, mechanics, natural philosophy, reading, writing, and even French and poetry? In the first case he would remain all his life a common 'Navvie'; in the second case, favourable talents & circumstances, and what is more important, a peculiar well directed industry would make him a 'Stephenson'. Now as regards the real extension of railways, a Stephenson is as valuable as perhaps a 100,000 navvies, for it is he that has led the whole theory and practise* of railway making in which so many hundred thousand persons are engaged in various parts of the world. This single man is probably more industrious than most but does not labour much above the average, yet see what education reflection & determination can accomplish. I need not refer to other names, such as Watt & Adam Smith to show how one man can even in a mere mechanical sense render himself worth millions of men, and it requires only a little more refined consideration to perceive that eminent men in every branch of knowledge & practical life, are really as valuable as Watt, Stephenson or Adam Smith, although they do not directly produce material wealth. Soyer[4] is worth a 100,000 other cooks, as Newton is worth 100,000 ordinary mathematicians and astronomers, because by due education, reflection, & industry he leads them all into new methods and raises their pursuit to a new level.

You will perhaps perceive the bearing of this in your own case; if you really wish to be useful, why not desire to be as useful as 100,000 other people, & lay yourself out accordingly. A woman's field of action

---

[3] In the original manuscript Jevons wrote 'Mills' but it may safely be inferred that he meant to write 'Mill'.

[4] Alexis Bênoit Soyer (1809–58), chef to the Reform Club, 1837–50; the British Government sent him to Ireland in 1847, where he organised soup kitchens in Dublin, and to the Crimea in 1855, where he reorganised the food supplies for hospitals and troops; he also developed the Soyer field stove. He was author of several works on food and cooking.

and her available means are considerably less than those of a man, but she has no reason to complain & remain idle, so long as the field is really so little occupied & still so wide, and while all her disadvantages are fully recognised & allowed for. Often, indeed, these very disadvantages when properly encountered become quite the reverse, as with Ida Pfeiffer,[5] Florence Nightingale and many others. I am using names in illustration of what I advance, which will perhaps dismay you; of course I do not in the least expect that you should follow in their footsteps, but that in your own chosen and natural way you should endeavour to be as confident, courageous & patient as they. You applied yourself for a time you say to teaching at schools. This is a very good thing but if you devote much time to it, aim at being as useful as 100,000 other teachers, by so studying the theory & practice of education, that you may be an original leader in that line. But the selection of your pursuit is a duty of your own, and if you feel no present inclination one way or another, be satisfied to reflect upon and learn what will in any case be useful.

For myself, as I have before stated, I have long felt the same desire for a useful life but while I was at school and college, it remained comparatively latent. I gave my attention chiefly to physical science feeling much interest in it and being sure that it could not prove useless. There is indeed almost an infinite field for work in the various branches of physical science but within the last few years I have become convinced that more is really to be done in the scientific investigation of *Man*. There are multitudes of writers of all degrees of eminence and cleverness who treat of every imaginable subject connected with Man. Take for instance the numbers of papers contributed to the Social Science Association.[6] But does it not strike you that just as in Physical Science there are general & profound principles deducible from a great number of apparent phenomena, so in treating of Man or Society there must also be general principles and laws which underlie all the present discussions & partial arguments? Is it not worth years of labour to dive into these inmost & obscurest principles, and after obtaining some good clue to follow it out with all the intense pleasure of mental success into a multitude of useful conclusions? Man is said to possess *free* will but however this be, he is at least a phenomenon in which *effect* is always connected with *cause*. All the investigations of Social Science must proceed on the assumption that there are causes to make people good & bad, happy & miserable, rich & poor, as well as strong & feeble. It follows that each individual man must be a creature of *cause & effect*.

[5] Ida Laura Pfeiffer (1797–1858), Austrian traveller; after her husband's death in 1842 she visited the Near East, then Scandinavia in 1845; she made two trips round the world, 1846–8 and 1851–4; her last long journey was to Madagascar, 1856–8.
[6] See above, Letter 115, n. 9, p. 322.

This has indeed been argued by Quetelet,[7] a German, but requires yet to be more completely proved. But the causes which operate in each man, letting alone a collection of men, are so very complex that their effects supply innumerable facts for many branches of knowledge. But why do these remain disconnected while the causes must have more or less connection. Men possess animal powers & functions; they have logical minds; they have a series of emotions; and they are placed in contact with definite but extremely variable external circumstances. A perfect consideration of all these data, in fact of all the causes in operation must result in a determination of all effects; for instance in the case of a single person it must explain every trait of his character, every action of his life, every word he has spoken, every thought he has conceived. Of course such is the infinite complexity of causes & of effect that we cannot treat them in detail. A few of the main features of Man & Society afford plenty of occupation. To attempt to define the foundations of our knowledge of man, is surely a work worth a lifetime, and one not excelled in usefulness or interest by any other.

Why then should anything beyond my necessary moral obligations debar me from it? While I should never consent to sacrifice them, why should I care to sacrifice my own present ease & amusements? Why should I care for money, for fine possessions, for present name and position, or even for the real pleasures of Scientific study, while there is such an important and interesting work evident to me? Others will not for years know or appreciate my real purposes, but it is not to be expected that they should. I do not profess to say what you should do with the long years before you; it is rather open advice to say – choose what is useful & good & therefore likely to be happy. Peeling potatoes, washing pans & plates, & mending stockings, are very useful employments & lead to much happiness – Cultivating flower gardens, working worsted slippers & making morning calls, are not profitless & it may be fairly supposed are highly agreable.* Painting Music and literature are indeed excellent pursuits for ladies, but they may even yet employ themselves with equal delight & propriety in branches of more serious learning which are not at all beyond their reach. To each individual the choice belongs, and so to yourself.

Excuse me if my letter is extremely heavy & serious; it is suggested by your own and while I cannot omit what I have said I have not time to

[7] Lambert Adolphe Jacques Quetelet (1796–1874), Belgian astronomer, meteorologist and statistician. Professor of Mathematics at Brussels Athenaeum, 1819, superintended the construction of the Royal Observatory there and became its director, 1828. Became Professor of Astronomy and Geodesy at the Brussels Military School, 1836, but is best remembered for his statistical work. See H. Westergaard, *Contributions to the History of Statistics* (1932). The work referred to is possibly *Sur l'homme et le developpement de ses facultés* (1835).

write much more on lighter subjects. A long time since I wrote about a small essay I was going to publish; perhaps you are surprised it did not appear, so I must briefly explain that the London Publishers Simpkin & Marshall said it would not pay its cost for printing, & referred the matter back to Mr Waugh[8] the Sydney publisher. I did not care to go on with it at the expense of perhaps £20 or £30 (the estimate of the total cost of 1000 copies being £82) but I did not see the least grounds for disencouragement,* as it is not at all usual for original essays by unknown writers on dry uninviting subjects to pay any profit. I am even glad now that it was not published as in years to come I can make use of the same conclusions free from a great many faults of style & mistakes which I expect exist at present in the essay.[9]

My days in Sydney are now drawing to a close, and I wish that they were over. To ship my boxes & my money, buy all my equipment and pack it up & close a hundred little affairs, is troublesome work and one is liable to become lazy when the whole day is at disposal. My present mail-dispatches will probably be the last from Sydney and I am preparing large packets of letters, photographs, specimens, papers, newspapers etc. I hope to send you a copy of my essay on the climate of Australia,[10] not that there is much in it of interest to you.

My books, music etc., are now packed up in the cases. I put the music & a few other things separate thinking you might like to have them opened at once but I have forgotten which case they are in, so you had better wait a few months longer until I am at home and all can be arranged, if ever such a long expected pleasure comes. I do not know whether anything will yield me more delight than to go over my favourite music with you; my part will be to expound the sentiment & principles of the composition, & perhaps to play the accompaniment; yours the vocal expression of the melody. – The Mount of Olives will be our first subject. My harmonium being sold I now cannot resist a little practise* on Mrs Millers piano, & am somewhat pleased at my progress. The piano is perhaps superior to the harmonium.

   I am
    Ever your affectionate Brother
      W. S. Jevons

Excuse me noticing that your handwriting is the reverse of good which is some disadvantage. You should be careful about it & you will soon improve. Mine used to be very bad but is getting better I think.

---

[8] James William Waugh (1820–67); son of an Edinburgh bookseller, he emigrated to New South Wales in 1840; published the *Sydney Magazine of Science and Art*, 1857–9, and *Waugh's Australian Almanac*. Cf. Vol. I, p. 23, and above, Letter 70, p. 174.

[9] The letter in which he mentioned this essay is not among the Jevons Papers. It seems possible that the 'dry uninviting subject' on which he wrote was the 'division of Labour'; he recorded having worked on this subject during 1857 in the Australian diary for that year.

[10] See above, Letter 121, n. 3, p. 340.

129. W. S. JEVONS TO LUCY JEVONS
[LJN, 119–21]

Double Bay, *February* 1859.

... It almost seems now as if my return to England were a reality very soon to happen, and it does not seem at all out of place to consider what must be done when it is accomplished. To build castles or even very moderate-sized houses in the air is absurd, but this is not the case with us.

You suggest very reasonably that it will be necessary for me to do something to earn a living in England, and that I ought not to be without settled plans. It is a fact which I do not mind confessing to yourself, that I wait very much 'for something to turn up', but I am pretty sure I can find some way of supporting myself, and perhaps others, which will not interfere with my own settled pursuits. . . . A preliminary, however, upon which I have almost decided is that of taking my B.A., not so much for the value of the title as for the sake of a little more study. . . .

Herbert's letter from Wayzata[1] is cheerful, and so far satisfactory. . . . I shall certainly try to reach his abode and see him. Travelling in the United States is, I believe, cheap, easy, and rapid, so that if I ever get into the country it will not be difficult. . . . Vessels to the west coast of America are now very scarce here. I shall have to take any that offers, whether it be Callao, Valparaiso, or San Francisco, but I understand there is such good steam communication along the coast that it does not much matter. I shall cross at Panama (where a letter might perhaps reach me), and enter the U. S. by one way or the other. I have no fancy for New Orleans and the yellow fever, but I should like to ascend the great Mississippi, the head of the navigation of which is, I believe, St. Paul's,* of which Herbert speaks.

I will now tell you that I have only just returned from a rough, hard-working, but fine excursion to the southern diggings. With the exception of the passage by the steamer, I walked all the way there and back, and to many places in the neighbourhood. I lived in a tent with Charles Bolton, Maurice O'Connell, and their mate, Frank Fuller, and saw and felt all the peculiarities of life in the diggings. My principal employment was photographing with my stereoscopic camera and tent, and my success exceeded all previous efforts, which, however, is not saying very much. I have about twenty pictures, many of which are almost professionally perfect, exhibiting not only general scenery, but

---

[1] Herbert Jevons had emigrated to Minnesota the previous summer. See Vol. I, p. 10.

all the principal operations of gold-digging and washing and incidents of tent life. The diggers were highly amused at being taken, and only required a hint to stand in any desirable attitude, so that my pictures seem almost alive with real diggers. I even got an aboriginal black with two black *gins* or wives, who sat still in the sun while I made four or five attempts at their portraits before I succeeded.

... When out in the field I am quite pestered with people wishing to buy views, and if I carried printing materials with me I might easily travel scot free as an itinerant photographer. It is one disagreeable thing in this country that a tourist is always mistaken for some sort of a tramp, because they are utterly unaccustomed to the tourist system, so highly developed at Snowdon, the Lakes, Mont Blanc, etc. However, it is pleasant to travel in places really primitive and unappreciated. I walked to the Valley of Araluen, a long narrow valley so entirely surrounded by steep mountain ranges that wheeled carriages of all sorts can neither get in nor out. Provisions are taken down the mountains on sledges. The place is occupied by none but gold-diggers and their dependent trades. A drawback to travelling there is that decent accommodation cannot be had. I had to beg and pray the only respectable landlady there before she would give me a bed in a loft. The valley, however, was highly picturesque, and the foliage of the trees along the sides of the creeks was delightful, at all events to an Australian eye. Here were fine large Casuarina trees, called swamp oaks, with a dark green foliage resembling the pine or fir of England, only more graceful. The shady natural groups of these trees were beautiful among the variety of fine old gum-trees to which we are here so much accustomed. The comprehensive view of the valley from the top of the mountains, with the distant wild ranges which hedge it in on all sides, was surpassingly beautiful. I made a desperate attempt to photograph it, with just a particle of success, but distant mountains as well as clouds are practically beyond the power of the photographer. The country surrounding the diggings of Janbecumberre, where I lived, was unlike other Australian country, being an unvaried wide and slightly undulating plain or tableland, entirely covered with fine green grass and shaded by fine scattered trees. It exactly resembled, in short, an unlimited English park. There were plenty of birds, including crows or ravens, magpies, many white cockatoos, and I also saw two magnificent black and scarlet cockatoos. Of course one apprehended the drawbacks of snakes and herds of wild cattle, the latter especially alarming to the timid, but being in fact very timid themselves. ...

130. W. S. JEVONS TO LUCY JEVONS
[LJN, 121–7]

Beechworth, Ovens Diggings, Victoria,
Sunday Evening, 13th March 1859.

. . . It is a pleasure to be able in the midst of my travels to spend a quiet hour in writing what you will soon read, and you will be glad to hear that I am as yet safe, well, and pleased with the strange and various scenes of life and nature which I meet.

I had set my heart on performing the overland journey to Melbourne, although knowing it to be exceedingly laborious, expensive, in most respects uninviting, and not altogether unsurrounded by dangers. As steam communication with Melbourne is so convenient and rapid, it is an unknown thing to go overland, except when there is necessary business on the road. I wished to gain a fair idea of what the interior of Australia is, although it be somewhat repulsive, and I had the further advantage of seeing two considerable gold diggings – viz., the quartz reef at Adelong, and the celebrated *Ovens District*. A journey of 600 miles overland is but a slight affair in a first-class railway carriage, but on a small mail cart, dragged by force of numerous horses over the uneven tracks and among the bush of Australia, it is really no matter of joke. The mail carts travel *day and night* at the rate of from 4 to 6 or 7 miles an hour, and during the whole twenty-four hours, awake or half asleep, you must hold on hard, lest an unexpected jerk should set you flying.

I do not mind admitting that I have scarcely met with a scene of beauty the whole distance. An eye accustomed, as mine now is, to the unvaried greenish brown or black of the distant bushy country, to the common shape of the mountain ranges, and to the foliage and other component parts of the foreground, is not again excited by similar scenes, although hundreds of miles away. The difference, too, of the coast and interior country is all against the latter in an artistic view. The varied scrub, forest, and flowers of Sydney, and the magnificent tropical vegetation of Illawarra and the coast ranges, are exchanged for a thin scattering of gum-trees and a partial covering of dry and straggling grass. The landscape is often like that of an ill-kept English park, but devoid of its variety, its interesting associations, the beauty of the tints and the noble roundness of English forest trees. The interior country of Australia may be classed into several kinds, over which you pass uneasily in dreary succession. The mountains are chiefly in the form of long ranges, with steep stony sides, but always covered with more or less gum-trees. In one place the trees upon some hills were so thinly scattered as to look perfectly ridiculous, indeed, like those in a Chinese painting. Again, at the foot of the ranges, generally occurs a large extent of undulating slopes, over which you travel roughly, with the sight of nothing but trees, grass and banks of sterile earth or coarse clay. Thirdly, there are alluvial lands or *flats*, as they are called, of rather more productive soil, but still a dull expanse, over which you are glad to pass at full gallop, swallowing, as you cannot help, your fair share of the dusty cloud which envelops the coach. The only places which are devoid of trees in Australia are what they call plains; these are level lands or gentle hills perfectly and naturally free from trees, and bearing only a carpet of grass which is generally so dry and burnt by the sun as to appear yellow like hay. The Goulburn plains extend some 20 or 30 miles, and this yellow expanse, bordered by dark brown bushy ranges, has a very remarkable appearance. On one end of these plains the town of Goulburn is laid out, not unprettily, as seen from a distance, but when inside it about noon the unshaded glare of the sunshine, and the abundance of white dust, are nearly insupportable. The town of Yass, again, is built on somewhat similar plains, but of less extent; here too is a river of decent pretensions, fringed with graceful trees; around are several remarkable mountains, while in the extreme distance is seen the gigantic and rugged range of the Australian Alps, the highest in Australia, but still not exceeding about 7500 feet, or half the height of Mount Blanc. The remarkable interior rivers, Murrumbidgee and Murray, great rivers as they are here called, have a very serpentine course between flat lands liable to inundation, but covered by clumps of trees are very picturesque.

The uneasiness and danger of the mountain roads of N. S. W. are now past, however, and I am in Victoria, and in the midst of one of those remarkable gold districts which are a new wonder of the world. Such a comfortless, unsightly but interesting place could not be found elsewhere. The greater part of this morning I passed in the Chinese camps here. They are collections of many hundred tents arranged close together in the form of rectangular streets. In the construction of these tents, canvas, split wood, old packing-cases, old tin, old clothes, old sacking, etc., are indiscriminately employed for the simple purpose of keeping out the sun and wind. You may imagine, then, how squalid and unsightly are a few hundred such tents, inhabited by swarms of the little ugly Mongolians, in their loose blue clothes, and often with their extraordinary basket hats. Often also you see them carrying water or transporting their earthly possessions in their own peculiar manner over their shoulders. In the centre streets of the camps are all manner of canvas shops, and a number of *temples*. They let me freely walk all round and examine the latter, which were the only places of worship

I had entered for a long time. The god himself was *shin* or *chin*, as they emphatically told me in answer to every question, and this god seemed to exist somewhere among an extraordinary collection of gimcracks, of pieces of drapery covered with Chinese characters, and probably close in the neighbourhood of a lamp which was burning. I also saw the old Chinese man prepare tea for this god: it was uncommonly weak, and offered in three teacups and three or four old eggcups. It was accompanied also by the burning of small sticks of incense and the beating of a drum and gong. In the shops I bought for you a Chinese fan, which fans very well, although it is decidedly ugly. For Henny I got a Chinese book, and Tommy may have the change in Chinese money. I greatly amused a little Chinaman who met me when seriously studying the volume, which I assured him I understood. The last 30 miles were travelled in company with a little Chinaman who was brought up in Glasgow and well educated; he dresses in the full style of a gentleman, and has the official title of interpreter and protector of Chinese for this district; still, he is all affability and condescension.

I should mention that in travelling the most solitary, flat, and tiresome part of the road, a distance of 120 miles, we came, among the dry grass and gum-trees, to a station called Kyeamba, where vines and fruit-trees grew luxuriantly. The proprietor, a funny old man named Smith, wanting a favour of the mail driver, took him, as well as myself and fellow-passenger, down into his vaults, where he stores his own made wines, and treated us to three or four kinds. They were light sweetish wines, but after a dry hot journey inexpressibly delicious and refreshingly cool. I drank two tumblersful, and yet preserved my right senses, and thought Kyeamba a true oasis in the Australian desert, where nothing better than water was to be found. For the present, however, good-bye, for I have booked my place for Melbourne, and start tomorrow at 5 A.M., consequently I must go to bed early.

Emerald Hill, Melbourne,
16*th March* 1859.

Since finishing the above account, the succession of dreary stages of monotonous objects and of tiresome delays and disappointments, has been exchanged for everything pleasing and convenient, and the rest of my letter will perhaps be a chapter of good luck. In travelling from the Ovens to Melbourne, a distance of 166 miles, we had curious but comfortable coaches drawn by four horses. The passengers were respectable and not disagreeable, and as companion I had a gold assayer, who chanced to be travelling from the Adelong gold-fields, where he had been with much the same object as myself, and whom I find to be very respectable. As we got towards Melbourne the roads improved, and the fresh coaches to which we changed were even more commodious. ... At distances of 10 or 20 miles we came to pleasant little towns with romantic-sounding names, such as Avenal, Violet Town, Seymour, Glen Rowan, Donnybrook, or peculiar native names, as Tarrawingee, Wangaratta. The country, however, was even more monotonous than anything I had passed before, in fact, one continued flat and lightly-wooded plain, intersected by several considerable river streams, and numerous devious creeks. Having left Beechworth at 5 A.M., we met with evident signs of the proximity of Melbourne at daybreak the next morning, and at eight o'clock found ourselves, covered as we were with a frightful accumulation of dust, in the busy streets of this great town. As yet I am charmed with Melbourne. It is totally unlike Sydney, and artificially as much greater as it is by the nature of its site worse than it. Built upon an expanse of land as nearly flat as can well be, nothing picturesque can be expected, but the fine straight regular streets, filled with handsome buildings and stored with every luxury, are the next best thing. But what chiefly charmed me was that on the very morning of my arrival I saw an announcement, by the Melbourne Philharmonic Society, of the oratorio *Israel*[1] for the evening. I instantly bought a ticket. I have often longed for an oratorio, but did not expect such a thing on this side of the world; moreover, with one exception, the *Mount of Olives*, there is no piece of music I more wished to hear than *Israel*. You will perhaps be surprised to learn that such a great and difficult mass of double choruses was very well performed here. The solo singers, indeed, were wretched, and the instruments were few and played with want of taste; but there was a good organ, and, what is more, the two choruses, making together some 120 or 130 people, sang with at least as much force and feeling as a similar number would in Exeter Hall. I found almost everything realised that I had expected of the *Israel*.

But I must spend what time I have in telling you of my progress here. Arriving at 8 A.M. from a journey of twenty-four hours, I had, before going to bed, not only heard an oratorio, but done the chief part of my business. I visited Mr. Hodgson,[2] an assayer here, and a pleasant little gentleman of my acquaintance in Sydney. Mr. H. took me round and showed me all the banks and assaying establishments; and when I asked his advice about means of living here, his chief assistant, a pleasant obliging man, said he had some rooms vacant in his cottage. ... I am well pleased with my lodgings, and I daresay I could stay with comfort longer than I at all intend to do. I shall be able to arrange my photographic things here with convenience, but there is a complete want of subject, for the view before the windows

[1] Presumably Hendal's *Israel in Egypt*.   [2] See above, Letter 127, n. 1, p. 357.

is a flat plain half covered with water, and a few short trees in the distance, said to be the Botanical Gardens.

I may perhaps compare Melbourne to Birkenhead. On entering it from the land side there are precisely the same wide well-formed streets, fine buildings, almost too large for their purposes, and preparations for all manner of parks and improvements. Then, on the other side, there is the same abundance of shipping, a forest of masts such as one sees at Liverpool, and there are railway trains with passengers and goods busily running in and out of town. Emerald Hill, where I am, is a quiet suburb $1\frac{1}{2}$ mile from Melbourne, but not far from Sandridge, *i.e.* Hobson's Bay, the port. It is called a hill, but I have hardly been able to detect any elevation above the general level of the plain.

I shall have much more to see in Melbourne, and to select a ship in which to leave Australia, then I shall spend at least two weeks in visiting the great gold fields of Bendigo, Ballarat, etc., which can be reached by coach in six hours. I shall not sail, then, probably under four weeks. More particulars I cannot give. As of course I no longer hear from you, I have not much to remark about home affairs, but it is needless to say how continually I have you and an English home in my thoughts. . . .

131. W. S. JEVONS TO LUCY JEVONS
[LJN, 127–30]

Emerald Hill, 9*th April* 1859.

. . . I am glad to say that my Australian travels are now achieved, and that I have safely returned from a rapid but satisfactory circuit of the Victorian diggings. They are almost entirely devoid of any picturesqueness, but such celebrated places as Ballarat and Bendigo are surrounded with extreme interest in both a scientific and social aspect. You can form no idea as to what strange scenes of life you meet. Thousands of very sturdy independent diggers raising daily from a wilderness of clay and gravel the much-sought gold, and rapidly adopting fixed habits, manners, and appearance. The digger dresses better than an English labourer, and generally in dark-coloured woollen clothes, discovering slight traces of the earth in which he works. He wears a straw or wide-awake hat, beneath which is a face rather stern and dark, and gravely bearded. You may always expect from him a rough, and rather familiar, but spontaneous civility, simply because from his independence of you, and little care for your superior position, he can easily afford it. Thousands of such men live in tents either with their families or with their 'mates,' that is, partners. In the latter case it is often amusing to see a big man going a round of marketing and carrying home chops, steaks, loaves, or perhaps a bundle of carrots. Again, there are the swarms of Chinese always pursuing a quiet kind of industry, and just alloying their own fixed habits with a tinge of the civilisation around them.

But the diggers only form a part of the population of the diggings, for gold that is raised must be spent, and whole townsful of greedy dealers collect together, offering the digger every kind of article which can draw from him his gold, but often giving in return, it must be said, the best products of other labour. . . . I stayed six days at Ballarat, of which I will only further say, that it was a very singular town with a first-rate hotel, where I lodged comfortably, but rather cheaply. I took some photographs, but no very good ones. There was an unlimited number of subjects in the peculiar style of life there existing, but I soon found it too laborious, time-consuming, and annoying a work, and despatched my apparatus back to Melbourne. Then I went by coach through Cresswick's Creek and Clunes (both alluvial or quartz reef diggings), to what is called the 'New Rush Back Creek.' Here some 30,000 diggers had literally rushed together in the space of a month or six weeks in consequence of rich new discoveries of gold just made. To describe the appearance of the mushroom town of canvas thus suddenly created among the ancient (and we may poetically imagine) terror-stricken gum-trees, would be impossible in a moderate-sized letter. There were full two miles of regular canvas streets, densely set with every kind of shop. There were five banks, of which one had offices in a draper's shop, while others, for instance the Great Oriental Bank, had small wooden or iron houses, of two or four rooms. There were photographers, doctors, dentists, lawyers, apothecaries, bankers, watchmakers, laundresses, libraries, in addition to every common kind of trade. I have an advertising newspaper published in the place within the few first weeks of its existence. You will perhaps not be pleased if I say too much of the grog shops, billiard-rooms, concert halls, and other questionable places of amusement, which perfectly abounded.

But I had no fancy to remain in the place, which even old stagers declared to be the most disagreeable hole on earth. Accordingly I went on to Maryborough, another old diggings, then, next day to Tarrengower, which is on a small mountain. Here I was excellently received by a gentleman I met on my overland journey, and he showed me the quartz mines, etc., in towhich we descended by perpendicular ladders, much to the benefit of my nerves.

After two days at Tarrengower, on to Castlemaine, a very pretty, clean, and model little town, which, with Forest Creek where the diggings are, forms a fine panoramic picture. Next day, again, to the celebrated Bendigo, and after another night home to Melbourne. Travelling here as elsewhere is full of amusing, but not at the time always agreeable, incidents, which will afford substance for much pleasant reminiscence.

Victoria is in the parts I have seen utterly unpicturesque, and little different from a wide poorly-wooded plain. I even now regret the deep dark gullies, the bold rocks, and the luxuriance of bush which New South Wales can certainly boast.

I may now state that on again reaching Melbourne I found a ship was almost immediately to sail for Callao, where my chosen route lay. On examining the ship I found her a sound, large, new one from Glasgow, rather dirty, but roomy, and as safe as any land. Accordingly I at once paid the passage money (£30), and have hurriedly provided myself with ship's bedding and a table, chair, etc., for berth. She was to have sailed to-day, but I am glad to find it will be Tuesday or Wednesday before she goes, and I have thus some time to spare for letter writing. This afternoon I called at the Melbourne Observatory upon the director, Professor Neumayer,[1] a rather new-comer. I was introduced to a little spare German, who received me with a tremendous bow, to which I was obliged to respond with interest. . . . With the greatest enthusiasm he at once commenced a complete round of his observatory, showing and discussing with me every instrument, meteorological, magnetic, and astronomical, of which at least the two former kinds, he had a numerous and very varied collection, all in active use throughout the twenty-four hours. Then he showed me many of the numerical results, explaining the methods of reducing them, and carefully taking my direction and name that he might post me his published reports, and even promising immediately to set his assistants to work to copy out a few barometer readings which I required, and had made the ostensible purpose of my visit. . . . How delightful it is to meet this enthusiasm for true and highly useful things, when one passes whole years together among those who are enthusiastic and greedy only about

---

[1] Georg Balthasar Neumayer (1826–1909), German hydrographer, oceanographer, meteorologist and scholar of earth magnetism. Ph.D. Munich, 1849; taught navigation and nautical astronomy at the Austrian School of Navigation, Trieste; decided to devote his efforts to research in the Southern Hemisphere and sailed to Australia in 1852, returning to Europe in 1854 to raise funds to establish an earth-physical observatory in Melbourne; Liebig was instrumental in obtaining financial backing from the King of Bavaria. Neumayer returned to Melbourne, 1857; the observatory was established and functioning by the following year, having obtained interest and support from the colonists and the Victoria Government, which took it over in 1859, appointing Neumayer director; he resigned in 1864 and returned to Germany. Hydrographer of the German Admiralty, 1872; President of the International Polar Commission, 1879; initiated the German South Polar expedition, 1901–3.

gold. One would be willingly snubbed each day of the year by the rich and addleheaded, if only received so well as this by the truly best of their race.

... I have lately formed an idea of collecting specimens of newspapers from all parts of the world, only a single copy, or at the most two, ot each, being admitted; I think that when I have got a good many they will be exceedingly interesting and useful, as presenting a peculiar insight to public and private matters of all people. A great part of the collection may be made without expense by getting old copies thrown away. I have already got nearly thirty Australian ones, of which some are curious, especially the *Back Creek Advertiser*, published at the New Rush. In America I shall meet with a multitude of papers – the date does not much matter, but should not perhaps be older than 1850, unless for papers which have ceased before that date. ...

132. W. S. JEVONS TO LUCY JEVONS
[LJN, 130–4]

Ship "Chrysolite,"
Latitude 19° 37′ South; Longitude 83·33° West.
600 Miles S. W. of Lima, S. America,
29*th May* 1859.

... I commence my letter anew, because my previous attempt was in such a solemn heavy style that I could not get far on with it, and even if I could have completed a few sheets in the same style, I should have dreaded their effect upon your general health and spirits. I believe I am blessed with what may be exactly described as a well-regulated mind, in which grave and gay are not incompatible; whose whole attention may for a time be given to any one subject or reflection without becoming so preoccupied that other things are inadmissible. ...

But you will wonder, perhaps, that I am in a ship and say nothing about the voyage. How I wish you could be here with me for a few hours, that you might go with me and look over the stern rail into the exquisite deep blue of the ocean water – a colour which seems to me in itself in the highest degree sublime, since it is the indication of perfect purity, of unfathomable depth and of almost infinite quantity of water. And then you would never be tired of looking round the visible horizon, although it is but a straight line every day, with an apparent dome-like sky above, and a plain-like expanse of heaving dark water below. By looking on the map for Port Phillip and Lima, or Callao (the port), in South America, you will see that the voyage between them lies across the greatest and most uninterrupted space of ocean which this globe possesses, and we passed certainly not far from the point where you are in the utmost possible degree remote from solid land. Add to this, that it is a part seldom traversed by any ships, and almost deserted by all living animals, and you would imagine the voyage to be gloomy and overpoweringly monotonous. But to me at least it has not seemed so.

Fortunately, as there was abundant room in the cabin, I obtained a berth all to myself, and I took care to furnish it with two little cheap tables in addition to other necessaries. With the aid of my closely-packed portmanteau, box, and bags, I find myself surrounded with books, instruments, and every little thing that I can want. The only unpleasantness is that I cannot do half what I wished and intended – books must remain unread, many things unwritten, and many experiments and observations untried. I have, however, got a good deal done of my journal or accounts of my tour in Australia,[1] having written, since I came on board, almost 170 large and closely-lined pages, illustrated with innumerable sketches or other figures of the most rough execution. I have as yet, too, deferred the general description of the diggings and of the modes of extracting gold, which might make another 100 pages. But I can assure you I will never require yourself or any one else to read it, nor do I myself venture to read what I have once written. Perhaps it may amuse me if ever I am an old man, and look back to the strange early days in Australia, when I was living in tents, sleeping in the air, exploring unknown and romantic mountain scenery, or jolting on the royal mail through bushy deserts at most dark and unearthly hours. Already I begin to regret Australia, and when I am holding yarns with the captain about it, I feel a slight tendency of water to the eyes, and an inclination to give most partial and 'rose-coloured' descriptions.

We are a very small, if not a very affectionate, party in the cabin here. The captain and I are perhaps the best friends aboard. The *Chrysolite* is from the Clyde, and he is consequently Scotch. I keep the Board of Trade meteorological log for him, and discuss or try various nautical observations. . . . I spend most of my day either writing in my berth or reading. To-morrow, however, I must begin to arrange and repack my boxes, as in three days we may possibly be in Callao. Winds, however, as I am fully convinced, are most contrary and capricious phenomena, and in spite of the many fine philosophers who write grandiloquently (in a quiet parlour with their feet on an English fender) about universal and inscrutable laws, proving the benevolence and wisdom, etc., the winds which we have had might certainly be

---

[1] These Australian journals were lost at Havana. See below, Letter 140, p. 398.

said to drive a coach and four through the most solemn and important laws and decrees of meteorologists. We repaired to high southern latitudes that we might benefit by the constant westerly winds which *always blow there*, but presently met a strong stormy east gale blowing right ahead of us, and delaying the voyage twelve or fourteen days. Now we are in the *trade winds*, which ought to be steady delightful breezes, but we find them to consist of heavy shifting squalls.

2nd June, 20 miles south of Callao. – This is one of those most cheerful days which occur in the lives of but few people, and then only at rare intervals – the first day in sight of a new continent after a long sea voyage. All day we have been lying becalmed 20 or 30 miles from the shore of Peru, and almost in sight of our port; but although this delay is provoking, it is not unpleasant to me. The coast is almost unequalled for boldness and grandeur, but is unfortunately shrouded for the most part in dense beds of cloud. The sky is gloomily clouded, and all around the atmosphere seems in a thick and hazy state. Yet below the layer of clouds peaked rocks or lofty precipices are seen rising from the water's edge, and above these are a confused multitude of mountain slopes, which seem to melt away into each other with that exquisite delicacy of outline and of tint which form the charm of distant mountain scenery. It was for a long time left to our imagination to trace the shapes and heights of the higher peaks, until for a short time we gained sight of an immense mass of mountains or tableland, probably that of *Pasco*, towering above the clouds, but scarcely distinguishable from them. The elevation of the loftiest summits, seen from here, does not exceed perhaps 12,000 feet, while Mont Blanc is nearly 16,000 feet in height. But then the *Andes* are a range of extreme length, and of immense proportion in every part. They are also situated close to the coast, so that the impression of loftiness must be all the stronger.

But we have had other novelties to-day to break the monotony of our monotonous voyage, for a whale was reported. I had never previously been so fortunate as to see the greatest of animals, and considered my chance quite gone; but here he was blowing away, that is, spouting out water just as the story-books describe him. We have also seen during the morning numbers of *pelicans*, great birds with large bills a foot or two in length, who coolly sit in the sea-water looking out for fish. For the last few days we have also seen numerous *booby birds*, who live on solitary rocks and islands, and also occupy themselves in fishing. Perhaps you have heard of Cape pigeons, who bear the sailor company in many a solitary voyage, but you can scarcely imagine what beautiful little birds they are, with white breasts, black heads and wings, most prettily diversified with black and white feathers; their shape is the plump yet elegant one of the pigeon or dove, and they can sit and swim in the water, which they do especially on a calm day, and they then look even prettier than when circling about, with their wings outspread and motionless, in the air. From ten to a hundred usually follow a ship day and night.

Marine Hotel, Callao,
9th June.

I have now been a week in Peru, and am already anxious to leave it – not that there is any want of interesting objects, but because everything and everybody is strange and unpleasing. Perhaps you have never before heard of Lima, the capital city of Peru, which is an old Spanish colony celebrated for its silver mines; yet it is a most remarkable place, and I have seen more novel sights in the last week than in any equal period of my travels. For instance, you will perhaps be shocked to hear that last Sunday afternoon I witnessed a true Spanish bull-fight in its full barbarity. Imagine a large rudely-constructed circus, open to the air of this delightful climate, where rain or storm is positively unknown except as a prodigy. It is overlooked by a bare lofty rock – the Sierra di San Cristobel, which bears a cross upon its summit.

. . . Two or three thousand of the Peruvian people are collected on its benches, while the richer and the fairer in complexion chiefly fill the highest range of galleries or the low series of sheltered boxes which enables them to be close to the wounded bull as he rushes round the circus and near him when he dies. The people are of all varieties, from Englishman or Yankee to negroes of unusual blackness and ugliness, but the dull dark faces of the native Indians are perhaps the most common.

Steamship "Medway," 29th June.

I must leave my description of a bull-fight for another time. . . . You must excuse this fragmentary, clumsy letter, but I find my faculty of writing almost deserts me amid the exciting or interesting scenes which I should wish to describe. . . . In my letter to Henny (of the 21st June)[2] I have answered her small epistle,[3] so happily received at Panama, and have given some account of progress since leaving Callao. . . . Curiously enough, I find in my desk some old English postage stamps which I have had since (on *this day five years*) I left home; now they serve to bear this letter which tells you how near I am to England. . . .

[2] See below, p. 377. These letters are reproduced in the order in which they appear in LJ.
[3] This letter is not among the Jevons Papers.

133. W. S. JEVONS TO HENRIETTA JEVONS
[LJN, 134-9]

Aspinwall Hotel, Panama,
21st June 1859.

... Some writer has said that a traveller's life is full of intense pleasures and intense disgust. This day seemed likely at first to be one chiefly of vexation and trouble, although indeed this strange little town excited in me no little interest. But when, in company with two fellow-passengers, I happened to pass a vacant-looking old building which serves as a post office, it occurred to me to enter, more with a view of finding something to do than because I had a faint recollection of once telling you to address a letter to me here. A board was pointed out in reply to my inquiry, covered over with slips of paper, variously aged and dilapidated, all written over with names in a nearly illegible and careless handwriting. All hope of success in my search vanished as I glanced over a few of these lists with their strange mixture of Spanish and English names – José, Pedro, Pablo, Antonio, Isidore, alongside of William, Henry, Thomas, John. But just escaping the edge of a mischievous tear, what do I see? my own name legibly, unmistakably written down, nay even correctly spelt to the last letter – this latter being an occurrence almost unprecedented during my lengthened experience among strangers. It was with a rare delight indeed that I received your little letter. . . . I hope to be at home in about three months, when it will indeed be pleasant to have a week's quiet life with my sisters, and it will then be time to discuss every plan; much there will be to discuss in so short a few days, for if I join the university again it will be necessary to settle to my study rather quickly.

My more immediate business now is to request you to write as quickly as possible, and give me intelligence of Herbert, whom I wish to visit before I return to England. Tell me if he is in the same place as according to the last account (Wayzata). The journey will be a rather long one of a few thousand miles, but will be easily performed with the aid of American facilities.

Steamship "Medway," Carribean Sea,
29th June.

Being unable to obtain a steamer from Panama to the United States without waiting nearly a week at the hot fever-breeding Isthmus, I determined to come on in this steamer, and with my previous fellow-travellers, as far as the Island of St. Thomas, West Indies, which, being a great port, will afford me a choice of routes to the States. We are within a day's sailing of St. Thomas, where, of course, I shall post this letter onwards. It will be tantalising to think that I am within fifteen or sixteen days of England, and see others proceed onward to that happy land, yet not to join them myself. But of course I must not be impatient and break off from my intended travels. At St. Thomas I shall either take a sailing ship direct to New York, or shall take the Havanna* steamer which touches at six or seven of the intermediate West Indian ports. I am now rather overrunning my time, and shall not leave sufficient for the wonders of the States.

You will perhaps like to hear a little about the places I have lately seen. Callao, where I first landed on the American continent, is a seaport of some consequence, six miles inland of which is the celebrated city of Lima (pronounced Leemā), the capital of Peru. I lived in a curious French hotel in the town of Callao for nine days, going up to Lima, when I desired, by means of the railway, which now connects them. The buildings there are quite unlike anything I had elsewhere seen, being built partly of sun-dried bricks, partly of laths and clay, for the climate is so dry and *rainless*, and the occasional earthquakes so severe, that this mode of construction is the most suitable. The houses are usually of one storey, and enclosed, according to the Spanish fashion, with an outer wall or range of buildings through which a gateway leads into the *patio* or courtyard. The most extraordinary love of ornament and of bright colours is shown by the people here, for they not only paint all the walls and houses of pink, sky-blue, light yellow, or other brilliant and pretty tints, but they also leave no vacant space without a fresco painting of some curious allegorical design, or of some landscape real or fanciful. The courtyards often contain fountains and small groves of potted plants and trees, so that the Lima houses, although very different from what the more substantial and reserved taste of the English would prefer, are often extremely elegant, and well adapted to the circumstances of the city. But the churches (of which there are sixty-seven) and the large old monasteries attached to many of them are the great points of interest in the place. The Roman Catholic religion, imported from Spain here, gained vast power, wealth, and extension among a population formed to a great extent of native Indians, low in the scale of intelligence, and of negroes who are worse. As a consequence the religion became debased into something which I can only regard as a bad form of idolatry. The churches are remarkable in an architectural point of view for an extreme and absurd abundance of ornament and colours, but the altars inside, before which the people worship, are what excite and disgust one most. They consist of large complicated erections, gilded and profusely covered with carving in every part. Often they are loaded with large quantities of pure silver, in the form of candlesticks and of ornaments of senseless and indescribable form. When silver was not to be had the commonest tinsel was substituted. The eyes are indeed attracted and dazzled by this tawdry and barbarous pile of decorations, but they rest with disgust upon the images which are placed in the niches and peep out from every side; the Virgin Mary with a gilded crown and a dress of bright yellow silk, embroidered with a mass of gold or tinsel lace; Christ himself represented by a barbarous wooden figure nearly naked, and showing wounds and streams of blood; and the Apostles clothed in robes of velvet, with the usual profuse and tawdry decorations. Such are the objects before which crowds of women, white, brown, or black in complexion, and even men, may be seen kneeling and praying at all hours of the day, while other women are murmuring their confessions to old priests who sit easily in the confessional boxes. But it would be impossible to give you a complete idea of the curious general aspect of these old Roman Catholic edifices, the gloomy vaulted naves, the ghastly images, the old and rude pictures, which startle you at every step, the antiquated organs, the great screens of double iron bars which separate off the chapel in which the nuns or monks attend the service. In the monasteries, again, you may roam through courtyard after courtyard, along gloomy long passages, and up great staircases, passing, every now and then, a small chapel enclosed by a lattice door, within which a solitary lamp burns before the tarnished old altar and its images, in evidence that it is not quite neglected. All these strange edifices, built of vast masses of sun-dried bricks, and tried by many an earthquake, have the evidences of decay, and one is almost glad to see that the tarnished altar-piece is not regilded, and the fallen image often not replaced. Where might one see idolatry if not in Lima? Who would be a Christian if this is Christianity? But I must tell you more about these things when I see you.

Leaving Callao by the Pacific Steam Navigation Company's steamer, we passed up the coast, stopping at three ports, and on the tenth day we landed in Panama. This is a curious old Spanish town of small size, but beautifully situated. Its inhabitants are chiefly negro, with a mixture of Indian blood; but the splendid churches and religious erections of the former Spanish colonists have now nearly passed away, for their ruins, overgrown with bushes, now encumber the town, and of a total number of seven or eight, only the cathedral and one or two more can be used for worship. I remained here two days in a good French hotel, then at 9 A.M. of the next day I started on the celebrated Panama railway, and in passing the Isthmus saw for the first time a tropical country of which every square yard is covered, nay, piled up, with a bright green luxuriance of vegetation in a multiplicity of elegant forms.

It took four hours to travel the distance of $47\frac{1}{2}$ miles across the land (the cost for fare and luggage being 43 dollars, or nearly £8 : 12s.), and we then went straight on board the *Medway* steamer, as Aspinwall, the railway station and port on this side, is a miserably hot and unhealthy place. Since leaving there we have touched in at Carthagena*, a Spanish seaport town of considerable beauty and interest, but we did not go ashore. Here a number of native Indians came off in their canoes and sold to the passengers many monkeys, parrots, marmosets, as well as shells, sponges, fruits, and other natural productions of this tropical place. The *Medway* is a steamer of considerable size, but old and extremely uncomfortable. The weather is intolerably hot and close in these tropical seas, as the thermometer never falls below 80°, so that travelling here is far from being a pure delight, and I now look forward to a quiet sooty room in London as very happiness itself.

It has rendered my journeys much more pleasant of late that I have been very fortunate in my travelling companions. From Melbourne I have been with old Dr. Fergusson,[1] an inspector-general in the English army, a very high rank, as he occasionally tells us. He is sometimes a great bore, being deaf and infirm, but he is a most plucky and excellent old man, so that I am glad to help and cheer him occasionally. He even went up a church steeple with me in Lima. Then at Callao we took on board several very intelligent and agreeable English gentlemen who have been a long time in Peru, and whose conversation is interesting and rational to an unusual extent. Lastly, there is Dr. Karl Scherzer,[2] the chief scientific traveller belonging to the *Novara* Austrian frigate, which has recently made a voyage round the world, and was for five weeks in Port Jackson. The doctor is an author and traveller of considerable German reputation, has spent twenty years in visiting nearly every part of the world, known almost every man of eminence, speaks six languages, has the rank of lieut.-colonel in the Austrian army, yet he is totally unassuming, and when not engaged in writing, spends the whole day in the most delightful conversation. Of course I am the best friends with him, and, either on scientific or political subjects, have much discussion at every spare hour of the day. Here every hour of the day is to spare. . . .

I can well remember how on this day five years ago I parted from

---

[1] Andrew Fergusson (1787–1870), M.D. Glasgow, 1819; Hospital Assistant, 1813; Assistant Surgeon, 1815; Surgeon, 1st West Indian Regiment, 1834; Staff surgeon, 1839; held local rank of Deputy Inspector General in China, 1847–50 and of Inspector General in Ceylon, 1855–8; Deputy Inspector General, 1850; Inspector General, 1858; retired on half pay, December 1858; died in Glasgow.

[2] Dr Karl Scherzer (1821–1903), Austrian explorer; travelled in North and Central America, 1852–5; led the Austrian *Novara* expedition, 1857–9 and the Austro-Hungarian expedition to the Far East, 1869.

you and Lucy, and also from my father. I have very often thought of the day with a feeling that was not far different from downright pain. Soon it might be buried and forgotten were it not that it was my father's last farewell. . . . But in about three months we will hope for a day as joyful as that was full of pain.

Hotel De Commerce, St. Thomas,
30th June.

I am again on land in a pretty seaside town with a very high temperature. But I must first think of posting my letters, then of breakfast. . . .

134. W. S. JEVONS TO HERBERT JEVONS
[LJP, 141–3]

Franklin Hotel. Philadelphia
July 25th 1859.

My dear Herbert

Having heard nothing to the contrary I assume that you have settled down upon the 40 acres of land which you were intending to purchase and I write to inform you that I have not only arrived safely in the great Union but am also intending to visit you in the far West – a journey indeed which will be very pleasant to me on more than one account. I cannot undertake to give you any written account of the countries I have lately seen, for when 'on the move', I am never in a mood for writing – My route has been simply this – From Sydney by mail coaches 550 miles across the country to Melbourne staying there 2 weeks – then a rapid tour of the Great Victorian Gold diggings. On returning to Melbourne found a ship just sailing for Callao in Peru – West coast of S. America. Took passage & after 47 days landed in Callao. Spent 9 days there & in the neighbouring extraordinary city of Lima. Thence by English mail steamer to Panama (7 days) calling at three intermediate minor ports. Spent 2 days in the strange old town of Panama – then crossing the Isthmus by railways took the steamer of the Royal W. I. Mail Company & in 7 days reached St Thomas WI. first calling at the port of Carthagena* in New Grenada. Stayed two days in the Danish island & town of St Thomas & then took a Spanish Mail steamer for Havana which called off the islands of Porto* Rico & St Domingo* – & then visited three minor ports of Cuba before reaching Havana (after 9 days passage). The great heat, the unhealthiness & the expense of living in Havana caused me to leave it by the first oppor^y which happened to be a small Screw Steamer leaving next day for Baltimore & after again passing 5 days at sea I found myself at last in a Yankee city.

My arrival there was about a week since for after spending several days in examining the Monumental city I 'took the cars' for Washington, scrambled over the Capitol, the Washington Monument, the Smithsonian Institute, Lafayette Square with Mr Sickles[1] residence, walked along the avenues & then seeing nothing more of the least interest in the American Capital abruptly took the cars back & came on here. Tomorrow morning I am again about to move to N. Y.

As far as I can now tell I shall wait about a week in N. Y. (at the Metropolitan Hotel) until I receive a letter from home in answer to mine from St Thomas. If I then hear that you are still in Minnesota, I shall take a route by Pittsburg,* thence by Steamer to Cincinnatti & Louisville, & St Louis & up to St Pauls,* which may occupy 9 or 10 days as I intend to stop one day in each of the considerable towns. You need scarcely expect me then under three weeks from the present time.

Of course I am deprived at present of any news from home, & unless I had luckily received a short note from Henny at the old Panama Post office by a lucky chance, I should be six months behind date. At present I am three months behind.

By such a lengthy travelling I have become more than ever accustomed to live independently so that it seems quite natural, and even to meet a relation will seem most strange yet pleasant. The return to England which has ever been my highest desire is now scarcely more than two months off, and I can hardly realize it.

In the list of passengers by the last English steamer from N. Y. I saw the name of F. Jevons. At first I was afraid it might be a mistake for your name, but found the same repeated in other papers. It is curious that I should so nearly have encountered Fred Jevons,[2] but perhaps we should not have known each other. Indeed I do not feel sure that we two shall very easily recognize one another.

I will give you my thoughts on American Affairs when I have more matured them and can converse with you. My Australian life has quite prepared me for that in the far west and a clean floor and a blanket will quite serve me as a bed.

I have throughout enjoyed the most surprisingly good health, having been often styled by fellow passengers 'the picture of good health'. A month in the very hottest tropical climate did not affect me, and I escaped the yellow fever of the W.I ports. [ ][3] I have almost lost two days of my stay in Phil^a. by a little illness from which I am today recovered.

[1] Daniel Edgar Sickles (1825–1914), American lawyer, army officer and politician. Member of the U.S. House of Representatives, 1857–61, 1893–5; U.S. Minister to Spain, 1869–73. In February 1859 he had shot and killed Philip Barton Key because of the latter's attentions to his wife, an act for which he was tried and acquitted, and which made him the centre of considerable public interest at the time.   [2] See above, Letter 56, n. 20, p. 132.
[3] The page is torn here.

The extreme convenience of American hotels renders travelling here easy & very tolerable so that I am almost becoming lazy. Opposite the bedroom where I now write at 10.30 pm is a free concert saloon whence every evening I can hear some really good vocal & concerted music, which is rather a treat.

Consider this to be the mere epitome of the letter which I should like to write and believe me to be

Your very affec. Brother
W. S. Jevons.

135. W. S. JEVONS TO LUCY JEVONS
[LJN, 143-4]

St. Nicholas Hotel,[1] New York,
1st August 1859.

... I have now been nearly a week in this great but not very amusing city. ... I shall start this evening for Pittsburg* on the Ohio River, which is the first step of my journey to Minnesota. It will be a splendid excursion, I have no doubt; but you may be sure I am beginning to be quite weary of travelling, and shall be delighted when I can give up all further thoughts of hotels, railways, steamboats, and that most terrible of bores, *baggage*. You can have no idea what a splendid hotel I have been living in here. It is perhaps the largest in the United States, which is saying a great deal. My bedroom, in which I am now writing, is No. 453; it is rather small, but fitted in a very superior way. ... Everything is at your service without question for the simple charge of $2.50, or about ten shillings per day: this is the uniform charge in nearly all hotels. Whatever I may say of the Yankees in other matters, certainly they are supreme in the management of their hotels.

The great towns which I have as yet visited are mere collections of great warehouses, shops, wharves and handsome dwelling-houses – in fact merchants' offices and merchants' houses. The alpha and omega of the whole is *trade*. The same is to a great extent the case with Liverpool – you know how devoid it is of things of higher interest – well, New York, Philadelphia and Baltimore are far worse. ...

[1] The St Nicholas Hotel opened early in 1853, 'a six-storey, marble-fronted edifice on Broadway between Spring and Broome Streets'. It was one of eleven large hotels to be damaged by fire in November 1864 as a result of Confederate sabotage against the North. Cf. *The Diary of George Templeton Strong*, edited by Allan Nevins and Milton H. Thomas (New York, 1952), vol. II, 114; vol. III, 522.

136. W. S. JEVONS TO LUCY JEVONS
[LJN, 145–6]

Wayzata, near Minneapolis,
Minneapolis, U.S.,
17th August 1859.

... You will be glad to learn by this letter that I have reached Herbert's location – the farthest point of my wanderings – safely, and have found him in very good health. It cannot be said that a log hut affords anything approaching luxurious comfort; but you must be aware that when you are hungry even potatoes and Indian corn bread are a comfort to the stomach, and when you are well tired it is delightful to rest upon any sort of a bed. People in this far West country live much more poorly than I should have expected, for as there are no butchers and no animals to butcher, fresh meat is almost unknown. On the whole, I am much pleased with Minnesota; and Minnetonka, which being translated from the Indian language means 'great water,' is a charming but by no means great lake. The numerous woody headlands, the bays, and a solitary island, have a very pretty appearance, and remind me somewhat of my excursions on the Parramatta river. Thus, just opposite to Wayzata is a sort of little peninsula running out and ending in a curious knoll. On the summit of this used formerly to stand an ancient stone which the Indian aborigines worshipped – the stone, indeed, has recently been removed to a museum, but the place is yet known as 'Spirit's Knob.' The fine woods here, with their bright green and abundant foliage, are very beautiful to my eyes, so long wearied by the stiff and monotonous brown gum-trees of Australia. The bushy dells through which the pathways lead you, and the very swamps with their thick green grass and rushes, are also beautiful in their way. ... Herbert has a fine piece of land, consisting of a sort of flat-topped hill surrounded by a small swamp, which is valuable for affording good logs and grass. At the same time the elevation of his future hut will be such as to render it very healthy. He has done very little towards clearing his own land as yet, but we are now living in a log erection belonging to, but deserted by, another man.[1] ...

---

[1] 'He continued his journey to Toronto, and then by way of Lake Ontario and the St. Lawrence he reached Montreal, where he walked into the Great Victoria Tubular Bridge, which was then almost completed. From Montreal he proceeded to New York, and found that he was just in time to take a passage by the Cunard steamer which sailed from Boston the next morning. ...' (LJ, p. 146).

The Victoria Bridge, Montreal, was completed in 1859 and marked one of the great engineering feats of the nineteenth century. Originally a tubular bridge 9184 feet long, it has since been replaced by one of cantilever design.

137. W. S. JEVONS TO F. B. MILLER

Cunard Steamship America
September 11th 1859.

My dear Miller

I cannot better spend the leisure of my last voyage than in writing you some account of my travels in order that I may post it as soon as possible after my arrival in England.[1] I have long looked forward to these few expectant days upon the rough Atlantic and now they are come and seem truly delightful. When there is so much to look forward to within the next few weeks, it is rather a task to recall the incidents of many past & tedious months, but I must make the attempt. The very accidents and annoyances too which occurred a short time since, now appear, as memory usually makes them, amusing occurrences, and scenes or employments which were pleasing at the time are now as it were distilled into something many times more pleasing.

I think you heard from Melbourne that on my return from Bendigo a vessel – the 'Chrysolite' of Glasgow was just about to sail for my intended destination, Callao, and that I at once paid the passage money (£30). I also took necessary provision for my comfort, such as tables & a chair, and had to buy a new set of bedding in lieu of the bundle which disappeared on the way from Sydney and for which I could not obtain compensation in spite of many stormy calls upon the agents (the more so as they got scent that I should leave in a few days). Of course the departure of the Chrysolite was put off day after day, but when I considered it no longer safe to remain on shore, the weather had become so bad that row boats would be swamped in Hobsons Bay and I had to be put off from Sandridge pier, which I had reached with all my goods in one of the exquisite Melbourne cars, in a stout little Cutter. As it was we did not sail the next day & indeed the captain was ashore all the time but late at night I was woke up by some noise, and presently heard the captain & mate settling all accounts for a hasty departure at daylight, which was happily achieved. It appeared indeed that so many consignees had made claims for damaged cargo upon the unfortunate Chrysolite and threatened to make her 'fast by the mainmast' that at last we had fairly to cut & run. We were two days beating down Port Phillip and through the channels at its entrance, but at last the pilot left us outside and the captain felt more easy about his claims.

The ship was a good well built one on her first round voyage and I had a good large cabin all to myself, as there were only three passengers on board including myself. Of the others one was a young man of American manners & tastes who did little except smoke and spit, but the third passenger was a poor old man who had spent his whole life in the Army

[1] Jevons did not send this letter. The original manuscript was never completed.

Medical Service, and having happily attained, as he was fold of telling us, to the *very high rank* of Inspector General of Hospitals, yet seemed to have little furthur* prospect of enjoying his position because by living in several of the worst climates upon the earth (West Indies, Ceylon etc) his health was quite gone and a dreadful cough indeed nearly caused his death during the voyage. He was also very deaf so that it is a mystery to me how the Circumlocution office of which he was the head in Ceylon could ever have been in motion at all for m^y years past. He told me sometimes that he was rich having a pension of £700 in addition to his savings; indeed he was fond of money and took much trouble in getting vouchers for all expenses that he might apply to the home Gov^t for repayment. Yet he was as good & mild an old man as you could wish and I was rather pleased to accompany him over these voyages.

The passage to Callao lasted 47 days including an extra nameless day which was added gratis to my lifetime on passing Long 180°, (a kind of premium to those who venture round the globe). After leaving the strange bare rocky islands of Bass Straits, and losing sight of the high mountainous outlines of Tasmania, we saw no land & no sign of land or of mortal thing (accepting* a single chance ship at a great distance) until we reached the coast of America. We crossed the largest unbroken surface of water on the globe which is nearly deserted by weeds, by fishes, or by birds, and it would be scarcely possible to pass six weeks in greater monotony. I had however plenty of books to read – and I occupied myself in writing very long accounts of my Australian excursions in a handsome journal book which I afterwards totally lost. I also kept the Board of Trade Meteor[1] Log for Captain MacIntyre who finding like many other captains that the mercury in his barometer behaved in an unaccountable manner, had abandoned the whole affair as useless, or at least beyond his comprehension. I accumulated a mass of figures concerning temperature, moisture, specific gravity etc etc & made many long remarks on sea & air, much to the amusement of Captain & mates, but I hope also to the enlightenment of Capt Fitzroy[2] of the Meteor[1] Depart^t of the Admiralty. We passed round the North end of N.Z. as strong South winds were then prevailing and got on so fast to the westward that we were confident of making the shortest passage on record & the Capt was in high & delightful spirits. But good fortune then strangely & apparently for ever deserted us; strong winds came right ahead of us and lasted nearly two weeks without the least cessation. Poor Capt MacIntyre now by degrees gave himself up to absolute

---

[2] Robert Fitzroy (1805–65), who had commanded the survey ship *Beagle* with which Darwin sailed to South America; he retired from active service in 1850, being appointed chief of the meteorological department of the Board of Trade in 1854; designed the cheap and serviceable 'Fitzroy barometer' and inaugurated a system of storm warnings; promoted rear-admiral, 1857, vice-admiral, 1863; F.R.S. 1851.

despair, feeling complete remorse at not having kept in more Southern Latitudes and declaring he could not meet his owners but must resign on account of his long voyages. At last even these two weeks were past and fair pleasant breezes soon carried us in sight of the Splendid mountainous coast of S America, so hidden however in close masses of cloud that it was for only a few minutes that I caught sight of the loftier summits towering above the region of clouds, & bearing traces of snow at an elevation of perhaps 15,000 feet.

We were here in the celebrated mild & stormless climate of Western Peru so that we beat but slowly up the coast and were a whole day to the Captains extreme vexation in entering the open bay which forms the harbour of Callao. This bay is enclosed by a long bare island, or detached mountainous ridge which stands boldly out into the ocean, as the last outwork of the Great Andes. Immediatly* round the shores of the bay lies a flat plain, delightfully green to the eyes of an Australian, and extending some 6 miles to the foot of the mountains which then rise abruptly in sublime pyramidal masses, piled more loftily & yet more loftily upon each other as the eye can penetrate furthur* between the clouds which in this season usually shroud them. The harsh reddish colour of their naked rocky sides is likewise mellowed by the atmosphere & the increasing distance into a series of the most exquisite tints, such as form the chief beauty of mountainous scenery.

But I was more interested perhaps by the curious aspect of Callao, the town being clustered round the more sheltered area of the bay, and my hopes were still more raised by the very numerous spires of the city of Lima which were just visible in the remoter part of the plain.

Although it was late in the afternoon I got my boxes into the Captains boat at once & went ashore, but was rather dismayed by the crowds of ugly Indians & negroes jabbering Spanish on the quay (or Mole as it is called) by the very curious character of the place altogether and the cheerless app^{ce} of the Hotal Marine (standing close upon the quay) to which I was advised to go, & where the only bedrooms were wooden cabinlike structures spread round a flat Peruvian roof, tobacconists & marine clothing dealers occupying the ground floor of the building while a dining room, billiard room & a corner devoted to the cook were on the second floor approached from outside by a staircase. I had to call to my aid what few French words I remembered for Hotel keepers in S America are nearly all French people. Having secured a room at last I was about to carry all my luggage up with the aid of the sailor boys when I discovered that the Resguardo or Custom house guard was just opposite the quay & the Hotel & there a crowd of Spanish officials examined all my photographic app^{s} & instruments with looks full of doubt & suspicion before they kindly allowed them to enter the country.

Poor old Dr Ferguson* was brought ashore the next day, & lodged in another of the wooden cabins on the roof, where the mild Peruvian air soon worked wonders in curing his cough.

Although I lodged in Callao, my time was chiefly spent about the streets of Lima which was easily reached by a railway connecting the city & its port.

138. W. S. JEVONS TO LUCY JEVONS
[LJN, 146–7]

Grove Park, Liverpool,[1]
18*th September* 1859.

... I awoke this morning in what appeared to me a new world, until upon consideration I found it to be the old and very dear one. Since daylight this morning I have been most pleasantly engaged in reviving recollections at every turn, and by every question and answer. Park Hill Road, indeed, looked dreary and forsaken beyond measure, and it is needless to seek our home where it used to be; but in Grove Park I have had as kind a welcome as I could possibly have looked for, and there are many things about it that remind me of home. Tommy is so much grown and changed in voice that I might not have known him, but I am gradually discovering that he is the same, except that he is as much a man now as a boy then. So much am I pleased with what I meet here, that I know not what it will be like to meet two sisters, or how I shall contain myself.

Unless you hear to the contrary, Tom and I shall leave Liverpool by one of the earlier trains on Wednesday, but I have not had time to consult *Bradshaw*.

It is needless to say more to-day, and what a pleasure it is to drop the old silver pen that has written you so many letters, and reflect that its use in that respect is gone. ...

139. W. S. JEVONS TO HERBERT JEVONS

Streatley, Berkshire
April 24th 1859[1]

My dear Herbert

It is now time to let you know that I have not only arrived quite safely in England but also find everything as I could wish. I was more

---

[1] The home of his uncle, Timothy Jevons.

[1] Jevons obviously dated this letter incorrectly. It was written in September 1859, during the weekend following his arrival home.

than satisfied with my reception in Liverpool perfectly delighted with the few days I have spent here with Lucy and Henny and I have yet some more to look forward [to][2] on reaching London. We have all come to the conclusion of taking a small furnished house in London but if a suitable one cannot be found in time there is the resource of lodgings or even of hiring a house and collecting what furniture we have got or can cheaply buy.

I had a long talk with Henry[3] in Liverpool and went over the accounts which were satisfactory. Tommys £250 had been nearly swallowed up by previous expenses but the accumulated untouched interest of my Fathers money amounts to £120 for Tommy & the same for me. I have an income of about £50 Tommy of £80 including £50 from J & Co. We have thus I think, plenty of means for living in London on a very quiet scale, and I am glad to find that Lucy entirely agrees with me on all points of economy and even urges them furthur* than myself. Tommy's & my College expenses will be about £35 each including the B.A. fees; we have reduced this sum by agreeing that Tommy shall attend Latin & myself greek* and that we then work up both Latin & Greek together. I had thought that I might make some immediate profit out of the work by getting a scholarship, but I believe I am excluded by the rules of age etc. Next Autumn will be the last opportunity for taking the B.A. in the old arrangement; Tommy will take it at the same time on the new arrangement.[4]

Lucy & I go to London on Tuesday (27th)[5] & probably stop for a few days with Mrs Enfield.[6] Henny & Tommy go soon afterwards to lodgings at Englefield which we shall probably keep until the house is ready. The college commences on October 12th.

Now that I am so comfortable here I scarcely care to recall the days when I was wandering alone, but will continue my account from the time I left Champlain after the vexatious Sunday detention. The Champlain steamer was the most handsome & comfortable American

---

[2] This word is omitted in the original manuscript.

[3] See above, Letter 21, n. 2, p. 38.

[4] 'One innovation in the traditional practice of Universities in awarding degrees in the Faculty of Arts was adopted from the first in the Matriculation Examination by the recognition of the English language as a necessary branch of study in addition to Latin and Greek. In 1859 special provision was made for including English Philology and Literature in the examinations for degrees and honours in Arts. The University also founded, for the first time in England, a Faculty of Science, and in the year 1860 began to hold examinations for the degrees of Bachelor and Doctor in that Faculty. An Intermediate examination in Arts was introduced in 1859. The candidate for the degree of B.A. was then required to pass two examinations and was no longer permitted to obtain a degree by a single examination two years after Matriculation . . .' *University of London. The Historical Record (1836–1926)* (1926) viii–ix.

[5] i.e. 27 September. This letter appears to have been written on the 24th.

[6] H. E. Roscoe's sister Harriet, who had married Edward Enfield in 1854.

one I had seen & the lake in some parts approached the beautiful. We reached the South End at Whitehall about 5 P M thence through pretty country to Saratoga where there was nothing at all remarkable to see but great crowds of people who filled several trains & rendered the furthur* travelling very unpleasant not to speak of complicated changes. A nice old American however took me under his guidance and put me on board the Hudson river boat Francis Skiddy from Troy, where they received my ticket although it was intended for the People's line from Albany. This steamer was one of the very largest of American river boats; it was very handsome & roomy but not particularly comfortable. It was too dark & I was too sound asleep to see most of the beauties of the river, but I was up in time next morning for the Palisade rocks and other sights at the lower end. Reaching N.Y at 8.30 a m on 6th I had a remarkable run of luck for about 3 hours & in that time completed everything I had to do, and secured a passage from Boston to Liverpool for £12.

A coach from the St Nicholas took me & the luggage to the 1 PM Newhaven* train; I reached Newhaven* at 4 PM. There I soon found the store of the Mr Towner who was to have brought my books & journals from Havanna.* It was rather shocking to hear that he had stayed there several weeks after me & there died of yellow fever in one of the hotels. Thus he was very far wrong when he joked upon the subject of the fever, telling me that I was very liable to it but that he himself was acclimated. I suspect however that he fell into the midst of the dissipation of Havanna,* & thus brought on his own death. My books however are gone.

I saw a little of the pretty 'city of Elms' & then went on by express train to Boston, reaching it at midnight. I slept at the U.S. Hotel opposite the station & was put on board the steamer by the Hotel coach before 8 a m the next morning (7th). As the mist had not yet risen from the town & Harbour I saw but little of them and the steamer went to sea before 10 am. We stopped at Halifax from 11 PM to 0.30 on the night of the 8th and I saw as much of the town as could well be done by walking about it at that time.

I was as well off on board as I could possibly expect having a large 4 berthed cabin to myself and was as well satisfied to be forard as abaft the crankhatches. A few of the 2nd Cabin passengers quarrelled with each other about slavery but I got on tranquilly with some dry old Americans. We reached Liverpool early on Sunday morning and were landed at 9 am. I took my luggage to Mary Bentley[7] who now lives by herself in the Park, from Mary Swain* having at last died[8] & Ann

---

[7] See above, Letter 20, n. 4, p. 36.
[8] See above, Letter 70, p. 176.

Bolton[9] having gone to a place in the country. I [was][10] sorry also to hear of Mrs Briggs[11] death a short time before; [she] left a number of little things to Lucy & Henny. Mary Bentley was [very] glad to see me & I did not think her much altered; her room was comfortable but she had not succeeded in keeping more of our furniture than a little lumber etc.

I was very kindly received at Grove Park where I found Uncle T. & Mary[12] just returned from a visit to Willy[13] in Scotland. Mary was rather melancholy after her mothers death[14] but not otherwise altered from what I remember her. Fred[15] was full of his American travels which greatly coincided with mine, including the trip from Niagara to Montreal. On the Monday I called at several places & in the evening was at Henry's. The next day I went to George's[16] house to meet Uncle William who was in town; Tommy generally accompanied me about having come up to Liverpool while Lucy & Henny remained in quiet lodgings at this small country village.

I said & intend to say nothing about the furniture unless they make some offer. Henry said that they would continue Tommy's £50 per ann. and would be glad to take him into the business. He spoke so openly that I was pretty well satisfied and did not enter on any business with Uncle Timothy. They would either take Tommy at once or after spending a few years in some other office as Fred has done,[17] and in the mean time Tommy would have at least £80 to live upon. Unless Tommy starts some practicable idea of his own, this is the only prospect he has, but he will continue a year at College in any case.

On Wednesday morning (20th) we left Liverpool by an early train and staid* 2 or 3 hours in Birmingham for the purpose of visiting Roscoe. He was stout & well in body, and was not without signs that he knew me, mentioning my name apparently of himself when asked. I believe he may be considered better and they say gives less trouble than before. I was not altogether pleased with the place.

[9] See above, Letter, 6, n. 9, p. 16.
[10] This page is torn and several words are missing.
[11] Possibly another of the family's former servants.
[12] His cousin Mary Catherine, eldest daughter of Timothy Jevons.
[13] William Edgar Jevons, who was an engineer with a firm in Glasgow.
[14] Timothy Jevons's wife Catharine died during 1859.
[15] See above, Letter 56, n. 20, p. 132.
[16] George Jevons (1818–1905), eldest son of William Jevons Junior. See above, Letter 21, n. 2, p. 38; also Vol. I, p. 12. In October 1853 he married Elizabeth Thornely (1820–83); they had three children, George Walter (b. 1854), Fanny (b. 1856) and John Daniel Thornely (1861–7).
[17] Frederick Jevons was employed by Rathbone Brothers, the Liverpool shipping and trading company; for an account of the firm at this period see S. Marriner, 'Rathbones' Trading Activities in the Middle of the Nineteenth Century', *Transactions of the Historic Society of Lancashire and Cheshire* 108, (1957) 105–27.

I reached Streatly* at 6 pm & found Lucy & Henny at the station. You will have been surprised to hear that Lucy's marriage was entirely broken off on her part but much better so than that she should marry a man she does not care for really. Russel* Martineau[18] appears to have acted very unwisely & unpleasantly in taking no refusal and pressing himself upon Lucy until he almost overcame her better judgement. One of his chief characteristics is known to be extreme perseverance and in this case it has had no [good] result. We shall perhaps have to live rather quietly in London [in] order that Lucy may not meet the Martineaus too much.

I may perhaps notice *privately* that Graham was heard to mention the place of some meteorological observer as just the thing for me, and to remark that the present holder would not live long.[19] This shows at all events that the Master of the Mint is favourably disposed.

I am sorry that our plans for the future cannot include yourself. Unless you have made one or other of the changes you mentioned, I fear the hut must be very solitary, which is a far greater objection than any want of comforts. Uncle T. & Henry almost expected you to return with me and at all events said that they should be glad to see you back. They were not aware too that you had only drawn £10 of the money in Mr Makins hand. In case of your moving we should be glad to do anything which you require & is in our reach, but otherwise I know that people are best left to manage their own affairs. After seeing the quiet & solid success with which you find yourself surrounded here, I am less than ever in love with Yankee manners & cleverness. There is a total absence of any profoundness or sincerity of mind among Americans in general while in England you may always find at least one man in a crowd who possesses better qualities.

We are now in lodgings at this quiet country place about 40 miles from London on the Thames beyond Reading – the fields & downs have a polished garden-like aspect and the cottages, inns & farm-houses are models of simplicity & picturesqueness. The children are numerous, pretty & happy looking – bobbing to you as you pass, a mournful proof of the servility of the lower classes. It is often surprising that English people cannot perceive the truth of the American idea that

[18] Russell Martineau (1831–98), eldest son of James Martineau, married Frances Bailey in 1861. Born in Dublin, he was educated at Heidelberg, University College London, and Berlin; B.A. 1850, M.A. 1854; lecturer in Hebrew Language and Literature at Manchester New College, 1857 (cf. below, Letter 147, n. 5, p. 421); Professor 1866–74; also in 1857 he joined the staff of the British Museum Library; assistant keeper, 1884; improved and catalogued the collection of Luther's works in the early printing department.

[19] John Welsh (1824–59), superintendent at Kew Observatory, 1852–9; he was known to be in bad health and died the following month. Cf. below, Letter 140, p. 402.

the noonday prosperity of England has past* over & is setting in the West.

Lucys Hennys best love & remembrances. Tommy is writing
   Ever your affectionate Brother
      W S Jevons.

Dearest Herbert – It seems hardly necessary for me to write, & add anything to these two most satisfactory letters from Stanley & Tom,[20] yet Stanley has offered the crossing of his letter, & I cannot resist the opportunity of adding just a few lines at this time of happiness in having dear Stanley back again in old England and with us here where we are having a nice quiet week together with nothing to do but talk pleasantly over the past & forward into the future. It would have been pleasant to have had you with us too dearest Herbert, however Stanley having been with you so lately & able to tell us about you[21] reconciles us here to y^r. absense,* especially as he brings a very tolerably good account of you and y^r. surroundings – Stanley tells you our plans for the future, so I will not add more about them but when we are settled I will write and give you a very particular account of our new house & style of life &c &c – let us hear from you soon dearest Herbert and how your hut gets on, and everything else. We think your sugar capital[22] & what is left of it we take with us to Harriet Enfields where Stanley & I go on Tuesday to look out for our new home. Good bye my dearest Herbert – Hennys love with mine, ever your very loving
      L A Jevons.

140. W. S. JEVONS TO F. B. MILLER
 [LJP, 139–41, 144]
      8. Porteus R^d. Fulham Place. London. W.
         5 Oct. 1859.

My dear Miller

I have already been two or three weeks in Old England, but am now for the first time in Lodgings which I hope to occupy for a continuance; this indeed is my first evening of quiet work and I devote it to the present Sydney-bound letter.

You must first be assured that I accomplished my intended journies* and even more in perfect safety and was well satisfied with what I saw. Nine months of perpetual hurry & change are now over, and my wish

---

[20] The letter from Tom is not among the Jevons Papers.
[21] Lucy actually wrote 'us' here in the note which she wrote across the first page of Jevons's letter.   [22] See below, Letter 149, p. 423.

for a quiet home, which by degrees grew horribly intense, seems now about to be fulfilled. By a strange illusory effect, too, I find myself walking the old crowded streets of London, and even the gloomy cloisters of the College, as if but a few days instead of years had passed since I left them. Excuse me when I say that Sydney and all that I have to remember & feel interest in there, have now a rather dream like and imaginary character, somewhat as if I had gone to sleep some night during the long vacation, and dreamt a great deal in a very short time, as people often do in tales. This letter however is to convince you that I do not really regard you as at all a fiction; I know also that you will be glad to hear that my rather adventurous change appears at present in as satisfactory a light as I could possibly expect.

I am scarcely inclined and yet must force myself to give a short account of my progress between Melbourne and London. We had a sufficiently prosperous passage on board the 'Chrysolite' to Callao, and I thus spent 47 days as monotonously & quietly as I shall ever do, reading or writing almost the whole day; as companions there were only Captain MacIntyre, a true Scotchman, with two Scotch mates, and two Scotch passengers. The Capt & I were the best friends, sometimes taking observ^s together, while I undertook the Gov^t Met. Log. which he had previously neglected entirely. One of the passengers was a poor old Army doctor (Dr Ferguson)* who often told me privately that he was rich and of high rank (Inspector-general of hospitals). But he had spent so much of his life in the tropics that his health was entirely gone and his cough so bad that we thought he would have died on the passage. He was a mild & excellent old gentleman and I was glad to be his companion both at Callao & in two subjequent steamer voyages. How plucky too it was for him to spend the last of his days in visiting the Australian Colonies in order to complete his knowledge of the globe.

Arrived in Callao, I was soon established in a most peculiar French Inn close to the wharf. My bedroom was a wooden cabin perched upon the flat Peruvian roof of a building which contained shops on the ground floor and the hotel parlours, kitchen etc on the first floor. But the place proved more comfortable than it seemed at first sight, and there was no objection to living rather out of doors because the Peruvian climate knows no such thing as rain or bad weather. The doctor was soon ensconced in an opposite cabin more pleased than otherwise by the peculiar novelty of the lodgings. It is impossible to describe to you in a letter of any moderate length, what a very strange place is Callao and still more, Lima, the capital city of Peru which was only 6 miles from Callao and easily reached by a railway. I spent five or six days in exploring the very numerous & extraordinary churches of Lima, the vast and strange old Monasteries, while every feature of the streets, the houses, and the people were entirely new. It is of course on the whole a Spanish City, but the larger part of the population consists of Indians (the aboriginal races) and of negroes, (emancipated slaves). The Spanish are unpleasing people: the Indians are short ugly & uninteresting; but the negroes were all disagreable* & ugly even as negroes go, and when of advanced age were usually startlingly horrid. Mrs Miller always used to declaim against the Catholic religion even when surrounded with all solemnity & beauty; I should like her to have accompanied me into any one of the Lima Churches, where she might indeed have witnessed a good deal of very undoubted idolatry. Each church contained a number of altars varying perhaps from 5 to 15, of which the principal was at the end, & that of the Virgin Mary, the one most attended to by far, near to it, the remainder belonging to various saints. These altars consisted of the most extraordinary & grotesque complication of images, pictures, symbols, gilt or silver ornaments, and architectural embellishments, supports, etc, that it is possible to conceive. The Virgin Mary in a yellow satin spangled ball dress, usually peeped out of an alcove of florid design; Christ naked & with abundance of bloody drops, laboured beneath an enormous cross in a glass case, which was filled up with artificial flowers; Peter and Paul, & the rest of the Apostles & Saints, appeared nearly the size of life, among the pillars & niches at the side, handsomely and appropriately robed in purple or scarlet velvet, while very bold if not pleasing impersonations of Angels, Archangels & other divine personages, hovered about in pink muslin, completing the living portion of the altar piece. But innumerable bunches of artificial flowers, lamps, candlesticks, glass chandeliers, and other articles of incomprehensible purpose, must be also added, until the altar is a mass of glare and bad taste that you could scarcely look upon; yet it was what crowds of Negroes, Indians, Spanish women & girls & even Spanish men were always worshipping. The architectural framework often from 20 to 30 feet in height was usually gilded from top to bottom, but on account of age the gilt was almost gone. The candlesticks, and other articles were often of solid silver, of which especially in the Cathedral, great masses were thus employed. Confessionals abounded in the corner of the churches, and it was often interesting to watch the young Spanish girls or *signoritas*, in their black mantillas grouped around kneeling on the marble floor in various fascinating attitudes and waiting their turn to be confessed; nor did they at all object to be watched by a foreigner.

The whole architecture of Lima is most unlike that of any other place; the material is sun dried bricks, like lumps of dry mud, these being very durable in the total absence of rain; the lower parts of buildings are always of great thickness to resist earthquakes and the upper parts for the same reason, of wood or cane wicker work plastered over with mud;[1] all the walls & buildings are coloured with various light & clear tints of blue pink or yellow; the fronts of the churches are painted so that their architectural beauty, such as it is, consists more in colour than form, while the court yards & entrances of the houses are embellished with large rude fresco paintings of allegorical or other design. These houses too are mostly of one story* in the Spanish form, i e with an outside wall or range of buildings, through which a wide gateway leads to an open *patio* or courtyard and to the principal sitting rooms, which are very open so that you can see the showy luxurious furniture within, and sometimes the spanish ladies themselves lounging uselessly about, or playing very brilliant noisy dances on their pianos. The brilliancy of the silks which these ladies wear, the absence of bonnets and gloves, the rigidity of their crinoline would be surprising to an Englishman, were he not dumbfounded by the coolness with which they smoke and spit, occasionally requesting or politely affording the convenience of a light to other ladies or Gentlemen near, this at all events I saw repeatedly at the bull fight. I have yet to mention that I spent a Sunday afternoon in watching a veritable Spanish bull-fight, in the course of which 10 or 11 animals were slaughtered in the mode usually described in books on Spain. I have heard you speak of the inhumanity of cutting the throat of a troublesome cur dog, but what would you think of a fine bull, a truly noble & courageous animal, enraged by the persecuting antics of the *toreros* with their bright coloured clothes, tormented by numerous hooked darts which are skilfully struck into his neck, and then slaughtered by a sword thrust through his body between the shoulder blades. Sometimes the first sword, missing the heart would not cause death, and the poor bull with the point of the blade projecting below and the hilt alone appearing above, would yet continue the chase rather lamely & with evident pain, until a second sword thrust caused the blood to pour from his mouth; then he would sometimes fall over heavily in instant death, but at other times lie down quietly to die, a most pitiable object, his fate being finally accomplished by one of the toreros sticking a dagger into the spine. The thousands of people, of every rank & race, who were present, greatly cheered & enjoyed the cruelest* parts of the performance, & occasionally they had the temporary but perfectly blissful excitement of seeing one or more of the toreros run a near chance of being gored tossed and perhaps killed. No accident happened this day. After the performance there was a rush of many persons to see the carcases, skinned & cut up into beef.

[1] Jevons then wrote '& whitewashed' but crossed it out.

One of the English Pacific S.N. Coˢ steamers fortunately left Callao for Panama within nine days, and I took a berth in company with the Doctor. We had a delightful & calm passage of 10 days touching at 5 intermediate ports on the strange Peruvian coast. I was pleased also to find on board a Dʳ Karl Scherzer, chief scientific member of the Novara Expedⁿ, a most pleasant German gentleman with whom I had much talk; there were also several Englishmen who had travelled a great deal among the Andes.

Panama is a curious little town of Spanish origin, now much ruined and degraded, but situated among tropical beauties, on a small rocky point projecting into the Bay of Panama, celebrated for its pearl fisheries and its charming little islands, which like the surrounding hills on the mainland are clothed in vivid green vegetation. Here was a French hotel in which we lived with comfort for two days and then entrusted ourselves to the Yankee railway train to be conveyed with extreme railway slowness, and at the huge cost of £8 (£3 for luggage) across the 45 miles of isthmus. The chief features of the country at first were steep hills of small height covered with luxuriant green forests & thickets; then we followed the banks of the Rio Chagre, & lastly passed over many swampy tracts where no whiteman can long resist the attack of fever.

As there happened to be no American steamer leaving for N. Orleans, or N. York for a fortnight I preferred to go on by the English Mail steamer to Sᵗ Thomas, West Indies; calling on the way at Cathagena.* This voyage occupied 7 days, a period of extreme discomfort caused by the bad accomodation* of the steamer, the tropical heat of the weather and the perpetual pitching of the ship against head wind & waves. The officers too from Captain down to Midshipman might be described as insolent conceited puppies who thought of nothing but their gold lace. We were all of us heartily glad to reach Sᵗ Thomas, a pretty little tropical island, with a curious little Danish town spread around the shore of the harbour, surrounded as it is by steep green hills rising almost from the waters edge.

The only vessel direct for the states was a small Yankee bark with a ruffianly crew; I preferred to take a Spanish steamer which in two days was to leave for Cuba. Ten days (I think) were spent in this most delightful voyage, the weather, glorious yet fiercely hot both day & night, being now delightful when every suitable comfort was afforded us; the day spent on the well shaded deck reading or watching the beautiful green islands as they came in sight or faded in the distance; sleeping at night upon a bed that was nothing but open cane work & a single sheet; enjoying fully the Spanish style of living, viz breakfast at 10 am with numberless dishes of meat & fish, flavoured highly with garlic, & succeeded by a fine desert,* nothing to drink but an abundance of claret wine; a similar meal for dinner at 4 PM, – iced lemonade at noon, & coffee at night; you may well believe then that this was a charming voyage. There were numbers of Spanish on board who are outwardly polite agreable* people. My only English Companion was Mr Stewart a Demerara sugar planter, who accompanied me to Baltimore in the States, but there were a Yankee engineer, a yankee merchant, and two operatic young ladies of English birth, American education & of the very romantic Italian names Francesca & Agnesa Natali. We stayed some hours at the Spanish town & island of Porto* Rico; again for some hours at a port in St Domingo. Thence we steamed for the port of St Jago de Cuba in the town of which I spent a day; we also touched at the less important places on the north coast of Cuba, and at last entered the striking and much praised harbour of Havanna.*

I shall never forget my visit to this port & town; – my determination to take everything with as perfect coolness as the tropical weather would allow, that the yellow fever might have a poor chance; the great beauty of some Spanish young ladies who came on board to meet their friends, in their walking dress, a kind of simple & elegant ball costume; the tremendous perspiration and confusion into which I suddenly fell when the Spanish Custom house officer refused for a long time to admit my photographic app^s into the country; the dispersion of my luggage by the time that the obnoxious articles were passed; my anguish next day on discovering that I had altogether forgotten & lost my Australian Journals, several valuable books etc which for use on board ship I had made into a separate parcel; the strange discomfort of the hotel Ferdinand which had floors of marble, doors of iron bars, & no real windows; the terrible still heat which pervaded everything; the drenching perspiration which rendered frequent changes of clothes necessary; the gay app^{ce} of the streets; the houses with doors & bow-window open to the street except as iron bars can close them; the ladies sitting publicly within, on rows of rocking chairs in large bare stony chambers; the innumerable cigar shops; the numbers of porters soldiers on guard, or others who in each corner were seated at small benches making thousands of the celebrated Havanna* cigars & paper cigarettes; the delicious ice creams which we had at the great Café Dominica; the coolness with which the ladies called at the Café in their volantes to take ices; the extraordinary & absurd form of the Spanish carriage or volante a kind of huge wheel barrow with one horse, immense long slender shafts, high wheels and a negro slave as postillion; the unfortunate breakdown which Mr Stewart & I had when we attempted to ride in one; the impassability of the narrow streets when all the fashionable ladies of the city rode out in the afternoon in full dress; the astounding discovery that they did their shopping at 9 oclock at night; my interesting walk over the town early next morning – into the churches also, & the cathedral in which Columbus is buried; the general sensation of yellow fever & uncertainty of life in new comers; our satisfaction on securing a passage during the day on board a small American Screw steamer; our enviable position on board her during the night, to leeward of a fever burying ground, near a fever hospital where some fires burning outside must have been consuming the clothes of those recently dead; the details of how many had died on the surrounding ships.

At daylight of the third day we steamed out of the narrow entrance of the harbour & passed the formidable *Morrs* or castle which guards it from American philibusters* & others.[2] The little screw steamer loaded with pineapples and bananas, made rapid *northing*, greatly assisted by the Gulf Stream. After 5 or 6 days at sea we steamed up the long Chesapeake Bay, and landing safely at Baltimore, I felt some exultation in at last entering the Great United States. A bare detail of my movements in Yankeeland is almost all that I can give. Four days I spent in Baltimore, one in Washington, 4 in Philadelphia and nearly a week of New York. Long straight rectangular streets, usually broad & handsome; huge business stores & shops rising 8 or 9 stories high covered with monster advertisement boards, and built in a style of architecture always thoroughly utilitarian yet seldom altogether inelegant; great hotels accomodating* many hundreds of guests and conducted on a uniform and mechanical system thoroughly American, & highly convenient to chance travellers; streets & avenues full of handsome mansion-like houses in which the richer American merchants adopt all the luxury & style of older countries; omnibuses carried quite to perfection & running through all the principal streets on iron rails; railways & railway trains which never think of going under the town by tunnels or over it by viaducts, but go in the most straightforward way, right through the streets; railway termini quite unenclosed so that every one takes the shortest path among the rails & carriages; people walking & children playing on the railway track, & taking no notice of a locomotive till

---

[2] Attempts to achieve a balance of power in Latin America between the United States and the European powers made the Caribbean a sensitive area during the nineteenth century. Cuba remained under Spanish rule but its strategic importance caused it to become the object of Anglo-American rivalry. The Americans attempted a number of filibuster raids during the 1850s, not only on the island but throughout the area, to precipitate British withdrawal from Central America. There were also three unsuccessful attempts by a renegade Spanish general to 'liberate' Cuba, 1849–51. Cf. K. Bourne, *Britain and the Balance of Power in North America 1815–1908* (1967), pp. 62–6, 178–81.

it comes close up with its warning bell dismally tolling – these are a few of the things which strike an Englishman when visiting these great eastern cities of the Union. In N. York I lived at the largest & finest of all American hotels, the St Nicolas* House, which can hold at least 800 people, the charge being $2.50. or about 10 shillings per day. Here I left the bulk of my luggage (which I found very useless & cumbersome) & then started on my tour through the western states. I reached Pittsburg* by rail, finding it an intolerable smoky manufacturing town; thence to the large town of Cincinnati (the Queen of the West) also by rail. I now embarked on one of the Ohio River steamers, a thing which in no way can be said to resemble any steamer seen in English waters – a kind of frail wooden barracks erected on the deck of a very flat barge, upon which also stand open to the air, the high pressure boilers and the rude engines; the passengers live in the second storey, their berths in two long rows with a dining saloon of equal  length between; the officers have a smaller storey to themselves above, & then the pilot (a very important person) has his steering wheel still nearer to the sky. Some boats have one large stern paddle wheel; most have two side wheels each worked by one cylinder. We made a slow tedious passage down the Ohio stopping to land or receive passengers & cargo every 5 or 10 miles; sometimes I was able to land and walk about a little; then we reached the Great Mississipi* River & made a still slower progress up its rapid turbid stream to St Louis. This town is large & important now but will soon be the western capital of the states; I left it the same afternoon in a better steamer, and the scenery of the upper Mississipi* becoming more nearly beautiful, I was better pleased. I had spent almost two weeks on this monotonous river life before I reached St Paul the chief town of Minnesota; but the same evening I succeeded in discovering my brother's settlement 22 miles away, and slept at night in his log hut. He had chosen a most beautiful & fertile part of the country near a pretty lake named Minnetonka, & had bought some land; he had commenced a little farming but from the low prices & bankrupt state of affairs in this State had not succeeded much. I had some good sport in fishing until at last I nearly caught a very big fish, upset the craft in the excitement, and ran a fair chance of drowning among the thick water lillies.*

After spending a few pleasant days with my brother, I started westward to Chicago, a large important but horribly dull place. Thence to

Detroit & through Canada to Niagara. There was nothing to disappoint me in the great falls the grandeur & interest of which cannot be exaggerated. I stayed a day & a half there and had scarcely time to see it fairly; I was also fortunate to witness Blondin[3] perform his terrible feat of walking across the ravine of the Niagara river on a rope; it was by night, he carrying fireworks upon his pole; it will be scarcely credible when I say that he stood on his head when partially across the rope.

I now took an excursion ticket which carried me to Toronto in Canada – along lake Ontario to Kingston; down the beautiful River St Lawrence, shooting down the rapids, to Montreal where I walked into the great Victoria tubular bridge;[4] then by way of Lake Champlain, and the Hudson River to New York, arriving here just in time to take my passage from Boston in the Cunard steamer America which sailed the next morning. But I found time to stay a few hours at the port of Newhaven,* where I was rather shocked to hear of the death at Havanna* of the Yankee Merchant who was a fellow passenger on the Spanish steamer and had promised to bring my lost books if they could be recovered. He had stayed at Havanna* several weeks, and taken the fever, which was then raging badly.

Turning economical after spending so much money, I took a 2nd cabin passage, (£12) but was very comfortable & had a large berth to myself. On the eleventh day I landed in my native town with feelings rather indescribable, and was very kindly welcomed by a variety of relations. I found I had spent £60 less on my journey than I had with me.

Two or three days were spent in Liverpool in revisiting old friends, & making acquaintance with newly born & newly married fresh ones. Then I met my sisters in quiet country lodgings on the Thames near Reading; the place a very beau-ideal of an English village, & of highly polished, cheerful smiling English country. Next I found myself for several days staying in an excellent London house, surrounded by everything that is comfortable & tasteful and engaged in finding lodgings. For some days more I was staying on the outskirts of Windsor Park, more than once visiting the fine old Castle itself & attending the beautiful service in the St Georges Chapel. I might describe others of the comforts & delights of the old country; for instance how my sisters have a country box of Mudies books[5] (10 volumes of the newest works)

---

[3] Charles Blondin (1824–97), the most famous of all tightrope walkers, achieved world fame by his crossings of Niagara Falls in 1859–60 on a rope 1100 feet long stretched 160 feet above the water. He did the crossing at varioustimes blind folded, wheeling a barrow, carrying a man on his back, and on stilts. Born Jean-François Gravelet at St Omer in France, Blondin eventually settled in London and died at Ealing.

[4] See above, Letter 136, n. 1, p. 384.

[5] i.e. books from Mudie's Circulating Library, founded in 1842 by a London bookseller, Charles Edward Mudie (1818–90).

sent down to them as often as desired in any part of the country. Here too one begins to feel of some importance & to realise the standing of a gentleman, especially when the country children, appear much astonished as you pass, drawing up in a line & bobbing or curtseying most respectfully.

I have not yet seen many London friends, but have called on Graham (the Master of your Mint). He as much as said that if I had arrived a little time ago, he would have recommended me for the Kew observatory, Mr Welch[6]* having recently died; I thought this rather encouraging although it was a miss.

I am now alone in lodgings in Paddington, in which my sisters & younger brother will also establish themselves in a few days. In company with my brother I shall attend the Univ. Coll. & pass the B A in a year from this.

If I have caused a twinge of regret in mentioning the pleasures of England I should also say that the weather occasionally is of an obscure, heavy smoky character, against which the best spirits cannot bear up. My present task of going into the city every day to look after my goods etc, is more horrible than anything which you have to do in Sydney. My boxes are all safe but I have to pay £2.10 duty on the books I bought in Australia.

Remember me most kindly to Mrs Miller – I am sure she still feels pride & pleasure in her adopted country. Remember me also to Hunt and my other friends in the Mint. How do you like your German colleague, who I fear has gone out with some ideas not likely to be fulfilled.

Oct 10th On Saturday I called at K. College & for the first time succeeded in seeing Dr Miller who sat at the same old table & was as kind as ever but made a great jump when a glass was heard to explode loudly in the laboratory. Mr Pisey[7] appeared to be in the highest degree flourishing and enquired much about you and the Australian climate.

I expect a letter in a few days by the Southampton part of the Aus^n Mail. Please direct to University College for the present

Ever yours sincerely
W S Jevons.

[6] See above, Letter 139, n. 19, p. 392.
[7] It has not proved possible to trace any biographical details of Mr Pisey.

141. W. S. JEVONS TO HERBERT JEVONS
[LJN, 148]

8 Porteus Road,
15th October 1859.

... I have only been at the college two days as yet, and feel rather strange. I have entered senior Greek and Latin, higher and lower senior mathematics, and senior German, in company throughout with Tom. This is rather a difficult enterprise on my part, since I was in none of these classes before except lower senior mathematics, while it is seven years since I was in Latin or Greek. De Morgan has started right away in differential calculus.[1] I think it would be impossible for me to keep up if I had not Tom's assistance, he having attended senior Greek and Latin last year. ... London is certainly a stirring place, but the atmosphere is appalling to one accustomed to the clear skies of Australia. ...

142. W. S. JEVONS TO HERBERT JEVONS
[LJN, 149]

8 Porteus Road, Paddington,
27th December 1859.

... A week since we had a rather sharp frost. Tom and myself had two good days' skating on the Serpentine and Kensington Garden pond. After six years' interval I was rather unsteady at first, but the second day skated, I think, as well as ever. Otherwise I cannot say that I find the slightest pleasure in going outside of the front door, and in consequence sit at home during these days (the Christmas holidays) in pretty constant work at mathematics, political economy, and such-like light occupations. ... I should uncommonly like to see a North American winter. I often feel seriously 'riled' at the thick atmosphere, mud, and gloomy streets of London, when I go over in memory the beautiful bright countries, or clean neat towns, I have lately seen, and a very good and sensible novel (*Geoffry Hamlin**)[1] which I read – exactly descriptive of Australian bush life – made me think very regretfully of the skies, waters, and woods of that land. My only resource is to turn my back to the window and plunge into De Morgan's differential calculus. ...

[1] On the relation of this work to Jevons's earlier studies in mathematics, see Black, *Ecomonica*, 38 (May 1972) 119–34. And cf. above, Vol. I, p. 15.
[1] *Geoffrey Hamlyn* (1859), a story of life among early settlers in Australia by Henry Kingsley (1830–76), younger brother of Charles. He spent five years in Australia almost at the same time as Jevons (1853–8).

143. W. S. JEVONS TO HERBERT JEVONS
[LJP, 149-51]

8 Porteus Road
Paddington. London. N.
Jan 27th 1860.

My dear Herbert

I was rejoiced to receive your letter a day or two since after so long an interval since the previous one. If you do not write very often I hope you will at least write regularly; otherwise it makes me think of instances I have known in Australia where letters have ceased and never been renewed, no one knows why. (Mrs Millers brother, George O'Connell – went to the Victorian diggings and has not since been heard of.)

I must confess that I forgot the fact that American rivers freeze in Winter – and that there is no railway yet to St Pauls.* I am sorry the carriage of the box should be so expensive to you as 10$ – but in fact I requested Henry to have the charges put down to my account. When you get the box, you will I think find the contents worth their carriage, and the books, violin, etc will render your [life]¹ but cheerful *to a degree* or *quite cheerful*, to use two Yankeeisms.

You must feel considerably satisfied in having a hut of your own, on your own land, of your own timber & your own construction, and now the chief impediment to the cultivation of your plot is removed. I suppose you will next summer get in some crops, and proceed with the completion of your little homestead, and we will hope that the returning cycle of prosperity and perhaps the influence of a new Republican Gov^{t2} will raise the fortunes of Minnesota and the profits of Wayzata farmers. If you will only write and tell us that the box full of articles³ and are useful to you, we will consider about sending a second box in the summer, as it can be done at little cost to ourselves beyond the transit-charges. For instance if you intend to stay a year or more in Wayzata, I think Meteorology would prove very interesting to you and it is just that pursuit which fills up leisure time and demands no more drudgery or severe work beyond the adding up of many figures. My set of instruments are now idle and with the addition of a small inexpensive aneroid barometer would be complete enough. So let me know if you would like them sent and also about other books, of which I could spare many.

¹ This word is omitted in the original manuscript.
² The election of a Republican administration, headed by Abraham Lincoln, did not take place until November 1860; but, as the Democrats were split on the slavery issue and the Republicans had made a strong showing in the 1856 elections, their victory was generally anticipated.   ³ Jevons appears to have left out some words here.

I have no wish to unsettle your plans but I often think how much better it would be if you were in New Zealand or Australia. You are already well accustomed to what they describe as the hardship of colonization, and would indeed find the mode of life in the Southern hemisphere luxurious compared with that of Minnesota. You would not hear of corn meal in the twelve-month, and would have abundance of the best beef and mutton. Arthur and Thomas Roscoe[4] as you know, sailed for Otago (?) and according to intelligence, are making very good wages as sawyers – some 10 shillings per day I believe. At all events you could not fail of making from 5 to 10s. Nor would it be a bad move to join my friends Maurice Oconnel* and Charles Bolton at the diggings – the work indeed is rather hard but sure to be paid at least moderately, and your good knowledge of business might turn to the best account in some of the small rising towns of N.S W, or NZ. Farming there is not the chief employment as in Minnesota, but if you preferred I dare say it would be possible especially in N.Z. Maurice was at one time nearly commencing a small farm near Sydney, but a gold digging rush took him off. You might not perhaps always meet with such a fine old neighbour as Mr Dudley, but then the people in general are more English, and in the country there is much of the same neighbourly feeling, mixed with some suspicion belonging to convict and other matters. It will be no harm to keep Australia in your mind. Money, I dare say, would not be wanting, for your own ground when improved and in better times would bring a good many $.

I may also mention, although it is perhaps raising false hopes, that there is a slight chance of a small legacy coming to our family – For a piece of forgotten property has been accidentally discovered in Liverpool as belonging to Grandpapa Roscoe's estate – and by will half of the value comes to our family, because £1000 was left to each of the daughters and has never been paid. The other half would have fallen to Aunt Jane but will now be divided among the Roscoes in general. The value is as yet unknown but perhaps rather over £1000 so that we perhaps *might* have a share of £100 each. William Alfred Jevons[5] is the lawyer; I have written to him on the subject and had a satisfactory reply. But it is very possible that the property might be contested, or sell badly, or from other unforeseen causes our hopes might be disappointed.

Time slips bye* with me most rapidly, and things sometimes appear not a little dreamy, although we have in our lodgings all the comforts of a house. I should feel very different perhaps, if I were paying my

---

[4] Jevons's cousins Arthur (b. 1825) and Thomas Stamford (b. 1826), second and third sons of William Stanley Roscoe, younger brothers of William Caldwell Roscoe.
[5] Another of Jevons's cousins. William Alfred Jevons (b. 1820) was the younger son of William Jevons Junior.

expenses and yet am not inclined to cut off from my future prospects by giving up the chance of study. I have no definite plan of earning money, but after my BA will try what can be done in the way of writing or teaching, so as to keep myself while working for my M A which I have a great desire to take in the Pol. Econ. and Mental Philosophy branch – as these are entirely the subjects I should follow in any case. Harry Roscoe whom I saw in London at Christmas is rather indignant that I am no longer a chemist and wants to know how I shall get my bread, which perhaps is quite a pertinent question.

Lucy is at present visiting all her friends in Liverpool, but I hope will not stay much longer. Henny is at times not quite well – but performs her duties of housekeeping with great success besides teaching at a Unitarian School and herself learning at the Ladies College. Tom of course is fully employed in the same classes with myself, and which are comparatively easy work to him.

I find the classes at college a little dull – the charm is rubbed off a few things – but then one learns more and more to adore De Morgan, as an unfathomable fund of mathematics. We were delighted the other day when in the Higher Senior, he at last appeared conscious that a demonstration, about differential equations, which extended through the lecture, was difficult; he promised indeed to repeat it. But then one is disappointed to find that the hardest thing he gives in any of his classes, is still to him a trifle, and that the bounds of mathematical knowledge are yet out of sight. I am working against such great odds in Mathematics, Latin & Greek that I have at present no time to give for Mental Philosophy in which my chief strength lies. Yet I spend much time in Pol. Economy as there is a small scholarship of £20 a year for 3 years to be competed for at the end of this year.

I have yet to mention the subject which is uppermost in mens minds here – viz the Rifle Movement concerning which the Queen in her Parliament speech expressed her 'Gratification and Pride'. Indeed Englishmen are now giving an unlooked for proof that they are at least as good a race as ever, and an actual army of 100,000 volunteers has been enrolled in the last few months, which I expect will be nearly doubled during this year. It is done in such a very sensible and bonâ fide manner, that I do not doubt the volunteers will be a permanent and most important institution, rendering invasion or alarm absurd, giving additional strength to all good government, and in some years to come perhaps rendering a reduction of the regular army possible. It is formed of all classes from noblemen and M P's down to shopmen, and some employées* of railways, works etc. but as a general thing there are none of the working classes. It may seem rather illiberal to say so, but I think it even thus a benefit, that the upper classes who possess the most intelligence, and are in a minority should be most armed. Altogether it is impossible to conceive a military force better adapted to ensure perfect peace than the present *volunteer rifles*. The Govt are put to no expense beyond that of *arms*; honorary or subscribing members pay the chief expenses of each corps while the effective members only subscribe a guinea and have to buy their uniforms.

I have myself joined the Queens Own Rifles – a corps in the Westminster Brigade, chiefly because Frank,[6] Dick[7] and Fred Roscoe[8] were already in it. It is also rather a good corps, being the Queens, and numbering already about 300 men, which will be increased to 500 or 600. The Westminster Brigade will be one of the chief – comprehending several other corps, and perhaps 1500 men. I have as yet been only twice to drill, which is carried on at night or on Saturday afternoon in Westminster Hall. And that grand old hall presents a very stirring not to say warlike and alarming scene when several hundred gentlemen in a number of squads or companies are going through their exercises, from the first awkward marching and facing, to the finished practise* with the Enfield rifle and a bright sword bayonet. For the present nearly all of the Queens drill in plain clothes and it is not necessary to appear in uniform until the summer when I dare say there will be a Grand field day in Hyde Park. Most other people one knows have also joined – For instance Mr Osler[9] is in the Lincoln's Inn lawyers corps, Harry E. Roscoe in a Manchester corps, and Will Jevons[10] in Napier & Cos corps, for it has become a custom for each great employer to equip a company of his own. In the summer we shall commence rifle firing at the Crystal Palace grounds. Yesterday we had a meeting at College in favour of a corps there, but I do not know whether it will prove very successful. The meeting at least was spirited for the Medicals mustered in force and the most amusing row was caused when a man who said he was a student 28 years since proposed an amendment and spoke disrespectfully of the English & their Government. Perhaps he was a little crazy – but it might have been rather unpleasant in consequences to him. For the medicals waylaid him and awaited his reaching the bounds of the college. Under these circumstances Mr Key[11] – the tallest strongest and vastest of the professors gave the poor man his protection and they were seen walking down Gower Street arm in arm, with a train of wild medicals after them – the populace being greatly taken by surprise.

[6] Francis James Roscoe. See Vol. I, p. 193, n. 6.
[7] Richard Roscoe. See above, Letter 70, n. 10, p. 176.
[8] Alfred Roscoe (1841–62), youngest son of Robert Roscoe. He died in February 1862 shortly after going up to Wadham College, Oxford. See below, Letter 157, p. 440.
[9] See Vol. I, p. 73, n. 1.
[10] William Edgar Jevons.   [11] See above, Letter 2, n. 2, p. 5.

You will hear that Mr Cobden has persuaded the Emperor of the French to introduce free trade and that a commercial treaty between France and England is the consequence.[12] Commerce perhaps is the best preventive of a war, and to tell the truth some preventive seems necessary – so open are the expressions of distrust and even hostility. But give us about a year more for preparation and between the volunteers, the surprising new Armstrong guns and general improvements and increase in the navy army, and fortifications – and England need have no fear of war; or at least not of invasion. But I cannot think Napoleon intends to fight us; for he has nothing to gain and all to lose. At present he is amusing himself with the Pope, and certainly he is at a summit of Imperial glory. Nevertheless he might like to have the upper hand of England too; but if he has any intention of invading why did he not do it, at the time of the Orsini affair[13] or after the Indian Mutinies when England was really defenceless. Still if the Emperor died, we know too much of the French to feel sure what would happen next.

The Queen in her Speech alluded rather sharply to the San Juan affair.[14] Americans, in fact are gaining themselves no credit just at present, and will have enough to do to elect a speaker and ward off a civil war. Nothing more occurs to me as worth saying at present and it being rather late I conclude.

I hope soon to have another letter from you.
Ever your affectionate Brother
W S Jevons

[12] The Cobden-Chevalier commercial treaty between Britain and France (1860) made free trade a reality in Europe. It extended the benefits of Gladstone's budgets of 1853 and 1860, which had freed foreign manufactures, by bringing easier access between British and French markets. The export of British manufactures to France was almost doubled. Cf. Checkland, op. cit., pp. 40, 359.

[13] Felice Orsini (1819–58), an Italian nationalist revolutionary who had taken refuge in England, attempted to assassinate Napoleon III in Paris in January 1858; he was executed the following March. Cf. above, Letter 97, n. 2, p. 259.

[14] Jevons is referring here to the dispute between Britain and the United States concerning the boundary between Canada and the Oregon territory, which the Oregon Treaty of 1846 had attempted to settle by accepting the 49th parallel as the frontier, with deviations to enable Britain to keep Vancouver Island. The boundary was defined as running midway down the channel separating Vancouver Island from the mainland, and through San Juan de Fuca Strait out to sea. However, there were three channels leading to the Strait and as a result the settlement left uncertain not only which channel was meant, but also the ownership of the San Juan Islands in Puget Sound. A joint occupation of the area by British and American troops had been begun to avoid a clash, pending settlement of the dispute. The increasing friction between the two countries in the period immediately preceding the outbreak of the Civil War increased the risk of incidents in the area. Cf. Woodward, op. cit., p. 306; Bourne, op. cit., p. 211.

144. W. S. JEVONS TO HERBERT JEVONS
[LJP, 151-2]

8 Porteus Road
Paddington W.
June 1   /60

My dear Herbert

We have just received your last and very satisfactory letter; as we are considerably in arrears I write at once, that it may go by the mail tomorrow. I like to hear of your progress in the clearing of your small farm, nor should I object to bear a hand in it and to enjoy some of the pure natural pleasures of Minnesota were these things not quite incompatible with other pursuits.

I should greatly fancy a little trolling on the lake, or a plunge into its clear water; indeed after the beautiful bathing I had at Sydney & a few times in America, I have no fancy for steamy dirty water tanks they call baths in London.

It is doubtless much more encouraging now that you live in your own hut upon your own freehold land, and sow your own crops. I hope you are perfectly satisfied at last with the simplicity bordering upon nature which you have attained; but it seems you are not free from social calls, and have been made school-trustee on account I suppose of your superior learning. If you intend staying at Wayzata I should strongly advise you to study *oratory* and democracy; to take the chair at public meetings of the inhabitants of Wayzata etc, and soon we shall hear of you as a Representative in the Minnesotan Legislature. Being an Englishman will not be a drawback if you renounce & blackguard your country a little. You wont injure England much in any case.

Your crops will serve I suppose, both to support you and to sell in some quantity if things should become more saleable* in Minnesota, and you are all the time adding to the value of your land in improvements. But your man must carry away a good deal of money; I suppose however that you would not have employment for him in winter, when everything is frozen. You tell us not to send another box this summer but I do not like putting it off till next spring. At all events in the mean time I will send you more frequent newspapers. I was obliged for your American Democrats[1] etc – one of which contained the amusing account of Mr Lovejoy[2] and his anti-slavery.

London is now in all the glory of the Season; there are countless exhibitions, meetings, etc, and the streets are full of grand carriages as

---

[1] According to the Library of Congress, there were several newspapers published in the United States with this title but none in Minnesota or surrounding areas, and as far as has been ascertained none of them were published around the year 1860.

[2] Owen Lovejoy (1811-64), abolitionist, politician; a congregational minister, he preached and lectured against slavery; elected to the Illinois legislature, 1844, and to Congress, 1856.

well as country folks spending their Witsuntide* Holydays.* But I am not at all lead* away from my work. In fact I have only made six visits to any kind of amusements since I came here and have not yet seen the inside of a theatre. I have neither time nor money and strive especially to save the latter that I may with a better conscience determine on my M A. study. We have now less than two weeks lectures remaining, – a great blessing since one gets intolerably weary of some four lectures per day. Then we have about a fortnight clear for work; lastly three days examinations for the two classes I shall enter and then comes the long vacation. After a walking tour of a couple of weeks with Tom we must nevertheless set to work again for the B A. in October. That fairly passed I must again work hard for a pol Economy scholarship in December, & then begin fairly at Mathematics & at the Metaphysical & Political subjects necessary for the M A. It is a tedious thing thus to spend so much time always in preparation; indeed it requires some courage but if I like to undertake the trouble & anxiety, I know of nothing to prevent it and the success which I may attain would repay it all. It would of course be an object of temporary ambition to get the M A. gold medal thus standing on a level with R. Hutton[3] & others nearly as high as the University of London can place you. But I should then have no idea of falling into the dilly-dally course which most of the Univ. Graduates appear to take.

During the last session I have worked a great deal at Pol. Economy; in the last few months I have fortunately struck out what I have no doubt is *the true theory of Economy* so thorough-going and consistent, that I cannot now read other books on the subject without indignation. While the theory is entirely mathematical in principle, I show at the same time how the data of calculation are so complicated as to be for the present hopeless. Nevertheless I obtain from the mathematical principles all the chief laws at which Pol. Econ^{ts} have previously arrived only arranged in a series of Definitions Axioms and Theorems almost as rigourous* and connected as if they were so many geometrical problems. One of the most important axioms is that as the quantity of any commodity, for instance plain food, which a man has to consume increases, so the utility or benefit derived from the last portion used decreases in degree. (The decrease of enjoyment between beginning & end of a meal may be taken as a rude example) And I assume that on an average the *ratio of utility* is some continuous mathematical function of the quantity of commodity. This law of utility has in fact always been assumed by Pol. Econ. under the more complex form and name of the Law of Supply & Demand. But once fairly stated in its simple form it opens up the whole of the subject. Most of the conclusions are of course the old ones

---

[3] See below, Letter 145, n. 6, p. 416.

stated in a consistent form – but my definition of Capital and law of the Interest of Capital are as far as I have seen quite new. I have no idea of letting these things lie by till somebody else has the advantage of them – and shall therefore try to publish them next Spring.[4]

I am extremely interested in Metaphysics; almost too much, in fact, so that I have had some doubts whether 21 months continuous work at them (for the M A) would not be rather too much. The ultimate question of philosophy that between idealism and materialism is necessarily an insoluble one, but one also on which we cannot avoid speculating with interest. Nor can I say that I yet feel bottom, I am somewhat as I was among the water lillies* & rushes out of my depth in a small Minnesota Lake when the fishes proved a too interesting sport for my prudence.

I find volunteering[5] an excellent antidote to Metaphysics; marching to a good band in full regimental order is really a most inspiring thing and when we form a battalion square bristling with bayonets the effect is most warlike. I generally go on Saturday afternoons in uniform for parade & battalion drill; also once a week before breakfast for skirmishing exercise in Hyde Park; on the latter occasions I have some 8 or 10 miles walking before breakfast with the addition of a rifle to carry and often a good deal of double-marching (running) For four hours every day of the week (morning & evening) some or other of our corps are at drill so that it is only a wonder that we do not make more rapid progress. We muster from 50 to 100 in the mornings & from 400 to 600 on Saturdays. Tomorrow afternoon we are to have a brigade field day in Hyde park when we shall be brigaded with The South Middlesex, West *do*, Six foot volunteer guards, Working Men's College Corps & perhaps others. The total strength of the above five[6] corps is perhaps 2500 men of whom about 1500 or 1600 may be expected to attend on any day. The volunteers altogether must be approaching about 150,000 and although there are some drawbacks, the success on the whole is quite beyond what any one could have expected a year or even 6 months ago. I like your idea of giving the franchise to volunteers above 21 years, I think they should also be exempted from serving on juries. Some regulations would be necessary as to attendance, but in a double way it would greatly tend to increase the numbers & regularity of attendance.

You will be glad to hear of the Sicilian Insurrection and of Garibaldi's feats. He is now the hero of Europe, and there is nothing at which

[4] Cf. the entries in Jevons's diary for February 1860, reproduced in Vol. IV, Part III. On the basis of these entries Professor J. A. La Nauze has claimed that 'young Jevons arrived on one identifiable day, February 19, 1860, at a comprehension of the "true theory of economy".' La Nauze, 'The Conception of Jevons's Utility Theory', *Economica*, xx (Nov 1953) 356–8.
[5] For details of Jevons's volunteer activities, see Vol. I, p. 36.
[6] Jevons first wrote 'London Irish' after 'West *do*' but crossed it out.

people here are more sincerely pleased than the defeat of the Neapolitans.⁷ Garibaldi has proclaimed Sicily a part of the King of Piedmonts Kingdom but the French Emperor will have a few words to say on this subject. The Emperor is also intriguing with the Russians who are again wanting Turkey so that politics are more uneasy than ever. I cannot the least agree with your opinions on non-interference – which is the Liverpool Manchester and Yankee doctrine and would soon place the whole world at the mercy of a few despots. England is now as it was 50 years ago the only check upon the French & Russians. As if we had not enough else to think about the house of Lords have just rejected a bill for the repeal of the paper duty thus imposing a tax of £1,400,000 on the people, when for hundreds of years it was thought to be the basis of the Constitution that taxation belonged to the Commons alone. People have as yet scarcely got over the first great surprise of such a breach in the constitution. But I have no doubt the Lords will hear and feel enough to bring them to their senses, and it is not unlikely the Gov^t may refuse to collect the tax.⁸ The English Constitution is not a subject to joke upon but really Lord Derby has brought us into a ludicrous position, at which no doubt the Americans will chuckle.

The visitors to London at this time are rather numerous; we have here at present Uncle Timothy & Mary C. who are sight seeing. Uncle T. came up with an American family who are all the go. Lucy & Henny are all well & full of sight seeing; soon they will go to Englefield relinquishing a part of one lodgings here, while Tom & I shall remain chiefly where we are, throughout the summer. It is fully arranged that Tom goes into the Office at completion of the B A. and it is likely but not sure that Lucy Henny & I will remain in these or other lodgings.

Ever your affectionate Brother.
W S Jevons

145. W. S. JEVONS TO HERBERT JEVONS
[LJP, 152–4]

8 Porteus Road. Pad^n. W.
July 25th 1860.

My dear Herbert

On returning home with Tom from a walk of 3 days in North Wales, I am glad to find a letter from you arrived in the meantime which I

---

⁷ 'In May 1860 Garibaldi and his thousand volunteers landed in Sicily, and overthrew the Bourbon Government.' Woodward, op. cit., pp. 302–3.

⁸ This situation was avoided the following year by including repeal of the tax on paper in proposals for the alteration of taxation for the year, which were contained in a single Bill; this passed through both Houses and the repeal took effect from 1 October 1861. At this time the tax yielded about £1,350,000. Cf. Dowell, op. cit., IV 342.

answer at once as it appears to me a long time since I last wrote. I would indeed write oftener were the postage not so high as a shilling for I am becoming more and more economical as I find the proofs of London expensiveness always thickening, and the time when I shall be earning my living again, always receding. Newspapers appear to be welcome to you and do not cost us more than the penny stamp since Uncle T. sends us the Spectator & Examiner. I will therefore post you at least one each week.

In the loss of most of the corn you planted, you experience some of the troubles of farming. It is doubtless not a cheering prospect to remain for many years in Minnesota, and I am somewhat sorry that you did not choose when you were making a change, an English colony, whether town or country, where the society would in the long run have proved more suitable. But it is, I should think, not very likely that you will now feel inclined to go a long distance and undertake a long and dreary separation from home. It is, I think, not practicable for you to farm in England, as you would have to compete with experienced farmers and to struggle against high rents in a manner almost unknown in Australia; in short you would require an agricultural education and considerable capital, and might even then be ruined by a bad season or by an unfortunate choice. As to whether you would again undertake a town life and a clerk's work depends entirely on your own feelings, but you should not forget after the hard but invigorating work of a settlers life how dispiriting a town life may be to those who are not strongly enough excited by the love of gain or some other love, and who have been once led to take wider views of the world than what are restricted within brick walls. For myself, if I were not affected by what I may almost call an unfortunate love of study & of particular pursuits, I would not long be in London, but would prefer labouring in some fine open wild country. And unless I can really succeed in what I have on hand, I shall never cease regretting that I ever left Australia. If I undertake the M.A. as I intend, there will be nothing but study before me for two whole years, and then there is no better prospect than before of earning a living. I feel really so much better suited to a literary life than any other that I shall lay myself out for it, perhaps beginning with much work and small pay in the newspaper line.

As regards your coming to London, we should all I am sure be glad to be reunited as far as possible, and if you could obtain a suitable place and make up your mind to the murky streets, super civilized manners and contracted notions of Londoners, nothing could be better. But you must be aware that we have no real home in London only Lodgings, that Tom will be fixed in Liverpool for five years at least and that Lucy & Henny are often away on visits. From our limited incomes and the uncertainties in which we are all placed, it is not possible to take a permanent house, and we are lucky in having found lodgings, comfortable and on reasonable terms, & kept by a family who are apparently anxious for us to remain. Until now we have had four rooms for £2 per week, now Tom is going we are to have three rooms for £1.10.0 so that the cost remains permanently at 10 shillings each per week. Provisions, especially meat (which is from 9 to 12 pence per lb) being very dear and Lucy not being quite so sparing as would best suit my circumstances, the weekly housekeeping expenses vary from 11 to 17 shillings per week, say an average of 13 shillings. Thus the yearly cost of board & lodging alone is £60 or £65. I spend very little on clothes, perhaps £15, but you may well believe that pocket money and extra expenses raise the total to about £100 without counting college & University fees. As my proper income is only £60 a year of course I have a large deficit to be filled from capital. Henny & Lucy have each as you know a pretty good income of £100 or £120 per annum, but I am really in some doubt whether they are not at present exceeding it, although Henry always recruits money when required. Tom has the best look out for when he enters Rathbones office at Christmas, he will receive £20 (on an average) per year from them; Jevons & C⁰ will allow him £50 per year as before, and he has £30 per year of his own. Hs is for the present to live at Uncle T's for only £30 per year so that he will have £70 for clothes, pocket-money, etc. If this turns out so he has suggested repaying me the £250 I sent for his college expenses, as far as convenient.

As you may not have heard of this arrangement concerning Tom I must state that he is to be engaged to Rathbones office for five years from next Xmas, and we are glad that he should be among such highly respectable people, and in an office where he will learn so much. It is to the latter that J & C⁰ look in recommending the office, and it is understood that he will join J & C⁰ at the end of the time as Fred[1] has done. Uncle T. wished Tom to come into their own office for the next five months previous to Xmas, but the B A stands in the way. You must allow I think that Henry & Uncle T. are doing for Tom as much as could well be done for him. They tried to make a bargain with the Rathbones for less than five years but this did not succeed; you will be glad I should think to hear of Tom joining such an office.

Lucy & Henny are now at Englefield where Lucy will remain all the Autumn while Henny in August goes for a considerable visit to Liverpool. After the prize giving at College, Tom & Will Jevons & I went down to Englefield also, and I was persuaded to stay some 12 days there, walking, bathing, playing quoits etc. Then I came up intending

---

[1] Frederick Jevons, his cousin.

to work at College for evermore, when Tom quickly following showed me that there was an excursion train to Llangollan for 11 shillings there and back. I was soon overpersuaded and we accordingly had three pleasant days in N Wales. On the first we walked from Ll. to Bala, on the second we ascended a high mountain 8 or 10 miles from Bala, called *Arreuig*, whence we had a magnificent view of the whole of N Wales (a finer view I should think than could be had from any other of the mountains). On the third day we walked back to Llangollan. The country pleased me much and the hotels were more comfortable than the American or Australian ones.

Now however I must attack in earnest the catalogue of work for the B A in October viz. Latin, Greek, Mathematics, Roman History, Greek History, English History, French, Animal physiology, Logic, Natural philosophy, Moral philosophy, all of which require looking up seriously and many to be learnt from the beginning.

In the College examinations I only went in for the Mental Philosophy and Political Economy. In the first the result came out

Equal prizes & certificates	{ Theodore Waterhouse[2] { W S Jevons.
2nd certificate	T. E. Jevons
3rd certificate	Francis Kossuth
4th certificate	Louis Kossuth

This is on the whole a satisfactory result since T. Waterhouse is certainly the first student of the College during the session and has carried all other prizes before him. I had hopes of beating him but am satisfied, considering that he attended better to the lectures than myself, to be equal. Tom had some hankerings after the prize but any disappointment on that score is assuaged by his conquest of the two sons of Kossuth[3] who thought they could beat everybody.

In Political Economy I had a sad reverse, such indeed as I never had before, for in spite of having studied the subject independently and originally and having read some dozens of the best works in it, almost

[2] Theodore Waterhouse (1838–91) was born at Aigburth, near Liverpool, of a Quaker family. He entered University College, London, in 1856, and graduated with honours in Mental and Moral Science in 1860; at the time when Jevons wrote this letter, Waterhouse had won twelve first prizes during his undergraduate courses, as well as an English essay and a Latin prose prize. In the session of 1861–2 he was awarded the First Certificate and Prize in Political Economy. In 1862 he was articled as a solicitor, and from 1864 onwards practised as such in London. He was engaged mainly in family business, but also in company flotations, most notably that of the Edison Telephone Company of London. See Edward [Lord Justice] Fry, *Theodore Waterhouse, 1838–1891; Notes of his life and extracts from his letters and papers* (printed for private circulation only, 1894).

[3] Lajos Kossuth (1802–94), Hungarian revolutionary who had declared his country's independence in April 1849, but was later forced to flee to Turkey and thence to France and Britain, where he was enthusiastically received.

neglecting other classes for the purpose, I was placed 3rd or 4th when I felt confident of the first prize.⁴ This I can only attribute to a diff^ce of opinion which is perfectly allowable having prejudiced the Prof^r. against my answers. However I shall fully avenge myself when I bring out my "Theory of Economy" and reestablish the Science on a sensible basis. The worst is that my chance of the Ricardo Scholarship of £60 to be awarded by the College next Decr in Pol. Econ. is naturally much endangered, since the Professor is one of the examiners.⁵ Richard Hutton⁶ is the other examiner, and it is not a little lucky that I am becoming pretty well acquainted with him, having accidentally met him at Teddington close to his house, & being invited, had dinner and much scientific conversation with him. R. Hutton is now much the same sort of literary & scientific hack as I am looking forward to being; he is a sub editor of the Economist, editor of the National review, Examiner in Econ. at the University, & so on, but he has been a long time in reaching what he has. Of course I should expect to strike out more original ideas than he favours the world with, although he may be a very good student & writer. The Autumn months will be in no small degree dull for Tom & me, dwelling in London & Cramming. Tom I do not doubt will often go to Englefield & so probably shall I occasionally. I have got a ticket of admission to the British Museum reading room, where I can spend my whole time, if I like, with a luxurious reading desk to myself, and the largest & finest library in the world entirely at my command. I do not know whether you have seen the new Reading Room, but it is certainly a perfect Paradise for readers, and by far the finest thing of the sort existing. I have as yet only been once but shall often go in future.

⁴ The Prize and First Certificate were awarded to Herbert H. Cozens-Hardy (1838–1920), afterwards Master of the Rolls, as Keynes notes (*Essays in Biography*, p. 293). The second place was given 'to a Student whose envelope was not returned to the Office' and Jevons was placed equal third with Marcus Nathan Adler (*Calendar of University College, London, 1860–61*, p. 74). This accounts for his use of the phrase 'third or fourth'.

The paper on which Jevons was examined was also reprinted in the *Calendar of University College, London, 1860–61*, at p. 167, and is reproduced in Vol. IV.

⁵ Jevons's fears in this respect were unjustified: he was in fact awarded the Ricardo Scholarship: cf. below, Letter 148, p. 422.

⁶ Richard Holt Hutton (1826–97). Born at Leeds, the son of a Unitarian minister; studied at University College, London, and afterwards at Heidelberg, Berlin and Bonn. Became editor of the Unitarian *Inquirer*, but his views (not now entirely Unitarian) gave offence and he resigned. Ordered to the West Indies for his health, where his first wife, Mary Anne Roscoe, contracted yellow fever and died.

On his return from the West Indies Hutton became joint editor with Walter Bagehot (a fellow student at U.C.L.) of the *National Review*, assistant editor of *The Economist* and professor of mathematics at Bedford College. In 1861 he became joint editor and proprietor, with Meredith Townsend, of the *Spectator*, and continued in that capacity until 1886.

His second wife was a cousin of his first, and both were grand-daughters of William Roscoe.

I should add that Tom went into two other examinations at College viz the Extra Greek class, & the senior Latin in both of which he got high certificates. His memory is very good and he can learn anything which he chooses with great ease, so that I am confirmed in my opinion that he has the best natural abilities in our family. It is only from his not applying himself with sufficient force to any one or more subjects that he fails to get prizes. I used to consider that I could myself get any prize for which I properly tried, but I am now beginning to feel less suited for conflicts in which memory and quickness gain the day.

I do not wonder at your objection to furthur* changes since I feel the same myself; a certain restlessness seems likely to be the ruin of our family. We are all of us rolling stones and gather no moss. I half suspect that I shall some time be again an emigrant, in which case I shall certainly make for the beautiful scenery and the English-like Colony of N. Zealand, but I will first have a fair try of a good many years here.

I had intended writing you a full account of our volunteer proceedings, but what with the Royal Review, the great Shooting match & many other exciting events, the Volunteers have for the last month been so extremely triumphant and the objects of such general admiration, that I am slightly surfeited. I have not recently attended much, but our Colonel seems very sensibly inclined to dispense with furthur* show and put us through a very thorough course of musketry instruction which is well attended every day, and which I shall also regularly attend. The movement is gradually extending to small places, & in North Wales we found that each small town either had or was about to have a company. Even if only half the enrolled members continue permanently (& a much larger proportion probably will), there will yet remain an army of 70,000 or 80,000, of the best made & most intelligent men of this English race, better armed and clothed than any other soldiers which is no small addition to the strength of the country. The companies too, which are now organised could easily be raised to double their strength on any emergency. The fleet is ever becoming larger & finer, and the Gov^t are just commencing the expenditure of £12,000,000 on fortifications, so that there is not the least fear of English supremacy being lost. The French Emperor has almost conferred a benefit upon us in thus raising our latent spirit. English diplomacy is much slanged by Englishmen but do you not see that the English & French combined rule the world, and effect much good, as in checking Russia, liberating Italy, overcoming the Chinese, not to speak of this Syrian business, while France is restrained by the English opinion from any very wrongful exertions of power?[7] When the two fall out, God help the weakest,

---

[7] This was the era of Palmerston's confident assertion of British power in foreign affairs. Palmerston and his foreign secretary, Russell, were at this time supporting the cause of the

for you may depend upon it that the English & French are as hearty enemies as ever. Few now attempt to keep up the humbug of "La Belle Alliance" "Fraterité"* and all that. We had 3000 French singers or Orphéonists lately at the Crystal Palace. 600 of them complained in the papers of their lodgings, & their leader got put into prison by his hotelkeeper. In spite of much palaver the whole thing fell very flat.

Fred Roscoe[8] has just passed the first B A Exam^n. and is likely to get very good honours in classics. He is the best classical student of our college & likely to do credit to the name of Roscoe. We see a good deal of the Robert Roscoes either in town or at Englefield, and I constantly meet Frank & Dick in my volunteer Com^y.

I have recently had a very good letter from Charles Bolton in Sydney; he had returned from the diggings and was again in the Mint as assistant in the Melting house at 8 shillings per day which although not so good as the 11 shillings he received under me, appeared to satisfy him. He was in decidedly good spirits.

Your letter has been posted to Lucy but we cannot have any answer in time to send with this. In your next will you show me how your cleared land is laid out, & where the hut is:

Ever your affectionate Brother
W. S. Jevons

146. HERBERT JEVONS TO W. S. JEVONS

nr Wayzata 6 Novr 1860
Hennepin County Minnesota

Dear Stanley

This is the great day of the Presidential election but I not being naturalized could not vote for President. I cannot tell you the actual result but it is considered certain that Honest old Abe as they call him will be elected, & that by means of all the free states against all the slave states. I will give you a few particulars about the present condition and future prospects of my beloved North star state. Winter is just about setting in the ground has been hard & frozen today & a clear bracing day after some cloudy raw weather. I have bought the first government statistical report of this state & will pick out a few items. In

---

Italians against Austria, and an Anglo-French expedition to Peking had forced the Chinese to open Tientsin and other ports to trade with the West. In 1860 civil war broke out in Syria, then a province of the Ottoman Empire, between Christians and Druses, an Islamic sect, and led to military intervention by France.

[8] See above, Letter 143, n. 8, p. 407.

Minnesota is the actual centre of the N. American continent. Emigration from New Orleans & Texas up to Minnesota has already reached the limits of the great desert of North America which begins about 98 of W.L. The great drought this season in Kansas shows that; – the inhabitants are now calling on the East for provisions to keep them alive. The only remaining territory of Emigration lies in Minnesota & the Saskatchewan & Red river valleys in B. America & there will be found to be the best farming countries in the continent. Almost the entire traffic to & from these two great valleys will have to pass through Minnesota to the Mississippi or lake Superior. The monthly means of F. Temperature at Fort Snelling at junction of Minnesota River with Mississippi are Dec 16.9 Jan 13.7 Feb 17.16. Mar 31.4 Ap 46.3 May 59 June 68.4 July 73.4 Aug 70.1 Sep 58.9 Oct 47.1 Nov 31.7. Rains cal: for 19 years at St Paul in inches Mar 1.30 Ap 2.14 May 3.17 June 3.63 July 4.11 Aug 3.18 Sep 3.32 Oct 1.35 Nov 1.31 Dec .67 Jan .73 Feb .52 November it is all snow. Minnesota wheat that has gone to Chicago has been found superior in quality to all the other states & we raise more to the acre at the same time. The national railway route & the only water route across the continent pass thro* Minnesota & thro* the Saskatchewan valley, which latter will be all settled with Yankees within the next 25 years.

The crops in Minnesota are surer by reason of regular rains than other states. The climate is far healthier than other parts of the United States, not a few who are living here have come on account of their health. Fever & ague leaves them when they come here & it helps consumptive folks. There is an advantage it has over Kansas & Iowa namely that it is better wooded.

When I came here in August 58 the financial state of the times was almost at their worst.[1] 99 out of 100 people you met were hard up & had a long complaining face. The first immediate circumstance that raised the inhabitants out of the slough of Despond was the arrival in the Spring of 59 of ginseng[2] buyers & all the time that people in the woods & some out of them could spare was spent in digging that root for which they got about 6 cents the pound green & at which they earned on an average $1\frac{1}{4}$ to $1\frac{1}{2}$ dollars per day. Then they have got over double I should think of land in cultivation, and the spirits of the community are generally much better. There comes however this fall a great blow

---

[1] He altered this sentence from 'the times were' without changing 'their' to 'its'.

[2] This is the common name of the genus Panax, a group of perennial herbs of the aralia family, native to woodlands in the Northern Temperate zone. The *Panax quinquefolia* was discovered in eastern North America after supplies of the *Panax schiseng* of Manchuria, which was widely cultivated by the Chinese, became insufficient. The dried root of the plant fetched a high price and was exported in large quantities to China, where ginseng was valued as a medicine.

to those squatters who have not & cannot pay for their lands. Last winter the Republicans did their best to pass a Homestead Bill giving each squatter, with certain limitations, 160 acres of land but the Democrat Senate first half spoilt the bill, & the president Buchanan afterwards vetoed it, & after that again ordered all the unpreempted surveyed lands of Kansas Iowa Wisconsin & Minnesota for sale. These sales were to have come off latter end of last month & this month but no speculators appear to have come forward. I dont know the cause but the squatters on lands west of us had determined on mobbing any speculator that dared to bid on any of their lands. In Sydney you wrote about reducing the price of government land. The Republicans here mean to do it with a vengeance namely make a gift of 160 acres on condition of occupation & cultivation by the party for 5 years.

What a mess your thick headed English colonel has made of the insurrection in New Zealand[3] that is the worst of living in an English colony you are sure to have some imbecile cowardly stuck up governor or commander to injure the colony in some way or to brow beat the colonists.

In B. Columbia they charge 10/– an acre in that out of the way region while here in a civilized region first sale land cheap conveyance from Europe, Electric Telegraph from the East to Minneapolis Mail in 3 or 4 days from New York & they charge you here 1:25 $ or just half of 10/–. The only way England can keep her territory on this continent west of lake superior* is to make a railway across it. If they are wise they will at once start a large independen[t] colony North West of this & call it Saskatchewan [and?][4] establish two or three towns on the best sites along the rivers by slips of land from the natives. The people here will put up a few saw & grist mills & two or 3 steamers & there would be a thriving colony in almost no time & [that?][5] in a climate natural and beneficial to the Saxon. He wont degenerate like he does in Australia. One of the great wants of the present day is a serviceable steam plough or machine to answer for a plough an idea occurred to me that one might be made in the following manner, namely a sort of Locomotive with 3 or 4 strong axles fixed near the ground underneath

---

[3] The Maori wars, which were mostly confined to the North Island of New Zealand, occurred intermittently, 1843–72, during which period the Maoris were under pressure from a rapidly increasing European population to alienate vast areas of land. The most serious fighting took place during the 1860s. Herbert Jevons is probably referring to Col. Charles Emilius Gold (d. 1871), who precipitated the outbreak of the first Taranaki war (March 1860–March 1861) by destroying Maori fortifications, crops, etc. He remained in charge of military operations until August 1860. The Maoris were skilled fighters and the conduct of the war reflected little credit upon the Europeans. For a detailed account see *Cambridge History of The British Empire*, VII, Part ii, pp. 120–142.

[4] The edge of the page is torn.

[5] A small piece of the page has been torn out.

armed with Iron prongs which being driven round by the Engine will go through the earth something like small paddle wheels. A great number of them would while tearing & mixing the earth fine a better way than mere ploughing, at the same time send the whole machine forward thus making the ploughing force the locomotive force as well. The advantage of this plan beyond the other steam ploughs now showing in this country is that in them the ploughs behind hold back, in mine my plough apparatus sends the machine forward. What do you think of this plan of mine. I am rather taken with it myself. By this time you & Tom will have passed your BA examinations and be glad that you have done so. It is about time that I should again hear from home; tho* I get a newspaper almost every week from you tho' they are far inferior in quality to the New York Tribune which I take along with my neighbour opposite and which is a better paper than any published in England.[6] There is more cleverness, information wit, & open frankness in it, tho' you must if you please continue to send me your papers as usual. I send you this week a Tribune. Your affectionate brother

Herbert Jevons.

147. W. S. JEVONS TO HERBERT JEVONS
[LJN, 155–6]

8 Porteus Road,
28th November 1860.

... I am now attending college again regularly. My classes are De Morgan's[1] higher senior mathematics, Potter's[2] senior mathematical natural philosophy, Malden's[3] extra Greek class, and Mr. Martineau's[4] mental philosophy class in the Manchester New College,[5] which is close

---

[6] The *New York Tribune* was founded in 1841 by Horace Greeley (1811–72), an influential supporter of Abraham Lincoln and fervent advocate of the emancipation of slaves.

[1] See Vol. I, p. 15; and cf. above, Letter 15, p. 29.

[2] See Vol. I, p. 65, n. 5.

[3] See Vol. I, p. 82, n. 7.

[4] James Martineau (1805-1900), younger brother of Harriet Martineau. Originally destined for a career as an engineer, he turned to theology and was trained for the Unitarian ministry at Manchester New College (see note 5 below). Minister of Eustace Street Presbyterian Meeting House, Dublin, 1827–32; of Paradise Street Chapel, Liverpool, 1832–48. Appointed Professor of Mental and Moral Philosophy and Political Economy, Manchester New College, 1840. Minister of Hope Street Chapel, Liverpool, 1849–57; resigned on becoming one of two full-time professors in the reorganised Manchester New College: Principal of the College, 1869–85.

[5] Manchester New College was, during the early nineteenth century, the principal institution of higher education in arts and theology for Unitarians. Founded in Manchester in 1786, it was moved to York in 1803 but returned to Manchester in 1840, and in the same year became associated with University College, London. In 1853 the College itself was transferred to London and set up in University Hall, Gordon Square.

at hand in University Hall. I am, of course, better up to De Morgan's brain-rackings this session, and shall devote much time to mathematics, yet, from having no natural talent for figures or quick memory, have no hope of becoming a practical mathematician. Besides, it is somewhat late in the day at twenty-six to learn mathematics, with which you will succeed from the first or never. The extra Greek class is a very pleasant one, being a lecture once a week for the elder students out of the regular course. We are now reading a Greek tragedy, and are soon to do some of Aristotle, which is what I chiefly desire. I have not much knowledge of Greek, but am gaining by degrees a proper admiration for Greeks, who, as philosophers, poets, generals, and so forth, certainly exceeded anything which individuals of all later time are likely to produce.

. . . Metaphysics is a rather too interesting study, and I am not inclined to pursue it so much as those, such as political economy and moral philosophy, which are equally in the clouds at present, but might become useful.

I expect every success from my theory of political economy, which seems to develop itself with that facility which is a proof of its soundness. It assumes the form of a complicated mathematical problem, from which all the common laws with due limitations flow. Independently, however, of the mathematical form, it has led me to a new view of the action of *capital*, which affords a determining principle for *interest, profits of trade, wages*; and I now perceive how the want of knowledge of this determining principle throws the more complicated discussions of economists into confusion. The common law is that demand and supply of labour and capital determine the division between wages and profits. But I shall show that the whole capital employed can only be paid for at the same rate as the *last portion added*; hence it is the increase of produce or advantage, which this last addition gives, that determines the interest of the whole.

I shall try to spare more time for this theory before long, and get it into form without much delay. . . .[6]

148. W. S. JEVONS TO LUCY JEVONS AND T. E. JEVONS
[LJN, 156]

8 Porteus Road,
9th December 1860.

. . . You will hear with pleasure, if not with surprise, that the Ricardo Scholarship[1] is actually within my reach, although it will not be formally

---

[6] Almost two years elapsed before Jevons 'resolved . . . at last to let out my theory of economy'; cf. below, Letter 165, p. 452.   [1] See below, Letter 145, n. 5, p. 416.

given me and published until the College Council meet again next January. The examination was for six hours last Tuesday, and proved a rather hard fight. The amount of lucre, you know, is £60, but the first £20 is not payable till February. . . .

149. HERBERT JEVONS TO W. S. JEVONS

Wayzata Hennepin C^{ty} Minnesota
1 April 1861

My dear Stanley

I received yours and Henny's letters[1] about three weeks since, & have been about to write an answer to them ever since but have got started only now.

I am at present engaged sugar making with a man from the prairie beyond St Anthony he lives with me & has been with me nearly three weeks already. We make the sugar from the sap of the Maple trees as you will no doubt be aware of, Spring is just commencing here & in about 2 weeks sugar making will be over, after that I think I shall put in enough crops to keep me in exercise & may be stay till they are grown & taken in. I think however that before the summer season is quite over I shall leave here. I may possibly go to a water cure establishment in New York State tho' that is yet only an idea I have got in my head & possibly I may go home to England again after that or go straight home but I am quite unfixed as to what I shall finally determine upon. I think I am as healthy altogether as I was when I left England perhaps more so but I am not in a good state of health. I dont see what course I ought to take, but perhaps if I wait a little my way may clear up.

I dont altogether dislike this place nor the people I have got amongst but my being brought up so differently to the people here is an obstacle to my being quite at ease among them & I dont know but what it is right for me to start being a *gentleman* again I am quite as hopeful for the future as I ever was & you must be satisfied with the above as to myself & my doings & intentions for the present.

As to the country I am living in I can only say that the way I like to regard their political prospects is to wait & see what happens. America is very different from England; the people I mean. The latter have a fixed character & seem to be changing & maturing slowly. Americans are forming & changing very quick* & very much. Their manners customs, & religious opinions are all changing & it seems to me best to leave them alone & let them work out their own salvation. but it will be very hard to avoid a war between the South & the North. The

[1] These letters are not among the Jevons Papers.

Gov^t are acting in a very careful & conciliatory manner towards the seceding states but Abe Lincoln considers himself bound to collect the revenue & that will exasperate the fire eaters very much. It is rather a sad event for James[2] to die from home & without even white people to attend to him in his last hours. People keep dying off one after the other & it is certainly a strange world this.

I note what you say about Harry Enfield. I suppose he is destined to make his mark in the world. He will I dare say be of use to you more than once but it is a mistake for you to compare yourself to him. It seems to me rather odd of you attending Martineaus metaphysical lectures. I never read Kant or knew what his explanations of things in general were but I am inclined to think they are merely a string of clever fancies. The truth about Metaphysics is not to be put in a book or treatise. I am inclined to think that the tendency of the present age is to deprecate the importance of Metaphysical studies & stick to exact science & practical knowledge & coming to that I wish I could give you & the rest a taste of our syrup & sugar.

The British Gov^t has been snubbing the [ ][3] I read in the papers. if I was them I [ ] out for all the priviliges* that were at [ ] as soon as they are reduced to milit [ ] spring & pride of volunteering is taken a [ ] of the honor.* You dont say anything a [ ] letter about y^r Political Economy disc [ ] you still believe that you have found [ ] correct principles of the science & are proceeding with the book you intended to write.

I strum on my fiddle every day now & it helps to ease my mind sometimes tho' my fingers are so thick and stiff that I cannot make any decent sounds, however my sugar making partner aids me to play now & then so I suppose it eases his mind too, & he has just had a disappointment in love. I suppose you or Tom have been us[ing][4] the skates I bought some time ago. I gave them t[o] Tom I believe. There are chances for skating here sometimes, tho' generally the ice is covered with snow. I have had a hard days work today, up before sunrise & working till past seven. I have a pack of cards now & lately the neighbours have come in & we have had some good games at fourhanded cribbage & such. My love to Lucy Henny & Tommy

Your affec. brother
Herbert Jevons

[2] See above, Letter 43, n. 7, p. 89.
[3] A square portion is missing from the top right-hand corner of this page.
[4] The edge of the page is torn.

150. W. S. JEVONS TO HERBERT JEVONS
[LJP, 157-8]

8 Porteus Road. Paddington
7 April 1861.[1]

My dear Herbert

A longer time than usual has elapsed since my last le[tter] and I am afraid we are both rather too apt to let newspapers take the place of letters. There is not much however even now for me to tell you, and to fi[ll] my paper I shall perhaps have to discuss politics which are interesting enough at present. We are here much as usual, having just got over the Easter holydays,* but without much holyday* work. Tom came up to see us for a few days imagining I suppose that London and our lodgings are every[thing] which is beautiful. Lucy and Henny are well and active although Lucy at least thinks she could not get on without a little medicine & medical advice now & then, and is in consequence forbidden at present beef, tea, coffee, & half the things which we generally esteem most wholesome. T[hey] are going next week to stay at Englefield with Patty who is troubled now with gall-stones, a painful but not a dangerous disease.

I am very busy at present with an apparently dry and laborious piece [of] work, namely compiling quantities of statistics concerning Great Britain which are to be exhibited in the form of curves, and if possible publish[ed] as a "Statistical Atlas".[2] The work will I think be very

---

[1] This letter, written on blue lightweight paper, is in a fragile condition, very frayed at the edges and considerably torn. Missing words and queries have been placed inside square brackets.

[2] Jevons did not in fact publish this work, but his plan of its contents has survived among papers now in the possession of the Royal Statistical Society, and is as follows:

'Contents
  Preface
  Introd.
  Ch. I On the Nature of Stat^l Science
    II On the graphical repres of Stat^l Data.
    III Sketch of the Commercial History of Great Britain.
    IV Conclusions to be [?drawn] from the Statistics presented in this Atlas.
    V Chronological table of events capable of affecting the Stat^l condition of the country.
Table of authorities referred to.
Note as to the construction of the diagrams.
28 Plates
  In front of each plate, a leaf of letter press containing a short Essay, and a table of contents and ref^{ces} for the plate.

Contents of the Plates

Plate I Population and its changes
  II Revenue and Expenditure of the U.K.
  III National Debt
  IV Chronology and Statistics of the Government

[*continued overleaf*]

interesting and important when done but the labour of rummaging the chaos of the Parliam[entary] Papers and then copying & calculating great columns of figures, is rather depressing to the spirits. I have been the last five days at the Muse[um] upon it but next week I shall have College work again to interfere w[ith] it. Almost the whole of the statistics go back to 1780 or 1800, a large part extend to 1700, or 1720, and some – for instance the price of corn as far back as 1400. The quantity of statistics which I shall exhibit in about 30 plates will I think rather astonish people – for instance there will be the population – births, deaths, marriages emigration etc as far as known. The revenue from various sources, – the expenditure – the Govt loans, the national debt, at different periods, property in savings banks, fir[e] offices etc – the operations of the clearing houses, bank of England retu[rns] since

    v Inventions – Literature of Economy and Biographical Chronology.
   vi (double) Funds, Price of Wheat, Rate of Discount and Bankruptcy
  vii Bank of England – Half Yearly Returns
 viii (double) Bank of England – Weekly Returns
   ix Transactions of the Banker's Clearing House. Bank Note Circulation, etc.
    x Bills of Exchange, Bank Note Circulation, Rate of Discount and prices of principal commodities.
   xi Miscellaneous Statistics concerning Capital.
  xii Price of Shares, Gold, Silver, Rates of Exchange and Coinage
 xiii Imports and Exports.
 xiv Shipping & Inland Conveyance
  xv Cotton
 xvi Wool and Silk
xvii Coal and Iron
xviii Metals and Minerals
 xix Building and other Materials
  xx Price, Imports and Exports of Wheat
 xxi Food, Pauperism, Change of Population, Price and Quantities of Wheat, Barley and Oats Sold.
 xxii Prices of Provisions and Fodder.
xxiii Wine, spiritous liquors.
xxiv Spiritous liquors, tobacco etc.
 xxv Tea, Sugar, Coffee
xxvi Trade with various countries.
xxvii Wages, Pauperism
xxviii Miscellaneous Statistics of Literature, Morals and Crime.'

On the back of the first sheet giving 'Contents of Plates' is written:
        The Commercial Atlas
        presenting in a series of
        Ten diagrams
    The Bank of England Returns
    The State of the Funds,
    the Rate of Discount, Bankruptcy
    the prices of the chief articles of commerce
    and other Commercial Statistics.

It seems possible that this title, with its reference to *ten* diagrams, may have related to the second attempt to produce a Statistical Atlas which Jevons made some eighteen months later. See below, Letter 168, p. 461.

1770, circulation since 1700, *weekly returns* of B of E since 1843, the price of the funds since 1723 – Imports, Exports, to different countries – supplies of cotton corn – wool & every principal article produce & prices of the metals, provisions materials etc. The [condition] as to pauperism – the rate of wages – strikes (perhaps) etc. [The naval] & military force of the country, the [num]ber of acts of Parliament [?] the number of patents, as a whole, and in various branches since 1623 the criminal condition of the country, – literature – etc etc. Railways, roads, shipping – –

The chief interest of the work will be in the light thrown upon the Commercial storms of 1793, 1815, 1826, 1839, 1847, 1857 etc the causes of which will be rendered more or less apparent. I find that the number of acts of Parliament, the number of patents, and the number of bricks manufactured are the best indications of an approaching panic, which arises generally from a large investment of labour in works not immediately profitable, as machinery, canals, railways etc. It is truly curious how [well] the curve of *bricks produced* shows this, bricks & mortar being the most enduring form of product. Most of the statistics of course is generally known but has never been so fully combined, or exhibited *graphically*. The statistics of patents, & some concerning literature will be quite new. The mode of exhibiting numbers by curves & lines, has of course [been][3] practised more or less any time on this side of the deluge. At the end of last century indeed I find that a book of 'charts of trade'[4] was published exactly resembling mine in principle, but in statistics the method never much used has fallen almost entirely into disuse. It ought I consider to be almost as much used as *maps* are used [in] geography. I have only properly undertaken the work since Christmas, and have now got nearly as much statistics as I require or can obtain but a large part of the more wearing work remains.

You did not say a word in your last letter about politics although you must [kn]ow how much we are interested in your American friends. I should like [to] have your opinion of the state of affairs. It seems to me that the North will have to knock under to the decision and readiness of the south – indeed where are there any forces to bring them under again. The only question is how long will Virginia, Maryland, Kentucky etc take to make up their minds for secession, and how long will your western states stand this rascally new Tariff. If Illinois, Michigan, Minnesota, Iowa, Missouri etc have any sense they will split from the Eastern states & form a Western Agricultural Federation, shipping their

[3] Omitted in the original manuscript.
[4] There seems no reason to question Keynes's identification of this work as William Playfair's *The Commercial and Political Atlas, representing, by means of stained copperplate charts, the exports, imports and general trade of England; the national debt and other public accounts; with observations and remarks* . . . (1786). See Keynes, op. cit., p. 267.

corn & other produce [by] the Mississipi* or the Great Western Railway of Canada, getting our [goo]ds duty free in return. New England, New York, & Pensylvania* will [th]en be left to their own devices. This tariff however cannot last long. [Fr]ed⁵[?] who is in London informs me that arrangements are already being made for extensive smuggling through the slave states. The Great Model Republic is evidently doomed and its stars are rapidly setting. Its [poli]tical power in the world, always very small, is now gone entirely, and [?] separate federations manage to agree and become wiser they can never again pretend to a rivalry with Great Britain.

We are here in a very placid prosperous state, or rather should be did not the affairs of America France Italy etc disturb our minds and depress trade. The Bank rate of discount has been at 8 per cent for a length of time – an unprecedented occurrence I suppose – it is only just reduced to 6 p.c.[6] Yet no inconvenience seems to result from such an extreme rate and I have little doubt that the Bank by its judicious action is saving the country from a crisis. Parliament is having an extremely dull session as yet – Parliamentary Reform is altogether voted out for the present[7] the bankruptcy bill is to be passed,[8] and it appears likely that the old Admiralty will be broken up[9] like a worthless old hulk and be repla[ced] by a Minister of the Navy. All hope for the French Emperor will then be gone. Our Navy now is of overwhelming power but unfortunately the French are getting ahead with these new Iron ships.[10] Of course when the admiralty can make up their mind that iron is better than wood we can easily build ten times as many iron ships as the Emperor and the advantage will ultimately be immensely

[5] See above, Letter 56, n. 20, p. 132.

[6] Bank Rate was raised to 8 per cent on 14 February 1861 and remained at that level until 21 March, when it was reduced to 7 per cent. The further reduction to 6 per cent came on 4 April. The 8 per cent rate was not unprecedented; Bank Rate had been at that level in December 1857, and as high as 10 per cent in November 1857. The 8 per cent rate in February–March 1861 was due to the secession of the Southern states producing fears of a complete cotton famine. Cf. Clapham, *The Bank of England* (1944) II 257, 429.

[7] 'The disinclination which the country had manifested to the subject of Parliamentary Reform in the preceding year, was assumed by the Government to be a sufficient reason for abstaining, during the present session from bringing forward any general measure for that object' – *Annual Register*, 1861 [24].

[8] The Bill, which systematised earlier legislation and extended its scope, became the Bankruptcy Act, 24 & 25 Vict. c. 134.

[9] Although a Select Committee was appointed to enquire into the workings of the Board of Admiralty it did not recommend any changes, and none in fact took place until 1869. Cf. *Report from the Select Committee on the Board of Admiralty, Parl. Papers*, 1861 (438), v.

[10] 'Within three years of the peace of Paris the rapid construction of armoured ships by the French caused a panic in England . . . in 1858, however, the admiralty decided to build an armoured and iron-hulled capital ship. This ship (the *Warrior*) was launched in 1860. A year earlier the French admiralty had changed the design of four large wooden line-of-battle ships in order to give them armoured protection. *La Gloire*, the first of these ships, was launched in November 1859 . . .' Woodward, op. cit., p. 293.

on our side. It is the declared resolution of Lord Palmerston, his Government and all Englishmen except some few fools that this country must always have far more naval force than can by any combination of other countries be brought against it [and] this you may depend we shall do for the few next centuries.

It is not easy to express what fools the Yankees have lately shown themselves to be, or how entirely the Southern men have outmanoeuvred them. It is perfectly evident that the secession movement was determined on so[me] time since, probably when the democrats found themselves not quite so strong as the Republicans. The bungling or treason of almost all the Gov^t off[icers?] enabled the southern men to accomplish all they had arranged and now wh[at] a pretty kettle of fish there is. The cool folly of the Northern men too is almost vexing; they scarcely seem to know how much their entire prosperity is endang[ered] by such a split. The movements of the Southern men quite astonish people [?] for their rapidity and wisdom – excepting the export duty on cotton wh[ich] is naturally not liked – Still I think the southern states have seen their best and will probably decline and sink into a state of degradation and anarchy like the Spanish slave colonies before very long. As to [the] ultimate prosperity of the northern & N W. states especially there cannot I [?] be the least doubt. Although the federation proves to be a mere fiction [the] [sta]te is I think pretty sound and united within itself – Even if a state [?] [?] every town & district would instantly have its own independent gov[ernment] [?] although some misunderstandings might arise between so many diff[erent] governments, they would on the whole get on very well. The army [and navy?] at least have not rendered much service in supporting the const[itution] indeed they seem to have entirely vanished off the scene. Cobden and Bright may [ad]mire a country[11] which only requires a revenue of £12,000,000 but I wonder whether they consider the states at present to be a good model for us. The English pay heavy, it is true, but it is half for old scores & deeds of which they may mostly be proud – with the remainder they support a fleet of more than 500 ships, of which 50 or 60 are screw ships of the line and an army which is continually doing the most useful and successful services in all parts of the globe. And now we have an army of 100,000, or 150000 volunteers, of whom a large part are well trained and practised riflemen.

It is an universal but ignorant mistake to suppose that the progress of the [Am]ericans is the most extraordinary & hopeful thing in the world. The progress of England, London, & many of the English colonies within this century is just as remarkable and more solid. From about the

---

[11] 'county' in the original manuscript.

period 1780-1800 as my curves show very strikingly everything in England took a start quite comparable and equal to that of the Americans while the English preeminence in intellect and good government and policy remains as distinct as ever. I observe that Minnesota has increased in population between 1850 and 1860 from 6,000 to 162,000 but this is in no way comparable to the progress of Victoria where Melbourne one of the most important and [pro]mising cities in the world has been almost entirely produced since 1851, and an English state of some 500,000 inhabitants has arisen. The progress of London as it goes on before our eyes is perhaps the most extraordinary. Whole districts have become part of the town which I can remember as fields, and the most magnificent squares & streets of mansions at the West End, rise like mushrooms wherever there is [a] little waste ground. One consequence is that the traffic in the City is rapidly approaching to a complete dead block up. The traffic however will be greatly relieved in a year or two when all the new Metropolitan railways & stations are finished. The great new Gov^t [of]fices will be commenced shortly I suppose, as also probably a vast Palace of Justice to contain all the various Courts now scattered about London. The Great Exhibition for 1862 is now just on foot. The building [wi]ll be a large affair, but having been designed by a Royal Engineer very ugly unoriginal & in some respects absurd.[12] The first steps towards [thi]s exhibition were[13] by many persons considered very injudicious but [no] doubt the spontaneous energy of the public will make it successful.

One of the most ingenious and excellent proposals ever made is [likely?] [this?] year to be carried out by Mr Gladstone; it is to turn the Post office [money] order offices into small savings banks.[14] In every village [and] [almos]t every street there will thus be a bank in which any person may [dep]osit a sum of money fr[om] a few pence to a few pounds with almost absolute security, and with a fair return of interest combined with the money order system already so successful no[thing] could promise greater advantages in promoting the accumulation of m[oney] by the poor. In America of course it would not do as every post master would go off with all the receipts towards the end of his time, when the next President comes in.

I observe this evening that the Emperor is going to have a new Loan

[12] The buildings for the Great Exhibition of 1862 were designed by Captain Fowke of the Royal Engineers and occupied an area of 24½ acres in South Kensington. In addition to the main building there were two large annexes, described by another contemporary observer as 'of unpretending ugliness' (*Annual Register*, 1862, pp. 78–9). In 1864 Fowke designed permanent buildings to be erected on the Exhibition site, which became the South Kensington Museum.

[13] 'we' in the original manuscript.

[14] Gladstone's Post Office Savings Banks Bill received the Royal Assent on 17 May 1861. *Hansard*, 3rd series, 162, 2191.

and raise more soldiers so I suppose Europe must look out. What between the French, Italians, Hungarians, Poles, Danes, Prussians & Americans, the English have no time to attend to their own affairs; during this year every one expects there will be a terrible blow up on the contin[ent] but there is some hope that Germany as well as Italy will be formed into a strong kingdom to resist the French – well – the English have got their powder dry and ready – the rifle shoot[ing] and volunteering this summer will be something surprising. Our [?] of musketry instruction and class-shooting begins next month and I am practising up pretty vigourously.* On Tuesday I had 40 shots and at the short range made 24 points out of 20 shots, being rather better than my previous shooting. Frank Roscoe however was there the same day and made 26 – sin[ce] then I have oiled the lock of my rifle and greatly eased it and will g[ive] me a much better ch[an]ce of a sure aim. Thus I think that there [will] be a pretty sharp match between Frank & myself for the best place in our company. As many however as 41 points in the 20 shots have been made by some London Volunteers and I expect that the display of rifle shooting at the Great Wimbledon meeting in the summer will be surprising and rather alarming to the Continentals. The Swiss have long been celebrated for rifle shooting – but some of their best shots who came over in a body last summer to compete at Wimbledon were quite distanced and gained only a few minor prizes. They confessed too t[hat] they had nothing at all to compare with our rifles. I observe that it [was?] a charge against Mr Floyd[15] that he purloined an English Westley-Rich[ards] breech loading Whitworth barrelled rifle,[16] belonging to the U.S. Gov^t. Knowing what a kick up there was going to be, he made a very wise move in [?] [the?] best rifle in the States.

You do not tell us about your affairs much. I almost wish you [would] leave the Americans to their fate and cast your lot in with us [aga]in. There is now, I should think, very little chance of much [prosperity?] [for?] some years to come in Minnesota and it seems a pity to s[pend?] [?] years among [such?] [inhos]pitable places We shall be glad to hear more from you soon, & especially your opinion [of?] Politics. I hope you get papers of some sort pretty regularly – I think not more than one or two weeks have been missed.

---

[15] John Buchanan Floyd (1806–63), American lawyer, politician, Confederate general; secretary of war, 1857–60, under President James Buchanan; in 1861, after his resignation from the cabinet as a secessionist, he was accused of having removed arms from Northern arsenals to the Southern states, in excess of their requirements, in preparation for war; he was exonerated by a Congressional Committee.

[16] The Whitworth rifle, invented in 1857 by the engineer Joseph Whitworth (1803–87), was manufactured by the Birmingham armaments firm founded by William Westley Richards (1790–1865). Cf. Rolt, op. cit., p. 217.

Uncle T. has lately discontinued the Spectator because it abused John Bright.[17] For want of more time I must close – Ever your affectionate Brother

W S Jevons.

I am going early tomorrow morning on a short excursion with Charles Thornely[18] till Sunday night to the Isle of Wight – which I rather want to set me up for the coming term.

151. W. S. JEVONS TO SIR JOHN F. W. HERSCHEL[1]
[HLRS]

University Coll. London
21 July 1861

Sir

I take the liberty to send you herewith copies of two papers which I published several years since.[2] I am lead* to do it at the present time from finding in your recently published treatise on Meteorology[3] such gratifying evidence that the opinions put forth on the subject of the Clouds, & bearing of course on the general problem of the atmosphere, are in substantial[4] accordance with your own, & therefore, I venture to say, are true.

At the same time I see no indications in your treatise that my experiments have yet fallen under your notice, or that you are aware how easily the *cirrose** form of cloud may be explained.

I am, Sir,
Yours with great respect
W. S. Jevons

[17] Although Jevons's cousin by marriage, Richard Holt Hutton, was soon to become joint editor and proprietor of the *Spectator*, North of England middle-class families like the Jevonses had a double reason for disapproving of the paper at this time; no friend to the Manchester School and its members, it was also a consistent advocate of the Northern cause in the American Civil War. Later in 1861, 'it welcomed John Bright as an ally in the Federalist cause' – W. B. Thomas, *The Story of the Spectator, 1828–1928* (1928), p. 191.

[18] Charles Thornely, artist, was probably a brother of Elizabeth, James and Susanna Thornely, all of whom had married cousins of Jevons's.

[1] Sir John Frederick William Herschel (1792–1871), chiefly known for his astronomical researches in which he greatly expanded the pioneer work of his father, Sir William Herschel, was also a distinguished mathematician and chemist. He served as Master of the Royal Mint from 1850 to 1855, carrying through a considerable reorganisation of its work, but was forced to resign because of failing health. See A. M. Clarke, *The Herschels and Modern Astronomy* (1895); H. Macpherson, *Herschel* (1919).

[2] 'On the Cirrus Form of Cloud, with Remarks on other Forms of Clouds', *London … Philosophical Magazine*, *XIV* (July 1857): 'On the Forms of Clouds,' *Sydney Magazine of Science and Art* (January 1858).

[3] J. F. W. Herschel, 'Meteorology', *Encyclopaedia Britannica* (Edinburgh, 1861).

[4] 'general' has been deleted here in the original manuscript.

An abbreviation of the second paper is in the L & E. Phil. Mag. for 1858.

Sir J. Herschel

*   *   *

Collingwood.

152. W. S. JEVONS TO T. E. JEVONS
    [LJN, 159]

8 Porteus Road,
23d July 1861.

... I have begun to read Mansel's Aldrich's *Artis Logicae Rudimenta*,[1] of which Aldrich makes 50 pages and Mansel 250, and the 250 are full of nothing but a jargon of five different languages, about the most useless and confusing historical points. I fear Sir W. Hamilton has thrown us back into scholasticism, judging from himself and his bright pupils. Nothing can be more devoid of interest or profit than this sort of learning. It only tends entirely to becloud us, as it did Sir W. H. to a great extent. Nevertheless I read the books as a good exercise in the five languages. I am also reading a little of Leibnitz, but it is great stuff; his pre-established harmony is about the best, and his *Monad Philosophy*[2] is just what you might expect. I have looked into Kant's Critique[3] (trans.), and shall read part of it some time. It is teeming with demonstrations, which are no demonstrations to me ....

153. SIR JOHN F. W. HERSCHEL TO W. S. JEVONS.

Collingwood
July 30/61

Sir,

I beg to thank you for your papers on Clouds. The experiments described are very satisfactory and afford I think a very pleasing and

---

[1] Henry Aldrich (1647–1710), Dean of Christ Church, produced his *Artis Logicae Compendium* in 1691, but it remained a popular textbook in the nineteenth century. Henry Longueville Mansel (1820–71), tutor of St John's College, Oxford, and follower of Sir William Hamilton in metaphysics, had produced a much modified version of Aldrich's work, under the title *Artis Logicae Rudimenta*, which reached a fourth issue in 1862.

[2] Gottfried Wilhelm, freiherr von Leibniz (1646–1716), *La Monadologie* (1714).

[3] Immanuel Kant (1724–1804), *Critique of Pure Reason* (1781); the translation used by Jevons was probably that by J. M. D. Meiklejohn (1852).

elegant illustration of many of the phenomena. When I wrote my article on meteorology I had not seen your papers or I should assuredly have referred to them. Being myself somewhat of a dabbler in Chemistry I have often noticed and been struck with the resemblance of finely dissolved precipitates formed by gradual mixture without agitation of mutually decomposing fluids to the forms of Cirrous and other clouds – as also to the parallel arrangement of the axes of minute specular crystals formed by precipitation in certain cases which afford an apt illustration of the explanation of haloes and parahelia by a parallel disposal of the crystals and this latter class of phenomenon, if my memory be correct, I have somewhere in that article mentioned.

Repeating my thanks for your obliging communication, I remain Sir
Your obedient servant
J. F. W. Herschel.

154. W. S. JEVONS TO HENRIETTA JEVONS

2. Fair View Avenue
Longsight
Manchester.[1]

My dear Henny

You may perhaps like to hear how I am getting on. Having fallen a little into the routine of the Assoc. & swallowed a little of the humbug, it begins to be rather amusing if not instructive. In the morning I go over to breakfast at Harrys between 8 & 9 am. Afterwards into town and getting the list of papers to be read during the day, choose the most interesting. The Sections begin at 11, and although you must not look for any very superlative discoveries, many of the papers are interesting & good and the discussions when they do take place are very amusing. When the sections end between 3 and 4 oclock, I get dinner in town; then go out to my lodging spend 2 hours in writing a little nonsense for the papers; get tea from my landlady and into town again at 8 PM to the Soirée or lecture. About 9 PM I go to the newspaper office & give in my copy, or get the reports and write a little more. About 11 oclock or sometimes later I correct the proofs & then home.

I dare say you were at the Liverpool meeting so as to know the sort of the thing it is, but I believe this meeting is about the most successful there has been (excepting perhaps the Aberdeen). The soirées of which one has been microscopic & the other telegraphic have been magnificent.

[1] This letter was written in September 1861, while Jevons was attending the meeting of the British Association held that year in Manchester, as correspondent of the *Manchester Examiner*. Mrs Jevons incorrectly gave the date of the Manchester meeting as September 1860, LJ, p. 156.

The telegraphic one last night was especially successful. Some thousands of people in a splendid Hall with some very good collections of objects. There was a short & very good address on the telegraphic exhibition; then messages were sent and answered at St Petersburg, Paris, Copenhagen, Moscow, & even Odessa & Nicolaieff.[2] The man at St Petersburg sent the temperature in degrees of Reaumur's thermometer,[3] & was asked to send it in degrees Fahrenheit. He sent back word to say that the Association might alter it themselves if they liked. My friend Clifton[4] had the getting up of the telegraphic exhibition & received the thanks of all the thousand philosophers present.

It has been very pleasant here for me to meet Dr Smith of Sydney, who has been in England a month or two but did not know where to find me in London. He has read a short paper. There are also two or three other people here that I know, and professors are as common as gooseberries. Harry has not had much company in fact no regular visitors except Mr Enfield & Harriet. None of their german friends has common* except a little German botanist who has been there a night to* two. I go in there just when I have time or feel inclined. Today they were to have some other men to dinner but I did not go as I had to walk through the rain to the newspaper office. Tomorrow night the great event comes off which is a lecture by the Astronomer Royal[5] on the Eclipse of the Sun, which will probably be the finest lecture ever delivered.

I have also been to some manufactories as a cotton-mill, a cotton machinery works, a flint glass works, & yesterday I went with Mr Enfield & a party of chemists to a chemical man^y at Warrington. Before leaving I shall go to some more manufactories & down a coal mine. You will perceive that members of the B. Assoc. are left in a state of unnatural activity and I shall be glad when it is all done. Most of the secretaries & lecturers have been ill with their exertions, Harry had to go to bed one day at 1 p.m and slept till next morning at 8 am. I have been invited by Uncle T. & Tom to Liverpool & shall probably go on Thursday or Friday and stay perhaps till Sunday or Monday and then home for good. I am rather better pleased with the people of the B. Assoc than I expected. There are many first rate people – the great majority are a sort of middle class sensible practical people and there

---

[2] The telegraphic messages are no longer with the manuscript.

[3] i.e., the scale devised in 1730 by René Antoine Ferchault de Réaumur (1683–1757), on the principle of taking the freezing point of water as 0° and graduating the tube of the thermometer into degrees, each one-thousandth of the volume contained by the bulb and tube up to zero.

[4] See Vol. I, p. 41.

[5] Sir George Biddell Airy (1801–92), Astronomer Royal, 1835–81. He completely re-equipped the Royal Observatory with instruments designed by himself.

is quite a small proportion of regular snobs. The worst thing is that they have Du Chaillu[6] down here talking about his Gorillas; he is the most insignificant little beast you ever saw. I believe a letter is soon to be read from his enemy Mr Gray[7] proving that he has told lies, which will be a rare treat if correct.

I enclose you portions of telegraphic messages received at the soirée last night.

Give my love to Lucy & Herbert & believe me ever yours affec.

W S Jevons

My head is too bothered with the Brit Assoc. to mention any other things.

155. FRAGMENT OF A LETTER FROM W. S. JEVONS TO
T. E. JEVONS
[LJP, 159–160]

[3 December 1861]

... Volunteering still prospers here ... last Saturday our prizes were distributed in Westminster Hall with considerable ceremony ... In our Company we had only the three regulation prizes of three[1] Enfield rifles – given according to the results of the class firing at 650 & 700 yards – Now it happened that Frank, another sergeant & myself made equal scores of 5 – out of 10 shots at 650 & 700 – hence an order was determined by the scores at 450 – 600 yds – which made Frank first & myself last – I however received a London Armoury Co^s Enfield rifle as the 3rd prize, which is so far satisfactory.

Our scores are as follows –

	150–300	450–600	650–900
F Roscoe	29	14	8
W S Jevons	25	12	10
			(650–700)
Carbonnel	22	13	5

[6] Paul Belloni du Chaillu (1835–1903), explorer, son of a French merchant in Gabon, where he was brought up; went to the United States in 1852, becoming a naturalised citizen; 1856–60, travelled 8000 miles through Central Africa on an expedition sponsored by the Philadelphia Academy of Natural Sciences, encountering anthropoid apes, at that time virtually unknown to Western Science, and bringing back several gorillas. His account of the journey, *Explorations and Adventures in Equatorial Africa* (1861), was received with great suspicion.

[7] Probably John Edward Gray (1800–75), keeper of the zoological department at the British Museum, 1840–74.

[1] These opening lines are taken from LJ, p. 159.

Thus my making 5 points out of 10 shots at 800 & 900 (the weather was favourable, & not so with Frank as he says) put me a long way in advance of him in the list of marksmen. I have now mounted my badge. A cup was presented to the 60 marksmen of our corps. I was unfortunate in the Competition chiefly I believe owing to being very cold at the time & without a top coat – I only made 7 out of 15 shots at 300, 500 & 600, whereas Frank made 12, & the winner 16.

I hope to beat Frank next spring entirely – It is not unlikely that the four first shots of our Co^y will have a sweepstakes of a guinea each – as the fourth man who missed one of his classes, & was thus shut out from all prizes, thinks he can beat us all. The competition you see is very sharp.

Our prizes were all presented by the hands of Lady Constance Grosvenor,[2] who is a celebrated beauty, & spoke and did it all with much grace, about which the papers give a great flourish.

She handled all the rifles cups etc so she must have good strong arms. Altogether she made considerable impression on the corps, & threw her husband our Commandant rather into the shade.

We are all very sorry to hear that Will[3] has been ill – But it must be considered that he arrived there in the autumn which is I suppose the worst time of the year – and there is no reason to suppose that he will have the fever again when once acclimatized. Every one has more or less fever, sooner or later in going to a tropical climate, & once over all the better.

I am beginning to get fairly into my MA work – Only lately the *additional* subjects for the MA were published – and are as follows –

"On the nature & principles of Social order, & Soc. progress, or of Civilization" and in the Hist. of Phil^y.

"Greek Speculation – the Theaetetus & Gorgias of Plato & the Nicomachean Ethics of Aristotle".

Is not this a pretty prospect – Just fancy learning the whole of Greek Speculation – in addition to reading Buckle – and buckling Plato & Aristotle.

The Ethics alone is no slight job – especially as Malden told us there were many parts he could not translate –

Then there is the whole of Mental & Moral phil. Logic Pol. Econ. etc. I am now partly engaged reading old fellows works more or less – such as Berkeley, Hobbes, Leibnitz, Descartes, Spinoza, Bacon etc. I am by degrees getting into the habit of reading the scholastic latin,

[2] Lady Constance Gertrude Sutherland-Leveson-Gower (1834–80), daughter of the second Duke of Sutherland. In 1852 she married Hugh Lupus Grosvenor (1825–90), later first Duke of Westminster, honorary Colonel of the 13th Middlesex Rifle Corps.
[3] Their cousin William Edgar Jevons had recently gone to Penang. Cf. Vol. III, Letter 199.

which will be a great convenience. I have also tried a little of Kant's German which is not quite so hard as one would expect – But he is for the most part full of wordy nonsense.

My statistical matters proceed slowly & the mere drawing of diagrams takes up an incredible deal of time.

Arthur[4] has pointed me out a notice in the Saturday Review of Rachel Jevon, who is mentioned in a new volume of the Calendar of State papers – Some time or other I will get a sight of her petition & may thus perhaps get a copy of her handwriting & some information concerning her family. It appears she is the daughter of a clergyman which is quite consistent with her being the Rachel mentioned in Shaws History of Staf^{re}.[5] since I know of more than one Staffordshire Jevon who was a clergyman.

Lucy & Henny probably keep you informed about many things that I shall pass over now –

Your affec. Brother
W S Jevons.

Herbert I am glad to say is strongly Anti American – He was at first somewhat inclined to think the North would beat the South, but does not maintain that now.

156. FRANCIS JAMES ROSCOE TO W. S. JEVONS

Victoria V.I.[1]
February 16/62

Dear Stanley

The last mail brought me your letter, which was very welcome, also the Volunteer Gazette – Before receiving your letter I had intended to write you a line to congratulate you on getting the MA medal which I hereby do – You do not tell me what you are thinking of doing now you have finished your University Course, probably you have not quite made up your mind. I hope however you will not go in for newspaper writing or editing; I dont think it would suit you & I think it is generally very unsatisfactory work, of which a man can never see the result.

I have put off writing this till the Steamer is in, & she goes off again very shortly, giving me little time, but it is not much matter as I have very little news further than what I have written Dick.

Business is very dull, & will be until the miners go up which will be in about a month.

---

[4] Arthur Jevons (1830–1905), engineer and artist, third son of Timothy Jevons.
[5] Stebbing Shaw, *The History and Antiquities of Staffordshire* . . . vols 1 and 2, part 1 (1798–1801).
[1] Vancouver Island. Cf. Vol. I, p. 193, n.6.

A few claims have been worked at Carriboo during the winter, & have turned out a good deal of gold – next year I believe a large quantity of gold will come from Carriboo, but it is *mining* there not *digging*, & no man can get an ounce of gold there before he has laid out capital in sinking shafts putting up flumes, pumps &c. Late in the autumn some very rich silver ore was discovered at Carriboo & they say there is plenty of it.

You kindly offer to look out for a photographic apparatus for me, but I dont think I could afford to get one, for strange as it may seem, I was never worse off for ready money than I am now, our business is increasing almost beyond our capital so we have to draw out as little as possible.

I was thinking some time ago of writing to you to ask you if you could lend me your camera for a few months – that is if you are not going to use it this summer. I think Messrs W Hunt & Co 160 Austin Friars will be sending some goods by express (ie via Panama) soon after you receive this – If you sent the Camera to their office to Mr Taylor he could send it with them – I should get it in May or June, & there are several of my friends here going back to England in the autumn, any one of whom would take it back for me, so you would have it back before the end of the year, accompanied by some negatives of the neighbouring country. I will tell Mr Taylor to let you know in case they send anything by express.

There is some very beautiful scenery near Victoria, & the scenery in British Columbia is as fine as any in the world.

I have seen very little of the island yet, but next August I intend to go up to Cowitchan* & Nanaimo & get a little shooting.

This last week I got some skating, a sharp frost having set in after a heavy fall of snow & my thermometer was down to 12° two nights; It has now however changed, & today it has been quite hot, & I expect we shall soon have Spring – the seasons here seem very much the same as in England except that there is more rain in winter & more settled fine weather in summer. It is a vast pity that we let the Americans have the country north of the Columbia; it was ours by right, & there is a good deal of fine agricultural land there to which Victoria is the natural market – the people on the other side of the sound even get their letters from San Francisco via Victoria, & they come over here to buy all their goods & to bring their produce.

A vast change has taken place in this town since I arrived last July; then the place was much more American than English, but now the Yankees are "played out" to use their own forcible expression, & everything is becoming strongly British – In July there were hardly any good brick buildings in the place, now there are many fine ones

Hotels, Stores &c. A month after I came here a wharf was sold for $7000 & people thought it sold pretty high it was sold again the other day for $20,000! I think however land has reached its maximum value & I should not like to invest at present prices.

I am sorry to hear such a bad account of No 5 company, but the corps generally seems very flourishing – there are two Queens men out here, one Blunt from No 13 & Robinson from No 2 both very good fellows & we often have a chat together about the old corps – I am going to try hard this spring to get up a corps, but so few fellows here are stationery* that I fear not many will join.

I hear the Str goes tonight so having other letters to write I must shut up, but will write you a decent long letter before very long & remain

ever Yours vy truly
F. J. Roscoe.

W. S. Jevons Esq.

157. W. S. JEVONS TO HENRIETTA JEVONS

8 Porteus Road
3 March. 1862.

My dearest Henny

There are a few points w^h require answering in your letter – besides a few things I may have myself to say. Fred's[1] sudden death is a very sad affair – It sometimes appears almost incredible that any one should die at the age of 21; and especially that the best should go first. Seeing him only at College, where he always appeared pretty lively & well – I had no idea that he was so ill during the autumn – and the doctor (Aikin) appears not to have known it either. His disappointment about the scholarship arose entirely from his health, but when he told me about it, I was almost afraid he would never get over it fully – so much was he set upon those kinds of successes.

Like yourself, I have also been thinking much about future arrangements but without any decisive result. What arguments has Mary[2] against a house? – Are they her own do you think or derived from Uncle T. & Henry? I do not intend to leave London & do not expect to – And I question whether a small house will be more expensive than lodgings.

Yesterday afternoon (Sunday) Herbert & I walked nearly all over Hampstead to see what chance there might be of getting a suitable house. Haverstock Hill just beyond the Camden Town Station seemed

---

[1] See above, Letter 143, n. 8, p. 407.   [2] i.e. Mary Catherine Jevons.

the most likely place & there was a small house there to let which might do. In Hampstead there were many small houses but few were to let. One, however, just at the entrance into the heath, was to let – and would probably do, if the rent were not too high. It was rather in a public position – but from the upper windows had a very wide view on *both* sides of the hill. It was built partly of wood & partly of brick, & with a nice small garden – name – *Vale Mount*. I think it probable, however, that houses will be more easily found in the Autumn – & do not propose to make any change till then.

I have no intention of taking Frank's Chambers w^h are too much in the town – He will probably give them up – & will sell his furniture, most of w^h I may buy – But he makes a condition that some of the things should be sold back again if he should desire.

The Quarry scheme[3] having come to an end, Herbert is hesitating between British Col., Nova Scotia and New Z. but inclines to the latter. Frank is mad after Nova Scotia at present & will perhaps go. I think Herbert will do best by going to N.Z. as he will never do any thing in England & may there. He has taken such a dislike to the Yankees that I do not think he will go near them again.

I really cannot understand how you can go on visiting all the year round as at present. It must continue I suppose for the present but when we take a house, we must come to some agreement – that for instance you shall stay at home at least four months out of the twelve.

I entirely agree that Mary B.[4] should not leave her present lodgings – If Tom can afford it [it][5] will perhaps be best for Lucy, you, Tom & myself to go equal shares in the whole expense – If not, for us three. It would never do to bring Mary up to London where she would be quite without her gossiping friends, & in a strange region – When I last saw her, she seemed very weak, & said she should not live long.

---

[3] Early in 1862 John Hutton had proposed a partnership between Herbert Jevons and himself to work a granite quarry at Gwylwyr, North Wales. Unpublished letters indicate that Herbert found it hard to make up his mind about the matter, which was by no means finally settled at this time, and this caused some concern among members of the family. On 14 April 1862 Herbert sent a memorandum of the proposed partnership agreement to Jevons and wrote '. . . I am moderately well pleased with what I have seen of the proposed quarry, and also John's quarry and if I can agree on terms with John, and raise £500 without too much difficulty I am prepared to undertake the quarry . . .' On the same day William Jevons, Junior wrote to Jevons '. . . I am very glad to hear that Herbert is likely to obtain suitable employment without going to the Antipodes. I hope he will succeed in obtaining the position in N. Wales . . .' On 17 April Herbert wrote to Henrietta Jevons '. . . If this quarry business comes to a mess it were better that I had gone to New Zealand . . .' On 27 April William Jevons, Junior wrote again to Jevons '. . . She [*Lucy*] speaks of Herbert as if he was again thinking of going abroad. I am afraid, then, he is disappointed of the situation you told us he expected . . .' The main difficulty appears to have been that of raising the necessary money to invest, and this was probably the decisive factor.

[4] i.e. Mary Bentley.

[5] Omitted in the original manuscript.

As John & Lucy⁶ (or ought one to say Lucy & John–? this is a knotty point that Lucy should settle once for all) will prob^y. be in Derby now – this letter may serve in answer to both of theirs.

John's indeed is suf^{ly} answered by his subsequent ones – but I may say that Herbert having taken up N.Z. again as likely to be the Britain of the South does not show much sign of disap^t at the end of the Quarry scheme – with w^h he was much taken up for some days.

I should perhaps tell you that in consequence of a note from Dr Smith I went to call on Graham last Friday – & he offered to get me a lectureship to the Andersonian Instit^n in Glasgow⁷ the subj. being Nat. Philosophy.

The salary appears to be only about £100 a year, but for practise,* & introd. to better places, this would form a very good beginning. I told him I should never make a popular lecturer – and that Nat. Phil^y was not the subject I was now following up. He seemed pretty well satisfied at my refusing it – & inserted my address in a book in case apparently, any more suitable should turn up.

Ever your affec. Brother.
W S Jevons.

Herbert will be writing to John shortly.

158. W. S. JEVONS TO HERBERT JEVONS
[LJP, 164–5]

8 Porteus Road W.
3 July 1862.

My dear Herbert

Whatever you do – dont do it in a hurry & all offhand. Whether you go to Melbourne or not there can be no need to go by the very next ship – Henny & I shall of course come down to Liverpool to see you off & we cannot come without some week or two of notice.

Both Henny & I find we have more to do than we can well manage – & we are for the most part putting off visiting the Great X until Tom can join us.

---

⁶ John Hutton and Lucy Jevons had been married the previous January. Cf. Vol. I, p. 11.

⁷ Anderson's Institution, constituted in 1796, had been founded under the will of John Anderson, Professor of Natural Philosophy in the University of Glasgow. The endowment included a museum, a library and a valuable collection of scientific apparatus. Thomas Graham had been Professor of Chemistry in Anderson's Institution, 1830–7. Anderson's College, as it was later known, was one of several institutions providing scientific and technical education that were later amalgamated to form what ultimately became the University of Strathclyde, which received its charter in 1964. Cf. *University of Strathclyde Calendar, 1968–9*, pp. 14–15.

We have had several letters from Lucy asking us into Yorkshire but we have not decided upon anything.

I have been much occupied of late in bringing out the Diagrams which were finished just at the time of my Examination.

As yet I am quite unaware of the number sold if any – and am very far from sanguine about the result – The total cost will be some £30 or £35 so that one cannot lose very much.

The distribution of prizes at College took place on Tuesday & I was mentioned in the report with reference to the MA. I was disappointed however with regard to a prize of £5 for an essay on Celtic literature. There were three competitors – each of them deserving of a prize, as Masson[1] the judge said, but a man now at Cambridge & a B.A. carried it off from having a considerable knowledge of Celtic, in which of course my acquaintance is as near zero as can well be imagined. The sympathies of the audience rather collapsed when a Cambridge man was announced successful – It is certainly not right that men who have all the rich prizes of Cambridge & Oxford should come back & steal our small rewards, when it is impossible for us to approach the other Universities unless by beginning from the beginning again.

On Saturday our regiment was inspected in Regents Park. There was a good attendance of some 800 or 900 men in all – & all the maneuvres* went off for the most part in a very satisfactory manner. There are no signs of decay about the Queens.

In firing my classes, I have had the misfortune to miss one of them – owing to using a new rifle with the sighting of which I was not acquainted. This loses me the marksman's badge next year. I am now however just taking the duties & badge of a sergeant.

Hoping to hear that you will not do anything hasty about leaving – & with love to Tom

Ever your affec.
W S Jevons

159. WILLIAM JEVONS JUNIOR[1] TO W. S. JEVONS

21 Cannon Place
Brighton July 14. 1862.

My dear Stanley

From an advertisement which I saw the other day in the Inquirer I learn that you have succeeded in obtaining the degree for which you

---

[1] David Masson (1822–1907), biographer and editor, Professor of English Literature at University College, London, 1853–65, in succession to A. H. Clough; Professor of Rhetoric and English Literature at Edinburgh University, 1865–95.

[1] For biographical details, see Vol. I, p. 183. n. 3.

have so long been studying, and I cannot refuse myself the pleasure of offering you my cordial congratulations. I have also to congratulate you on having at last brought out your statistical Diagrams, which I hope will bring you profit, as I am sure they will bring you fame. It does not appear from your advertisement that the Diagrams are accompanied with any Treatise pointing out the conclusions to which they lead. But I presume you intend to publish something of the kind, as the Diagrams alone will be insufficient to convey to every mind the instruction they contain –

I think I wrote last to you from Lewes. We stayed there six weeks; but I cannot say that we enjoyed our visit, for your aunt and I were both laid up with influenza which pulled us down very much. Your aunt, indeed, has hardly yet got over the effects of it. We were all very glad to get back to our old quarters which we found cleaned, renovated, and garnished, and where we were received again with a hearty welcome. We are now enjoying the company of George[2] and all his family, who are come here for a month. They have lodgings in the same street, and of course we see them every day. I hope George will benefit by his visit, for he was much overworked and needed rest and change –

Give our love to Henrietta and to Herbert, if he is with you, and believe me,
  my dear Stanley
    your affectionate Uncle
      W. Jevons

160. WILLIAM JEVONS JUNIOR TO W. S. JEVONS
          21 Cannon Place, Brighton
          July 17. 1862

My dear Stanley,

I am exceedingly glad to hear that you have not only obtained your degree, but also won high honours, and a gold medal, which I have no doubt you richly deserved. I am also exceedingly gratified and obliged by your kindness in sending me three copies of each of your Diagrams. You have been really too generous. But I suppose you meant that I should dispose of two of the copies wherever I might think them likely to be acceptable; and accordingly I have given one copy to your cousin George who desires me to say, with his love, that he shall value it very highly. The other copy I thought of sending to my son William.[1] But on second thoughts, it occurs to me that it could not be so well bestowed on any one as on the celebrated writer and first-rate economist

[2] See above, Letter 139, n. 16, p. 391.   [1] See above, Letter 143, n. 5, p. 405.

John Stuart Mill, and if you have not already sent him one, I will endeavour to obtain his address from one of his sisters whom I know, and forward it to him either in your name or my own, as you judge best. One copy of each Diagram I will keep for your sake and for my own instruction, and I shall value it very highly, though the subjects to which your researches relate are not familiar to me. I have read the notes at the foot of the Diagrams, and they partly supply what I supposed was wanting to make them useful. But doubtless it would require a Treatise of considerable length to unfold fully all the instruction with which your Diagrams are fraught I do not much wonder that men of business do not appreciate the value of your labours. Those who are intent upon gain alone, though they may be keenly alive to mercantile and financial fluctuations of their own time by which they hope to profit, are not likely to philosophize upon past fluctuations. But students of political economy and social science will surely be willing to avail themselves of your researches, and in time, I have no doubt your Diagram will engage *their* attention. It was not to be expected that they would sell rapidly: so do not, I beg you, be disheartened by the little success you have yet met with.

I am afraid I am not very competent to advise you on the subject of your future pursuits. But I fear that you would obtain but a very precarious income from your scheme of literary and scientific agency. It would be mere drudgery, and you are qualified for something far higher than the work of a literary hack. Could you not do better by writing for the periodical press? Our numerous newspapers, reviews, and magazines must require the constant employment of a large number of talented writers, and you have already shown that you can do good service in that way. Writers so employed are generally, I believe well paid, in proof of which I may mention that the writer who contributes the short articles on chess which regularly appear in the Illustrated London News receives, as I have heard, a salary of not less than £300 a year. W. J. Fox,[2] when he wrote political articles for the Times, received, if I am rightly informed, more than double that pay. But a more certain source of income, though it might not suit your taste so well, would be *private tuition*. You are very well qualified to prepare young men in classics and mathematics for the universities, and your degree alone

---

[2] William Johnston Fox (1786–1864), leading Unitarian preacher; radical politician: M.P. for Oldham, 1847–52, 1852–7, 1857–63; edited the Unitarian theological periodical, the *Monthly Repository*, 1828–36, becoming its owner in 1831 and transforming it into a vehicle of social and political reform and literary criticism; published the *Finsbury Lectures* (1835–40), a series of sermons which had attracted large congregations; leading editorial writer on the *True Sun*, 1835; for many years contributed to numerous periodicals and newspapers. Cf. F. E. Mineka, *The Dissidence of Dissent. The Monthly Repository, 1806–1838* (University of North Carolina, 1944).

would go far to recommend you in that line. But I speak from experience when I say that the employment of a private tutor in families, to assist young ladies and gentlemen to complete the education they have received at school, is a very pleasant and sufficiently lucrative employment, and in London you could not fail to obtain as much of such employment as would bring you a tolerably good income. You have all the linguistic qualifications, and your manners and address would soon render them available.

Your aunt and cousin Annie join me in love to yourself and dear Henny, and they desire me to say how much gratified they are to hear of the honours you have obtained. Remember me very kindly to your brothers when you see them, and to all at Grove Park, particularly Mary Catherine.

Believe me.
   My dear Stanley
     Your affectionate Uncle
      W. Jevons.

P.S. Since writing the above I have learnt that Mr J. S. Mill resides somewhere in the South of France, so that there would be some difficulty, and perhaps not much use, in sending him your diagrams.

161. W. S. JEVONS TO HERBERT JEVONS
 [LJN, 166–8]

Beaumaris,
Sunday, 17*th August* 1862.

... As it is so few days since you started, it is of course unlikely I should have much to tell you of here. We were sorry to find from the *Mercury* that the *Champion* did not get clear away on the first try, but was driven back with loss of an anchor and cable. On hearing this Tom and I went down and ascertained the position of the *Champion*; but Baines and Co.,[1] to more than one inquiry, told us there was no steamer going to it, and no means of communication. We intended, indeed, to go off and see you by sailing boat. On getting down to the stage, however, the wind seemed to be blowing so fresh, and the ship lay so far from New Brighton, that we thought it more prudent to give up the plan.

Your letter, sent back by the tug-boat, gave us much pleasure, as it seemed to show you would have a cheerful voyage in spite of some

---

[1] See above, Letter 60, n. 3, p. 146.

discomforts. By the time you get this you will feel disposed to forget the voyage, and set to the disagreeable work of finding employment in a large city like Melbourne. . . .

Our family enjoy some blessings, but also lie under certain curses – one of which is a certain stupid simplicity of character which continually mars their undertakings. A little wiliness, and a rather thicker skin, would make us succeed far better in this world; and I really cannot believe that success in this world is always to be sacrificed. We have between us so much good-nature and inflexible honesty, that it sometimes seems as if we can none of us ever be of the least use to friend or foe.

There is nothing more necessary than to remember that everybody you meet is more or less imperfect and apt to do wrong. Take this as a matter of course, and make the best of it. You will have hard enough work to keep yourself always right.

I write down a few such reflections, which have often occurred to me before, because it is now most necessary that you should take some active steps to secure good success in a new continent. A still greater fault, and one more peculiar to yourself among our family, is a want of deliberation in planning an undertaking, and then a want of resolution in carrying it through the first slight difficulties. Everything that is worth doing must be commenced with some degree of painful exertion, only to be recompensed by the *hope* of success. It is only as work actually proves successful and easy from practice that it can be agreeable and spontaneous. The theory which you once propounded to me, that everything should be done spontaneously, that is, without exertion, is not only totally false but fatally so, if it could really ever be carried out in practice. It is like expecting fruit to fall into your mouth as you spontaneously sit upon the ground; it might do so by chance, but most people who waited for it would die of starvation. A man of any sense climbs the tree at the cost of much labour and some risk, but is rewarded by as much fruit as he requires. The life of a civilised man is distinguished from that of a savage chiefly by the rule that the former exerts himself for future, the latter only for present purposes. The degree in which a man studies the future, and sacrifices present ease to probable future satisfaction, is the best measure of his ability as a builder of his own fortune, apart, of course, from all consideration of what he esteems good-fortune.

I shall probably leave Beaumaris in a day or two, and return almost straight to London, but it will be time enough in succeeding mails to tell you of our affairs in England. . . .

162. TIMOTHY JEVONS[1] TO W. S. JEVONS

Sydenham House
nr B'water, Aug! 18. [1862]

Dear Stanley

I left home on Saturday to come here for a few days. Before leaving I rec^d, on that morning, a letter from Mr Sage, of Melbourne, replying to a letter I wrote to him a few months ago about Herbert. I will inclose* his letter for your perusal; & I am sorry it is not more encouraging. In one respect it w^d seem to offer some prospect for an increase of business, in *Iron*, for Mr Sage; as he tells us that one of the houses in the trade is giving up the business. As I shall hold out to Mr S. when I write, the inducement of an increased credit if he can make room for Herbert with the view of extending his business, I am in hopes it will be the means of accomplishing what we all desire. At all events I have no doubt Mr S. will do his utmost to assist Herbert:[2] & if nothing desirable offers itself he can but go on to New Zealand afterwards. I shall write to Mr S. by the next Mail, on the 25$^{\underline{th}}$, to acknowledge his letter, & tell him of Herbert's departure. – With respect to the Diagrams, it has occurred to me to suggest to you to send a copy of each to the Editor of the *Economist*, which is a paper particularly connected with all Commercial & Financial subjects, & statistics; a favourable notice in such a paper will help the sale very materially.[3] I shall return home at the end of this week, & I hope you will then return to Grove Park to finish your visit, which was cut off sadly too short before. With my kind regards to Lucy & Mr H. and love to Henny, believe me

Yours sincerely
Tim^y. Jevons

Please return Mr Sage's letter to Liverpool in a few days.

[1] See above, Letter 21, n. 2, p. 38.

[2] In two unpublished letters written to Jevons in October and November 1862, Herbert Jevons gives an account of the hospitality he received from this Mr Sage when he arrived in Melbourne and of his assistance in finding lodgings and providing introductions to possible employers. He encouraged Herbert to accept the job in a Sydney bank obtained for him through F. B. Miller. Sage did not feel able to offer Herbert a partnership in his own iron business, which he did not consider large enough, particularly at a time of economic difficulty. His letter is not among the Jevons Papers, and no biographical information about him has come to light.

[3] The diagrams did receive a notice in *The Economist*, through the assistance of R. H. Hutton; see below, Letter 167, p. 459.

163. W. S. JEVONS TO THE PRINCIPAL LIBRARIAN,[1]
BRITISH MUSEUM

8 Porteus Road
Paddington W.
29 Aug. 1862.

The Principal Librarian
of the British Museum.
Sir,
I beg to offer for the Museum Library a collection of printed & MS documents relating to the Thames Tunnel – forming a pretty complete history of that undertaking – In addition to the Acts of Parl.[t] it contains the Reports of the Engineers & Directors, proceedings of meetings, circulars, notices, receipts & other business documents – with pamphlets, figures etc. Some MS correspondence is added comprising Autographs of both the Brunels –

The whole are bound in one volume of small folio size. The collection was formed by my father Thomas Jevons one of the Shareholders –

Were you willing to accept them, I could also add the following works which I believe are not in the Museum Library.
The Melbourne Directory – 1859.
  Ballaarat* Directory
Sydney Post off. Direc. 1857.
Directorio de la Habana 1859
The Sydney Magazine of
  Science & Art 1857–9
nearly complete except as to the last few numbers pub.[d]
An Enquiry into Deposits of Gold – by W.[m] Gardner
  Maitland N S Wales. 1856.

Sydney University Magazine No 1. January 1855.
Account of the 'Rush' to
  Port Curtis –
  by Fred.[k] Sinnett.
    Geelong. 1859.
  I am Sir
      Your Obedient Servant
          W S Jevons.

---

[1] At this time Sir Anthony Panizzi (1797–1879), an Italian lawyer forced into exile for his political activities; arrived in London in 1823, becoming naturalised in 1832; after teaching Italian in Liverpool he became Professor at the University of London, 1828–37; assistant librarian in the British Museum, 1831; Keeper of printed books, 1837–56; Principal Librarian, 1856–66; designed the Reading Room, which was opened in 1857.

P.S. I may also add –
The Life Exp^{ce} etc of N. Pidgeon
City Missionary – Sydney. 1857.

Smiths Brooklyn Direc. N.Y. 1856–7
Trows New York Direc. 1860.[2]

164. W. S. JEVONS TO RICHARD H. HUTTON
[LJP, 165–6]

8 Porteus Road W
Sept 1 1862

Dear Richard,

The diagrams which you are so good as to intend noticing in the Economist,[1] accompany this

They are designed not so much to allow of reference to particular numbers, which can be better had from printed tables of figures, as to exhibit to the eye the general results of large masses of figures which it is hopeless to attack in any other way than by graphical representation.

My diagrams not only shew the minutest details given in the tables, but also supersede the taking of averages, since the eye or mind of itself notices the *general course* of a set of numbers.

It is only be representing large masses of statistics in this manner that any sure foundation can be laid for Pol^l Economical arguments. Most statistical arguments depend upon a few figures picked out at random.

In the latter part of the Funds diagr. it is very obvious that a rise in the price of corn is followed by a rise in the rate of interest & by increased bankruptcy. This is remarked in one of the *notes* at the foot where I also speak of corn as forming part of the capital of the country. It perhaps sounds rather odd, as we are accustomed to think of capital as so much money, but the expression is theoretically correct.

---

[2] Although the original manuscript of this letter is among the Jevons Papers, the information it contained appears to have been communicated in some way as several of the items listed are now in the collections of the British Museum: *A collection of miscellaneous documents relating to the Thames Tunnel, comprising Acts of Parliament, reports, views, manuscript letters, etc.* (1824–53); *Tanner's Melbourne Directory for 1859* (Melbourne, 1859); *Huxtable's Ballarat Commercial Directory for 1857* (Ballarat, 1857–8); *Cox & Co.'s Sydney Post Office Directory, 1857* (Sydney, 1857); *The Sydney Magazine of Science and Art* ... 2 vols (Sydney, 1858–9); F. Sinnett, *Account of the 'Rush' to Port Curtis* ... (Geelong, 1859); N. Pidgeon, *The Life Experience and Journal of N. Pidgeon, City Missionary* ... (Sydney, 1857).

[1] See below, Letter 167, n. 7, p. 459. Richard Hutton, editor of *The Economist*, 1858–61, had by this time taken over *The Spectator* but he apparently still did reviews for *The Economist*. Walter Bagehot, its editor 1826–77, was a close friend and it seems likely that Hutton would have persuaded him to provide space for a review of Jevons's diagrams. Cf. A. Buchan, *The Spare Chancellor. The Life of Walter Bagehot* (1959) p. 127; also Vol. I, p. 182, n. 3.

The Bank Diagr. when properly studied throws light on many questions especially that of the circulation of B of E notes which is seen to be comparatively little variable *but always rises slowly for two or even three years after a large accumulation of bullion has taken place, as in 1852 & 1858.* The same seems *now to be taking* place even in a greater degree, the present circulation being nearly £1,500,000 over that of this time last year so the Times says.

It is all nonsense to ascribe a rise of prices to bank notes being increased in numbers. It is a superabundance of *gold* that raises prices & perhaps quickens business & the increased circulation of notes is the *result*, as clearly shown on the diagram.

I send these few lines because the *purpose* of the diagrams is not stated upon the face of them.

Ever yours truly
W. S. Jevons.

165. W. S. JEVONS TO HERBERT JEVONS
[LJP, 168–70]

8 Porteus Road W.
14 Sept 1862.

My dear Herbert

Although I am somewhat tired by writing most of the day and reading the rest, I must at least make a beginning of a letter to you as for the present at least I shall certainly not let a mail go without a letter.

Both the letter you sent ashore by me & that by the tug-boat tended greatly to diminish the trouble which we could not but feel at losing you again for a series of years. The members of our family do not always agree together perfectly in little things of common life – but they never cease to regard each other in everything that is of greater moment. And as I was the one so frequently thought of when in your distant position, so will you be now.

Some two weeks ago I received a newspaper from Sydney posted by Ch^s Bolton. I was glad to find on your account chiefly that my predictions of their downward course were not quite correct & that the Colony was becoming decidedly prosperous again. The yield of gold is now many times greater than when I left – Trade was somewhat improving; protection was losing favour & the ministry was becoming more & more settled. The N S Wales Railways however, which I always opposed as certain to fail & drag the country into difficulties[1] were still as far from completion as ever – The roads accordingly were in a wretched state, & they were going to spend no end of money on them.

[1] See above, Letters 90 and 98, pp. 235 and 262.

I do not know so much about Melbourne, but things seem improving there almost as much as at Sydney. Mr Sage indeed sent home a rather discouraging letter which arrived soon after you left. But people are so apt to grumble that I do not wonder at it & hope you will not let him discourage you. I would certainly have a fling at the iron selling if it can possibly be done, & I think Sage will be acting against his own interests in not carrying out Uncle T's proposals & extending his trade if it can be done.

As it is impossible for us here to anticipate what you may be doing in Melbourne, I do not like to talk much about your affairs. But in case you do not like Melbourne I hope you will remember that Sydney is a very agreable* place & that Miller & Mrs Miller would welcome you there in the kindest manner you could want, & that all whom I knew so well in the Mint will be more or less ready to help and advise you. Of course if you prefer to push your way in Melbourne or New Zealand without resorting to Sydney it is all the better.

Landing in a Colony is very gloomy anxious work, as far as I had any exp^{ce} of it, and it can scarcely be so well for you as it was for me. As you know, however, I was very short of money on getting to Sydney, – & the Mint prospects altogether were in a state of uncertainty.

I am now in no enviable position here, as my college work being entirely finished I must look for money making employment. To make money by writing is so very severe an employment that I am almost afraid of it, & yet it seems the only one I could thoroughly take to.

I am beginning some articles in the Spectator – one in this weeks number[2] – I am also finishing some very laborious statistical calc. what in fact you copied out for me – the bank Returns, & shall probably offer them to the Economist.

I may also undertake some other articles. I have resolved however at last to let out my theory of Economy, & have accordingly written a short paper entitled "Notice of a general mathematical theory of Economy" which will I hope be read at the Brit. Assoc. meeting at the beginning of next month. Although I know pretty well the paper is worth perhaps all the others that will be read there put together, I cannot pretend to say how it will be received, whether it will be read at all, or whether it wont be considered nonsense.[3] Our family have not half enough humbug. One part of our composition with five of humbug would make a first character. If I had even a small percentage of HER'S ways, I should by this time have been soaring up in the regions of fame ease & fortune, instead of labouring away in obscurity & without a

---

[2] 'The Clerk of the Weather Office', xxxv (12 September 1862) 1020–1.
[3] Cf. Vol. I, p. 188, n. 1.

half penny of profit. I quite agree with Shakespeare when he wrote in disgust in one of his sonnets.

> "Gilded honour shamefully misplaced
> and right perfection wrongfully disgraced
> and Strength by limping sway disabled,
> and art made tongue-tied by authority,
>
> * * *
>
> and Captain Good attending Captain ill."[4]

I send you a portion of a portrait I have had taken – but do not like.[5] The first spare money you gain in Australia must be spent in having your portrait taken, an indispensable operation which you omitted here. With the powerful sun of Australia you may however be taken even better where you are.

I am very curious indeed to know what effect my theory will have both upon my friends & the world in general. I shall watch it like an artilleryman watches the flight of a shell or shot, to see whether its effects equal his intentions.

You will be interested & surprised by the American news. The Northerners are outgeneralled in the most extraordinary manner & instead of the South being invaded both Washington & Cincinatti* are in danger, & all such advantages as the North ever gained in the South are being rapidly lost. It seems impossible to conceive a more utter disgrace than the Northerners have incurred in their two campaigns already ended. After fifty years of brag that they would whop creation & so on: after spending a million of men & 200 million pounds sterling their own capital is actually in danger of capture. I hope to goodness it will be taken & burnt, & Lincoln, Seward, Stanton, Mac-Clellan,*[6] & the whole set of ignorant fools carried south, to be hung or shut up for the rest of their lives.

It still seems impossible to say what will become of either North or South. If the North still goes on drafting men & sends half a million

---

[4] See Vol. I, p. 182, n. 4.   [5] See Plate 5, facing p. 45.

[6] William Henry Seward (1801–72), Secretary of State, 1861–9; a dominant figure on the American political scene during the Civil War, notorious for the belligerence of his conduct of foreign relations, particularly at this period when the possibility of European intervention in the war appeared to be increasing; he was consequently unpopular abroad, especially in Britain: Palmerston had described him as a 'vapouring, blustering, ignorant man' (quoted Bourne, op. cit., p. 213).

Edwin McMasters Stanton (1814–69), Secretary for War, 1862–8; a versatile and energetic administrator, although he eventually had to be dismissed from office by President Johnson on account of his duplicity and disloyalty to the administration; a lawyer of national repute, he had defended Daniel Sickles (q.v.), p. 382 in 1859; appointed Attorney-General in President Buchanan's administration, 1860.

General George Brinton McClellan (1826–85), appointed officer commanding the army of the Potomac, July 1861, after much publicized successes against the confederacy in West Virginia; promoted general-in-chief of all the Northern armies, November 1861, but proved more South it is hardly possible to see how the South can any longer keep up their wonderful resistance. Another campaign must surely exhaust the South if not the North – It is the financial crash however that will bring the North up & that must come soon although the lies & oppression of the Gov^t & the foolish credulity of the people keeps it off longer than any body could have expected.

15th Sept. Furthur* news from U.S. today are even more adverse. The Federals are actually more closely surrounded by rebels than they were before the first Campaign & before Bull run – There have now been altogether three great battles on Bull Run, two of them decided defeats, & the third certainly not a conquest for the north.[7] But I must leave you to read the news either in the Melbourne papers or in one which I shall probably post you.

Fred[8] is in London now & tomorrow night is coming to stay here for a few days. I shall be going to the Exhibition and a few other places, which will relieve the present dullness of London.

Hoping that you will have another letter either from Lucy Henny or Tom –

    Believe me
     Ever your affec Brother
      W S Jevons.

Mind that you write pretty fully as to how you go on

As it is not quite certain whether we shall continue long at Porteus R^d you had better direct my letters to College for the present: Gower Street.

---

unfit for the supreme command owing to lack of experience; relieved in March 1862; continued to command the army of the Potomac and organized the defence of Washington; relieved of all commands by Lincoln in November 1862 and never again employed in the field.

 [7] The fortunes of the Confederacy were at their zenith at this period. The first major engagement of the Civil War, the First Battle of Bull Run, fought near Manassas, Virginia, on 21 July 1861, had been a decisive victory for the South. During the spring and summer of 1862 the Confederate commanders had successfully out-manoeuvred McClellan in defence of their stronghold, Richmond, Virginia. The Second Battle of Bull Run (30 August 1862) resulted in a further major defeat for the Northern army, which retired to Washington, pursued by the Southern forces under General Robert E. Lee who, by 2 September, was threatening the capital. On 3 September Lee moved towards the Potomac; in the face of a superior force he detached a portion of his army which captured Harper's Ferry on 15 September, under General 'Stonewall' Jackson. McClellan, commanding the defence of Washington, moved to take advantage of the division of Lee's forces and after several preliminary actions the two forces met at the Battle of Antietam (17 September 1862), in which the Confederate forces were defeated. McClellan's failure to follow up this victory led ultimately to his dismissal. The North suffered a further setback at the Battle of Fredericksburg (13 December 1862) and by the beginning of 1863 military and civilian morale had sunk to a low ebb, resulting in widespread dissatisfaction with the Lincoln administration.

 [8] i.e. Frederick Jevons.

... to⁹ raise independent bodies of volunteers & such things indicate that the States will not stand any more blundering at Washington. It is now in the highest degree likely that the Federal gov^t will come to an end, and the Northern States be for a time at least broken up & perhaps finally separated into several fragments. This is what I have predicted all along. I will allow that if the Federals could begin another Campaign with the same money & number as the last they must temporarily overpower the South – but I do not think this is possible – The South are striking a decisive blow to avoid another campaign.

Fred is now stopping with me here & we are very dissipated – At Cremorne Gardens last night until after 12 PM. & tonight & the following night we are also going on the loose.

Ever yours
W S J.

Yesterday[10] I had the satisfaction of seeing my Diagrams in a pub^rs window in the Royal Exchange – I persuaded Stanford to send them on sale, as he promised to several places, but I do not yet know how many are sold.

... According[11] to some of the last news there is a general war commencing on the part of the Red Indian all along the U S boundaries beginning in Minnesota by a massacre of 70 whites. It is very lucky you left Minnesota for if you were not drafted for the southern war you would have been in danger from the Indian & probably have had to join in measures of defence. I would much rather be a volunteer in England or Australia than in America.

There is some slight chance of a cessation of the war by a Secession of the Western States – for the Southern Congress is offering or about to offer a guarantee of the free navigation of the Mississipi* if they will take no furthur* part in the war.

This seems the only present chance of peace, and if the western States have any sense they will surely accept it.

---

⁹ This undated passage, written on a separate half sheet of paper, appears to be part of an addition Jevons made to the letter a day or so later.

¹⁰ In LJ, p. 169, this passage follows immediately after the paragraph ending '... I shall watch it like an artilleryman watches the light of a shell or shot, to see whether its effects equal his intentions' (above, p. 453).

¹¹ The two following paragraphs appear to be a further undated addition to the letter, written on both sides of a quarter sheet of paper.

166. WILLIAM JEVONS JUNIOR TO W. S. JEVONS

21 Cannon Place, Brighton
Oct 11. 1862

My dear Stanley

My M.S., together with your note relating to it, came safely to hand yesterday evening. I have attentively read your remarks upon my treatise, and hope to benefit by them when I again turn my attention to the subject. In some instances you seem not to have quite apprehended my meaning. But that must be because I have failed to express myself with sufficient clearness. What puzzles me most in your letter is what you say of my views concerning the planetary system. You remark that you cannot see in my treatise any proof that matter is distributed through space upon any symmetrical system. What this refers to I do not understand, as I do not remember to have used the word 'symmetrical' in speaking of the planetary system. My leading idea is that life under an infinite variety of forms is essential to the system to which our earth belongs, but that there is a distinction between planetary and solar life, the former being individualized and distributed, while the latter is the grand result or combination which gives unity to the whole. But I will not trouble you farther with these speculations, which require, I admit, to be more fully matured before they are fit to be presented to the public.

I am glad to find that you have better hopes concerning my other work on Christianity.[1] What you say encourages me to proceed in that work with more concentrated attention, and were I not afraid of withdrawing your thoughts too much from your own studies, I would solicit your examination and judgment of what I have written on that subject.

I was glad to see in the Times that your paper has been read in the Statistical Section of the British Association, though it was only a bare notice of the fact – In a previous number of the same paper it was stated that a M^r McLeod*[2] had read a paper in which he attempted to apply mathematics to the investigations of Political science. I should like to know how far his notions coincide with yours.

I was not at all aware that you were "somewhat gloomy" during

---

[1] Cf. Vol. I, p. 184 and Vol. III, Letter 175.

[2] Henry Dunning Macleod, 'On the Definition and Nature of the Science of Political Economy', *Report of the Thirty-second Meeting of the British Association . . . held at Cambridge in October, 1862.* Transactions of the Sections, 160–61.

In this paper Macleod developed the idea of political economy as a 'science of exchangeable relations of quantities', contending that 'it was already implicitly acknowledged that it was a mathematical science'; but there was no actual application of mathematics to economic questions in the paper. Cf. Black, *Manchester School*, 30 (September, 1962) 205.

For biographical details of Macleod, see Vol. III, Letter 429.

my late visit with you. You certainly did not show it in your behaviour. It grieves me much to hear that you have any cause for being gloomy, and that your prospects at present are not very cheerful. I really think you need not despond. Your talents and acquirements, with the help of what you earned in Australia, must surely, if properly directed, secure you a competence, in such a field of employment as London –

With many thanks for the trouble you have taken in inspecting my M.S. and with the best love of all of us to yourself and sister, I remain,
My dear Stanley
Your affectionate Uncle
W. Jevons.

I hope that the stamps which I inclose* will be sufficient to indemnify you for the posting and registration of my M.S.

167. W. S. JEVONS TO HERBERT JEVONS

8 Porteus Road W.
18 Nov. 1862.

My dear Herbert

Another month has gone & we still write without the advantage of knowing how you are doing. It must even be a couple of months yet before we hear.

If you can only get into some place moderately satisfactory, I hope you will stick to it, & trust to improving your position by degrees. Any progress however slow & interrupted is yet sufficient to give that hope which I am convinced is the only source of true satisfaction in life. No progress can well be slower than mine now is; nothing can be more indefinitely difficult & desperate than to make ones way in literature here, and yet I will try it for a little. At present I am in pretty good spirits – during parts of the autumn I was in dreadfully low spirits which indeed always seize me at intervals, so regular & certain that I know their approach & calculate upon it.

Lately I have made some attempts to overcome what I always considered a simple impossibility; that is to become a public speaker. I spoke several times at the last meeting of our debating society,[1] about as well as could be expected for a first attempt. I shall have to speak three times at least on the next meeting. It is not altogether impossible that I might make a rather good speaker in time – If so it would greatly

[1] Cf. Vol. I, p. 187.

improve ones prospects. For in almost any scientific or literary place one requires to be able to speak.

There is not very much to tell you of here. Henny keeps up her spirits pretty well; goes often to the schools,[2] & I favour her going out as much as possible. At present both she & I have colds not improved by going to a concert last night at St James Hall, where Joachim,[3] Halle[4] & Sims Reeves[5] all performed, the last singing Beethovens songs very finely. After much deliberation we agreed for the present to defer any change of lodgings or house, chiefly I believe because the Bryants shed a few tears on learning our intentions of leaving. But I am also desirous of not incurring any charges until I begin to make the money to pay for them. My schemes are continually deferring this. But the results though so slow will I hope appear in due time.

Lucy & John I am sorry to say, [are][6] pressed hard by the want of orders & John will be driven to discharge his men. Lucy however reports herself strong & well – & seems happy and there are I may add hopes of a small nephew for you early next year. John seems to have exerted himself much about his business but without any present success whatever.

Tom is all right in Liverpool, full of music & other amusements – also learning Italian.

I have just begun to take lessons on the organ. I get one hours lesson per week & one hours practise* after it, on a good large organ with two rows of keys, pedals & 24 stops, for one guinea per quarter. It is from a little man who keeps this organ for the purpose in a small house in Bermondsey 6 miles away. It is very agreable* both learning & playing; in time I may make a tolerable player. After once becoming acquainted with the management I should be able to take advantage of any opportunities of playing large organs, or even of playing some Chapel organ regularly. The little organist teaches very carefully though he gets so little for it.

I have had some very favourable notices of my diagrams – in the

[2] Henrietta Jevons taught at a Unitarian School in London. Cf. above, Letter 143, p. 406.

[3] Joseph Joachim (1831–1907), violinist, composer and friend of Brahms, who wrote much music for him. He was accounted the best interpreter of the work of Bach and Beethoven of his day.

[4] [Sir] Charles Hallé (1819–95), German-born pianist and conductor; studied at Darmstadt and in Paris, where he established his reputation by concerts of classical music; came to England after the 1848 Revolution and ultimately settled in Manchester. He and his orchestra became well known throughout the country and did much to raise the standard of musical taste by making the public familiar with the works of the great composers; knighted, 1888.

[5] Sims Reeves (1818–1900), English tenor, son of an Army musician; began his singing career at the age of ten when he entered the choir of the Royal Artillery band; after studying in Paris, Bordogni and Milan he returned to England to follow a successful career in opera and oratorio.   [6] Omitted in the original manuscript.

Spectator, Economist,⁷ by R. Hutton – they were *just noticed* in the *Times* City Article⁸ through Stanford's influence. But what is best they were noticed with almost extravagant praise by the Exchange Magazine,⁹ quite spontaneously. I have since opened communication with the Editor & offered to send him some papers, which probably I shall do some day. He seemed agreable* to receive them. I am thinking of undertaking another diagram scheme – of much better design – on a small scale – in form of an atlas¹⁰ & restricted to last 20 years – to be called "the Merchants' Atlas of Commercial Fluctuations" As I intend it the labour would be enormous, but the work when done so good that I think it could not fail to command success. At the same time I would not make it a large work, & keep the expense within two or three times that of the diagrams, which is not considerable. I am going by Stanfords advice to send out another circular concerning the Diag. with the opinions of press – to London Merchants Stockbrokers & others & hope to sell a number more, before the half yearly acct at end of year when I look for some returns. Henny has probably written you much other news, & so being much tired I conclude.

Please let us hear fully of your proceedings. I have written a long letter to Miller at Sydney, sending him the Diagrams. It is the second letter since you left – so if you go to Sydney they will be quite looking for you.

Ever your affec. Brother
W S Jevons.

⁷ These were the two diagrams published by Stanford. The notice appeared in *The Economist*, 15 November 1862, xx 1267, and included the following comments:

'. . . Mr. Jevons' idea is simply a picturesque development of the diagram illustrating the weekly prices of wheat which appears in the agricultural journals, but it is certainly very effective, and those not well versed in the subject may learn a great deal in a short time from his diagrams . . . To the student who wishes to study the law of connection between the state of trade, for example, and the state of the currency, these tables will [be] found of the greatest value, and on their accuracy and completeness our readers may implicitly depend.'

⁸ '. . . among purely statistical publications have been two elaborate diagrams by Mr. W. Stanley Jevons, 1, showing the price of the English funds, the price of wheat, the number of bankruptcies, and the rate of discount monthly since 1731; and, 2, all the weekly accounts of the Bank of England since the passing of the Bank Act in 1844 . . .' *The Times*, 8 October 1862, 4.

⁹ *The Exchange: a Home and Colonial Review of Commerce, Manufactures and General Politics* (1862) I, 412:

'We have never met with so much valuable and interesting information, set forth in so clear a manner, and in so small a compass, as is contained in Mr. Jevons's beautifully-executed diagrams. It would be impossible, in a short notice, to convey an adequate idea of the multitude of facts brought together by our compiler, and of the immense amount of labour which must have been expended in collecting them. There is much food for the reflective political economist, and a storehouse of data of great practical value to our bankers, merchants and brokers. We have at a glance the effects of all the great political movements of the last century and three quarters upon the value of property, the price of food, and the general industrial progress of the country.'

¹⁰ See above, Letter 150, n. 2, p. 425; also Vol. I, p. 179.

168. W. S. JEVONS TO T. E. JEVONS
[LJP, 172–3]

8 Porteus Road
28 Dec. 1862.

Dear Tom

I suppose I must write you another note before the end of this old year. I have not very much to say as I dont like talking about things until they are done. We spent an agreable* Christmas day at the Worsleys,[1] of course not so entertaining as a Liverpool Christmas day – being very quiet yet not stiff like most London parties. I envy you the run down to Beaumaris & a sight of the Welsh mountains. The dreariness of London of late makes one long for the country.

How are Volunteer matters in Liverpool – Here they are still alive. A certain number stick to it through thick & thin, and there are numerous recruits so that there is no fear of the corps failing in general. Our company and one or two more however in the regiment are I am afraid little more than nominal just at present. Boxing day was not a general field day here but our Reg^t was out at noon. There were not however more than 400 or 500 men. We marched in capital order from West^r Hall to Hampstead – Arrived on the heath we commenced operations by storming Jack Straw's Castle which was taken in the twinkling of an eye. Refreshed by the plunder we then extended over the heath in skirmishing order – The place is perfect for the purpose being covered with gorse bushes & gravel pits which serve for rifle pits. Our men skirmished rather wildly & without a rigid observance of the field exercise book. Still it was a good lesson as regards the real purpose of light infantry movements. With the fineness of the day we got our spirits up and we contributed greatly to the amusement of a numerous crowd of people who regarded us and our band with great favour. The work done the Colonel informed us that a van of provisions etc were in attendance to which the men rushed off. A slight mistake arose in the fact that half the men thought they were not to pay – while others thought they were. Some fellows finding large jars of port wine went off with them into quiet corners & discussed it in tumblers among circles of peculiar friends. Before we marched off the provision men had discovered that they were minus a gallon of wine and an inquiry resulted in one or two men having to fork out a pound or two. But the rest were all the better for it, and while some few perhaps reached home rather fresh and oblivious the rest declared they had had a glorious day.

I rather like my sergeants duties which I am now beginning to exercise a little. I looked well after my section – one of the privates of

[1] Cf. above, Letter 35, n. 7, p. 65.

which was Calder Marshall R A the Sculptor[2] – but some of my men would get mixed up in other Companies & not even the Sculptor had any clear ideas about good cover.

I think the new order restricting the number of V C will operate beneficially in filling up the ranks of those which already exist. The new regulations which are to come out may rather alter the composition of the force but all the true men will remain. I am convinced however that the force can only be kept up to its present amount by numerous new men. But now expense will no longer be so much an obstacle many will perhaps join who were before prevented. I think the popularity of the force increases.

I must say I am interested when we are in Hyde Park Wimbledon, Hampstead or elsewhere to think how often the same ground was covered by the Old Volunteers.

You will be inquiring about my Volunteer Hist.[3] This has rather come to grief. For after almost completing the information necessary I found I had not the light imaginative pen necessary for making a book popular in the present day. The history would have proved little more than a series of historical notes – Yet it is a pity to let so many interesting facts go waste – I have some notion of writing to the Editor of the V. S. Gazette, asking if he knows of anyone who would go partnership & make a book out of it that would sell well. What do you think.

I am at present going on with my old work of diagrams. I find that more than 200 of my former diag. have been sold including the Liverpool sale, which will return me nearly £20 of the £25 spent on printing. I am now thinking of a *small atlas* with plates about 6 × 8 inches from 1844–62 comprising monthly quotations of prices exports imports etc etc all fully reduced, analysed etc so as to make quite a small gem of a work – which cannot fail to be successful – & comprising the bank accounts as usefully as the large diagram. It is somewhat the same idea with which I first began nearly 2 years ago[4] but I have learnt so much by experience that my first diag. are quite laughable beside the little gems I now produce. I have just begun drawing to day a glorious one of the cotton trade comprising prices of 5 kinds of cotton, also of yarn, twist, two kinds of cloth, with imports, exports, consumption & stock of cotton. The atlas would contain perhaps 12 plates including

1. Bank Accts, 2. Money Market – Stock Market, Corn of several

---

[2] William Calder Marshall, R.A. (1813–94), the sculptor, was born in Edinburgh and trained under Chantrey. He became A.R.S.A. in 1842, A.R.A. in 1844 and R.A. in 1852.
[3] Cf. Vol. I, p. 186.
[4] See above, Letter 150, n. 2, p. 425.

kinds, Agricultural produce, butchers meal, the principal exports & imports – prices etc all the fluctuations during the year & the seasons are to be fully worked out. A good deal of the work is done but of course infinite labour will be necessary for finishing it satisfactorily.

Will you be so good as early in January to call on Benson & Mallet,[5] *to get what they owe me – and take away such of the diagrams as remain unsold.*

We are anxiously awaiting a letter from Herbert but I am afraid we shall not have any till near the middle of January.

Monday. The news just arrived surprised but gratified us much. It is especially satisfactory on Lucy's account. It is of course the beginning of a new chapter in the history of the family & shall be duly recorded in my genealogy book this evening.[6]

Ever yours
W S Jevons

[5] Benson and Mallett, a firm of stationers and printers, then in business at 10 and 12 Castle Street, Liverpool; cf. Gore's *Directory of Liverpool*, 1862.

[6] Lucy's first child, Thomas Grindal, was born on 26 December 1862. He died of diphtheria in 1875. See LJ, p.345.